Date Due

D1260615

MODERN ECONOMIC SOCIETY

MODERN
ECONOMIC SOCIETY

BY

SUMNER H. SLICHTER

PROFESSOR OF BUSINESS ECONOMICS
AT HARVARD UNIVERSITY

NEW YORK
HENRY HOLT AND COMPANY

TO MY WIFE

TO MY WIFE.

PREFACE

The rapid development of economic life compels a constant restatement of economics. This restatement is bound to lag more or less behind the reality which it purports to describe because, by the time economists are able to discover what the new reality is, it has partly ceased to be and a still newer reality has taken its place. In the field of specialized and monographic studies, the science of economics has kept fairly close behind the rapid development of industry. However limited has been the success of economists in reducing the description of modern industrial activity to laws, there are few developments in modern industry which have not been investigated and described by the specialists in the various branches of economics. Nevertheless, the enormous monographic output during the last two decades has had relatively little influence upon general descriptions of economic processes which, somewhat unfortunately, have acquired the traditional name of " principles of economics."

Such claim as this book makes upon the reader must rest largely upon the fact that it represents an effort to reduce the lag between the specialized and monographic work and the more generalized descriptions of our industrial system. Every economist will appreciate the enormous difficulty, if not the impossibility, of incorporating the work of a wide variety of specialists into a general description of modern industry. But it is not enough to say that the task is impossible. Whether possible or not, it must be attempted, and done as well as can be. No one man, of course, can hope to acquire familiarity with all of the enormous number of special researches in the fields of finance, labor, international trade, public utilities, agricultural economics, public finance, and others. Although this book has been in process of writing for ten years, the author does not pretend that he has been able to do justice to the work of the specialists.

It will be observed from the above remarks that this book makes no pretense at great originality. At some points, it is true, a refinement or a new turn has been added to theory. But the main reason for the existence of the book is precisely the fact that it does *not* pretend to be original. If there is any originality in it, it must be largely in the synthesis which it presents rather than in its treatment of specific topics.

All but the last several chapters of the book have been in use at Cornell in substantially the present form for a number of years — much of it for as many as nine. Many past and present members of the Cornell staff have been exceedingly generous in offering suggestions for the improvement of the manuscript. Particularly great is my indebtedness to Professors M. A. Copeland and P. M. O'Leary, and to W. C. Beatty, P. L. Clark, Horace Davis, H. B. Dolbeare, C. D. Edwards, W. L. Farman, L. A. Froman, F. R. Garfield, S. M. Jaquith, W. R. Leonard, P. S. McGuire, E. B. McNatt, and Elmer Pendell. Major and Mrs. L. K. Underhill have read the book in a preliminary edition, have offered many discriminating criticisms, and have corrected a number of historical, legal, and mathematical errors. Mr. D. M. Keezer has also gone over the book in preliminary form and made numerous suggestions. Specialists in certain fields have read and criticized all or most of some chapters — Professor H. L. Reed, Chapters XI, XX, and XXI; Mr. W. D. Pence, Chapter XVIII; Dr. J. S. Davis and Professor J. G. Knapp, Chapter XIX; Dr. J. B. Hubbard, Chapter XX; Mr. F. J. Schlink, Chapter XXII; Professor M. Slade Kendrick, Chapter XXVIII; Mr. L. R. Edminster, Chapter XXIX; Professor J. F. Ebersole, Chapter XXX. In preparing the chapter on trade unionism, I have been helped by the advice of O. S. Beyer, Jr., and M. H. Hedges. Needless to say, at certain points these experts dissent from opinions or interpretations which I have seen fit to retain. Nevertheless, I am under great obligation to them for many penetrating criticisms. My father, who has read several of the preliminary editions, has helped me with many constructive comments. Greatest of all is my indebtedness to my wife who has read the entire manuscript at several stages with minute care. Every page bears the impress of her numerous suggestions. She has also prepared the index.

Acknowledgment is made to Alfred A. Knopf, Inc., for permission to use in Chapter IV, in slightly altered form, extracts from my paper, "The Organization and Control of Economic Activity," contributed to *The Trend of Economics*.

S. H. S.

HARVARD UNIVERSITY,
May, 1931.

PART ONE
INTRODUCTION

PART TWO
SOME BASIC CHARACTERISTICS OF THE EXISTING ECONOMIC ORDER

PART THREE
THE OPERATION OF THE EXISTING ECONOMIC ORDER

xi

PART FOUR

SOME CONSTRUCTIVE SUGGESTIONS

PART I

INTRODUCTION

CHAPTER I

THE CONTROL OF ECONOMIC ACTIVITY

I. OUR IMPERFECT CONTROL OF INDUSTRY.   II. THE POSSIBILITY
OF ACHIEVING CONTROL OF INDUSTRY.   III. THE SCOPE AND PUR-
POSE OF THIS BOOK.

I. OUR IMPERFECT CONTROL OF INDUSTRY

At the end of the seventeenth century, the mining of coal had scarcely begun; iron was made in small charcoal-burning forges which produced only two to three hundred pounds a day; steel was almost a precious metal, being usually made by heating iron bars of good quality with charcoal for twelve days at a cost of several hundred dollars a ton.   Cloth was woven on hand looms in the cottages of the weavers, whose wives and daughters spun the yarn.   The steam engine had not been put to use; the cast-iron plow, the reaper, the thresher, the sewing machine were yet to be invented; the horse was still, as he had been for centuries, the fastest means of transportation available to man; no use was made of electricity.   Agriculture was the occupation of nine-tenths of the people.   As late as 1800, only six towns in the United States had a population of 8,000 or more.

Probably never before has industry changed so rapidly as it has been doing during the last two hundred years.   This change, because of its quickness and completeness, is called "The Industrial Revolution."   So profound and manifold have been its effects upon all branches of human activity, that it is undoubtedly the most important development in history since the disintegration of the Roman Empire.

The technological essence of the revolution in industry, the very kernel of the revolution, so to speak, has been the substitution of mechanical power, especially power from mineral fuels, for animal muscle in the production of goods.[1]   Between 1870

[1] Prior to 1850, mineral fuels furnished less energy than work animals.   Even as late as 1880, minerals provided less energy in the United States than firewood.   But

3

and 1926, the energy consumption of the United States increased about fifteen times — five times as rapidly as the population.[2] It has been estimated that we now possess in non-human sources of energy the equivalent of sixty slaves for every man, woman, and child in the United States.[3] Had a person living in 1700 known that two centuries later we should possess such great sources of energy, he would no doubt have been confident that economic problems would no longer exist. Were such a person to return to earth today, he would undoubtedly be amazed at the multitude of economic problems which confront us. Some of these problems exist *in spite of* the Industrial Revolution; many more *because* of it.

Most astonishing of all perhaps is the fact that two centuries of Industrial Revolution have left the problem of production still far from solution. One might have expected that the marvelous technological development of the last two centuries would at least have solved the problem of poverty. Between 1850 and 1928, per capita output in the United States — corrected for changes in the purchasing power of the dollar — increased nearly fourfold, but in 1928 it was still only $749.[4] However large that would have seemed to the man of 1850, it seems pitifully small to us when we consider how much — or how little — $749 will buy. A good test of the sufficiency of production is furnished by how adequately a lifetime of work enables men to provide for their old age. In 1911, the Pennsylvania Commission of Old Age Pensions found that 43 per cent of the persons fifty years of age or over investigated in their homes had no means of support except their own earnings and that approximately 27 per cent of these were not working.[5] The Massachusetts Commission on Pensions

---

in 1923, they contributed 87 per cent of the total energy consumed in American industries. Tryon, F. G., and Mann, L., " Mineral Resources for Future Populations," *Population Problems in the United States and Canada,* p. 124.

[2] Tryon, F. G., " An Index of Consumption of Fuels and Water Power," *Journal of the American Statistical Association,* September, 1927, v. XXII, p. 277.

[3] U. S. Department of the Interior, " Power Capacity and Production in the United States," *Water Supply Paper 579,* p. 1.

[4] Based on the estimates of Dr. W. I. King in *The Wealth and Income of the United States,* p. 129, and *The National Income and Its Purchasing Power,* p. 87.

[5] The Pennsylvania Old Age Pension Commission. Epstein, A., *The Problem of Old Age Pensions in Industry,* p. 20.

in its 1925 report states that nearly a fourth of the persons of sixty-five years or over interviewed by the Commission had incomes of $100 a year or less and that one-third had incomes of less than $400.[6]

Despite the pressing need for more output, modern industry fails to operate even at its existing capacity. Among the most extraordinary economic phenomena of the age are the periods of unemployment and depression which recur at frequent intervals. Goods are needed as much as ever, men are anxious to work, there are factories and machines ready to manufacture the needed products, and business men eager to obtain orders. Yet despite these things, our economic system for some reason balks and produces only at a greatly diminished rate. It is as if some magic hand had applied brakes to the wheels of industry. Business men, for all their trying, secure orders only in much smaller quantities, and thousands of men who ask nothing but the chance to work are unable to obtain employment. The machines stand idle and consumers receive a smaller volume of goods. Thus far our efforts to end or prevent these periods of stagnation have had only limited success. Eventually the depression ends and prosperity returns. But never to stay. Factories do not continue indefinitely to operate full time nor workmen to be relatively well employed. After a few years, economic strains accumulate; they prove too much for some enterprises; there are failures, a collapse of credit, a crisis, and another period of stagnation.

It is not, however, merely in times of depression that industry fails to produce to capacity. Under existing economic arrangements, most enterprises must *normally* restrict output in order to maintain solvency. Consequently, even in busy and prosperous years, our mines and factories turn out far less than their equipment or supply of labor permits. In 1928, the Portland cement mills of the United States had an annual capacity of approximately 243,252,000 barrels. But although output in that year broke all records, it was only 176,195,000 barrels, or 72.4 per cent of the capacity of the industry.[7] In the twenty-two years from 1907 to 1928, the annual output never reached 90 per cent

[6] *Ibid.*, p. 20.
[7] Portland Cement Association, *Concrete and Cement*, 1929, p. 4.

of the capacity of the industry and exceeded 80 per cent in only six years. The following diagram shows the estimated capacity and production of the industry for the nine years, 1919 to 1928:[8]

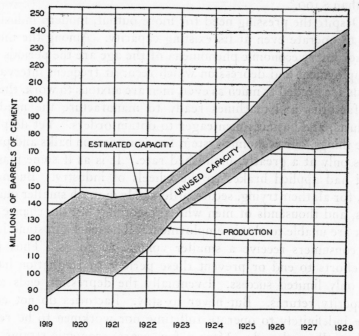

The chronic underproduction which is found in the cement industry exists in practically every industry concerning which we have information. The committee of the Federated American Engineering Societies which studied waste in industry estimated that the shoe industry operates at little more than half its capacity, the men's clothing industry at less than three-fifths, printing plants at two-thirds, metal working plants at about five-sevenths.[9] Were our bituminous coal mines to operate steadily at capacity, their output would be about twice our present consumption. The capacity of our *cane* sugar refineries alone, based on 300 working days a year, is approximately one-third more than our normal consumption and exports of sugar.[10] Three per cent of our flour mills, employing 44 per cent of the workers, would, if operated full time, make practically all of the flour that we use. The

[8] Adapted, with permission, from a diagram in *Concrete and Cement*, p. 6.
[9] Federated American Engineering Societies, *Waste in Industry*, pp. 17–18.
[10] American Sugar Refining Company, *Annual Report*, 1926, p. 5.

automobile industry in 1923 was equipped to turn out approximately 4,500,000 cars, but though the demand for cars in that year was unprecedented, the output was not more than 4,000,000. In 1923 the paper industry had the second best year in its history, but the output was over 2,000,000 tons below the industry's capacity of 9,519,800 tons.[11] During the ten years ending with 1922, the sales of structural steel averaged only 56 per cent of the industry's capacity. In 1916, when sales came closest to capacity, the percentage was only 70.[12] Indeed every industry concerning which we have information appears normally to produce far below its capacity.

An accurate estimate of the extent to which industry *as a whole* underproduces cannot be directly derived from the figures for specific industries because the estimates for individual industries are based upon the amount of idle equipment rather than the number of idle men. If all industries were simultaneously to attempt to operate at capacity, there would probably not be enough labor to run all of the existing equipment. But that industry as a whole does underproduce is indicated by the fact that unemployment is *always* large — even in prosperous years. It has been estimated that the annual minimum unemployment among non-agricultural wage and salary earners in the United States between 1920 and 1927 varied from 5.1 per cent in 1920 to 15.3 per cent in 1921 and averaged 7.8 per cent for the eight year period.[13] These figures are probably too large because they include idleness caused by sickness, accidents, and strikes as well as by lack of work. But the figures do not include time lost by men who had jobs but who did not have full-time employment at them. Counting idleness caused both by inability to find work and by lack of full-time employment, it is probable that the number of unemployed between 1920 and 1927 averaged in excess of 6 per cent of the gainfully employed population.

But most of the economic problems of the day exist, not in spite of the Industrial Revolution, but because of it. This is

[11] *Paper Trade Journal*, April 10, 1924, v. LXXVIII, p. 79.
[12] *Commercial and Financial Chronicle*, January 20, 1923, v. CXVI, p. 228. The figures on sales are those reported to the Bridge Builders and Structural Steel Society down to April, 1922, and those reported to the Bureau of the Census since then. The estimated capacity of the industry was based upon a special survey conducted by the Bureau of the Census. [13] *Recent Economic Changes*, v. II, p. 879.

scarcely surprising. Human cupidity and stupidity are dangerous in proportion to the power which men have at their disposal. Precisely because the Industrial Revolution has placed immense power in men's hands, it has created the problem of controlling that power. Thus, before the days of modern machinery, it was not of vital importance that employers have strong incentives to guard their employees against accidents. The workers, by exercising caution, were fairly well able to avoid injury. Today, when the industries of the United States annually kill through industrial accidents approximately 23,000 employees and disable 575,000 for four weeks or more and 3,000,000 for a day or more, powerful incentives to encourage employers to fight accidents are urgently needed. Likewise the problem of conserving natural resources is important today simply because modern industry, with its machines and artificial power, consumes raw material so rapaciously. In the last twenty years the world has exploited more of its mineral resources than in all previous history.[14]

An important aspect of the Industrial Revolution has been the application of scientific methods to many branches of business administration. This creates numerous problems of control because it greatly increases the ability of business managers to accomplish their purposes, regardless of whether these are desirable or undesirable from the standpoint of the community. Consider, for example, the significance of improvements in the art of marketing. Science aids business in its dealing with consumers by analyzing the mind of the buyer, pointing out the numerous desires, hopes, fears, prejudices, ambitions, and impulses which lead people to purchase and suggesting ways of appealing to each, explaining how to disarm suspicion and arouse confidence, how to meet objections, how to organize advertising campaigns and to prepare advertising copy. As long as enterprises exerted little influence upon how men spent their money, there was no serious problem. But as soon as business enterprises gain substantial influence over our choices, a problem of control is created because the knowledge and skill of the marketing experts are devoted to making men desire, not necessarily the things which are beneficial

[14] Leith, C. K., "Exploitation and World Progress," *Foreign Affairs*, October, 1927, v. VI, p. 3.

to them, but the things which it is profitable to industry for them to demand.

The Industrial Revolution has led to the creation of gigantic business enterprises which count their capital by tens of millions and their employees by tens of thousands. The immense power of these enterprises over their customers, employees, and competitors, and even over the government itself, raises many perplexing problems of control. To what extent and by what devices should immense organizations, such as the United States Steel Corporation, General Motors Corporation, or the American Telephone and Telegraph Company, be held responsible to the community for their activities? And what voice should the employees of a large concern possess in determining the policies of the enterprise? Trade unions have been struggling to introduce into industry the principle, well recognized in the field of government, that those who must obey laws or rules should have a voice in making them. Possibly the trade unions are wrong; possibly it would be unwise to apply the democratic principle to the internal control of industry. One thing, however, is clear: the problems of industrial organization which confront us, the problems of how authority within industry and over industry should be distributed, subject to what controls it should be exercised, are no less momentous than the great constitutional issues which were created during the seventeenth and eighteenth centuries by the demands of the merchants and manufacturers for a greater voice in the control of the state. Indeed, it is probable that our problems of industrial organization are more difficult than the problems of political organization because, in the case of industry, it is a matter of giving a balanced representation to a broad range of interests without seriously impairing the efficient operation of complicated and delicate economic machinery.

When we observe modern industry failing to give steady employment and to produce to capacity even when millions of people urgently need more goods; unnecessarily killing and maiming thousands of men each year; wasting irreplaceable natural resources simply because it is more profitable under existing economic arrangements to waste them than to conserve them; employing thousands of experts for the purpose of making men desire certain things, not because they are good for men to use, but because they are profitable for business enterprises to sell; denying to wage earners an opportunity to participate in making the rules under which they work; when we observe all these things, it is difficult to avoid the conclusion that man, in no small degree, is a slave to his creations, dominated by industry instead of making it serve his ends — that, in the words of Emerson, "Things are in the saddle and ride mankind." How to make industry more of a tool and less of a tyrant, how to prevent the process of making a living from interfering with the opportunity and the capacity of men to lead the good life, how, indeed, to make the process of getting a living a part of the good life itself, these are the supreme economic problems, and at few stages in human history have they been more acute or more fascinating than they are today.

II. The Possibility of Achieving Control of Industry

That any good can come of subjecting economic phenomena to conscious control has been bitterly disputed. During the nineteenth century a curious philosophy of economic fatalism attained great influence in the United States and Great Britain and, to a less extent, in other countries. The philosophy of economic fatalism, it is true, enjoyed little credence among economists, but it did have, and still does have, considerable vogue among business men. The doctrine has had several forms. One form — the one which was most popular in the United States — was based upon the idea that economic phenomena are governed by natural law and that efforts to control them are attempts to interfere with the inexorable working of nature; that, at the best, such efforts are bound to be futile, at the worst they may do much harm.

More penetrating reflection would have shown the error in this reasoning. As long as man can alter conditions, he can "interfere" with nature — just as he "interferes" with the law of gravitation every time he constructs elevators and drinking fountains. It is extraordinary that in no realm except that of social relations are we told that we must passively accept the fate which nature metes out to us. In hundreds of ways, from wearing clothes to building smudges and sprinkling lawns, we endeavor to control the effect of the weather upon us and no one tells us that our efforts are useless. Only when we seek to control human beings are we told that we are interfering with nature and attempting something which is vain, if not vicious.[15]

The success of our efforts to control industry depends largely upon how completely we can foresee their results. Of the infinite consequences of any deed, we can, of course, know but a few. This, however, does not justify inaction, which also has its effects, infinite in number and for the most part unpredictable; but it does mean that our ability to exercise control over industry will always be extremely limited. To improve our ability to foresee results, and thus to enlarge our control over industry, we need to know how industry works and why it works as it does. For this information we must turn in the main — though not entirely — to economics.

The subject matter of economics is industry, the process by which men get a living, but economics is not the only science or art which studies industry. Physics, chemistry, geology, psychology, business administration, and the numerous agricultural arts and sciences, all study at least some aspects of industry — such problems as how to burn coal with less waste, how to transmit power more economically, what crops are best suited to certain soils and climate. What distinguishes these numerous arts and sciences from economics?

The answer is that economics studies industry, not as a technological process, but as a complex of human practices and relationships. It analyzes how we get a living, not in terms of machines or chemical reactions, but in terms of the human practices, relationships, and organizations which are involved. It is not concerned with the chemistry of steel production or with how much the life of railroad ties is prolonged by creosoting; but it is vitally concerned with how human interests are affected by the institutions of slavery, serfdom, or the wages system, with what results we obtain when we organize production by permit-

---

[15] But even the business men who assert that governmental interference with business is harmful or futile expect the government to provide a coinage, mail service, a consular service, roads, a protective tariff, and perhaps to subsidize a merchant marine.

ting everyone to make almost anything he chooses in almost any way that he pleases, or when the state intervenes by imposing a protective tariff upon certain commodities, forbidding certain competitive practices, or fixing certain prices by law. Economics is also concerned with how the process of getting a living is affected by buying on credit, by the attempts of trade unions to regulate wages and working conditions, and by the efforts of associations of business enterprises to control the competitive methods of their members. In brief, economics is simply the study of industry from the standpoint of the human practices and organizations which make the process of getting a living what it is.

But granting that some degree of deliberate guidance of economic activities is neither impossible nor necessarily undesirable, it may well be doubted whether the desires of a very large part of the population will ever play much part in determining what control is exercised over industry. Are not the problems of economic policy so technical, so multitudinous, and so rapidly changing that the public is likely to be incapable of deciding what policies it wishes pursued? Consider the startling rapidity with which industry changes. We accept the telephone, the central power plant, the street car, the automobile, moving pictures, wireless telegraphy, and the skyscraper as matters of course, as if they had always been. Nevertheless, New York City obtained its first telephone exchange in 1879 and its first central electric-power distributing plant about forty years ago,[16] and its first high steel building was erected well within the memories of men now living. The motorman who is reputed to have run the first electric street railway car was in 1923 still running a car in Richmond, Virginia.[17] The automobile, the phonograph, moving pictures, and wireless telegraphy have each been important commercially for less than twenty-five years. Twenty years ago a 5,000-kilowatt turbo-generator was revolutionary; in 1927 the General Electric Company was building a turbine for the State-Line Generating Company with a capacity of 208,000 kilowatts — the muscular energy of two million men, or half the population of

---

[16] General Electric Company, *Thirty Year Review of the General Electric Company, 1892–1922*, p. 6.

[17] *Motorman and Conductor*, June, 1923, pp. 1–2.

the United States at the time of the Revolutionary War. Can we hope to invent and to put into effect new methods of controlling industry as rapidly as its amazing evolution creates the need for them?

There is grave danger that we cannot. In the first place, the so-called natural sciences and the technologies based upon them, which largely determine the rate of industrial change, are able to make discoveries more rapidly than economics because they employ the method of experiment under controlled conditions — an investigative device for which economics and the other social sciences have no adequate substitute. In the second place, technological research is heavily subsidized by industry itself, but the study of how to control industry is not. Some of the largest and best equipped laboratories in the country are owned by business establishments. The National Industrial Conference Board estimates that more than 1,000 enterprises have research departments or laboratories and that about $200,-000,000 is spent annually in the United States for industrial research. In 1926, one of these concerns spent over $5,000,-000 on industrial research and another about $13,000,000.[18] The American Telephone and Telegraph Company has several thousand people at its headquarters and laboratories who do nothing but make new inventions and develop new methods of operation. No comparable support is given to research in the social sciences. In the third place, changes in industrial technology do not require popular approval — they can be made at the order of the manager the instant he is convinced that they will pay. Many methods of controlling industry require governmental action. But governments in democratic countries do not usually act until public opinion demands it.[19] It usually takes the public some time to decide what it wishes. Aside from the time required for thousands of people to become acquainted with

[18] *Law and Labor*, December, 1927, v. IX, p. 318.

[19] The inability of the democratic state to act as promptly as the rapid development of industry requires suggests that we may be steadily forced to rely more and more upon non-governmental methods of controlling industry. Of course we must not overlook the possibility of inventing new governmental machinery which will operate with far greater speed and effectiveness than any which we now possess. There is no reason for supposing that it is less possible to improve upon the political inventions of the eighteenth century than it has been to improve upon the mechanical inventions.

the conditions that need correction, there is the serious difficulty that the methods of correcting them conflict with time-honored conceptions of individual responsibility, the rights of property, and the functions of government. Some of the problems created by the corporation, for example, can be dealt with only by modifying traditional notions of business privacy; and to cope with the problems of unemployment, industrial accidents, and occupations disease, we must sacrifice deep-seated conceptions of individual responsibility. By the time that the public has finally decided what it wishes, it may be too late to undo what has already happened. Thus industry is likely to go on confronting the public with one *fait accompli* after another and the public is likely to remain in a more or less bewildered state of indecision concerning what steps, if any, should be taken to protect its interests.

Doubt concerning the public's ability to control industry is further enhanced by the possibility that industry may succeed in controlling the desires and the opinions of the public — or at least in so befuddling issues that men cannot decide what public policy they prefer. Here we encounter one of the chief differences between the problems of the social sciences and those of the natural sciences. The material with which the chemist or the physicist deals does not fight back — it makes no carefully planned and generously financed efforts to resist control, *it does not employ science itself to prevent control from being achieved.* But industry resists as soon as we attempt to regulate it. Just as it endeavors to persuade us to accept its wares, so it seeks, by influencing legislatures, courts, political parties, and newspapers, to impose upon us its scales of value, its ideas of wise and unwise public policy. In all of this there is nothing inherently objectionable. The danger simply is that industry will exercise *too much influence.* Here we are undoubtedly face to face with the kernel of the problem of industrial control — namely, how to prevent industry from unduly molding our opinions, how to prevent our ideals, our scales of values, from being too much affected by the standards of the market place, how, in short, to protect life itself from being too completely dominated by the process of getting a living.[20] Industry's growing skill in molding men's minds

[20] Should the man in the street prove unable to resist in reasonable degree the efforts of special interests to mold his opinions, it is not improbable that we may be

makes this problem both increasingly important and increasingly difficult.

But possibly the public is less helpless than it at first appears to be. Control of industry is far from being merely a matter of formal legal enactment. Indeed, it is probable that the most effective methods of control are the informal and the indirect ones — not laws so much as customs and ethical standards, the raising of new generations of business men who possess broader conceptions of their responsibilities. The mere discussion of what policies should be pursued and the airing of facts which occurs during controversies over public policy are capable of producing profound changes in the ethical conceptions both of business leaders and of the entire community. The result may be, not the enactment of laws, but voluntary changes in the methods of business enterprises themselves. The discussion of the problem of unemployment during the last decade has resulted in little legislation in the United States, but it has deeply affected the thinking and the policies of the business leaders of America. In this instance at least, the public has influenced the leaders of industry as much as the leaders have influenced the public.

But whatever the role that the general public plays or is capable of playing in determining economic policies, it is unquestionably true that never before have so many experiments in the control of economic activities been under way in various parts of the world. Consider merely the far reaching guidance that is exercised over industry by four of the great boards and commissions in Washington — the Interstate Commerce Commission, the Federal Reserve Board, the Federal Farm Board, and the Federal Trade Commission. Here we find the major policies of four great divisions of industry — transportation, banking, farming, and general manufacturing and wholesaling — determined in large degree by bodies which the government has especially created for the purpose. The numerous and ambitious attempts to guide the actions of industry which are being made in all parts of the world lend to the study of eco-

---

compelled to make drastic changes in our political machinery. It is too early, however, to judge how the man in the street will behave. High pressure publicity methods are so new that he still reacts to them in an unsophisticated way. Probably he will not always remain such pliable clay.

nomics today an interest and an importance beyond that which it has ever enjoyed before.

III. THE SCOPE AND PURPOSE OF THIS BOOK

Fifty or even twenty-five years ago, one could have written a description of economic society which would have been more or less applicable to all countries of western civilization. But, in their efforts to grapple with economic problems, the leading industrial countries of the world have each developed peculiar and distinctive economic arrangements. No longer is it possible to give a picture of economic society which more or less accurately fits Australia, Germany, Italy, Russia, Great Britain, and the United States. Consequently, in this introduction to economics, we shall not attempt a general survey of economic society in countries of European civilization but shall center our attention upon the industrial system of the United States.

Our analysis will begin with a description of certain basic characteristics of modern industry in terms of which its operation is to be explained. After this survey of fundamentals, we shall endeavor to describe how the economic system works. In doing so, we shall be as concrete and realistic as possible. In studying the operation of industry, we may encounter some laws or principles of more or less general validity. To a large extent, however, we shall find that economic phenomena are to be explained in terms of particular circumstances, many of them more or less peculiar to our own time and country.

But we cannot be content with simply explaining how industry functions. Our ultimate concern is with the problem of social control, with how to bring our methods of making a living into harmony with our conceptions of the ideal life. Consequently, in the course of examining the operation of industry, we shall raise some general questions concerning what features of its operation are desirable and what ones are undesirable and we shall inquire what general steps might be taken to make industry serve us more satisfactorily. In doing so, we shall, of course, be reaching out beyond the strict limits of economics, for it is not the peculiar function of economics, or of any other science, to determine what is good and what is bad. Nevertheless, the analysis of our economic system can be made most fruitfully by pointing out, in conjunction with the description, tests by which the functioning of industry may be appraised and by showing how the operation of modern industry gives rise to practical problems of public policy.

REFERENCES

Chase, Stuart, *The Tragedy of Waste*, 1926.
Clark, J. M., *Social Control of Business*, 1926. Ch. IV and V.
Dewey, John, *The Public and Its Problems*, 1927. Ch. III, IV, and VI.
Godkin, E. L., *Unforeseen Tendencies of Democracy*, 1903.
Hamilton, Walton, *Current Economic Problems* (third edition), Chicago, 1925.
Lippmann, Walter, *Public Opinion*, 1926.
Tawney, R. H., *The Acquisitive Society*, 1920. Ch. II, III, and IV.
Young, A. A., " English Political Economy," *Economica*, March, 1928, No. 22.

CHAPTER II

SOME FUNDAMENTAL ECONOMIC CONCEPTS

I. GOODS. II. THE THREE BASIC ECONOMIC PROCESSES. III. THE NATURE OF PRODUCTION. IV. COST OF PRODUCTION. V. SOME ACCOUNTING CONCEPTS, TERMS, AND DEVICES.

I. Goods

If we could obtain as much of everything as we wanted without effort, there would be no economic problems and no science of economics. Nature provides a few things without labor by man and in excess of the quantities required to satisfy all desires for them. Such goods are called *free goods*. Air is usually a free good. So sometimes is water. Whether or not a good is free depends upon circumstances of time and place. Nature supplies water in many places greatly in excess of the desire for it *at those places,* but it is brought into houses only at the expenditure of human labor. Hence, although water in the ocean or in many streams is a free good, when it comes out of the kitchen faucet it is not.

The goods which concern the economist are those which need to be economized, that is, those which are obtained only by human effort or which, if supplied freely by nature, are not provided in sufficient quantities to satisfy all desires for them. Such goods are known as *economic goods*. Clothing, houses, automobiles, food are, of course, economic goods because labor is required to produce them. Land in its natural state. virgin timber, or minerals in the ground, which have been entirely produced by nature, may be economic goods simply because they are too scarce to satisfy all the desires for them.

The services yielded by some goods are appropriable but those provided by others are not. By " appropriable " is meant that the possessor can confine the benefits of the good to himself to the exclusion of other persons. There is no inherent difficulty in appropriating the benefits of many things — such as chairs, oranges, hats, shoes, houses — but this is not true of all goods. The rays of a lighthouse, for example, guide every passing boat and it is not practicable to withhold them from some vessels and let them shine for others. So also the protection afforded by an army or a fleet extends to everyone in the land; dikes and levees benefit not only those upon whose land they stand but all whose property might be flooded; a public health department, by reducing contagious disease, inevitably serves everyone in the community. Sometimes part of the benefits yielded by a good are appropriable and part are not. Schools are principally advantageous to the children who attend them, but they provide some gain to everyone who profits from a higher level of knowledge in the community.

The extent to which goods are appropriable is important because it determines in large degree the respective spheres of public and private enterprise. Private enterprise can exist only where the possessor of a good can withhold a substantial part of the benefits yielded by it from persons who are not willing to pay for them. Where this is impossible, there is likely to be no profit in producing the good and it must be provided, if at all, by the state or by philanthropic agencies.

II. THE THREE BASIC ECONOMIC PROCESSES

Every economic system, no matter what its nature, must do three things. First of all, obviously, it must provide for the production of goods. Because we cannot produce enough to satisfy all of our desires, we are confronted with the problem of how to make the best use of our limited supplies of labor, equipment, and natural resources. What things shall we make, in what quantities, and by what methods? Shall we produce more food or more ornaments, more amusement or better medical care? Whose labor shall be used to make this and whose to make that? All of these questions must be settled in order to organize production and every economic system must furnish some way of deciding them. The second thing that every economic system must do is to provide a way of determining how the members of the community shall share in the output of industry. More for

A means less for B. How shall we decide whose desires shall go unsatisfied? What tests shall be used? Shall each person receive an equal share in industry's output or shall some receive more than others; if the latter, who shall get more and who less and how shall the size of the shares be determined? Finally, the economic system must provide a way of regulating the consumption of goods. Shall everyone be permitted to consume whatever he chooses, shall some goods be withheld from some classes or offered to some classes upon especially favorable terms?

These are the basic functions which every industrial system must perform. Consequently, the analysis of any economic system must consist very largely of an inquiry into how it regulates the fundamental economic activities of producing goods, dividing the product of industry, and consuming goods — or, as the economist says, of *production, distribution,* and *consumption.* Is it a good method of getting human desires satisfied? Does it make possible a large production? Does it permit some men to make a living in ways which detract from rather than add to the total satisfaction of human desires? Does it get the things produced which will yield the maximum satisfaction and by the methods which entail the least sacrifice? Or does it lead to the use of wasteful methods of production and the expenditure of much labor upon making things which yield little or no satisfaction? Does it get goods distributed fairly? Do those who deserve rewards get them and others get none? Is it a satisfactory method of regulating consumption? What habits of consumption does it encourage, and what does it discourage?

III. The Nature of Production

Economists at one time believed that men who added to our stock of visible, material things — farmers, miners, manufacturers, fishermen — were productive but that those who simply rendered intangible services — merchants, transporters, warehousemen, lawyers, actors, policemen, engineers, servants — were not. These distinctions, however, have long been abandoned. For it is obvious that the essential thing in which we are interested is having our desires satisfied and it is equally plain that the suppliers of intangible services satisfy our desires no less than the makers of concrete articles. For example, our ability to use goods depends not only upon the characteristics of the goods themselves but upon their being available for use at the time and place desired. Hence the railroad which brings coal from the mine to the city and the merchant who holds it until the consumer needs it are no less productive than the miners who dig it from the earth. And it is clearly ridiculous to regard the men who make the instruments with which the surgeon operates as productive, but not the surgeon who performs the operation; or the workmen who build theatres, but not the actors who play in them. The essential thing is whether something is being done which directly or indirectly contributes to the satisfaction of human desires. Any activity which produces this effect is productive regardless of whether it results in the creation of material things or in the creation of intangible services.

The man in the street is in the habit of regarding production as something which is inherently and essentially desirable. He distinguishes more or less unconsciously between production and predation. But it is clear that if we define production as any activity which directly or indirectly satisfies human desires, we cannot regard it as desirable in itself. Men may be employed to slug, kill, steal, bear false witness, adulterate goods, ruin a competitor's business, fight much needed legislation, discover how laws can be circumvented with impunity, falsify or color the news. In each case some one's desires are being satisfied no less than when a physician is employed to heal or an artisan to build. Evidently production and predation are not mutually exclusive categories — many activities are both. One of the outstanding economic problems of the day is how to establish a closer relationship between those things which are profitable to do and those which are socially desirable and how to diminish the number of activities which are detrimental to the community but profitable to individuals.

Nature provides a few things, such as fruits, nuts, and honey, but in most parts of the world it does not provide them in large quantities unless stimulated by man. And even in the tropics where nature is most prodigal, its gifts must be gathered and that involves human effort. Human effort employed in production is known by economists as *labor*. Labor, according to the economist's usage, includes the services of all workers from the highest executive to the common laborer.

Of the various tools, instruments, and materials which man uses in production, it is convenient to distinguish those which are furnished immediately by nature and those which, in part at least, are man-made. The contributions of nature consist of sunshine, rainfall, air, land in its natural state (including the metals, minerals, oil, gas, and rock), the animals, fish, and birds in their natural state, virgin timber, and water power — in short, everything which nature, unaided by man, provides. The contributions of nature to the productive process may be grouped under the general head of *natural resources* or *natural capital*.

Man-made and material instruments of production — tools, machines, boats, equipment, buildings, bridges, dams, fences, levees, canals, technological books, and raw materials upon which human labor has been expended — constitute a third factor of production. They are known as *artificial capital*. Many things are partly natural resource and partly artificial capital. This is true of cultivated land, because, though nature made it, man has cleared it, fertilized it, and often drained and graded it.

For these three groups of productive factors to function effectively, they must be brought together into proper relationship. Men who are to produce lumber, steel, wheat, or what not must be brought into touch with the proper natural resources, furnished with the proper tools and equipment. The manner in which the necessary relations are established between these various factors of production is determined by our *economic organization,* which, therefore, must itself be regarded as a factor of production. The economic organization consists of a vast variety of practices, customs, organizations, and legal rights — such things as property rights, the partnership, the corporation, the trade association, trade unions, franchises, patents, credit instruments, the numerous rules, legal and extra-legal, regulating the process of making a living.

IV. Cost of Production

All goods which men produce cost something to make. There are two principal conceptions of cost: human cost and money outlay. Human costs and money costs are often in conflict — that is, low money costs are frequently achieved only by incurring high human costs and low human costs are often made possible only by high money costs. This conflict between money and human costs lies at the bottom of many economic problems and we shall have frequent occasion to refer to it.

Human costs fall into two general classes: those connected with labor and those connected with waiting. The former class includes fatigue; exposure to heat, cold, dust, noxious fumes and gases, disagreeable odors, and unwelcome discipline; and the loss of life, health, and limb which are incident to producing goods. Waiting is a cost because men as a rule prefer to have things now rather than later. Yet all production takes time and this means that men must wait to get their desires satisfied. Frequently we are compelled to choose between the sacrifice involved in working harder and that represented by waiting longer. Shall we work faster and get a good finished sooner or shall we labor less intensely and wait longer for the completed article? Often the quality of goods depends upon the time consumed in their production. For not only does careful and painstaking labor require more time but the product may need aging to reach the best quality, as in the case of cheese, beer, meat, wine, tobacco, wood used for violins and pianos. Hence we must choose between less waiting and poorer quality or more waiting and better quality.

Economists and business men differ somewhat in their conceptions of pecuniary costs. They agree in regarding as costs all forms of money outlay which an enterprise incurs in producing an article — such as wages, salaries, commissions, raw material, rent, taxes, advertising, insurance, postage, telephone, telegraph, power, heat, light, water, office supplies, freight, express, cartage, royalties to owners of patents, interest on borrowed funds, and allowances for depreciation, cancellations, and bad debts. But in addition to all these items, the economist also includes the profit necessary to induce business men to make the good in a given quantity over a long period of time. The business man, however, does not regard profits as part of his costs. The reason for this difference is that business men and economists look at costs from different points of view. The business man, who is constantly facing the problem of how much he must charge in order to make a profit, regards costs as the payments which must be made *by* him to others and the allowances which he must make for bad debts and depreciation. The economist, taking the standpoint of the community, conceives of cost as the amount which must be paid *to* business men in order to get a certain output.

Pecuniary costs fall into two general classes — those which fluctuate more or less directly with the volume of output and those which, despite small variations in production, remain relatively fixed. The former are known as *direct, prime,* or *variable* costs; the latter as *indirect, fixed, supplementary,* or *overhead* costs. It is obvious that the raw material actually entering into an article and the labor directly expended upon its fabrication tend to vary closely with the number of units produced. These two expenses are the principal variable costs.[1] Most expenses, however, are little affected by small changes in the volume of output. No expenses, of course, are *absolutely* fixed. But a *small* increase in production, for example, would not require that more executives or janitors be hired, a larger building be constructed or rented, or more light or heat be purchased. The distinction between fixed and variable costs is of great importance in explaining economic phenomena, and we shall refer to it frequently.

Depreciation is an item of pecuniary cost which warrants some explanation. Suppose that a manufacturer pays $10,000 for a machine which is expected to last for ten years. At the end of that time, it either will be worn out or will have been rendered obsolete by the invention of better machines. At any rate, it will be worth only its scrap value, which we shall assume to be negligible. Obviously the cost of the machine is part of the cost of the goods which it produces, and, unless the manu-

---

[1] The right to use a patented process may sometimes be paid for on the basis of so much per unit of output. In this case it becomes a variable cost. There is much to be said for classifying losses from cancellations and bad debts as variable expenses.

facturer gets back within ten years the $10,000 which he paid for the machine, he will lose. In selling his goods, therefore, he must collect enough, over and above all other costs, to yield him $10,-000 in ten years. If we disregard the possibility of realizing compound interest, this would be $1,000 a year. We call this charge *depreciation*. It goes on whether the machine is running or not.

An important characteristic of depreciation is its uncertainty. The manufacturer cannot know *precisely* how long the machine will last before it wears out or becomes obsolete. The best that he can do is to make a guess based upon past experience. If he guesses that the machine will last longer than it actually does, he of course underestimates the amount which he should allow each year for depreciation.

V. Some Accounting Concepts, Terms, and Devices

In analyzing the operation of industry, it is helpful to be familiar with the principal devices by which the financial condition of enterprises is indicated. There are two devices which are of fundamental importance — the *balance sheet* and the *income statement*.

An obvious way of throwing light on the financial condition of an enterprise is to draw up a list of its assets and a list of its debts and other obligations. This is essentially what a *balance sheet* is. It consists of two columns — one showing the assets of the enterprise, with the value of each, and the other enumerating its liabilities — that is, the claims against the assets. Below is the balance sheet of an imaginary corporation:

Assets

Fixed assets	
Real estate and plant	$1,000,000
Machinery and equipment	400,000
Patents	10,000
Current assets	
Cash	60,000
Marketable securities (at cost or market price, whichever is lower)	100,000
Raw material (at cost or market price, whichever is lower)	125,000
Finished product	50,000
Accounts receivable	175,000
Notes and bills receivable	60,000
Total assets	$1,980,000

Liabilities

Claims of creditors
  Fixed liabilities
    Bonded indebtedness $500,000
  Current liabilities
    Accounts payable   115,000
    Notes and bills payable   70,000
Claims of owners
    Capital stock   1,000,000
    Surplus   210,000
    Undivided profits   85,000
Total liabilities $1,980,000

It will be noticed that the assets do not consist only of physical property, such as land, buildings, machinery, raw material, finished product, and cash. They include also non-physical forms of property. For example, the corporation owns $100,000 of securities (stocks or bonds) in other corporations and it has patent rights which it values at $10,000. It is also owed money by its customers who have bought goods but have not yet paid for them. These legal claims against its customers are, of course, part of its assets. They are represented in the balance sheet by the two items " accounts receivable " and " bills and notes receivable." To some customers the corporation is willing to sell without requiring special documents to give evidence of the buyer's obligation to pay. Such debts are listed in the balance sheet as " accounts receivable." But in some cases the corporation is unwilling to sell goods on credit unless the buyer gives special evidence of his indebtedness. The evidence may take the form of a promissory note or a bill of exchange.[2] Promissory notes and bills of exchange which the corporation holds as evidence of money owed to it appear in the balance sheet as " notes and bills receivable."

It is a characteristic of the balance sheet of a solvent enterprise that it always balances. This may seem surprising. Why should the liabilities of a successful concern always exactly equal its assets? Why should it not be possible for a prosperous enterprise to possess assets greatly in excess of its obligations? Of course, it is possible for enterprises to own more than they owe.

   [2] Definitions of promissory note and bill of exchange and a description of how they are used in extending credit will be found in Chapter XI.

In fact, every successful concern does own more than it owes. It is obvious, however, that any excess of resources over the claims of the creditors belongs to the owners of the enterprise. To the claims of the creditors against the assets of the enterprise, therefore, we must add the claims of the owners who are entitled to any assets which would remain after the claims of the debtors had been satisfied. The relationship is expressed by the equation:

$$\text{assets} - \text{claims of creditors} = \text{claims of owners}$$

This is why the assets of a solvent enterprise and the claims against them — including the claims of the owners — must always balance. In case the claims of the creditors exceed the assets, the business, of course, is insolvent.

In our imaginary balance sheet, the claims of the creditors are represented by the items " bonded indebtedness," " accounts payable," and "notes and bills payable." What do these items mean? The item " bonded indebtedness " means that the enterprise has obtained part of the capital required for its business by the sale of bonds, which are simply promises to pay, made in a certain legal form.[3] " Accounts payable " and " notes and bills payable " are the opposites of " accounts receivable " and " notes and bills receivable." Just as the firm sells goods on credit, so it also buys on credit. When it purchases without giving special evidence of its obligation to pay, the claims of its creditors appear as " accounts payable "; when a promissory note or a bill of exchange is used to evidence the debt, the creditors' claims are called " notes and bills payable."

In the case of unincorporated enterprises, the claims of the owner against the resources are sometimes represented by a single account called "proprietorship," " owner's equity," or " net worth." In the case of corporations, however, the proprietory claims are often indicated by several accounts. The outstanding stock represents, in theory at least, the amount directly invested in the business by the original stockholders. It is included in the balance sheet usually at its par value.[4] If

---

[3] The use of bonds in raising capital will be explained in Chapter VIII.

[4] When stock is issued by corporations, it is customary for each share to have a " face " or " par " value. The actual value of the stock in the market, of course, may be above or below its par value. The law forbids corporations from issuing stock for less than par. It has not proved possible, however, to enforce this rule, because stock can be issued in return for services or property other than cash. These

the enterprise has been profitable, some of the profits may have been reinvested in the business. When this has been done, it is often indicated by a special account known as " surplus." [5] Finally, there are profits which have been earned but which have been neither reinvested in the business nor distributed to the proprietors. They are usually shown by an account called " undivided profits."

It will be noticed that the claims of the creditors and the assets are divided into two classes — fixed and current. This distinction is of great importance. Fixed assets consist of the permanent equipment of the business, such as land, buildings, and machinery, which cannot be readily converted into cash or which could not be sold without interfering with the ability of the business to continue operation. Current assets, on the other hand, include the resources which are available on short notice for the payment of debts. Besides cash, they include readily marketable securities, raw materials, and finished product. Because accounts receivable and notes and bills receivable as a rule represent debts which will be paid in the near future, they are usually, though not always, current assets. Fixed liabilities are claims which run for a considerable period before they must be paid; current liabilities are those which must be met a short time after they have been incurred. Ordinarily the period of one year is used to distinguish between fixed and current liabilities. Bonds and long-term promissory notes are, of course, fixed liabilities; accounts payable and notes and bills payable are usually current liabilities.

---

can be valued arbitrarily at the par value of the stock given for them. Thus there is ostensible compliance with the rule that a dollar of value must be received for every dollar of stock issued.

If the stock is included in the balance sheet at par when it actually was sold for assets that are worth less than this amount, how can the balance sheet be balanced? If the claims are inflated, evidently the assets must be inflated also in order to bring the two into equality. There are several ways of inflating the statement of assets. Property acquired in exchange for stock may be listed at the par value of shares given for it even when this far exceeded its worth in the market at the time of purchase. Such items as " patent rights " and " good will," which at best have a more or less indeterminate worth, offer convenient opportunities for inflating the value of the assets.

[5] The surplus account, however, does not invariably represent the entire amount of reinvested profits, for stock is sometimes issued to represent reinvested earnings. In such cases, outstanding stock stands for both original investment and reinvested earnings and the surplus account only for the portion of reinvested profits against which stock has not been issued.

It was said that the distinction between fixed and current assets and liabilities is of great importance. The reason is that it throws light upon the ability of an enterprise to meet its current obligations. When an enterprise seeks a loan from a bank, one of the first things that the banker wishes to know is the ratio of its current liabilities to its current assets. Unless the current assets substantially exceed the current liabilities, the banker will probably refuse the loan. The total resources of the concern may greatly exceed its total indebtedness, but unless its current assets are substantially larger than its current liabilities, it may get into trouble because of inability to pay cash when cash is due.

But the balance sheet is not an entirely adequate indicator of the financial condition of an enterprise. In the case of our imaginary firm, for example, the value of the assets is $1,980,000 and the claims of creditors are $685,000. Apparently the worth of the enterprise to its owners is $1,295,000. As the amount of stock outstanding is $1,000,000, the value of each $100 share, according to the balance sheet, is $129.50. And yet the stock may actually sell for substantially above or below $129.50. Why is the value of a stock as reported by the balance sheet — called the book value of the stock — often far different from the price which prevails in the market?

There are two principal reasons. One is that the balance sheet does not necessarily report the present worth of property. The usual practice is to report either the present market value or the price originally paid for it — whichever is lower. Thus a piece of real estate which is now worth $100,000 may be listed in the balance sheet at $50,000 because it cost only $50,000. In this case, of course, the balance sheet understates both the value of the assets and the worth of the business to its owners.[6]

[6] Below are listed the market values and the book values of the stocks of some leading companies on December 31, 1925. Union Trust Company, Cleveland, Ohio, *Trade Winds*, November, 1925, p. 19.

	Book value	Market value
F. W. Woolworth and Company	$ 34	$213
Eastman Kodak Company	46	111
General Motors	69	117
General Electric	91	328
Beech-nut Packing Company	30	68
May Company	58	136
Sears Roebuck	111	236
Timken Roller Bearing	22	54
R. H. Macy and Company	51	103

In making use of balance sheets, therefore, one should ascertain how the values given for the assets compare with their real values.

The second reason why the value of a stock as reported by the balance sheet often differs from the market price is found in the fact that the value of an enterprise to its owners is affected by its present and prospective net income as well as by the excess of its assets over the claims of its creditors.[7] The assets of an enterprise may greatly exceed the claims of the creditors because the concern was highly profitable in years gone by and these past profits may have been invested in the business. But the enterprise may not be making money today. Or the converse may be true — even though the assets of an enterprise exceed the claims of its creditors by only a small amount, its net earnings may be large. Likewise the net income of a business may change greatly without affecting the difference between the value of its assets and the claims of its creditors. An exceptionally efficient management, for example, may substantially increase the profits of a firm without affecting either the value of the assets or the claims of the creditors. A similar result may be produced by other causes — tariff legislation favorable to the enterprise, the formation of a monopoly, a general rise in prices. On the other hand, an inefficient management, the development of cutthroat competition, or a sudden drop in prices may cause net income to drop rapidly even though the proprietary interest, as shown by the balance sheet, is little changed in value.

Because the value of an enterprise depends upon its net income as well as upon the excess of assets over indebtedness, the balance sheet needs to be supplemented by the *income statement.* This reports the income and expenses of an enterprise *over a*

---

[7] It might seem that the present and prospective income of an enterprise would be the *sole* determinants of the value of the stock. But it is obvious that an enterprise which has little income and little prospects for an increase in income may have assets which make its stock of great value. The profits of a street railway may be almost completely destroyed by automobile competition and there may be little likelihood that the street railway will ever earn large profits. But expansion of the business district of the city may cause the car barn sites of the company to have high value for office building purposes. The great value of the company's real estate may give its stock a value that is high in proportion to present or prospective earnings from street railway operations.

period of time. Below is an imaginary income statement, show-ing the sources of income and expense and the disposition made of the net income.

Income from sales [8]		$1,230,000
Operating expenses	$970,000	
Earnings after operating expenses		260,000
Depreciation	100,000	
Interest on bonds	20,000	
Taxes	30,000	
Net earnings		110,000
Non-operating income		20,000
Total net income		130,000
Dividends paid	70,000	
Added to surplus		60,000

In drawing up an income statement, it is extremely important not to confuse *current* and *capital* gains and current and capital outlays. Not all of the receipts of an enterprise are part of its current income. Current income is that which is the result of ordinary, current operations; capital gains are those which are attributable to relatively long periods. Suppose, for example, that an enterprise on moving to new and larger quarters sells its former place of business at a substantial advance over the pur-chase price. A profit has evidently been realized, but clearly it is not properly attributable to the operations of the year in which the sale occurred. To include it in current profits would seri-ously exaggerate the prosperity of the enterprise.

Just as it is important to distinguish accurately between capi-tal gains and current income, so also it is equally important to distinguish accurately between expenditures which represent cur-rent operating expenses and those which represent investments. For if expenditures which really represent investments are counted as operating expenses, the profits of the firm are under-stated and it is made to appear less prosperous than it actually is. On the other hand, if operating expenses are classified as capital expenditures, the profits of the enterprise are overstated. Assume that a manufacturer purchases two hundred tons of coal,

---

[8] Most enterprises are anxious to conceal the fluctuations in their sales and operat-ing expenses. Consequently the items "income from sales" and "operating ex-penses" are omitted from most income statements which are intended for publication. Such statements usually begin with the item "earnings after operating expenses." Sometimes even the allowance for depreciation is not reported separately.

a safe, and a drill press. The coal will be consumed in the course of current operations; it is, therefore, a current expense. But the safe and the drill press will last for many years. At the end of the current earning period, they will be assets in the possession of the enterprise. The expenditure for the safe and drill press, therefore, is an investment. Of course, it is also true that the outlay for the safe and drill press is part of the cost of making goods and must, therefore, sooner or later find its way into the costs of the enterprise. But since the safe and drill press are expected to last for some years, their cost should be distributed over the period of their expected life. This is done through the device of the deduction for depreciation — which has already been explained. The original outlay for the safe and drill press is classified as an investment rather than as an expense but a portion of this outlay is included in the expenses for each year in the form of a depreciation charge. The depreciation charge, therefore, simply represents the portion of the total outlay which it seems reasonable to charge against the business done during that year.

The income statement should throw light upon the operating efficiency of the management. Current income does not necessarily all come from operations — for example, our imaginary corporation owned $400,000 of securities from which it presumably derived some return. Likewise some current expenses, such as depreciation, interest on indebtedness, and taxes, are not immediately determined by operations. In order that the income statement may throw light upon operating efficiency, it is desirable that it show separately the operating and non-operating income and operating and non-operating expenses. This, it will be noticed, is done in our imaginary income statement.

REFERENCES

Carver, T. N., *Essays in Social Justice*, 1915. Ch. II.
Clark, J. M., *The Economics of Overhead Costs*, 1923. Ch. III.
Hobson, John A., *Work and Wealth: A Human Valuation*, 1914. Ch. V, VI, VII, and VIII.
Goldmark, Josephine, *Fatigue and Efficiency*, 1912.
Lincoln, E. E., *Applied Business Finance*, 1923. Ch. XIII.
Reed, H. L., *Corporation Finance*, 1925. Ch. XV, XVI, XVII, and XIX.
Saliers, E. A., *Financial Statements Made Plain*, 1919.

PART II

SOME BASIC CHARACTERISTICS OF
THE EXISTING ECONOMIC ORDER

CHAPTER III

FREE PRIVATE ENTERPRISE

I. POSSIBLE FORMS OF ECONOMIC ORGANIZATION. II. HOW FREE
ENTERPRISE ORGANIZES PRODUCTION. III. HOW SHARES IN THE
OUTPUT OF INDUSTRY ARE DETERMINED. IV. HOW CONSUMPTION
IS REGULATED UNDER FREE ENTERPRISE. V. SOME CLAIMS ON
BEHALF OF FREE ENTERPRISE. VI. SOME ASSUMPTIONS OF THE
THEORY OF FREE ENTERPRISE. VII. THE SIGNIFICANCE OF COM-
PETITION. VIII. SOME ISSUES RAISED BY FREE ENTERPRISE. IX.
THE EXTENT TO WHICH GOVERNMENTS INTERFERE TODAY. X.
CAN FREE ENTERPRISE BE RETAINED?

I. POSSIBLE FORMS OF ECONOMIC ORGANIZATION

We have seen that every economic system must provide some
way of doing three fundamental things: (1) getting goods produced; (2) determining what share each person shall have in the
total product; and (3) regulating the consumption of goods, that
is, determining who shall consume this good and who that. The
manner in which these three basic economic processes are performed stamps the economic system with its most essential characteristics. How does the existing economic order organize and
regulate the production, distribution, and consumption of goods?

There are several ways in which these activities *might* be
organized and regulated:

1. On the basis of family autonomy. Each family might
produce everything which it uses, relying upon others for nothing. In such a society there would be no trade.

2. On a communistic basis. What is produced and what
each person does might be determined by the group as a whole
and the product might be the property of the group, to be divided in accordance with socially determined rules.

3. On a despotic basis. The things produced and the tasks
of each person might be decided by a despot or a despotic class,

the product in all or in part being the property of the despot to be shared with the others as he saw fit.

4. On the basis of custom and heredity. Instead of choosing his own work or having it selected for him by the group or a despot, each person might be born into his occupation. He might be expected to do the thing which his father did, and other occupations might be closed to him. Likewise the share of each person in the product and the things which he is permitted or forbidden to consume might also be determined by custom.

All of these methods of organizing and controlling economic activities have been more or less prevalent in the past and, indeed, instances of them still exist. They are not, however, the methods which prevail today in the United States. It may seem a strange way of doing, but we organize industry by, in effect, saying to each individual, " Choose your own occupation. Produce what you like. What you do, to whom you sell, what or from whom you buy, the prices you get or give, are all your own concern. You are free, subject to a few restrictions, to produce whatever you wish regardless of whether or not it is needed, regardless of whether or not too much of it already exists. You are likewise free to refrain from engaging in any occupation no matter how acute may be the shortage of goods or how pressing the need for your help. You are free to buy from whoever is willing to sell and to sell to whoever is willing to buy. You are equally free to refuse to buy or sell whenever you please and for any reason or no reason."

This is what we mean by *free private enterprise.* Under it the government confines itself in the main to the suppression of fraud and violence and to the enforcement of contracts. It does not itself engage in or attempt to guide the course of industry. It pursues a " let alone " or " hands off " policy. Let us now see how, under free enterprise, the three fundamental economic processes of production, distribution, and consumption take place.

II. How Free Enterprise Organizes Production

Why does not a system of freedom, in which each person is at liberty to pursue whatever occupation he pleases and to produce whatever he wishes, result in hopeless chaos? Why do not many essential articles fail to get made and why does not the output of many things far exceed the demand for them? How can we get along without a central directing body to discover how much different things are in demand and to tell each of us what to produce?

To put the problem concretely and specifically, how does New York City each day obtain about the quantity of milk that it demands? The city's daily consumption in 1922 was approximately 2,000,000 quarts. This was supplied by 450,000 cows and came from 1,150 creameries and 40,000 farms in New York, New Jersey, Connecticut, Massachusetts, Pennsylvania, New Hampshire, and Canada. Of the thousands of people engaged in supplying New York with milk, almost none knows either how much the city consumes or how much is being produced. And yet, despite this ignorance, New York each day receives about the amount of milk that it demands. There is neither a great surplus nor a shortage. Milk does not spoil because there is no one to consume it, and babies do not go without it because too small a supply reaches the city on some days. At the same time, other cities in the neighborhood are also receiving their daily supply from the same territory. Each uses a different quantity, yet each receives about the amount that it demands.

This comparatively simple case illustrates our problem. What determines the relative quantities of each and everything produced — how much cotton, corn, oats, wheat, or oranges we raise, how much steel, lumber, coal, or cloth we produce? What tells us when to make more and when less of each commodity?

The guide upon which we rely is the profit in making different goods, which, of course, depends upon the prices which they command and the cost of producing them. Suppose, for example, that New York failed to receive enough milk to satisfy the demand. Rather than go without milk or drink less, many people would be willing to pay more. Consequently the price would promptly rise. This would tend to end the shortage. More milk would be shipped to New York and less to other places. This would continue until there was no greater profit in selling milk in New York than elsewhere.

Just as price regulates the distribution of milk between cities, so it also determines the total amount produced in the country as a whole. Failure of the supply to keep pace with the demand would cause the price to rise. The greater profit to be had from the sale of milk would cause farmers to produce more of it. Some farmers, who had been separating their milk and selling the cream to be made into butter, might turn to the sale of whole milk. Others might abandon raising grain, stock, or fruit and enter dairy farming. As the output of milk increased, the price, of course, would drop. This would continue until producing milk was no more attractive than alternative branches of farming. If, furthermore, the demand for milk were to fall off or the supply to increase faster than the demand, farmers, in order to dispose of their supply, would be compelled to lower the price. Milk production would become a less profitable occupation, men would be deterred from entering it, and some of those already engaged in it might be led to abandon it or at least to reduce their output. And this would continue until the price rose and milk production became no less attractive than alternative occupations.

Innumerable illustrations could be given of the guidance of production by prices. A striking instance is supplied by the effect of changes in the price of wheat upon wheat acreage. During the fifteen years immediately preceding the war, the acreage planted to wheat in the United States remained substantially stationary. The European war caused the price of wheat to rise rapidly. On December 1, 1914, the average farm price in the United States was 98.6 cents a bushel, the highest in over forty years. In consequence, the area planted increased from 53,541,-000 acres in 1914 to 60,169,000 in 1915, the largest in the history of the country. The weather in 1915 was so favorable that the yield per acre was the largest on record. The result of the record-breaking acreage and the record-breaking yield was a crop of over a billion bushels — the first in the country's history — and a drop in the average farm price by December 1, 1915, to 91.9 cents, causing the acreage for 1916 to decline to 52,316,000. But in 1916 the weather was so unfavorable that the yield per acre was the lowest since 1900. The small crop led to a pronounced advance in price. On December 1, 1916, the farm value was $1.60 per bushel.[1] In August, 1917, after the United States had entered the war, Congress passed the wheat guarantee bill. The President fixed the price for the 1917 crop at $2.20 for No. 1 spring wheat or its equivalent. Stimulated by the high guarantee, acreage increased in 1918 to 59,181,000 and in 1919 to 75,694,000, an unprecedented amount. In 1920, the guarantee expired and a general business depression set in. The result was a rapid fall in both price and acreage. The average farm value, which was $2.15 on December 1, 1919, was $1.44 a year later, and the acreage for 1920 was 61,143,000, or over fourteen and a half millions less than in the previous year.

Price also determines in large measure where and how goods are made. Because living in New York City is expensive, it might seem a poor place in which to locate a factory. But the great stream of immigrants who for many years entered the country at New York and who were reluctant to undertake a long journey through a strange country provided the city with a bountiful supply of cheap labor. To take advantage of this, many industries, such as the needle trades, grew up in or near the East Side. At one time, the Genesee valley in western New York was an important wheat region and Rochester, at the falls of the Genesee, was a great milling center. As the urban population in the East has grown, the greater profits in dairying and in fruit and truck raising have driven wheat raising to the west. The same is true of sheep raising. At one time, New York State contained nearly 5,000,000 sheep; now it has less than one-tenth that number. The growth of urban population has made dairying so profitable that most farmers cannot afford to raise sheep in New York.

Whether goods shall be made by hand or by machinery is often a question of money costs. Shall houses be built of wood or brick? As long as our immense forests were far from exhaustion, wooden houses were the almost universal rule. In Europe, where timber is less plentiful, frame dwellings are the exception. We still use timber to a greater extent than do most countries, but the cost of certain woods, such as white pine, has caused us to use cheaper varieties — Norway pine, hemlock, spruce, Douglas fir.

---

[1] The rise in price, however, was in part due to the rapid rise in the general price level which occurred during 1916.

Shall land be farmed intensively or extensively? The English obtain about twice as many bushels of wheat per acre as do the Americans, but we obtain about twice as many bushels per man. The reason is that in England, where land is relatively expensive, it is economized by the use of more labor and less land. Here, where labor is expensive in comparison with land, labor is economized by the use of more land and less labor.

III. How Shares in the Output of Industry Are Determined

In our highly specialized society, each of us, at the best, contributes to industry's output very few things. One man may produce wheat, another wool, another milk, another cattle, another corn. In fact, most men do not contribute even one complete product. Hundreds of workers combine their efforts to make a suit of clothes, a pair of shoes, an automobile, or a telephone.

Although each individual makes a very specialized contribution to the product of society, each wishes to obtain from that output hundreds of articles. The man who produces only wheat desires flour, butter, sugar, clothing, shoes, hats, magazines, furniture, services of doctors, dentists, lawyers, and much else. If he contributes 2,000 bushels of wheat to society's stock of goods, how much is he entitled to withdraw?

Just as prices determine what things are produced, in what proportions, and by what methods, so, under free enterprise, they also determine the share of each person in the output of industry. If our imaginary wheat grower, who has produced a crop of 2,000 bushels, obtains $1.25 for each bushel, he is thereby enabled to purchase articles valued at $2,500. Just how much this is, will depend upon the price of shoes, hats, sugar, and the various other things which he desires. The next year he may work harder and produce 2,400 bushels. In the meantime, however, the price of wheat may drop to 75 cents a bushel. Hence, despite the fact that he has worked harder and raised more wheat, he has only $1,800 to spend for goods. And if, perchance, prices in general have risen, each of his dollars will buy him less than the year before. In a word, what share a man receives in the product of industry is determined by the prices of what he has to sell quite as much as by how industriously and efficiently he labors.

IV. How Consumption Is Regulated under Free Enterprise

There are many ways in which we might determine what goods each person shall consume. We might undertake to ascertain the peculiar needs of each and see that he was afforded some special opportunity to obtain the things which would satisfy them. Or we might study the ability of different persons to use goods to the advantage of the rest of us and arrange for men of outstanding ability to receive the things which they require in order to be of greatest service to the community.

To a limited extent, we do regulate consumption upon the basis of either needs or ability to use goods advantageously. Schooling is considered so important that many governments supply a certain amount of it free or below cost. Police and fire protection, parks, playgrounds, and, to some extent, transportation, communication, and insurance are also considered so essential that they are provided by the government. Fellowships and scholarships, awarded to students of special promise, are among the few attempts which we make to place goods within reach of those who can use them to special advantage.

Under a system of free enterprise, however, which permits men to buy whatever they can get on the best terms that they can obtain, neither need nor ability to use goods for the benefit of others necessarily has much to do with determining how goods are consumed. Of far greater importance are the prices of different commodities and the ability of different persons to pay these prices. Goods go to those who are able and willing to pay the most for them — not to those who have the greatest need for them or who will do the greatest good with them.

In some respects, the control of consumption by price and ability to pay works out very satisfactorily. Suppose, for example, that unfavorable weather or blight made it likely that the potato crop would be exceptionally small. It is obvious that we should need to consume potatoes sparingly, making more than customary use of substitutes. If, on the other hand, the outlook were for a large crop, it would be to our interest to use more potatoes than usual. In each case, price produces the desired effect. If the prospects are for a small crop, the higher price induces spar-

ing consumption; if a large crop seems probable, the low price encourages larger consumption. Because skilled labor is scarce, it
is desirable that we economize it by using its products sparingly.
The high wages of skilled craftsmen make their products expensive and encourage consumers to avoid wasting them. Commodities which can be made only at great risk of accident or industrial disease should also be used sparingly. In so far as these
hazards cause workmen to demand higher wages, they increase
the price of the products and limit their consumption.[2]

Although the regulation of consumption by prices usually encourages the economizing of scarce goods, it does so in a manner
not altogether satisfactory. If consumption must be reduced,
this should perhaps be accomplished by those using less who can
do so with the smallest inconvenience and sacrifice. As a matter
of fact, the well-to-do, who are best supplied, are least induced
by higher prices to curtail their purchases. It is the poor, who
can least afford to reduce their consumption, who get along with
less when the supply falls short. In periods of severe food shortage, such as often occur during war time, the regulation of consumption by ability to pay works such hardship that it is sometimes superseded by a system of rationing.

V. Some Claims on Behalf of Free Enterprise

Since free enterprise is the principal method by which our
economic activities are organized and controlled, our study of
modern industrial society must very largely consist of an inquiry
into how freedom works under present-day conditions — such as
machine industry, huge corporations, and science applied to business. But before we proceed further with our analysis, it will
be helpful to become familiar in a general way with some of the
claims which have been made in behalf of free enterprise. The
" obvious and simple system of natural liberty," as Adam Smith
called freedom of enterprise,[3] has been regarded as the one and

---

[2] But price does not invariably encourage the use of cheap and discourage the use
of expensive things. When a good is purchased for display, the very fact that it is
dear causes it to be desired. Were it to become cheap, the demand would fall off. Diamonds, for example, are in demand because, being costly, they are a means of display-
ing wealth. Were they to become plentiful and cheap, they would be less desired.
For this reason, the monopoly which controls the South African mines carefully
limits the output.

[3] *Wealth of Nations*, Bk. IV, Ch. IX.

only way in which men might attain the maximum satisfaction of
their desires with a minimum outlay of sacrifice. It is true that
this extreme view has been accepted by few economists of repute
and that since the middle of the last century it has been increasingly under attack. Nevertheless it has had and still does have
wide acceptance by the general public and by certain schools of
politicians, and it is appealed to frequently in political controversies. And even though we no longer spend much time discussing
whether or not we can *always* trust free enterprise to regulate
economic activity better than any other method, we are frequently
compelled to decide whether or not it is the best way of controlling a specific economic activity under specific circumstances.
Consequently the claims which have been made on its behalf are
still very live issues.

The reasoning in support of the belief that freedom of enterprise results in the maximum of satisfaction at the minimum of
cost is very simple. Each individual, it is said, is better able
than any one else to judge his own interests. If men are at liberty
to spend their money as they choose, they will naturally purchase those things that will yield them the most satisfaction.
Consequently the very commodities which give consumers the
greatest pleasure are the most profitable for business enterprises to produce. Likewise, if men are free to use such methods of production as they wish, they will select those which involve the least cost per unit of output. With the goods which
give the greatest gratification being made by the methods
which are least costly, it follows, according to the theory,
that there will be the maximum surplus of satisfaction over
sacrifice.[4]

VI. Some Assumptions of the Theory of Free Enterprise

But if this result is to follow, two things would appear to be
necessary: (1) goods must go to the consumers who will derive
the greatest pleasure from them, and (2) the tasks of making
goods must be assigned to the workers who can perform them
with the least sacrifice for each unit of product. Does freedom

---

[4] But it is not true that the largest net *individual* satisfactions add up to make the
largest possible *total* satisfaction, for one man's pleasure may be achieved at the
cost of another man's pain.

of enterprise cause either goods or jobs to be distributed in this manner?

We have already seen that under a system of free enterprise goods tend to get into the hands of those who offer the best prices for them. But how then can they be consumed so as to yield the maximum of satisfaction? Are the people who are willing and able to pay most for goods also those who will derive the most satisfaction from using them? If they are not, it would appear possible to increase the surplus of satisfaction over sacrifice by causing goods to be distributed more in accordance with needs and less in accordance with ability to pay. We have no way of comparing the amount of pleasure which two persons derive from consuming an article. And yet it seems ridiculous to assert that ability to derive satisfaction from goods is proportionate to ability to pay for them. Assume that A and B each wish a pair of shoes. A, who is well-to-do, is willing to pay $12; B, who is poor, will offer only $7. Obviously A will get the shoes. But because he is rich and well supplied with shoes, an additional pair is only a slight convenience to him. B, poor and scantily supplied, has urgent need for another pair. It seems clear that the sum total of satisfaction would be greater if B obtained the shoes, and yet it seems equally clear that under freedom of enterprise they will go to A.

We are no better able to compare the pains suffered by different persons than we are the pleasures which they enjoy. Nevertheless it does not appear probable that freedom of enterprise necessarily causes jobs to be distributed so as to result in a minimum sacrifice for each unit of output — so that, for example, persons who can do heavy work with least fatigue will be given heavy work. Rather jobs tend to go to those who are willing to do the most work for the least money. Now the fact that X is willing to do a job for a dollar a day less than Y does not necessarily mean that X finds the task less onerous or unpleasant than Y. It may simply mean that he needs the money more and is willing to work at a lower rate in order to get it.

In face of the fact that ability to derive pleasure from goods does not appear to correspond to capacity to pay for them and that jobs are not necessarily given to the men who can do them with the least sacrifice for each unit of product, how can it be asserted that industrial liberty results in a maximum of satisfaction over sacrifice? But the exponents of free enterprise are not without a reply. To interfere with liberty in order to bring about a distribution of goods upon the basis of needs rather than ability to pay, or in order to cause jobs to be assigned to those who could perform them with least sacrifice, might have the *immediate* effect of increasing the surplus of satisfaction over sacrifice. But this result, it is said, would be short lived. Men have the greatest incentive to improve their efficiency when they are free to compete for any jobs which they desire and to spend their income as they see fit. Were this incentive diminished by distributing jobs to those who could perform them with the least sacrifice and goods to those who would derive the most pleasure from them, output would inevitably decline. What would be gained by a different distribution of goods and jobs would be lost through smaller production.

VII. The Significance of Competition

But how is it possible for us to trust business enterprises with so much freedom? In other branches of human relations, laws to regulate conduct seem to be quite essential. Why should industry be an exception to this general rule? If we leave business concerns free to make anything they like by any methods which they see fit, what is to prevent them from supplying the public with poorly made or adulterated goods or from using methods that are cheap in terms of dollars but expensive in terms of human sacrifice? Might not the sum total of pleasure be greater and of pain be less if the state enforced certain standards of quality or prohibited the use of certain methods of production?

The theory of free enterprise does not, it is important to emphasize, assert that restraints upon human selfishness are not needed. It simply assumes that they are provided by *competition*. This, according to the theory, is the great regulative force which establishes effective control over economic activities and gives each of us an incentive to observe the interests of others. Thus business establishments are deterred from furnishing adulterated or poorly made goods by the fear that customers may shift their patronage to rivals. Likewise the enterprises which fail to protect their men against accidents or industrial disease or which work them unusually hard, are penalized by the refusal of laborers to work for them except at a higher wage than other employers pay.

The mere existence of competition, however, is not enough. For it to perform satisfactorily the protective function attributed to it, certain very definite conditions must be present.

To begin with, an appreciable proportion of buyers and sellers must be willing to discriminate against those sellers or buyers who ignore, and in favor of those who take account of, the welfare of others. Otherwise, of course, no one has an economic incentive to pay attention to the well-being of his fellows. Assume, for example, that an enterprise pollutes a stream by dumping refuse and chemicals into it. From the standpoint of the firm, this may be an economical method of production. But from the standpoint of the community it is an expensive one, because it kills the fish, spoils the stream for bathing, and makes it foul and ill-smelling. But competition will not stop the pollution unless an appreciable number of consumers, wage earners, or investors refuse to deal with the firm which is responsible — that is, unless a substantial number of consumers refuse to buy from it, or wage earners to work for it, or investors to put money into it. But if the enterprise charges no more than its rivals for goods of equal grade, offers equally attractive conditions of employment, and pays as high dividends, who has an interest in discriminating against it? Perhaps the very fact that the enterprise pollutes the stream enables it to offer better terms than its rivals.[5] Or take the case of child labor — another method of production cheap in dollars and cents but expensive in terms of human cost. If the firms which employ children are able, *because of that very fact,* to sell for less or to pay higher wages to adults or higher profits to investors, who is going to discriminate against them? Under these circumstances, does not competition positively encourage the employment of children?

But willingness to discriminate between those who consider

---

[5] During recent years, for example, there has been a rapid increase in by-product coke ovens which discharge phenol and other industrial wastes into the Ohio River and its tributaries, rendering the water unpalatable and unhealthful. Because competition cannot be expected to check the practice, Congress has been asked to authorize the prosecution of concerns dumping phenol or other wastes into navigable streams. Washington *Daily News,* January 16, 1928, p. 10.

the interests of others and those who do not is insufficient. Competition protects consumers against inferior ware only when they know good quality from bad; it protects laborers from unguarded machines only when they know which employers have and which have not guarded their machines. In other words, competition is an efficient protective agency only when buyers or sellers have the information necessary to make intelligent choices. It fails, for example, to protect consumers against milk from tubercular cattle because the ordinary buyer of milk has no way of distinguishing the milk of healthy cows from that of diseased.

The information needed for intelligent choices may be available, and yet many buyers or sellers may be too ignorant, too careless, too neglectful of their own interests to use it. If, for example, workmen show no disposition to shun plants which are notoriously dangerous or unsanitary, what incentive have employers to improve conditions?

Discrimination can have an effect only when those who are its objects realize that it is being practiced. For years, wage earners, by quitting and seeking work elsewhere, have discriminated against employers who gave poor treatment. But all of this produced little effect upon working conditions and labor policies because employers were not aware how many men were quitting. As soon, however, as enterprises began to keep track of the number of resignations, great improvements occurred in the treatment of labor.

Finally, competition works well as a protective force only when there is not great disparity in bargaining power between buyers and sellers. If workmen are so numerous and jobs so scarce that competition among laborers for jobs is more intense than competition among employers for men, conditions of employment are bound to be unsatisfactory. Likewise in boom times, when goods are scarce and deliveries are slow, competition fails to protect consumers against poor ware. In the clothing industry, for example, it is notorious that in busy years the quality of garments goes down.

VIII. Some Issues Raised by Free Enterprise

It would be premature at this stage of our inquiry to undertake an appraisal of free enterprise as a method of organizing and controlling economic activity. But in studying how industrial liberty works under modern conditions, it will be helpful to know some of the principal issues which are raised by the claim that it results in a maximum net satisfaction.

It is, of course, perfectly plain that one might believe that free enterprise does produce a maximum of satisfaction over sacrifice without believing it to be the best method of organizing industry. Possibly the economic system should serve higher ends than gratifying, with the least cost, whatever desires different individuals happen to have. Perhaps certain wants or the wants of certain people should have preference over others, perhaps no labor or materials should be expended to gratify some desires. These possibilities suggest that industrial freedom may not be desirable even if it *does* produce a maximum of pleasure with a minimum of pain. But does it necessarily bring about this result?

The whole theory that industrial liberty results in a maximum net satisfaction rests, it will be recalled, upon the assumption that each individual knows his own interests better than any one else and consequently can make his own decisions better than any one can make them for him. Is this true? May not free enterprise fail to yield the greatest possible satisfaction precisely *because* it results in choices which are molded too much by impulse, habit, prejudice, ignorance, or clever sales talk and too little by reflection, investigation of facts, or comparison of alternative opportunities? Under the system of economic freedom, choices are largely a matter of individual decision. This means that they are usually made in a hurry and by amateurs who have little opportunity to obtain expert advice. This situation may not be inevitable, but it exists. And yet millions of individuals, each attempting to decide for himself about the purchase of scores of articles concerning which he knows little, are an easy prey for ingenious selling and advertising experts. It may be true, as the theory of free enterprise asserts, that each individual knows his own desires better than any one else, but of what good is this if he has time to investigate neither what he is buying nor what he might buy, or if he is prevented by a skillful salesman from reflecting very much as to what he really does wish after all. Hence, when we find the United States spending more for tobacco than for education, the explanation may be, not that we desire tobacco more than education, but simply that the facilities for getting people to buy tobacco are more efficient than those for persuading them to pay for education. A representative body which could employ experts to investigate people's needs and desires and to test products might be able to spend a considerable portion of consumers' money with greater satisfaction to them than they could obtain by spending it themselves.

Perhaps the most striking aspect of the theory of free enterprise is its assertion that intervention of the government in economic activities is unnecessary. The theory, as we have already said, does not deny that restraints on human selfishness are needed. It simply asserts that we can trust competition to provide them. But closer inquiry reveals that the defenders of free enterprise do not trust competition to do all things. However much they trust it to guard the lives and limbs of workmen against dangerous machinery or to protect consumers against injurious foods, they do not rely upon it to enforce contracts or to prevent fraud. But the same reasoning which is used to prove that the government need not intervene on behalf of wage earners and consumers can be employed to show that laws are not required to guard business men against fraud or breach of contractual obligations. Would not a customer who refused to pay his bills soon experience difficulty in getting dealers to sell to him, and would not an enterprise which violated its contracts find other concerns unwilling to deal with it? Is not the aid of the courts in these matters as superfluous as laws to protect workmen against dangerous machines or consumers against adulterated wares?

This inconsistency in the theory of free enterprise is to be explained by its origin. The theory was invented several hundred years ago to justify the demand of business men for release from oppressive legal restrictions. That the makers of the theory should have had greater faith in the capacity of competition to protect workmen against loss of life or limb than in its capacity to protect business men against bad debts is not surprising. When the rights of business were involved, it seemed quite proper for the government to lend the aid of its courts; only when the interests of consumers or wage earners were at stake did competition become a perfect protective instrument and intervention by the government "paternalistic" and "an unwarranted invasion of private rights."

Because the theory of free enterprise assumes that competition is needed to prevent freedom from being abused, it must also assume that competition is a more economical method of production than monopoly. Otherwise the claim that freedom results in the greatest satisfaction and the least sacrifice could not be correct. In many instances, however, it seems reasonably certain that monopoly is more economical than competition. The clearest cases are the so-called "octopus" industries, such as gas, electric light and power, water, railway, and street railway, which must run wire, pipe, or rails close to each consumer in order to deliver the service. It is the cost of duplicating this part of the plant which makes competition in these industries so uneconomical. In the oil industry, the desire of each landowner to obtain as much of the oil as possible causes him to put down an excessive number of wells along the edge of his property, thus diminishing the pressure under which the oil is held, substantially reducing the quantity which can be recovered, and greatly increasing the cost of getting it. Or consider the wastefulness of competition in distributing milk. With only a few customers in each block, a driver must travel many miles to reach several hundred customers. A study of competitive milk distribution in Rochester, New York, indicated that 2,509 miles of travel were necessary to distribute milk which a monopoly could deliver with 300 miles of travel.[6] Competition required 356 men, 380 horses, and 305 wagons; a monopoly, it was estimated, would need 90 men, 80 horses, and 25 horse-drawn trucks. In most other industries, the case against competition is less clear, but undoubtedly there are many in which monopoly would be more economical.

The exponents of economic freedom answer that, even though monopoly is more economical at any given time, it may be less so in the long run. The search for new and cheaper methods of production needs, it is said, the spur of competition. In other words, competition more than makes up for its wastes by stimulating the development of better technique.

Although the theory that government intervention in indus-

[6] Williams, John R., *The World's Work*, February, 1913, v. XXV, p. 456.

try is unnecessary presupposes the existence of competition, the very absence of state interference often results in monopoly. This is not surprising. Indeed, it would be strange if business men, left at liberty to do as they like, should not frequently combine to exploit the public rather than compete to serve the public. Consequently the government may find itself compelled to intervene either to enforce competition or to regulate monopoly. Either policy, of course, is a departure from the principle of free enterprise.

IX. The Extent to which Governments Interfere Today

Although our industrial system is still predominantly one of free enterprise, the steady extension of the government's control over economic activities has been one of the major political trends of the last several generations — comparable in importance with the rise of representative government and the growth of imperialism. Every day it is becoming increasingly true that one of the principal functions of government is the guidance of economic activities.

As a matter of fact, the state has always exercised more control over industry than most men have suspected. The government is in reality guiding the course of industry when it punishes violence and fraud, protects property, and enforces contracts. If enterprise were *perfectly* free, everyone would be at liberty to make a living in *any* way that he saw fit. When the state says, "You shall not make a living by fraud or violence," it is being no less paternalistic than when it forbids men to employ child labor or to sell adulterated food. But notice that the government is doing more than prohibiting certain methods of making a living. It is positively subsidizing other methods. Why not let each person protect his own property and enforce his own contracts? When the state lends the aid of its police and courts to protect property and enforce contracts, it is encouraging men to make a living by accumulating property and entering into contracts.[7] It is sometimes suggested that when the state limits com-

---

[7] This becomes especially clear when it is recalled that the state not only enforces contracts but also prevents interference, even peaceful interference, with opportunities to make contracts. This is what the courts do when they issue injunctions against peaceful picketing in labor disputes.

petition — as when it restricts the hours of labor — it interferes with the survival of the fittest and helps weaklings to subsist. The same objections may be made to the restraints which the government imposes on fraud and violence. Do not such restraints help the less fit — the timid and the weak — to survive in competition with the courageous and the strong? What could be more paternalistic? Is there not danger that such artificial protection to the weak and cowardly will result in racial deterioration?

The efforts of the government to guide the course of industry fall into two principal groups: (1) the imposition of restraints; and (2) the positive encouragement of certain industries or industrial practices.

Of the many restraints which the government imposes upon industry, the most important undoubtedly is the prohibition of slavery. In a system of perfect industrial freedom, everyone would, of course, be free to sell himself as well as his property. But today in the United States men have less control over themselves than over their clothes or real estate. Not only does the state refuse to enforce contracts involving the sale of human beings but it positively forbids the institution of slavery.[8] The purchase and sale of human labor is hedged about with many other restrictions. Most states forbid the employment of children under fourteen years of age in non-agricultural occupations and thirty-six limit to eight hours the working day of children under sixteen employed in factories.[9] Only four states in 1928 placed no restrictions upon the employment of women.[10] Nine states limit the minimum wages which may be paid to women in certain occupations.[11] A few states regulate the working

[8] Property in human beings is by no means completely abolished. The League of Nations Slavery Commission reported that slavery exists in nineteen countries. The two principal centers are Abyssinia and China in each of which it is estimated that there are roughly two million slaves.

[9] Report of Professor Samuel McCune Lindsay to National Child Labor Committee. New York *Times*, December 15, 1929, Section II, p. 20.

[10] Alabama, Florida, Iowa, and West Virginia.

[11] California, Colorado, Massachusetts, North Dakota, Oregon, South Dakota, Utah, Washington, and Wisconsin. Despite the fact that the United States Supreme Court held the minimum wage law of the District of Columbia to be unconstitutional, the present laws in these nine states have not yet been successfully questioned. *Monthly Labor Review*, November, 1929, v. XXIX, pp. 1069–1071. The Colorado law is ineffective because of lack of appropriations.

hours of men in certain occupations, and the Federal government
limits the working hours of certain railroad employees.

There are a multitude of restrictions upon the entrance into
occupations, the buying and selling of goods, and the use of
property. Not everyone who cares to may in most states be a
plumber, barber, physician, pilot, stationary engineer, lawyer,
pharmacist, dentist, or chauffeur. As a rule, it is necessary to obtain a license or to satisfy other legal requirements to practice any
of these occupations.[12] Numerous restrictions surround the sale
of drugs, intoxicants, and firearms. Pure food and drug acts,
meat and milk inspection acts, and " blue sky " laws further limit
the things that may be bought and sold. The state defines the
units of weight and measure and has a corps of inspectors to
check the scales and measures in use.[13] Many prices, such as the
charges for gas and electricity and for telephone, telegraph, railroad, and street railway service are not left to be settled by buyers
and sellers but are fixed by the government. In the Federal Reserve system, as we shall see in later chapters, the government
has created an instrument for regulating, in a general way, interest rates on short-time loans and for even exercising some
control over the general price level.

Especially numerous are the restrictions which the government imposes on the use of property. In order to build a railroad, gas plant, street railway, or electric plant, it is necessary in
most states to obtain from the public service commission a certificate of convenience and necessity certifying that the public is not
being adequately served and that the proposed enterprise is
needed. The man who erects a building must conform to many

---

[12] Massachusetts recently passed a law requiring automobile drivers to carry
accident liability insurance. To obtain an automobile license in Massachusetts, one
must guarantee his liability for damages on account of personal injury or death of
others to the extent of $5,000 in the event that one person is injured or killed and
$10,000 in case two or more persons are injured in a single accident. In the year
1925, some 20,000 people were killed and 1,250,000 injured by automobiles in the
United States. The property loss was approximately $750,000,000. In the vast
majority of cases, the driver who caused the accident was without financial responsibility.

[13] In August, 1924, Mr. George Warner, chief of the Wisconsin department of
weights and measures, reported that the inspections of his department showed that one
out of every three filling-station pumps in the State gave short measure of gasoline.
Wisconsin State Journal, August 16, 1924.

The government also defines the meaning of certain trade terms. For example,
it is culpable to call a metal " sterling " that is not 98.01 per cent fine silver.

rules concerning height, materials, plumbing, lighting, ventilation, exits, fire escapes, stairways, elevators, window space. Factory owners must observe many regulations concerning the guarding of machinery and dangerous equipment. Cities are beginning to prescribe the uses to which different areas may be put and soon it will not be possible in most large places to construct a store, warehouse, factory, or office building wherever one pleases.[14]

But governments do not merely impose restraints upon industry; they also encourage and guide its development. The colossal business enterprises of today have been made possible largely by incorporation statutes which exempt the owners of corporations from unlimited liability for the debts of their enterprises. The tariff is undoubtedly the device which governments have most frequently used to stimulate the development of particular industries. Subsidies and exemption from taxation are often used for the same purpose. Many countries subsidize shipping, the construction of railroads in the West was encouraged by huge land grants, and the development of agriculture was stimulated by the Homestead Act. More recently the government has sought to help agriculture by creating land banks which provide farmers with cheap credit. By establishing the Federal Reserve system, the government has assumed a large part of the responsibility for administering the nation's fund of commercial credit and for determining the credit policies of the banking system; for providing industry with sufficient, but not too abundant, credit. One of the most ambitious attempts of the government to intervene in the direction of industry is represented by the recently created Federal Farm Board. With a working capital of $150,000,000 supplied by Congress, the Board is endeavoring to stabilize the prices of the principal agricultural products. As part of its program, the Board is seeking to make revolutionary changes in the marketing of farm products by establishing a large national coöperative organization to handle each of the major crops.

Not only does the government guide industry by imposing restraints on some practices and encouraging some branches of

---

[14] The first *comprehensive* zoning ordinance was adopted by New York in 1916. So rapidly has the movement grown that within a decade substantially three-fourths of the largest cities had adopted zoning ordinances.

industry and some business methods; the government itself furnishes many goods and services. It provides currency systems, highways, and postal service; it constructs and maintains parks, roads, harbors, and canals; and frequently it operates waterworks, railroads, telegraph and telephone lines, street railways, and gas and electric plants. The municipal enterprises in Great Britain employ about 1,000,000 wage earners.[15] Many governments gather and distribute market information, often in competition with commercial agencies. Education, though partly provided by commercial and philanthropic schools, is in the main furnished by the government. In the United States, the government is the most important single supporter of scientific research.

X. CAN FREE ENTERPRISE BE RETAINED?

The theory of free enterprise grew up during the eighteenth century as an attack upon the oppressive regulation of industry by stupid and despotic governments. Since the time when the theory was invented, industry, as we have seen, has gone through a revolution. Science, now extensively used in all branches of production, was then only beginning to be applied to industry. Machinery, today the dominant technique in many industries, had not yet come into general use. The corporation was an exceptional form of organization which Adam Smith, the foremost of the eighteenth century economists, did not regard as serviceable under most circumstances. The trade union existed but was not important, and the credit system was still in a rudimentary stage. Trade associations, as we know them, did not exist. Quite clearly a method of organizing and controlling industry which might have worked well before the days of machinery, science in industry, corporations, employers' associations, trade unions, and a highly developed credit and banking system, may be far from satisfactory today.

Before we can judge the adaptability of industrial freedom to modern economic conditions, we must become familiar with what these conditions are. Nevertheless there are certain general circumstances which strongly suggest that freedom of enterprise is likely to mean increasing domination of human beings by the

[15] Webb, S. and B., *A Constitution for the Socialist Commonwealth of Great Britain,* p. 11.

economic machine. We have learned, for example, that free enterprise assumes the existence of competition. In many branches of industry, however, competition is non-existent or has become so limited in its effectiveness that it is of little use as a protective agency. Where this is true, some other device — the government, or organizations of consumers or wage earners — must be employed. The technological development of industry indicates that the field within which competition is suppressed or restricted is likely to become steadily broader. Machine methods and large business units are becoming more prevalent. Each of these things, as we shall discover, increases the ratio of fixed expenses to total costs, and this, as we shall also learn, is likely to cause either the limitation or the elimination of competition among business enterprises. Finally, even in those fields where competition still exists, the systematic study of business methods is causing both consumers and workmen to be confronted with expert specialists who are better and better able to manipulate them and outbargain them.

All of these things and others which we shall encounter later suggest that free enterprise may not provide effective control of industry under present day conditions and that new methods must be devised. The pioneers who opened this continent handed down to us a strong faith in the efficacy of unhampered private initiative. It is not easy to abandon the time-honored philosophy of our fathers, but we must face the realities of the day. If we are unwilling to give up machinery, large business units, the corporate form of organization, and the credit system, which appear often to prevent free private enterprise from working satisfactorily, then possibly we must abandon in some degree the economic philosophy of the pioneer and the frontier and develop one fitted to the facts of modern industry. As we have already pointed out, it is precisely because the industrial revolution has rendered traditional methods of organizing and controlling economic activities more or less obsolete that economics is today a particularly important and a particularly interesting study.

It should be observed that abandonment by the government of its hands-off policy toward industry does not inevitably mean a loss of real freedom. The unregulated buying and selling of goods does not necessarily represent a state of freedom. Buying and selling are simply ways in which human interests find expression; they may be good ways of giving expression to some interests and bad ways of giving expression to others. Many human interests, as we have seen, fail to find adequate expression in the market place — for example, the interest of the community in unpolluted streams, or in scenery that is not defaced by bill-boards. Can it be reasonably maintained that the sum total of human freedom is diminished by laws which forbid the polluting of streams or restrict the erection of bill-boards? And even free private enterprise, as we have seen, presupposes that restraints will be imposed upon individuals by competition. But under some circumstances, competition may be a more onerous method of control than regulation by public authority, for undoubtedly there is such a thing as the tyranny of unrestrained competition.

Real freedom consists in having the conditions and the institutions which are satisfactory to the greatest number.[16] Consequently, it is especially misleading to regard the rules which the state prescribes for industry *merely* as restrictions. It is more realistic to regard the state as an instrument for creating freedom, and the restrictions which it imposes upon industry as a means to that end. Consider, for example, the effect of a zoning law. By restricting the uses to which property in residential sections may be put, it creates freedom from the noise, dirt, and congestion which are produced by factories or stores. Laws against the sale of milk from tubercular cattle create freedom from tuberculosis. If the government could not legislate concerning milk from tubercular cattle, we should have no choice as to the kind of freedom which we had. But because the government can act, we are able to choose whether farmers shall be free to sell milk from tubercular cattle or whether babies shall be free from the danger of being fed infected milk. Far from

[16] The institution of money illustrates clearly the fact that freedom is not essentially a matter of laws or absence of laws but a matter of having institutions which serve our purposes. Probably no single economic arrangement makes a greater contribution to real freedom than money. Consider the tremendous gain in freedom of choice which was achieved when barter was superseded by a universal medium of exchange. In a state of barter, one's ability to obtain what one wanted was limited by one's success in discovering some one else who not only possessed what one desired but who also was willing to accept what one had to offer.

merely imposing restrictions, *the government gives us an opportunity to choose the kind of freedom that we shall have.* The issue is not control versus no-control but the particular kind of control which free enterprise provides versus other kinds.

REFERENCES

Carver, T. N., *Essays in Social Justice,* 1915. Ch. III, IV, and V.
Clark, J. M., *Social Control of Business,* 1926. Ch. II, VI, and IX.
Hamilton, Walton, *Current Economic Problems* (third edition), 1925.
Hobhouse, L. T., *Liberalism.* Ch. III, IV, VII, VIII, and IX.
Keezer, D. M., and May, Stacy, *The Public Control of Business,* 1930.
Mill, J. S., *Principles of Political Economy.* Bk. V, ch. I, X, and XI.
Sidgwick, Henry, *The Principles of Political Economy,* 1883. Bk. III.
Smith, Adam, *The Wealth of Nations,* 1776. Bk. IV.

CHAPTER IV

MODERN INDUSTRY A CAPITALISTIC ORGANIZATION

I. THE MEANING OF CAPITALISM. II. WHY THE CONTROL OF IN-
DUSTRY MATTERS. III. THE INFLUENCE OF WAGE EARNERS IN
THE CONTROL OF INDUSTRY. IV. THE INFLUENCE OF CONSUMERS
IN THE CONTROL OF INDUSTRY. V. THE INFLUENCE OF THE
GOVERNMENT AND TRADE ASSOCIATIONS IN THE CONTROL OF IN-
DUSTRY. VI. ARE WE LIKELY TO RETAIN CAPITALISM?

I. THE MEANING OF CAPITALISM

The production of all goods which man makes requires the coöperation of at least nature and labor and also, in most cases, the use of artificial capital. The necessary natural resources and equipment *might* be supplied by the persons who use them and, in the case of agriculture, the professions, and retailing, this is the rule. It is an outstanding characteristic of modern economic society, however, that in most industries the capital is owned by persons other than those who use it. From this fact arise many of our most momentous economic problems.

When labor and capital are not supplied by the same person, some one must take the lead in organizing the two into producing enterprises. Under a system of free enterprise, there is no reason why the initiative in organizing production might not be taken by laborers, consumers, or the government as well as by the owners of private property. Laborers might hire capital just as property owners now hire workers. Or consumers or the government might take the lead in forming producing organizations. In the handicraft industries, where each producer owns his own tools, laborers and capitalists are not differentiated. As a matter of fact, all of these forms of industrial organization do exist to a limited extent. In an overwhelmingly large proportion of cases, however, the decision to start a business is made by those who contribute all or part of the capital — that is, by capitalists. They select the officials, choose a location, have buildings erected, equipment installed, and workmen engaged. The officials, being hired by the capitalists, are responsible to them and removable by them. Their job is to run the business in the interests of the capitalists and to pursue the policies which will yield the maximum advantage to them. Today then, instead of goods' being made largely by persons who also sell them in the market (as was the case at one stage of handicraft industry and is still largely true of agriculture) goods are made by wage earners who use capital which they do not own and who work under the direction of supervisors who are responsible to the owners or capitalists. Because the vast majority of present-day enterprises have been organized by capitalists and are controlled by them, we refer to our economic order as *capitalism,* or as a capitalistic organization or system.

When it is said that modern business establishments are controlled in the main by property owners, it should not be inferred that all capitalists possess a voice in the direction of the enterprises to which they furnish funds. Many investors purchase securities which give their owners a share in the income but, under ordinary circumstances, no direct share in the control of the enterprise. Nor is the actual influence of capitalists who do possess at least a formal voice in the direction of a concern necessarily proportionate to their investment. Mr. Gary, long the dominant man in the United States Steel Corporation, was not even a large stockholder. Often property owners find it advantageous to act through directors and hired managers, and these agents frequently become in large degree independent of those to whom they are nominally responsible. The ascendency of management over ownership in modern industry is a recent development of great significance to which we shall give more attention later. The direction of industry is largely in the hands of capitalists and their agents, but the agents are becoming increasingly powerful and independent.

II. Why the Control of Industry Matters

If competition were a perfect regulative device, it would be a matter of indifference whether enterprises were organized and managed by capitalists, wage earners, or consumers. The regulative force of competition would compel whoever was in control to have due regard for the interests of others. Competition for the custom of buyers would cause business enterprises to sell honest goods at reasonable prices; competition for labor and for capital would compel fair treatment of workmen and investors.

It is indicative of how far competition falls short of this ideal, that the objectives which industry pursues, the methods and policies which it uses reflect so largely the interests of those who control it. When capitalists control industry, it is naturally operated for their advantage; when wage earners control, it is run primarily to benefit them; when consumers are dominant, it is managed to suit their interests. It is important to bear in mind this relationship between the control of industry and its aims and methods. Capitalistic control, for example, is often praised on the ground that it is more efficient than control by labor, consumers, or the state. This may or may not be true. But *unless the aims and methods of capitalistic industry are socially desirable,* its very efficiency is a curse rather than a blessing, for what is gained by having industry highly efficient in pursuing harmful ends or in using vicious methods? [1]

How the aims and methods of industry are affected by the interests of those who control it is well illustrated by the present economic order. It is frequently referred to as a " price system." By this is meant that industry is organized upon a price basis and that it is managed, as a rule, so as to produce the maximum profits. It produces, not necessarily the things which are most needed and which will do the most good, but those which promise the largest pecuniary gain. Its methods and policies are determined primarily by price considerations. Managements are constantly endeavoring to lower the cost of production. But the costs which they are striving to reduce are money, not human, costs; the outlay in terms of human sacrifice causes most managers little concern. The aim of the large staffs of technical experts which are engaged in industrial research is, not to develop methods that make the jobs more psychologically satisfying and

---

[1] Popular and prevailing conceptions of industrial efficiency are products of capitalistic control of industry. So accustomed are we to appraising the results of industry in terms of dollars and cents that we uncritically assume that a saving in dollars and cents represents a gain in industrial efficiency, without stopping to ask by what process and at what cost the saving has been achieved.

worth while from the standpoint of the workers, but to reduce money costs. To keep track of pecuniary costs, firms install elaborate accounting systems which require an expensive personnel to operate. When money costs increase, satisfactory explanations must be forthcoming or somebody's job is in jeopardy. But there are no elaborate systems and no expensive personnel for keeping track of human costs, and, when these increase, department heads are not called into the front office to explain. On the contrary, if money costs can be reduced by methods which increase human costs — such as speeding up, longer hours, night work, failure to guard machinery properly or to protect workmen against heat, dust, fumes, or industrial poisons — the money-saving method is usually adopted without hesitation.

It is somewhat startling to find the desire for money playing such a dominant part and other human needs and desires such a feeble and incidental rôle in the determination of industrial policies. The reason why price is the supreme guide and organizer of production, the medium in which costs and benefits are computed, is *because it accurately reflects the interests of the class which, under existing economic arrangements, directs and controls production,* — that is, the propertied or capitalist class. Those who contribute property to industry are interested in the money returns and, in so far as they determine industrial policies, they select the ones which promise the largest pecuniary gains; they make the goods, whether adulterated or honest, which promise the largest net money income; and they employ the methods of production, whether injurious to the community or not, which entail the least money cost.

In an economic order controlled by consumers or jointly by consumers, workers, and capitalists, price would play a much less important rôle than it does now. Suppose, for example, that consumers participated in choosing the management and that the management were responsible to them as much as to the investors. In the handling of labor there might be no great change, for consumers, like capitalists, are interested in low money costs rather than in low human costs. But undoubtedly the kind and quality of goods produced would be substantially changed. Pecuniary considerations would no longer be dominant. The representatives of the consumers would insist that only serviceable goods be made; that adulterated goods, goods of extremely poor quality, goods which could not render the service expected of them, should not be produced at all. They would insist that paints be made to protect wood as well as to color it, that fabrics be made to wear, that furniture be stoutly built, that clothing be made correctly, not ironed into shape for purpose of sale. They would insist upon honest labels. To the plea of capitalists that it is sometimes more profitable to use barytes and chalk in paint instead of lead, to make flimsy chairs instead of well constructed ones, or that honest labels would injure the sale of many commodities, consumers would be deaf. In short, they would be guided, not solely by price considerations, but by service considerations as well. Price would be important but no longer would it be dominant.

But it does not follow that the control of management by wage earners instead of capitalists would diminish the importance of prices and of pecuniary considerations in economic life. It might, but also it might not. It is true that laborers, like capitalists, are interested primarily in the money return from their work rather than in the benefit that it confers on consumers. Consequently a change to labor control of industry might not benefit consumers. But more doubt attaches to the effect of labor control of enterprises upon the methods of production. One possibility is that a far more vigorous effort would be made to keep down the human costs of production. The workers might not consent to speeding up, long hours, unsafe or unsanitary conditions, simply because they were cheaper. Possibly they would not permit the employment of women and children at night work or at hazardous occupations simply because they would work for less. On the other hand, so difficult is human behavior to predict, that it is possible that *less* attention would be paid to human costs and more to pecuniary considerations under labor-controlled industry than under present capitalistic industry. Which result followed labor control would probably depend upon whether or not there was competition between the different labor-controlled enterprises. We know that when men work for themselves, they are likely to work longer hours, take greater risks, and drive themselves harder than they are willing to do as employees. Consequently, if manual laborers controlled the policies of industrial enterprises and if the profits of each enterprise depended upon success in competition, the working day might be longer, the pace of work faster, and the protection to life and health less adequate than they are today under capitalism.[2]

Not only does capitalistic control of production make price and pecuniary considerations of peculiar importance, but it is responsible in no small degree for the acute conflict between capital and labor which is such a conspicuous characteristic of modern industry. Had we deliberately planned an industrial system which would create intense conflict between capital and labor, we could scarcely have devised one which would have achieved this result more completely than does the existing economic order. As industry is now organized, the business owners receive, as a rule, not a fixed return but the entire difference between receipts and expenses. Everything over and above costs belongs to them. This means that labor can ordinarily get more only at the expense of the owners. Not by coöperating to increase output or to reduce costs, not by devising labor-saving methods or by working harder, do the employees of an establishment gain higher pay. By doing these things, they simply increase the profits of the proprietors. Only by gaining income which would otherwise go to the capitalists, can workers raise their own compensation.

The conflict which arises when wage earners seek to increase their income at the expense of business owners is intensified by the fact that the net return over and above costs is often small in comparison with the wage bill. In such cases a small advance in wages produces a disproportionate drop in profits. To illustrate the conflict which results, let us imagine an enterprise with a gross annual income of $1,000,000; total expenses, exclusive of return on the investment, being $900,000; and, of these, $400,000 being labor costs. Net profits evidently are $100,000. Suppose that the employees seek an advance of 10 per cent in wages. This would increase the total wage outlay by $40,000. Assuming that the volume of business and the expenses other than wages are constant, profits would be reduced to $60,000.

---

[2] The experience of producers' coöperatives tends to bear out this conclusion. Trade unions have difficulty in compelling the workers in producers' coöperatives to limit their hours of work to those enforced by the unions upon capitalistic enterprises.

In other words, giving the employees 10 per cent more would reduce the return to the owners by 40 per cent. Is it to be wondered, when a moderate advance in wages means such a disproportionate reduction in profits, that managements so stubbornly resist the demands of workers for more compensation? Neither party can be blamed for the difficulty of adjusting wage rates, because the trouble arises out of the customary form of industrial organization. It results from the fact that, in order to give a proportionately small amount more to the workers, it is necessary to take a relatively large amount from the business owners. If part of the capital of the enterprise were in the form of bonds, the clash would be still greater. If the interest on the bonds were $30,000, there would remain $70,000 for the stockholders. Giving the workers 10 per cent more under these circumstances would reduce the return of the stockholders by over one-half, — from $70,000 to $30,000, or by 57 per cent.[3]

If capital were hired by workers instead of workers' being hired by capital, the investors in each enterprise would undoubtedly receive a fixed, instead of a variable, return. The wage earners, having procured the needed capital by agreeing to pay a stipulated return on it, could not then increase their wages at the expense of the investors. To advance their wages they would have to raise the net income of the enterprise. But having done this, they would have no difficulty about increasing their compensation. Quite obviously, conflict between capital and labor would be greatly reduced in intensity. Likewise, if the consumers hired the capital, the investors would again receive a fixed instead of a variable return. The $40,000 necessary to raise wages 10 per cent would, in this case, come out of the consumers, who would be compelled to pay 4 per cent more for their goods. Clearly there would be a distinct conflict of inter-

---

[3] The New York Factory Investigating Commission found that in the making of work shirts the contractor's cost per dozen was 79.13 cents, of which 50.33 cents was labor and 2.41 cents profit. In other words, to make a profit of less than $2\frac{1}{2}$ cents, the employer had to incur a labor cost of over 50 cents. A charge of 5 per cent in labor costs would more than wipe out the entire profit. *Fourth Report of the New York Factory Investigating Commission,* v. II, p. 228.

One reason why the conflict between employer and employee is peculiarly acute in the so-called " sweat " shops is because the labor cost is unusually large in proportion to total costs and profits. This is because the employer ordinarily has no outlay for raw materials. These are usually supplied by the jobber for whom he is making the goods.

est between consumers and wage earners, but it would be less severe than that between stockholders and wage earners. In the one case, to give the workers 10 per cent more, 40 per cent must be taken from profits; in the other, 4 per cent must be added to price.

III. THE INFLUENCE OF WAGE EARNERS IN THE CONTROL OF INDUSTRY

The principal way in which wage earners exercise a voice in modern industry is that which the theory of free enterprise assumes they will use — by shunning those employers who give low wages, poor working conditions, or bad treatment, and by preferring those who offer the best terms and conditions. Consequently the employers who offer the best wages, conditions, and treatment get the pick of the job seekers and experience least difficulty in holding their men. By thus discriminating among employers, workers give each one an incentive to offer better and better wages and conditions. But the effectiveness of this method of controlling conditions of employment depends, as we learned in the preceding chapter, upon the existence of certain circumstances. There must be competition among employers for labor; the workers must be well informed concerning wages, conditions, and managerial policies in different plants; they must be willing to take the time and trouble to discriminate against the enterprises which offer the least favorable terms of employment; and finally, employers must know that workmen are discriminating. To what extent do these conditions exist?

A detailed discussion of the bargaining situation of wage earners can better be reserved for a later chapter, but it is desirable at this point to notice in a general way the ability of wage earners to influence industrial policies. Competition for labor is fairly general, but it is often subject to some restriction. Occasionally there are definite agreements among employers concerning wage rates and the length of the working day. In other cases, wages and, to a less extent, hours are affected by the strong disapproval which business men manifest toward any one who ventures to offer substantially higher wages or shorter working hours than have been customary. It will be recalled with what intense hostility business men greeted Mr. Ford's high wage policy. The golf clubs, rotary clubs, trade associations, and chambers of commerce, through which business men are knitted together, all facilitate the creation of conventional standards of fair wages and hours which employers voluntarily observe. Social pressure, however, is not ordinarily brought against the employer who simply offers safer or more pleasant conditions of work.

Among the circumstances which make it difficult for wage earners to exercise a strong influence upon industrial conditions and policies, perhaps none is more important than inability to obtain the information needed to compare jobs in different plants. Even information concerning wages in different plants is not easy for the ordinary worker to obtain. Some countries have public labor exchanges at which employers list their vacancies. These exchanges, of course, greatly facilitate comparisons between plants. A few of our states have such exchanges, but they are little used by most employers. Although national and state governments and a few private organizations collect wage statistics, the figures fail to give the information which is of vital importance to the wage earner — namely the rates which different employers are paying. The result is that the ordinary worker is left dependent upon hearsay and visits to plants. Hearsay is not accurate and does not usually provide information about many jobs. Visits to plants give most workers little opportunity to exercise choice. By the time the job seeker has investigated several plants and returned to the best-paying job, it is almost sure to have been filled.

In noting the difficulty which workers encounter in comparing wages in several establishments, emphasis should be placed upon the fact that many jobs are paid by the piece.[4] Piece rates in different plants can be compared only in terms of the amounts yielded by them per day or hour. Some pieceworkers earn more, others less, and the earnings of all fluctuate greatly as conditions change. In busy times, when the flow of work is good, earnings rise, but they fall when work comes through in small lots. They are affected also by the condition of machines,

---

[4] Figures gathered by the writer show that of 220,536 workers employed by 175 manufacturing establishments, 78,837, or 35.8 per cent, were paid by the piece, 28,173, or 12.7 per cent, were paid a bonus or premium, and 113,526, or 51.5 per cent, were paid on a time basis. *American Economic Review,* v. XV, No. 1, Supplement, March, 1925, pp. 94–95.

tools, and raw materials and by many other factors. Some firms are generous about crediting workers with extra time at day-work rates when their piecework earnings fall off. Other enterprises are less liberal. When, therefore, a job hunter is offered a piecework place at which he is told that he should earn $35 a week, what does this mean? Do the best or the average men earn this amount? Is $35 the average for good weeks and bad or can it be earned only during the busy season? In how many weeks of the year is it impossible to earn $35? The extreme indefiniteness of the statement that at a particular operation a pieceworker should earn $35 is self-evident. Perhaps a job in another plant, which a more conservative management estimates will yield only about $30, is actually more remunerative.

Even more difficult than the comparison of wages in different plants, is comparison of the agreeableness of the work, the nature of managerial policies, the effect of different jobs upon the length of working life, and the risks of accident, industrial disease, and unemployment. The relative agreeableness of the work and the nature of managerial policies are difficult to compare because they cannot be reduced to quantitative terms. The only way to get information about them is by hearsay or by working in the different plants. The limitations of hearsay have been indicated. Working in different plants is, of course, a slow and inconvenient way of discovering where the work is most attractive and the management fairest, and after a man has worked in several places and decided which he prefers, he is likely to find difficulty in getting a job there.

Information concerning the physical and nervous strain of the different tasks in different plants is almost totally lacking. A little, but not much, is known concerning how fast men wear out in a few *occupations,* but practically nothing is known of the length of trade life at *specific jobs in specific plants.* So many factors affect trade life — speed of work, hours, amount of overtime and holiday work, opportunities to rest, presence or absence of helpers, use of fatigue-saving devices, ventilation, temperature, light, and noise — that to compare different plants is difficult in the extreme. This means that, in choosing between jobs, workmen cannot accurately take account of the human depreciation rate and it means, furthermore, that most employers have little incentive to reduce the rate at which men wear out. It is serious enough when business men, in estimating costs, must guess at the depreciation rate of their equipment. How much more serious is the ignorance of workers concerning the rate at which the managerial policies and the working conditions of different enterprises wear out employees.[5]

Until the passage of workmen's compensation acts, little was known concerning the accident hazards of industry. Many risks were, of course, obvious, but there was little precise quantitative information concerning the seriousness of the hazards in different industries.[6] Workmen's compensation laws have resulted

[5] Although workers are able to exercise little influence over the speed of work and, consequently, the length of trade life by discriminating in favor of some employers and against others, they are often able to affect the rate of work by other methods. For the management to control the pace effectively, it must be able to measure the output of individual employees. Many operations in modern industry do not lend themselves to measurement. In the case of non-repetitive work, such as special order and repair work, measurement is usually impracticable because there is no common unit of performance. In other cases, the contribution of each workman becomes indistinguishably merged in a common result. This is illustrated by many assembling operations, by building construction, maintenance of track, operation of railway trains, and the work of yard gangs. A rough indication of the extent to which individual output is measurable in manufacturing is provided by figures on the use of different methods of wage payment. As a rule, whenever measurement is feasible, piecework or a bonus or premium system is used. The figures given in a previous footnote show that out of 220,536 employees in 175 establishments, 35.6 per cent were paid by the piece, 12.7 per cent were paid a bonus or premium, and 51.5 per cent were paid on a time basis. From these data, it is a conservative estimate that, under the existing state of managerial technique, determination of individual performance is impossible or impracticable in the case of one-third of the jobs in the manufacturing industries. Since repetitive work is found principally in manufacturing, it is probable that in other industries measurement of individual output is even less practicable.

Whenever the management cannot keep track of individual output, it is, of course, easy for the men to exercise a high degree of control over the speed of work, and we find them giving expression to their desire that the rate should not be too fast. And even where individual output can be readily ascertained, it is often possible for the men to retain substantial control over their output. For, although it may be possible to determine how much each man actually does, it is less easy to discover how much he *might* do and to make him do it. Workers can make life unpleasant for a man who, in their opinion, does too much. Consequently, even where the management keeps track of individual output, the men often exert a pronounced restraint upon production.

[6] In the absence of definite information, only the conspicuous, dramatic dangers which make a vivid popular impression, such as the risk of explosion in coal mining or in the manufacture of explosives, and of falls in the erecting of structural steel, greatly influence the choice of occupations. Cave-ins and rock-falls kill and injure more coal miners than catastrophic explosions, but the latter is the risk popularly associated with the industry. Working in a junk yard is not regarded as particularly dangerous but the likelihood that the cuts frequently received in handling

in the collection of voluminous statistics on industrial accidents, but workmen are still unable to control hazards by discriminating in favor of the safe plants because the available data show only the relative hazards of different industries and occupations. As for the risks of industrial disease and unemployment, data are as scanty as was information concerning industrial accidents before the passage of workmen's compensation acts. No matter how desirous wage earners may be of taking these hazards into account, they can do so only in the crudest fashion. Even the experts have only the most uncertain notions concerning the amount of unemployment and occupational disease in different industries and callings, and, as to the rates in individual plants, *nothing* is known. Here are dangers of the first magnitude which workmen are practically powerless to control by the method of discrimination, for the simple reason that, even if they desire, they cannot show preference for those enterprises in which the dangers are least.

In view of the fact that wage earners have never had the information needed for intelligent choices between jobs, no one knows how much they would use it if they had it. If they now seem strangely indifferent to many conditions which are of vital importance to them, this may be due to the lack of accurate and easily accessible facts about jobs. But even if the information were available, workmen would never make full use of it and to this extent their control over industry would be limited. Often they would be too busy, too careless, or too lazy to find out about alternative jobs. Particularly important is the predisposition, which wage earners share with most of us, to be optimistic. This is plainly shown in their attitude toward positions which are notoriously dangerous or which offer extremely irregular employment. The hazards seem so remote and unreal that when it comes to deciding between a higher paying position at which the risks are great and a lower paying one at which they are small, most men accept the greater risk for an insufficient differential in pay.[7]

jagged material will be infected renders this among the most hazardous of occupations.

[7] The hazards of window washing in New York City make it so difficult for the employers to obtain workmen's compensation insurance, as required by the state law, that the firms in the industry have been compelled to provide their own insur-

But grant that workmen have the information needed for intelligent choices and that they are not too careless or too optimistic to use it. They may still be prevented from showing preference for the best jobs by the cost and trouble of doing so. Acceptance of some jobs would require that the worker change his residence. For the man with a family, the expense and trouble of moving may outweigh the advantages of a better position. Then too, labor, it must be remembered, is the most perishable of all commodities — more perishable even than fresh flowers or vegetables — for no one has discovered how today's labor can be sold tomorrow. Under the circumstances, the job seeker is strongly tempted to take what he can get rather than to speculate on the possibility of finding a better job later. And finally, it should be noted that, even though it might pay a man to wait several weeks or months to get an exceptionally desirable position, many workers cannot afford to go long without an income.

For all of these reasons — because competition among employers for labor is restricted, because the necessary information about working conditions is almost completely lacking, because wage earners, like nearly every one else, are inclined to be careless and optimistic, and finally because the exercise of choice is often costly — wage earners find that their ability to affect industrial conditions and policies is severely limited. And yet, despite these obstacles, they do discriminate between jobs and employers and, by so doing, they exert substantial influence over industry. Labor turnover is a standing manifestation both that workers do discriminate and that they have great difficulty in doing so.[8] Since information about jobs is scanty and difficult to obtain, and since waiting without employment for a good position is expensive, the job seeker, without spending much time on investigation, is inclined to take the best position available, trusting to luck that it will prove satisfactory. Once on the job, he discovers how much he can earn at it, how onerous the work,

---

ance. Nevertheless, it is easy to obtain plenty of window washers at wages of about $60 a week.

[8] Labor turnover may be defined as the change in personnel due to men's quitting. It includes all terminations of employment whether due to resignation, layoff, or discharge. Only resignations, however, are indicative of an effort on the part of workmen to discriminate between employers.

how fair the treatment by the foreman. Often enough the place proves unsatisfactory, for experience shows that nearly two out of three newly hired men give up their jobs within a year.[9] Because it costs money to train new men, the employer who finds many of his workers leaving after a few weeks' service is likely to investigate the reasons and, if he can, do something to remove them.[10]

The fact that wage earners exert such limited influence upon industry by the method of individual discrimination has led them to establish trade unions. Of the 14,321,000 manual laborers engaged in manufacturing, mining, transportation, and building construction in the United States in 1927, 3,276,000, or 22.9 per cent, were union members. Unions influence industry by directly bargaining with employers concerning wages, hours, and working conditions. The bargaining strength of a union depends, of course, upon its ability, in case of failure to reach an agreement over the terms of employment, to withdraw from an employer's service more men than he can promptly replace. If even a short interruption to operations would be a serious loss to him — as it is in the case of a newspaper — the union's bargaining power may be great.

It is customary for employers and unions to record in black and white the terms of employment. These agreements are known as trade agreements. They have been described as industrial constitutions, for they mean that, within their scope, each side is governed, not by its own selfish preferences, but by rules which have been mutually accepted.[11] In content and scope, trade agree-

---

[9] In seven typical plants, the percentage of newly hired men who quit before the end of the calendar year was 87.0, 72.0, 71.0, 70.5, 67.1, 62.5, 57.2. Slichter, S. H., *The Turnover of Factory Labor*, p. 50.

[10] And yet the influence of labor turnover upon industrial policies has been important for little less than two decades. In order for employers to be affected by turnover, they must know its extent and its cost. But only since about 1913 has labor turnover received much attention. Even today thousands of employers are so uninformed about it that they do nothing to prevent it. It is one of the great ironies of modern industrial life that the very method of discrimination which the workmen can most easily practice should so long have been ineffective because managers did not realize that the men were using it on an extensive scale.

[11] The legal status of these agreements is somewhat nebulous. The traditional view has been that there is no contract between the employer and the union because the union does not agree to furnish labor to the employer. Consequently, the agreement is not enforceable by the employer against the union or by the union against the employer. It is, however, a memorandum governing the terms of the individual con-

ments vary considerably. The first one made between an employer and a union usually specifies little more than rates of pay and hours of work. As time passes, the agreement tends to become broader and more detailed in its provisions. Having raised wages and shortened hours, a union may concentrate upon changing the method of wage payment, such as replacing piecework with daywork. Or it may seek to regulate overtime or holiday employment, the number and training of apprentices, the selection of new workers, the reasons for discharge, the methods of promotion, the sequence in which men shall be laid off when business is slack, or the way in which employment during dull times shall be divided among the force.

When we notice how trade agreements steadily become broader and more detailed in their provisions, it is apparent that they represent a tremendously significant process. They are a way by which the foundations of the economic order are slowly being altered and, almost without our realizing it, a new economic order is being created. They are an encroachment upon the essence of capitalism — the control of industry by property owners — because they mean that decisions concerning many matters are made, not exclusively by property owners or their agents, but jointly by property owners and the representatives of the workers. Every new trade agreement and every extension of an old one is a step in the supplanting of capitalism by a new economic order.

The fear of employers that their workers may organize extends the influence of trade unions far beyond the plants in which they have members. An important result of this fear has been the establishment of large numbers of employee representation committees. These have been organized at the suggestion of the employers, but the members are usually elected by the workers. There are now several hundred of these committees representing over a million wage earners. Because they increase the influence of non-union workers upon the terms of employment and

---

tracts between the individual workmen and the employer. Of late years there has been some tendency for the courts to treat the agreements as contracts legally binding upon both sides. Many persons have long been of the opinion that this would be desirable. There is danger, however, that the effect would be to introduce a legalistic spirit into industrial relations which would do much harm.

upon shop conditions, these committees are an important factor
in the control of industry.

Employee representation committees are usually entitled to
discuss with the management any matters which in their judgment should receive attention.   Because the committee members
are selected from the regular force, they are not, as a rule,
experienced negotiators.   And since they depend for their jobs
upon the management with which they deal, they are less as-
sertive, vigorous, and persistent than independent representatives
in pushing the interests of the men.   Nor do they have funds to
finance strikes or an organization to assure them the support of
workers in other plants, should a strike occur.   For these
reasons, their bargaining power is inferior to that of union
workers who have professional leaders, defense funds, and nation-
wide organizations.

In spite of these handicaps, however, the more active employee representation committees exercise real influence.   On
many matters, such as minor improvements in physical conditions, there is no conflict of interest between men and management.   It is good business to maintain certain standards of
cleanliness and safety, but, unless some one brings matters to
the attention of officials, bad conditions may long remain un-
remedied.   Sometimes employee representation committees obtain
concessions by giving guarantees or promises which individual
workmen could not.   A committee in a Cleveland plant got hours
reduced from ten to nine a day by promising that there would
be no decrease in output.   Later, by the same promise, it obtained
a reduction from nine to eight.   Employee committees are a
means of organizing public opinion in the plant behind certain
demands.   When plant opinion is strongly organized behind a
request, the employer may consider it wise to give in.   When the
Colorado Fuel and Iron Company offered its men the *basic* eight
hour day, the employees' committee requested, and was granted,
the *actual* eight hour day.[12]   When the company desired to
change the hour for beginning work, it met such determined
opposition from the committee that it abandoned the project.

[12] By the basic eight hour day is meant that all time over eight hours is considered
overtime and paid for at overtime rates but that more than eight hours is regularly
worked.   The actual eight hour day means that the working day is regularly eight
hours and that it is the exception rather than the rule to work longer.

Finally, employee committees give the men opportunity to persuade the management that a given action is or is not wise or fair. A large employer, who suffered severely by the drop of prices in 1920, decided to reduce wages 15 per cent. So convincingly did the employees' committee argue against the cut that the employer decided to make it 12½ per cent instead of 15.

A few business enterprises are controlled, not by capitalists, but by the workers in them. They are known as producers' coöperatives. They are more numerous in Great Britain than in the United States, but there have been a few here in the foundry, cooperage, shingle, window glass, and other industries. The funds for these enterprises are supplied either by the workers in them or by outsiders — sometimes in part by trade unions. The management, however, is selected not by those who supply the funds but by the workers, and the profits, after a limited return on the investment, go to the workers. Many coöperatives have failed, but many have been successful. And yet, strange to say, the number of establishments which are really controlled by their employees has been diminished by success almost as much as by failure. When an enterprise is profitable, the temptation is strong for the original force to keep the control and the profits for themselves. As the business expands or as old workers leave or retire, new men are hired as ordinary wage earners. They are given no voice in the enterprise and no share in its profits. Thus from establishments which were controlled from below by all of the workers and in the profits of which each had a share, there develop concerns in which control and profits belong to a small group of original employees and in which these insiders have the same relation to the other workers as do the investors in an ordinary enterprise.

The tendency for successful coöperative enterprises to grow by a natural process of evolution into capitalistic enterprises is of great significance because it shows how deeply rooted capitalism is in human nature. Capitalism is simply a manifestation of the tendency for the direction of production to gravitate into the hands of the minority who possess property and superior initiative and ability — or at least the *particular kind* of ability needed by business managers. It represents the desire of these persons to keep for themselves the profits which result from their property, initiative, or ability.

IV. The Influence of Consumers in the Control of Industry

Just as wage earners influence industry by discriminating in favor of the employers who offer the best terms of employment, so, according to the theory of free enterprise, consumers exercise an influence by purchasing from the sellers who offer the best goods at the lowest prices. But the consumer experiences much the same difficulties in influencing industrial conditions and policies by the method of discriminative buying as does labor by the method of discriminative selling.

The market information which the consumer needs in order to get the most for his money is often lacking or obtainable only at great expense or trouble. Or the consumer may be too careless, too busy, or too ignorant to use the information that is available. Consider to what extent consumers possess the information which they need in order to purchase where they can get the most for their money. Business enterprises can buy through specialists who spend much time and money investigating prices, quality, and the existing and prospective condition of the market. But what does the average consumer know concerning the prices asked by different dealers? A few prices are published in advertisements, but most of them can be ascertained only by inquiry at each store — a method so laborious and time-consuming as to be impracticable for the average shopper with many things to purchase and little time in which to buy them. Far more difficult to obtain is information concerning the quality of goods. How is one to decide which pair of shoes or suit of clothes or piece of furniture is best? The statements of sales clerks are often worse than useless. Experts can sometimes appraise quality by inspection, but the ordinary buyer is not an expert. In many cases quality can be discovered only by elaborate tests. Even if the consumer could make the tests, it would do him little good, because, in order to make them, it would be necessary for him to buy the article, and testing it might destroy its usefulness

All of this means that consumers exercise very imperfect control over both the prices and the quality of goods. In so far as buyers pay little or no attention to quality, inferior ware tends to drive out the better; in so far as they fail to compare prices of competing sellers, merchants have little incentive to sell goods at the lowest prices which operating costs permit.

In so far as the customer buys where he finds prices lowest and quality best, he is prevented from exerting an influence upon many important industrial conditions and policies. Consider, for example, his ability to affect the advertising and selling methods of business enterprises. In some respects these methods are open to serious objection — as, for instance, when establishments push sales by fostering the love of invidious distinctions. But what can the consumer do who disapproves of the efforts of business concerns to stimulate competition in consumption between him and his fellow consumers? If he refuses to deal with the firms which use such methods, he must probably give up, to some extent, purchasing where he can do best. Reflecting that his own refusal to deal with a given firm would exert no influence, he is likely to buy where terms are most favorable. Under these circumstances, consumers can offer little effective resistance to the efforts of business to create intense rivalry in consumption. Nowhere, as was said before, does man's domination by his economic institutions appear more conspicuously than here, where we see the immense resources of business devoted to shaping men's desires in the interest, not of human happiness, but of business.

Just as wage earners sometimes establish industrial enterprises under their own control, so consumers have also organized to do things which are ordinarily done by capitalists. In the United States, the most important consumer-controlled concerns are mutual life and fire insurance companies and building and loan associations. In other countries, the organization of industrial enterprises by consumers has gone much farther. In Germany there has been a noteworthy development of consumer-controlled banks. Most important of all, however, are consumer-controlled stores, known as coöperative stores. These are numerous in most countries of Europe. The membership and sales of the retail coöperative stores in the principal countries of Europe in 1928 are shown in the table which follows.[13] The move-

---

[13] *Monthly Labor Review*, October, 1929, v. XXIX, p. 872.

ment, it will be observed, is particularly strong in Great Britain, Finland, Switzerland, Hungary, and Denmark.

Country	Number of societies	Number of members	Number of coöperators per 1000 inhabitants [14]	Sales in dollars
British Isles	1,267	5,579,000	473	$973,786,000
Germany	1,361	3,686,000	203	250,294,000
France	3,388	2,212,000	217	129,863,000
Italy	3,333	827,000	82	84,876,000
Sweden	824	366,000	248	76,891,000
Finland	535	412,000	490	71,342,000
Denmark	1,785	321,000	374	68,806,000
Switzerland	826	375,000	444	61,062,000
Czechoslovakia	1,058	776,000	228	55,075,000
Norway	439	100,000	152	26,580,000
Belgium	110	420,000	225	26,254,000
Poland	2,658	672,000	99	25,793,000
Hungary	1,763	856,000	429	24,777,000
Netherlands	227	203,000	118	22,485,000
Austria	175	342,000	209	22,241,000

The rapid rise in the cost of living during and immediately following the war stimulated the growth of most consumers' coöperatives. Membership in the British retail societies, for example, grew from 3,054,297 in 1914 to 4,504,852 in 1920.

In many countries, the retail societies have formed wholesale coöperative societies. In 1927, the sales of the English wholesale society were $423,242,000 and of the Scottish $86,313,000. The German wholesales in 1928 did a business of $106,255,000.[15] Some of the wholesale societies conduct extensive manufacturing operations. The flour mills, boot and shoe factories, and textile mills of the English wholesale society are among the largest in Great Britain. The society also has factories making cocoa and chocolate goods, soap, candles, preserves, shirts, underclothing, caps, umbrellas, overalls, drugs, pinafores, blouses, leather bags, cigars, flannels, blankets, corsets, hosiery, paints, varnish, brushes, mats, hardware, butter, and margarine. It has creameries in Ireland, tallow and oil factories in Australia, bacon

[14] In computing the number of coöperators per 1,000 of population, the number of actual members was multiplied by four. This was done because each member, as a rule, represents a family.

[15] *Monthly Labor Review*, October, 1929, v. XXIX, p. 873.

factories in Denmark and Ireland, tea plantations in Ceylon and India. From a concession of 300 square miles in West Africa, it obtains palm oil for its soap works. Its packing plant at Denia, in the heart of the Spanish raisin district, employs 600 persons. Its own ships ply between England and France; it has its own foreign buying depots in New York, and in Canada, Denmark, Greece, and Sweden.[16]

Coöperative retail stores have made much less progress in the United States than in most European countries. The U. S. Bureau of Labor Statistics was able to obtain returns from 457 retail societies — including not only stores but bakeries, laundries, gasoline filling stations, and restaurants. In 1925, the membership of 432 of these societies was 131,205 and the sales of 451 of them were $43,404,716.[17] The contempt of Americans for small economies, the individualistic tradition, the weak development of class consciousness among wage earners, the numerous racial groups, the mobility of the population, the large chain stores, department stores, and mail order houses with their extraordinarily effective marketing methods and their " bargain counter " appeals, the aggressive hostility of jobbers and retailers, all have hindered the development of coöperatives. They seem to flourish best in the midst of more or less distinct social or racial groups to which they can cater — in the mining towns of Illinois, for example, and among the Finns in the upper peninsula of Michigan, northern Wisconsin, and Minnesota. As class consciousness among American workingmen grows, as the individualistic tradition and the disdain for petty economies weaken, and as the labor movement becomes stronger, coöperative stores may possibly fare better in competition with chain and department stores.

V. The Influence of the Government and of Trade Associations in the Control of Industry

The preceding chapter described in a general way how the government intervenes in the conduct of industry. This intervention is more than a departure from the principle of free

---

[16] Based upon the accounts by E. P. Harris in *Co-operation, the Hope of the Consumer*, pp. 222–224 and by Albert Sonnichsen in *Consumers' Coöperation*, Ch. IX.

[17] U. S. Bureau of Labor Statistics, " The Coöperative Movement in the United States in 1925," *Bulletin No. 437*, pp. 37, 41, and 47.

enterprise; it is also a departure from the essential principle of capitalism, for it means that decisions concerning many industrial policies and conditions — what prices shall be charged, how machinery shall be safeguarded, what the length of the working day shall be, how buildings shall be constructed — are made by the government rather than by the investors or their representatives. The government, it is true, often does not precisely decide these matters; it simply sets limits to the discretion of business men — as when it restricts the height of buildings, the length of the working day for women, or the age below which children may not be employed. But since the self-interest of business men usually impels them to go as far as the law permits, the state is practically determining precisely what shall be done.

The willingness of an enterprise to pursue a certain policy or to observe certain rules may depend upon the willingness of its competitors to adhere to the same rules and policies. Thus a retailer may be willing to close his store at noon on Saturdays provided his competitors do likewise. The establishment and enforcement of policies and standards which represent the common interests of competing firms has been an important activity of organizations of business enterprises known as trade associations.[18] Concerns often compete by offering wider choice of sizes and grades of goods than rival enterprises. The result is a wasteful multiplication of sizes and varieties which increases manufacturing costs,[19] discourages enterprises from producing to stock during dull seasons, and enhances the cost of marketing by compelling retailers and wholesalers to carry a supply of little-used sizes and varieties.[20] No competitor, however, is willing

[18] A trade association may be defined as an organization of enterprises or business owners in an industry for the purpose of promoting their common interests. The numerous activities of trade associations are discussed in Chapter VIII.

[19] The economies which often, though not always, accompany specialization among business enterprises are discussed in Chapter VI.

[20] The savings through reducing the number of sizes are strikingly illustrated in the report of the standing committee concerned with the simplification of steel reinforcing bars, which states: "Whereas many of our warehouses were being compelled to carry some 16 to 20 different sizes we have now reduced to 11 sizes. About 600,000 tons of reinforcing bars are sold annually in the United States. Dealers under the old arrangement carried in idle stock between 150,000 and 200,000 tons. With the 11 simplified sizes it is our judgment that this business can be more efficiently handled with a stock of about 75,000 tons. In other words, the reduction in sizes to be carried means a saving in idle stock of approximately 100,000 tons, which at an

to reduce the variety represented by his line unless his rivals do the same. Trade associations have played an important part in persuading competitors to confine their production to certain standard dimensions and grades.[21] The inability of many buyers to distinguish the quality of goods has led some trade associations to regulate quality themselves or to assist consumers in recognizing it. The purpose, of course, is not primarily to protect the consumer, but to prevent some concerns from degrading quality in order to undercut prices. The association of cement manufacturers refuses to admit enterprises unless their product is of a certain quality. Some associations of lumber manufacturers employ inspectors to see that the product of members actually is of the grade represented.

Trade associations, being composed of capitalistic enterprises, are not a departure from the control of industry by property owners. But because they make industrial policies very different from what they would be if each enterprise pursued its own interests regardless of those which it has in common with other firms, trade associations may be regarded as a separate influence in the control of industry. In fact, the restrictions which they impose, though supported by no legal sanction, are often similar to those enforced by the government.

VI. Are We Likely to Retain Capitalism?

Evolution applies to economic organizations and institutions no less than to animal structure. Hence it is reasonably certain that capitalism will not always endure. But how long it will last and what will succeed it, no one knows. At present the voice of property owners in the control of industry seems to be diminishing. This is occurring in three principal ways — through

---

average cost of about $45 per ton means a saving in capital investment of $4,500,000 for the industry." *Thirteenth Annual Report of the Secretary of Commerce,* p. 22.

[21] In determining what sizes and grades are unnecessary, it is usual for an agreement to be reached between the users, distributors, and manufacturers of the commodity, each interest, as a rule, being represented through its trade association. Occasionally a great many associations are represented. For example, no less than thirty-two national technical and trade associations were represented on a joint committee engaged in the standardization of pipe flanges and fittings; twenty-one on a similar committee on the dimensions of bolts, nuts, and rivets. Agnew, P. G., " How Business is Policing Itself," *The Nation's Business,* December, 1925, v. XIII, p. 42.

the growth of state intervention, of trade unionism, and, probably most important of all, of professional management which is more or less independent of control by investors. The first two are a result of the disposition of farmers, wage earners, and many others to become increasingly critical of the operation of economic institutions and to demand somewhat the same voice in the affairs of industry that they possess in the affairs of government. The growing independence of management is simply the result of large concerns owned by thousands of investors who do not follow the affairs of their enterprises or attend the annual meetings of the stockholders. None of these three tendencies, it is to be noted, affects the title to the property used in industry. But mere private ownership of capital, as we have seen, is not capitalism. Capitalism is the control of policies by private property owners. In the degree that this control passes from their hands to the government, consumers, wage earners, or hired managers, the economic order ceases to be a capitalistic one.

But in response to the tendency of consumers and wage earners to become more critical and self-assertive, business men have experimented with ways of allaying discontent and criticism. A striking illustration is provided by the revolutionary changes in methods of handling labor — sometimes called " the welfare offensive." Within the last decade it has become customary for large enterprises to provide themselves with a personnel manager whose duty is to gain the good will of the workers just as the task of the sales manager and the advertising manager is to gain the good will of customers. Physical conditions have been greatly improved, willingness to hear and adjust complaints has superseded the practice of telling dissatisfied men to quit if they dislike their jobs, regular avenues of promotion have been created, and safeguards have been provided against arbitrary and unjust discharge. Many enterprises have offered employees opportunity to purchase stock on favorable terms.[22] Employee rep-

[22] Illustrative of such stock purchase plans is that of the Standard Oil Company of California. Each employee was permitted to set aside, through monthly pay roll deduction, up to 20 per cent of his compensation for the purchase of stock. For every dollar so invested by the employee, the company added 50 cents to assist in the acquisition of stock. During approximately five years, some 12,000 employees purchased nearly $26,000,000 worth of stock. Of those eligible for participation

resentation plans have been established by over 200 concerns, employing in excess of a million workers, and hundreds of employers have awakened to the outstanding importance of steady work to wage earners and have gone to some pains to provide it.

Equally significant have been the efforts of public utilities to diminish the demand for more effective regulation and particularly the agitation for public ownership. Large public service companies now commonly have a public relations manager who has the responsibility for adjusting complaints, handling publicity, and generally fostering public good will. Especially important is the customer-ownership movement. Between 1914, when it began, and 1926, electric light and power companies alone sold $300,000,000 worth of stock to 1,200,000 customers.[23] As the stock usually carries no voting rights, the customers gain no voice in the affairs of the companies. It is significant how quickly agitation for lower rates or for public purchase is followed by a customer-ownership stock-selling campaign.

The immediate prospects of state intervention and trade unionism in the United States appear thus to hinge largely upon the success of business enterprises in allaying the critical and self-assertive attitude which wage earners and consumers have shown signs of developing. During the next several decades we are likely to witness an extraordinarily interesting test — a test of whether a people, fairly prosperous and well supplied with cheap amusements, can, by tact, liberality in adjusting minor complaints, skillful publicity, employee representation, customer-ownership, and such other schemes as experts can contrive, be induced to permit capitalists or their representatives a relatively free hand in the direction of industry. But to the tendency of management to become independent of ownership there is no check in sight. It may be objected that the shift in power from owners to managers represents no real change in the control of industry, that professional managers are guided by essentially the same pecuniary standards which business owners accept. This, however, is true only in part, because professional manage-

---

— employees of less than a year's service being ineligible — 86 per cent took advantage of the plan.

[23] Report of the committee on customer-ownership to National Electric Light Association, 1926.

ment develops standards of its own to which it tends to adhere even in violation of the interests of investors. By influencing these professional standards, the public has an excellent opportunity to affect the conduct of industry.

REFERENCES

Fay, C. R. *Co-operation at Home and Abroad*, (revised edition), 1920.
Gide, Charles, *Consumers' Co-operative Societies*, 1922.
Hobson, J. A., *Work and Wealth*, 1914. Ch. IX, X, XIII, XIV, and XVI.
Marshall, L. C., *Industrial Society*, 1918. Ch. III and XIV.
Sée, Henri, *Modern Capitalism*, 1928.
Veblen, Thorstein, *The Theory of Business Enterprise*, 1904. Ch. I and III.

CHAPTER V

MACHINE INDUSTRY

I. THE REVOLUTION IN TECHNOLOGY. II. MACHINERY AND PRO-
DUCTION. III. MACHINERY AND SPECIALIZATION. IV. MACHINE
INDUSTRY AND LARGE BUSINESS ENTERPRISES. V. MACHINERY
AND THE POSITION OF LABOR. VI. MACHINE TECHNIQUE TENDS
TO MAKE INDUSTRY DYNAMIC. VII. MACHINERY AND MODERN
INDUSTRIAL COSTS. VIII. MACHINERY AND INDUSTRIAL RISKS.
IX. MACHINE INDUSTRY AND LARGE FORTUNES.

Our economic order, we have seen, is one of free capitalistic enterprise — free because each individual is at liberty in the main to make his living as he sees fit, and capitalistic because the initiative in organizing production and determining industrial policies is taken by capitalists or their representatives. How this system of free capitalistic enterprise works depends largely upon the nature of industrial technique and of current economic organizations and institutions. In this and the immediately following chapters, we shall examine some of the features of modern technique and of the economic organizations and institutions which most affect the operation of industry. The topics which we shall discuss are machine technique, the high development of specialization, the prevalence of large business units, certain forms of modern business organization — especially the corporation, the coöperative association, and the trade association — the organization of labor, the widespread practices of producing goods in advance of orders and of doing business on credit. Because machine technique has been of such basic importance in making our economic order what it is, we shall begin with a discussion of machinery.

I. The Revolution in Technology

We have said that the very kernel of the Industrial Revolution has been the production of goods by mechanical power instead of animal muscle. The application of mechanical power to production has been made possible by machinery. Because tools which are not in machines must be guided by human intelligence, only in rare instances can we apply non-human power to them. The movements of tools in machines, however, are mechanically determined — in fact, machines are simply devices for substituting mechanically controlled force for humanly controlled. An ordinary needle is a tool and must be guided by hand, but when we construct a mechanism to operate the needle we have a sewing machine. So also a bit and augur, a hammer, and a plane are tools, but when we make apparatus to guide them mechanically, we have a drill press, a trip hammer, and a planer. Because tools in a machine require no guidance by intelligence, it is possible to move them with energy from non-human sources.

Machinery makes possible not only the use of more power but an intense concentration of power at certain points. It is inconceivable, for example, that human energy could be substituted for that of a huge blooming-mill motor of 22,000 horse power capable of reversing many times a minute. The motor represents the muscular power of 176,000 men.

It is somewhat strange that not until the middle of the eighteenth century did power-driven machinery begin to be used on a large scale. Why was so little use made of machinery before that time, and why, once machine methods began to be substituted for hand methods, did they spread with such amazing speed?

Machine industry first developed on a large scale in Great Britain and spread from there to other countries. Its origin and growth, therefore, must be explained largely in terms of British conditions and experience. The explanation has two principal parts. In the first place, for the use of machinery to be profitable, certain conditions must be present. These conditions existed with more or less completeness for the first time in eighteenth century Britain. In the second place, there was at this time a rapidly growing demand for more product and, therefore, for a more productive technique.

First, as to the favorable circumstances. Machine industry requires a large market. This means that transportation must not be obstructed by customs-barriers; that it must not be too costly or hazardous; and that there must be a commercial organization capable of handling wholesale trade. In these respects, important progress had been made in Great Britain by the middle of the eighteenth century. Great Britain, in contrast with France and Prussia, had no provincial customs-barriers. Transportation, though leaving much to be desired, was slowly improving. By the beginning of the eighteenth century, numerous "wagoners" were operating teams and wagons on regular schedules between the larger cities. Early in the century a number of rivers were made fit for navigation, and by the end, 3,000 miles of canals had been constructed in England.[1] The development of the coal and iron industries during the eighteenth century was largely made possible by the improvements in inland water transportation. Great improvements were also made in roads. Early in the century Parliament began to charter turnpike trusts which were authorized to build roads and to collect tolls. Not until the middle of the century did the turnpike trusts become numerous, but between 1748 and 1770 the number increased from 160 to 530 and the mileage under their control quadrupled.[2] The commercial organization which wholesale trade requires was well developed. Specialized wholesalers with widespread market connections were numerous, particularly in the textile trades, which were among the first to adopt machine methods; banks for financing wholesale operations had been established; and a beginning had been made with insurance.

Once transportation became cheap and safe, the accumulation of funds in the hands of business men was greatly accelerated because it was possible to make large profits from the price differences between the home and remote markets. From the standpoint of the rise of machine industry this was important. Machinery is so expensive that its use is not likely to spread rapidly unless there are large accumulations of funds available for investment in it. Such accumulations existed in eighteenth century Britain, where foreign and wholesale trade had created a class of well-to-do merchants who had capital for venture in commercial and industrial enterprises.

The force which, in the midst of these favorable circum-

[1] Hammond, J. L. and B., *The Rise of Modern Industry*, p. 78.
[2] Trevelyan, G. M., *British History in the Nineteenth Century*, p. 9.

stances, produced a revolution in technique was the rapid growth in the demand for manufactured goods. For this there were several causes. One was the British capture of the Dutch carrying trade, which gave Britain the most favored position in markets that had formerly belonged to the Dutch. A second was the growth of population in the colonies, where the abundant opportunities to make a living caused population to increase with extraordinary rapidity. A third was the substantial expansion in the population of Ireland, produced by the introduction of potato raising in the seventeenth century. But by far the most important cause of all was the revolution in British agriculture. The old practice had been to plant a piece of land for two years and to let it lie fallow the third. Under the new method, or Norfolk system, as it was called, the fallow was eliminated by planting turnips or other root crops the third year, feeding them to stock, and using the manure for fertilizer. This was equivalent to a great addition to the arable land of the country. By making it possible to keep more stock, the new method also added to the supply of manure and resulted in larger crops. Simultaneously with these changes went great improvements in animal breeding — at the end of the century, the oxen and sheep at the Smithfield market were two to three times as heavy as at the beginning.[3] The revolution in agriculture resulted, to a large extent, in more people rather than in a higher standard of living, but it did enable the agricultural classes to increase substantially their demand for manufactured goods.

It was the pressure of the rapidly growing demand for manufactured goods which stimulated the invention of machines. The relationship between the inadequacy of old methods and the invention of new ones can be traced in industry after industry. When exhaustion of the forests made it difficult to get charcoal for smelting iron, and the iron industry was beginning to migrate to the forests of Scandinavia and North America, a furnace was invented which used coal. This invention revolutionized the iron industry. Perhaps cotton manufacturing most clearly illustrates the relationship between the new inventions and the pressure for more output. Even before the invention of the flying shuttle in 1738, the spinners had trouble in keeping pace with the weavers.

[3] Ashley, W. J., *The Economic Organization of England*, p. 135.

The flying shuttle increased the speed of weaving and made it still more difficult for spinners to keep the weavers supplied with thread. The next inventions, however, helped to relieve the pressure upon the spinners. In 1764, James Hargreaves, a master weaver, invented a machine, called, in honor of his wife, the " spinning jenny," with which an operator could spin eight threads at once. Improvements soon increased the capacity of the jennies to thirty threads. In 1769, Richard Arkwright patented a spinning machine which could spin a finer and stronger thread than the jenny and, in 1779, Samuel Crompton devised the spinning mule, which combined the good points of Hargreaves' and Arkwright's inventions.

These improvements enabled the spinners to meet the demand for thread and shifted the pressure to other parts of the production process. Before cotton is spun, it must be " carded " — that is, the fibres must be brushed or combed so that they lie parallel. Soon a machine for doing this was invented. The methods of dyeing cloth were also greatly improved, and in 1787 was invented the power loom, which was operated by water or steam power and could weave with unprecedented rapidity. The thing which now held back production was the removal of the seed from the fibre preparatory to carding. Under the methods in use, a day was required for a man to remove the seeds from four or five pounds of cotton. The cotton gin, invented by an American, Eli Whitney, in 1792, greatly reduced the time and labor. The problem now was how to grow enough cotton. This was solved, not primarily by the invention of machinery, but by the use of slave labor. When the cotton gin was invented, slavery in the South appeared to be slowly dying out. The revolution in cotton manufacturing created a great demand for cheap labor to grow cotton and caused slavery to flourish more than ever before. Hence our Civil War may be justly regarded as a product of the Industrial Revolution.

II. Machinery and Production

Perhaps the most obvious result of machine industry is the extraordinary increase in output for which the new machine technique is largely responsible. A hundred years ago, a skilled workman could make about thirty needles in a day. Now a semi-skilled girl with the aid of a machine makes 500,000 in the same time. On the Great Lakes, ore vessels are loaded with 10,000 tons of ore in twenty minutes and unloaded in a little more than three hours. One can conjecture how long a gang of laborers would require to perform these operations by hand. It is estimated that the entire population of the world would be needed to produce by hand methods the amount of cotton cloth which is turned out by 1,500,000 workers using machinery. Agriculture is not ordinarily regarded as an industry in which machine technique is dominant, yet the greater part of our principal crops may be attributed to machinery. By comparing the quantity of labor necessary to produce the crops by hand methods with that actually used, the percentage of each crop attributable to machinery was estimated as follows: [4]

Barley	95.7
Wheat	94.5
Oats	89.2
Hay	81.3
Rice	72.5
Potatoes	65.1
Cotton	64.8
Corn	60.9
Rye	60.0

As these estimates were based upon the methods in use about 1895, long before the advent of the tractor and the automobile, the proportions today are doubtless distinctly larger.

Care must be taken, however, not to overestimate the productivity of machinery. That a worker aided by machinery can turn out ten times as much as by hand does not mean that the machine method is ten times as productive. Account must be taken of the labor used in making the machine, supplying it with power, and keeping it in repair. The smoke which is produced in making power for machines defaces buildings, damages furnishings, and is deleterious to health. The smoke nuisance in London has been estimated to cost $21,000,000 annually, exclusive of the waste of fuel which it represents. [5] Heavy

[4] Quaintance, H. W., "The Influence of Farm Machinery on Production and Labor." *Publications of the American Economic Association, Third Series*, November, 1904, v. V, p. 29.

[5] The People's Gas Light and Coke Company, *Yearbook*, 1927. Estimates of this kind are, of course, extremely rough. The loss was divided as follows: extra washing and wear of linen, $10,750,000; depreciation of clothing, curtains, carpets,

machines or those whose operation is accompanied by vibration or shock must usually be housed in stronger and more expensive buildings than are needed for hand operations. Because of the superior productivity of machines, their output must be transported farther in order to dispose of it. Selling in distant markets means more than heavier freight charges; it means greater railroad fares for salesmen, larger telegraphic expenses, and higher cost of supervising the sales force.[6] In so far as machine production means large plants, it means city production. Even small cities, however, have many expenses which in smaller places are less or absent altogether. Street car service, for example, is unnecessary in small towns; sewage and garbage disposal, fire and police protection all cost less *per capita*. Machinery has made noise, crowds, and dirt the usual conditions of life for most city dwellers, and quiet, sunlight, seclusion, and cleanliness luxuries which must be purchased. Finally, there are the millions of accidents which are attributable directly or indirectly to machinery and which go far toward diminishing the net advantage derived from it.[7]

Despite the heavy offsets which must be charged against machinery, it is clear that production *per capita* has been greatly

---

and other textiles, $5,000,000; increased mortality, impairment of health, and lessened working capacity, $1,600,000; other losses and wastes, $3,650,000. The Mellon Institute has estimated the smoke loss of Pittsburgh at $10,000,000, and the smoke abatement commission of Chicago puts the annual loss there at $42,500,000. The latter two estimates, however, include, not only the damage done by smoke, but the wasted fuel which it represents.

[6] The growing proportion of workers required in transportation and distribution as markets expand is indicated by the increase in the percentage of gainfully employed persons in the United States engaged in trade and transportation from 4.13 in 1840 to nearly 10 in 1870 and 17.6 in 1920. *Twelfth Census; Special Reports, Occupations*, p. xxx; *Statistical Abstract of the United States*, 1924, p. 47. In England and Wales, the proportion of all gainfully employed engaged in retailing increased from 5.3 per cent in 1841 to 9.5 in 1891. Although the total gainfully employed in England and Wales less than doubled from 1861 to 1891, the commercial group — clerks, accountants, brokers, agents, auctioneers, travelling salesmen, and persons engaged in banking and insurance — nearly trebled. Hobson, J. A., *The Evolution of Modern Capitalism*, pp. 384 and 386.

[7] Not all industrial accidents, of course, are directly due to machinery. The *immediate* cause of most of them is carelessness on the part of the injured man. But whether or not negligence results in an accident depends upon the conditions under which it occurs. A man who is careless in a factory is likely to get hurt. Since carelessness is in some degree inevitable, the responsibility for accidents due to it appears to rest as much upon the environment which the new technique creates as upon human nature.

augmented. This is indicated by a rapid increase in income *per capita*. Extremely accurate estimates are impossible, not only because of the paucity of statistical data but because the quality of goods has greatly changed and because many articles in daily use now were not made seventy-five or one hundred years ago and many things produced then are not used now. Bowley believes that in the fifty year period, 1850–1854 to 1900–1924, the purchasing power of wages in England doubled,[8] and King has estimated that, in the period 1850 to 1910, *per capita* income in the United States practically trebled and that, from 1910 to 1928, it increased nearly 29 per cent, making it in 1928 nearly four times that of 1850.[9] It is not intended to suggest that production is at all adequate, for we have seen that it averages only about $749 per person. But power-driven machines — and the rich natural resources of the United States — have made possible an indulgence in war and armaments on a scale beyond the imagination of our forefathers, the substantial elimination of the labor of small children, a grade school education for nearly all children,[10] an automobile and a telephone for every six persons, 12,000,000 houses wired for electricity, and, as items of ordinary diet, white bread, butter, milk, oranges, bananas, and many other things which a century ago were distinctly luxuries. And most important of all, machinery has made a tremendous difference in the death rate — both directly, by enabling people to live better and to employ more medical aid, and indirectly, by enabling the community to support scientific research on a larger scale. The result has been a remarkable increase in the population of all countries of European civilization — an increase which has occurred despite the fact that in those countries the birth rate

[8] *Dictionary of Political Economy* (Palgrave ed. 1908), p. 801.

[9] *The Wealth and Income of the People of the United States*, p. 129; *The National Income and Its Purchasing Power*, p. 87. Carl Snyder has estimated that the physical volume of production in the United States increased nearly fivefold between 1870 and 1925. *Business Cycles and Business Measurements*, p. 239.

[10] From 1870 to 1924, the percentage of children between five and seventeen years of age enrolled in public schools increased from 57 to 83, the percentage of those in attendance to those enrolled from 59.3 to 79.3, and the days attended per pupil enrolled from 78.4 a year to 132. Between 1890 and 1924, the enrollment in public high schools increased nearly seven times as fast as the population, the enrollment in colleges, universities, and professional schools five times as fast as the population. *Monthly Labor Review*, October, 1927, v. XXV, p. 745. The expenditure per person in elementary and secondary schools increased from $5 a year in 1850 to $62 in 1924.

has been falling. No fact illustrates more clearly how close even today is the connection between production and survival than this drop in the death rate as production increases.

III. Machinery and Specialization

Not only is machinery responsible for our present standards of living, but, as has already been suggested, it is also responsible for many of the most outstanding characteristics of modern economic society. For example, to machinery is largely traceable the minute specialization of labor which is so typical of modern industry.[11] The artisan of two centuries ago not only often made a complete product but, in addition to being a tanner or cobbler or nail maker or blacksmith, he was frequently a small farmer supplying his family with a large part of its food. To-day there are few workers, except those in agriculture, who make even one complete product. There are about ninety operations in making a pair of shoes, a hundred and fifty in making a man's coat, and thirteen in making a strip of steel into a spring leaf for an automobile spring. A worker's task may consist solely in making buttonholes, picking out sheets of tissue paper from between sheets of paper money, or watching for dents in tin cans as they pass before him on a moving belt. Professor Commons describes specialization in the meat packing industry as follows:

" The animal has been surveyed and laid off like a map; and the men have been classified in over thirty specialties and twenty rates of pay from 16 cents to 50 cents an hour. The 50-cent man is restricted to using the knife on the most delicate parts of the hide (floorman) or to using the ax in splitting the backbone (splitter); and wherever a less skilled man can be slipped in at 18 cents, $18\frac{1}{2}$ cents, 20, $22\frac{1}{2}$, 24 or 25 cents, and so on, a place is made for him and an occupation mapped out. In working on the hide there are nine positions at eight different rates of pay. A 20-cent man pulls off the tail, a $22\frac{1}{2}$-cent man pounds off another part where the hide separates readily, and the knife of the 40-cent man cuts a different texture and has a different ' feel ' from that of the 50-cent man. Skill has become specialized to fit the anatomy." [12]

For this minute specialization, machinery is largely responsible. It pays to divide the making of an article among many workmen only when there is enough work to keep each man

[11] Machinery is also, of course, a manifestation of specialization.
[12] " Labor Conditions in Slaughtering and Meat Packing," *Trade Unionism and Labor Policies* (first series), p. 224.

busy doing solely one thing. A clothing manufacturer can divide the making of a coat among 150 workers only when his sales of suits run into many hundreds a week. And if Mr. Ford could not sell several thousand cars a day, he could not keep one man busy tightening up a certain bolt. All of this means that the minute specialization of labor depends upon the size of the market within the reach of each enterprise. But large markets presuppose cheap transportation and cheap transportation is largely a product of the locomotive, the steamship, and the automobile — in other words, of machinery.

IV. Machine Industry and Large Business Enterprises

To machinery also is attributable the rise of huge business enterprises employing thousands or even tens of thousands of men each and with annual sales running into the tens or hundreds of millions. These immense enterprises are largely, though not entirely, a result of the fact that it is often more economical to produce goods in large plants than in small ones. But large plants, as we have seen, are possible only when markets are large, and it is the application of machinery to transportation which has placed vast markets within the reach of any plant.

Wherever we find large business enterprises, we find also the corporate form of organization and the problems which go with it — such as the concentration of power into a few hands and the exploitation of stockholders by insiders. Few men can supply from their own pockets the capital needed by a large modern enterprise and those who can do not care, as a rule, to put so much of their wealth into a single business. To provide the immense amounts of capital needed by large enterprises, resort has been had to the business corporation, which is essentially a device to facilitate the raising of large amounts of capital. It is not a new invention, for it was used several hundred years ago in the conduct of foreign trade, where the risk was great and the capital required was considerable, but it has become common only since the development of machine technique. Today it is the typical form of business organization in all industries in which machinery is extensively used.

V. Machinery and the Position of Labor

When business enterprises were small, it was not unreasonable for wage earners to look forward to becoming employers. As long as they had this expectation, they did not feel that they belonged to a distinct and separate wage-earning class. Nor did the masters regard their apprentices and journeymen as members of a different class. In fact, the sons of masters were usually apprentices or journeymen and many an apprentice married his master's daughter. It is noteworthy that there is no evidence of enduring labor organizations among medieval artisans. Expecting soon to become masters, they apparently felt no pressing need for organizations to protect the interests of journeymen. But how ridiculous it would be for the modern industrial worker to expect to become the owner of a railroad, a shoe factory, a steel works, or a cotton mill![13] Of course he has some chance of obtaining a supervisory position, but even that is remote, for the simple reason that such positions are few in comparison with the number of employees.

As soon, however, as the average laborer has no hope of becoming either an employer or a supervisor, he tends to become class conscious. Feeling that he will be a member of his class for life, he identifies himself with it and becomes interested in organizations for the purpose of protecting and helping it. Thus, even before the days of machinery, as soon as the development of wholesale markets led to large enterprises in some industries,

---

[13] A study of occupational statistics might lead to the conclusion that the chance of rising out of the wage-earning class is improving. From 1870 to 1920, the number of proprietors and officials in the United States increased slightly more rapidly than the number of industrial wage earners — 545 per cent as compared with 521 per cent. The professional class, however, increased 665 per cent and the lower salaried class 1,288 per cent. In 1870, there were 2.55 industrial wage earners for every person falling in the group of proprietors, officials, professional men, and lower salaried employees, but in 1920, only 1.78. Coincidently with the remarkable increase in the number of professional and salaried workers has gone a decline in the size of families in these classes, necessitating that the increase in the professional and salaried workers come largely from other classes.

What these figures really mean, however, is better opportunity for the *children* of wage earners rather than for wage earners themselves. The technical knowledge required in professional work and in many salaried positions is so great that it requires special schooling. The above calculations are based upon A. H. Hansen's analysis of occupational distribution in his "Industrial Class Alignment in the United States," *Quarterly Publication of the American Statistical Association*, December, 1920, v. XVII, pp. 417–425, and his supplementary note in December, 1922, v. XIX, pp. 503–506.

we find the workers in those industries developing class consciousness and forming trade unions. It is machinery, however,
and the large business establishments which it has created that
are primarily responsible for the sharp class cleavage in industry.
Today in the United States about one-fifth of the manual laborers in non-agricultural pursuits belong to trade unions and, did
not employers bitterly oppose labor organizations and destroy
them wherever possible, the union membership would be much
larger.

We have seen that the way in which a system of free enterprise operates depends very largely upon the distribution of
bargaining power among classes and individuals. Obviously
such a revolutionary change as the substitution of machine
for hand methods could scarcely occur without profoundly
affecting the relative bargaining power of wage earners and
employers. In the main, machinery seems to have made labor
relatively weaker, but this result has not by any means been
universal.

Machinery has weakened the bargaining power of labor in
several ways. It is largely responsible, we have seen, for the
minute specialization of labor. Specialization tends to reduce
the bargaining power of labor because, the more minutely work is
subdivided, the less each laborer has to know and the more
easily, therefore, he can be replaced with an inexperienced man.
By increasing the size of the business enterprise, machinery has
reduced the importance of the individual workman. One worker
is less important to an establishment employing 500 or 1,000 men
than to a firm employing 5, 10, or 20. In most cases, machinery
seems to reduce the proportion of skilled men required by industry. It is easy to see that the work of the handicraftsman,
who guides the movements of his tools, frequently demands great
skill. Whether or not machinery, in relieving workers of the
necessity of guiding their tools, renders skilled men less necessary
depends upon how the tasks which machinery creates compare
in difficulty with those which it eliminates.

Machinery creates the tasks of (1) repairing and maintaining the machines; (2) setting them; (3) putting the work in and
removing it when completed; (4) starting and stopping the machines and regulating their operation. The first two usually

require considerable skill, but a very few men can ordinarily do the repairing and the setting of many machines. By far the largest group of laborers needed in running most types of machines are the operators, the men who put the work in and start the machine, regulate its operation, stop it, and remove the work. A few machines, such as the locomotive or the automobile, require skilled operators. *In these cases, however, the operator does more than merely start and stop the machine.* In the case of the locomotive and the automobile, he regulates its speed and its internal working. But when the duties of the operator consist simply of putting in and taking out the work and of starting and stopping the machine, they demand little skill. This is particularly true when the operation is repetitive, for it then becomes practicable to provide jigs and fixtures which assure that the work will be held in proper position. When the tasks of the operators are thus simplified, the introduction of machinery almost invariably reduces the general level of skill needed among wage earners.

In two important ways machinery has tended to increase the relative bargaining power of labor. In the first place, the application of machinery to transportation has rendered accessible vast areas of unoccupied land and rich stores of natural resources. The opportunity of wage earners to take up land in the Mississippi Valley, Western Canada, or Australia and become their own employers has greatly improved wages and working conditions by compelling employers to offer as attractive terms as nature; and the demand for railroad construction, mining, and lumbering in the new regions which machine transportation has rendered accessible has still further improved wages and working conditions. In the second place, machinery has increased the bargaining power of labor by enhancing the cost of labor turnover. Every machine, as will be explained presently, imposes on the employer certain fixed costs which go on whether the machine operates or not. Assume that an employer has a machine on which the fixed costs are $10 a day and on which an experienced operator turns out twenty pieces. This gives a fixed cost of 50 cents each. Suppose now that the experienced man quits and is replaced by a new employee who, during the first two weeks, produces only ten pieces a day. This is a fixed cost of a dollar each, or, on ten pieces, a loss of $5 a day compared with the performance of an experienced man. The more elaborate and expensive machinery becomes and the heavier the fixed costs connected with it, the greater are the losses suffered by employers when experienced workers must be replaced by green men. Obviously, when it costs $5 or more a day for several weeks to break in a man, it may pay employers to make concessions in order to hold old employees.

VI. Machine Technique Tends to Make Industry Dynamic

When methods of production are determined by the persons who use them, industrial technique has a tendency to become fixed. Men dislike to change their ways of working because things usually go more smoothly when the habitual routine is faithfully followed. Furthermore, long adherence to the same methods prevents workers and employers from seeing the possibility of others. They come to regard every step in the customary procedure as necessary; and their intimate knowledge of the difficulties of doing the work, of the precautions which must be taken to achieve satisfactory results, makes them see objections to any new process. Thus there gradually grows up a stock of trade beliefs or superstitions which discourage experimentation and innovation in certain directions. Finally, each worker or employer tends to keep to himself such improvements as he discovers. Business men do not care to have their innovations in technique become known to competitors, and the laborer who discovers a way of doing more or better work feels that by keeping it to himself he will make his job more secure. Thus the spread of better methods is impeded and much knowledge dies with those who discover it.

Although the attitude of producers toward changes *in their methods of production* tends to be intensely conservative, this is much less true of their attitude toward changes *in their products*. The best way of increasing sales is to offer the consumer something better than he can obtain from any rival enterprise. The easiest way for machine makers to sell more machines is to improve on the old ones. If the new machines are sufficiently superior, most users of the old ones will be compelled to discard their old equipment and replace it with new. Thus machine builders have a tremendous incentive to develop new and superior machines. This is why machinery makes industry dynamic — it causes the technique to be determined largely by the *makers* of machines rather than by their *users*. Were it left to machine-*users* to invent new machines or to improve existing ones, industrial technique would probably change almost as slowly as in the days of handicraft.

VII. MACHINERY AND MODERN INDUSTRIAL COSTS

One of the most important results of machine industry is its effect upon industrial costs. Pecuniary costs, we have learned, fall into two classes, direct and fixed, direct being those which fluctuate closely with small changes in output, and fixed costs those which are affected little or not at all by such changes. Now it is quite apparent that, in the degree that costs are fixed, small fluctuations in sales will produce great changes in profits. Assume that there is an increase in the sales of an enterprise with relatively large fixed costs. The total expenses do not increase in proportion. Consequently, profits expand even more rapidly than sales. Thus fixed costs create a tremendous incentive to increase sales, even by cutting prices, if necessary. On the other hand, if sales decline, all expenses do not drop in proportion. This means that profits fall even more rapidly than the volume of business. To the importance of fixed expenses may be ascribed many phenomena which are characteristic of modern industry, such as the high development of marketing methods, the extraordinary sensitiveness of business to fluctuations in demand, the quickness with which changes in demand plunge industry into depression or restore it to prosperity.

Machinery tends to increase the relative importance of fixed costs because it replaces variable labor costs with the fixed costs that go with machines. Suppose that a manufacturer uses only hand methods. His operating expenses will then vary quite directly with his volume of output. If his sales increase, his costs will rise in proportion, because he must hire proportionately more men. If sales fall, he can promptly cut his expenses by laying off workers who are no longer needed. Quite otherwise when machines are used. Once a machine is purchased, most of the costs connected with it continue whether it is used or not. When demand declines, the manufacturer cannot eliminate the costs connected with the machine by laying it off. He can, of course, sell it if he thinks that the drop in his market is permanent, but that is not practical if the decrease is only temporary.

What are the expenses connected with the machine which go on whether it is running or not? One of them is depreciation, with the meaning of which we are already acquainted. If the machine cost $10,000 and is expected to be worth nothing at the end of ten years, the manufacturer must get back enough each year to give him $10,000 in the course of ten years. This would be $1,000 a year — if we disregard the possibility of getting interest on the money in the depreciation fund. If he had not put his money into the machine, he could have lent it at interest, receiving say, 6 per cent, or $600 a year. He must, therefore, expect to get from the machine $600 to compensate him for what he might have obtained had he invested his money in another way. This interest charge goes on whether the machine runs or not. The machine should be insured against fire, and the insurance premium must be paid whether or not the machine is used. We may assume the premium to be $10 a year. Finally, he must pay taxes on the machine. These may also be assumed to be $10 a year. Thus, by installing the machine, the manufacturer has incurred the following costs, all of which continue whether it runs or not:

Depreciation	$1,000
Interest	600
Insurance	10
Taxes	10
	$1,620

It is apparent that the proportion of these expenses which must be borne by each unit of product depends upon how many units are produced. If 1,000 units are turned out a year, each unit must bear $1.62 of the total cost. If 2,000 are made, the share of each is only 81 cents. Evidently it may be more profitable for the manufacturer to sell more units at a low price than a few at a high price.

VIII. Machinery and Industrial Risks

By increasing production and cheapening transportation, machinery has eliminated the food famines which were a great dread of the Middle Ages, but it has greatly increased the seriousness of the job famines which are typical of modern industry. To the artisan-farmers who were so numerous both in England and New England during the eighteenth century, unemployment could have no great terrors. Even though work in the mechanical trades might be scarce, the laborer still had some food from his land and shelter for himself and his family. Machine industry, however, has no place for the artisan-farmer because it demands laborers who will be in the factory every day that they may be needed. Furthermore, by compelling them to live in large cities where land is expensive, it also makes it difficult, or at least inconvenient, for wage earners to become home owners. To workers with nothing to sell but their labor, dependent for goods upon purchases from the grocery store and for shelter upon a rented tenement, a general business depression is in a rough way comparable to the medieval famine. And, as we shall learn when we study business cycles, the present economic system is peculiarly subject to general depressions.

The new technique has brought into industry large, swiftly moving apparatus, elevators, high voltages and steam pressures, cranes lifting immense weights over the heads of workmen, and many other features which greatly enhance the danger of industrial accidents. Man has in large degree subdued the wilderness, but he has created the modern factory, which probably is almost as dangerous as the jungle. In 1919, there occurred in American industries about 23,000 fatal accidents, and about 575,000 non-fatal ones causing four weeks or more of disability. The industries of New York kill about 1,500 of their employees a year, or about four a day, and those of Pennsylvania kill 2,500 to 3,000 workers each year.

Capitalists as well as laborers find their risks increased by machine industry. For one thing, the machine technique increases the losses which investors experience when an enterprise proves unprofitable. As long as a business pays no return to its owners, their investment in it is for the time being practically lost. If there is no prospect for profits later, the only way to recover part of the investment in the machines is to sell them. But second-hand machinery must usually be sold at a heavy sacrifice, particularly if it was designed to meet the peculiar needs of a certain firm. Suppose, however, that the investors had put their money into a business using no machines whatever. In this case, it is likely that the money would have been used to buy raw materials and to make advances to wage earners. From raw materials and the work of laborers, a finished product results, which, if not defective or out of style, should be salable at comparatively small sacrifice, because it is not secondhand ware. Hence, the investors would probably be able to recover a large proportion of their money.

As long as costs are largely variable rather than fixed, the problem of predicting what unit costs will be next week or next month is primarily a matter of forecasting changes in the prices of labor and raw materials. But machinery, by enhancing the importance of fixed costs, such as depreciation, interest on investment, taxes, and insurance, introduces another element of uncertainty. In order to know unit costs, the business man must know, not only the prices of labor and raw material, but *how many units he will produce during a given period*. This depends upon how many orders he obtains, which, of course, is a matter of much uncertainty. In expectation that sales will be large and unit costs low, he may quote low prices. If sales are small, he may discover that he is selling below cost. Thus machinery increases the risks of business by making it more difficult to estimate future costs of production.

Finally, machine technique enhances financial risks by increasing the losses imposed upon business houses by dull years and dull seasons. Attention has been directed to the fact that, when hand methods are used, enterprises can cut their costs promptly, simply by laying off superfluous men. This ability to adjust expenses to unfavorable business conditions naturally aids concerns in maintaining solvency. Machine technique, however, imposes costs which business establishments cannot escape when sales decline. Machines go on depreciating, taxes on them must be paid, and insurance must be carried whether sales are above or below normal. If the machines were purchased with borrowed money, interest on it must be paid. All of these unavoidable fixed expenses add to the difficulty of tiding over periods of slack business.

IX. MACHINE INDUSTRY AND LARGE FORTUNES

Many current economic problems center about the enormous fortunes which are characteristic of modern economic society. It is important to realize that these fortunes are products of machinery, no less than of the genius of those who have acquired them. In order to amass a huge fortune, one needs a large market in which to do business. Had Mr. Field and Mr. Wanamaker lived in 1750, they could scarcely have made such vast sums, for the simple reason that cities large enough or wealthy enough to provide the necessary market did not exist. As long as the expense of transportation made immense factories impossible, no business man, irrespective of how superior his ability, could make scores of millions in manufacturing. Or consider the huge incomes often obtained by the owners of patents, trade names, or advertising slogans, the writers of successful novels or popular songs, eminent singers or actors. Not simply because of their talents, but because the application of machinery to transportation puts within their reach a market of a hundred million instead of ten million, do these persons obtain such large incomes. As population increases, their incomes may be expected to rise, just as the value of land mounts as men multiply.

REFERENCES

Hobson, John A., *The Evolution of Modern Capitalism* (new and revised edition), 1916. Ch. III, IV, XII, and XIII.
Marshall, L. C., *Industrial Society*, 1918. Ch. VII.
Usher, A. P., *A History of Mechanical Invention*, 1929. Ch. IX, X.
Veblen, Thorstein, *The Theory of Business Enterprise*, 1904. Ch. II.

CHAPTER VI

SPECIALIZATION

I. THE NATURE OF SPECIALIZATION. II. SOME REASONS FOR SPE-
CIALIZATION. III. SPECIALIZATION AND THE OPTIMUM DENSITY
OF POPULATION. IV. SPECIALIZATION MAKES GETTING A LIVING A
MATTER OF BUYING AND SELLING. V. SPECIALIZATION AND IN-
TERDEPENDENCE. VI. SPECIALIZATION AND SPECULATIVE PRO-
DUCTION. VII. SPECIALIZATION AND FINANCIAL RISKS. VIII. SPE-
CIALIZATION AND THE WORKER'S JOB. IX. SPECIALIZATION AND
THE DISTRIBUTION OF INCOME.

I. THE NATURE OF SPECIALIZATION

Each family, locality, or country might, if it chose, undertake
to make everything that it needed, to strive for self-sufficiency.
But most persons today, except in agriculture, do not even produce a complete product, and regions which approach self-
sufficiency scarcely exist outside the so-called "backward countries."[1]

Specialization is of three principal kinds: occupational, of
business units, and territorial. Occupational specialization is
that which the individual practices. It is represented by the
doctor, lawyer, bricklayer, machinist, or farmer who pursues
one line of activity for a living. The degree of occupational specialization varies greatly. A man may be engaged in diversified
farming, which means that he is pretty much a jack-of-all-trades,
or he may be a buttonhole maker in a clothing factory, which
means that he does nothing but make buttonholes.

Business enterprises, as well as individuals, specialize. The
1929 commercial telephone directory of New York City lists
4,338 distinct kinds of business and this, of course, is far from
complete, for many things are not made in New York City.

---

[1] Even a country so large and diversified in climate and resources as the United
States is dependent upon other countries for articles of such common consumption
as diamonds, rubber, coffee, tea, silk, cocoa, bananas, tin, and a large proportion
of its wood pulp, wool, and sugar.

Within industries, the enterprises specialize. A producer of machinery usually makes only certain varieties — possibly only lathes or drill presses — and probably only certain sizes and types of those. A shoe factory does not make all kinds of shoes but confines itself to men's or women's shoes of a certain general grade; men's suits are made in some factories, women's in others, collars, shirts, gloves, hats in others.

Finally, cities, localities, and countries specialize. Akron, Detroit, Lowell, Brockton, Troy, Fall River, Pittsburgh are all associated in our minds with certain products. " Corn belt," " wheat belt," " cotton belt " are familiar expressions. A survey of the agriculture of the country would show a multitude of small areas of specialization — some devoted to different varieties of fruit, others to butter, cheese, garden truck, potatoes, or tobacco. Thirty mineral districts, according to Professor C. K. Leith, account for three-fourths of the world's mineral production — three-fourths of the world's iron comes from six districts in the United States, England, France, Sweden, and Spain; two-thirds of the world's copper from about half a dozen districts in the western United States and Chile; and over one-half of the gold from the Union of South Africa.[2] Over three-fifths of the world's cotton is produced in the southern United States, about two-thirds of the coffee in Brazil, and half of the rubber in British Malaya. An extreme case of localized production is furnished by the gilsonite industry. Gilsonite, a brilliant, black asphaltic substance used in making telephone mouthpieces, electric switch handles, varnish, paint, knobs, and buttons, is sold all over the world but is mined only in Utah.[3]

A man cannot confine himself solely to producing one thing unless others devote themselves to producing the many other things he needs. And he cannot spend his whole time making part of an article unless others perform the remaining operations. When we say then that our economic society is characterized by a high degree of specialization, we are also saying that it is a highly coöperative society. The coöperation is largely unconscious, but it is none the less real. The farmer who raises corn

[2] " Exploitation and World Progress," *Foreign Affairs*, October, 1927, v. VI, p. 129.
[3] *The United States Daily*, June 7, 1928, p. 5.

is probably not aware that he may be coöperating in the production of cosmetics or mattresses, but both cosmetics and mattresses are among the hundreds of commodities made from corn. The way in which the unconscious coöperation among specialists is created is by buying and selling. It is important to realize that, functionally considered, buying and selling are a method of creating and organizing coöperation among specialists. The thousands of individuals and firms that coöperate in making automobiles, for example, are brought together by automobile manufacturers' buying labor, coal, steel, tires, glass, carburetors, magnetos, bodies, hair, leather, paint, varnish; by the producers of these things in turn purchasing labor, equipment, and materials; and so on indefinitely. Probably every gainfully employed person in the country is directly or indirectly a maker of automobiles, and, for that matter, of most other things.

Besides this basic way of creating coöperation, there is a secondary method which may be called the authoritative one. Fundamentally the employees of a business enterprise are brought into coöperation by having their services purchased by the same employer. They are not, however, in the same position as independent producers who sell their services or products to the same buyer. How the work shall be divided among them and what each person shall do is decided, not by the specialists themselves, but by the management. In other words, *within the enterprise,* coöperation is established, not by buying and selling, but by authority.

II. Some Reasons for Specialization

How long would it take the reader to make the articles which he uses in one day? Possibly close to a lifetime and certainly many years. Yet, by concentrating upon making or doing one thing, he is able to produce enough each day to buy what it would take him years to make.

Whence comes the superior productivity of occupational specialization? Partly from the fact that it enables men to concentrate upon doing the things which they can do best. The man who has great strength and endurance but little dexterity can do work requiring strength and leave to others tasks which primarily demand dexterity; the man of superior intellect can devote himself to work requiring thought and let others do the routine jobs.[4] But proficiency is a product, not merely of natural aptitude, but also of knowledge and practice, and specialization enables workers both to learn more about their work and to acquire greater practice at it. The physician who specializes upon certain diseases and the production manager who gives his full attention to increasing output become more expert because their time is not taken by other things. Specialization avoids waste of time. In changing from one job to another, the materials and tools used on the first must be put away and the things needed for the second must be found and assembled. Possibly a machine used for the first job must be reset for the second. Then there is always a warming up period during which the worker is getting into the swing of the task and his production is not up to normal. Finally, specialization often economizes equipment. If work were not minutely specialized and if each employee required separate tools and machines for each operation which he performed, a much larger investment in equipment would be necessary. It is, of course, possible for several men to use the same equipment but this is likely to cause some idleness by forcing some of them at times to wait for a tool or machine. Consequently, when work is not specialized, a choice must be made between idleness of men and idleness of equipment. The men can be kept constantly busy only by having as much equipment of each kind as may be needed at any moment. When work is specialized, however, no more tools and machines are needed for each occupation than there are specialists in it.

All of these advantages are independent of particular forms of industrial organization. Because of them, we would have specialization even were there no division of producers into employers and employees. But there are effects of occupational specialization which are important largely because of the existence of employing and wage-earning classes. Because occupational specialization is peculiarly advantageous to employers, it is probably

---

[4] Specialization, of course, creates the problem of finding the job for which each person is best fitted and giving him an opportunity to prepare for the work and, after having prepared himself, to do it. These things are all most unsatisfactorily done at present, in the main, probably because psychologists are so little able to determine what aptitudes a given task requires or a given person possesses.

carried further in modern industry than it would be in a non-capitalistic society. For one thing, it enables employers to economize the scarcer types of ability by the use of unskilled or semi-skilled labor. Certain operations in the making of shoes, for example, require considerable skill. If there were no specialization in shoe making, each worker would have to be a skilled man. Subdivision of work makes it possible to have the difficult operations performed by a few skilled men and to use children, women, or unskilled workers, who otherwise could not be employed in the industry, for the less exacting work. Professor Commons found in meat packing that a gang of 230 men killing 105 cattle an hour included but eleven men who were paid 50 cents an hour and three paid 45 cents, while the number getting under 20 cents was 144.[5] Minute subdivision of work usually lessens the employer's dependence upon individual employees. Each job is more quickly learned and, if a worker leaves, a new man is more easily trained for the vacancy. Not only does this facilitate the task of maintaining production in the face of a changing personnel but, as was explained in the preceding chapter, it obviously enhances the bargaining power of the employer. Specialization also helps the employer control the rate at which his men work — an effect which has received inadequate attention from economists. One specialist does the first operation, a second the next, a third the next, and so on. Obviously this gives the employer an opportunity to control the speed by making a pace setter of the first worker. If any man fails to maintain the established pace, this at once becomes evident by the piling up of unfinished work beside him, and the employer can put pressure upon him to speed up. If the men are paid by the piece, even more effective pressure may be exerted upon each slow worker by his fellow employees. Those who perform operations subsequent to his find their earnings limited by his failure to supply them with more work. Naturally they insist that he speed up, and they make life unpleasant for him if he does not. From the standpoint of the broad interests of the community, the terrific pace which many enterprises are able to enforce through the combination of specialization and piece work is undoubtedly undesirable. Finally, specialization sometimes

---

[5] These are the wage rates which prevailed in 1904 and were, of course, much lower than those which now exist.

facilitates the allocation of responsibility for faulty work. Defects in the product are often traceable to particular operations. If all the men in a department perform the operation, it may be impossible to discover who caused a given defect, but if the work is specialized and only one or a few men do each operation, the discovery may be easy.

Some reasons for specialization among business enterprises are closely analogous to the advantages of occupational specialization. For example, a firm which makes only one product or a group of closely related products can learn better how to manufacture and market its ware. It can also adapt its machinery, equipment, layout of plant, and personnel to the making of that one thing. If, however, it produces several articles, its men, machines, and plant layout may not be ideally suited to the manufacture of any of them. A plant devoted to only one product is likely to be easier to manage than one making several. Routing and scheduling work through the shop is obviously simpler when there are not several products which may interfere with one another. The Knox Hat Company, for instance, in 1922 made 9,720 varieties of soft hats. This meant frequent shutdowns in machines in order to change from one kind of hat to another. After studying the savings which might be expected from greater specialization, the company reduced its line, first to 3,684 varieties, and later to about 2,000.[6] Specialization of business enterprises reduces the stock of raw materials which must be carried, the capital tied up in carrying them, and the warehouse space devoted to storage. Small stocks of raw materials are particularly advantageous during periods of falling prices. The so-called simplification movement — that is, the reduction in number of items made by a plant — which has recently made such rapid progress in the United States, has been greatly stimulated by the precipitous drop in prices in 1920 and by the subsequent downward price trend.[7] Finally, specialization of business enterprises

[6] Basset, W. R., *Taking the Guesswork Out of Business*, pp. 32–34.

[7] A small degree of specialization greatly reduces the inventory which must be carried. For example, a certain shoe company concentrates on five standard lasts with standard variations of double-soled, blucher, black or tan leather, and Oxford or high shoes, making about twenty models in all. The shoes are all made of calfskin. If an additional type of leather were used, it would mean doubling the number of models. The average shoe manufacturer produces from twenty to thirty lasts and 100 to 150 models.

helps plants to gain the advantages of occupational specialization. A firm which makes small quantities of many products is likely to find difficulty in keeping each of its employees busy doing one job and one only. It can do so more easily if it produces a large quantity of only one thing.

It is worth noting that in agriculture specialization is largely by *groups* of products rather than by *individual* products. For example, dairy farming is likely to involve raising corn, small grain, and hay. In cultivating the corn, the land is being prepared for the small grain crop and when the land is used for the small grain, it is being prepared for the clover. With dairying also often goes the raising of hogs and possibly calves. If the milk is taken to a cheese factory, hog production is carried on to consume the whey. If the farmer separates his milk and sells his cream to a butter factory, hogs and calves may be raised to consume the skimmed milk. A grain farmer is likely to raise horses as a side line in order to consume the unsalable roughage. In all of these cases, there is specialization, but it is specialization of groups of products.

Just as some persons are peculiarly well fitted to do certain things, so some localities, on account of soil, climate, or proximity to power, raw materials, supplies of cheap labor, and markets, are exceptionally well adapted to the production of certain goods. Because electricity can be produced so cheaply at Niagara Falls, the city is a center for industries using large quantities of power. Chicago, Pittsburgh, Buffalo, and Duluth are important producers of steel because they are well located for assembling the raw material and for reaching certain markets. Climate, topography, and soil cause the farmers in large parts of New York, Wisconsin, and Minnesota to specialize in dairying. Since Wisconsin and Minnesota are remote from the large markets, they make butter and cheese, which can be easily shipped great distances; New York, being near many large cities, finds it advantageous to concentrate upon the production of milk. Steel towns, which usually have a surplus of women workers, tend to attract industries employing a proportion of female labor.[8] Often the by-

---

[8] An increasing number of cities are realizing the desirability of a planned diversification of industry. Where broad diversification of industry does not exist,

product of one industry is the raw material of another. Soap factories are likely to locate in meat packing centers.

But it would be a mistake to assume that industries are always located where goods can be produced most economically. Accident, as well as economic advantage, often determines their location. The first plant making a new product or using a new process is likely to be built where the inventor of the articles or the process lives. The location may be good or poor; rarely, however, is it the best possible. Once an industry gets started at a place, other plants tend to grow up there too. There are several reasons for this. New enterprises are usually started by those who have had experience in the industry. Such men, of course, are to be found where the industry already exists. The initiators of a new enterprise find several advantages in building their plant at the place where they themselves live and where there are other plants in the same business. They need not change their residence in order to keep in close touch with their business; capital and bank credit are more easily obtained where both the industry and the promoters of the new enterprise are known; a force of technical men and skilled workers is more readily recruited; and there are usually auxiliary industries, furnishing machinery, raw materials, parts, and repair service, near which it is advantageous for new plants to locate.

Notice that our analysis of the advantages of specialization sheds some light upon the desirability of protective tariffs. No individual thinks of making everything for himself. Why should a region? But regions, and particularly nations, are reluctant to become part of a larger economic system. Independence, self-sufficiency, is their goal. The principal device for checking regional specialization is the protective tariff. By creating barriers to trade between several regions, protective duties prevent commodities from being made in the particular places which are most favorable for their production. And so intimately are the sev-

---

some groups of workers, such as women and youths seeking to enter industry, may find employment difficult to obtain. Cities with diversified industry are likely to have less distress during business depressions. If several members of a family work in different industries, it is less likely that all will lose their jobs and the family income is not cut down so drastically. Furthermore, sales of the stores do not fall off so much and the stores lay off fewer employees.

eral forms of specialization related that, in limiting territorial specialization, tariffs also limit occupational and business specialization. The reason, of course, is that tariffs restrict the market within the reach of each plant. One reason why industry is more productive in the United States than in Europe is because we have an area within which one can travel east and west four days, or north and south two days, without encountering a tariff barrier. Europe, which has about the same area, is divided into twenty-seven regions each separated from the others by a tariff wall. In fact, it is only because we have such an immense free-trade area that our high tariff does not disastrously affect our standard of living.

III. Specialization and the Optimum Density of Population

The fact that specialization tends to make possible larger per capita output is of significance in determining what is the optimum amount of population for a country. Other than merely economic considerations, of course, (such as the requirements of national defense) affect the density of population which is most desirable. From the standpoint of economics, however, the optimum may be defined as the density which, under a given state of technique, makes possible the maximum per capita output. In some respects, as will be explained in detail in Chapter XV, an increase in population tends to reduce the output per capita. The essential reason is that labor produces, not alone, but with the help of capital. If population becomes more numerous relative to the resources of the community, each worker has a smaller quantity of resources to help him produce and his output tends to be less. To this extent, an increase in population tends to diminish per capita output. But a greater population also makes possible more minute specialization and this, as we have seen, tends to increase per capita output. The net effect of an increase in population depends upon which tendency predominates.

Instructive illustrations of the intimate relationship between specialization and the optimum density of population are afforded by the dismemberment of some European countries following the

World War. Probably Austria-Hungary was overpopulated even before the War. Nevertheless there is no doubt that the degree of overpopulation is far greater now than it was in 1914 because the dismemberment of the country has led to the erection of tariff barriers which have partially destroyed the advantageous system of specialization which existed within the boundaries of the old Austro-Hungarian Empire. It is probable that few parts of the United States are seriously overpopulated, but it is certain that, if the several states were permitted to destroy our existing system of specialization by imposing tariffs, our population, though no greater than it is now, would be far too large. In a word, the density of population which a country finds advantageous depends upon the degree to which political and other conditions permit men to specialize.

IV. SPECIALIZATION MAKES GETTING A LIVING A MATTER OF BUYING AND SELLING

Specialization means that the process of getting a living in modern economic society is largely a matter of buying and selling. Most of us produce very little for our own consumption but sell our labor or the products of our labor and, with the money thus obtained, buy what we desire. Even the farmers, who produce for themselves to a greater degree than any other class, purchase about two-thirds of what they consume, and most city dwellers buy a much larger proportion. This means that buying and selling are far more important in modern economic life than at any time in the past and that prices and price changes affect the average man far more than ever before. Because getting a living today is so much a matter of buying and selling, our study of modern economic society must consist very largely of an inquiry into how buying and selling work under existing conditions, how prices are made, and what determines the conditions of bargains.

V. SPECIALIZATION AND INTERDEPENDENCE

If eastern Europe, suffering from war and revolution, buys less from England, England is unable to purchase as much from America. This is likely to mean that farmers here must take less for their crops and that thousands of factory workers lose their jobs. The effect, of course, extends all over the world, for a depression in this country means that we can afford to buy less tea and silk from Japan and China, coffee from Brazil, rubber from Malay, bananas from Costa Rica, olives, olive oil, and lemons from Spain and Italy, currants from Greece, or sugar from Cuba. The crash on the New York stock exchange in the fall of 1929 caused the Amsterdam diamond cutting shops to go on half-time; the drop in the price of silver during the latter part of 1929 and the early part of 1930, which reduced the buying-power of silver-standard countries, such as China, accentuated the agricultural depression in the South by forcing down the price of cotton.

These illustrations, which could be multiplied many times, indicate the interdependence which has been introduced into modern economic society by specialization. When individuals, groups, and sections specialize, their prosperity depends upon their ability to sell what they make and this depends upon the ability of other individuals, groups, and sections to buy. The prosperity of one class or country tends to make other classes and countries better off, and the misfortunes of one class or country tend to spread to other classes or countries. When the southern farmers get a good price for their cotton, the southern merchants and the manufacturers who make goods for the South are likely to be well off, the employees of those manufacturers will probably have fairly steady work at relatively good wages, and merchants in the factory towns will have large sales. A slump in the automobile, the steel, or the textile industry will very quickly affect the sales of beef in Detroit, Pittsburgh, or New England and thus the price which the western cattle raiser or feeder can get for his stock, and his ability to buy clothing, automobiles, and agricultural implements.

An extremely important result of the high degree of interdependence in modern economic society is the extraordinary liability of the industrial system to derangement. The unconscious coöperation which buying and selling establish between specialists is by no means easy to maintain free from interruption. Let an important part of the community, through crop failure, misjudging the demand, or other cause, suffer a severe loss in purchasing power, or let it refuse to buy because of belief that prices are about to fall, and the resulting breakdown in demand spreads far and wide throughout the economic system, causing a substantial drop in production and severe unemployment for both labor and capital. How to protect ourselves from these frequent breakdowns in exchange — that is, in buying and selling — is one of the outstanding economic problems of the day.

VI. Specialization and Speculative Production

If one needs a suit of clothes in a hurry, a merchant tailor can make it as a rush job in two or three days. In an up-to-date clothing factory with minutely subdivided operations, several weeks elapse between the time when a piece of cloth is cut up and that when the finished suit emerges. If the factory, with its highly subdivided labor, can make garments for less than the tailor, why does the factory take longer to make a suit? If its cost is less, must not the factory make the suit in fewer hours of actual work? But if this is so, why does it not finish the suit more quickly?

The reason can be learned by visiting any plant where operations are subdivided. On either side of each employee one will notice a stack of parts, the first consisting of those on which he has not yet performed his operation, the other of those on which he has but which have not yet been taken to the next worker. What do these piles mean? Simply that when goods are produced by highly subdivided labor, each article is being worked on for but a small part of the time. The article may be in production for several weeks and yet the number of hours of work applied to it may be very few. During most of the period, the article is in one of the piles beside a worker.

This simple case illustrates a most significant effect of specialization. Though it enhances the productivity of capital and labor, it usually lengthens the productive process. It does this in three ways. First, as we have just seen, it increases *within plants* the period which elapses from the time when raw material is started through the factory until the finished product is ready. Second, just as each worker must have a supply of unfinished parts waiting for him to work on, so each plant, in order to make quick deliveries and to avoid interruptions of production, needs a stock of raw materials.   The more numerous the plants through which raw materials must pass before a completed product emerges, the larger is the total stock of partly finished goods constantly on hand and the longer is the period required for raw materials to become finished commodities.   Finally, the transportation which specialization makes necessary may add weeks or even months to the period which elapses before raw materials get into the hands of ultimate consumers.   Consider such cases as cotton grown in the United States, spun and woven in England, and sold in India or China; or wool produced in Australia, converted into cloth in England, and sent to various parts of the world for manufacture into clothing.

VII. Specialization and Financial Risks

Increasing the time required to produce goods is not the only way in which specialization affects business risks.   A firm which makes only one thing puts its eggs into one basket.   If demand suddenly collapses, as did the demand for wheat in 1921, if the industry becomes overdeveloped, as the copper, rubber, and coal industries have been, if better and cheaper methods of production are discovered, the concern which makes only one thing may find itself in serious financial difficulties.   When an enterprise produces several commodities, it scatters its risks.   Changed conditions may destroy the profit from the sale of one article but income may be more or less sustained by sales of other products.   Specialization also increases the risks of the workmen because, the narrower a worker's training and experience, the greater the likelihood that changes in industrial technique will render his skill and knowledge unnecessary.   If, however, he is an all-round mechanic, there is less danger that new methods will render *all* of his skill obsolete.   Notice also that minute specialization, at the same time that it exposes the specialists to severe losses of income because of price changes, also makes such losses peculiarly burdensome because, as has been pointed out, the family of today, thanks to specialization, must obtain by purchase the things which it needs.

If each person produced only for his own consumption, he would not limit output because of uncertainty of demand.   In a specialized society, however, where everyone produces for sale, the fear of not finding a market at a profitable price creates a tendency to restrict production. Each business man fears that he may turn out more than he can sell at a profit. Consequently, many concerns *normally* operate at less than capacity. There are, of course, times when optimism is so great that enterprises do not hesitate to produce all that they can. As a rule, however, the fear of not finding a profitable market for their wares causes business establishments to restrict output. By so doing they give only part time employment to labor, limit labor's ability to purchase the product of industry, and thus limit their own ability to dispose of their output. One of our great economic problems is how to introduce enough certainty into business so that enterprises can afford to produce more nearly at capacity. Could this be accomplished, the output of industry would probably increase as much as one-fifth.

VIII. Specialization and the Worker's Job

Specialization causes industry to produce more, and possibly even better work, but does it cause industry to turn out better men? "The main branch of the education of human beings," it has been said, "is their habitual employment." At any rate, the job occupies half of the waking hours of most workers. Consequently, if men's mental habits and characteristics are in large degree products of the conditions under which they live, then the job is a most important part of the environment. What kind of environment is produced when work is divided into minute little tasks which each man performs over and over again? William Hard and Ernest Poole have described specialization in the meat packing industry as follows:

" A month ago we stood with a superintendent in a room of the canning department. Down both sides of a long table stood twenty immigrant women, most of them visibly middle-aged and mothers. ' Look at that Slovak woman,' said the superintendent. She stood bending slightly forward, her dull eyes staring straight down, her elbows jerking back and forth, her hands jumping in nervous haste to keep up with the gang. These hands made one simple precise motion each second, 3,600 an hour, and all exactly the same. ' She is one of the best workers we have,' the superintendent was saying. We moved closer and glanced at her face. Then we saw a strange contrast. The hands were swift, precise, intelligent. The face was stolid, vague, vacant. ' It took a long time to pound the idea into her head,' the superintendent continued, ' but when this grade of woman once absorbs an idea she holds it. She seems to have no other thought to distract her. For much of our work this woman is the kind we want. Her mind is simply all on the table.' " [9]

Undoubtedly it would be unfair to hold specialization responsible for the mental characteristics of this particular immigrant woman. Probably she was given the job because she was not fitted for anything better. It is worth while speculating, however, upon what is going to be the ultimate effect of the policy of making every job as simple, mechanical, and foolproof as possible and of relieving the workmen, as far as can be, of the necessity of exercising initiative, ingenuity, or judgment. On the frontier, where initiative, self-reliance, and ability to make one's own decisions are most essential, men tend to develop these qualities. Can we expect such characteristics to flourish in an environment in which every movement that the worker makes has been planned and taught to him by some one else and every act requiring initiative, self-reliance, and ability to think has, in so far as possible, been taken away from him? We are confronted with the conflict, which we meet again and again in the study of industry, between man's interests as the end of production and his work as a means of production. If we accept the Greek ideal that the good life is the expression and use of many faculties, the rapid transformation of tasks demanding knowledge, thought, judgment, and initiative into routine operations requiring only physical exertion must impress us as a dire calamity. Not least among the merits of trade unionism is the fact that, in a world which tends to reduce manual laborers to automatons, unions offer a means by which workers can retain some opportunity for self-expression, a chance to participate in deciding how their daily work shall be done.[10]

[9] Hard, William, and Poole, Ernest, " The Stock Yards Strike," *Outlook*, August 13, 1904, v. LXXVII, p. 887.

[10] Although subdivision of labor reduces the demands made on men's knowledge and intelligence, it often increases the demands upon their physiques. One reason is that, as we have seen, it helps the employer speed up his men. Another is that the physical strain is not distributed over a large number of muscles, as in the case of nonspecialized jobs, but is concentrated with little relief throughout the working-day upon a few muscles and a small part of the nervous system. In consequence, a person who does light but highly specialized work, such as a girl who does nothing but pick out defective ball bearings with a magnet or a man who does nothing but put a small part into a punch press 30,000 times a day, may be more fatigued at the end of the day than an old-fashioned blacksmith.

IX. Specialization and the Distribution of Income

Among a number of shoemakers, each of whom made complete pairs of shoes and was paid by the piece, there would be some inequality of income, for some would make more shoes than others. But if the work were divided by specializing the most skilled men upon the most difficult tasks exclusively and the less skilled men upon the easier, the differences in income would be increased. The most skilled workers, who would now be exercising their rare ability *all* instead of only part of the time, would be able to command higher wages than before. On the other hand, the less skilled men, who would do less exacting tasks all of the time, could scarcely retain their original wages.

This illustration indicates how specialization affects the distribution of income throughout industry. By permitting men of rare ability to concentrate upon doing the things for which they are peculiarly well fitted, it enables them to earn more than they otherwise could.[11] To the men of the common types or degrees of ability are left tasks from which the most difficult elements have been extracted and which are correspondingly less remunerative. In other words, if specialization enables some men of extraordinary executive capacity to get high salaries by directing the labor of others, it compels others to do the work and accept the pay of semi-skilled or common laborers — not because they are incapable of anything else but simply because they are *less* capable than other persons. Specialization, in short, is one of the ways in which we get more product by accepting greater inequality of income. The more minute the subdivision of labor, the greater tend to be the incomes of those who do the work requiring the rarest ability and the lower (relatively) the incomes of those who do the tasks from which the difficult elements have been taken away.

Specialization leads to great increase in production but it also leads to great inequality in bargaining ability. Some men specialize upon buying and selling — they know the wheat market, the stock market, or the real estate market, or they are

---

[11] It is not intended to imply that those who get the best paying jobs are always those who are best fitted to perform them. Often enough those who hold such jobs are the ones who are best fitted by ability or position to get and retain them rather than the ones who are best at performing them.

specialists in selling goods at retail or in buying labor or agricultural produce. Other men are skilled only in raising crops, operating machines, curing disease, or writing poetry. What is the effect, in a society where incomes are competitively determined, of having some people who are expert at buying and selling dealing with others who are not?

The existence of a class of expert buyers and sellers is one reason for doubting the claim that freedom of enterprise results in the maximum surplus of satisfaction over sacrifice. The claim is based, it will be recalled, upon the assumption that each purchaser knows better than any one else what goods will yield him the greatest pleasure and that he will spend his money accordingly. But when the amateur buyer is confronted with an expert salesman, is it not likely that choices will be determined more by the skill of the salesman than by the capacity of the goods to gratify the desires of the purchaser?

Another question raised by the existence of a body of expert buyers and sellers is whether freedom of enterprise is compatible with fair distribution of income. Industrial freedom enables many persons to make a living simply by becoming expert in forecasting the movement of prices. The farmer, for example, who is skilled in raising crops, not in selling them, sells to middlemen who make buying and selling their business, who are constantly studying the market tendencies, and who know far better than he when to buy and when to sell.

Is it not inevitable that those who are expert in buying and selling will get more than their share of the income and that those who make far more important contributions to the life of the community but who lack skill in buying and selling will get very inadequate rewards? At first glance this would seem to be true and probably it is true to some extent. In the long run, however, it is unlikely that the exceptional skill of the specialists in buying and selling brings them much more income than they would obtain in other occupations. As soon as the rewards received by these experts exceed those obtained by men of about equal ability in other occupations, there tends to be an influx of men into buying and selling. The result is that the incomes of specialists in buying and selling are brought down to the level of other occupations requiring equally rare ability. *But this is accomplished by an in-*

crease in the number of expert buyers and sellers beyond that which is needed and which would exist if their expertness did not enable them to get the better of amateur buyers and sellers. In other words, although the ability of the expert to get the better of the amateur may not enable him to get a larger income than men of equal ability in other occupations, it does cause the community to be burdened with an unnecessarily large number of persons in the buying and selling occupations.

REFERENCES

Basset, W. R., *Taking the Guesswork Out of Business*, 1924. Ch. II and III.
Black, J. D., *Production Economics*, 1926. Ch. V, VI, VII, VIII, IX, and X.
Goodrich, Carter, *The Miner's Freedom*, 1925.
Marshall, L. C., *Industrial Society*, 1918. Ch. VI.
Weld, W. E., and Tostlebe, A. S., *A Case Book for Economcis*, 1927. Pp. 158–171.

CHAPTER VII

LARGE BUSINESS UNITS

I. THE PREVALENCE OF LARGE BUSINESS UNITS. II. SOME AD-
VANTAGES OF LARGE BUSINESS UNITS. III. LIMITATIONS ON THE
SIZE OF BUSINESS UNITS. IV. WHY THE SMALL FIRM STILL PER-
SISTS. V. LARGE BUSINESS UNITS AND FIXED COSTS. VI. LARGE
BUSINESS UNITS AND THE PROFESSIONALIZATION OF MANAGE-
MENT. VII. LARGE BUSINESS UNITS AND INDUSTRIAL LIBERTY.
VIII. LARGE BUSINESS UNITS AND THE RELATION BETWEEN INDUS-
TRY AND THE STATE.

I. THE PREVALENCE OF LARGE BUSINESS UNITS

When the Pennsylvania Railroad distributed its quarterly
dividend in December, 1926, the checks filled thirty-eight government mail sacks. The preparation of the checks required a clerical force varying in number from twenty to one hundred for three
weeks' time.[1] In 1928, the gross receipts of the General Motors
Company were nearly a billion and a half dollars, almost as
much — allowing for the change in the price level — as the
receipts of the government itself in 1914.[2] In 1929, the American Telephone and Telegraph Company and its subsidiaries
spent on plant extensions and service improvements more than
$550,000,000 — one and a half times the cost of the Panama
Canal. Two companies — General Motors and the American
Telephone and Telegraph — pay over $100,000,000 a year
each in dividends and at least seven others pay over $40,000,000
a year each.[3]

Such facts as these give us an impression of the size which
business units have attained in the United States. But such spec-

[1] Pennsylvania Railroad, *Information*, December 17, 1926.
[2] *Annual Report*, 1928, p. 8.
[3] The seven are: United States Steel Corporation, E. I. Du Pont de Nemours
Company, Standard Oil Company of New Jersey, Kennecott Copper Company, General Electric Company, Anaconda Copper Company, and Standard Oil Company of
Indiana. There may be others.

tacular examples of size must not cause us to overlook the importance of small business units in American industry. It still remains true that half of the factories in the United States employ not more than five wage earners each. Nevertheless, over one-half of the wage earners engaged in manufacturing are employed in establishments with more than 250 workers and over one-fourth in establishments with more than 1,000. The Federal Trade Commission recently estimated that six companies control about one-third of the developed water power in the United States, eight companies about three-fourths of the unmined anthracite coal, thirty companies over one-third of the immediate reserves of bituminous coal, two companies over half of the iron ore reserves, and four companies nearly one-half of the copper reserves.[4]

The size of business enterprises in most lines of business is increasing. In manufacturing, for example, the average number of wage earners per establishment increased 38 per cent between 1898 and 1919. Until 1919, the growth in manufacturing was so rapid that, despite the increase in the size of plants, the number of factories also increased. Between 1919 and 1927, however, factory output (in physical terms) increased about 25 per cent but the number of factories decreased over 10 per cent. In a few growing industries the concentration of production has been so great that the number of plants has been diminishing for many years. Thus the number of salt works decreased from 282 in 1869 to 86 in 1919; the number of woolen and worsted mills from 2,066 in 1879 to 852 in 1919; the number of leather tanneries from 7,569 in 1869 to 680 in 1919; and the number of boot and shoe factories from 1,959 in 1879 to 1,449 in 1919.[5] In retailing, municipal utilities, and banking, the concentration of business into larger establishments appears to be going on even more rapidly than in manufacturing. Between 1919 and 1928, for example, the national income increased about 43 per cent but the sales of chain stores, according to the index of the Federal Reserve Board, increased 525 per cent in wearing apparel, 366 per cent in groceries,

[4] Federal Trade Commission, "National Wealth and Income," *69th Congress, 1st Session, Senate Document No. 126*, p. 4.

[5] Thorp, Willard, "The Integration of Industrial Operation," *Census Monographs III*, pp. 48, 56, 63, 64.

159 per cent in drugs. It is estimated that about 18 per cent of the retail sales in the country are now made by chain stores.[6] In banking, the total loans and investments of all banks in the United States (other than savings banks and private banks not under state supervision) increased between June, 1923, and December, 1929, from $37,359 millions to $58,417 millions, or nearly 54 per cent, but the number of banks decreased from 29,242 to 24,360 or about one-sixth.[7]

II. Some Advantages of Large Business Units

The size of business enterprises depends upon how many operations it is profitable to combine under central direction. If there were no limit to the advantage in combining different operations under one management, all of the industry of the country would eventually be combined into one huge business enterprise. But every concern finds it advantageous to purchase many of the services which it needs. Most establishments, for example, find it desirable to buy nearly all of their transportation. The advent of the motor truck has diminished the relative amount of transportation which many enterprises purchase and has increased the amount which they find it advantageous to supply themselves. And special cases can be found of enterprises which find it advantageous to supply an extraordinarily large part of their own transportation. A striking instance is the United Fruit Company which operates over 1,000 miles of railroad and over 100 ocean vessels. The company is primarily engaged in producing bananas, but circumstances have caused it to become both a large railroad and an important steamship company.

Business enterprises become large in four ways: (1) by small plants' growing into large ones; (2) by simple combination — that is, by separate plants of the same sort being combined under a single management; (3) by integration — that is, by plants performing successive steps in the productive process being combined under the same management; and (4) by com-

---

[6] Nystrom, P. H., *The Economics of Retailing* (revised edition), v. I, p. 376.

[7] *Federal Reserve Bulletin*, July, 1924, v. X, p. 567, and April, 1930, v. XVI, pp. 147 and 151.

plementary combination — that is, by several plants which make different products being united under one management. In order to explain the prevalence of large business enterprises it is necessary to explain when and why each of these four forms of growth is profitable. By "profitable," of course, is meant, not beneficial to the community, but remunerative to the owners. Possibly large business units are detrimental to the community, but, if they are more profitable than small ones to business owners, they will tend to multiply.

Large plants are in great degree the product of machine technique and of occupational specialization. Many of the costs connected with machinery, we have seen, go on whether it operates or not. This means, of course, that machines are most profitable when they are operated continuously. Consequently, machine technique tends to concentrate production in plants which do a sufficient business to keep the machines busy a large part of the time.[8] The advantages of occupational specialization also can be realized most completely by large establishments. Of course, if it were not advantageous to combine specialists under a single management, the advantages of the minute division of labor would produce many small but highly specialized enterprises rather than a relatively few large concerns. Indeed, there are many instances in which large markets produce great specialization without producing large business units. The reason why the advantages of minute specialization often produce large business establishments is that these advantages can often be most completely realized when specialists work under central direction. What are the advantages of uniting specialists under central direction? There is an obvious saving in the transporting of raw material from one specialist to another and a saving in the amount of raw material in process of fabrication at all

---

[8] But the economy of machinery depends upon the *number* of plants as well as upon the *size* of them. Small plants may find it advantageous to use machinery in case the number of the small plants is large and in case, therefore, they can obtain machines at relatively low prices. The economy of tractors in agriculture arises very largely from the fact that there are so many farms. With many tractors demanded, they can be produced at prices which make them more economical than horses. The economy of machinery in small shoe repair shops is a result of the large number of shops. Many other examples might be cited — the widespread use of cash registers, typewriters, or adding machines in small businesses as well as large.

times, since each specialist need not have such a large amount of material waiting for him to work on. Even one specialist must have shelter, light, and heat; the cost for ten is not ten times the cost for one. If there are a number of specialists, they must be supervised, and it is little more difficult to supervise 50 or 100 than it is 25. The advantages of specialization among the executives are of great importance, but these can be achieved only when the enterprise is large enough to have several executives. A large plant can have purchasing, credits, production, labor, selling, advertising, accounting, each supervised by an expert who gives his attention to nothing else. If the volume of business is small, however, each executive must supervise several branches of the business.

But opportunity to make greater use of machinery and ability to subdivide labor more minutely are not the only advantages of large plants. In the making of some goods, raw materials are left over from which it is possible to manufacture valuable by-products. It is not usually profitable, however, to provide a special force and special machinery to work up waste materials unless they are available in fairly large quantities. Hence a large plant is usually able to manufacture more by-products than a small one. For example, one of the commodities produced by the large meat packers is an extract from the adrenal or suprarenal glands of cattle which has great value in the stoppage of bleeding in surgical operations and as a remedy for hay-fever. Over 16,000 cattle are required to furnish one pound of this substance.[9] Obviously the small-town butcher, killing a few cattle a week, could not turn out this by-product. Nor could he afford to make combs, buttons, knife and cane handles from the horns and hoofs; glue from parts of the bones and cartilage; pipe stems, chess men, dice, artificial teeth, crochet needles, or electrical bushings from the bones; pharmaceutical supplies from the glands, artists' brushes from the soft hair in the interior of the ears; or to market the dried blood as fertilizer. In fact, to the small butcher, from 40 to 60 per cent of the animal is waste. To the large

[9] Swift and Company, *Year Book*, 1924, p. 46. An interesting case of by-product manufacture is furnished by a large maker of soap. This company purchases cottonseed and presses the oil from it. A slight amount of the cotton fibre adheres to each seed. This fibre is reclaimed and made into paper pulp. The pulp made each year from the reclaimed fibre is worth about a million dollars.

packer, a steer yields over a hundred commodities which together are worth 10 to 40 per cent as much as the meat.

Closely related to the manufacture of by-products is the reclamation of materials used in the process of production. A special salvage squad and special apparatus for recovering materials are profitable only when there is much to be saved. Several years ago the Ford Motor Company was recovering about 2,000 gallons of oil daily by running twenty tons of steel turnings through centrifugal wringers. The oil was cleaned of grit and foreign matter and returned to the factory to be used again. Obviously it would not pay the company to purchase the wringers unless it had large quantities of turnings from which oil could be recovered. The salvage operations of the Ford Company are an excellent illustration of what is possible when reclamation is on a large scale. In 1923, the salvage squad consisted of over 400 men and saved nearly $1,000,000 worth of materials a month. Each day, over 390 tons of steel trimmings, 190 tons of steel-stamping waste, and 153 tons of cast-iron borings were reclaimed. Silver valued at $5,000 was recovered from the photographic laboratories. All of this meant a saving of more than $5.00 on each car produced.[10]

Because large plants purchase in greater quantities than small ones, they usually obtain special prices and preferential treatment. It is easy to imagine the buying advantages of an immense shoe factory, such as the Endicott Johnson, that uses each day 4,100 miles of thread and 14 tons of tacks and nails.[11] A recent review of the market for steel sheets and plates reported: " For the past five months concessions — say $2 to $4 or $5 a ton — have been made on very large lots from the small lot prices." [12] Another review of the Pittsburgh sheet steel market said: " For the first quarter of this year Ford had bought at from 4.90c to 5.10c while other buyers paid 5.35c or close to that figure." [13]

---

[10] *New York Evening Post*, January 3, 1924.

[11] Weld, W. E., and Tostlebe, A. S., *A Case Book for Economics*, p. 419.

[12] *New York Evening Post*, April 26, 1924, Sec. II, p. 1.

[13] *New York Evening Post*, April 26, 1924, Sec. II, p. 3. The disposition of sellers to give preferential treatment to large buyers is naturally accentuated by the existence of fixed costs which go on unchanged regardless of whether the volume of business is large or small. But it is encouraged also by the fact that direct labor and material costs too are often less when goods are turned out in large lots. It takes no longer to set a machine for a run of 1,000 pieces than it does for a run of 500.

But favored treatment of large buyers takes forms other than special prices. Banks are more eager to secure their accounts, and extend credit to them somewhat more liberally than to equally sound but smaller enterprises. This is particularly true when the concern is large enough to maintain accounts at several banks. Railroads make a special effort to supply large customers promptly with cars and to give them unusually good switching service — an important advantage in times of traffic congestion, when cars are difficult to obtain and deliveries are slow. The favored treatment of large shippers by the railroads in distributing coal cars is a noteworthy chapter in the history of the coal industry.

The power of the large business organizations in the market enables them to take unfair advantage of other enterprises with less than ordinary danger of retaliation. Large buyers, knowing how greatly their future patronage is desired, are less hesitant than small ones about cancelling orders when market changes make this profitable. The manufacturers of knit underwear report that they are more liable to receive cancellations from large department stores than from small merchants.[14]

The head of a huge steel company is reputed to be paid a million dollars a year. If this salary were paid by a small plant, it would substantially increase the cost of each ton of steel but, when it is paid by a plant making millions of tons a year, the additional expense per ton is small — far less than an executive of outstanding efficiency is able to save. Thus we see that an establishment can afford to hire exceptionally capable and, therefore, unusually expensive managers and technical experts only when its output is large. Indeed, large plants (and, for that matter, large business enterprises) may be regarded as devices for economizing the relatively limited amount of high-grade managerial ability. Because a few men are far superior to the majority in administrative skill, it pays to have large plants in order to place a larger number of workmen and larger amounts of capital under the direction of the few, superior managers. Where

---

Often the spoilage is less. In plain printing, for example, the spoilage rate on a run of 25,000 or over is less than one-sixth that on a run of 200 or less and no more than half that on a run of 1,000 to 2,500.

[14] Bureau of Foreign and Domestic Commerce, " The Knit-Underwear Industry," *Miscellaneous Series, No. 32*, p. 145.

production is carried on by a large number of small enterprises, as in the case of agriculture or retailing, the average level of managerial ability is bound to be low.

Large plants can afford to make large expenditures for experimentation and research. The possibility of conducting elaborate research at a small cost per unit of product, when output is large, is illustrated by the proving ground of General Motors Corporation. It happens that General Motors Corporation is a combination of large plants rather than a single large plant but this does not impair the value of the example for our purposes. The proving ground is the largest in the world; every kind of road — mud, dirt, sand, gravel, and concrete — is represented; there are hills with grades up to 24 per cent, a four-mile speedwell banked at the ends to 45 per cent, and a complete service garage. And yet the cost of operating the proving ground in 1926 amounted to only a few cents per car sold by the company.

Large plants are more likely than small ones to have among their managers and principal owners men of important and extensive business interests. These men, because of their wide connections, are often able to impart to the management information which might not otherwise reach it in time to be of much use and they are also able, because of their prestige and influence, to assist materially in getting preferential treatment for the enterprise.

The second way in which business organizations become large is by combining a number of plants under one management. The plants themselves may not be large. The individual stores operated by the Great Atlantic and Pacific Tea Company are small, but it has over 10,000 of them. What are the advantages of combining a number of like establishments under single management?

Combinations of plants possess many of the advantages of a large plant — the ability to buy in large quantities, to take unfair advantage of other enterprises with less than ordinary danger of retaliation, to hire exceptionally able managers, to spend large sums upon experiment and research at a low cost per unit of output, and to profit from the presence of important business men among the executives or on the board of directors. But other important advantages can be realized only by uniting several like plants under common management.   Combination is particularly useful when some aspects of a business require a much larger organization than others.   The size of the organization that is best for fabricating or growing may not be best for buying or selling or carrying on research.   Combination enables some branches of the business to gain the advantages of largeness and other branches to retain the advantages of smallness.   Combination is a way of getting the best managerial ability when the most economical plant is small — too small to be able alone to hire expensive managerial talent.   Combinations have an excellent opportunity to stimulate efficiency among plant managers by keeping accounts in a uniform way and comparing regularly the costs in the different establishments.   Substantial savings can also be made by extending to all plants the technical improvements discovered in each one.   If each plant has been making several products or several styles or sizes of one product, the combination may achieve the gains of plant specialization by concentrating the production of certain articles, sizes, or styles in certain plants.   In industries where part-time operation of a plant is almost as expensive as full-time, a combination can save money during slack periods by closing some of its plants and operating the others full time.   Likewise, if one plant is tied up by fire, flood, or strike, the combination can promptly supply its customers from other plants.   The possibility of filling orders from any one of several plants makes it possible for each plant to carry a smaller stock of raw materials and finished goods than would otherwise be necessary and hence makes the amount of working capital less than would be needed if the plants were operated by independent enterprises.   Finally, combinations are often able to make large reductions in marketing expenses.   This they do by consolidating the branch offices, warehouses, and service stations of the plants in the combination; by reducing the number of salesmen and having only one of them call on each customer; by eliminating duplication in advertising; and by filling each order from the nearest plant.[15]

[15] A combination may grow simply because one enterprise has a chance to acquire the plant of another at a bargain price.   Such an opportunity may occur because the second firm has become involved in financial difficulties.   For the first enterprise to expand by building another plant might not pay but expansion by purchase may be profitable provided the price is low.

Integration is the third way in which business enterprises grow. The International Harvester Company manufactures not only agricultural implements, but also steel and lumber from which to make them, and it produces coal with which to make the steel. The American Telephone and Telegraph Company, in addition to controlling enterprises which give telephone service, owns the Western Electric Company, which makes telephone instruments, cable, and other things used in the telephone business. Some large newspapers make their own paper; the Pennsylvania Railroad builds many of its locomotives; numerous steel manufacturers produce the ore, coal, coke, and limestone used in making iron and steel; and the American Sugar Refining Company owns forests and lumber mills and makes its own barrels.

When the enterprise which uses the raw materials owns the plants in which they are produced, good and uniform quality and reliable delivery are assured. These are the most obvious and in many cases the most important advantages of integration. But integration also often reduces costs. The expense of selling the raw material, which may be considerable, is saved. Sometimes there are special reasons why an enterprise can produce certain materials at a great saving. The Baltimore and Ohio Railroad has found it advantageous to manufacture over 1,500 varieties of forgings and bolts used in repairing its locomotives and cars. It can manufacture at very low cost because it makes the parts from scrap. More prompt and reliable delivery has led to further saving for the road. Since steel mills had taken six to eight months to fill orders, the railroad had been compelled to carry a several months' stock of parts and often to pay fancy prices to jobbers for material which was immediately needed. Now a thirty to sixty days' supply of parts is sufficient and it is no longer necessary to pay emergency prices to jobbers. A large and unexpected increase in the demand for a commodity may cause the price to soar far above the cost of production. This naturally leads some firms to make the commodity for themselves. When the sudden shift from open to closed cars caused the price of plate glass to rise rapidly, the Ford Motor Company, which was using about one-fourth of the country's output, discovered that it could make its glass for less than it was paying. It therefore purchased a glass factory and built another. An enterprise which produces raw material for itself is often able to make it more steadily than a firm which produces for the open market. Most coal mines, for example, operate with great irregularity, but a public service company which owns a mine can run it rather steadily because the company is sure to be needing coal. A comparison of the days operated by the independent mines and the so-called " captive " mines — that is, those owned by the users of the coal — revealed that in every state the " captive " mines operated more regularly than the independent ones.[16]   In industries with heavy fixed costs, the economy of steady operation is substantial. Finally, an effort to purchase raw materials or to sell by-products at more advantageous prices may lead to integration. A few years ago the great fluctuations in the price of leather led several large shoe manufacturers and large packers to enter the tanning industry.[17]   The shoe manufacturers hoped to gain from buying their hides when prices were low, and the packers from selling their hides as leather, which is more stable in price than hides.

Business enterprises also grow by combining under one management plants making different commodities. This form of growth we have called " complementary combination." The International Harvester Company, which in the beginning was primarily a manufacturer of harvesting machinery, now also makes cream separators, gas engines, trucks, plows, hay balers, manure spreaders, tractors, and other farm machinery. The large meat

[16] The United States Coal Commission found that in 1920 the days operated by " captive " and independent mines were as follows:

	" Captive "	Independent
Pennsylvania	272	244
West Virginia	223	199
Kentucky	226	183
Virginia	305	264
Ohio	191	188
Illinois	238	213
Indiana	211	193

The Commission found that about one-fourth of the bituminous coal is produced by " captive " mines. *Report of the United States Coal Commission*, p. 225.

[17] National Bank of Commerce, New York, *Commerce Monthly*, January, 1928, v. IX, pp. 25–26. Periods of extreme currency inflation are likely to encourage integration because buying and selling are thus to some extent avoided. The recent inflation in Germany greatly stimulated integration. With stabilization of the currency, the principal reasons for these combinations disappeared and there has been a tendency to abandon them.

packers have of late years added eggs, poultry, butter, and cheese to their products. The Canadian Pacific Railway operates steamships on the Atlantic, the Pacific, and the Great Lakes, and a large chain of hotels.

In so far as the plants making different products use the same raw materials, such as coal, lubricants, steel, lumber, and paint, combination increases their buying power and thus gives them the advantages of large-scale buying. Many of the principal gains from combining the production of several commodities or services under one management are in the field of marketing. Sometimes the sale of one commodity helps the sale of another, as when a railroad stimulates traffic by establishing hotels at scenic spots or by operating boat lines to connect with its trains. Meat packers find it advantageous to sell poultry, butter, eggs, and cheese because, with their refrigerator cars, their branch houses equipped with refrigerating facilities, and their salesmen already calling on butcher shops and delicatessen stores, they can distribute these commodities at little additional expense. Likewise, the International Harvester Company, with its salesmen already calling on implement dealers, can market a full line of agricultural implements at not much greater cost than part of a line. General Foods Corporation and Standard Brands are two recently formed complementary combinations which are advantageous primarily because of economies in marketing. Each is a combination of enterprises making packaged and trade-marked food products. General Foods Corporation includes the manufacturers of Walter Baker Chocolate, Jello, Postum, Maxwell House Coffee, Calumet Baking Powder, Log Cabin Maple Syrup, Blue Ribbon Mayonnaise, Minute Tapioca, and other products; Standard Brands, the manufacturers of Royal Baking Powder, Fleischmann's Yeast, Chase and Sanborn Coffee. All of these products are sold to the public through the same jobbers and retailers. Instead of each manufacturer's having his own salesmen to call on the jobbers and retailers, there are obvious economies in having each salesman sell a number of non-competing products. In the case of yeast, the Fleischmann Company had built up an elaborate delivery system under which deliveries were made to bakers and retailers at frequent intervals. This was necessary in order to assure delivery while the product was fresh. Complementary combination makes it possible to use this delivery system to handle other products, such as coffee, which it is also desirable to deliver promptly and at frequent intervals.

III. Limitations on the Size of Business Units

It has been pointed out that if every increase in size meant a decrease in unit costs, nearly all of the business in the country might become concentrated in the hands of one gigantic enterprise.[18]   But largeness has its disadvantages as well as its advantages.   Enterprises tend to expand, therefore, until the gains of greater size are balanced by its disadvantages.   This point, of course, is not necessarily reached at the same time in all branches of the enterprise.   Greater size may be an advantage in purchasing or in marketing but a disadvantage in manufacturing; or it may be an advantage in manufacturing but a disadvantage in marketing.   Every enterprise, therefore, is a compromise between the advantages of largeness or smallness in some departments and the disadvantages in others.   Experimentation is constantly going on in the structure of enterprises and in the distribution of authority and functions in order to gain largeness where that is an advantage and smallness where that is desirable. The combination of plants, as has been pointed out, is partly an attempt to gain largeness in some branches of the business and smallness in others.   So also, as will be explained in Chapter VIII, are the coöperative concern and the trade association.

Before pointing out the positive disadvantages of largeness, it is desirable to direct attention to the fact that, after a given point, the advantages of largeness are realized only in diminishing degree.   Consider, for example, the gains from the subdivision of labor.   In cutting up work and assigning different operations to different specialists, the divisions first made are naturally those which are expected to produce the greatest additions to output.   The process of dividing the work more and more minutely among an increasing number of specialists can go on almost indefinitely, but if the management was right in choosing which subdivisions to make first, the successive ones will result in smaller

---

[18] Not necessarily *all* of the business because, as will be pointed out presently, small enterprises might survive because of special advantages or because the owners might be willing to accept less than the usual return upon their investment.

and smaller gains. It is important to observe that even a relatively small plant can obtain a high degree of specialization, at least among *manual* workers. A clothing factory or a shoe factory, employing only 400 or 500 men, can obtain exceedingly minute division of labor among its manual workers — about as high a degree as is profitable. Of course, further growth makes it advantageous further to subdivide functions among *executives* and this is sometimes highly profitable. On the whole, however, a plant need not be very large in order to exhaust most of the advantages of specialization among manual laborers. Nor is the subdivision of labor pure gain, for it creates the problem of coördinating the activities of specialists. Where operations are purely mechanical, this is usually not difficult, but good coördination between the activities of specialist executives is not easily achieved and the difficulties mount as the number of specialists increases.

Up to a certain point, growth in size enables a plant to use larger, more automatic, and more specialized machines and equipment. But after the plant has become large enough to use the most efficient sizes, further growth simply compels it to duplicate equipment which it already has. Furthermore, after a plant has become large enough to receive the preferential treatment and prices which very large buyers obtain, further growth has little effect upon the treatment which it receives. After a combination has five or six plants, the addition of others adds little to the possibility of either stimulating managerial efficiency by comparing costs in different plants or of gaining the advantages of plant specialization. And if the plants controlled by a combination are fairly well distributed, the acquisition of more does not greatly increase the saving made by filling each order from the nearest plant.

But the mere fact that increasing size eventually yields diminishing advantages would not itself check the growth of enterprises, were there not positive drawbacks to largeness.[19]

---

[19] At precisely what point the most advantageous size is to be found is partly a matter of business conditions. Small enterprises are likely to excel in the power to adjust themselves to changes in the business situation. Because their fixed costs are, as a rule relatively small, they are especially able to cut their expenses in periods of poor business. Large enterprises, with relatively heavy fixed costs, are less able to adapt themselves to times of slack business. They are likely to gain, relative to small

The most serious are administrative difficulties. A large concern, as a rule, is more difficult to manage than a small one. *In other words, a net advantage from largeness can usually be achieved only by the use of exceptionally able managers.* The reason is that, as a business grows, the principal executive finds it increasingly difficult, first, to make wise and prompt decisions and, second, to maintain effective control over his force.

The first difficulty arises largely because the chief executive has less opportunity to become familiar with the internal working of his enterprise. The growth of the concern compels him to become more and more a specialist on its external relations — its relations with the government, with the rest of the industry, with the banks, and with the market. More and more of his time must be spent with bankers, attorneys, and large customers. Thus a situation develops in which those who are in intimate touch with conditions and the manner in which operations are going — that is to say, the workmen and the lesser officials — lack authority to make needed changes and improvements, and the executive who determines policies, who has the authority to decide what shall be done and how money shall be spent, is more or less out of touch with conditions and not in a good position to appreciate what is needed. Precious time may pass before the chief executive finds an opportunity to look into a recommendation and make a decision. Hence it is characteristic of large enterprises that they are lacking somewhat in flexibility and in power to adapt themselves to sudden changes in markets or conditions.

Nor does the delegation of authority to subordinates solve the problem. For growth of the enterprise creates the same difficulties for the principal department heads as for the chief executive. The larger the plant, the larger are most of its departments. Each department head has more matters claiming his attention and more conditions to supervise. Furthermore, he often must give more time to relations with other departments. So, like the chief executive, he is compelled to make many decisions on the basis of inadequate information or to delay action until after the time when it should have been taken.

ones, in a comparatively stable business situation such as prevailed in the main between 1922 and 1929.

The situation would be relieved if workmen and minor officials were more interested in increasing output and lowering costs, and more willing to communicate to department heads their knowledge of wastes and to suggest better methods of production. But the existing control of industry, by its very nature, tends to diminish the interest of workmen and small officials in efficiency. Is it discovered how to produce in eight hours what formerly required nine, or how to reduce or eliminate certain expenses? No reduction of hours or relief from the swift pace of production, no improvement in wages or working conditions automatically follows. Wages and working conditions are no better than managements, in view of the economic strength of the wage earners, find it expedient or necessary to grant. But if wages and conditions in each enterprise depend, not upon how much or how cheaply the business produces, but upon the men's bargaining power, why should the workers help the management increase output or reduce costs? Must not their efforts, under the circumstances, center upon increasing their own bargaining power rather than industry's producing power? All of this suggests that capitalism may be inherently unadapted to the administration of large concerns, and that the advantages of large-scale production will not be fully achieved until changes in the government of industry give workmen and minor officials a more intimate interest in output and costs.

The second administrative difficulty which impedes the growth of enterprises is that of maintaining effective control over the force. There are two general methods of administrative control — first, personal contact and observation, and second, statistical measurement of the performance of individuals and departments. The method of personal observation and contact is obviously most effective when enterprises are small and it becomes steadily less effective as they grow in size. Statistical measurement of performance is only profitable on an intensive scale when production is large — indeed, the possibility of measuring performance in detail is an important advantage of large firms over small ones. But after a concern has attained a considerable size, further growth does not enable the management to improve the statistical controls. And these controls, of course, are never perfect, for almost invariably there are some things which elude measurement. Judged by operating costs, a department may be highly efficient, but it may achieve its good record at the expense of other departments. The foundry may make a good showing by furnishing the machine shop with poor castings; a laborer may work rapidly but be hard on machines and tools, wasteful of material, and careless about the quality of his output. Employees and department heads, it must be remembered, are often more interested in how efficient they *appear to be* than in how efficient they *are;* they often use more ingenuity in covering up their shortcomings than in improving their efficiency. Consequently, it is always necessary to supplement statistical controls by observation and personal contact and this, as we have seen, becomes increasingly difficult as the enterprise grows larger.[20]

IV. Why the Small Firm Still Persists

In many fields, such as professional services, retailing, farming, repairing, and the making of women's suits and dresses, small enterprises predominate and in many others they exist side by side with the large firms. In the boot and shoe industry, for example, 227 factories make nearly two-thirds of the product and 1,343 slightly more than one-third; in flour milling, 228 mills produce over three-fifths of the output and 6,838 only twelve per cent.[21] If the large enterprises have so many advantages, why are small ones able to exist in such great numbers?

[20] Not only does the lack of contact between the chief executive and his subordinates make it difficult for him to hold them to the highest efficiency but it sometimes prevents him from adopting the policies which he believes would be advantageous to the enterprise. To be successful, a policy needs the cordial support of the officials responsible for its execution. Not infrequently, however, new policies are strongly opposed by officials who have become used to other methods. Were the chief executive in closer contact with his subordinates, he might persuade them to give the new policy a fair trial. As it is, the knowledge that a certain policy would receive only grudging support from subordinates prevents many a chief executive from experimenting with it. This is simply another way in which large enterprises are lacking in flexibility and adaptability.

[21] *Monthly Labor Review*, October, 1925, v. XXI, pp. 695–696. It is interesting to compare the annual product per laborer in plants of different sizes:

Number of establishments	Average number of wage earners	Annual product per wage earner
Boot and shoe factories		
227	488	$5,133
738	89	4,205
605	11.5	3,153

At the outset, it should be noted that a small firm may have higher *average* costs than a large firm and yet have no difficulty in competing, provided only that the large concern cannot *add* to its product for less than the cost to the small enterprise. Suppose, for example, that a large firm can produce 1,000,000 units a month at an average cost of $1.00 each but that making 100,-000 additional units a month would cost $1.25 each. Suppose also that a small firm could manufacture at a cost of $1.15 per unit. Obviously, if consumers would take 1,100,000 units at $1.15 each, the small firm, despite its higher average cost, could compete.[22]

But many small firms undoubtedly have as low average costs as large enterprises in the same industry. In some instances, these low-cost enterprises remain small simply because expansion involves risks which the owners do not care to incur. Or they may remain small simply because the management, though unusually efficient, is not ambitious to expand the business, or because the owners do not care to share control with other capitalists, as would be necessary in order to obtain funds for expansion. In many instances, however, it is possible for an establishment to have low costs only by remaining small; if it grew, its costs would rise. It has already been emphasized that large enterprises are usually more difficult to administer than small ones. This means that a mediocre man at the head of a small concern may be able to produce at no higher cost than an exceptionally able man at the head of a large establishment. Smallness, in many instances, therefore, is a prerequisite to good management. Other small enterprises may have low costs because they have unusually cheap waterpower, raw materials, or labor. But the amount of water power that is available may be only sufficient for a small plant and the raw material may be limited by the fact that it is the by-product of another plant in the city. Many small

---

Flour mills

228	66	$8,764
953	11	5,234
6,838	1.5	2,498

The difference in the product per wage earner would, of course, be compensated in part by the smaller fixed costs in the smaller plants.

[22] The larger enterprise could drive the smaller out of business but it would lose money by so doing.

family enterprises, such as small stores or farms, obtain a large part of their labor for nothing by utilizing the spare time of the wife and the out-of-school hours of the children. But only the labor of the family, of course, is available on such terms. Small sweat shops exist largely because they can purchase labor more advantageously than large plants. The shop owner is scarcely more than a workman himself. He lives in the working class district, speaks one or more of the languages of the wage earners, and has relatives and friends among them. Through his contacts with workers, he is able to hand-pick a force of the most docile, least informed, and most poverty stricken laborers — persons who can be had for less than large enterprises, less intimately in touch with the labor market, find it necessary to give. Sweat shops are most likely to flourish in highly seasonal industries where the non-continuous employment creates a favorable opportunity for employers to enter into special bargains with their employees. The small shop, in which the owner himself hires the labor, is better able to profit by this opportunity than the larger enterprise which deals with workers through salaried officials.

Many of the fields in which the small concern flourishes are ones in which the advantages of machinery and occupational specialization are not readily realized. Retailing, professional services, custom tailoring, the making of women's suits and dresses, are examples. In all of them machinery is relatively unimportant and in most of them, minute occupational specialization is not practicable, either because the product is not standardized, as in the case of repair work or custom tailoring, or because the number of styles is large and the size of orders small, as in the women's suit and dress industries.

Some industries in which small establishments abound are characterized by exceptionally great administrative difficulties. Such is true of agriculture. A farmer cannot readily oversee the work of many laborers working on different parts of the farm, and it is not usually practicable, as it is in coal mining, to avoid the necessity of such supervision by paying by the piece. The repair industries and the manufacture of women's suits and dresses also have extraordinary administrative difficulties. Wherever, indeed, it is impossible to reduce the work to a routine by standardizing operations, close and interested supervision is peculiarly necessary. The small enterprise is exceptionally well adapted to such situations, because only when an establishment is small can the owner manage it himself with little or no assistance from hired executives. No management is quite so vigilant or painstaking as that of the man who himself receives the entire benefit of every dollar saved or gained and who bears the entire loss of every dollar unwisely spent.

When it is important for consumers to have goods available close at hand and on short notice, small *plants* are likely to predominate. This is why there are so many small neighborhood drug stores and grocery stores and why the country store competes with the mail order house even when charging higher prices. It is, of course, possible that the small stores may be part of an immense chain. So reluctant, however, are most business men to surrender their independence that small business units abound wherever small plants have advantages over large ones.

Market conditions may make small enterprises more successful than large ones even though bare manufacturing costs are lower when production is on a large scale. The tanning industry is an example. Sudden and radical changes in shoe styles have caused sudden shifts in the demand for upper leather. " Because of the uncertainty and the changeableness of fashion, tanners of most kinds of upper leather have found it profitable to reduce the unit of production to a comparatively small figure, even though this increases the cost of carrying on business. This prevents an accumulation of unwanted stock should the style change, and the tanner can shift quickly and easily to another variety more in demand. It has been found that a small plant . . . is really better fitted to meet such conditions than a large tannery. . . . The smaller organization, concentrating on a few kinds of leather, has a decided advantage over the larger factory turning out several sorts and thereby compelled to be conversant with style trends in many lines of finished goods." [23]

In many industries where small enterprises flourish, considerations other than price are important in determining from which seller consumers purchase. The professions are an ex-

[23] National Bank of Commerce, New York, *Commerce Monthly*, January, 1928, v. IX, pp. 23–24.

ample. Retailing is another. The personalities of the dealer and his clerks, the atmosphere of the store, and the quality of the service may be more attractive than the lower prices but impersonal atmosphere of a larger store. The quality of the work in the repair industries and in custom tailoring, and the design of the garments in the women's suit and dress industries are more important than small differences in price. Under such circumstances the low cost enterprises do not necessarily win out.[24]

Finally, the prevalence of small enterprises in many branches of industry must be attributed in large degree to the intense desire of millions of men for independence. So dearly do many men love independence that they are content to remain in business as heads of small concerns for substantially less than salaried managers or even skilled workmen receive. Larger enterprises may be able to produce goods at fewer hours of labor per unit of output, but even so, they may not be able to undersell the small enterprise if the owner is willing to accept less than the large concern must pay its hired labor. In agriculture, for example, large farms, operated in the main by hired workers, must be able to produce at substantially fewer man-hours per bushel than the independent farmer before they can undersell, and thus displace, him.

A word concerning the future of the small enterprise may not be amiss. One hears it frequently asserted that the days of the small concern are numbered, that the development of automatic and semi-automatic machines and the spread of mass-production are bound to destroy most of the small concerns. No one knows whether or not this prediction is correct. A strong reason for doubting it, however, arises from the steadily growing productivity of industry. An ever-decreasing proportion of the population seems destined to be engaged in producing the necessities of life and an ever-increasing proportion in producing luxuries. Some luxuries, such as automobiles and radios, can be made by the methods of mass production. But is it not likely that a large part of the demand for luxuries will be demand either for personal services or for articles which possess distinctiveness and

[24] Strictly speaking, it is inaccurate to speak of low cost and high cost enterprises where the product of each is more or less unique.

individuality and which, therefore, cannot be made by automatic or semi-automatic machines? No one can say, but the certainty of an enormous increase in the demand for luxuries should make us cautious in predicting a decrease in the number of small concerns.

V. Large Business Units and Fixed Costs

We have already learned that machinery increases the importance of fixed costs in modern industry and that this is an effect of profound significance. Large business units do the same thing because they need, as a rule, a relatively larger staff of permanent supervisory, technical, and clerical employees than do small enterprises. There are several explanations of this. In small businesses, operations can be controlled by observation; in large ones, more or less elaborate records and reports are needed to show how efficiently different departments are being conducted. This means a staff of accountants, bookkeepers, and clerks. Since the records must be kept and the reports made whether the enterprise is busy or not, this part of the staff is little affected by fluctuations in the volume of business, and the cost of maintaining it is a relatively constant expense. Large establishments, as we have seen, can afford to have more functions performed by experts than can small enterprises. They can afford, for example, to hire purchasing agents to do their buying; chemists, physicists, and metallurgists to test materials; traffic managers, credit men, advertising men, claim agents, employment managers. In a small firm such experts could not save enough to pay their salaries. Not only are these experts needed in both slack and busy times, but in the course of their work they acquire such familiarity with the problems of the business that it would be poor economy to dismiss them in dull times and replace them when business revived. A similar situation exists in the case of research, which, as we have learned, large enterprises often support on an extensive scale. The research workers accumulate so much special knowledge that it would be wasteful to discharge them when sales fall off, in expectation of hiring others when times improve.[25]

---

[25] But when severe business depression threatens the solvency of enterprises, immediate necessity may compel drastic reductions in the salaried staff despite the fact that

VI. Large Business Units and the Professionalization of Management

When a man operates a small business of his own, he can manage most departments himself. As the enterprise grows and as more managers are needed, men are hired for such positions as advertising manager, sales manager, production manager, and department heads. Usually the chief executive of a large concern is an important owner — often he is the founder or the son of the founder — but as these owner-executives die or are retired, the tendency is for the other owners to replace them with professional managers. Thus the growth of large business units causes a gradual gravitation of management from the hands of business owners into the hands of hired professionals. The highest development of this tendency is to be found in railroading, where immense business units have existed longer than in almost any other industry. In railroading there are no founder-presidents left and very few sons-of-founder presidents. Railroad officials now are usually professional experts and any one of them who makes an outstanding record on one road is likely to be hired by another.

The professionalization of management undoubtedly means more expert, though somewhat less interested, administration. It also introduces possibilities of conflict between the owners and the managers. For example, the owners — especially the less well-to-do ones — usually desire as large a return upon their investment as possible. The professional managers wish a larger and more important business to administer. Furthermore, they desire to make the business easier to manage by improving the equipment. Hence, while the owners wish the highest possible dividends, the managers prefer that a large part of the earnings be reinvested in the business. A conflict may arise between the interests of the owners and the policies of the manage-

---

this procedure is not economical in the long run. For example, the Census of Manufacture shows that between 1919, a year of prosperity, and 1921, a year of severe depression, the number of salaried officers and employees engaged in manufacturing decreased by 20.2 per cent, or nearly as much as the number of wage earners, which decreased 22.8 per cent. But salaries were more stable than wages. Although the total wage payments decreased 21.6 per cent between 1919 and 1921, the expenditures for salaries decreased only 10.1 per cent. *Census of Manufactures, 1925,* p. 7.

ment because the managers may be more interested in smashing a union than in making money for the stockholders. The managers may desire the luxury of a free hand. A union may be troublesome to deal with but expensive to destroy — so expensive that it is more profitable to tolerate the union than to destroy it. Nevertheless the management may spend hundreds of thousands or even millions of dollars to get rid of it. And after having smashed it, the management may be compelled to pay practically the union scale in order to keep the men from organizing.

Of very great importance is the possibility that the professionalization of management will lead to the development of professional standards and that managers will be governed in their policies by these standards as well as by the desire to make profits for business owners. It has already been suggested that if standards could be made to reflect the interests of the community, the professionalization of management might become an important instrument in the social control of business. Experience with professionalized management is still too scanty to afford a satisfactory basis for prediction. It is true that in railroading, where management has longest been on a professional basis, there is some evidence that officers feel responsible to a wider constituency than the business owners. But the evidence is none too plentiful and in any event a public service industry is not a safe basis for generalization. It is also true that the difficulty which business owners experience in controlling management when the ownership of an enterprise is widely diffused — a difficulty which will be discussed in the next chapter — sometimes gives officials considerable latitude in their choice of policies. But when there are a few large owners or when powerful banking houses are represented on the board of directors, the independence of the officials may not be great. Then there is the fact that many officials sooner or later become shareholders in the concerns which they serve. Such men may represent the interests of ownership quite as completely as the old fashioned owner-manager. One thing, however, seems certain. The rise of the hired executive confers upon the rapidly growing schools of commerce an opportunity to assist in creating professional standards of management by sending out men who visualize their life work as something more than making the maximum number of dollars for business owners.

VII. Large Business Units and Industrial Liberty

In the early Middle Ages sovereignty and property were not separated — the ownership of land carried with it many powers which have since become part of the authority of the state. The gigantic business units of modern industry appear to be bringing about a reversion to the days when sovereignty was an attribute of property. With property now goes the power to prescribe rules which affect employees as intimately as do the ordinances of the city or the statutes of the state in which they live — rules prescribing when work shall begin, how long the men shall have for lunch, when work shall cease, for what reasons and how long employees may absent themselves without losing their jobs, whether payment shall be by the day or by the piece, by whom and for what reasons men may be discharged, how promotions and lay-offs shall be made. The workers have a right to vote for the officials of the government. If they dislike the way in which the town or the state is governed, they can use their votes to change the government. But the only way in which wage earners can influence the rules of the shops is by their bargaining power. It is fantastic, however, to imagine any one of the 250,000 employees of the United States Steel Corporation or of the 175,000 employees of General Motors Corporation bargaining over the rules which govern the company's shops. Many enterprises have their own private police forces. They do not, it is true, have their own courts but, in their control over discharge, they have a rough equivalent.

Wage earners have sought, through their trade unions, to resist the tendency of property to acquire sovereign or quasi-sovereign powers. Whenever the workers have organized trade unions, they have sought to make shop rules a matter of joint determination and their administration a matter of joint control. Some employers regard this as an invasion of the rights of property and an interference with their right to run their businesses as they see fit. But can a concern employing 5,000, 10,000 or 250,000 men be regarded simply as private property? It employs enough men to make a good sized town. Can the managements of such enterprises expect to promulgate rules affecting the lives of thousands of people with the same freedom as that possessed by absolute despots?

Thus far the problem of industrial government which has been created by the rise of gigantic business enterprises has aroused little interest outside of trade union circles. Quite possibly it will never command widespread attention. But if the public ever becomes deeply interested in industrial liberty, it may seriously question whether a huge steel works is private property in the same sense as a peanut stand or whether the form of industrial government which is suitable for a grocery store or a shoe-shining parlor is also fitted for an automobile factory employing 10,000 or 25,000 men.

VIII. Large Business Units and the Relation between Industry and the State

Finally, and perhaps most important of all, large business units, more than any other feature of our economic arrangements, create the problem of the relationship between industry and the state. The history of government shows that whenever powerful extra-political organizations arise, the relationship which shall exist between them and the state becomes a major political issue. It was so in the Middle Ages when the power of the Papacy made the relationship between the church and the state perhaps the supreme political problem. Today the development of huge business enterprises has made the relationship between industry and the state *the* political issue of the age. It occupies much the same position in modern political life as did the problem of the church and the state in the Middle Ages.

REFERENCES

Clark, J. M., *The Economics of Overhead Costs*, 1923. Ch. VI and VII.
Dewing, A. S., *The Financial Policy of Corporations*, 1920. V. IV, ch. II and III.
Jones, Eliot, *The Trust Problem in the United States*, 1922. Ch. XIX.
Lincoln, E. E., *Applied Business Finance*, 1923. Ch. XXI.
Marshall, Alfred, *Industry and Trade* (second edition), 1919. Bk. II, ch. III, IV, and VII.
Thorp, Willard L., " The Integration of Industrial Operation," *Census Monographs III*, 1928.

CHAPTER VIII

MODERN BUSINESS ORGANIZATIONS

I. HOW THE CORPORATION FACILITATES THE RAISING OF CAPITAL. II. THE CORPORATION AND THE INCIDENTS OF OWNERSHIP. III. THE CORPORATION AND THE CONCENTRATION OF POWER IN MODERN INDUSTRY. IV. THE EXPLOITATION OF CORPORATIONS BY INSIDERS. V. THE DIFFUSION OF OWNERSHIP AND PRIVATE PROPERTY. VI. THE COÖPERATIVE CONCERN. VII. THE TRADE ASSOCIATION.

I. How the Corporation Facilitates the Raising of Capital

Activities in modern economic society, we well know, are to a large extent conducted, not by unattached individuals, but by organizations. It is evident that this fact must profoundly affect the operation of industry. Even when individuals buy and sell for themselves, their decisions are often governed by rules or standards which organizations have set. In this and the following chapter, we shall examine the leading characteristics of several outstanding organizations in modern economic society — the corporation, the coöperative association, the trade association, and the trade union.

One hundred years ago, corporations were so few that they were created only by special acts of the legislature. Today nearly one-third of the national wealth is owned by corporations.[1] They employ five-sixths of the wage earners engaged in manufacturing and over nine-tenths of those engaged in mining and they produce nearly 40 per cent of the national income.[2] The individual firm and the partnership are far from extinct because in 1925 there were over ten million independent business men. This is one-fifth of the total number of gainfully employed. But the number of independent business men was slightly less in 1925 than in 1920 and only 200,000 more than in 1909.[3]

[1] Federal Trade Commission, "National Wealth and Income," *69th Congress, First Session, Senate Document No. 126*, p. 136.
[2] King, W. I., *The National Income and Its Purchasing Power*, p. 74.
[3] *Ibid.*, p. 62. Over three-fifths — 6,317,000 — of the independent business men

The corporation, we have learned, is a product of large-scale industry, a result of the fact that neither of the two traditional types of business organization — the individual firm and the partnership — is adapted for raising the huge amounts of capital needed by large concerns. It is the legal device which makes possible the gigantic business enterprises of modern industry. And since the employees of many corporations outnumber the working population of many cities and states and since the financial transactions of many corporations greatly exceed the financial operations of many states, the internal government and operation of corporations are quite as worthy of study as the operation of the government itself.

The trouble with the individual firm as a device for raising capital obviously is that few persons possess the immense funds which large business establishments require. At least fourteen enterprises in the United States have assets of over a billion dollars,[4] and many others have assets of over half a billion. Even our wealthiest men could not individually provide the capital needed by these enterprises. Nor is the partnership suitable for raising large amounts of capital. One dare enter into partnership only with persons concerning whose honesty, ability, and financial responsibility one is certain. For this there are two reasons. Any member, acting on behalf of the partnership, can bind it by the agreements which he makes. More serious still, each partner is liable without limit for the debts of the concern. It makes no difference how little a partner has invested. Suppose that he has put in only $10,000 and that the debts of the firm are $100,000. He may be sued for the entire $100,000. Of course, he may recover from the other partners for their shares, but perhaps they have little property upon which a judgment can be levied. After one has entered into a partnership, withdrawal is difficult. Naturally, a member can be permitted to sell his

---

were in agriculture. The number in manufacturing and mining is diminishing rapidly — from 301,000 in 1909 to 176,000 in 1925.

[4] The United States Steel Corporation, the Southern Pacific Company, the Pennsylvania Railroad, the American Telephone and Telegraph Company, the New York Central Railroad, the Standard Oil Company of New Jersey, the Union Pacific Railroad, the Atchison, Topeka and Santa Fé Railway, the Standard Gas and Electric Company, General Motors Corporation, the Baltimore and Ohio Railroad, the National City Bank, the Chase National Bank, and the National Bank of Commerce.

interest only to a purchaser who is acceptable to the other partners. If no satisfactory buyer can be found, either the remaining members must buy the share of the retiring one or the business must be terminated and its assets sold. Frequently the
remaining partners buy out a retiring member only at the expense of their working capital — that is, by selling part of their
stock of goods at sacrifice sales. If the number of partners is
large, withdrawals, because of death or desire, are bound to be
frequent.[5]

How does the corporation make it possible for thousands of
investors who are scattered over the whole world and who know
nothing about each other's honesty, ability, or financial responsibility, to combine their capital in an enterprise? Before answering this question, let us see exactly what a corporation is. To
become a corporation, a group of persons must first go through
the formality of obtaining a charter from the state — a very
simple matter; in fact, *too* simple in most states.[6] This charter
confers on them certain privileges which we shall describe presently. Corporations acquire capital by selling shares of stock,
and investors become members of a corporation by purchasing
some of these shares. But thousands of stockholders, scattered
possibly from Maine to California, obviously could not manage
the enterprise and make the multitude of decisions which are
every day required. They must act through representatives.

[5] Although the corporation started as a device for raising large amounts of capital, recent practices in stock distribution have given the corporation other advantages.
The possibility of dividing the shares of ownership into many thousands of small
parts enables corporations to gain good will for their products by distributing the
stock among possible customers and to gain more loyal and interested service by distributing shares among employees. It is not feasible to make partners of customers
or of large numbers of employees, but it is practicable to make stockholders of them.

[6] Corporations may be established by specific legislative enactment or under general incorporation laws which prescribe the conditions upon which charters will be
granted. The former method, once the only one, led to favoritism and other serious
abuses and has been superseded. Corporations now come into existence when the
articles of incorporation are filed in the proper public office. The articles of incorporation state the name of the corporation, the business which it proposes to pursue,
its place of business, the amount of its capital stock, the par value of the shares, the
names and residences of the stockholders, and the names of the directors. The powers
of corporations are limited by the terms of the charter or of the statute under which
the charter is issued. For example, a corporation formed to operate a steel foundry
would not be authorized to run a candy factory. But the courts hold that a corporation may perform lawful acts necessary to its existence or to accomplish the objects
of its formation. The laws authorizing the establishment of corporations reserve
the right of the legislature to amend, alter, or repeal the charter rights granted.

Once a year there is a meeting of the stockholders at which a board of directors is elected. The board, in turn, selects the officials who give full time to the management of the corporation.

The reason why the corporation makes it possible to raise capital from thousands of persons who are total strangers to one another is to be found in the special privileges which the charters confer. What are these privileges? For one thing, the corporation cannot be bound, as can partnerships, by the acts of any member. It acts only by vote of its stockholders or directors or by decision of its officers or employees. Furthermore, the stockholders are not responsible without limit for its debts. Their liability is usually limited to the par value of the stock held by each, which means that if the stock was fully paid for when originally sold by the corporation — that is, if the corporation received for it money or goods equal to its par value — the owner has no further liability for the debts of the enterprise. Since a mere member cannot bind a corporation and since the liability of shareholders is limited, it is not necessary to restrict the freedom of members to sell their stock. Any stockholder may withdraw simply by selling his shares to anyone who will buy them, and this may be done without the consent of the other stockholders. And because the shares are issued in small denominations and because the owner need not sell all of them to any one person, the disposal of stock is greatly facilitated.[7]

It is desirable to bear clearly in mind that corporations are

[7] If the advantages of the corporation over the individual proprietorship and the partnership are so pronounced, why are not all enterprises incorporated? Yet in both agriculture and retailing, there are relatively few corporations and, even in manufacturing, the unincorporated enterprises are half again as numerous as the corporations.

Compared with the corporation, the individual firm and the partnership have two principal superiorities. In the first place, they avoid the expense and trouble incident to incorporation, and the special taxes or supervision to which corporations in some states and in some lines of business are subject. The Federal government imposes a special income tax upon corporations and many states impose special taxes upon them. Investigations of the Treasury Department indicate that about 92 per cent of the corporations reporting net income pay higher taxes under the Federal law than they would have had to pay had they been partnerships. *Annual Report of the Secretary of the Treasury*, 1927, p. 49. In banking, the regulation of corporations is so minute that many enterprises operate as individual firms or partnerships in order to escape supervision. In the second place, unincorporated enterprises often enjoy better credit standing than they would if incorporated. The limited liability of the owners of a corporation for its debts may render dealers in raw materials less willing to sell to the corporation on credit or bankers to lend it money.

privileged bodies which exist in large numbers only because the state exempts them from rules of law which apply to both the individual firm and the partnership. It is also desirable to notice that, in fostering the existence of corporations, the state is sponsoring the creation of economic power in highly concentrated form. Indeed, in many instances the state is making possible the establishment of organizations which, as was pointed out in the last chapter, practically exercise sovereign powers. Hence it is peculiarly fitting that the state should grant the right to be a corporation subject to certain conditions designed to prevent abuse of the immense power which large combinations of capital possess. For example, it might be required that, in return for the privilege of limited liability, corporations must recognize the right of their employees to organize themselves into trade unions or that every corporation employing 100 workers or more must establish a works council to represent the employees in dealing with the management. It might be stipulated that the factory rules and regulations and the rates of pay must receive the approval of the works council before taking effect and that this approval may be withdrawn upon a specified notice.

II. The Corporation and the Incidents of Ownership

A man owns a farm. He has the right to decide how it shall be operated — what shall be raised, what methods of cultivation shall be used. In other words, the management is under his control. Because he owns the farm, the income from it is his. But instead of an income there may be a deficit. Just as the owner is entitled to the income, so he is liable for the deficit. These three accompaniments of proprietorship — control of management, right to income, and risk of loss — have been called " the incidents of ownership."

The preferences of investors concerning income, risk, and control vary widely. One may desire the possibility of a large income above everything else and be willing to risk great losses in order to get it. Another may desire most of all a voice in the control of the business. Still another may be ready to sacrifice control and the chance of a large return in order to obtain a small but certain income. An important advantage of the corporate form of organization is that it permits the combinations of risk, income, and control in almost any proportions and thus enables enterprises to raise funds by appealing simultaneously to investors of widely different preferences.

Three principal types of securities — *bonds, preferred stock,* and *common stock* — are issued by corporations in order to meet the varying tastes of investors. But within each of these general classes there are many varieties. The owners of bonds, preferred stock, and common stock might be regarded as forming a sort of cafeteria line. The bondholders come first and are entitled to the first share in the income of the corporation; the preferred stockholders are entitled to the next share; last of all come the common stockholders who are entitled to whatever is left — *provided there is something.* If the corporation is prosperous, the amount which remains for the common stockholders may yield them a far greater return than that received by the other security owners.

Bonds are interest-bearing certificates of indebtedness. The bondholder, therefore, is a *creditor,* not an owner, of the corporation. The interest which he receives on his bonds is one of the expenses of the enterprise and, with rare exceptions, must be paid regardless of whether the concern has made any profits. As long as the interest is paid, the bondholder has no voice in the affairs of the corporation. A bond is naturally more attractive to investors when some assurance is given that the interest and principal will be paid. This may be done by pledging specific pieces of property as security for the debt represented by the bonds. Then, even if the corporation has insufficient property to pay all of its debts, the bondholders will not lose, provided enough property has been pledged to satisfy their claims. The most common form of security for bonds is a first mortgage upon real estate of the issuing corporation. In case interest or principal is not paid when due, the bondholders may foreclose the mortgage. Bonds thus secured are known as first mortgage bonds. Sometimes the security may be a second mortgage,[8] in which case

[8] When two mortgages are issued against one piece of property, the claim represented by the first one must be satisfied before the second claim is paid. If the property does not yield enough to satisfy both claims, the holders of the second mortgage lose.

the bonds are known as second mortgage bonds. Some enterprises own little real estate but possess large holdings of stocks or bonds in other corporations. These stocks and bonds may be pledged as security for a bond issue by being deposited with a trustee which is authorized to sell them for the benefit of the bondholders whenever the corporation fails to pay interest or principal. Bonds thus secured are known as collateral trust bonds. Two kinds of bonds, debenture and income, have no specific security; they are simply general claims upon the assets of the corporation. The difference between them is that interest on debentures must be paid whether it has been earned or not, whereas income bonds are entitled to interest only when there is income from which to pay it.

Preferred stock, as the name indicates, receives dividends before the common stock, but the preferred stockholder has no right to dividends if the directors do not declare them and his return is limited to a specified rate — usually about 6 or 7 per cent. Sometimes missed dividends on the preferred stock become claims against the corporation which must be paid before the common stock receives any return. In this case, the stock is known as *cumulative* preferred in contrast to *non-cumulative.* Occasionally the preferred stock is *participating* — that is, it is entitled to an additional share in profits after a certain dividend has been paid upon the common stock. If the corporation ceases business and distributes its property among the owners, the preferred stockholder may have a prior claim, as against the common stockholders, upon assets equal to the par value of his holdings.[9] Sometimes the preferred stockholders have a vote in the selection of directors, but often they have none unless the corporation has failed to pay dividends on the preferred stock for a stipulated period.[10] Upon questions which directly affect the value of the preferred stock, such as the issuance of bonds, the holders often have a vote. In rare cases, the preferred stockholders have exclusive voting rights. A company

[9] This is the usual provision, but sometimes the claim of the preferred stockholder is more than the par value of his holdings and occasionally less.

[10] Examination of 157 preferred stocks showed that one-fifth gave no voting power, one-fourth full voting power, and the remainder conditional voting power. Keister, A. S., "Recent Tendencies in Corporation Finance," *Journal of Political Economy*, April, 1922, v. XXX, p. 264.

may make its preferred stock more attractive by including in its contract with the preferred stockholders a provision that no dividends shall be paid on the common stock unless the remaining surplus is not less than a year's (or several years') dividend requirements on the preferred stock. Or the company may contract to set up an annual sinking fund with which to retire part of the preferred issue each year. This protects the preferred stockholders against conditions which might reduce the competitive ability of the enterprise and against changes in management which might reduce its earning power.

The *common stock* is entitled to whatever profits may remain after the claims of the bondholders and preferred stockholders have been met. Usually the common stockholder has a vote for each share — often, as we have seen, when the preferred stockholders have no vote — but, within recent years, there have been many cases in which the common stock has been divided into two classes — ordinarily designated " A " and " B " — only one of which has voting rights.

This great variety of securities indicates what a wide range of choice corporations offer to investors. In selecting a security, however, the investor must remember that income, risk, and control are affected by the prosperity of the issuing concern and by the proportions in which securities are issued, as well as by the rights which they confer. The common stock of a well established and profitable enterprise which has only a small bonded indebtedness may offer a more certain income than the first mortgage bonds of a new company of unproved earning power. And the amount of control represented by a share of stock depends upon how many shares possess voting rights and to what extent the capital of the corporation was raised by the sale of non-voting securities.

To illustrate how the incidents of ownership are affected by the relative amounts of different types of securities, let us compare the issues of three corporations, X, Y, and Z, each capitalized at $1,000,000 and each having a net income of $80,000 a year. The capital of X is represented by $400,000 of 5 per cent first mortgage bonds and $600,000 of common stock; that of Y by $400,000 of 6 per cent, cumulative, non-voting preferred stock and $600,000 of common stock; that of Z by $1,000,000 of common stock. The income in these three cases would be distributed as follows:

	X	Y	Z
Net income	$80,000	$80,000	$80,000
Interest on bonds	20,000	—	—
Dividends on preferred stock	—	24,000	—
Remaining for common stock	60,000	56,000	80,000
Dividend possible on common stock	10 per cent	9.33 per cent	8 per cent

The common stock of X obviously represents the greatest command over income and that of Z the least. The Z common also represents the least control of property and the least risk. To control an investment of $1,000,000, there would be needed $500,100 of Z common but only $300,100 of X or Y common. There are preferred claims ahead of both the X and Y common but none ahead of the Z common. As between the X and Y common, the risk is difficult to compare. The claims ahead of the X common are slightly smaller, but they are interest charges which must be met regardless of what earnings may be, whereas the claims ahead of the Y common are preferred stock dividends which need not be paid every year. It is probable that the X common represents the greater risk.[11]

The wide variety of security issues is convenient to those in control of corporations no less than to investors. Suppose that a company capitalized at $1,000,000 needs $500,000 in order to expand and to improve its plant. The present owners desire to retain control and are willing to assume some risks in order to do so. But the sales of the enterprise may be subject to great ups and downs. Hence the owners desire to avoid saddling it with fixed charges that must be met regardless of earnings. Or the concern may already have substantial fixed charges in the

[11] It must not be deduced from this illustration, however, that, when part of the necessary capital is raised through the sale of bonds or preferred stocks, the common stockholders invariably obtain more net income for each share of common stock. Whether or not this is true depends upon whether the rate of profit on each $100 invested turns out to be above or below the rate of return that must be paid on the bonds or the preferred stock. Suppose, in the above instance, that the net income was $30,000 instead of $80,000. The amounts remaining for the common stock would be $10,000 in case of X, $6,000 in case of Y, and $30,000 in case of Z. The dividend possible would be: X, 1.6 per cent; Y, 1 per cent; and Z, 3 per cent. Z, with no bonds or preferred stock, could pay the highest dividend.

form of interest on bonds or notes or of rentals on leased property. Either situation might be met by issuing non-voting preferred stock. Or the corporation may have a reasonably stable income which warrants the incurrence of the fixed charges that bonds impose, but its property may consist largely of intangibles, such as trade names and good will. In this case, the capital might be raised by issuing debenture bonds. A new enterprise with doubtful earning prospects might experience trouble in selling bonds. It might remove the difficulty by offering the bondholders an opportunity to share in the gains in case the venture is successful. This could be done by making the bonds convertible into preferred or common stock within a stipulated period at the option of the bondholder.

III. The Corporation and the Concentration of Power in Modern Industry

It is somewhat paradoxical that the nineteenth century, which witnessed in politics the triumph of the democratic philosophy, of the idea that government should be based upon the consent of the governed, should witness in industry a rapid concentration of power. The simultaneous spread of the democratic philosophy in politics and the concentration of power in industry are profoundly significant because it seems scarcely possible that so marked a discrepancy between our ideals and our institutions can permanently persist. Whether the difference will be eliminated by changes in ideals or by changes in institutions cannot be foreseen, but substantial alterations in one or both appear inevitable.

In facilitating the concentration of power in industry, the corporation has played a prominent part. To control a corporation, one need only own in excess of half the voting stock. Thus a company with an invested capital and outstanding stock of $1,000,000 could be controlled by a man owning $500,100 of its stock. Had he put his money into an unincorporated firm of his own, his control would extend over only $500,100 of property. The corporation practically doubles the amount of property which he can control.

But the concentration of control may go far beyond this. Some capital may be raised by the sale of bonds, which, of course, confer no voting rights, or by the sale of non-voting preferred stock. If an enterprise sells $500,000 worth of bonds, $500,000 worth of preferred stock, and $1,000,000 of common stock, $500,100 invested in common stock will control $2,000,000 of property.

Because both bonds and preferred stock impose obligations on the company, the proportion of capital which it is safe to raise by them is limited and this, of course, restricts their usefulness as devices for concentrating control over wealth. Unless a business has a stable or a steadily growing income, it cannot safely raise more than half of its capital by bonds and preferred stock. In many cases, even this proportion would be too large. When, however, a concern has issued all of the bonds and preferred stock that it safely can, there are several devices by which control can be further concentrated. One is the *holding company*. A holding company, as its name implies, is nothing but a corporation, which, instead of owning land, buildings, and equipment, holds securities in other enterprises.[12] Its income is derived from the securities which it owns. If a holding company had a capitalization of $1,000,000 and if its shares were sold at par, a man with $500,100 could control it. The holding company could control an enterprise having $2,000,000 of common stock — assuming that the stock could be purchased at par. The company might, however, have raised $2,000,000 additional capital by the sale of bonds and preferred stock. In this case, $500,100 would control $4,000,000 of property. By forming a second holding company to own securities in the first one or by raising part of the capital of the holding company through the sale of bonds and non-voting preferred stock, concentration of control would be still further increased. The old American Tobacco Company, which was dissolved in 1912 by the Supreme Court as a combination in restraint of trade, affords an extreme illustration of the control of vast properties through holding companies and non-voting securities. Through these devices, a few large stockholders in the American Tobacco Company controlled eighty-six other companies capitalized at nearly half a billion dollars.[13] Professor W. Z. Ripley has estimated

[12] Most holding companies are not purely such. In addition to securities they have physical property of their own.
[13] Marshall, L. C., *Industrial Society*, pp. 729–730.

that in the case of twelve large public service companies $150,-
000,000 of common stocks control an investment of approximately ten times that amount.[14]

In recent years a new device for concentrating control has
arisen — the separation of common stock into two classes only
one of which carries voting rights. As a rule the voting shares
are but a small proportion of the total and often they are not
offered to the general public but are kept by insiders in " payment " for their " services " in organizing or reorganizing the
enterprise. Thus the bankers who reorganized Dodge Brothers
offered to the public $160,000,000 of bonds and preferred stock
and 1,500,000 *non-voting* shares of Class A common, but kept
for themselves 500,000 of Class B *voting* common shares. Industrial Rayon issued 598,000 shares of non-voting Class A
common and 2,000 shares of Class B carrying exclusive voting
rights.[15] The Southern Gas and Power Corporation has outstanding a note issue of $2,000,000, preferred stock of $5,000,-
000, and 250,000 shares of Class A *non*-voting common stock.
Voting power is concentrated in 100,000 shares of Class B common. As the corporation is itself a holding company owning
local utilities in eight different states, the concentration of control
is doubly great.[16]

Thus far we have assumed that, in order to control a
corporation, it is necessary to possess more than half of the
voting stock. Much less, as a rule, is sufficient, especially if the
enterprise is large and the holdings small and scattered. A
stockholder who possesses possibly thirty or forty shares of stock
in a corporation can scarcely afford to attend the annual meeting.
Doing so would probably involve a trip of several hundred miles.
The expense of this trip and the value of the time lost would
probably equal the return on his investment for a year. But
even if the expense were not prohibitive, what would be the
object in his attending? He knows too little about the affairs of
the enterprise to do more than ratify the policies which the
managers recommend. And, should he by chance feel inclined

[14] *World's Work,* December, 1926, p. 128.
[15] Ripley, W. Z., *Main Street and Wall Street,* pp. 86–87.
[16] The criticism of non-voting common shares became so severe that late in 1925
the New York Stock Exchange adopted the policy of refusing to list them in the
future.

to oppose some policy of the management, what influence could he exert with thirty or forty votes out of possibly several hundred thousand? Hence it is not surprising to find the annual meetings of the stockholders sparsely attended. Only one shareholder — outside of officers and directors — attended the meeting of the Standard Oil Company of New Jersey on August 15, 1919, at which it was decided to issue $100,000,000 of preferred stock.[17] Often stockholders are not sufficiently interested even to be represented by proxy and those who do send proxies usually sign the printed form which the management sends out and which authorizes some officer to vote the signer's shares. It is evident that under these circumstances ownership of a very small fraction of the stock would enable those already in control of a corporation to keep control. The recent tendency for the ownership of corporations to become more diffused has been hailed as a step toward the realization of industrial democracy. As a matter of fact, it simply means more small stockholders, who know little about the business and its problems and who, even if they desired to, could not afford to attend annual meetings. In other words, diffusion of ownership facilitates concentration of control.[18]

IV. The Exploitation of Corporations by Insiders

The corporate form of organization raises interesting questions concerning the validity of the theory of free enterprise. That theory asserts, it will be recalled, that the pursuit of his self-interest by each person will produce a maximum surplus of satisfaction over sacrifice. Self-interest, of course, may be anything which the individual conceives it to be, but in business

---

[17] New York *World*, November 17, 1926, p. 20.

[18] Most large corporations now number their stockholders by the tens of thousands. The American Telephone and Telegraph Company on December 31, 1926, had nearly 360,000 stockholders. No stockholder owned as much as one per cent of the stock and the average holding was less than twenty-seven shares. *Annual Report*, 1926, p. 12. Among the 47,000 stockholders of Swift and Company in 1925, the average holding was thirty-one shares. To vote a majority of the shares would have required the entire holdings of over 1,400 of the largest stockholders. Swift and Company, *Year Book*, 1927, p. 12. The General Motors Corporation, at the end of 1929, reported 198,600 stockholders. New York *Times*, January 1, 1930, p. 49. Pennsylvania Railroad reported over 196,000. New York *Times*, April 1, 1930, p. 49. United States Steel Corporation, at the end of the first quarter of 1930, had 124,069 common stockholders. New York *Times*, April 8, 1930, p. 37.

transactions it is usually identified with pecuniary advantage. Suppose, however, that the officers and directors of large corporations were carefully and efficiently to seize every opportunity to profit at the expense of the stockholders. It is plain that corporate enterprises would be seriously handicapped in competition with the individual proprietorship and the partnership and that we should be prevented in large measure from obtaining the advantages of large business units. In other words, we are able to obtain the advantages of large-scale production only because the officers of corporations either do not conceive of their interests in narrow pecuniary terms or because their actions are largely determined by traditional standards of commercial integrity rather than by deliberate pursuit of self-interest. The truth of the matter is that the successful operation of large corporations requires a high level of commercial honesty. Among many peoples of the earth, it is probable that large-scale production could be only incompletely developed because their standards of business integrity make it difficult to operate large corporations.

But thousands of widely scattered stockholders who are unable to keep in close touch with the affairs of their enterprises and who cannot easily unite to protect their interests are obviously a tempting prey to unscrupulous managers, directors, and cliques of large stockholders. Although our standards of business practice are high enough to make it possible for us to operate large corporations, they are not high enough to prevent the history of corporate enterprise from being sprinkled with many disgraceful episodes such as those associated with the names of " New Haven," " Alton," " Erie," or " Rock Island."

The methods of exploiting stockholders are numerous. One of the simplest and most common is the payment of exorbitant salaries to officials. In investigating the affairs of the Chicago, Rock Island, and Pacific Railway a few years ago, the Interstate Commerce Commission found high officials being paid large secret additions to their regular salaries. Another simple method is for the corporation to purchase materials and supplies at exorbitant prices from other companies in which the insiders are interested. Officers and directors sometimes purchase other enterprises or land which they resell to their company at an immense profit to themselves. It has been a common practice for insiders in railroad companies to build short feeder lines which are sold to the principal company at a high price. Now that the large chains of gas and electric plants are expanding rapidly, we find those in control buying small plants and reselling them to the chain company for a comfortable profit. Occasionally insiders exploit an enterprise by forming a special selling agency through which the company agrees to market its products — paying well, of course, for the service. In September, 1898, officials of the Standard Rope and Twine Company formed such an agency known as the Union Selling Company to which the Standard Company paid 7½ per cent commission on all sales — increasing its selling expense by about 50 per cent.[19] More recently Colonel Robert W. Stewart was ousted as chairman of the board of directors of the Standard Oil Company of Indiana because, in collaboration with the executives of several other companies, he formed a dummy company which purchased 33,000,000 barrels of oil at $1.50 a barrel and immediately resold it to his company and several others at $1.75.[20]

Officers and directors naturally come into the possession of inside information which enables them to purchase the stock of the company before it rises or to sell it before it falls. Sometimes facts which would materially affect the value of the stock are deliberately withheld in order that insiders may profit. In other cases, misleading information is published. About a year before the failure of the Baltimore and Ohio Railroad in 1896, the president stated: " I can safely say the road has not been in so strong a position as now for at least fifteen years." Shortly after, the dividend on the common stock was passed. When a company is not prosperous, there is a strong temptation for the officers to conceal this fact because it may cause the efficiency of the management to be questioned. We know that the line between operating expenses and capital expenditure is often difficult to draw. This creates an opportunity to conceal losses by classifying some operating expenses as investments of capital. After the failure of the Baltimore and Ohio Railroad, the accountants for the receiver found that for some years the income

---

[19] Lough, W. H., *Business Finance*, pp. 533–534.

[20] After the transaction had been exposed several years later, Colonel Stewart turned back his share of the profits to the Standard Oil Company of Indiana. He said that he had been keeping the amount " in trust."

of the company had been overstated to the extent of $11,204,858 by charging certain operating expenses to capital accounts.[21] The income of the Atchison, Topeka, and Santa Fé Railroad was deliberately misrepresented for at least three years prior to its failure. In this instance, the overstatement was about $7,000,000.[22]

The problem of how to protect stockholders against exploitation by insiders is extremely difficult of solution. It is now the practice of corporations to have their books audited by firms of certified public accountants but these audits seem to have slight value, especially when it is to the interest of insiders to understate the value of assets and the amount of income. Some good could be accomplished if corporate charters were granted subject only to certain safeguarding conditions. Among such conditions might be included: (1) relatively complete and frequent publicity of accounts comparable to that now required of the railroads; (2) prohibition of the issuance of non-voting stock; and (3) authorization of the cumulative voting of the stock. The last provision would assist minority interests to gain representation on the board of directors. If nine directors were to be elected, it would be optional for a stockholder owning one share to cast one vote for nine men or nine votes for one man.

Thus far, however, the states have attached few safeguarding conditions to the right to be a corporation. This is partly because the fees which corporations pay have made the states eager to issue as many charters as possible. Consequently there has grown up a disgraceful traffic in corporation charters, with many states striving to outdo each other in the leniency of the terms on which charters are granted. Indeed, the New York Stock Exchange, a purely private organization, does more to protect the interests of the small stockholder than any state government. Although many states permit the issuance of non-voting common stock, the New York Exchange will not list new issues of such stock, and more publicity of finances is required to get an issue listed on the New York Exchange than to obtain a corporate charter from any state. But in so far as it is possible to protect stockholders through the terms of the charter, little progress is likely to be

---

[21] Lough, W. H., *Business Finance*, pp. 548–549.   [22] *Ibid.*, pp. 549–550.

made until competition of the states for fees is ended by the federal government's requiring all corporations doing an interstate business to obtain federal charters.

V. The Diffusion of Ownership and Private Property

One of the most important questions raised by the corporation is that of the effect of the diffusion of ownership and concentration of control upon the property rights of the stockholder. Can he be considered the owner of a piece of private property in the same sense as a man who is the sole owner of a farm, store, or factory? Rights involve responsibilities. But just what responsibility are the small and scattered owners of a large corporation able to assume? What, for example, does the ordinary stockholder know of working conditions in his enterprise? What facts could he discover if he endeavored to inform himself? He cannot compel the management to enlighten him and he probably cannot afford to make a personal investigation. But suppose that he does discover what the working conditions are and that he believes they should be improved, even at some sacrifice of profits if necessary. What can he do about it? Unless the management is willing to furnish him a list of the other stockholders and their addresses, he cannot effectively communicate with them for the purpose of creating concerted action. And if he did communicate, what response could he expect? Would the other stockholders feel that he or they knew enough about either the working conditions or the competitive situation of the enterprise to override the policies of the management?

In view of the almost complete inability of the stockholders to assume responsibility for conditions in their enterprises, what rights can they claim against interference by the state? Suppose that the state intervenes and says that, since the stockholders cannot act, it will insist upon decent working conditions. Do the rights of private property protect the shareholders from having the state assume responsibility which they themselves cannot shoulder? None of these questions have been presented to the courts in the precise form in which they are here asked. It seems inevitable, however, that the growing size of business enterprises and the growing diffusion of ownership will compel the courts to re-define the rights of stockholders in the light of the inability of stockholders to assume responsibility.

VI. The Coöperative Concern

We have seen that coöperative retail stores are relatively less important in the United States than in many European countries. In the selling of agricultural products, however, and in the buying of farm supplies, coöperative associations are of great and rapidly growing importance. In 1928, 12,000 marketing and purchasing coöperative associations transacted a business of nearly $2,500,000,000, about four-fifths of which represented the sale of farm products and one-fifth the purchase of farm supplies.[23] Between 1919 and 1924, there was an increase of about 73 per cent in the number of farms selling all or part of their products coöperatively and an increase of 85 per cent in the physical volume of farm products thus sold.[24] In 1924, about 14 per cent of all farms sold some or all of their crops coöperatively.[25] During the last few years, there has been a rapid growth of large-scale coöperatives and many farm-controlled coöperatives are now in the "big-business" class. Some of these large coöperatives are federations of small ones. Among the largest are twelve associations affiliated with the National Live Stock Producers' Association of Chicago which handled livestock to the value of $138,000,000 in 1928; the California Fruit Growers' Exchange which sold $96,500,000 of citrous fruit during the year ending October 31, 1928; the Dairymen's League Coöperative Association of New York with 71,000 members and sales of $82,500,000 in the year ending March 31, 1928; and Land O'Lakes Creameries, Inc., of Minneapolis, a federation of more than 400 creameries with annual sales of about $50,000,000.[26] There are many others with annual sales in excess of ten millions. Indeed, the rapid growth of coöperatives in agriculture is comparable to the rise of the corporation in other fields. The coöperative movement, and particularly the tendency to form

[23] United States Department of Agriculture. *Agricultural Coöperation*, January 26, 1929, v. VII, p. 19.
[24] *Ibid.*, October 1, 1925, v. V, pp. 377 and 397.
[25] *Ibid.*, October 1, 1925, v. V, p. 377.
[26] *Ibid.*, February 9, 1929, v. VII, p. 37.

large-scale coöperatives, is likely to receive a strong impetus from the creation of the Federal Farm Board in 1929 because a principal function of the Board is the encouragement of coöperatives. In fact, it is the policy of the Board to establish a national coöperative for marketing each of the principal crops. Such large-scale coöperatives have already been established under the Board's direction for grain, wool, and cotton, and the organization of others is being fostered.

Corporations, as we have seen, being primarily devices for attracting capital, are naturally organized in such a manner as to be as attractive to capitalists as possible. Voting power and profits are both distributed in accordance with the number of shares held. But the success of enterprises depends upon their ability to attract patronage and their ability to obtain efficient service from their employees, as well as upon their success in obtaining capital. The coöperative association is based upon this fact — it represents an effort to attract patronage or to gain unusually efficient labor by giving control and profits to the patrons or the employees instead of to the investors.

Membership in coöperative associations is usually acquired in the same manner as membership in corporations — by the investment of capital. Some coöperatives, however, have no capital. In such cases, membership is obtained by the applicant's being accepted by other members. Coöperative associations are usually governed by a board of directors who are selected by the members and who appoint the manager just as do the directors of a corporation. In two important respects, however, the coöperatives differ from corporations: (1) each member of the association, no matter how much money he has invested in it, has only one vote; and (2) the funds invested in the enterprise receive only a limited return.[27] After this has been paid, the remaining profits are distributed among the members in accordance with some other principle than the amount of money invested. In the case of coöperative workshops, it is usual for the workers to

---

[27] Some "coöperatives" are incorporated under general corporation laws which provide that each shareholder shall have one vote for each share of stock that he owns. When a "coöperative" is incorporated under a general incorporation law, it may be difficult to prevent the sale of stock to persons who are not active members. At the end of 1925, all but two states had passed special laws providing for the organization of coöperatives.

share in the profits in proportion to the amount of their wages; in the case of buyers' or sellers' coöperatives, the profits are distributed in proportion to patronage, that is in proportion to the amounts purchased or sold through the association. In short, the dividend is based upon wages or patronage instead of upon investment.

Many coöperative enterprises deal only with members — that is, many buyers' coöperatives, such as coöperative retail stores, sell goods only to members; many sellers' coöperatives, such as creameries or cheese factories, sell only the product of their members; many coöperative workshops hire only workmen who are willing to become members. Refusal of sellers' coöperatives to market the product of non-members, of buyers' coöperatives to sell to non-members, or of coöperative workshops to employ non-members may at first seem a narrow and arbitrary policy, but violation of this rule almost invariably causes the coöperative enterprise to lose its democratic character and transforms it into an organization for the profit of the few rather than for the service of the many. If a coöperative store, for example, sells to non-members, an incentive is at once created for the members to refuse admission to all applicants, in order that they may keep for themselves the profits made on the sales to outsiders. A similar temptation exists in the case of other types of coöperatives. This is why the principle of doing business only with members is so frequently abandoned.[28]

Because the coöperative associations offer less attractive terms to investors than does the corporation, they do not flourish in industries where the capital required is large and where raising sufficient funds is a major problem. Furthermore, the very democracy of coöperative associations and the fact that their members are mainly men of small resources have handicapped them in obtaining competent management. To men who have never earned more than two or three thousand dollars a year, salaries of five to twenty-five thousand dollars seem sheer extravagance. Yet such salaries are often necessary to attract

---

[28] Although one of the basic rules of the coöperative movement is that coöperatives should serve members only, about 85 per cent of the farmers' coöperatives reporting to the U. S. Department of Agriculture for 1925 were serving patrons in addition to their own members. *Agricultural Coöperation*, October, 1925, v. IV, p. 421.

capable executives.[29]   Finally, coöperative enterprises suffer because the principle of industrial control and profit distribution for which they stand causes them to be fought bitterly by business organizations of the traditional types.   Discrimination confronts them on all sides.   Coöperative coal mines have found that railroads delayed in supplying them switch tracks and, when at last the tracks were in, the car supply, a vital thing to a coal mine, has been irregular and unreliable.   Coöperative retail stores find their supplies of goods shut off by the threats of retailers to boycott any jobber who sells to a coöperative.   Large manufacturers of dairy products bid up prices in local markets temporarily in order to cause farmers to break away from coöperative creameries.   But despite these obstacles, the coöperative seems destined to become increasingly important, especially in the marketing of crops and in the purchasing of farm supplies. It peculiarly suits the needs of the small farmer because it gives him the advantages of a large business unit in buying and selling but permits him to retain his independence as a small cultivator of the soil.

VII. The Trade Association

It has been suggested that evolution applies to industrial organizations and institutions no less than to animal structure and that it would be an error to regard the existing forms of business organization, such as the corporation, as in any way final.   A question of intense interest in the study of industrial organization is whether the making of the principal decisions in industry and the determination of major policies will remain indefinitely in the hands of the individual business enterprise or whether it will be transferred in large degree to associations of enterprises representing the industry as a whole.   Will the unit of administration, in other words, become less and less the *individual firm* and more and more the *industry?*

The rapid spread of trade associations during the last several generations and the increase in the number and importance of

---

[29] For example, the Secretary of Agriculture reports that there are over 150 agricultural coöperative associations in the United States each doing a business exceeding $1,000,000 annually.   Enterprises of this size need thoroughly capable executives.   *Report of the Secretary of Agriculture,* 1927, p. 17.

their functions make these far from academic questions. The first national trade association in this country, the United Brewers' Association, was organized in 1862. The Carriage Builders' National Association was founded in 1872, the Laundryowners' National Association in 1883, the National Wholesale Lumber Dealers' Association in 1894. Now almost every industry has its trade association. There are over 900 national trade associations in the United States and in addition many local and sectional ones.

The principal functions of the first trade associations were to afford members of the trade an opportunity to discuss common problems and to represent the interests of their members before legislative bodies. There are so many things, however, which trade associations can do better than individual concerns acting independently that the functions and activities of trade associations have steadily increased.

Some things are almost impossible for an individual enterprise to do. For example, a single firm cannot collect certain types of market information, such as statistics on the volume of shipments, the amount of unfilled orders, the stocks of goods on hand, or the prices being paid or received. Few concerns would be willing to divulge this information to one of their competitors. They may be willing, however, to give the information in confidence to a trade association, which, by combining the data from different enterprises, obtains totals that give a clear picture of the general market situation but betray nothing concerning the business of individual firms. Statistics concerning the volume of production, unfilled orders, stocks on hand, shipments, and current prices are obviously of great usefulness in enabling enterprises to adapt their production and selling policies to market changes and are gathered by many trade associations.

Some activities which would be almost prohibitively expensive if carried on by each concern for itself can be conducted through a trade association at little expense to each firm. In this way the trade association places within the reach of small enterprises many of the advantages of large business units. The collection of credit information is an example. The National Wholesale Lumber Dealers' Association has on file over 40,000 reports on wholesale buyers.[30] The Electrical Board of Trade of New York City has over 17,000 folders of credit information on firms in the electrical industry.[31] Only very large enterprises could afford to assemble such vast quantities of credit information. Furthermore, its collection is an activity which can be performed better by an association than by individual concerns acting independently. Consider, for example, the monthly reports of all accounts ninety days or more past due which are issued by some trade associations. These reports are made possible simply by arranging with the members to report such accounts to the association office. When a trade association receives a credit inquiry concerning a firm for which it has no file, a request to all members for a report of their experience with the firm is likely to bring the needed information.

Industrial research which may be prohibitively expensive to individual concerns can often be conducted economically through a trade association. It is estimated that trade associations are spending $35,000,000 a year for industrial research.[32] Much of the work is carried on in coöperation with educational institutions and government bureaus. About 400 university fellowships are supported by trade associations, and sixty-one research associates are maintained at the Bureau of Standards.[33] The investigations cover all manner of problems. The American Institute of Baking operates four complete baking units. Part of its work consists in developing a certified list of acceptable baking ingredients.[34] The Laundryowners' National Association has been studying the properties of textiles with a view to eliminating laundering weaknesses and the effect of laundry supplies on textiles; the National Canners' Association has studied the types of tin plate most suitable for food containers, the effect of the canning process upon the vitamin content of foods, the protection of canners' crops against pests and plant diseases; the Warm Air Heating and Ventilating Association has a house as a laboratory in which are studied the advantages and disadvantages of heat-

[30] U. S. Department of Commerce, " Trade Association Activities," *Domestic Commerce Series, No. 20*, p. 121.

[31] *Bulletin of the Electrical Board of Trade of New York*, March, 1928, p. 6.

[32] " Trade Association Activities," *Domestic Commerce Series, No. 20*, p. 3.

[33] *Ibid.*, p. 3.

[34] *Ibid.*, p. 69.

ing equipment of different design and the methods of increasing the efficiency of furnaces.[35]

There are some activities which the individual enterprise can ill afford to finance because the benefits accrue to the whole industry rather than to the enterprise which bears the expense. This is one reason why the cost of training apprentices is often borne in part by the trade association. Many boys, on completing their training, change their employer. Thus the firm which bears the expense of training frequently does not obtain the services of the apprentices which it has trained. Some trade associations have worked out apprenticeship courses and either have established schools of their own or coöperate with public school authorities in giving the courses. The United Typothetae of America conduct a correspondence course for apprentices; the New York branch of the Employing Printers of America contribute to the support of schools for compositors and pressmen which are conducted in coöperation with the unions; local contractors' associations coöperate with the building trades' unions and the public school authorities in conducting classes for apprentices.

Certain types of advertising can be better conducted by trade associations than by the individual enterprises because the benefits accrue to all the concerns in the industry. Suppose, for example, that it is desired to induce the public to use more of a certain commodity, say cypress, cement, or sauerkraut. A single producer or even a small group of producers could ill afford to bear the entire expense of advertising the merits *of the commodity* rather than the superiority of particular *brands* because the benefits would be shared by every enterprise in the industry. Consequently, the advertising of *products,* as distinguished from *brands*, has frequently been undertaken by trade associations — witness the advertising of brick, cement, sheet steel, mahogany, cypress, flowers, sauerkraut, leather, tile, by organizations of producers in those industries.[36] It is estimated that trade associations are now

---

[35] *Ibid.*, pp. 68–72.

[36] Sometimes the consumption of a commodity can be increased by providing expert information concerning its uses. The Portland Cement Association maintains a service staff of over 200 engineers, distributed among twenty-four district offices, who give free advice and suggestions concerning the use of cement and concrete. The cement manufacturers are also interested in preventing the improper use of

spending about $10,000,000 a year on commercial advertising.[37] Advertising by trade associations has been greatly stimulated by the fierce competition between many commodities — ice fights electric refrigerators; silk battles cotton; lumber struggles with cement, brick, and stone; green tea with black tea; leather with rubber; paint with wall paper.

If the workmen in an industry have a union, it is often advantageous for the employers to act together either in fighting it or in dealing with it. Some associations of employers maintain their own secret service organizations to discover attempts to unionize the plants of the members, and keep corps of armed guards and staffs of professional strike breakers ready at a moment's notice to take the places of men who quit. They have large defense funds to assist any plant which has labor trouble and they arrange, if necessary, to have the orders of a struck establishment handled by other plants.

An association of employers is also advantageous if the employers prefer to work with the union rather than to fight it. It strengthens their bargaining power by enabling them to meet the union with a united front. It also makes possible a single trade agreement between the union and all the enterprises in the association. The terms can be arranged so that no concern has an advantage over the others. Furthermore, when there is an agreement between the union and an association of enterprises, the latter stands behind it to prevent unscrupulous employers from gaining an advantage by violating it and to protect any enterprise from being handicapped by its employees' demanding more than the agreement gives them.[38]

Among the most important activities of trade associations are those which may be regarded as relating to the government of industry — standardization of raw materials, equipment, and prod-

---

cement or concrete because the failure of a concrete structure naturally tends to give a bad name to cement.

[37] "Trade Association Activities," *Domestic Commerce Series, No. 20*, p. 3.

[38] Organizations for fighting or dealing with trade unions exist in nearly every industry. Prominent among the fighting type are the National Founders' Association, the National Erectors' Association, the National Metal Trades' Association, and the Employing Printers of America; among the organizations cultivating friendly relations with unions, the American Newspaper Publishers' Association, the Stove Founders' National Defense Association, and the American Photo-Engravers' Association.

ucts; the regulation of trade practices, such as the maximum period for which credit will be granted; the establishment and enforcement of standards of business practice and "codes of ethics"; and the prevention of unfair competition and of trade abuses, such as the misbranding of goods or the cancellation of orders. Standardization is necessarily a coöperative undertaking and trade associations have played an important part in getting agreements in regard to standards. The paper makers, through their association, have induced rag dealers to sell rags in accordance with standard grades and classification; the cement manufacturers have brought about the adoption of a standard specification for cement; in the automobile industry more than 600 standards relating to engines, electrical systems, parts and fittings, and materials have been formulated and widely adopted.[39] As a general rule, however, trade associations are interested in helping to standardize articles which their members buy rather than the articles which they sell. In fact, trade associations may fight hard to prevent the standardization of articles which their members sell.

Many trade associations have established codes of business ethics but most of these codes are extremely general and the provisions are sometimes inimical to the public. The Chamber of Commerce of the United States, in examining the by-laws and codes of ethics of over 400 trade associations, found only sixty-seven which were sufficiently definite to be regulations of business practices. Forty-three associations had adopted a standard practice toward cancellations and the return of goods; thirty-four, standard interpretations of terms of delivery; seventeen, a uniform contract of sale; and forty-two advocated uniform credit practice.[40]

The inability of many buyers to distinguish accurately between superior and inferior goods tempts producers to skimp on quality and to attract buyers by shading prices. Naturally no business man wishes his competitors to do this. Hence, controlling the quality of the product is an important activity of certain trade associations. Several associations of lumber manufacturers employ inspectors to check the grading of lumber by the mem-

[39] "Trade Association Activities," *Domestic Commerce Series*, No. 20, p. 91.
[40] *Ibid.*, p. 110.

bers. The Portland Cement Association admits no manufacturer who does not guarantee his product to meet the standard specifications for cement. Sometimes fierce competition causes the production of poor quality with the result that the commodity acquires a bad name and the users turn to substitutes. Such was the situation several years ago in the malleable castings industry. To remedy it, the trade association established a testing laboratory to which each member sent a specimen casting from every heat. The association established certain tests of quality which must be met by the product of every member and it engaged foundry experts to visit the plants of members and show them how to produce better castings.

The most important activity of many trade associations is the discouragement of price cutting. This is significant because the heavy fixed costs in modern industry, as we shall see later, create a strong incentive for enterprises to sell below cost when business is slack. Some of the activities which have been described have the discouragement of price cutting as one of their purposes. The collection of statistical information, for example, is intended to prevent the overproduction which makes cutthroat competition practically inevitable. Many trade associations encourage their members to acquire a better knowledge of costs in hopes that this will discourage price cutting and some associations even endeavor to induce their members to adopt a uniform system of cost keeping. Most important of all is the opprobrium which is constantly and persistently heaped upon the price cutter in the bulletins and publications of trade associations and in the addresses at the annual meetings. Occasionally more direct devices for raising or maintaining prices are employed and the trade association comes into conflict with the anti-trust laws, as did an association of hardwood lumber dealers.[41] The influence of trade associations upon prices will be discussed further in Chapters XIV and XVI.

In addition to the matters with which trade associations have already sought to deal, there are many others which might be handled advantageously by them. Many costs lie beyond the control of the individual firm and can be reduced only by joint

[41] See *American Column and Lumber Company, et al.*, v. *United States*, 257 U. S. 377 (1921).

action or by an organization capable of controlling the policies of all or most of the plants in an industry. In so far as labor turnover is due to differences in wages and conditions for the same class of work in different plants, it can be eliminated only by coöperative action. The invention of new machinery produces great waste because the competition of the enterprises which possess the new machines compels other concerns to scrap equipment prematurely. If it were possible through trade associations to regulate the rate at which new inventions are installed, the cost of progress, to both business enterprises and wage earners, could be substantially reduced. During recent years advertising and selling expenditures have shown an alarming tendency to mount. Yet they cannot be kept down by the independent action of competitors. Just as one nation dare not reduce its armaments unless its rivals do likewise, so a single firm cannot ordinarily cut its outlay for advertising and selling unless its competitors do the same. Possibly trade associations may be the means of placing some limit upon advertising and selling outlay. Because trade associations can do so many things which the individual establishment cannot, they are likely to grow steadily in importance and to acquire more functions and power. This gradual acquisition of functions by trade associations may, in the course of time, create material changes in business organization. Individual enterprises will still exist, but in many industries they will be distinctly less important than they now are. By a slow process of evolution, the principal form of business organization may become one representing each industry as a whole.

REFERENCES

American Institute of Co-operation, *American Co-operation*, v. I to IV, 1927.
Britain's Financial Future, 1928. Ch. VII and VIII.
Dewing, A. S., *The Financial Policy of Corporations*, 1919. V. I.
Elsworth, R. H., " Agricultural Co-operative Associations," United States Department of Agriculture, *Technical Bulletin, No. 40*, 1928.
Hibbard, B. H., *Marketing Agricultural Products*, 1924.
Lough, W. H., *Business Finance*, 1922. Ch. IV, V, VII, VIII, XXIII, and XXIV.
Reed, H. L., *Corporation Finance*, 1925. Ch. I, II, IV, V, XXII, and XXIII.
Ripley, W. Z., *Main Street and Wall Street*, 1927.

CHAPTER IX

THE ORGANIZATION OF LABOR

I. THE EXTENT OF UNIONISM. II. THE CAUSES OF UNIONISM. III. TRADE UNION STRUCTURE. IV. THE GOVERNMENT OF TRADE UNIONS. V. TRADE UNION POLICIES. VI. THE SIGNIFICANCE OF TRADE UNIONISM.

I. The Extent of Unionism

Strikes and revolts of workers are found far back in history. So also are organizations of small employers, such as medieval gilds. Only within the last several hundred years, however, and particularly within the last century, do we find wage earners maintaining on an extensive scale more or less continuous organizations for the purpose of representing their interests in dealing with employers. Now, for the first time in history, we find the manual laborers, the people who have passively done the dirty, disagreeable, and dangerous work and who have allowed other classes to guide government and industry, organizing for the purpose of exercising some conscious control over their destinies. Trade unionism is just as much a distinctive feature of modern economic society as the corporation, the coöperative society, or the trade association, for wherever we find industry conducted by modern methods under the control of capitalists — whether in Europe, Mexico, Australia, South Africa, China, India, the Argentine, Canada, or the United States — we find trade unions. Of the seventy separate countries in the world, associations of wage earners have attained some importance in over fifty and great importance in over twenty. In the United States in 1927, approximately 3,900,000, or 14 per cent, of the 27,300,000 non-agricultural wage earners were organized.[1] In the year 1897, the number was less than 450,000 which means that, in a generation, trade union membership in this country has increased over eightfold. The degree of organization is, of course, much

[1] Wolman, Leo, in *Recent Economic Changes*, v. II, p. 480, and King, W. I., *The National Income and Its Purchasing Power*, p. 56.

greater in some branches of industry than in others. The extent of union membership in four leading branches of industry in 1927 was as follows:

	Number of wage earners	Number of trade unionists	Percentage of organization
Construction	1,421,000	1,014,000	71.5
Manufacturing	9,100,000	906,000	9.9
Mines, quarries, and oil wells	1,251,000	406,000	32.4
Transportation and utilities	2,540,000	950,000	37.4

In the United Kingdom, Germany, Sweden, Australia, and Belgium, the degree of organization is greater than in the United States. The British unions, with approximately five million members, embrace about one-half of the manual workers in manufacturing, mining, and transportation, and the German unions have more members, both absolutely and relatively, than the British. We cannot understand our economic order unless we know why, wherever it appears, it provokes such a strong tendency among wage earners to form trade unions.

II. The Causes of Unionism

There is a more or less prevalent belief that unionism is solely a product of the factory system, that it began when the factory system began and that it has spread with the spread of machinery. This view is far from true. Although machinery has greatly affected the growth of unionism, sometimes helping and sometimes even hindering it, trade unionism antedates the factory system. In England, unions preceded the factory system by about seventy-five years. In the United States, the first unions were established among the printers and the shoemakers late in the eighteenth century. The printing shops might be regarded as small factories but there were then no factories in the shoe industry.

The prerequisite to the existence of unionism appears to be a class of manual laborers who are free, who work for wages, and who have little hope of being anything but wage earners. There is, of course, scant possibility of organization among workers who are not free. Nor are unions likely to develop among wage earners who have a good chance of becoming independent business men. As long as this chance exists, the wage earner is interested in getting ahead *as an individual*. Only when he sees little or no prospect of rising out of his class, does he feel that his welfare depends upon the welfare of the class and does he become interested in organizations for improving the condition of the class.

The opportunity to rise out of the wage earning class did not disappear simultaneously in all occupations. In fact, in some industries, such as agriculture, the hired laborers still expect to become employers and hence are not interested in unionism. The earliest instances of unionism in Great Britain appear to have been in the woolen industry and in the London tailoring industry late in the seventeenth century. In the woolen industry, the improvement of transportation led to the rise of wealthy clothiers or wholesalers who purchased wool wherever they could obtain it cheapest and then gave it out, first to be carded and spun and then to be woven into cloth. The cloth was " fulled " in the wholesaler's mill, given out to be " dressed," and finally sold by the wholesaler.[2] It is obvious that the wholesaler required far more capital and business skill than the ordinary weaver could hope to possess. The rise of the wholesalers, therefore, practically meant that the manual laborers in the woolen industry were doomed to remain wage earners for life. We find organizations of woolen workers springing up simultaneously with the wholesale clothier. The creation of a permanent wage-earning class in the London tailoring industry was a result of the rise of the " shopkeeping tailors " who, instead of making up the customer's own goods, furnished the cloth and in addition gave long credits to aristocratic customers. The shopkeeping tailor also required more capital and more ability than the average journeyman possessed. Furthermore the business tended to gravitate into the hands of the most skilled workers, the cutters, who employed sewers to make up the garments.[3] Among these sewers, who had little chance of becoming employers, we find trade unions arising. As the development of modern market organization and of modern technology has deprived the workers in industry after industry of the expectation of being anything but wage earners, unionism has become more and more universal.[4]

[2] Webb, S. and B., *History of Trade Unionism* (revised edition), pp. 32–35.

[3] For a more detailed account, see Webb, S. and B., *Ibid.*, pp. 30–31.

[4] It should not be inferred, however, that unionism is most prevalent in those industries where the wage earners have the least opportunity to become employers.

But the expectation of the average manual laborer that he will always be a wage earner is not an entirely satisfactory explanation of trade unionism because there are a number of other circumstances which also have encouraged modern wage earners to form labor organizations. Among the most important of these is the fact that during the nineteenth century, for the first time in history, ability to read and write became almost universal among the manual workers in the principal industrial countries. This was a revolutionary change and one of greatest importance in making it possible to reach the wage earners with the message of unionism.

The union movement has been greatly helped, moreover, by the fact that, throughout all classes of society, the last century and a half has been a period of criticism and dissent, that during this time conscious revolt against established manners, philosophies, and beliefs has been almost a social custom. Unionism, being a challenge to the existing control of industry, naturally prospers when dissent in general flourishes and when the habit of frowning upon change is less pronounced than usual. Of special significance in paving the way for unionism has been the widespread democratic movement in politics. It has helped the labor movement because it has demanded in the field of government essentially the same thing that unionism has demanded in industry — control of the government by the governed. When men are taught that they should have a voice in making the laws of the land, and especially when they are given the vote and urged to use it, they find difficulty in understanding why they should not participate in making the rules of the shop or of the industry. And trade unions have profited also because, during the last century, social reform has become the religion of many men — it has attracted much of the idealism and devotion which, in other ages, would have sought expression in the church. This has given unions scores of leaders whose zeal and self-sacrifice can be matched only by the missionaries of the church.

Although the manual laborer is far better provided for today

The ability of unions to exist depends upon the relative strength of the employers and the workers. In many industries where the workers have the least chance of becoming employers, unionism is extremely weak simply because the employers have been strong enough to keep it out or to destroy it. The steel industry is an example.

than at any time in history, his hold on what he has is often precarious.   Contrast his situation with that of the villein on the medieval manor.   The villein had a wretchedly small income, but he had a job which would be his for life.   And although subject to the vicissitudes of weather and war, his share in the product of his land and labor was fixed by custom.   He had no reason to hope for or to fear changes in it.   The modern wage earner lives in an industrial order in which wages and conditions of employment are determined by bargaining power.   He deals with powerful and aggressive enterprises which search diligently for ways of cutting expenses.   Consequently the modern worker stands in constant peril of having his pay lowered or his working day lengthened.   Any foreman who takes a dislike to him can deprive him of his job; in many industries there are several slack seasons each year when a large part of the force is laid off; every few years there are periods of general business depression which throw hundreds of thousands out of work; and finally, the management is ever striving, by devising jigs, fixtures, and automatic machines, to replace skilled artisans with women, children, or semi-skilled specialists.   Against the constant possibility that his wages will be lowered, his working day lengthened, or his job taken away from him, the wage earner seeks protection.   Many a man who is too bound by inertia to make much effort to *improve* his condition, will fight vigorously *to keep what he already possesses*.   Unionism is to be interpreted in part as an effort of workers to introduce greater security into an economic order which makes their hold on everything they have peculiarly precarious.

In this connection it is significant that labor organizations first became numerous in the United States when customary standards of wages, hours, and speed of work were imperiled by cheap transportation.   This occurred in the main during the second and third decades of the last century.   As a result of the steamboat and the turnpike, there grew up a class of wholesalers whom we know as merchant capitalists.   They had their goods made by contractors in small shops — for, outside of the textile industry, there were then almost no factories in this country.   Usually the merchant capitalist furnished the raw materials.   In order to get his goods made at rock bottom prices, he played different contractors against each other.   Since competition among the contractors was almost purely on the basis of price, they strove strenuously to reduce costs by cutting wages, lengthening the working day, increasing the speed of work, and subdividing operations so as to replace skilled craftsmen with women, children, unskilled and semi-skilled men. In an attempt to protect themselves against these changes, the skilled workers established unions and, by 1834, labor organizations were to be found in nearly every industry of importance.

Trade unionism has undoubtedly been encouraged by the selling and advertising activity of modern business. It may seem strange that business men, who do not desire industrial unrest, should spend millions upon millions each year in creating it. Nevertheless, the salesman and the advertising man are probably more formidable fomenters of discontent than the walking delegate. Business houses constantly seek to extend their sales, and to do this they must make people desire things which they do not possess — in other words, render them dissatisfied with their lot, get them to aspire to a more expensive standard of living. The result is to make the worker dissatisfied with his wages. His standard of living, influenced by salesmen, advertising experts, and emulative consumption — which in turn is skillfully stimulated by business enterprises — rises more rapidly than his earnings. Feeling keenly the need for greater income, what is more natural than for him to regard his wages as unfairly low? As long as business enterprises spend vast sums on carefully planned efforts to make people discontented, they must not be surprised when their employees organize for the purpose of obtaining more pay.

III. TRADE UNION STRUCTURE

In order to illustrate the structure of trade unionism in the United States, let us assume that you are a machinist living in Chicago and a member of the local branch of the International Association of Machinists. The local union has its own constitution and by-laws, officers, and funds. It is affiliated with the International Association of Machinists, called " international " because it has local branches in Canada as well as in the United States. Part of the monthly dues paid by the members of the Chicago local go into the treasury of the international, and the local is subject to the constitution and by-laws of the international. The Chicago machinists' local is also a member of the Chicago Federation of Labor and of the Illinois Federation of Labor. The former is a federation of local unions, representing many different crafts and industries, within the city of Chicago, and the latter of local unions within the state of Illinois. Each state has a federation of unions similar to the Illinois Federation of Labor, and about 600 cities have federations similar to the Chicago Federation of Labor.

In 1929 there were 146 national and international unions in the United States. One hundred and six of these, comprising about 81 per cent of the members, were affiliated with the American Federation of Labor.[5] The International Association of Machinists is one of these affiliated unions. The Federation is the labor organization about which the public hears most, but it does not possess much power. For example, contrary to popular belief, it has no authority to order strikes among the members of the affiliated national or international unions. It is simply a loose federation of autonomous unions — the mouthpiece but not the governing body of the labor movement. The state and municipal federations are also members of the American Federation of Labor, but the voting is so arranged that control is possessed by the nationals and internationals.[6] Within the Federation there have been formed several departments of unions which have more or less common interests. The building trades' unions, for example, have formed the Building Trades' Department; those in the railroad industry the Railway Employees' Department; and the metal working crafts, the Metal Trades' Department. A union may be affiliated with several departments. The International Association of Machinists, for example, is affiliated with both the Metal Trades' and the Railway Employees' Departments.

In the American labor movement, the principal economic powers and functions are concentrated in the hands of the national or international unions and their locals. As a rule, it is these

---

[5] U. S. Bureau of Labor Statistics, " Handbook of American Trade-Unions," 1929 edition, *Bulletin No. 506*, p. 3.

[6] Local unions are not admitted to the American Federation of Labor unless there is no national union for them to join or unless the national which they would naturally join is not itself affiliated.

organizations which conduct negotiations with employers, which declare and call off strikes, which control finances, and which administer the death and sick benefits provided by many unions. In early days, when national unions were weak and when in many trades there were no nationals, the local unions leaned rather heavily for support upon the city federations, and these organizations were correspondingly important. At present, the city and state federations and the American Federation of Labor itself are primarily political and publicity agencies. They distribute publicity material; they afford the unions of the city, state, or nation an opportunity to record their stand on public questions; and their officials are active in working for and against legislation before city councils, state legislatures, or Congress. The work of the industrial federations — the Railroad Employees', Building Trades', and Metal Trades' Departments of the American Federation of Labor — lies more largely in the field of economic action. The federations in the building and railroad industries are important agencies for joint bargaining with employers and, to a less extent, this is true of the Metal Trades' Department. Much has been done by the industrial federations to bring about simultaneous expiration of the agreements which the affiliated unions negotiate with employers. This means that, if several trades strike over the terms of the new agreement, the strikes will come at the same time. In this there are two advantages from the standpoint of the unions: the employers' plants are more completely tied up, and men who are not striking lose less employment because the plants are not closed by strikes so frequently.

A much mooted question among trade unionists is whether organization should proceed along craft or industrial lines. Should all workers in the automobile industry, for example, regardless of whether they are machinists, molders, painters, electricians, or upholsterers, belong to one industrial union, the workers in the agricultural implement industry to another, and so on; or should all machinists, regardless of the industry in which they work, belong to a craft organization of machinists, all molders to a union of molders, all carpenters to a union of carpenters? The skilled trades usually prefer the craft form of organization, because it permits each trade to pursue its interests unhampered by the weaker, unskilled men; the workers in the less skilled occupations, on the other hand, usually desire the industrial form of organization because it gives them the help of the skilled crafts in the industry. The most radical unionists, who look forward to a social revolution, oppose craft unionism on the ground that it fosters narrow craft consciousness instead of class consciousness and focuses the attention of the workers upon the welfare and prosperity of their particular craft rather than of labor as a whole.[7]

Trade union structure is a product of industrial technique and naturally varies and develops with differences and changes in technique. Craft unions can exist only where there are more or less sharply defined occupational lines. They have their basis in the fact that the members of a trade are more concerned with each other's wages and working conditions than with those of other crafts. Molders in the stove industry, for example, are more interested in the wages of molders in the machine tool industry than in the wages of stove mounters or of metal polishers in the stove industry. If they strike, they need to have the

---

[7] When we study the actual state of trade union organization, we find that pure craft or pure industrial unions are somewhat rare. Instead of only these two basic types, we find many variations of them. Besides pure craft unions, embracing workers from one craft only, there are *compound craft* unions admitting men from two or more closely related trades, and *craft and specialist* unions which include both members of a skilled craft and the semi-skilled specialists who do not know the entire trade but who do know a branch of it. The bricklayers and masons' union and the plumbers and steamfitters' union are examples of compound craft unions. The machinists', the sheet metal workers', and the carpenters' unions, in addition to all-around mechanics, also admit specialists. There are also several variations of the industrial union. The *departmental industrial* union confines its membership to one industry but, instead of embracing all occupations in it, includes only those in one department or branch — examples are the bookbinders' and the photo-engravers' unions. The *quasi-industrial* union limits itself to one industry and embraces all employees in it with the exception of a few auxiliary workers engaged in plant repair and maintenance, such as janitors, window washers, plumbers, electricians, carpenters. Of this class are the boot and shoe workers', the street railway employees', and the textile workers' unions. Finally, there is the *compound industrial* union which includes all workers in several industries — the soft drink and cereal workers' union, which has jurisdiction over the flour, soft drink, and yeast industries, is of this type.

In many cases, actual practice does not square with rules of admission. Some craft and specialist unions, for example, are composed in the main of skilled tradesmen and make little effort to organize the semi-skilled specialists. Such is true of the machinists' union. Many quasi-industrial unions, although nominally admitting almost every one in the industry, confine their membership largely to the skilled. This is true of the iron and steel workers' and some of the textile workers' unions.

molders in other industries refrain from acting as strike breakers. Molders in other industries have an interest in helping the stove molders because, if stove foundries pay more for molders, other foundries in some degree feel the necessity of doing likewise.

Many industrial unions are not essentially different from craft unions. They are industrial simply because the craft happens to be found in one industry only and because the craft happens to be predominant in that industry and is strong enough to compel all employees in the industry to belong to one union. Although *nominally* industrial organizations, they may be devoted primarily to advancing the interests of the dominating craft. The miners' union is an example. Although *nominally* an industrial union, it has, until very recently, been practically a craft union.[8]

An industrial union is likely to be less cohesive than a craft union because it contains a diversity of occupational groups. Sometimes friction between occupational groups causes an industrial union to split into a number of craft unions. This happened to the International Typographical Union in the nineties. Originally it embraced compositors, pressmen, electrotypers and stereotypers, and bookbinders — practically all of the workers in the printing industry. But the other groups felt that the union was being run too largely by and for the compositors. Consequently, they broke away and formed unions of their own. The International Typographical Union today is a craft union composed almost exclusively of compositors.

But although industrial unions may possess less solidarity than craft unions, they may be the only kind of organization which can effectively tie up a plant and win strikes. This is especially true when minute subdivision of labor and the development of automatic machinery replace the craftsmen with semi-skilled specialists. These specialists *might* form unions along departmental lines — for example, in the clothing industry the pressers might organize one union, the operators, who perform the sewing operations, another, the cutters another. But because it is relatively easy for employers to replace specialists in case of a strike,

[8] Changes in the methods of coal mining are reducing the relative numbers of skilled miners. But when the union was formed, the skilled miners made up the bulk of the workers in the industry and the union was essentially a craft union confined to one industry simply because coal miners are found only in coal mining.

it is advantageous for these workers to organize in larger groups in order to be able to tie up the plants more effectively.

The tendency to form industrial unions appears even where technical changes have not destroyed crafts but where a single craft has difficulty in winning strikes. Suppose that the truck drivers of a plant strike but that the machine operators remain at work. Rather than settle the strike promptly by granting the men's demands in whole or in part, the employer can possibly afford to pay high wages to a few non-union drivers until his men are willing to come back at their old wages. But if all of his men, including both machine operators and truck drivers, quit, it may not pay the employer to spend the amount necessary to replace his force. It may be cheaper for him to compromise. Consequently, whenever an occupational group finds that it has great difficulty in winning strikes, it acts as does the individual worker who finds his bargaining power insufficient to gain him good terms — it joins with other groups to form a bargaining group of greater size and power. In other words, it takes a step in the direction of industrial unionism. In 1875, a strike of boilers and puddlers in the Pittsburgh iron industry failed because the heaters and rollers were kept at work with muck iron made by non-unionists elsewhere. As a result, this group of highly skilled workers was convinced that an industrial union was necessary to enable them to tie up the iron mills effectively, and an amalgamation of the three national unions of iron and steel workers into a quasi-industrial union occurred in 1876. For years, the lasters were the aristocrats among the boot and shoe workers, because machinery had reduced the skill needed by the other workers in the industry. As long as the lasters were strong enough to win strikes, they maintained their own independent unions. About 1890, however, the invention of new lasting machinery weakened the bargaining power of the lasters and in 1895 they joined with the other boot and shoe workers to form a quasi-industrial boot and shoe workers' union.

IV. THE GOVERNMENT OF TRADE UNIONS

The early national unions possessed little authority over the locals and many local unions would still be glad to be free from control by the national officials. But, reluctant as many locals have been to give up their freedom, most unions have found it desirable to concentrate the union's funds in the national treasury and to impose upon the national organization the responsibility for financing strikes. Centralization of finances is advantageous because a strike, like a fire, may come at any time. It may come before a local has accumulated more than a small defense fund, it may last so long that it exhausts even a large fund, and then, before another has been accumulated, a second strike may occur. It is not surprising, therefore, that many unions have placed the financing of strikes largely in the hands of their national organizations. This has usually involved stipulating minimum dues which the locals shall collect — the sum usually being larger than previously collected by many locals — and the diversion of a larger part of local receipts into the national treasury.

Some organizations, however, have gone much farther than others in centralizing finances. A few have done next to nothing. Whether or not unions have proceeded far in centralizing finances appears to be determined by whether or not their members produce for local or for national or sectional markets. It is easy to see why this should be so. Suppose that the barbers in a given city seek a wage increase which would raise their compensation distinctly above that of barbers in neighboring towns. If the union embraced substantially all the barbers in the town, the employers would not find it profitable to spend much money resisting the wage increase. As the barber shops in one city do not compete with those in others, the owners could pass on all or most of the increase to the public in the form of higher prices for shaves and hair cuts. Assume, however, that the workers in the men's clothing industry in a certain city sought a wage advance. Even if the rates asked were lower than those paid by competitors in other cities, it might pay the manufacturers to make a long and costly fight against raising them. Since the price of the finished product is determined by what competitors in other markets charge, the entire cost of a wage increase must fall upon the employers. They could not pass it on in the form of higher prices. If the union demanded higher wages than were paid elsewhere, the resistance of the manufacturers would be more stubborn than ever because the increase would put them at a serious competitive disadvantage.

These two imaginary cases help us to understand why some unions have centralized finances and others have not. Because the master barbers can easily pass higher operating costs on to the public, the local barbers' unions do not meet such determined resistance to their demands and, consequently, do not need the help of a strong national to win strikes. For the same reason, there has been little centralization of power among unions in the construction industry. Because buildings are not made in one place and shipped to others, the contractors in Cleveland are not prevented from passing on a wage increase to the public by the fact that wages may be lower in Pittsburgh or Toledo. But in the clothing or coal industries, where the employers in one place compete with those in others, any local which seeks better conditions is likely to be faced by a longer fight than its treasury can finance. Help from the rest of the organization is needed. Consequently the unions in these and similar industries have more and more concentrated finances in the hands of the national.[9]

With the financing of strikes in their hands, the national officials naturally gain considerable control over negotiations

[9] Some unions which deal with employers among whom there is no inter-city competition have centralized authority simply because they deal with exceptionally large and powerful enterprises against whom it is difficult to win strikes. The street and electric railway employees are an example. Were the barbers and the building trades not favored by peculiarly advantageous bargaining conditions, it is possible that they also might concentrate great authority in their national officials. The barbers deal with employers who are scarcely more than workmen themselves, who possess little capital and cannot easily bear the losses which a strike inflicts. No large investment is required to start a barber shop and the master barbers cannot ignore the possibility that some of their employees might seize the opportunity afforded by a strike to set up shops of their own.

The bargaining advantages of the building trades are numerous. Many of the crafts are highly skilled and, even if unorganized, would be well paid. Thus they are easily able to stand the loss of work which strikes impose. Small repair jobs assist the men in some crafts — such as painting or carpentry — to support themselves during strikes. Work in the building trades is so intermittent and the men are so used to being out of a job that a strike does not worry them nor reduce their morale as it does in the case of men accustomed to more steady employment. If the employees of a manufacturer strike, he can often have his orders filled elsewhere or hire guards, barricade his factory, and operate with strike breakers who eat and sleep in the plant. The contractor cannot have his contracts filled elsewhere. His jobs are scattered, and this, combined with the fact that the work is usually exposed, renders it difficult to carry on operations with strike breakers and guards. A delay in the completion of a building is likely to be costly to the contractor, for the building season is short and construction during the winter is usually somewhat more expensive. It is even more serious, however, to the owner who loses rent for every month that completion is delayed. It often pays the owner to make almost any concession to the men in order to have the building done at a certain time.

with employers and acquire authority to decide what strikes shall occur and what shall not. To prevent the dissipation of the national funds on unwise and hopeless strikes, it is usual for the union laws to provide that national support shall be given only in cases approved by the national officers. This means that before ordering a strike the local officials refer the dispute to the national officers. If they decide to support the local, the strike will probably occur. Most locals, however, need national financial help so badly that denial of it means practically denial of their right to strike.[10]

Concentration of power in the hands of national officers undoubtedly tends to reduce the number of strikes. A local union which becomes involved in a controversy with an employer is likely to have difficulty in deciding wisely upon the advisability of a strike. Smarting under real or fancied wrongs, incited by well meaning but visionary and emotional radicals or possibly by agents of the employer who seek to provoke an inopportune strike in order to destroy the union, the members are likely to be guided too much by the desire to punish the employer and to vindicate their rights and too little by considerations of expediency. But the national funds are rarely adequate to support all the strikes which locals would like to call. Consequently before granting financial aid to a local, it is usual for the national office to send out a representative to interview the employer and to see if a compromise is not possible. This officer is likely to be far more successful than local leaders in settling the trouble. In the process of local negotiations, personal feeling may have developed between the employer and the local officials. Consequently each side may lack the spirit of compromise, the willingness to study how conflicting demands can be adjusted without sacrifice of vital interests. The national representative, coming in calm and collected, without animosity toward the employer, is obviously better able than the local officers to continue the negotiations. Most important of all, he has the will to agree. He is sent out to prevent a strike and, unless he does so, he fails in his mission. If there is a way to avoid trouble, he wishes to find it. And he is not afraid to be moderate. Local leaders often fear

---

[10] About thirty unions go a step farther and forbid their locals to strike before obtaining the consent of the national officers.

to compromise on certain points about which their constituents feel strongly. The national representative, being largely independent of the votes of the local, is more likely to meet the employer half way when points of vital importance to the union are not involved. And he is likely to be more resourceful and ingenious than local leaders in seeking a basis for compromise. But although concentration of authority in the hands of national officials tends to reduce the number of strikes, those which occur are likely to be serious, involving important issues, participated in by many men, hard fought, and often of long duration.

The success of unions, like that of corporations, depends upon the possibility of obtaining officers who are willing to subordinate their own pecuniary interests to the interests of the members. Indeed, if every man pursued the dollar with such singleness of purpose as some statements of the theory of free enterprise assume, unions could scarcely endure. It is probable that the centralization of power assists labor organizations in obtaining more loyal and honest leadership. For example, it discourages employers from attempting to disrupt unions by the use of stool pigeons. When locals can call strikes, an agent of the employer, who has acquired influence in the local, may destroy it by stampeding it into striking at an inopportune time. But this is more difficult when strikes must be authorized by the national officers. Of course, agents of employers do at times become national officers of unions, but such places are less easily won than local offices, and, furthermore, it is difficult to persuade the national executive board, which usually passes on strikes, to approve an obviously unwise strike.

V. Trade Union Policies

Possibly the most conspicuous characteristic of union policies is their dissimilarity. For example, some unions insist that foremen be members; others prohibit them from holding membership. Some unions go to great trouble and expense to get the closed shop; others, such as the railroad brotherhoods, are not interested in it and make no effort to obtain it. Some organizations, the United Garment Workers or the International Boot and Shoe Workers' Union, for example, attach great importance

to the union label; others, such as the Amalgamated Clothing
Workers, believe that the label has pernicious effects. Some
unions strenuously oppose piecework, others prefer it and even
strike to obtain it or to keep it; some have strict apprenticeship
rules, others oppose such requirements. Sometimes the same
union will pursue diametrically opposite policies. The molders'
union, which has fought many a strike to drive piecework out
of the jobbing and machinery foundries, has threatened to strike
in order to obtain piecework in the furnace foundries. The
electrical workers and sheet metal workers, which insist upon
the closed shop in building construction, do not advocate it in the
railroad shops. Because trade union policies are so numerous and
so divergent, we shall confine ourselves to a general survey and an
explanation of several of the most important ones — the policies
relating to (1) the admission of members; (2) the closed shop;
(3) standard rates and conditions; (4) output and costs; and
(5) strikes.

Union admission requirements are criticized because they are
too liberal and because they are too strict. Those who make the
first objection assert that labor organizations should make membership a certificate of competency and should admit no one
who has not passed an examination testing his trade skill. Union
members would then have no difficulty, it is said, in obtaining
steadier work and higher wages than other workmen, and strikes
would be unnecessary. Those who believe that union admission
requirements are too strict point to the high admission fees or
to the excessively long apprenticeships required by some organizations, and to the restrictions upon the number of apprentices.

Doubtless a union which admitted only superior workers
could, without resort to strikes, secure better wages and conditions than those received by the average worker. But such
organizations, however useful, would differ materially from
the present unions. Their purpose would be to improve the wages
and conditions of the *best* workers in each occupation. The existing organizations, however, aim to improve the wages and
conditions of *all* members of a calling. In order to compel employers to pay certain rates, unions must prevent them from getting their work done on less favorable terms. To accomplish
this they must admit every one whom employers might hire to

avoid conceding the organization's terms. Instead of imposing their standards of competency, *most unions allow each employer to establish his own tests of fitness and trade skill.* The carpenters' union, for example, simply says to employers, " If a man is a carpenter to you, he is a carpenter to us. If you are willing to employ him as a carpenter, we are willing to admit him to our organization. Our concern simply is that every man whom you hire as a carpenter shall receive a carpenter's wages."

Even if unions were to admit only the superior workers, they would probably not long adhere to this policy. After the better men had obtained a certain differential over the wages of the less efficient, they would find their ability to get more limited by the competition of the less skilled. Only as the wages of the less competent went up, could the superior workmen obtain more. But they would scarcely be willing to wait passively for the wages of the ordinary laborers to rise. They would wish to make them go up. To do this they would probably organize the less competent — in other words, abandon the practice of admitting only the best workmen.

Undoubtedly each union, if it could, would substantially restrict the number of workers entering its trade, just as American manufacturers seek to exclude foreign competitors from the American market by a high tariff wall and as the merchants of many towns keep out transient dealers, peddlers, and traveling representatives of out-of-town firms by persuading the city council to impose a license tax. But the cases where unions have actually succeeded in restricting the entrance into a trade are rare. Many organizations limit the number of apprentices which employers may hire, but employers rarely hire even as many as the union rules permit. And few unions have been able to insist that no man shall work as a journeyman unless he has served an apprenticeship. Many thousands of journeymen have almost literally " picked up " their trade by working at it in different shops. But a labor organization, as has been explained, can compel employers to meet its terms only when it can prevent them from getting their work done for less. Hence it must admit to membership the men who otherwise would underbid its members. Special circumstances may enable a union temporarily to pursue an exclusive policy, but such a policy sooner or later creates the cause for its own abandonment. It brings into existence a body of non-union workmen whose competition prevents the organization from getting better conditions and even threatens its existence. The union has no alternative except to let down the bars and to take in the unorganized.

But although most unions find themselves compelled to admit any workmen to whom employers are willing to pay the union scale, it is an advantage to the union to have every member thoroughly competent and able to command high wages. Consequently many unions, such as the electrical workers', the sheet metal workers', the bricklayers', the pressmen's, the photoengravers', the typographical union, and others, are greatly interested in improving the training received by apprentices. In many cities, these unions have succeeded in bringing about the establishment of apprenticeship classes which all apprentices are required to attend. The electricians and the pressmen have also established classes for journeymen.

Few union policies have been more criticized and less understood than the demand for the closed shop. If a man can obtain the same wages and working hours as union members without joining the organization, naturally he has no strong inducement to join. And naturally too the members feel that no worker should enjoy the wages and conditions which the union achieves unless he is willing to share in the cost of obtaining them. But strong as is the feeling against the " dues dodger," it is not the principal reason why unions demand the closed shop. Some organizations, we have seen, manifest little interest in the closed shop, and the conditions which accompany their indifference indicate that the chief reason behind the demand for the closed shop is the fear that employers will destroy the union. From the very outset, unions have been compelled to fight in order to exist. Employers have refused to accept them as legitimate economic institutions made necessary and desirable by the industrial life of the time. Business men have refused, except where compelled, to meet union representatives and, whenever possible, have destroyed the organization. They have fought not merely the demands of unionism but unionism itself.

Most national unions have reached the stage where they no

longer fear complete destruction, but the fight for the right to organize goes on. The extension of unionism is accomplished only by struggle, and during every period of depression, employers drive unionism from many shops where, in prosperous times, it was tolerated. Unions still enjoy security only to the extent that they are strong enough to repel attack.

As long as this conflict over the right to organize goes on, compelling unions to be militant organizations, with a militant psychology, a militant point of view, and a militant tradition, labor organizations are bound to attach great importance to such defensive devices as the closed shop. Unionists are certain that if non-members were permitted to work in the shop, the employer would hire them in preference to union members and that furthermore, by favored treatment, he would induce some employees to drop out of the organization. In this way he would gradually build up a skeleton force of non-unionists and then, at the first slump in business, he would sever relations with the union. Against such tactics, labor organizations seek to guard by insisting that only their members shall be employed.[11]

Some unions, we said, are indifferent toward the closed shop. But wherever this is so, there is some reason why the union need not fear attacks upon its existence or why it is able to repel such attacks with unusual effectiveness. Why, for example, is the molders' union, which in many instances has fought stubbornly for the closed shop, indifferent to it in the stove industry? For one thing, the union and the Stove Founders' National Defense Association have dealt together without a break in their relations for nearly forty years and neither desires to end this arrangement. In this industry, therefore, the union regards collective bargaining as institutionalized. The agreement is between the union and a national association of employers, rather than between the union and individual employers. As no member of the association wishes his competitors to gain an advantage by driving out the organization, the union knows that it would have

---

[11] As a matter of fact, there is considerable variation in the terms of trade agreements which establish closed shops. Some require that only union members be hired, others permit the employer to engage any worker who is a member or who is willing to join. A very large proportion — possibly a majority — permit the employer to hire non-members if, after a stipulated period, — usually about forty-eight hours — the union has failed to supply sufficient union members.

the support of the association in dealing with any employer who attempted to destroy the local in his plant. Finally, stove molding is paid by the piece. Spoiled castings are paid for if the employer is at fault but not if the worker is responsible. Naturally disputes over who is to blame are frequent. The men join the union in order to gain the aid of its grievance committee in these controversies. Hence the closed shop is not needed in order to get men into the organization.

A somewhat different set of circumstances explains the attitude of the railroad brotherhoods. Because their work requires ability to read orders written in English, the closed shop is unnecessary to protect these workers against the competition of immigrants who often are not interested in joining a union because the wages here seem high to them. Promotion is by seniority, which means that there is no floating supply of railroad workers, many of them non-union, who could be employed by the companies in an effort to drive out the organizations. The hazardous nature of the employment makes insurance important to the men but it also makes commercial insurance expensive. The brotherhoods attract members by furnishing cheap insurance. Of special importance is the fact that promotion by seniority makes discharge a peculiarly severe form of discipline. A discharged engineer must begin again as a fireman and a discharged conductor as a trainman. Safety, however, requires that discipline be strictly maintained. Consequently, the men join in order to get the benefit of the union grievance committee. And those who do not join are likely to find their breaches of discipline carefully reported to the management.

Workmen compete for jobs by accepting lower wages, working longer hours, putting up with dangerous or unsanitary shop conditions, turning out more work. This competition, if unrestricted, is likely to result in low wages, a killing speed of work, an excessively long working day, and hazardous and unhealthy shop conditions. Unions seek to check these tendencies by agreeing with employers upon the least favorable terms at which any worker may be employed in the shop — the minimum rates of pay, the maximum number of hours, the least favorable shop conditions and sometimes the maximum speed of work. This policy is known as the policy of standard rates and conditions. It is important to notice that it establishes only conditions of *minimum* favorableness to the employees. It does not preclude employers from offering better wages or working conditions. Unions usually insist that the standards also apply to non-unionists. Were an employer permitted to hire non-unionists on any terms, he would strive strenuously to replace the union men with non-members and the organization would soon be driven from the shop.

The policy of the standard rate of pay is frequently criticized on the ground that, in the words of the late President Eliot, it deprives the members of the union " of all motive for improvement " and " represses ambition for excellence." [12] This criticism is based upon the mistaken assumption that the standard wage is a maximum as well as a minimum wage. It is true that many employers pay no more than the standard wage — just as many employers operating non-union plants pay a standard rate to all workers in a given occupation — but there is nothing in the standard rate itself to prevent the reward of efficiency. As a matter of fact, there are several ways in which the standard rate promotes industrial efficiency. For one thing, by preventing employers from increasing profits by decreasing wages, the standard rate encourages them to increase the efficiency of their plants. In other words, by eliminating hard bargaining as a source of gain, it compels employers to rely upon better management. Most unions undertake to apply more or less the same standard rate in all plants. But if several competing plants must pay the same wages, it is evident that that concern will have the lowest costs which is best managed, equipped, and situated. The result is that the standard rate aids the concentration of business into the plants which can produce most advantageously.[13]

No criticism of unionism makes a deeper impression on the public than the one that unions are indifferent or hostile to pro-

---

[12] Eliot, C. W., *The Future of Trades-Unionism and Capitalism*, pp. 25 and 27.

[13] It is often asked why unions do not classify their members according to skill and provide for the recognition of merit by establishing several rates, one for first class men, one for average men, and another for sub-average men. There are several reasons. If employers desire to establish graduated wage scales of their own, there is nothing to prevent them, for it is nearly always permissible to pay more than the

duction. That men should organize to increase their wages or to lessen their hours, the public can readily understand, and with such aims it is inclined to sympathize. But that the very organizations which seek higher wages and fewer hours at the consumer's expense should disclaim all responsibility for production and sometimes even impose positive impediments upon it, seems to the public the height of unfairness.

Trade union policies are difficult for most of us to understand because we are accustomed to thinking of industrial efficiency in terms of money cost. That method of production is most efficient which yields a given product with the least expenditure of dollars, that enterprise is most efficient which has the lowest money costs. This way of looking at things is a result of the fact that industrial enterprises are usually initiated and controlled by property-owners or their representatives. This means that methods and policies are determined primarily by price considerations. Managements are constantly endeavoring to lower the cost of production. But the costs which they are striving to reduce are money, not human, costs. Business executives are not studying how to alter industrial processes in order that jobs may be made more pleasant; they are simply hunting for ways to save money, regardless of how the men in the industry are affected. If expenses can be reduced by methods which increase human costs — such as speeding up, longer hours, night work, failure to guard machinery properly or to protect workmen against heat, dust, or industrial poisons — the money-saving method is usually adopted. Even such important life-saving devices as air brakes and automatic couplers were brought into general use only by penal statute twenty years after their value had been demonstrated.[14]

Trade unions are just as much interested in decreasing costs

union scale. But if workmen are to be classified and paid on the basis of skill, unions prefer the classification to be made by the employer. For the union to attempt it, would create internal dissensions and weaken the organization. The experience of unions in this country with classified wage scales has not been favorable. In times of prosperity, the demand for men is so great that all workers get the highest rates; in times of depression, even the best workers have been compelled to accept the wages of the lowest class. Instead of a variation in wages as between the superior and inferior workmen, classified scales have produced fluctuations in the wages of all workmen in point of time.

[14] Downey, E. H., *Workmen's Compensation*, p. 131.

and in raising industrial efficiency as are the employers, but the costs in which unions are primarily interested are human costs instead of money costs, and the efficiency which they strive to promote is efficiency which is measured in terms of human costs. Naturally they challenge the efforts of managers to reduce the money costs at the expense of human costs. For example, if employers are left free to hire whom they please, they will take the men who appear to be most efficient. This means that the burden of unemployment is concentrated upon the older and the less competent men. The workers believe that the burden is not so onerous when it is more or less equally divided. Consequently, when they are able, they insist that the employer engage his help through the union and that the man longest out of work be hired first. In reducing the staff, the employer, if given a free hand, would dismiss the least efficient workers. Again we find the unions objecting to imposing the burden of unemployment upon a small class. They usually demand either equal division of work or lay-off in accordance with seniority. Employers could undoubtedly turn out more and better goods if they were free to discharge workers for minor faults or even for suspected faults. Unions seek to introduce the principle that no workman shall be deprived of his job except by due process of law. In practice this means the abolition of discharge as a penalty for minor offenses and as a device for putting fear of the boss into the minds of workmen. Possibly the result is a lower quantity and quality of product but a security is introduced into the jobs which workmen find attractive.

But besides more or less indirectly interfering with production in order to reduce human costs, unions, under some circumstances, directly and deliberately endeavor to restrict output. For this there appear to be two principal reasons — the fear of unemployment and the fear of being speeded up.

Insecurity of job tenure is part of the price which the laborer pays for industrial freedom. When serfdom was abolished, he won relief from the *duty* to work. But although millions of persons depend for their living solely upon the sale of their labor, we do not yet recognize the *right* to work. Neither the need of workless men for jobs nor the need of an insufficiently provided public for goods imposes on industry an obligation to employ all the available labor, no matter how willing or how competent it may be.

Not only are wage earners dependent for work upon the willingness of industry to offer it, but industry, even in periods of prosperity, does not customarily provide as many jobs as there are men to fill them. Just how much the number of wage earners usually exceeds the number of positions is more or less conjectural, but it is estimated that in no year during the period 1920 to 1927 was the average number of non-agricultural wage earners out of work in this country less than a million and that in three out of the eight years it was well over two millions.[15]

If we bear in mind the limited number of jobs and the temporary character of many of them, it is apparent that one of the principal problems of the wage earner is how to make the limited amount of work yield the largest possible volume of employment. This he attempts to do by going slowly. By working rapidly, he simply brings closer the time when he no longer will be needed, but if he works slowly enough, he may not lose his place at all, for new orders may come in which will prolong his employment. Restriction of output, then, is one way by which workmen, both organized and unorganized, seek to introduce security into an industrial order which does not provide as may jobs as there are workers and which throws large numbers out of employment every day because it has nothing for them to do.[16]

Unions naturally reflect the universal desire of wage earners to economize the supply of work, and many of their rules which seem inexcusably burdensome have this for their primary purpose. One reason why restrictive practices are especially rife in the building trades is because unemployment in these trades is exceptionally severe. The irritating jurisdictional rules and the wasteful disputes which these rules engender represent the competition between the various crafts for a larger share in the limited volume of work. Could steady employment be assured to all proficient men, this competition would cease and the rules

[15] *Recent Economic Changes*, v. II, p. 478.

[16] It is possible to show — as will be done in a subsequent chapter — that the restriction of output does not increase the total amount of employment in the community, but it often does prolong the employment of the workers who practice restriction This, of course, is what they are interested in.

and disputes which arise from it would become less numerous and burdensome.

The fear of being overspeeded is a product of the peculiar nature of the employment contract. The methods of buying and selling labor are different from the methods of buying and selling anything else. No one would think of purchasing coal or sugar or what-not with the price to be paid specified but not the quantity to be delivered. Nevertheless this is the way in which labor is customarily bought and sold. The employer agrees to pay a given price for an hour's or a day's labor but nowhere is it stated what an hour's or a day's labor is. This means that it is settled by a struggle. As soon as the wage earner begins work, a contest sets in over the rate of output — a contest which continues as long as his employment, the man ever ingeniously concealing his productive capacity, the management constantly alert to discover evidence of restriction.

Nor is the situation essentially different if payment is by the piece instead of by the hour or day. When a pieceworker earns an unusually large day's wage, it is often difficult to determine whether he did so because he worked exceptionally fast or because the price per piece was set too high. Employers have been accustomed to assume the rate to be too high. High earnings, therefore, have caused the rate on the operation to be cut. Realizing this, the workers consciously restrict output; employers, aware that the men are holding back, endeavor to speed them up. So again the rate of work becomes the subject of a struggle; and all because no agreement exists concerning what should be regarded as a fair day's output.

There is a widespread impression that trade unions are really functioning only when they are striking, that this is the essential reason for their existence, and that their officials, in order to hold their jobs, must stir up trouble between the members and their employers. It is true that, although unionists comprise less than one-fourth of the wage earners engaged in transportation, mining, and manufacturing, 78 per cent of all strikes during the period 1916–1921 were ordered by trade unions. It is also true that the strike is the principal weapon of labor and that, in order to drive good bargains *without actual resort to it,* labor organizations must not be too reluctant to use it.

But it is not true, as a general rule, that unions are eager to strike. Not only is the strike an enormously expensive weapon and one which imposes severe hardships upon the strikers and their families, but it is a dangerous instrument for, in case of defeat, many of the strikers are likely to lose their jobs and the organization in the plants involved is likely to be destroyed. Hence, unions usually prefer a reasonably liberal compromise to a strike. We have already noted that many unions have guarded against hasty and ill-advised strikes by transferring the control of finances from the locals to the national organization, and, in many instances, forbidding locals to strike without the consent of the national officers; and we have seen that the national officials, far from spending their time stirring up trouble, are constantly engaged in adjusting disputes. During 1919, a year of numerous strikes, the local unions directly affiliated with the American Federation of Labor and seventy-seven of the nationals spent $3,347,143.31 on strikes and $4,247,725.71 on death, sick, unemployment, and traveling benefits and tool insurance — in other words, nearly a million less for strikes than for various beneficiary features. The strike record of individual unions for 1919 further reflects the desire of most organizations for peace:

The bookbinders' union reached 87 agreements with employers by negotiation or arbitration and 17 by strike.

The boot and shoe workers' union, with 46,700 members, had 3 strikes involving a total of 300 men.

The cigar makers had 63 strikes but obtained 164 increases in wages without striking.

The leather workers had 2,017 of their 11,700 members engaged in 14 strikes, and negotiated 25 agreements peaceably.

The meat cutters and butcher workmen had 23,000 members out of a total of 65,300 involved in strikes. They made 175 agreements and had 17 strikes.

The painters had 143 strikes involving 24,000 out of 103,000 members. The union secured about 600 agreements with employers.

The potters had one strike in which 48 of their 8,000 members took part.

The printers and color mixers in the wall paper industry had one strike affecting 70 of their 5,000 members.

The pulp, sulphite, and paper-mill workers entered into 6 agreements without striking and had 6 strikes involving 5,000 of their 9,500 members.

The quarry workers with 3,000 members had 2 strikes in which 200 men were engaged.

The street and electric railway employees made 105 agreements through negotiation, 41 through arbitration, and 31 as a result of strikes. Their 75 strikes involved about 60,000 out of their membership of 98,700.

The stove mounters made 114 agreements through negotiation or arbitration and 5 by strikes that affected 250 of their 1,800 members.

The teamsters and chauffeurs secured 480 agreements and had 103 strikes in which 48,000 out of 110,800 members participated.

The tobacco workers secured 11 agreements and had 6 strikes involving 700 men out of about 15,200 members.

But even unions which are slow to strike may carry on the struggle with great vigor and persistence once the decisive step has been taken. The International Typographical Union, for example, has been noted for its conservative policy. Nevertheless, when the job printers, who had promised to introduce the forty-four-hour week on May 1, 1921, took advantage of the industrial depression to violate their agreement, the Typographical Union, despite the unfavorable business situation, did not hesitate to initiate a nation-wide strike to enforce the agreement, spending over $14,000,000 to push the struggle through to a generally successful conclusion.

VI. The Significance of Trade Unionism

One of the most significant effects of trade unionism is its influence upon freedom within the shop and the protection which it gives to the personalities of the workers. Unionism prevents men from being crushed into mere obeyers of orders. It gives them a chance to express themselves without fear of the management; to discuss their aspirations, their ideas, and their grievances openly, without dread of being overheard by the foreman and being disciplined. It even gives them an opportunity to criticize the management, to find fault with the way the plant is run, and to talk freely about how they think the plant should be run — in short, to express the same sort of ideas about the management of the plant that free citizens are accustomed to express about the government of the country. Mr. Otto S. Beyer, Jr., has well said: " Labor organizations guard workers in industry against developing a general feeling of inferiority, futility and despair, and so prevent apathy and servility, with its blighting effect on industrial and community morale, from permeating the rank and file of wage earners." [17]

[17] *Interborough Rapid Transit Company* v. *William Green,* p. 431.

More important, however, is the effect of trade unionism upon the government of industry. In place of an oriental despotism under which the word of the manager is final, unionism seeks to introduce the principle that decisions should be based upon rules and that rules should be based upon the consent of the governed. Whether men shall be paid by the day or by the piece, what the working hours shall be, in accordance with what rules men shall be promoted or laid off, what reasons shall justify discharge, how much work a man must do in a day, what precautions shall be taken against accidents and industrial diseases, all of these questions and scores of other matters should be decided, unions insist, not by the management alone, but *jointly* by the management and the union.

The fight of trade unions for a voice in the control of industry has often been compared with the fight for parliamentary government. The comparison is not without merit. Trade agreements are similar in some respects to constitutions — they guarantee rights which are similar to those which are guaranteed by constitutions. And it is true without question that the problems of the distribution of authority within industry are no less important than the problems which confronted the constitution makers of the seventeenth, eighteenth, and nineteenth centuries. The fight for parliamentary government extended over several centuries. The fight of trade unions for a voice in the direction of industry has already lasted more than a century and it is likely to continue much longer.

During the next century trade unionism may become an exceedingly useful instrument for decentralizing the regulation of industry, or at least for preventing the state from becoming overburdened with regulating activities. It seems likely that the state will continue to assume more and more direction over industry. In this event, it may become increasingly important to protect the state against assuming more work than it can effectively perform. This would necessitate developing, wherever possible, other agencies and other methods of control and, in particular it would necessitate encouraging self-regulation within industry. It may be found that trade unionism provides a foundation which can be advantageously used in building up our future machinery of industrial control.

It is often said that unionism of the type prevalent in the United States is essentially conservative, because it does not seek to overthrow the existing economic order but accepts the basic institutions of private property and the wage system and strives merely to substitute collective for individual bargaining. It is true that nearly all American unions are conservative in the sense that they are satisfied to proceed step by step. But examination of the changes which they are making in the government of industry indicates that they are revolutionary and, in fact, are nibbling at the very foundations of the economic order. For they contest the control of industry by property owners and assert that government in industry should rest upon the consent of the governed. But the very essence of private property is the right to make decisions, and when unions limit that right and divide it between the property owners and the workers, they are making a fundamental change in private property itself. It is a delusion to pretend that this is not revolutionary. But most revolutions are accomplished by men who know not what they do.

REFERENCES

Commons, J. R., *Trade Unionism and Labor Problems* (first series), 1905. Ch. I, IV, and X.

Commons, J. R., and Associates, *History of Labour in the United States,* 1918.

McCabe, D. A., " The Standard Rate in American Trade Unions," *Johns Hopkins University Studies,* v. XXX, 1912.

Perlman, Selig, *A Theory of Trade Unionism,* 1928.

Tannenbaum, Frank, *The Labor Movement,* 1921.

Webb, S. and B., *Industrial Democracy,* 1902.

Webb, S. and B., *The History of Trade Unionism* (revised edition), 1920.

CHAPTER X

SPECULATIVE PRODUCTION

I. PRODUCTION IN MODERN INDUSTRY IS SPECULATIVE. II. DIFFICULTIES IN FORECASTING DEMAND. III. DIFFICULTIES IN FORECASTING SUPPLY. IV. ERRORS IN FORECASTING SUPPLY AND DEMAND CAUSE SOCIAL WASTE. V. REDUCING THE RISKS DUE TO SPECULATIVE PRODUCTION. VI. THE TRANSFER OF THE RISKS DUE TO SPECULATIVE PRODUCTION.

I. Production in Modern Industry Is Speculative

If one wishes a pair of shoes, a load of coal, a pound of coffee, or a sack of flour, it is not necessary to wait for it to be produced. It will be found ready for delivery in the possession of the retailer. And even though we have the article made to order, as we sometimes do in the case of suits or shoes and as we usually do in the case of houses, most of the steps in the productive process have been taken in anticipation of our demand. The merchant tailor has a supply of cloth on hand, the shoemaker a stock of leather, and the materials which go into a house — bricks, lumber, cement, paint, glass, furnace, radiators, hardwood, plumbing fixtures — can be obtained ready-made from dealers who keep them in stock. This tendency to produce goods before finding buyers for them has always existed, but it is more universal today than ever before. It is, as we have seen, one of the inevitable results of specialization. From this marked tendency to produce in anticipation of demand, follow results of great significance.[1]

Could the demand and supply of goods be foretold, production in advance of demand would be no more speculative than

[1] The great drop in prices which occurred in 1920 caused business enterprises to lose heavily on goods which they had purchased or produced in advance of orders. Since that time, business has developed a tendency to avoid producing or buying greatly in advance of immediate needs. Steel, for example, which was formerly ordered three to six months in advance, is today ordered and produced as needed. For an excellent discussion of changes in purchasing policies, see L. S. Lyon's *Hand-to-Mouth Buying*.

production in response to definite orders. But even in the case of staple articles, such as coal, wheat, or meat, estimates of the future demand and supply often prove to be seriously in error. The result is that the producer who makes goods before selling them runs the risk that they will not bring enough to cover the cost of production. The pervasiveness of production in advance of orders, combined with the difficulty of forecasting supply and demand, means that speculation permeates the entire economic system. It is not confined to the stock market, the wheat pit, or the cotton exchange. Practically *all* producers, *whether they desire to be or not,* are speculators, for they incur expenses without knowing what return they will receive. The North Dakota wheat grower who rails against the speculators in the grain exchange is himself a speculator, for, in effect, he gambles that the price of wheat next fall or winter will cover the cost of raising his crop; the retailer who in August orders a stock of fall suits and overcoats is speculating that weather, style trends, and business conditions will enable him to sell his goods at a profit; the boy who spends four years learning to be a plasterer is speculating that for the next thirty-five or forty years wages and working conditions in that trade will be satisfactory to him.

II. Difficulties in Forecasting Demand

In the fall of 1923, when the demand of retailers for suits was quite below normal owing to stocks carried over from spring, the men's clothing manufacturers put their hopes for a good fall business on overcoats. Mild weather, however, held up the demand so that both overcoating materials and made-up garments were unloaded at price concessions. Mills reduced the price of piece goods by about 30 per cent. Had the clothing trade been better able financially to cope with the delayed demand, values might have been sustained, but the poor spring season, following the conditions created by the depression of several years before, impaired the credit of many manufacturers and compelled them to convert merchandise into cash.

This very ordinary experience illustrates the world of uncertainty in which the business man must plan his operations. Men's ability and willingness to pay for goods change rapidly. These changes are partly independent of the economic order and partly products of it. The ability of farmers to demand goods, for example, depends upon the size of crops, which in turn depends upon the weather. Frequently, of course, a small crop, by reason of the higher price which it commands per unit, yields a greater total return than a large crop, but it is none the less true that the farmer's purchasing power is largely determined by the weather. The willingness of consumers to buy many articles also depends upon weather conditions. Fruit or fresh vegetables which reach market on a cool, raw, summer's day bring less, assuming the supply to be the same, than on hot, sultry days. A mild and pleasant autumn hurts the fall trade in many articles — although lighter fall buying may lead to heavier winter purchasing — and a cold and unpleasant spring and summer reduce the sales of spring and summer goods.

Uncertainty in demand is also produced by economic institutions. The disposition of consumers to purchase on the basis of whim and fancy, suddenly to take up new styles and quickly to drop them, is in great measure a creation of competitive profit seeking. The very efforts of enterprises to strengthen the demand for their own products often render the market *as a whole* less certain. To enhance the demand for their output, business establishments offer the consumer a greater variety and a swifter succession of styles and encourage him — or her — to demand something new, distinctive, different, and more expensive than that possessed by others. But all of this makes it more difficult to judge what particular styles will prove most popular.[2] It is certain that people will be wearing hats, shoes, and clothes three or four months hence, but no one knows what colors, shapes, or materials will be in demand.

A most important way in which the economic order creates uncertainty in demand is through the wave-like variations in business activity known as the business cycle. During the boom phase of the cycle, when prices are rising, demand is abnormally large because buyers, expecting that prices will go higher, tend to purchase in excess of their immediate needs; during periods of

[2] The committee of the Federated American Engineering Societies which investigated waste in industry found that in the men's clothing industry " the trend in recent years due to the desire of the manufacturers to stimulate additional demand and their fear of losing ground to competitors, has been toward an increasing number of styles of young men's suits and of varieties of cloth." *Waste in Industry*, p. 96.

depression, demand is reduced by the fact that many buyers are using up supplies which they accumulated during the boom period, or are waiting for prices to drop still lower. The speculative buying which accompanies rising prices leads many producers to believe that the permanent demand is greater than it really is and causes them to overexpand the capacity of their plants. Estimating the long-run demand is made more difficult by the fact that during boom periods many purchasers, fearing that they can obtain prompt delivery of only part of their orders, ask for more than they really desire. And, of course, no one knows when the boom will end. The risk is most acute in the case of articles, such as crops or live stock, which require a year or more to produce. The intense demand and high prices prevailing at the peak of prosperity stimulate an enlarged output which may not reach the market until the crest of prosperity has passed and the country is in the depths of depression.

Fluctuations in demand are likely to be greatest for products which are most remote from the completed stage. Assume that an article passes through four stages before final consumption. During the prosperous phase of the business cycle, retailers, instead of buying at the rate of actual ultimate consumption, may purchase at 5 per cent above this, or at the rate of 105 instead of 100, accumulating stocks in expectation of higher prices. Wholesalers, likewise anticipating higher prices, may also purchase 5 per cent in excess of their sales. As their sales are at the rate of 105, their rate of purchase becomes 110.25. If manufacturers, also foreseeing higher prices, buy raw materials at 5 per cent above their rate of consumption, their purchases of raw materials will be at the rate of 115.7625. Thus, by the time the demand reaches the raw material, it is far above the rate at which the finished commodity is being consumed. The farther removed the product is from the completed stage, the more pronounced also is likely to be the drop in the demand for it when prosperity turns to depression. Because of stocks accumulated during prosperity, the retailer, in the early stages of depression, need not buy as much from the jobber as he sells to consumers, nor the jobber as much from the manufacturer as he sells to retailers, nor the manufacturer as much from the producer of raw materials as he sells to wholesalers.

Last of all, competition enhances the difficulty of forecasting sales, because it makes the demand for the output of any single enterprise far more uncertain than demand in the market as a whole. However steady the total demand for a commodity, no firm dare count on buyers for its own output, because the volume of its sales depends upon the outcome of a competitive struggle.

III. DIFFICULTIES IN FORECASTING SUPPLY

To the risks produced by uncertainties in demand must be added those created by uncertainties in supply. The quantity of many things — crops, water-power, oil, natural gas, and other natural products — is in considerable degree beyond human control. Consider, for example, the experience of the petroleum producers and refiners. In 1923, their profits were greatly reduced by a large and sudden increase in the production of petroleum due principally to oil discoveries in California. Although the consumption of gasoline during the first four months of 1923 was 35 per cent above 1922, stocks on hand May 1, 1923, exceeded those of the year previous by over 55 per cent. Again in 1927 there was a sudden increase in petroleum production, this time because of new wells in the Seminole field in Oklahoma. At the end of June, 1927, crude petroleum was selling for nearly a third less than the year before and gasoline had dropped over a fifth.

Probably no group of producers suffers more from inability to forecast supply than do the farmers. The speculative character of farming was dramatically illustrated in the fall of 1926 when, following the government's forecast of an unusually large crop, the price of cotton dropped one-third in a month — on September 4th, it was 18.7 cents a pound; by October 8th, it had fallen to 12.5 cents. The decrease chopped approximately $400,000,000 from the value of the crop in one month. The uncertainties of other branches of farming are equally great. In 1924, for example, the corn crop was smaller than in a dozen years. The next year, however, it was exceptionally large — the seventh largest in the history of the country. But the small crop of 1924 had caused a great reduction in the number of hogs. Consequently, when the immense crop of 1925 was produced, there were not enough hogs to consume it, and the price of corn, which had averaged $1.11 a bushel on the farms in June, 1925, dropped a year later to less than 66 cents, putting many farmers in severe financial straits. The meat packers too were affected. Cheap corn in 1926, following the bumper crop of 1925, and a scarcity of hogs, resulting from the poor corn crop of 1924, caused hogs to be fed longer and marketed at heavier weights in 1926. But fatter hogs meant relatively more lard per hog. In the midst of this situation came the bumper cotton crop of 1926, resulting in a heavy production of cottonseed oil, an important competitor of lard. Consequently the packers found themselves with a large quantity of lard on hand — their stocks on August 31, 1926, were more than double those of the year before — and with prices falling.

To a great extent, of course, uncertainty regarding supply is unavoidable. But in no small degree it is simply the result of inadequate statistical information. If one knows how rapidly a commodity is being produced, at what rate it is being consumed, what the productive capacity of the industry is, how much new capacity is under construction, how large are the existing stocks of the commodity, and what is the volume of unfilled orders in the hands of producers, it is often possible to make fairly satisfactory estimates of future supply. But, despite the fact that, during recent years, trade associations and the Department of Commerce have made splendid progress in publishing regular information on many of these points, the available data are still seriously incomplete.

Until recently, when farmers decided what to plant, they had no figures on the acreage which was being put into different crops. A year of shortage and high prices might be followed by a year of great overplanting and low prices. Or precisely the opposite effect might occur. Anticipating that the high prices might lead to great overproduction, farmers might reduce their acreage and the shortage might be greater in the second year than in the first. Recently the Department of Agriculture has attempted to remedy this situation by the publication of " intention to plant " reports.

Accurate statistics on supply are often difficult to obtain and sometimes serious mistakes are made. A notable instance occurred in 1923 in connection with the government estimate of the cotton crop. In November the price of cotton went to 37 cents a pound on the expectation that the yield would be nearer 9,000,-000 than 10,000,000 bales. The final government estimate in December was 10,081,000 bales and this proved remarkably close to the actual size. Before the end of February, 1924, the spot price of cotton had fallen below 30 cents a pound.

IV. ERRORS IN FORECASTING SUPPLY AND DEMAND CAUSE SOCIAL WASTE

When producers accurately forecast supply and demand, they tend, under ordinary competitive conditions, to produce neither more nor less of an article than they can sell at what they regard as a satisfactory profit. Errors in estimating demand or supply, however, usually result in a larger or smaller output than can be sold at a gain. What disadvantages, if any, are involved in either of these situations? Does either inherently and inevitably involve loss to the community?

The answer depends upon how accurately prices reflect men's desire for goods and the human cost of producing them. If the prices of goods do not accurately represent the satisfaction which they give or the sacrifice which they cost, then we cannot assume that because there is a deficit in dollars and cents, there is necessarily a deficit in terms of human pleasure and pain. A commodity may fail to command a remunerative price simply because it appeals in the main to persons who have small incomes and cannot afford to pay high prices, but it may yield far more satisfaction in comparison with its cost than an article which brings a good profit because it appeals to the well-to-do. For example, on account of miscalculating the demand, the manufacturer of a cheap automobile might make far more cars than he could sell at a price which covered his costs and yet these cars might yield far more satisfaction in relation to the expense of making them than a fine car for which there might be a profitable market.

But although mistakes in estimating supply and demand do not *necessarily* mean loss to the community, it is probable that in most cases they do and that more accurate forecasts would be a gain to the community as well as to the individual business man. A man decides that a town needs a new hotel or office building and erects one so large that it is never more than half occupied;

farmers raise so much corn or wheat that it does not pay to ship part of it to market; a rubber company erects an immense tire factory which, because of insufficient demand, stands idle for several years. In each case the waste from maladjustment between supply and demand is clear. No less real, though possibly less obvious, is the waste consequent upon an underestimate of demand or an overestimate of supply. Suppose that farmers underestimate the demand for wheat. As a result, consumers are unable to obtain as much as they would eagerly purchase at prices which would yield the farmers a handsome profit. Because farmers put less land into wheat, they may have raised an unusually large amount of corn. But the consumers, we have seen, prefer more wheat to more corn. The waste caused by the farmers' erroneous forecast is that consumers must take corn when they would prefer wheat.

We have already called attention to the fact that, despite the pressing need for more goods, modern industry ordinarily produces at substantially less than its capacity. This is partly because the demand for everything fluctuates and industry is equipped to meet the periods of peak demand. But why do not enterprises keep busy during slack periods by producing in anticipation of future orders? Some goods, of course, cannot be economically stored, but this is not the principal difficulty. The truth of the matter is that, although industry does, to a substantial extent, produce in anticipation of demand, the difficulties in forecasting supply and demand prevent production from being carried on any more in advance of orders than the exigencies of competition compel. In competitive industries, the individual enterprise possesses too slight control over prices and over the designs, styles, and models which are offered to the public to go very far in producing to stock.

The most important way in which erroneous estimates of supply and demand produce waste is by causing interruptions to buying and selling and a general curtailment of production. We have learned that the interdependence introduced into modern industry by specialization makes it exceedingly difficult to avoid serious breakdowns in buying and selling and, consequently, in production. Let us see what happens when business men quite generally overestimate the willingness and ability of the public to purchase goods. Goods are produced at such costs that high prices must be obtained for them. The public proves unwilling or unable to pay the expected prices and the goods must be sold for less. At once the wheels of production slow down and business stagnation sets in. The public, anticipating lower prices, refuses to buy even as much as it has been purchasing. Business enterprises, confronted with a smaller demand, lay off superfluous workers and postpone adding to or renewing buildings and equipment. Their profits being lessened or wiped out by a smaller volume of business at low prices, many of them reduce or suspend dividends. All of these steps decrease, of course, the demand for goods and compel a still further curtailment of production. Eventually, as we shall see later, forces are set in motion which cause demand to revive, but the first effect of a general overestimation of demand is a curtailment in production causing a drop in demand, further curtailments of output, further decreases in demand, and a serious breakdown of the economic machine.

V. Reducing the Risks Due to Speculative Production

The most obvious way to reduce the risks of speculative production is to diminish the necessity for producing in advance of orders. One way of doing this is by improving the speed and reliability of transportation. The stocks of goods which retailers and wholesalers find it desirable to carry and the quantity of raw materials which manufacturers keep on hand depend largely upon how quickly and surely they can replenish their supplies in case of a sudden and abnormal demand. Since the great drop in prices in 1920, many business concerns in the United States have been endeavoring to operate with smaller inventories in relation to their output. They have been assisted in reducing inventories by a remarkable improvement in the speed and dependability of railroad service — stimulated by good roads and motor truck competition. The stocks which business establishments must keep are also affected by the number of sizes and varieties of each article. The recent movement, sponsored by Mr. Hoover, to eliminate unnecessary sizes and varieties has made possible great reductions in the stocks of many distributors. It has been pointed out that before the number of sizes of steel reënforcing bars had been reduced from twenty to eleven, the warehouses in the United States normally had on hand in idle stock from 150,000 to 200,000 tons. With eleven standard sizes, it is believed that a stock of 75,000 will be entirely ample.[3]

Since the risks of producing in anticipation of demand arise largely from ignorance of the present or prospective states of supply and demand, one way of making production less speculative is to enlarge and improve market information. It would be difficult to overestimate the importance of the statistics on production, consumption, the volume of accumulated stocks, and the amount of unfilled orders, now published by the government and by many trade associations.

In forecasting the prospects of an industry, account must be taken, not only of data which pertain directly to it, but also of the general business outlook. As this is too technical a problem to be handled by the ordinary business man for himself, a number of forecasting services have grown up. Thus far, attempts to forecast business developments have met with only indifferent success. As knowledge of the business cycle develops and as business men become more critical of forecasting, the services should improve. Eventually they may be a substantial help in reducing business risks.

The replacement of competition by monopoly naturally diminishes the hazards of production in anticipation of demand. A monopoly, of course, avoids the uncertainty which, under competition, exists because of the very fact that each enterprise is attempting to increase its sales at the expense of its rivals. A monopoly is also able to acquire more complete and accurate market information than competitive enterprises. Its own records tell the rate of production in the industry and the volume of unfilled orders. It can only estimate the size of stocks in the hands of middlemen, but it knows the size of its own stocks and, since the middlemen purchase almost entirely from it, it should be able to estimate their holdings with precision. Being the sole or almost the sole enterprise in the business, it can keep accurate track of additions to productive capacity. Its control of supply enables it to produce to stock during dull seasons without fear of glutting the market or having its output rendered obsolete by

[3] See footnote 20 on pp. 80 and 81.

the creation of new styles. Should it overestimate demand, it can easily correct its error by temporarily curtailing output.

Trade associations are somewhat less effective than monopolies in reducing the risks of speculative production. A trade association which embraces most of the firms in the industry, is able, of course, to give its members the same information concerning the rate of production, the amount of unfilled orders, additions to productive capacity, and the volume of existing stocks as a monopoly obtains from its own books. By inducing members to standardize their products, trade associations diminish the danger from unsalable stocks. Possibly trade associations may eventually succeed in establishing some control over the number of styles and the frequency of style changes. To do so, however, they would need considerably more influence over their members than most associations now have. And even if an association were able to control the number of styles and frequency of style changes, it is doubtful whether it would do so, for style changes, though they enhance the hazards of business, compel consumers to purchase more than they otherwise would.

Finally, trade unions are often of importance in reducing the risk of speculative production, at least when a union controls most of the plants in a competitive area. Unions, we have learned, enter into agreements stipulating the minimum rates of pay for a given period. Every employer then knows what wages his competitors will have to pay and he can produce in anticipation of orders with the assurance that his rivals will not be able, by cutting wages, to flood the market with cheap goods.

VI. THE TRANSFER OF THE RISKS DUE TO SPECULATIVE PRODUCTION

The rapid fluctuations in prices which characterize our economic society give rise to a class of specialist speculators who make a living by buying when they expect prices to rise and selling when they expect them to fall. Specialized speculation extends to only a few commodities — grain, coffee, cotton, and provisions are the most important. It does not extend to other commodities primarily because contracts to accept or deliver given quantities of a good at a future date cannot be satisfactorily made unless the quality of the good can be accurately and easily specified. And although the volume of speculative trading on commodity exchanges runs from two to ten times the amount of produce on which it is based, most of the speculation is carried on by a relatively few professionals. Professor Boyle estimates that less than 150 professionals account for four-fifths of the speculation on the Chicago Board of Trade.[4]

Because professional speculators do nothing but buy and sell, not even keeping a store or a warehouse and thus not making goods more physically available to consumers, the belief has gained currency that speculators are parasites. Especially does the man in the street find his sense of propriety shocked by " short " selling — that is, the selling of something, say wheat, which one does not possess.[5] Nevertheless, the professional speculator in grain, coffee, cotton, sugar, provisions, and many other articles is extremely useful. He probably lessens the hazards of speculative production and he assumes part of them himself, thus enabling other business men to avoid taking chances which he is better able than they to assume.

The professional speculator may diminish the hazards of speculative production by reducing the fluctuations in price which create the risks. Obviously, if prices never changed, there would be no risk in producing in advance of orders, and the more closely prices approach stability, the less risk there is. Attempts to furnish conclusive statistical proof that professional speculation diminishes price fluctuations have not met with success. Consequently it seems probable that the effect of specialized speculation upon commodity prices is less than most economists assume — too small, apparently, to be distinguished from the many other conditions which affect prices.[6] Nevertheless it is possible that professional speculators slightly reduce the fluctuations in prices because they buy and sell on the basis of more accurate and complete information than non-specialists. Suppose, for example,

---

[4] Boyle, J. E., *The Chicago Board of Trade*, pp. 42–43. About forty of these are pit scalpers — men who make their profits on price changes during the day but who each day sell as much as they buy and buy as much as they sell and do not go overnight with unsold grain or uncovered contracts to deliver grain.

[5] As a matter of fact, short selling is by no means confined to the wheat pit or the stock exchange. It extends throughout industry. Manufacturers and jobbers frequently accept orders for goods which they do not possess.

[6] In the case of stock prices, it is probable that speculation enhances rather than diminishes price fluctuations.

that the prospects are that the wheat crop of the world will be exceptionally small. Because professional speculators in wheat are constant students of the market, they are likely to foresee the impending shortage sooner than others. Convinced that a shortage is coming, they purchase wheat with the intention of selling it later at a higher price. But the " wheat " which the speculators buy is not actual wheat; it is a contract by which the seller agrees to deliver wheat at some time in the future and it is known as a " future contract " or a " future." [7] The demand of the speculators causes the price of futures to rise. This, of course, causes the spot price, or the price for immediate delivery, to advance also, because the spot price can never be less than the future price by more than the cost of holding and storage. The advance in the spot price naturally tends to lessen consumption. Thus more of the present supply of wheat is carried over to relieve the future shortage and the short crop produces a smaller rise in price than it otherwise would.[8]

[7] The future delivery date is not any date but one of several customary dates. In the grain trade in the United States the futures traded in are May, July, September, and December. Few buyers of futures accept delivery of the actual commodity. Suppose that A buys 10,000 bushels of December wheat from B. Instead of holding his contract until December and receiving grain on it, A expects to sell his contract before December. But B, in selling to A, probably sold grain which he did not own. Consequently, B and others, who sold December wheat short, must purchase either wheat futures or actual wheat to fulfill their contracts. A finds a ready market for his future contract among those who have sold short. When December arrives, the December wheat contracts are largely held by previous short sellers who settle among themselves by delivering contracts instead of wheat. But the holder of a contract who wishes actual wheat may demand and receive it. Cornering of the actual wheat supply is rendered more difficult by the fact that the rules of the Chicago Board of Trade make twenty-one grades of wheat deliverable on future contracts. There are also other rules which make a market " squeeze " more difficult. See Boyle, J. E., *The Chicago Board of Trade*, pp. 53–54.

[8] But the notion that professional speculators are *necessarily* performing a social service when they tend to stabilize the price of cotton, wheat, or other crops must not be uncritically accepted. It is true that a stable price means smaller risks for the people who are dealing in the commodity. Surely it is to the advantage of cotton and flour mills to have the prices of cotton and wheat stabilized. But from the standpoint of the *growers*, a too stable price would be undesirable. The reason is that it would create instability of incomes. In the case of cotton, the available evidence points to the conclusion that somewhat greater stability of prices would make for greater stability of income for cotton growers, because large crops appear as a rule to sell for less than small ones. In the case of wheat, however, the contrary appears to be the case. The American output is only a small part of the world output. Consequently, a large crop in the United States usually brings growers here more than a small crop. The conclusion follows that stability in the income of wheat growers would be promoted by more violent, rather than less violent, fluctuations in the price. This topic is discussed further in Chapter XIX, p. 441. For more detailed discussion of the rela-

If the outlook were for an exceptionally large crop, specula-tors, instead of buying, would sell short — that is, they would enter into contracts to deliver in the future wheat which they do not now possess but which they expect to purchase later. They are willing to do this because they expect the price to decline and thus count on being able to buy for less than they have sold. The eagerness of speculators to sell wheat for future delivery forces down the future price, the spot price goes down with it, and the consumption of wheat is encouraged. Consequently, when the large crop is marketed, stocks of wheat are low and the large crop does not depress the price so much as it might otherwise have done.

It is obvious that a speculator reduces price fluctuations *only in event that he correctly forecasts future demand and supply*. If he erroneously expects a small crop and by pushing up prices in-duces a large carry-over, the fall in price will be greater than ever in case the crop is large. If, by short selling in expectation of a large crop, he brings about a small carry-over, the rise in price will be greater than ever, should the crop be small. All of this means that the *amateur* speculator who buys or sells on the basis of inadequate knowledge is likely to accentuate rather than dimin-ish price fluctuations. It means furthermore that even the pro-fessional speculator may at times accentuate price movements. The conclusion that speculation based upon correct market in-formation tends to stabilize prices assumes that speculators who believe that the price is high will sell futures and that those who believe that it is low will buy futures, but is this assumption necessarily correct? Suppose that a speculator believes that wheat is higher than it should be but suppose that he also sees that the market is in control of the " bulls," that is, of the speculators who are buying for a rise, and that the price is rising and is likely to continue to rise.[9] Will this speculator sell short and thus help check the unwarranted rise in price? Is he not more likely to

tionship between price fluctuations and stability of farmers' incomes, see Black, J. D., *Agricultural Reform in the United States,* pp. 95–151.

. [9] This situation is not uncommon because the " public," that is the amateur specu-lators, almost invariably speculate for a rise. The amateurs come into the market when the price is rising and because it is rising and they are likely to continue to come in after the price has risen more than fundamental conditions warrant.

buy, thus reënforcing the tendency for prices to rise? Later, when he believes that the rise in price has nearly reached its limit, not only may he sell all the wheat that he has purchased but he may also sell short. In this way he makes a profit on the rise and another profit on the decline. But notice that he has increased rather than reduced the fluctuations in prices. For this reason, it is a mistake to assume that professional speculators, even when correctly informed of market conditions, *invariably* tend to stabilize prices. But it is largely the presence of ignorant speculators in the market, or the willingness of ignorant speculators to rush into the market when the price exhibits a distinct tendency to rise or fall, which gives the professional speculator an opportunity to make profits by deliberately seeking to create large fluctuations in prices.

Far more important than the service which professional speculators may perform by diminishing slightly the risks of production in anticipation of demand is the service which they render by assuming a large part of the risks, thus permitting manufacturers and wholesalers to concentrate more exclusively upon the problems of their businesses. Many manufacturers of cotton or woolen cloth or of flour desire to avoid speculating in the raw material which they use. They prefer to make only a manufacturer's profit and to transfer to others the possibility of gaining or losing from changes in the value of raw materials.

But how can a manufacturer transfer to a speculator the risk from changes in the price of his raw material. This can be done by an operation known as *hedging*. The nature of hedging can be made clear by several illustrations. Suppose that a mill receives an order for several thousand barrels of flour to be delivered over a period of ninety days. The mill does not have space to store enough wheat to fill the order and yet the manager fears to purchase wheat only as he uses it lest the price should rise and he should suffer a heavy loss on the contract. To avoid such losses, he purchases wheat *futures* — that is, he buys contracts calling for the delivery of the wheat to him at some future date. Then, as he buys spot wheat to manufacture into flour, he sells an equal amount of futures. If the price of wheat rises, his loss on his flour contract is substantially balanced by his profit on the sale of the futures. But if the price of wheat drops, the loss on the future contract is balanced by the profit on the flour.

Some mills, especially those remote from wheat-growing areas, find it desirable to store wheat in excess of the amount needed to fill their contracts for flour. Often too they have large quantities of wheat in transit. Such a mill wishes to protect itself against a drop in the price of wheat.[10] To do this it sells futures — that is, it agrees to deliver at some future time an amount of wheat equal to that which it has purchased. In order to fulfill these contracts, the mill must buy wheat. As it enters into contracts to sell flour, it buys a corresponding amount of wheat to cover its sale of futures. If the price of wheat goes up, the mill gains on the wheat which it has manufactured but loses on its sale of futures. If the price goes down, the mill makes a profit on the future contract but loses on the wheat which it has converted into flour. In either case, the gain and the loss about balance each other.

In each of these two instances, the mill is in the position of an enterprise which manufactures a commodity that does not greatly change in price. Its profits come, not from fluctuations in the price of the raw material, but from the margin that exists between the price of the raw material and that of the finished product. But it is only possible for the mill to attain this position because somebody else is willing to bear the risk of changes in the price of raw material. This " somebody else " is the speculator. When he buys futures, he is assuming the risk that the price will drop; when he sells them, he is running the risk that it will rise.

It is important to notice that the success of a hedger in transferring risks to speculators depends upon whether or not the spot and future prices move precisely together — the future price rising by the same amount as the spot price and falling by exactly the same amount. Suppose that a mill purchases, at $1.00 a bushel, 10,000 bushels of wheat to be manufactured into flour, and hedges the purchase by simultaneously selling 10,000 bushels of December futures at the prevailing price, which we shall as-

[10] Hedging may not be purely a matter of choice with the mill for if it borrows money with which to buy wheat, the bank probably insists that the purchase be hedged in order to protect the loan.

sume to be $1.05. Suppose also that, when the mill sells its flour, the spot price of wheat has dropped to 95 cents a bushel and that flour is selling at a corresponding price. On the wheat that the mill purchased for manufacture into flour, it loses $500. But if the price of December futures has also dropped by 5 cents, the mill can buy December futures to cover its short sale at $1.00. It therefore makes $500 on the future sale — precisely enough to balance the loss on its purchase of wheat for manufacturing. But if the price of December futures fell by only 4 cents, to $1.01, the mill would make only $400 on its future sale and would fail by $100 to balance its loss on the wheat consumed in manu- facturing.

As a rule, the spot and future prices of wheat rise and fall by almost precisely the same amounts.[11] From time to time, how- ever, the spread between the two changes appreciably and this prevents hedging from being a perfect method of transferring risks. The future price can, of course, never exceed the spot price by more than the cost of storing and holding, but the cost of stor- ing and holding is itself subject to slight changes as interest rates and elevator or warehouse charges rise and fall. Furthermore, the future price may be considerably less than the spot price plus the cost of storage because the future price is affected by the har- vest prospects. The spot price may be held fairly high by a small carry-over from the previous year's crop but the outlook for a bumper harvest may cause the future prices to drop. At times the prospect of a bumper crop drives the future price below the spot price.[12]

REFERENCES

Basset, W. R., *Taking the Guesswork Out of Business*, 1924. Ch. V and VI.
Brace, H. H., *The Value of Organized Speculation*, 1913.
Hardy, C. O., *Risk and Risk-Bearing*, 1923. Ch. I, II, III, IV, XI, and XII.
Lyon, L. S., *Hand-to-Mouth Buying*, 1929.

[11] But this has been much less true of cotton. The principal difficulty in the case of cotton has been the problem of equitably and precisely determining the grades of cotton which may be delivered on a future contract which runs in terms of middling cotton.

[12] The possibility of transferring risks by the process of hedging is, of course, not affected by whether the future price is above or below the spot price provided only that the spread between the two remains unchanged. In the case of wheat, the future price has been below the spot price about one-fifth of the time during the last several decades.

Marshall, L. C., *Industrial Society*, 1918. Ch. VIII.
Pigou, A. C., *Industrial Fluctuations*, 1927. Ch. VI and VII.
Weld, W. E., and Tostlebe, A. S., *A Case Book for Economics*, 1927. Pp. 184–201.
Wright, Charles, and Fayle, C. Ernest, *A History of Lloyd's*, 1928.

CHAPTER XI

MODERN INDUSTRY A CREDIT ECONOMY

I. THE NATURE OF CREDIT.   II. HOW COMMERCIAL CREDIT IS
GRANTED.   III. THE EFFECT OF COMMERCIAL CREDIT UPON THE
VOLUME OF PURCHASING POWER.   IV. THE SOCIAL UTILITY OF
COMMERCIAL CREDIT.   V. SOME PROBLEMS WHICH COMMERCIAL
CREDIT CREATES.   VI. THE NEED FOR THE CONTROL OF COMMER-
CIAL CREDIT.   VII. THE FEDERAL RESERVE SYSTEM.

I. THE NATURE OF CREDIT

In modern economic society more goods are sold in exchange
for promises to pay later than for cash down. And even when the
buyer pays at once, he may pay with borrowed money. Over
four-fifths of the business in the United States is done by check
rather than by cash, and checking accounts, as we shall see presently, mainly represent money borrowed from the banks.[1]

Selling or lending something in exchange for a promise to pay
later is known as extending credit. Credit itself may be defined as
the confidence in the intention and ability of a purchaser or borrower to pay later which makes the seller or lender willing to give
him something in exchange for his promise. From this practice of
doing business on the basis of credit, follow consequences of un-
suspected significance. Exchange and production are facilitated,
men of ability but of little capital are aided, business risks are sub-

[1] In recent years there has been a rapid extension of the use of credit in retail
transactions. A recent investigation of the Bureau of Foreign and Domestic Commerce covering 6,832 stores in various lines of retailing, with annual net sales (exclusive of returns) of $2,501,637,000 in 1927, disclosed that credit sales were $718,-
458,000, or 28.7 per cent of the total, and installment sales $203,833,000, or 8.1 per
cent. U. S. Bureau of Foreign and Domestic Commerce, "National Retail Credit
Survey, Part I," *Domestic Commerce Series*, No. 33, pp. 3, 7, 10, 16, 22, 29, 34, 39,
43. The proportion of credit and installment sales varied greatly in different lines
of retailing. Among 124 fur stores, 51.5 per cent of the sales were on credit and 11.2
per cent were installment sales; among 726 furniture stores, 27.1 per cent of the
sales were for credit and 57.7 per cent were installment sales. On the other hand,
89.5 per cent of the sales of 2,000 boot and shoe stores and 78.4 per cent of the sales
of 1,616 general clothing stores were for cash.

stantially increased, and the fluctuations of business activity are greatly accentuated. But in order to understand why credit produces these results, we must learn something of its nature and of how it is granted.

We know that more or less time usually intervenes between the incurrence of the expenses of production and the receipt of the returns from the finished article. The length of time that intervenes varies greatly. In the case of permanent plant and equipment, such as land, buildings, and machines, the waiting period may be very long. An enterprise buys a machine for $10,000. It does not get the $10,000 back at once. Over a period of years the machine produces goods which gradually pay for it. Possibly fifteen years elapse before the machine has paid for itself — that is, before it has returned its entire purchase price over and above operating expenses, repairs, interest on the investment, insurance, and taxes. In this instance, it is clear that the *average* waiting period required to get back each dollar invested in the machine is about seven and a half years.

In the case of other costs, such as raw materials, labor, advertising, rent, interest, taxes, and the like, the period between the time when the expense is incurred and the time when payment is received for the finished product is much shorter — usually not longer than three, six, or nine months. A merchant stocks his store with fall or spring ware. Several months elapse before most of it is sold. In the meantime, clerks must receive their salaries, rent and light bills must be met and the goods themselves paid for. A contractor spends three or four months erecting a building. He will not be paid until it has been completed. In the meantime he must pay his men, buy supplies, pay rent on his office and storage yards, and meet sundry expenses. Often weeks or months elapse between the time when a manufacturer receives an order and the day when he makes shipment on it. He too must purchase labor and materials, pay rent, and meet many miscellaneous expenses. The farmer plants his crop in the spring but does not harvest it until months later. Seed, fertilizer, insecticides, and labor must be purchased, the living expenses of his family must be met, and, if he is a tenant, he may have to pay rent each month.

This analysis indicates that business enterprises need two sorts of credit — long-term and short-term. Obviously it is extremely risky, under ordinary circumstances, for a concern to obtain the funds needed to erect a building or to purchase a machine by a loan repayable in three or six months or even a year. The loan would fall due long before the building or machine had yielded sufficient income to pay for itself. To finance the acquisition of things which pay for themselves very gradually — land, buildings, machines, horses, cattle, and many so-called permanent improvements — business establishments need loans running from five to fifty years and even more. By the time such loans mature, the accumulated return from the land, building, or machine should make payment of the debt possible. Long-time loans of this sort are known as *investment credits*. They are usually represented by bonds, mortgages, and long-term notes.

To pay for things which are quickly turned into cash, such as labor, materials, rent, light, heat, power, advertising, insurance, taxes, transportation, it is necessary to borrow only for short periods — thirty, sixty, and ninety days, or perhaps six months. Short-term loans needed to supply funds for current operations have been traditionally known as *commercial credits*. To some extent, however, business enterprises use short-time loans to finance the acquisition of permanent equipment. We shall, therefore, understand by commercial credit *any* short-term loan, regardless of whether it is used to finance current operations or to acquire permanent equipment.

Of course, it is *possible* to obtain funds for current operations — working capital, the business man calls them — by long-term loans, and to some extent it is done. As a rule, however, working capital — in so far as it is borrowed at all — is obtained by short-term loans instead of by the sale of bonds or of long-term notes. For this there are two principal reasons. One is that the amount of working capital required is constantly changing. The output of most firms fluctuates greatly from month to month and even from week to week. An exceptionally large order today may be followed by a temporary lull of business. Nearly all industries are in some degree seasonal and it is not unusual for the production of a firm in the busy season to be four or five times the volume in the off-season. Equally large are the fluctuations caused by the periods of general prosperity and depression. Were enterprises to provide sufficient funds to meet their peak needs from the sale of long-term securities, much of the time they would be paying interest on funds for which they have no immediate need.

But why do not business enterprises raise enough capital for their peak needs by selling long-term securities and, during periods of slack business, lend any surplus funds which they have on hand? Some concerns follow this practice but it has several disadvantages. It is necessary for the enterprise to lend its surplus funds in such a way that it can terminate the loan and obtain cash on very short notice. But the rate of return on such loans is likely to be less than the concern must pay on its own long-term securities. This is especially true during periods of general business depression, which are precisely the times when most enterprises would have surplus funds to lend. Furthermore, the ability of enterprises to obtain investment capital is limited. Ordinarily it is easier to borrow for a short period than for a long one. The more distant the maturity of a loan, the greater is the danger that something may destroy the borrower's ability to pay. Consequently, even after a firm has obtained all that it can by long-term loans at moderate interest rates, it usually can still borrow for three or four months in order to finance the making of goods for which it has orders. Especially in those industries in which large production units are more economical than small ones, is it advantageous for the owners to use their own capital and all that they can borrow for long terms to build large and economical plants, relying upon short-term loans to supply most of the working capital.

Besides these two outstanding reasons, there are innumerable others why enterprises negotiate short-term loans. Notes, interest, rents, taxes, may fall due when a concern, for some unforeseen reason — a strike, slow collections, or what not — is short of ready cash. A merchant may be unable to pay his bills because unseasonable weather has retarded his sales or because general business depression has suddenly set in and reduced demand. In fact, general business depressions invariably force thousands of enterprises to borrow in order to meet debts which they had expected to pay out of sales. Transportation tie-ups, due to floods, storms, strikes, or simply congestion, embarrass many concerns because customers do not pay for shipments until they receive them. In times of rising prices, business houses may borrow in order to stock up with raw materials before prices go higher. Or they may accumulate supplies out of fear of strikes among the producers of raw materials or on the railroads. For example, expectation of a strike of miners or railroad workers causes thousands of establishments to store coal and they may need to borrow to pay for it.

II. How Commercial Credit is Granted

Wholesalers and manufacturers grant huge volumes of short-term credits. Indeed, liberality in extending credit is an important competitive device. In the language of the business community, these sales are made " on open book account." There is no specific acknowledgment of indebtedness by the purchaser but he is simply charged on the books of the seller with the price of the goods sold to him. But to the extent that some enterprises extend credit to others, they are likely to find it necessary to borrow from commercial banks. In the last analysis, therefore, these institutions directly or indirectly supply most of the short-term credit. The commercial banks are not to be confused with savings banks or investment banking houses which specialize upon making long-term loans. Many commercial banks, it is true, engage to a considerable degree in extending long-term credits, because many of their loans which *appear* to be for brief periods are renewed several times before they are finally paid. Nevertheless, the principal business of commercial banks is extending short-term credits — usually running six months or less. In order to understand the operation and problems of our credit system, we must know how commercial banks lend money.

Let us assume that a retail shoe merchant has purchased part of his fall stock of shoes for $5,000. He cannot pay for them until they are sold, but the manufacturer needs funds at once in order to pay his workmen and to meet his bills for raw materials and other operating expenses. How can the manufacturer obtain his money promptly and how at the same time can the retailer be given time to pay for the shoes? There are three principal ways.

One method involves the use of a *promissory note*. This is simply a written promise, conforming to certain legal requirements, to pay money at a certain time. Either the retailer or the manufacturer might obtain funds from a bank in exchange for his promissory note. If the retailer borrows the money, he pays the manufacturer at once, and later, when he has sold his shoes, he pays the bank. If the manufacturer does the borrowing, he uses the funds thus obtained to meet the expenses incurred in making the shoes. He obtains money with which to repay the bank when the retailer, having sold the shoes, pays him for them. Strictly speaking, in each of these cases the bank simply *buys* the merchant's or the manufacturer's promise to pay. Since the note is not payable until some future time, the bank does not buy it at its full face value but deducts enough to allow itself interest on the funds which it advances. In other words, the bank purchases the note at a discount. For this reason, the operation is often known as *discounting* and the percentage of the face value which the bank deducts as the *discount rate*.

In some cases, a business enterprise may borrow on its promissory note, not from its bank, but in the open market through a commercial paper house. The commercial paper house is simply a middleman that buys notes from borrowers and resells them. The customers of commercial paper brokers are in the main banks, so that a firm which borrows through a broker is ultimately borrowing from a bank.[2] The reader may wonder why an enterprise should sell its notes to a commercial paper house rather than borrow directly from its own bank. The principal reason is to be found in the provision of the national banking law which prohibits any national bank from lending to any one borrower an amount in excess of 10 per cent of its capital and unimpaired surplus. A large enterprise which is situated in a small town may be unable to obtain enough credit from the local banks. It should be observed that only well known enterprises of good credit standing can borrow in the open market because the paper of other concerns is not readily salable.[3]

[2] Commercial paper houses charge a commission of one-fourth of one per cent. They do not add their endorsements to the paper which they sell. In order to make this unnecessary, the notes are not made out to the broker. The borrower draws a promissory note payable to himself and endorses it in blank.

[3] The commercial paper houses find a market for their paper among banks

A second method of extending credit involves the use of a *bill of exchange* or, as it is also called, a *time draft*. This is simply an order drawn by one person upon a second person to pay money at a stated time. In the use we are considering, however, the bill is drawn, not upon a bank, but upon an ordinary business enterprise. Such bills are known as *trade bills,* in distinction from banker's bills, which are drawn upon banks.

How might a trade bill be used to finance the sale of shoes? The shoe manufacturer draws a bill ordering the retailer to pay the price of shoes (in this case, $5,000) on a stipulated date. The time of payment is determined by the conditions of the sale. The manufacturer sends the bill to the retailer who, by writing " accepted " across the face and signing, indicates his willingness to pay it upon maturity. Such a bill, accepted by a business house other than a bank, is known as a *trade acceptance*. The retailer returns the accepted bill to the manufacturer, who endorses it and obtains funds by selling the bill to his bank.[4] Before the acceptance falls due, it is expected that the retailer will have sold his shoes and will thus be in a position to pay the bank which has purchased the acceptance.

A third method of advancing credit is by a *banker's bill*. This, as we have seen, is simply a time draft or bill of exchange which is drawn against a bank instead of against an ordinary business enterprise. Such a bill, after acceptance, is known as a *banker's acceptance*. Prior to the passage of the Federal Reserve Act in 1913, national banks were not permitted to accept time drafts drawn against them. The power of the banks to accept time drafts is still restricted to a few types of transactions. But despite legal restrictions, the use of banker's bills has grown rapidly in the United States during the last decade — far more rapidly than the use of trade bills. More than half of the banker's bills outstanding in the United States arise out of the importation and exportation of goods. But banker's bills are also

---

with idle funds. The pronounced seasonal fluctuations in industry cause the demands on the banks for credit to be much larger at some seasons than at others. And, of course, the times of large and small demand vary according to the industries in the community.

[4] The trade bill may be discounted by a bank *before* as well as after acceptance by the drawee.

used to a substantial extent in the marketing of staple commodities and this use is likely to grow.[5]

It is not likely that a banker's bill would be used to finance the purchase of shoes in our illustration, but it might be used to finance the purchase of a staple commodity by a manufacturer, such as a purchase of cotton by a cotton mill. When a banker's bill is used, the credit may be arranged by either the buyer or the seller of the goods. Suppose that a cotton mill purchases $20,000 of cotton to fill an order for cotton cloth and that the mill wishes ninety days in which to convert the cotton into cloth. The mill arranges with its bank for a credit authorizing the seller of the cotton to draw on the mill's bank for $20,000 at ninety days sight. The law requires that shipping documents conveying or securing title to the goods must be attached to the draft when it is accepted. The seller ships the cotton and sends the draft with the attached documents to the mill's bank. The bank accepts the draft, sells it in the market,[6] and credits the proceeds to the mill, which uses them to pay the seller of the cotton. In ninety days, when the bill falls due, the mill's bank, of course, must pay it. But the contract of the bank with the mill requires that the mill put the bank in funds to meet the bill one day before maturity. The mill obtains the funds to meet this obligation from the sale of the cotton cloth.

[5] There are four classes of transactions against which national banks are permitted to accept time drafts. They are:

1. the shipment of goods between the United States and foreign countries, between the United States and its dependencies or insular possessions, between foreign countries, or between dependencies or insular possessions of the United States and foreign countries;

2. the storage of readily marketable staples, provided the bill is secured at time of acceptance by a warehouse receipt conveying title to such staples and issued by a party independent of the customer;

3. the shipment of goods within the United States, provided shipping documents conveying title are attached at the time of acceptance;

4. the creation of dollar exchange. A brief explanation of this use will be found in footnote 13 on page 242.

The banks are also limited in the amount of liability which they may incur by acceptances to 50 per cent of their paid up capital and unimpaired surplus, except that the Federal Reserve Board may give a bank special permission to accept up to 100 per cent of its capital and surplus.

[6] The buyer of the bill is likely to be an acceptance dealer, who like the commercial paper house, is a middleman. The acceptance dealers sell to other banks most of the acceptances which they purchase. In the future, many corporations are likely to invest temporarily idle funds in banker's acceptances.

The credit may be arranged by the seller, instead of the buyer, of the cotton. In this case, both a banker's bill and a trade bill are used. The seller arranges with his own bank to accept a draft drawn by him and payable in ninety days. The bank sells the acceptance in the open market and credits the proceeds to the account of the seller. In this way the seller is paid. When the seller draws the bill against his bank, he also draws a second draft — this one upon the buyer of the cotton. The second draft, with shipping documents giving possession of the cotton, is also delivered to the seller's bank which sends the draft and the documents to a correspondent bank in the city where the mill is situated. The correspondent bank presents the bill to the mill for acceptance. Only after accepting the bill does the mill obtain from the correspondent bank the shipping documents which enable it to obtain the cotton from the transportation company. The trade acceptance is held by the seller's bank. It provides, when paid, the funds to enable the bank to meet the draft which it accepted for the seller of the cotton.

In the United States, commercial transactions are usually financed by the sale of promissory notes to banks. On the continent of Europe and in Canada, the bill of exchange is more commonly employed. Of late years, its use has been slowly spreading in the United States. It has several advantages from the standpoint of the seller of goods, the banks, and the community. It is especially convenient to sellers who are engaged in foreign trade or who are making sales at a great distance. The seller can draw the bill and discount it with a banker at the same time that the goods are shipped, attaching the bill of lading to the bill of exchange to give the discounting banker title to the goods until the buyer has accepted the bill or paid it. Thus the seller is not compelled to wait for his money until the buyer receives the shipment. In case the time of transit runs into weeks or months, as it often does in foreign trade, the advantage to the seller is considerable.

To the bank, the trade bill, after acceptance, has the advantage of always being " two-name paper " — that is, two persons are responsible for payment because the law requires the drawer to pay in case the acceptor defaults. A promissory note can be made two-name by having a second person endorse it, but fear of offending a customer and losing his business may prevent a bank from requiring an endorser in some cases where one is really desirable. Furthermore, the acceptance itself gives some indication of the transaction out of which it grows. A bill drawn by a shoe manufacturer upon a retailer of shoes obviously grows out of a sale of shoes by the manufacturer to the retailer. When the bank advances funds on the bill, therefore, it has some assurance that it is financing a legitimate commercial transaction. Bills of exchange often bear upon their face a statement that the obligation of the acceptance arises out of the purchase of goods by the drawee. This indicates that the acceptance is not being used in settlement of past-due accounts. There is nothing on the face of a promissory note, however, to reveal what gives rise to it. For all the bank may know, the borrower may use the funds for purposes quite other than he represents when he offers the note to the bank. Thus the bank may unwittingly finance a highly speculative venture, which, if unsuccessful, will render the maker of the note unable to pay.

The advocates of the trade acceptance assert that it is a valuable device for discouraging reckless buying. When a merchant buys on open book account, there is generally an understanding that he will pay within a stipulated period — thirty days, sixty days, or possibly ninety days. But the seller may be somewhat lax in holding the buyer to the agreement. The seller wishes the future business of the buyer and he may be willing to wait a little longer for his money in order to retain the buyer's good will. Or suppose that the buyer paid cash but that he borrowed the money from his bank on his promissory note. Assume that, when the note falls due, he cannot conveniently meet it. Quite probably he can gain an extension of time by asking his bank to accept a new note in payment for the old one. Loath as the bank may be to do this, it may be even more reluctant to refuse, because he might take offense and transfer his account elsewhere. The ease with which buyers can obtain extensions of time either from sellers or from banks encourages some of them to purchase less conservatively than they should, to purchase more than they can be sure of selling before the expiration of the loan. It is estimated that the overdue accounts of jobbers and manufacturers normally

average about 30 per cent of sales.[7]   Trade bills, on the other
hand, discourage overbuying because they compel the purchaser
to pay for his goods at the stipulated time. It will be recalled
that, when the purchase of shoes was financed by an acceptance,
the funds were advanced by the *manufacturer's,* not the retailer's,
bank. The retailer is under obligation to pay a bank of which he
is not a customer and with which he has no account. He therefore is in no position to request an extension of time and, even
if he did request it, the bank, having no fear of losing an account,
would not hesitate to refuse. Indeed, the retailer does not know
who will present the bill for payment.[8] It may be sold several
times before maturity and it is likely to be held by some one who
has no interest in gaining or retaining the acceptor's good will.[9]

The banker's bill has several important advantages. One
advantage is that it enables a bank to extend credit at times when
it is not able to expand its loans. This is particularly important
in marketing crops. The heavy seasonal movements of crops
often create a demand for more loans than the banks in the agricultural regions can satisfy. Some buyers of wheat who have
need for special grades find it advantageous to supply most of
their needs during the early fall months when the crop is first
coming to the market. Such a buyer may need $50,000 to finance
a purchase of wheat. His bank in Minneapolis may be unable at
this particular time of the year to lend him this amount. But

---

[7] Treman, R. H., *Trade Acceptances* (American Acceptance Council), p. 43.

[8] It is customary to permit the drawee, that is the person upon whom the bill is
drawn, to designate the bank or trust company *at* which the bill shall be payable;
but this does not mean the money is owed *to* the bank at which the bill is payable.

[9] But the very fact that the trade acceptance compels the buyer to be ready to
pay at a definite date has restricted its use in the United States. Competition among
sellers partly takes the form of granting easy and liberal credit terms. Consequently many sellers are reluctant to ask buyers to accept a bill which would compel the customer to make payment without fail at a certain date. They prefer to
treat buyers somewhat more liberally by selling to them on open book account.

The argument that the trade acceptance discourages reckless buying is probably
sound under most circumstances. Nevertheless, it is desirable to notice that the
abuse of the trade acceptance in 1920 positively encouraged reckless buying and
led to excessive accumulations of goods by many merchants. Concerns which had
purchased to the limit of their credit pointed out to sellers that trade drafts could
be discounted on favorable terms. But the advocate of trade acceptances can reply
with some justice that the abuse of the trade acceptance in 1920 was made possible
only because banks and business enterprises in the United States were unfamiliar
with it and did not appreciate the importance of ascertaining the financial condition of drawees.

it can and will accept a draft drawn by him against it and secured by warehouse receipts. By selling the acceptance, the bank enables the customer to obtain the needed funds without advancing them itself.

A second important advantage of the banker's acceptance is that it is more readily salable than the notes or trade acceptances handled by the commercial paper houses. One reason for this is that the credit standing of a bank is better known than that of most business enterprises.[10] The ready marketability of banker's acceptances makes them an extremely important element in the creation of a national discount market — that is, a national market for short-term paper. Such a market is extremely desirable, particularly in a country such as the United States where the seasonal movements of business are pronounced and where agriculture is such an important part of the national economy. A national discount market enables the banks in any section of the country which have idle funds to invest them promptly, to diversify their risks by purchasing paper which arises out of many industries, and to select their paper so as to obtain maturities at the season when they must be ready to meet an increase in the demand for cash. Furthermore, a national discount market enables any bank which has a sudden need for cash to meet it by selling paper in the open market. Because of their superior security and marketability, banker's acceptances are more useful than any other class of paper in making possible a broad and active national discount market.

III. THE EFFECT OF COMMERCIAL CREDIT UPON THE VOLUME OF PURCHASING POWER

When a bank lends on a promissory note or a bill of exchange, it does not usually advance cash. It is more convenient to both

---

[10] Another reason is that the Federal Reserve Banks, in order to develop a market for banker's bills, have stood ready at all times to purchase all the banker's acceptances offered to them provided that the acceptances meet certain requirements. Furthermore, the Reserve Banks have purchased bills at a high price in comparison with the discount rates on other classes of paper. It is also important to notice that the ready marketability of banker's acceptances depends partly upon the fact that only a relatively few of the larger and better known banks offer acceptances. Indeed, despite the rapid increase in the total volume of bank acceptances, there has been a tendency for the number of banks which offer such acceptances to decrease. In 1917 and 1918, approximately 500 banks in the United States were offering acceptances. By 1922, the number had dropped to about 375 and late in 1927 to about 165. *Commerce and Finance*, December 14, 1927, v. XVI, p. 2563.

bank and borrower for the bank to give credit on its books in the form of a deposit account against which the borrower can draw checks. From his standpoint, of course, a checking account is equivalent to cash. This custom of giving checking accounts instead of cash for promissory notes and bills of exchange seems a trivial detail and yet probably no practice in the conduct of modern business has more momentous consequences.

It creates, for example, a peculiar relationship between the deposits of a bank and its loans. The man in the street is accustomed to think that banks lend *out* their deposits, that they lend money which has been deposited in them for safe-keeping or convenience. To some extent this is done, but it is more accurate to say that banks lend *in* their deposits, because deposits are mainly the *results* instead of the *sources* of loans. A bank buys a promissory note for $1,000 payable in four months. It pays $980 for it, giving the seller a checking account for that amount. On the asset side of the bank's balance sheet, the item " loans and discounts " is increased by $1,000 and on the liability side, the item " deposits " is increased by $980. The difference between the two is credited to " profit and loss." When the balance sheet is drawn up, the profit balance in this account appears as " undivided profits." Because of this dependence of deposits upon loans, it will be found on examining the balance sheets of commercial banks that, as business activity increases or decreases, loans and deposits rise or fall together. Because too of this relationship between loans and deposits, a law requiring banks to maintain a minimum reserve against *deposits* limits the amount which banks may lend.

But far overshadowing all other results of the practice of giving checking accounts in exchange for promissory notes and bills of exchange, is its effect upon the volume of currency. If banks simply lent the money deposited in them by their customers, the extension of credit would not increase the number of dollars in circulation. But when banks grant credit by creating or adding to deposits subject to check, more is involved than a transfer of dollars already in existence. *New dollars are created.* Suppose, for example, that a number of banks possess a total of $1,000,000 in cash. If every borrower insisted upon taking with him the money which he borrowed, it would obviously be impossible for the loans of these banks to exceed $1,000,000. But if borrowers are willing to accept checking accounts instead of cash, the way is paved for the banks to lend more than they possess. Assume that the banks lend $5,000,000, giving the borrowers checking accounts for that amount and keeping their $1,000,000 in reserve to meet demands for cash. Evidently there has been a net increase of four million in the number of dollars. It is true that the new dollars are not stamped out of gold. They are *credit* dollars and they are created by the stroke of the pen rather than by dies and stamping machines, but their purchasing power is no less than that of the dollars coined at the government mint. In other words, the principal way in which dollars are created in modern economic society is by borrowing. This means that the number of dollars in existence at any particular time depends upon the willingness and ability of business men to borrow and the willingness and ability of banks to lend. The volume of purchasing power fluctuates with men's state of mind; the growth of pessimism may suddenly throw millions of men out of work or the growth of confidence may create thousands of jobs over night.

But by what sleight of hand is it possible for banks to create dollars by the stroke of the pen? Let it be repeated that it can be done only because borrowers are willing to accept checking accounts instead of cash. But why does this make it possible? Will not the borrowers, by drawing checks against their accounts, quickly exhaust the bank's funds? It is true that the borrowers soon draw against their accounts, *but their checks do not necessarily cause the bank to lose cash*. For the recipients of the checks, in many cases, prefer a checking account in a bank to cash in their own possession. Hence, instead of cashing the checks, they deposit them in the bank. Every bank, therefore, is constantly having checks drawn against it but is also receiving from its customers checks drawn in their favor. To illustrate how the disbursement of cash is avoided, let us suppose that A borrows $1,000 from his bank and receives, as a result, a credit for that amount on its books. He draws a check to pay a debt of $1,000 which he owes B. B happens to have his account at the same bank. He deposits the check which A has given him, the bank debits A on its books for $1,000 and credits B with the same amount. Simply by entries in the books, A has been able to use his loan to pay his debt, and the bank has not been compelled to advance a cent of cash.

The process is essentially the same if A and B keep their money in different banks. B deposits the check in his bank which credits him with the amount and presents it to A's bank for payment. But A's bank does not necessarily give B's bank cash for the check. In all probability, it has received from its depositors many checks drawn against B's bank. Each bank presents all the checks which it holds against the other, and the difference, usually a small fraction of the total, is settled in cash.

How much more than their cash resources banks can safely lend depends upon circumstances which are beyond the scope of a general and non-technical inquiry such as we are making. Our banking system *as a whole* can ordinarily lend from seven to ten times its cash resources. This, however, does not mean that *each bank* can immediately lend from $7,000 to $10,000 for every $1,000 addition to its cash. This is an important fact and it is desirable to see why it is so. Suppose that it is considered desirable to maintain one dollar of reserve for every eight dollars of loans. Suppose also that all banks have lent up to this limit. Bank A now obtains an addition of $2,000 to its cash. It does not follow that bank A can now expand its loans by $16,000. But the gain of $2,000 in cash may enable the banking system as a whole to add $16,000 to its loans. In order to explain the difference between the ability of a single bank and of the banking system as a whole to expand loans, let us assume that the bank A, after receiving the $2,000, makes a loan of $2,000. The borrower draws three checks of $500. One is deposited in bank B, the second in bank C, the third in bank D. Bank A has lost $1,500 of the $2,000 addition to its cash. Obviously the gain of $2,000 in cash does not enable the bank to expand its loans by $16,000. But banks B, C, and D each have gained $500 in cash and bank A still has $500 of the $2,000 which it gained. Assume now that bank A expands its loans by another $500 and that each of the other three banks, because of its gain of $500 in cash, increases its loans by $500. Assume also that the borrower of bank A draws a check which is deposited in bank B, the borrower of bank B a check which is deposited in bank C, the borrower of bank C a check which is deposited in bank D, and the borrower of bank D a check which is deposited in bank A. Each of the four banks has increased its loans by $500 but none of the four has lost any cash. Since a ratio of one to eight between reserves and loans is considered safe, each of the four banks is still in a position to expand its loans. If each does so simultaneously and if the checks drawn against them are deposited in about equal amounts in all of the banks, the expansion of loans can go on until each of the four has increased its loans by $4,000 — or $16,000 for the banking system. At this point the ratio of one to eight between reserves and loans will be reached.

This hypothetical case makes clear why an individual bank does not have the same power to expand its loans as does the banking system as a whole. No bank can for long expand its loans faster than do the other banks — it soon finds itself checked because the more rapid increase in its loans causes it to lose cash to the other banks. But if all banks expand their loans more or less simultaneously and at about the same rate, the expansion may continue for some time before the limit of safety is reached. The increase in loans causes the banking system to lose some cash to the rest of the country but, if most people are in the habit of keeping their money in banks, the decrease in the cash holdings of the banks is not likely to be large.

In places where banks are numerous, it is cumbersome for each to settle claims with every other one separately. Clearing houses have, therefore, been established to which each bank brings its claims against the others and at which the amounts due to and from each are determined. For the difference between the amounts due to and from it, each bank pays or receives cash. When the banks are in different cities, the machinery for cancelling claims is more complicated, but the principle is the same. A national clearing system recently established by the Federal Reserve Banks greatly improved the facilities for cancelling claims originating in different parts of the country.

By lending far more than their holdings of cash, banks impose upon themselves the necessity of keeping their assets highly liquid. Borrowers are constantly drawing upon their checking accounts.

This means that the banks are receiving a certain demand for cash. They cannot meet this demand indefinitely unless checks and cash are deposited with them as fast as claims for cash are presented for payment.

To assure that they will receive cash and checks about as rapidly as checks are presented for payment, conservatively managed banks *make most of their loans for short periods only and in most cases require payment and not merely renewal on maturity*. The shorter the average duration of loans, the more rapidly cash and checks flow back into the bank. Assume, for illustration, that a bank has lent a total of $900,000, that each loan is for three months, and that an equal amount of the loans matures on each day. Evidently the loans would be repaid at the rate of $300,000 a month or about $10,000 a day, and the process of repayment would enable the bank to meet a daily demand for cash of about $10,000 without diminution of its cash resources. If, however, the loans ran twelve instead of three months, they would be paid back at the rate of $75,000 a month or $2,500 a day and the bank would be in a position to meet a daily demand for cash of only about $2,500.

Of course, the fact that a loan runs for only three or four months does not necessarily mean that it will be repaid in that time. To assure that their loans are really liquid, banks must make certain that the loans are used to buy goods which can be turned into cash quickly and without great loss or that they are secured by readily marketable stocks or bonds. Of late years there has been a conspicuous increase in the latter type of loan — loans secured by stocks or bonds. Between December, 1921, and December, 1929, about 700 large banks which have nearly half of the banking resources of the country increased their loans on securities from $3,765,000,000 to $7,968,000,000, or 112 per cent. All other loans increased about 24 per cent.[11] Loans to provide working capital are not as a rule secured by stocks or bonds. The rapid increase of loans on securities probably meant in the main an increase in borrowing for stock market and real estate speculation. But it is also probably true that commercial banks are financing the acquisition of large amounts of permanent equipment. Banks could not afford to make short-term

[11] Federal Reserve Board, *Sixteenth Annual Report*, 1929, p. 110.

loans directly upon the equipment itself, because it turns itself into cash too slowly. If, however, an enterprise can furnish easily salable stocks and bonds as security, it may finance the purchase of machines or other equipment by a series of short-term loans, a new one being negotiated in time to provide funds with which to pay off the maturing loan.[12]

It has been pointed out that when a bank deals with regular customers, it sometimes finds it difficult to insist upon liquidation of loans at maturity and to avoid granting renewals. The customer expects to be accommodated and will take his business elsewhere unless he is. For this reason, banks do not necessarily achieve sufficient liquidity by restricting their loans to short periods. To assure that they can add substantially to their cash on very short notice, banks invest part of their resources in high-grade and readily marketable bonds, in bank acceptances, or in commercial paper purchased from commercial paper houses. In addition, country banks protect themselves by keeping funds on deposit in other banks in the large financial centers. On these deposits, a small rate of interest is received. Finally, the banks in the financial centers and, to a less extent, other banks lend money at "call" on the speculative exchanges. These loans are terminable at a moment's notice on the demand of the lender. All of these forms of investment may be regarded as a secondary reserve which the bank can use to increase its cash reserve whenever necessary.

IV. The Social Utility of Commercial Credit

In examining how banks reduce the necessity of paying out cash, we incidentally became familiar with an important service performed by commercial credit. What an intolerable nuisance it would be if it were necessary, whenever one had a payment to make, to send actual cash! By the use of checks which are cancelled against one another to settle indebtedness between banks,

---

[12] Many concerns regularly plow back a considerable proportion of their earnings into the business. Short-term loans to be spent for permanent equipment are frequently obtained for the purpose of anticipating the reinvestment of income. They are paid off with the income which it has been decided shall be put back into the business. But purchasing new equipment with borrowed money in anticipation of a reinvestment of earnings means that at any given moment industry has more permanent equipment than it otherwise would have. Hence short-term loans in anticipation of the reinvestment of earnings add to the equipment of industry.

vast payments are made possible with a minimum of trouble, risk, and expense.

Not only does the credit system make it possible to do a vast volume of business within a country with a small transfer of cash, but it does the same thing between nations. The several methods of making payments in international trade need not be described in detail. The essential point is that the banks of each country maintain accounts with banks in other countries against which they issue drafts and letters of credit to persons who wish to send funds abroad. As the banks are constantly diminishing their balances abroad by the sale of drafts and letters of credit, they need a way of replenishing them. They might ship bullion, but this expense can usually be avoided by purchasing bills of exchange drawn by domestic exporters upon foreign importers. An American exporter, for example, who sells cotton to a British importer probably obtains his money by the use of two drafts — one, a banker's bill drawn against his bank in New York (or elsewhere in the United States), and the other, a trade bill drawn against the British importer. After shipping the cotton, the exporter presents the two bills, with the bill of lading and other shipping documents attached, to his bank — the banker's bill for acceptance and the trade bill for collection. The bank accepts the first bill, sells it in the open market, and credits the exporter with the proceeds. The bank sends the trade bill, with the documents attached, to its London correspondent, which presents it to the importer for acceptance. After accepting the bill, he is given possession of the cotton. If the American bank wishes cash in its London account at once, it instructs its correspondent to sell the bill immediately after it is accepted. Otherwise the British bank holds the bill until maturity when it presents it to the cotton importer for payment, crediting the sum received to the account of the American bank. In this way the bank obtains the funds to meet the payment on the acceptance.

But the funds which the bank obtains are not in the United States, where it must make payment on its acceptance, but in England. From the standpoint of our present discussion, this is the interesting part of the transaction. After the bank has paid its own acceptance and received payment from the British importer on his acceptance, it has (disregarding the commission it receives for its services) the same amount of cash as before, but it has less cash in New York and more in London. It has used the transaction as a means of increasing its balance in London without shipping bullion and thus it has put itself in a position to sell more drafts and letters of credit to Americans who wish to make payments abroad.[13]

Most important of all, however, is the effect of commercial credit upon the production of goods. In some ways commercial credit retards output because, as we shall see presently, it both increases the susceptibility of the economic system to business depressions and intensifies the severity of depressions when they come. At the moment, however, we are concerned with the ways in which credit tends to increase production.

It seems strange that merely creating more dollars should affect the output of industry. Production appears to be a matter of the number of men employed and of the technical equipment at their disposal. Does commercial credit affect either? Suppose that it were not possible to obtain working capital by short-term loans. Would fewer wage earners be employed or would employment be more intermittent? Possibly the workers would have to take lower wages in *dollars* than they now do.[14] But is there any reason to suppose that the mere lack of commercial credit would prevent workers from finding employment with *somebody* at *some* wage, even if very low in dollars?

There are at least four general ways in which commercial credit affects the output of industry. It increases the output of seasonal industries by enabling plants to produce in anticipation

[13] The seasonal movements of both exports and imports are pronounced and do not necessarily coincide. Consequently American importers may be demanding funds to make large payments abroad at times when American exporters are furnishing few bills with which the banks here can build up their balances abroad. Banks may meet this situation without the shipment of bullion by drawing time drafts against their foreign correspondents. Upon acceptance, the bills are sold abroad and the proceeds credited to the accounts of the American banks abroad. Several months later the American banks must provide their foreign correspondents with funds to meet the acceptances. By this time the American banks expect that the seasonal increase in American exports will create a large supply of trade bills drawn by American exporters upon foreign importers. By purchasing these bills, the American banks make the necessary increases in their balances abroad.

[14] The lower money wages might not have lower purchasing power because, as will be pointed out presently, creating credit dollars tends to make all prices higher.

of future orders. Were it not possible to borrow on a considerable scale in order to purchase raw materials and labor, many enterprises could not operate during the dull season. Both men and machines would be idle until orders came in and the community would lose the production.

It is very common for business enterprises to be confronted with difficulties which seriously reduce production but which can be eliminated by the expenditure of a few hundreds or thousands of dollars. A farmer's crop may be threatened with ruin by a pest. If he lacks funds to buy poisons and cannot borrow from a bank or obtain poison on credit, his crop will be lost. Credit, either from his bank or from a merchant, will enable him to save his crop. The community, as well as the farmer, is a gainer.

Commercial credit affects the output of goods by opening business opportunities to men who could not otherwise take advantage of them because of lack of funds. This is not an unmixed gain, however, because the possibility of entering some businesses with a small amount of borrowed capital causes them to become crowded with more enterprises than are really needed. The overdevelopment of some branches of retailing, such as the grocery business, is partly attributable to the fact that stocks of goods can be easily obtained on credit. But there are also advantages in having productive opportunities open to a large number of people. It reduces the danger that men will be compelled to work as employees when they would be more efficient as independent business men. In addition, the more people who enter a business, the abler are likely to be those who survive in the competition and in whose hands, therefore, the direction of production becomes concentrated.

Of great importance is the effect of commercial credit upon the quantities of tools, machines, and other equipment available for the production of goods. Commercial credit increases the equipment, and hence the output, of industry in two ways. In the first place, short-term loans, as we have seen, are often used by business enterprises to finance the acquisition of permanent equipment, and, during recent years, it has become increasingly common for investors to buy securities with money obtained by short-term loans and then to pay back the loans out of current income. The practice received an impetus during the War, when

Liberty bonds were bought and paid for in this way. To the extent that enterprises use commercial credit to purchase equipment or investors use it to purchase securities, industry has a greater number of buildings, machines, and tools. In the second place, commercial credit releases funds for investment in permanent equipment. If enterprises could not obtain working capital by borrowing the dollars created by the banks, they would be compelled to rely upon the savings of investors. To this extent the savings would not be available to purchase the technological apparatus of industry, and the quantities of buildings, machines, and tools which industry could purchase would be less.[15]

V. Some Problems Which Commercial Credit Creates

We have already learned that prominent among the characteristics of our economic order are the great dependence of the economic fortunes of each person and enterprise upon the prosperity of other persons and enterprises, and the great risks of doing business. Interdependence, we have seen, is largely a product of specialization, and business risks are in great degree a result of the difficulty in forecasting supply and demand. But both interdependence and business risks are made more pronounced by the practice of doing business upon the basis of promises to pay instead of cash down. Obviously, when an enterprise sells goods on credit, it assumes a risk of not being paid. Furthermore, when the funds used by a business establishment for working capital are largely borrowed on short-term loans, there is risk that the enterprise may fail because of inability to convert goods promptly into cash. And when the assets of nearly every concern consist, in substantial degree, of the promises of others to pay, it is plain that the solvency of each firm depends upon the ability of other firms to pay their debts.[16] B's solvency depends upon A's ability to pay, C's upon

---

[15] The relation between commercial credit and the creation of capital will be discussed in more detail in Chapter XXVI on The Accumulation and the Reward of Capital.

[16] At the time that credit is extended, the debtor's ability to meet his obligation usually appears to be good. But in the several months which intervene before the maturity of the indebtedness, many things can happen which affect the debtor's ability to pay. In prosperous times there are few failures among firms of good credit standing, but in years of depression many enterprises fail which, up to the time of insolvency, were regarded as good risks. The figures of a leading credit agency show

whether B can pay, D's upon whether C can pay, and so on. Thus the use of commercial credit binds the whole business world closely together. If one enterprise miscalculates supply or demand and purchases more raw material than it can use or makes more goods than it can sell at a profit, other concerns which have sold it goods on credit or have lent it money may find their solvency affected. The interdependence introduced into modern industry by commercial credit causes every miscalculation of business managers to have far-reaching repercussions and makes our economic system extraordinarily subject to derangement. Plainly every business enterprise has an interest that credit shall not be granted too liberally. Every period of extravagant credit extension ends in a general crash which affects the conservative enterprises as well as the others, for, when the firms which granted credits most liberally cannot collect from their debtors and pay their creditors, the concerns which were more conservative also find difficulty in meeting their obligations.

Few characteristics of modern economic society have attracted more attention than the alternating periods of boom and depression which are known as the business cycle. These periods would occur even if transactions were all for cash, but commercial credit makes both the ups and the downs of business far greater than they otherwise would be.

It is obvious that if enterprises had to pay cash and had to pay with their own rather than with borrowed money, they could not greatly increase their demand for goods at times when a rise in prices seemed imminent. Demand would be limited by the amount of cash which business men had to spend. They might, it is true, spend dollars faster at some times than at others, but, nevertheless, demand, being limited by the amount of cash on hand, would be relatively stable and prices would be correspondingly steady.

Credit, however, makes possible large and sudden increases in the demand for goods — and, consequently, in prices — be-

---

that in 1889, 1890, 1891, years of good business, concerns with good or very good credit comprised 7.8, 7.9, 8.8, and 7.0 per cent of all failures. In 1893, 1894, 1895, and 1896, years of crisis or depression, 30.3, 29.0, 27.7, and 28.3 per cent of all failures were firms of good or very good credit standing.

cause it makes possible on a moment's notice an enormous increase in the number of dollars. It is not necessary to dig down into the ground for the gold out of which to make more dollars. All that is necessary is that the banks possess enough cash to warrant a substantial expansion in their loans. In case the banks are able to make large increases in their loans, business men who acquire the conviction that prices are about to rise and that it is an advantageous time to buy, can almost instantly obtain from the banks millions of dollars with which to act on this conviction. But the banks, creating dollars by the stroke of the pen, can add to the currency far faster than factories and farmers can add to the supply of goods; consequently prices are likely to rise. Output soon reaches the limits set by plant capacities, but business men do not cease demanding credit. On the contrary, the large profits which they have made from the advance in prices renders them more optimistic than ever concerning the immediate future, and leads them to expect still higher prices. Consequently, they continue to demand more dollars from the banks. With the output of goods more or less stationary and with more and more credit dollars being placed at the disposal of business men, prices are likely to increase more rapidly than ever. It is extremely important to notice that the cumulative increase in prices is made possible largely because business men, when in a mood to buy more goods, are able to obtain dollars from the banks with which to make the purchases. Were it not for commercial credit, business men might have the *desire* to spend more but not the *ability* to do so.

Sooner or later, for reasons which will be discussed in Chapter XX, prosperity turns into depression. Now we find credit, which had previously accentuated the intensity of the boom, increasing the severity of the depression. During the period of prosperity, enterprises borrowed heavily from banks and made large purchases on credit. But the money was borrowed usually for short periods. As long as demand is active, business establishments have no difficulty in selling goods promptly enough to pay their debts. If demand were to continue brisk, the debts would cause no trouble. But demand and prices do not increase indefinitely and as soon as they show signs of falling, the large credits extended during the boom period cause trouble.

Buyers, anticipating lower prices, delay purchasing as long as possible and take only enough for their immediate needs. Sellers, finding difficulty in selling, and needing funds to meet maturing loans, cut prices. This, however, simply encourages buyers to hold off longer in hope of still lower prices. Were it not necessary for business enterprises to pay for goods purchased on credit or to repay money borrowed from banks, they could take their time about selling. The supply of goods thrown on the market would not rise so suddenly, and buyers would be less strongly disposed to delay purchasing. As it is, the very credits which made possible the increase in business activity and the rise of prices now help bring about business stagnation, precipitous decline of prices, and unemployment. The drop in prices is so great that many firms are unable to realize enough from the sale of goods to meet their obligations and hence become insolvent. Other enterprises pay their debts only by drawing upon their capital. Concerns often find themselves with less capital after a cycle of prosperity and depression than before. Their ability to produce may be impaired for some time because they lack the funds to make full use of their equipment and because their impaired credit limits their ability to borrow.

The drop in prices and the severity of the depression are accentuated by the fact that, during the period of rising prices, business enterprises purchased goods in excess of their immediate needs with the expectation of selling later at higher prices. This speculative hoarding is made possible, of course, largely by the credit system. It is easy to see how the hoarding of goods during prosperity intensifies the subsequent depression. In the first place, it accentuates the drop in prices and the losses of business houses because it increases the quantity of goods which must be converted into cash in order to meet outstanding indebtedness. In the second place, it increases the volume of unemployment and hence decreases the rate at which goods are consumed. Because retailers purchased beyond their immediate needs when prices were rising, the depression finds them with large stocks of goods on hand. Not until retailers have nearly emptied their shelves can wholesalers get large orders. But the warehouses of wholesalers were also filled during prosperity, and not until the wholesalers have nearly emptied their warehouses can manufacturers obtain large orders. During all this time, while retailers are emptying their overloaded shelves and wholesalers their over-crowded warehouses, manufacturers can give employment to only a small part of their forces. In other words, thousands of men must go without work because, during the period of pros-perity, retailers and wholesalers, by purchasing goods on credit or paying for them with borrowed funds, were able to fill their shelves and warehouses too full. And the very fact that many men are out of work makes it take longer for wholesalers and retailers to sell their surplus goods.

VI. The Need for the Control of Commercial Credit

It is perfectly clear that there is such a thing as overexpan-sion of credit, but it is not easy to say just where the line between legitimate expansion and overexpansion should be drawn. The test of what is overexpansion and what is not varies with business conditions. Because credit is used to finance the production of goods, an increase in the volume of credit is usually necessary in order to make possible an expansion in the output of industry. In general, however, any tendency for credit dollars to increase more rapidly than the physical production of industry is to be viewed with great suspicion. For if dollars for buying goods are created faster than the supply of goods is increased, prices are likely to rise and the speculative hoarding of commodities which usually has such a disastrous aftermath is likely to set in. This does not mean that an expansion of credit may never be desirable when the physical volume of production is stationary or diminishing, but it does mean that in such cases there should be special reasons to justify the expansion.

Prior to the establishment of the Federal Reserve system in 1914, the amount of credit granted by banks was restricted prin-cipally by the legal requirement, imposed by the federal govern-ment upon the national banks and by the states upon the state banks, that a certain reserve be maintained against deposits.[17] The national banks were divided into three classes, known as country banks, reserve city banks, and central reserve city banks. The central reserve city banks were the national banks in New

---

[17] The ratio of reserves to deposits is known as " the reserve ratio."

York, Chicago, and St. Louis; the reserve city banks were the national banks in about forty cities known as reserve cities; and the country banks were all other national banks. The country banks were required to keep a cash reserve of 15 per cent against deposits but were permitted to keep three-fifths of it on deposit in reserve city or central reserve city banks. The reserve city banks were required to keep a reserve of 25 per cent, half of which might be kept on deposit in central reserve city banks. The central reserve city banks were required to keep a reserve of 25 per cent in their own vaults.

With the important exception of a legally required reserve, control of the volume of credit was left to freedom of enterprise.[18] But freedom of enterprise cannot be trusted to prevent the overexpansion of credit. As banks derive their profits principally from lending money, they are strongly disposed, when left to themselves, to lend as much as they safely can. If they are to be restrained from expanding loans when the situation demands that credit be restricted, some group — depositors, borrowers, investors, or seekers of employment in banks — must have an interest in discriminating against the banks which disregard the need for restriction. But who has an interest in doing this? Certainly not investors or depositors. Their interest simply is to obtain the best possible return on their funds and they will invest or deposit money in the bank which offers the largest and surest return regardless of the policy which it pursues in extending credit. Job seekers are interested in salaries and conditions of employment and are quite ready to work for the bank, whatever its credit policy, which offers the highest salaries and the best conditions. Least of all are prospective borrowers likely to discriminate against banks which fail to restrict credit. On the contrary, borrowers are likely to discriminate in *favor* of them. Indeed, the fear that customers will take their business elsewhere if loans are not granted liberally has caused many banks to exercise less caution during times of great credit expansion than they otherwise would. Consequently, under the old national banking system, the banks had every incentive to lend as much as the law permitted and no incentive to limit the expansion of credit as soon as the general business situation demanded it.

[18] There were other restrictions on the *kind* of loans which banks might make.

The tendency of the banks to lend nearly all that their reserves permitted created two difficulties. The less serious but the more frequent was a seasonal shortage of funds which occurred nearly every year in the fall and sometimes at other seasons. The harvesting and sale of crops and fall buying caused people to withdraw money from the banks. This, of course, by reducing their reserves, diminished the ability of the banks to lend. At precisely this season of the year, however, the demand for credit increased, because manufacturers were producing for the fall and the Christmas trade, and wholesalers and retailers were laying in their fall and winter stocks. The result was that many business men were unable to obtain as much credit as they needed and that they were compelled to pay higher rates for loans. In order to meet the seasonal demand for cash and credit, banks were compelled to reduce the amount of money loaned on the stock exchange. This compelled speculators who had purchased stocks with borrowed funds to sell their securities. The result was often a sharp and sudden drop in stock prices which was alarming to owners of securities and to many business men who were accustomed to regard the stock market as a barometer of business prospects.

The tendency of the banks under the old national banking system to lend all that the law permitted prevented them from temporarily extending loans during the critical periods which usually follow the collapse of a general boom in business. This was the second and the more serious defect in the old national banking system. Temporary expansion of credit is needed after the collapse of prosperity in order to save firms from bankruptcy by giving them loans upon goods which, in the prevailing condition of the market, could not be sold except at ruinously low prices. It will be recalled that the essential difficulty of most concerns during times of crisis is inability to sell goods fast enough to obtain the funds needed to meet maturing obligations. It is this difficulty that creates the desperate desire to sell which, in conjunction with the general disinclination to buy, drives prices down to ruinous levels. Clearly one way to alleviate the crisis and to reduce the drop in prices is to enable enterprises to meet their obligations without immediately selling their goods. Banks can do this by granting them loans. Thus it is apparent that our credit machinery should be so constructed that it is able to meet the extraordinary demand for credit which accompanies every period of crisis.

But the difficulty under the old national banking system was even more serious than the failure to make possible an expansion of credit when prosperity ended. Not only were the banks unable to expand credit *but some of them felt compelled to contract it.* They feared that, in the general suspicion and mistrust which prevails during such times, their solvency might be doubted and runs might start on them. Consequently, they endeavored to increase their reserves beyond the legally required amounts. This they did by curtailing loans and by accumulating cash. During the crisis of 1907, some banks went so far as to advertise how much their reserves exceeded the legal minimum.[19] The situation was aggravated by the pyramiding of reserves. It will be recalled that the law permitted the country banks to keep part of their reserves on deposit in banks in reserve and central reserve cities. This made it possible for a dollar to count as part of the reserves of two banks — of the bank which had deposited it and of the bank which held it. When the crisis occurred, the country and reserve city banks, fearing runs, withdrew some of the money which they had on deposit in other banks. This did not increase the reserves of the banks which withdrew their money but it did decrease the reserves of the banks which had held the money and it compelled these banks to reduce their loans.

VII. THE FEDERAL RESERVE SYSTEM

The control over the volume of credit which was lacking under the old national banking system is now provided, to some extent, at least, by the Federal Reserve system. This represents one of the most notable attempts of the day to substitute conscious control of economic activity for the unplanned results of unguided forces.

[19] In order to conserve their reserves, some banks suspended cash payments and met demands for cash with some form of scrip — such as clearing house certificates that would be honored as cash by other banks in the clearing house and by some merchants. The suspension of cash payments naturally tended to intensify the alarm and also to make it more difficult for the banking system to increase its reserves by making many persons unwilling to deposit their cash in banks.

The Federal Reserve system consists of three principal parts: twelve Federal Reserve Banks and their branches, the Federal Reserve Board which supervises and coördinates their activities, and the member banks. Every bank which operates under a charter from the national government must be a member of the Reserve system, and state banks and trust companies may join by complying with certain requirements. Although less than one-tenth of the state banks and trust companies are members, these possess over half the resources of all such institutions.

The country is divided into twelve Federal Reserve districts each with its own Reserve Bank.[20] Each Reserve Bank is owned by the member banks in its district. But although the banks own all of the capital stock of the Reserve Banks, they do not completely control them.[21] Three of the nine directors of each Reserve Bank are appointed by the Federal Reserve Board and the activities of the Reserve Banks are subject in many respects to control by the Board. Six of the nine directors of each Reserve Bank are elected by the member banks. In voting, the banks are divided into three groups, one composed of the smallest banks, a second of the middle-sized banks, and a third of the largest banks. Each group elects two directors. Thus the small banks are assured representation. Only three of the directors may be officers or directors of other banks. At least three, and usually a majority, are representatives of manufacturing, commerce, or agriculture. The directors elect the officers of the Reserve Bank, determine its policies, and establish, subject to approval by the Federal Reserve Board, the rates which it charges member banks for loans. All profits, after setting aside the surplus provided in the law and after paying the member banks 6 per cent on their stock, go to the United States Treasury.

Individuals may neither deposit money with the Reserve Banks nor borrow from them — they are bankers' banks. They receive deposits from banks which are members of the Federal Reserve system and they lend money to them. It is from their

[20] Federal Reserve Banks are located in the following cities: Boston, New York, Philadelphia, Cleveland, Richmond, Atlanta, Chicago, St. Louis, Minneapolis, Kansas City, Dallas, and San Francisco. In addition, there are over twenty branches of Federal Reserve Banks and several foreign agencies.

[21] Each member bank may be required to invest 6 per cent of its capital and surplus in the Reserve Bank of its district.

function of holding the reserves of the member banks that the Reserve Banks derive their name. The law does not permit a member bank to count cash in its own vaults as part of the reserve which it must keep against deposits. Only funds on deposit in the Reserve Bank of its district count as its reserve.[22] Member banks which wish to increase their reserves or to obtain more cash may do so by borrowing from the Reserve Banks. This they do by rediscounting with the Federal Reserve Bank commercial paper — promissory notes and bills of exchange — which they have already discounted for their own customers. The paper must conform to certain requirements concerning the date of maturity and the nature of the transaction which gives rise to it, and the borrowing bank must, of course, make itself liable for payment by endorsing it.[23] But the business of the Reserve

---

[22] All member banks must maintain a reserve of 3 per cent against time deposits. The Federal Reserve system retains the old distinction between country banks, reserve city banks, and central reserve city banks. Against demand deposits, country banks are required to keep a reserve of 7 per cent; reserve city banks, of 10 per cent; and central reserve city banks, of 13 per cent.

[23] The paper must arise out of " actual commercial transactions." Commercial transactions are so defined that notes, drafts, or bills covering merely investments or issued or drawn for the purpose of carrying or trading in stocks, bonds, or other investment securities, except bonds and notes of the government of the United States, are ineligible for rediscount. At the time that the paper is rediscounted, it must have a maturity not to exceed 90 days, except that agricultural paper may have a maturity not to exceed nine months. Only about one-fourth of the paper held by the member banks meets these requirements.

The theory back of the rules of eligibility is (1) that the volume of eligible paper should rise and fall with seasonal and cyclical changes in the physical volume of production but that it should not be affected by changes in the volume of speculation and (2) that the paper should be " self-liquidating " — that is, that it should be used to finance the purchase or production of goods which could be readily sold in order to provide funds to pay off the paper. In other words, the theory is that when more credit is needed to finance an increase in production, the banks should automatically be in a position to provide it but a rise in the volume of speculation should not automatically provide the banks with a supply of paper which might be rediscounted to finance a still larger volume of speculation.

It is obvious that in at least one important respect the eligibility requirements are not consistent with the theory. Notes on which customers have borrowed to hold or to deal in government securities may be rediscounted by the bank which holds them provided, of course, the date of maturity is not more than 90 days. But it is obvious that the volume of obligations issued by the government has no close connection with the currency needs of the country. And however desirable somewhat narrow eligibility requirements may be, it is important to realize that the eligibility requirements alone can do little to assure that the volume of credit will rise and fall with the rise and fall of physical production. The volume of credit must always be controlled in the main by other devices. Indeed, it is practically impossible, merely through general eligibility rules, to prevent the rediscounting of paper which is used

Banks is not exclusively with the member banks, for, in addition to rediscounting commercial paper for member banks, the Reserve Banks are permitted to buy and sell obligations of the government and banker's and trade acceptances in the open market.[24]

Just as the law requires member banks to keep a certain reserve against deposits, so it also requires the Federal Reserve Banks to maintain reserves of not less than 35 per cent against *their* deposits. These reserves must consist of gold or lawful money.[25] To enable the Reserve Banks to meet the demands upon them for cash without making great inroads upon their reserves, they are permitted to issue notes, known as Federal Reserve notes, which circulate as hand-to-hand money. In fact, these notes are now the most common variety of paper money in circulation. They are secured by commercial paper equal to 60 per cent of their face value and, in addition, by a 40 per cent gold reserve.

The general direction of the Federal Reserve system is in the hands of the Federal Reserve Board. It is composed of eight members appointed by the President with the approval of the Senate. Six devote their entire time to the work. The other two are the Secretary of the Treasury and the Comptroller of the Currency.[26] The Board must approve the rediscount rates established by the directors of each Reserve Bank before they are put into effect;[27] it passes upon the salaries of the officers and em-

---

to finance speculation. One of the most widespread and dangerous forms of speculation is, as we have seen, the accumulation of large inventories in anticipation of higher prices. And yet paper used for this purpose may be eligible for rediscount.

[24] But they are not permitted to purchase corporate securities or promissory notes in the open market.

[25] That is, money which is legal tender.

[26] It is regarded as unfortunate by some students of the Reserve system that the Secretary of the Treasury is a member of the Board. In fact, one of the members of the board, Mr. Miller, testified during 1928 before the House committee on banking and currency that the Secretary should not be a member. The Secretary is interested primarily in the fiscal problems of the government rather than in the needs created by the general business situation. When the government is contemplating large borrowing or refunding operations, the Secretary is under great temptation to use his influence for low interest rates, even though the general business situation demands that the expansion of credit be discouraged.

[27] There has been doubt as to precisely what authority the Federal Reserve Board possesses over rediscount rates. Does the Board simply have authority to veto changes of rediscount rates which the Reserve Banks initiate or may it order the

ployees of the Reserve Banks and under certain conditions may remove any officer and director; it defines the classes of loans which the law, in general terms, says Reserve Banks may make; it may require one Reserve Bank to lend to another which is short of funds. But the Board does not pass upon the individual loans which a Reserve Bank makes, or prescribe when, how much, or how little it shall lend to a member bank. Nor can the Board compel a Reserve Bank to lend to a member bank or prevent it from doing so.

The policies which the Federal Reserve system has developed in the course of nearly two decades naturally include some which could scarcely have been contemplated by most of the persons who participated in creating the Reserve system. In fact, it is probable that few of the persons who were most active in planning the system had a clear vision of the possibilities of the machinery which they were bringing into existence. Most of them believed that they were simply creating an instrument which would prevent the acute shortages of credit at certain seasons of the year and at times of financial crisis. It did not occur to them that they were creating an instrument which might also be used to stabilize business by checking the excessive expansion of credit during periods of prosperity. The idea that business could and should be stabilized commanded almost no popular attention when the Federal Reserve Act was passed in 1913. During the early years of its existence, the Reserve authorities made little attempt to check the expansion of credit during times of prosperity — in fact, during the war period, the Reserve Banks made credit easier rather than more difficult to obtain. The disastrous results of this policy have led the Reserve authorities to attempt what many people regard as an unauthorized function — to check the expansion of credit when the expansion is being used to create dangerous speculation in commodities or securities and dangerous inflation in prices. Today, in 1930, there is far more doubt

---

Reserve Banks to raise or lower their rates even against their will? The law provides that the Reserve Banks shall determine rediscount rates weekly, subject to " review and determination " by the Federal Reserve Board. In 1919, the Attorney General formally advised the Reserve Board that it was authorized to fix rediscount rates. The matter came to a head in September, 1927, when the Chicago Reserve Bank was compelled by the Reserve Board to reduce its rate from 4 to $3\frac{1}{2}$ per cent.

concerning the ability of the Reserve system to control the volume of credit than there was five years ago when the policy of stabilization was newer. But although the efforts of the Federal Reserve system to check the excessive expansion of credit in boom times have been less successful than its most sanguine supporters had hoped (and predicted), the Reserve system remains, as was stated above, one of the most notable attempts of the day to subject economic activities to conscious control.

There are two principal ways in which the Reserve Banks (or the Federal Reserve Board acting through the Banks) seek to prevent overexpansion of credit. One is by raising the charge which Reserve Banks make for rediscounting commercial paper — the rediscount rate, as it is called. It will be recalled that the member banks are permitted to count only funds on deposit in the Federal Reserve Banks as their legally required reserves. Suppose that the member banks have lent all that they can without increasing their reserves. If the Federal Reserve Banks now advance their rediscount rates, the member banks must pay more for additional reserves against which to make further loans. But if it costs the banks more to obtain the reserves for loans, they are likely to increase their charges to customers, and if loans cost more, business men find it less profitable to borrow and a check is placed upon the tendency for credit to expand.

This assumes, it will be noticed, that, at the time when the rediscount rate is raised, the member banks have lent nearly all that their reserves permit and that they must rediscount with the Reserve Banks to obtain additional reserves. Suppose, however, that the Reserve Board decides that the expansion of credit should be checked at a time when the member banks have lent substantially less than their reserves permit. Not being compelled to rediscount with the Reserve Banks in order to expand loans, why should the member banks raise their discount rates, and why, therefore, should an increase in the rediscount rate affect the expansion of credit? Those who believe that the Reserve Banks and Board should control the expansion of credit hope that advances in the rediscount rate will be accepted as a signal that the expansion of business activity is on the point of going too far. It is expected that the advance in the rediscount rate will induce banks, even though possessing idle reserves, to scrutinize applications for credit more carefully and to be less liberal in making loans. It is hoped, furthermore, that the more conservative enterprises, fearing an early decline in prices, will cease buying in advance of immediate needs. This in itself would diminish the demand for credit. It would also diminish the demand for goods and hence the tendency for prices to rise, and this in turn would discourage less conservative enterprises from buying in advance of immediate needs and still further reduce the demand for loans.

The second method by which the Federal Reserve system seeks to check the overexpansion of credit is by the sale of securities in the open market. During times of slack business, when member banks are not seeking credit on a large scale, the Federal Reserve Banks invest a considerable part of their idle funds in acceptances and in short-term obligations of the government. When these securities are sold by a Reserve Bank, they may be purchased either by a member bank or by an ordinary business enterprise or business man. Suppose that a member bank is the buyer. When the bank pays for the securities, it reduces either its credits on the books of the Reserve Bank or its cash. The former constitute its reserves, which determine how much it may lend, and the latter is a means by which it can increase its reserves without borrowing. Quite clearly the bank by its purchase has reduced its capacity to lend without borrowing from the Reserve Bank. The same result follows if the securities are bought by an ordinary business enterprise or an individual. The purchaser pays by giving the Reserve Bank a check upon his bank. This reduces either the bank's deposits in the Reserve Bank or its cash and thus its ability to lend without rediscounting. Thus, if the Reserve Banks only have enough government obligations and acceptances to sell, they may succeed in largely wiping out the surplus reserves of the member banks and thus may cause them to increase their charges for loans or at least to grant credit more sparingly.

Perhaps it would be more accurate to regard the rediscount rate and open-market operations as two parts of a single method of credit control rather than as two distinct instruments of control. The reason is that the member banks may counteract the effect of sales of government obligations or acceptances by the

Reserve Banks simply by borrowing from the Reserve Banks —
that is, the member banks, by rediscounting, may borrow back the
money which they lose when the Reserve Banks sell securities in
the open market.   Consequently open-market sales may fail to
raise interest rates and, therefore, to check the expansion of
credit unless they are accompanied by an increase in the rediscount rate.   On the other hand, an advance in the rediscount rate
may have little effect unless the member banks find themselves
compelled to borrow from the Reserve Banks.   Open-market
sales, therefore, may be necessary to compel member banks to
borrow and thus to make the rediscount rate effective.   *Together*
open-market operations and the rediscount rate may be an effective instrument of credit control; the use of either one *alone* may
have little effect in many situations.

In times of crisis, when business enterprises have difficulty in
selling enough goods to meet their maturing obligations, we have
seen that expansion rather than restriction of the volume of
credit is needed.   Under the old national banking system, it will
be recalled, the banks contracted loans and hoarded cash during
times of crisis because they feared a demand for cash and had no
source from which to get it.   The Federal Reserve system makes
it possible for the member banks to expand credit at such times
because it enables them to obtain cash or to increase their reserves
on short notice simply by rediscounting commercial paper.   But
what assurance is there that the Reserve Banks will be able to
rediscount the large amounts of commercial paper that are likely
to be offered to them in periods of crisis?   Under the old national
banking system, the banks lent so much during boom times that
crises found them unable to expand credit.   Is the same thing
not likely to occur in the case of the Federal Reserve Banks?

There are several reasons for believing that it is not.   In
the first place, the Reserve Banks do not attempt to earn the
highest possible profits, because, after they have paid their stockholders 6 per cent, the remaining profits go to the government.
In the second place, as the Reserve Banks compete neither with
each other nor with member banks, they have no incentive to keep
down their rediscount rates in order to get business which might
otherwise go to rivals.   Finally, the rediscount rates of the Reserve Banks are under the control of the Federal Reserve Board,

which is appointed by the President to represent the public interest. Should the Reserve Banks not maintain adequate surplus reserves, it is expected that the Board would order an advance in rediscount rates.[28]

But suppose that, despite these safeguards, the Reserve Banks so expanded their loans during boom times that the period of crisis found them with no surplus reserves. How could the situation be met? There are several ways. As the commercial paper which they have rediscounted matures and is paid, the Reserve Banks receive cash. They are also being called upon to pay out cash. By retaining the cash received as rediscount paper matures, and by meeting the demands for cash by issuing Federal Reserve notes — which require a cash reserve of only 40 per cent — the Reserve Banks can gradually increase their reserves. If this method is not sufficiently rapid, the Reserve Banks can sell securities in the open market. And finally, if these methods fail to provide the needed reserves, the Federal Reserve Board may suspend the requirements that a cash reserve of 35 per cent must be kept against deposits and of 40 per cent against the Federal Reserve notes. The suspension may not exceed thirty days but it may be renewed for periods of fifteen days. The Reserve Banks, however, must pay a tax upon the amounts by which their reserves are deficient.

REFERENCES

Burgess, W. Randolph, *The Reserve Banks and the Money Market*, 1928.
Goldenweiser, E. A., *The Federal Reserve System in Operation*, 1925.
Marshall, L. C., *Industrial Society*, 1918. Ch. V.
Moulton, H. G., *The Financial Organization of Society* (second edition), 1925. Ch. VII, XVIII, XXI, XXII, XXIV, and XXVI.
Reed, H. L., *The Development of Federal Reserve Policy*, 1922. Ch. IV, V, VI, IX.
Rodkey, R. G., *The Banking Process*, 1928.

[28] It may happen, as it did in the crisis of 1921, that though the reserves of the entire Reserve system are sufficient to meet the credit needs of the time, those of certain Reserve Banks are not. To meet this contingency, a Reserve Bank may borrow from another on the security of paper which it has rediscounted or it may sell commercial paper in the open market. Should one Reserve Bank be unwilling to loan to another, the Reserve Board may compel it to do so.

PART III

THE OPERATION OF THE
EXISTING ECONOMIC ORDER

CHAPTER XII

THE DETERMINATION OF PRICE UNDER COMPETITION —PRELIMINARY ANALYSIS

I. THE PIVOTAL RÔLE OF BUYING AND SELLING IN MODERN ECONOMIC SOCIETY. II. THE INTERDEPENDENCE OF PRICES. III. PRELIMINARY ANALYSIS OF PRICE DETERMINATION UNDER COMPETITION. IV. THE MEANING OF CHANGES IN SUPPLY AND DEMAND. V. GRAPHIC REPRESENTATION OF SUPPLY AND DEMAND. VI. FURTHER ANALYSIS OF THE DETERMINATION OF PRICE UNDER COMPETITION. VII. WHY SOME PRICES ARE HIGH AND OTHERS ARE LOW.

I. THE PIVOTAL RÔLE OF BUYING AND SELLING IN MODERN ECONOMIC SOCIETY

In modern economic society, getting a living, as has been pointed out, is largely a process of buying and selling — selling what one has in order to purchase what one desires. Even the farmer, who is more self-sufficient than any other producer, buys about two-thirds of what he and his family consume. And not only is buying and selling the way in which each of us gains his livelihood, but, as we have seen, it is also the principal method by which the industrial activities of the community are organized. No central planning board directs our economic activities, telling us to produce more of this or less of that and assigning this capital and these men to the making of shoes and that capital and those men to the making of hats. What consumers choose to buy determines what industry makes; and it is by purchasing labor and by purchasing or renting capital that business men assemble the labor and equipment needed to produce goods. The prices created in the process of buying and selling regulate our lives far more minutely than could an efficient despot — and often as arbitrarily as a capricious tyrant. They determine the quantity of each good that enterprises produce, where goods are made, and what methods of production are most profitable; they even determine in large degree which of us are well-to-do and which of us are poor.

When getting a living is so largely a process of buying and selling, understanding how our economic system works is, in large degree, a matter of discovering what fixes the terms on which goods are exchanged. We shall begin our analysis of the operation of modern industry by examining how prices are determined. Our study of prices will fall into two principal parts. To begin with, we shall ask how individual prices are determined. What are the principal ways in which prices are fixed in modern economic society? Are they satisfactory ways? What results do they produce? It has been pointed out that prices organize production, determine the distribution of income, and regulate consumption. Do some methods of price determination lead to a more advantageous organization of production than others, to a fairer distribution of income, to a better regulation of consumption? What problems, if any, are produced by each method of determining prices?

The second part of our study of prices will deal with influences which cause the whole system of prices to rise and fall. An economic system such as ours, in which minute specialization creates a high degree of interdependence, in which production is carried on in anticipation of demand and largely through the use of credit, is likely to experience violent upward and downward movements of the general price level. The fluctuations may start in certain industries in which supply or demand has been badly miscalculated, but they soon spread to all prices. These sharp changes in prices, according to their nature, either stimulate or discourage industrial activity and profoundly affect the distribution of wealth. What are the causes of these general price movements, what are their effects, and what is the possibility of controlling these movements?

In addition to influences which produce violent short-time fluctuations in the price level, there are others which create a long-time upward or downward trend in prices. These long-time trends have many important consequences. After we have examined the short-time fluctuations in the price level, we

shall study the causes and the effects of the long-time movements.

But understanding how our economic system operates involves far more than understanding how prices in general are
determined. In the preceding chapters, modern industry has
been described as a system in which production is guided by the
choices of consumers and carried on by enterprises that are controlled by capitalists, are operated for profit, and use hired labor
and enormous amounts of capital. In order to understand the
operation of modern industry, we need to examine in some detail
the guidance of production by consumers, the working of the
wages system, how capital is created, what rôle it plays in industry, and how production for profit operates.

Is it true that consumers guide production? Do consumers
really determine what industry makes, or does industry determine
what consumers desire? Do the current methods of determining consumers' choices make for well-formed and well-considered
decisions? Does the consumer know accurately what he or she
is purchasing? Does it pay business enterprises to prevent the
consumer from making careful and well-informed choices, to prevent him from knowing accurately what he is buying? If so, to
what extent and under what conditions?

From the standpoint of business enterprises, wages are a
means of making men willing to work. Are they an efficient
incentive? What are their merits and weaknesses as an incentive? From the standpoint of the worker, wages are a means
of procuring a living. The laborer of today, unlike the slave or
serf of yesterday, does not have to work for any particular employer but he must work for *some* employer because, in most
instances, he does not possess enough property or credit to start
a business of his own. For nearly four-fifths of the gainfully
employed people in the United States, wages are almost the sole
source of income. What determines whether wages are high or
low? Why are they higher in the United States than in other
countries? What is the possibility of raising them? How are
they affected by trade unions, tariffs, machines? Can they be raised
by law? The bargain between wage earners and employers is
also a method of determining the conditions under which

men work. Is it a satisfactory method? Are there important interests which are not easily taken into account in bargaining and which fail to obtain adequate consideration in the
market place?

How are the huge amounts of capital used by modern industry created? What conditions govern the rate of capital accumulation? Under what circumstances is accumulation accelerated,
under what circumstances retarded? Are the current methods
of raising capital economical or are they unnecessarily costly?
And are they fair or unfair? In order to have capital accumulated, it is necessary, of course, for some resources of the community to be devoted to making capital goods rather than goods
for ultimate consumption — that is, consumers' goods. In other
words, in order to have more capital, it is necessary for some persons to consume less today than they otherwise would. In the
degree that men prefer to use goods now rather than later, the
limitation of consumption today in order to produce more capital for use tomorrow involves sacrifice. Does the limitation of
consumption, which makes possible the creation of capital, occur
among those persons who can limit their consumption with the
least sacrifice? The restriction of consumption today in order to
have more capital for use tomorrow may not be worth while unless the additional capital makes possible a sufficient gain in the
output of consumers' goods tomorrow. By whom and how are
the decisions to create more capital made? Are the decisions so
made that the sacrifice involved in postponing consumption receives proper weight; so that the production of new capital is
controlled by the cost of creating it? Or do those who must
limit their consumption have little or nothing to say concerning
how much capital shall be created? It seems reasonable that
the persons whose reduction or restriction of consumption makes
possible an increase in capital should partly own the capital which
they have helped to create. To what extent is the process of capital creation of such a nature that the abstaining is done by some
persons and the resulting capital owned by others? And finally,
what determines the reward which the owners of capital receive
and to what extent is the rate of accumulation affected by the size
of the reward?

It is the expectation of gain which, in the main, induces men to organize business establishments. What determines the rate of profit that business concerns obtain and how well does the institution of private profit perform the function of encouraging enterprise? This is a particularly pertinent question today because the growing separation of ownership and management causes profits to go largely to persons who have little direct control over industrial operations.

There is one conspicuous exception to the general rule that in modern economic society things are obtained by buying and selling. The government does not usually sell goods in order to obtain money for its support. It obtains most of its funds simply by taking them from the members of the community — in other words, by taxation. And since one-tenth of the national income of the United States goes to support the national and local governments, it is evident that the kind of taxes which the government imposes must profoundly affect the prosperity of the country. In examining the operation of modern industry it is important for us to inquire how the government obtains its income and how these methods affect industry.

Industry in the United States is, of course, part of a world economic system. The government pursues policies which are intended to improve our position in the world economic system. Other nations endeavor to improve their positions. The aspirations of many countries to develop manufacturing, attempts to control the movement of capital and the sources of raw material, and the legacy of debts and reparations left by the war, all create many outstanding problems of international economic policy. What are the principal international economic policies pursued by nations today and what are the effects of these policies? Does the scramble for national advantage leave all nations worse off? What are the prospects for more coöperation and less rivalry in international economic relations, for a more intelligent organization and direction of the world economic system, an organization which will adequately represent the common interests of all nations and which will help each nation prosper through the prosperity of all? We shall close our examination of the operation of modern industry by a survey of current international economic policies.

II. The Interdependence of Prices

Any explanation of how prices are determined must consist very largely of an explanation of how they are interrelated. For every price, it must be remembered, is related to every other price. The relationship between prices may be compared to the relationship between bodies in a gravitational field. Just as a change in the position of any body in the field affects every other body, so a change in the price of any good starts a multitude of changes running throughout the whole system of prices. For this, there are two principal reasons. In the first place, the amounts which buyers are willing to spend upon different goods depend upon the relative prices of the goods. A change in the price of any one commodity, therefore, alters the amounts which buyers are willing to spend for a myriad of other goods. In the second place, the distribution of income among different persons in the community depends upon prices. Any change in price is almost certain to increase or to decrease the incomes of the sellers of the good and likewise to decrease or increase the incomes of the sellers of other goods. But no two persons have precisely the same desires. Consequently, every shift in the distribution of income produces changes in the demand for goods. Thus each change in the price of a good causes other prices to change and these in turn cause still other prices to change.

In order to illustrate the interdependence of prices, let us suppose that there is a rise in the price of coal. This will increase the demand for coal substitutes and will cause their prices to rise or, as we shall see later, possibly to fall. If consumers must pay more for coal, many of them will have less to spend for other goods.[1] This will tend to diminish the demand for, and hence the prices of, goods in general. Coal is used in producing many articles. Hence the rise in its price tends to increase the cost, and therefore the price, of these commodities. The smaller output of coal means that there is less need for the goods — such as drills, powder, timber, and the serv-

[1] It is possible, however, that the higher price of coal will cause people to reduce their consumption of coal so drastically that they will have *more* to spend for other goods. This will tend to raise the prices of other things.

ices of miners — used in producing it. Consequently, the prices of these goods tend to drop. The advance in the price of coal is likely to mean that mine owners will have more money or less to spend. If the advance produces little change in the quantity of coal demanded, the mine owners will undoubtedly have more to spend; if it causes a large drop in the quantity demanded, they will have less to spend. In any event, their ability to purchase other goods will be changed and consequently the demand for the things for which they spend their money will be altered.

Can the constant and confusing movement of prices be explained? Are there laws which describe it? Are there principles which explain when a price moves up rather than down? Do price movements have any definite direction — do prices gravitate toward any particular point? To these questions the answer is: "Yes." Prices do have regularity and order; there are definite conditions under which they move upward and others under which they move downward; they gravitate toward a definite point. In this and the immediately following chapters, we shall analyze the principles of price movements.

III. Preliminary Analysis of Price Determination under Competition

The maker of a recently patented automobile lock negotiates with a huge automobile manufacturer for the sale of his product; the Interstate Commerce Commission holds hearings on coal rates from West Virginia to New England; in the wheat pit excited brokers struggle to buy or sell while the price changes from minute to minute; retailers from one end of the country to the other continue to sell chewing gum for the same price that has prevailed for a generation. Clearly no single formula will explain all of these prices. In one instance the price is fixed by a monopoly, in another by a governmental body, in another by competition among both buyers and sellers, and in the last it is greatly influenced by custom. These four cases do not represent all of the ways in which prices are determined but they illustrate the most important ones. Most prices, indeed, appear to be products of a *combination* of conditions — competition modified by custom, competition with a degree of monopoly, or monopoly tempered by fear of governmental interference.

Most frequently of all, prices are the result of competition among both buyers and sellers. In order to illustrate how prices are determined in this case, let us inquire what fixes the price which grocerymen obtain for berries. Suppose that on a certain day the prevailing price for berries is 25 cents a box. Earlier in the season they may have sold for 40 cents; perhaps the day before they were 20. What makes the price today 25 cents instead of more or less?

The dealers are guided in setting prices upon their berries by their estimates of supply and demand. They know that a few persons who are well-to-do or unusually fond of berries will, if necessary, pay a high price in order to get them. They also know that the quantity which these persons will buy is limited and that large quantities cannot be sold at a high price. *What each merchant attempts to do is to get the highest possible price and still dispose of his stock before it spoils or before a new supply comes into market.* This naturally involves an estimate of the demand for berries, and the estimates of different merchants are likely to vary. One dealer may decide that he can sell his supply at 26 cents a box, another may ask 25, and a third may ask only 24 cents. The day may open with berries selling at almost as many prices as there are merchants.

How long these differences remain will depend largely upon how quickly the buyers and dealers discover them. If the buyers notice them promptly, the dealers who are selling for least will find their stock diminishing rapidly and they may decide to raise their prices. The merchants who ask the highest prices, however, finding their berries going very slowly, are likely to ask less. Thus when buyers are quick to discover and act upon price differences, the charges of competing concerns for a given grade of product have a strong tendency to become uniform. But even if the buyers are slow to discover the price differences, dealers are likely to learn of them promptly and this creates a tendency for prices to become uniform. Most merchants are anxious to avoid creating the impression that their charges are higher than those of their competitors. Consequently, some dealers may lower the price on their berries as soon as they discover that it is above the average. They may do this even though sales at the higher amount have been satisfactory. On the other hand, some

of the dealers asking the lowest prices may raise them on discovering that rival firms are finding good demand at higher prices.

When the merchants put prices on their berries, they are
guessing what demand will be. They have, of course, their previous experience to guide them. They know in a general way
what the demand for berries was yesterday and the day before
and last week. Nevertheless they are compelled to *guess* about
the demand, and their guesses, even though made carefully and
intelligently, may be wrong. Possibly the demand proves unexpectedly large and by early afternoon the berries are nearly all
sold. In this case the dealers are likely to raise the price a cent
or two. On the other hand, if the berries sell slowly, the price
is likely to be cut, for the fruit must be sold before it spoils. But
the reduction may not come until the berries are on the verge of
spoiling. For if consumers are slow to discover that one merchant is asking less than others, each dealer may decide that a
lower price would produce such a small increase in sales that it
is more profitable for him to allow a few boxes to spoil rather
than cut his charge. If, on the contrary, buyers are quick to discover where berries are cheapest, a small reduction will produce
a big increase in the sales of the first dealers who make it. Under
these circumstances, merchants are likely to cut prices as soon as
they notice that their berries are selling slowly.

Our analysis of how dealers put prices on their berries has
indicated that: (1) when a seller finds that he can obtain more
for his supply than he is asking, he tends to raise his price; (2)
when he finds that he has a greater supply than he can sell at
the prevailing price, he is likely to ask less rather than not sell
all of his product. Consequently, when more product is demanded than is offered, price tends to rise; when more is offered
than is demanded, price tends to fall — *in other words, when
there is competition among both buyers and sellers, price tends to
be fixed at the point where demand and supply are equal.* No
matter how keen the competition among sellers, there is no need
for them to sell below this equilibrium price because everyone who
is willing to accept it is able to find a buyer at it. Likewise, there
is no need for purchasers to offer more, because every one of
them who is willing and able to pay the equilibrium price — that
is, the price at which supply and demand are in equilibrium — is

able to find a seller at that price. It is desirable to observe that in one important respect any other price would be less advantageous than the one established by competitive buying and selling. At any other price, a smaller volume of goods would be sold. If the price were higher, the sales would be less because a smaller quantity would be taken; if it were lower, the sales would be less because a smaller quantity would be offered. At any other price, therefore, fewer persons would be able to satisfy their desire to buy and fewer persons would be able to satisfy their desire to sell.[2] In this respect and to this extent, the prices established by competition are ideal prices. In other respects, as we shall see, they may not be ideal.

IV. The Meaning of Changes in Supply and Demand

Before proceeding further with our analysis of price determination, it is desirable to notice the two senses in which demand or supply may be said to increase or decrease. At 10 cents, the demand for an article may be 1,000, at 9 cents 1,100. We may say, therefore, that, as price drops from 10 cents to 9, demand increases from 1,000 to 1,100. *Strictly speaking, however, demand has not changed.* The willingness and ability of consumers to pay for the good are the same. They are still willing to purchase either 1,000 units at 10 cents or 1,100 units at 9 cents. The expressions *increase in demand, decrease in demand, increase in supply,* and *decrease in supply* are better used to refer to changes in the ability or willingness of buyers to purchase or sellers to supply a good. For example, the demand for the commodity might increase so that at 10 cents people were willing to buy 1,100 instead of 1,000 and at 9 cents 1,200 instead of 1,100.

V. Graphic Representation of Supply and Demand

It is often helpful in the study of price determination to represent the state of supply and demand graphically. In doing this,

---

[2] But this statement is subject to an important qualification. It is possible that the costs of production under monopoly may be so much less than under competition that the monopoly may find it advantageous to sell for less than competitive enterprises could sell. In this event, the number of units sold will be greater under monopoly than it would be under competition. This matter will be discussed in Chapter XVI.

it is customary to let the vertical, or Y, axis of the diagram represent the prices at which different quantities of the article will be bought or sold, and the horizontal, or X, axis the quantities which will be bought or sold at the different prices. Suppose that it is desired to represent the following state of supply and demand for wheat:

Price	Bushels demanded at respective prices	Bushels supplied at respective prices
$1.05	950	750
1.10	900	800
1.15	850	850
1.20	800	900
1.25	750	950

Lay off scales along the X and Y axis. The origin of the scales, where the X and Y axes intersect, might be zero. In this case, however, it is more convenient to begin the price scale on the Y axis at $1.00 and the quantity scale on the X axis at 700. We now have the following scales:

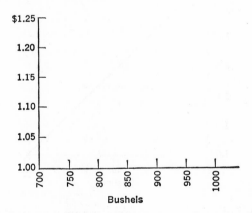

Let us first represent the state of demand. The fact that 950 bushels will be demanded at $1.05 is indicated by a dot at the 950 point on the quantity scale opposite the $1.05 point on the price scale. To show that, at $1.10, 900 bushels will be demanded, a dot is made opposite $1.10 on the price scale and opposite 900 on the quantity scale. Plotting the remainder of the demand data in this way, we obtain a row of dots showing the quantities which will be taken at different prices:

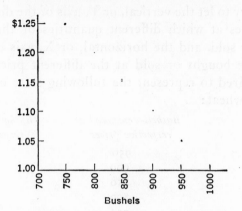

The data do not tell us how much wheat will be demanded at intermediate prices, such as $1.01, $1.02, $1.03, $1.04, $1.06. The dots which we have put down, however, indicate the general trend of demand. By connecting them with a line, we obtain a close estimate of the demand at the intermediate prices.

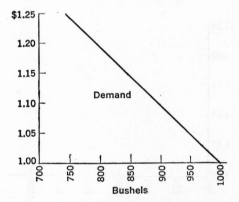

Supply is indicated in the same manner as demand, by dots showing what quantity will be supplied at each price. By connecting these dots we obtain a line showing the amounts which will be supplied at the prices for which we lack data. (See next page.)

The price which will theoretically prevail is, of course, the one which equalizes supply and demand. The point at which demand and supply are equal is the point at which the demand and supply lines intersect. Reference to the price scale indicates that

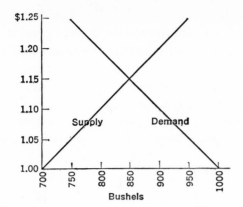

equality occurs at $1.15 and that this, therefore, is the price which
will theoretically prevail.

Frequently it is impossible to represent supply and demand
by unbroken lines or curves. Suppose, for example, that the
commodity is hats and that the numbers which will be offered
and demanded at various prices are:

Price	Demand	Supply
$1	4	2
2	3	3
3	2	4

As the price rises, the quantity demanded declines and that offered increases. But neither, of course, changes by fractions of
a hat. The data do not tell us precisely at what points the
changes occur. We know simply, for example, that somewhere
between $1.00 and $2.00 the demand for hats drops from four to
three. These sharp breaks in the number of hats offered or demanded cause the demand and supply lines to form a series of
disconnected parallel lines. Assume that quantities demanded and
supplied change at $1.01 and $2.01. At $1.00, demand for
hats is four and supply two; at $1.01 to $2.00 inclusive, demand is three and supply three; and at $2.01 to $3.00, demand is two and supply four. To indicate a demand of
four at $1.00, we place a dot opposite $1.00 on the price scale
and opposite four on the quantity scale. Since at $1.01 and
up to $2.00, three hats are demanded, we draw a vertical
line opposite three on the quantity scale and extending from
$1.01 to $2.00 on the price scale. Opposite two on the

quantity scale is another vertical line beginning at $2.01 and ending with $3.00. As for supply, a dot opposite $1.00 on the price scale and two on the quantity scale shows that at $1.00 there is a supply of two. A vertical line opposite three on the quantity scale and extending from $1.01 to $2.00 indicates that, from $1.01 to $2.00, the supply is three. At four on the quantity scale another line extends from $2.01 to $3.00, showing a supply of four within this price range. The diagram is as follows:

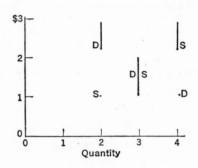

Notice that in this instance it is impossible to determine the theoretical price except within the limits of $1.01 and $2.00. At these two prices and at all others between them, demand and supply are equal. Any one of these amounts, therefore, *may be* the market price. Which *is* the price is largely a matter of the bargaining skill of buyers and sellers. For this reason, the range of prices within which demand and supply are equal and price indeterminate is known as a *higgling area*.[3]

VI. Further Analysis of the Determination of Price under Competition

In the market which we selected for illustrating the operation of supply and demand under competition, the sale of berries at retail, prices are quoted almost exclusively by the sellers. This is true of retail trade in most parts of the United States. It does not follow, however, that the sellers *make* the price, because in

---

[3] Since, in the case of all goods, there is a certain unit which is the smallest quantity for which prices are quoted, the state of demand and supply should, strictly speaking, always be represented by a series of dots or very short parallel lines rather than by a continuous line. But when the number of units in terms of which prices are quoted is very large, it is much more convenient to represent demand and supply by continuous lines.

deciding what to ask they are guided by what they find buyers willing to pay. Probably changes in price occur less promptly than they would if purchasers actively bargained for goods, because the sellers, absorbed with the details of their businesses, may be slow to notice changes in demand. The ultimate determinants of price, none the less, are supply and demand. In other markets, of which the labor market is an example, prices are customarily quoted by the buyers. At least this is true as far as most manual labor in non-agricultural industries is concerned. A job seeker who is so bold as to bargain over terms thereby eliminates himself from consideration. But the employers of labor no more fix the rate of wages than fruit dealers fix the retail price of berries, because, just as the merchants must take account of the consumer's willingness to buy, so must employers take account of the laborer's willingness to work. In other markets — the stock exchange, the board of trade, and wholesale markets generally — both buyers and sellers make offers. Such offers, because of their definitely quantitative character, are the best way of indicating changes in demand and supply. Consequently the adjustment of price to changes in supply and demand is likely to occur more promptly in markets where the price quotations come from both buyers and sellers.

In describing how the price of berries is determined, we pointed out that all berries are sold at one price only when buyers are quick to discover differences in the quotations of the different dealers and when each merchant promptly ascertains whether his price is above or below the equilibrium price. How soon these discoveries are made depends upon the facilities for collecting and distributing market information. In the case of the stock and grain markets, these facilities are highly efficient. The stock market tickers, for example, report the price paid in every sale involving 100 shares or over, and for the tickers to be as much as five minutes behind the market is a matter for newspaper comment. In most markets, however, the arrangements for providing information are extremely inadequate. Consequently there is likely to be a considerable range in the prices at which sales are made and much of the product may be sold for distinctly more or less than the equilibrium price.

To see more clearly how scanty market information affects price, let us analyze the situation of a wage earner seeking to sell his services. There is no single place comparable to the stock exchange or the wheat pit where he can make the sale or learn either of specific vacancies or of the general state of supply and demand. From talks with other workmen and the " help wanted " advertisements he probably gains some idea of the state of the market and of prevailing wage rates. Then he starts to peddle his labor from plant to plant. After several failures to find a vacancy in his occupation, he is offered a job at 55 cents an hour. A few blocks away another plant may be offering 60 cents for the same work. But he does not know this. He does not even know very definitely whether 55 cents is above or below the current rate in the occupation. If he turns down the opening, he does not know how soon he will get another or what the wages will be. If he is optimistic, or if he has not been out of work long and is not financially pressed, he may decide to take a chance on getting more than 55 cents. But if he is cautious, discouraged by his search for work, or near the end of his savings, or if he has heavy family expenses, he may accept the 55 cent job even though he suspects that other plants are paying more. If, however, he were supplied with market information indicating that at 55 cents the number of positions exceeded the job seekers and telling him where vacancies existed, he might hold out longer for more than 55 cents. If enough men did this, the enterprises trying to hire workers for 55 cents would be compelled to offer more. In short, readily available market information tends to overcome the effects of differences in bargaining power and negotiating skill and to enable all buyers and sellers to get the same price. *Absence of easily obtained market information tends to cause differences in bargaining power and higgling skill to become fully reflected in price.*

VII. Why Some Prices Are High and Others Are Low

Before leaving this preliminary analysis of the determination of prices, it is desirable for us to ask the meaning of prices. What do prices signify? Why is cotton worth less than silk and platinum worth more than steel? Does a high price mean that a commodity is highly useful and a low price that it is less useful? Is an expensive commodity, such as platinum, more useful than an inexpensive commodity, such as steel? A crop of 75,000,000 bushels of wheat sells for $1.00 a bushel; the next year, when the crop is 100,000,000, wheat may sell for 70 cents a bushel. Does the fact that the public pays $70,000,000 for the crop of 100,-000,000 bushels and $75,000,000 for the crop of 75,000,000 bushels mean that the community would prefer a small crop to a large one; that the farmers are rendering a greater service when they raise 75,000,000 bushels than when they raise 100,000,000?

In order to answer these questions, it is necessary for us to ask why it is generally true that less of a commodity will be purchased at a high price than at a low one. In explaining how the price of berries is determined, we took it for granted that if the price were high, a smaller quantity would be sold than if the price were low. This seems a commonplace fact, but it will bear looking into.

The explanation is to be found in the fact that, after a given point, successive quantities of any good yield a diminishing amount of satisfaction. One pair of shoes is a necessity in a northern climate, a second is a great convenience, but a sixth or seventh would be of little use. If shoes were extremely expensive, many people would limit themselves to only one pair, because they would obtain more satisfaction by spending their money for other things than for a second pair of shoes. At a lower price, however, some persons would decide that they would obtain more satisfaction by buying a second pair of shoes and smaller quantities of other things. At still lower prices some persons would purchase a third pair. The point, however, would eventually be reached — and, in the case of shoes, it would be reached very soon — when an additional supply would be a nuisance rather than a convenience and when most people would be unwilling to increase their stock of shoes at any price.

The matter may be put in another way. Different goods may be regarded as competing for the dollars of consumers. The amount that it is advantageous for the consumer to spend for any commodity is limited by the fact that additional quantities of the good yield less and less satisfaction. But the lower the price, the more of the commodity it pays the consumer to buy rather than spend his money for other things.

It is not intended to suggest that the persons who are willing to pay the highest prices for any commodity or to buy the largest quantities of it are necessarily the persons who desire it most intensely and who derive the greatest satisfaction from it. The power of a good to satisfy desires does, of course, affect the demand for it. But demand is partly a matter of ability to pay. No matter how intensely one may desire an article, he does not exercise demand for it unless he is able to offer a price for it. The persons who are willing to pay the highest price for a good and to buy it in the largest quantities are likely to be persons who are exceptionally well-to-do rather than persons who desire it most intensely. Nevertheless it is true that *all* consumers, both rich and poor, are willing to buy additional quantities of any article only at a steadily diminishing price.

This helps to explain something that has seemed paradoxical to many persons — the fact that many of the most useful things, to which we attach most importance, such as wheat or steel, are cheaper than less necessary things, such as tea or platinum. When there is a competition among both sellers and buyers, the price of every unit of the supply sold tends to be the same. No seller is likely to accept less than he can obtain from some other buyer and no buyer is likely to pay more than he has to pay some other seller. *This means that the price of every unit sold is fixed by the willingness of the public to purchase the last unit sold.* If the producers have 1,000 units of an article to sell, the price of *every one* of the 1,000 units tends to be no more than the public is willing to pay for a 1,000th unit. From this view it follows that prices do not indicate the relative demand for different commodities, and much less the relative desire for them. Prices simply indicate the willingness of the public to pay for the last unit that is sold. Or, to put it slightly differently, prices indicate the willingness of the public to pay for one unit *of a given supply*. If a crop sells for $75,000,000 when there are 75,000,-000 bushels and for $70,000,000 when there are 100,000,000, this means, not that the public prefers small crops, but that when there are 75,000,000 bushels, the importance which purchasers attach to one bushel is measured by $1.00 and when there are 100,000,000 bushels, the importance which they attach to one bushel is measured by 70 cents.

A relatively high price, therefore, *may* mean that a good is in greater demand than other goods. But it may *also* mean that the commodity, although in less demand than other commodities, is so scarce that the public is willing to pay a high price to obtain the last unit of the supply. A low price may mean that the good is in small demand, but it may also mean that the good, although in great demand, is so plentiful that the public is unwilling to pay much to obtain the last unit of the supply. In the following table, for example, it will be observed that commodity B is in greater demand than commodity A — at *every* price the public is willing to purchase more of B than of A.

| Quantity | demanded | Price | Quantity | supplied |
A	B		A	B
1,000	1,100	$1.20	1,400	1,700
1,100	1,200	1.10	1,300	1,600
1,200	1,300	1.00	1,200	1,500
1,300	1,400	.90	1,100	1,400
1,400	1,500	.80	1,000	1,300

Nevertheless, an inspection of the points at which supply and demand reach equilibrium indicates that the price of B is less than the price of A — 90 cents instead of $1.00. The reason why the commodity which is in greater demand commands the lower price is found in the supply situation. At any given price, producers are willing to supply more of B than of A. The public demands B more than it does A, but it is unwilling to pay as much for a *1,400th* unit of B as for a *1,200th* unit of A.

REFERENCES

Henderson, H. D., *Supply and Demand*, 1922. Ch. II and III.
Knight, F. H., *Risk, Uncertainty, and Profit*, 1921. Ch. III.
Marshall, Alfred, *Principles of Economics* (eighth edition), 1920. Bk. V, ch. II–VI.
Mitchell, W. C., *Business Cycles. The Problem and Its Setting*, 1927. Pp. 108–115.
Rufener, L. A., *Principles of Economics*, 1927. Ch. V and VI.
Taussig, F. W., *Principles of Economics* (third edition), 1924. Ch. VIII–X.

CHAPTER XIII

THE STABILITY OF PRICES UNDER COMPETITION

I. SOME FACTORS INFLUENCING THE STABILITY OF PRICES. II. THE ELASTICITY OF SUPPLY AND OF DEMAND. III. THE EFFECT OF THE ELASTICITY OF DEMAND AND OF SUPPLY UPON PRICE MOVEMENTS. IV. THE DETERMINANTS OF THE ELASTICITY OF DEMAND. V. THE DETERMINANTS OF THE ELASTICITY OF SUPPLY. VI. THE EFFECT OF FIXED COSTS UPON THE ELASTICITY OF SUPPLY. VII. THE EFFECT OF PRICE MOVEMENTS UPON THE LEVEL OF SUPPLY AND DEMAND.

I. Some Factors Influencing the Stability of Prices

Everyone knows that the prices of some goods rise and fall far more than the prices of others. Some prices are stable because they are fixed by the government or by a monopoly or because they are influenced by custom. But especially among prices which are fixed by competition, some fluctuate much more than others. What are the reasons for these differences?

Fluctuations in prices naturally reflect changes in supply and demand. But a given change in supply or demand may produce little change in the price of one commodity and yet a very pronounced change in the price of another. Much depends upon whether changes in supply or demand can be foreseen far enough ahead to do much about them. In middle-class residential districts, the Sunday demand for cream is about three times that of week days and the demand for milk is less.[1] But this does not produce differences in the prices of cream or milk on Sundays and week days, because the changes in demand can be foreseen and prepared for. Likewise the great increase in the demand for toys every December produces no appreciable increase in price. Occasionally little can be done about changes in supply and demand even when they can be foreseen. For example, the sea-

[1] U. S. Department of Agriculture, *Marketing Activities*, August 17, 1927, v. VII, p. 207.

sonal variations in the supply of cattle are easily predicted, but the price fluctuates considerably. Range cattle are marketed when the grass season is over, dairy farmers thin out their herds in the fall, corn-fed cattle are marketed in greatest quantities three to four months after the corn crop is harvested. In September and October, cattle receipts are usually about twice those of February and March, which, as a rule, are the lightest months. Yet because Americans dislike frozen meat, the price must be adjusted so that the beef from these cattle will be sold within several weeks after they are slaughtered. Still more frequently, changes in supply and demand cannot be foreseen. Crops are perhaps the best illustration of commodities which are subject to great and largely unforeseeable changes in supply. In 1916, the wheat crop was over one-third less than the crop of 1915; in 1916, the output of potatoes was small, but in 1917 it was large — more than half again as large as in 1916. The 1920 apple crop was 50 per cent larger than the one of 1919, but the 1921 crop was less than half that of 1920. In 1924, the yield of corn was the smallest in over a decade, but in 1925 it was the seventh largest in our history. A variation in the size of a crop is not, of course, precisely the same thing as a variation in the quantity offered for sale, because, when the crop is large, part of it may be stored, and when it is small, there are usually heavy withdrawals from storage. Nevertheless large changes in output are ordinarily accompanied by pronounced changes in the supply which will be sold at a given price. The demand which is most subject to sudden and unpredictable changes is that dependent upon weather, fads, and fashions — the demand for meat, fruit, and vegetables, which changes with the temperature from day to day, and that for wearing apparel, which is affected by the severity or mildness of the season and by the fads of the moment that cause overnight shifts in preferences for color, design, and material.

II. The Elasticity of Supply and of Demand

But the stability of prices is not merely a matter of the stability and predictability of supply and demand. It is greatly affected by the extent to which a given change in price is accompanied by an increase or decrease in the quantity of the

commodity offered or demanded. At any given time, differ-
ferent quantities of a good would be supplied and demanded at
different prices. In the case of some goods, the quantities which
would be demanded at high prices would be relatively small in
comparison with the quantities which would be demanded at low
prices; in the case of other commodities, almost as much would
be demanded at high prices as at low ones. At a 10 per cent
higher price, the quantity of one good demanded might be 5
per cent less; of another, 10 per cent less; and of still another,
15 per cent less. The fact that goods differ greatly in the degree to which the quantities supplied or demanded vary with
the price is of great importance in the analysis of many economic problems. It is particularly important in explaining the
relative stability of some prices and the relative instability of
others.

When, at any given instant of time, the quantity of a good
which would be taken at a high price is substantially less than
the amount which would be taken at a low price, the demand is
said to be *elastic;* it is said to be *inelastic* when the amount which
would be taken at a high price is almost as large as that which
would be taken at a low price. Likewise, supply is said to be
elastic when the amount which would be offered at a high price
is large relative to the amount which would be offered at a low
price, and inelastic when the quantity offered at a high price
is little larger than that offered at a low one. In the following
diagram, the nearly horizontal line D represents elastic demand
and the nearly vertical line D_1 inelastic demand.

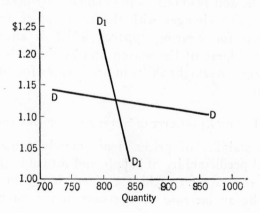

More precise definitions of elasticity and inelasticity of demand can be constructed by defining as an *elasticity of unity* that degree of responsiveness to price change which causes the total amount spent for a commodity to be the same at all prices. If, for example, at $1.00 the demand is for 1,000 units, at $2.00 for 500 units, and at $4.00 for 250 units, the elasticity of demand is unity because, at every price, the total amount spent for the commodity would be $1,000. An elastic demand is one which is so responsive to price changes that the total expenditure for the commodity would be greater at a low price than at a high one; an inelastic demand is one which is so unresponsive to price changes that the total expenditure for the commodity would be greater at a high price than at a low one. The following brief table illustrates these distinctions:

| | *Quantity demanded* | | |
Price	Elasticity of unity	Elastic demand	Inelastic demand
$1.00	1,000	1,200	800
2.00	500	500	500
4.00	250	200	300

The elasticity of demand, of course, need not be constant throughout all price levels; in fact, it usually is not. At high prices, as will be explained presently, the demand is likely to be more inelastic than at lower prices.

In the case of supply, an elasticity of unity is that responsiveness to price changes which causes a given rise or fall in price to be accompanied by a proportionate rise or fall in the quantity supplied — that is, which causes a 10 per cent increase in price to be accompanied by a 10 per cent increase in the quantity supplied or a 25 per cent increase in price to be accompanied by a 25 per cent increase in the quantity supplied. Supply is elastic when a given change in price would be accompanied by a more than proportionate change in supply — a 10 per cent increase in price by more than a 10 per cent increase in the quantity supplied or a 5 per cent decrease in price by more than a 5 per cent decrease in the quantity supplied; supply is inelastic when a given change in price would be accompanied by a less than proportionate change in supply, as when a 10 per cent drop in price would be accompanied by less than a 10 per cent decrease in the quantity supplied.[2]

III. The Effect of the Elasticity of Demand and of Supply upon Price Movements

How do the elasticity of supply and the elasticity of demand affect the stability of prices? There are four possible combinations:

demand elastic — supply elastic
demand elastic — supply inelastic
demand inelastic — supply elastic
demand inelastic — supply inelastic

Prices are likely to be most stable when both supply and demand are elastic, and least stable when both supply and demand are inelastic. It is easy to see why this is so. Suppose that there is an increase in the supply of an article. The price will tend to drop. But how far will it go? Obviously this depends upon how a given change in price affects the quantity demanded — that is, upon the elasticity of demand. If a small drop in price produces a large increase in the quantity demanded — in other words, if demand is elastic — the price will not fall far before the quantity demanded is equal to that offered and the price will drop no farther. But if the demand is inelastic, a substantial decrease in price must occur before the quantity demanded is equal to the supply. Assume now that the demand for a good increases. If supply is elastic — that is, responsive to price changes — the price will not have to rise far before the quantity supplied is equal to that demanded. If, however, the supply is not sensitive to price changes, a large advance in price will be

---

[2] This definition of elasticity of supply is based on the assumption that, at any instant of time, the quantity which will be forthcoming at a high price is greater than the quantity which will be supplied at a low price. This assumption is generally true but it is also sometimes true that, if only a very small quantity of a good is demanded, the price which must be paid to get it produced is higher than the price which would induce the production of a larger quantity. The reason, of course, is that the unit cost of making a very few units is often exceedingly high.

It is also true that, after a large and permanent increase in demand, producers may be willing to supply a large quantity for less than they formerly supplied a smaller quantity. The reason is that, when an industry is equipped to produce a large quantity, the cost of production per unit may be less than when the industry is equipped to produce a smaller quantity. A permanent change in demand, therefore, may change the general level of supply. This point will be discussed more fully in Chapter XV.

necessary to bring supply up to demand. Thus it is evident that when both demand and supply are elastic, a small movement in price will bring the two into equilibrium, but when both are inelastic, a large price movement is needed.[3]

The violent price movements which are characteristic of commodities that are inelastic both in demand and in supply sometimes create difficult economic problems. The most noteworthy is undoubtedly the problem of stabilizing the prices of agricultural staples, such as wheat. In the United States, wheat is less elastic in demand than in most countries, and, for short periods, it is relatively inelastic in supply because the output, as far as the immediate future is concerned, is determined by the weather rather than by the price.[4] It is partly because an unusually large crop often produces a severe drop in price (and also because wheat is largely raised by specialists who derive almost their entire incomes from this one crop) that there is great interest in plans for stabilizing the price of wheat.

IV. The Determinants of the Elasticity of Demand

What determines whether demand and supply are elastic or inelastic? Let us first consider demand. Matches, salt, shoe laces, soap, bread, potatoes, electric light bulbs, are a few commodities which are highly inelastic in demand. Why is this so?

[3] This can be shown graphically:

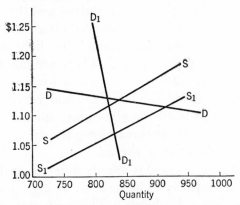

In this case there has been an increase in willingness to sell the article represented by the change in the supply curve from S to S_1. It is evident that the drop in price produced by this change is much less when the demand is elastic, as represented by D, than when it is inelastic, as represented by D_1.

[4] In continental countries where most people eat rye bread, the demand for wheat is more elastic because, when wheat is expensive, rye bread is more heavily consumed.

Each of these articles, it will be noted, costs very little. Even a big change in the price would not greatly affect the consumer's total expenditures. The smaller the price of an article, the less is the demand for it likely to be affected by a given percentage change in price — doubling the price of an article selling for 5 cents is likely to have less effect on demand than doubling the price of a commodity selling for $5.00. Most of the goods in our list are necessities according to the prevailing mode of life in the United States and for most of them there are no satisfactory and less expensive substitutes. There are, it is true, substitutes for potatoes and wheat bread, but the use of both bread and potatoes is so largely a matter of habit that consumers are not easily persuaded to use the substitutes. When the potato crop was short in 1916, efforts to induce housewives to buy more rice met with surprising opposition. There were riots on the East Side in New York and the cry arose that an attempt was being made to introduce a Chinese standard of living. Finally, the commodities in our illustration cannot be economized by being used longer or by being repaired. One reason why the demand for shoes and clothing falls off when they become expensive is because it is easy to economize them by repairing them.

A special word should be said concerning electric light bulbs. Electric lighting is not a necessity and there are inexpensive substitutes for it. But if one wishes electric lighting, one must have bulbs. In a sense then, they are necessities and there is no substitute for them. Consequently, however elastic the demand for electric lighting may be, the demand for light bulbs is little affected by changes in their price. There are hundreds of commodities of the same sort — the demand for nails depends primarily upon the demand for buildings and very little upon the price of nails, the demand for plate glass upon the demand for closed cars, the demand for thread upon the demand for clothing rather than upon the price of thread.

The elasticity of demand is usually different at different price levels — demand is likely to be inelastic at high price levels and more elastic at low price levels. This may seem to contradict the statement that the demand for articles which cost little tends to be inelastic and the demand for expensive articles tends to be elastic. But it is not a contradiction because it is a different proposition. Most articles are demanded by many different persons, some of whom are rich and some of whom are poor. But the proportion of the demand which comes from poor persons is much larger when the price is low than when it is high. If the price drops, the rich are not likely to increase their consumption of the good because they are probably already using all they care for, but many poor persons are likely to increase their consumption. On the other hand, if the price rises, the rich are less likely to reduce their consumption substantially because they have so much money that a few dollars more or less do not mean much to them. But a rise in price causes the less well-to-do to curtail their consumption. As the rise continues, the poor reduce their demand more and more. Eventually, the price may get so high that practically all of the demand for the commodity comes from the rich. After this point further increases in price are likely to have less effect upon the quantity demanded because, as explained above, the rich are less disposed to reduce their demand for an article simply because the price has risen. To put the matter slightly differently and more briefly: the part of the demand which comes from the poor is more elastic than the part of the demand which comes from the rich. At low prices, the proportion of the demand which comes from the poor is much larger than at high prices. Consequently, the demand for an article at low prices is likely to be more elastic than at high prices.

Thus far we have used elasticity of demand simply to refer to the fact that *at any given instant of time* different quantities of any good would be demanded at different prices. If we alter our concept of elasticity of demand to mean, not that different quantities of a good would be demanded at different prices at a given instant of time, but the responsiveness of demand to changes in price *during a short period of time,* we encounter the interesting fact that the elasticity of demand is affected by the size or the rapidity of price changes. If, for example, sellers, who have been receiving $1.00, begin to hold out for $1.05 and then the next month for $1.10 and the next for $1.15, the demand may respond to all of these increases as an inelastic demand. If, at $1.00, 1,000 units were demanded, at a price of $1.05 the demand may be 975; at \$1.10, 950; and at \$1.15, 925.   But if the sellers suddenly raise the price which they ask from \$1.00 to \$1.15, the demand may be distinctly more elastic.   It may drop from 1,000 to 800 units.   The explanation is that the ways in which men spend their money are, to a great extent, determined by custom.   As long as prices remain about the same, consumers go on purchasing the things that they have been in the habit of using.   In other words, a succession of *small* price changes does not jolt consumers into experimenting with substitutes.   A large and sudden price change, however, is likely to alter long-established habits of consumption.   The result is that, for very small price changes, the elasticity of demand may be little, but for larger changes it may be pronounced.   This means that, when the elasticity of the demand is conceived as the response of demand to price changes during a brief period of time, the elasticity cannot be represented by a single curve but must be represented by a *number* of diverging curves—a *sheaf* of curves—each curve representing the elasticity for a different rate of price change.   In the following diagram, the curve D represents the demand when the price rises by small increments in response to a slow change in supply; the curve D_1 represents the more elastic demand which is caused by a sudden drop in supply sufficient to produce a sudden jump in price from \$1.00 to \$1.15 and then from \$1.15 to \$1.30; and curve D_2 represents the still more elastic demand which results from a change in supply sufficient to produce an initial jump in price from \$1.00 to \$1.20 and a subsequent jump from \$1.20 to \$1.40.

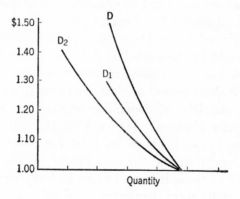

It is important to bear in mind that price jumps of not less than 15 cents are necessary to produce the elasticity represented by curve D_1 and jumps of not less than 20 cents to produce the elasticity represented by curve D_2. Strictly, there should be unbroken gaps between \$1.00 and \$1.15 and between \$1.15 and \$1.30 in the case of the curve D_1 and between \$1.00 and \$1.20 and between \$1.20 and \$1.40 in the case of curve D_2. In other words, there should simply be a series of points representing the elasticity of demand for different rates of price change. It is convenient, however, to connect the points in order to indicate the trend of demand and to show which points form part of the same series. Were the price, after jumping suddenly to \$1.15 or to \$1.20, to fall slowly, the quantities demanded would probably correspond to those indicated by the curves D_1 and D_2.

V. The Determinants of the Elasticity of Supply

It is impossible to discuss the elasticity of supply without reference to the time allowed for delivery. A supply curve represents, of course, the willingness and ability of producers to supply a good at a given time. But the willingness and ability of producers to make delivery within twenty-four hours may be different from their willingness and ability to deliver in thirty days. Small orders which could be filled in twenty-four hours without great difficulty may be accepted on a day's notice for little higher price than would be asked when a month is allowed for delivery. Large orders, however, can be filled quickly only by working men overtime and possibly by postponing other work — at the risk, of course, of offending the customers whose goods are delayed. For doing this, producers naturally expect a higher price. On November 1st, a printer might be willing to supply 10,000 copies of a small circular for delivery on November 30th at 10 cents a copy. On November 29th, however, he might refuse to supply the same number for delivery the next day at less than 20 cents each. In other words, *supply tends to be more elastic as the delivery date becomes more remote.* This is illustrated by the following diagram in which S represents the amounts which will be offered at different prices for delivery within twenty-four hours and S_1 the quantities which will be offered for delivery in thirty days:

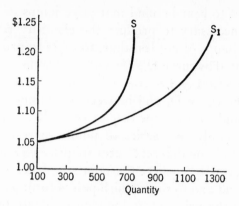

For very small amounts, there is no difference in the price; but, as the quantity increases, the price necessary to induce immediate delivery rises rapidly. In each case, after supply has been increased to a certain point it becomes impossible to add to it *within the stipulated time period* except at great expense.

In considering the elasticity of supply, we shall assume that a short delivery period is involved. When this is so, the elasticity appears to depend largely upon: (1) the possibility of storing the commodity at small expense; (2) the availability of stocks of the good which can be quickly drawn upon; (3) the existence of idle productive capacity; (4) whether the production of the good requires highly specialized equipment or specially trained workmen or whether enterprises which make other things could make it also; (5) whether or not the good is produced as a by-product in connection with some more valuable good; (6) whether or not the production of the article entails pecuniary costs.

Commodities which are perishable and expensive to store are offered for sale more or less regardless of the price — in other words, the supply is inelastic. Once the commodity has been produced, there is nothing to do but sell it for what it will bring. But goods which can be stored at moderate cost are likely to be held back to a considerable extent whenever the price is low. Then, when the price is high, large amounts are likely to be withdrawn from storage. The effect of perishability is well illustrated by the prices of pork loins and of ham. Pork loins, being marketed fresh, must be sold promptly for whatever they will bring. Since many more hogs are brought to market in some months (January and February) than in others, the price of loins fluctuates greatly. The highest wholesale price in any year is usually from 50 to 100 per cent above the lowest. Hams are in greatest demand in the summer, when hog receipts are low, but, because hams are easily stored, the price fluctuates much less than that of loins. The peak price of the year is rarely more than one-half and usually not more than one-third above the lowest.

Lard is an example of a commodity which is relatively elastic in supply because there are sources from which the output can easily be increased. Fat hog backs contain about 80 per cent of lard. If lard is high relative to hog backs, it pays to render them for their lard. This was done during the war when the price of lard was unusually high. The supply of cattle under most circumstances is elastic because it is possible to market them earlier if the price is favorable or to hold them back if it is not. Furthermore, about half the cattle of the country are dairy cows. A high price for cattle encourages dairy farmers to sell their older and less productive cows. The availability of existing stocks of goods is often a matter of transportation cost. Hence, the less expensive a commodity is to transport, the greater is likely to be the elasticity of its supply.

As long as an industry has idle producing capacity, a small advance in price is likely to induce a large increase in output. In fact, the additional supply may be forthcoming at no increase in price whatever. After the capacity of the industry has been reached, however, the supply becomes much more inelastic, unless the article can be easily and cheaply made by plants in other industries. The possibility of making a commodity economically in plants not especially designed for its production tends, of course, to make the supply more elastic. When, for example, an article can be easily manufactured with the ordinary lathes, planers, and drill presses found in almost any machine shop, a small increase in price is likely to bring about a large increase in supply.

Commodities which are by-products are usually inelastic in supply because their output depends primarily, not upon their price, but upon the demand for the principal product. Silver is inelastic in supply because the bulk of the production is obtained as a by-product of copper, lead, and zinc ores. Hides are another example. As the value of a hide is about one-tenth that of a steer, the price of hides has almost no effect upon the number of cattle offered for sale. A large increase in the price of leather has little effect upon the supply beyond stimulating care to reduce the number of spoiled skins. It is, of course, possible to store hides, but the very variability in their price discourages this.

Farm flock eggs are an illustration of a commodity which is inelastic in supply because its production entails little pecuniary outlay. The hens are fed largely with scraps rather than with purchased feed and they are cared for by the farmer's wife in her spare time. Consequently, the number of hens and the production of eggs is little affected by changes in the price of eggs. In fact, agricultural commodities in general may be classed as goods which are inelastic in supply because their production does not involve large out-of-pocket money expenditures. Farming is a family industry in which only about one-fourth of the work is done by hired employees. When demand drops, factories reduce their staffs of hired employees more quickly than farmers cut production. In fact, as long as farmers remain in farming, it is profitable for them to produce as much as they and their families can make their land yield. Over-production in agriculture has been slow in correcting itself during the last decade partly (though not entirely) because farming is carried on by independent enterprisers rather than by hired employees.

VI. The Effect of Fixed Costs upon the Elasticity of Supply

An exceedingly important characteristic of the supply of many commodities is that, when demand is less than the capacity of the industry, supply is likely to be far more elastic in responding to increases in demand than in responding to decreases. In other words, below the capacity of the industry, supply has a one-sided elasticity — it stretches more readily than it contracts. The explanation of this peculiarity of supply is to be found in the nature of modern industrial costs. Pecuniary costs, it will be recalled, fall into two principal divisions — variable or direct costs, which fluctuate closely with the volume of output, and fixed or overhead costs, which are little or not at all affected by small changes in production. Machinery and large business units, it has been pointed out, have made fixed costs far more important than ever before in the history of industry. To fixed costs is attributable the fact that, below the capacity of the industry, supply tends to be inelastic in response to decreases in demand and elastic in response to increases in demand.

Let us first inquire why fixed costs tend to make supply inelastic in response to decreases in demand provided that the industry is operating at less than capacity. Suppose that a firm produces at a cost of $5.00 a unit and that its expenses are *all* direct — which means that, for every unit of goods which it turns out, its costs are increased by $5.00. Clearly if this firm agreed to sell 1,000 units at $4.00 each, it would lose $1,000, because its expenses would increase $5,000 but its income would increase only $4,000. Assume now that the direct expenses are only $3.00 per unit of output and that the enterprise has fixed costs of $40,000 a year. Suppose also that it can turn out 25,000 units a year but that it is producing only at the rate of 19,000 units. It has an opportunity to sell 1,000 units at $4.00 each. How would its net income be affected by the acceptance of this contract?

Clearly the enterprise would lose $1.00 on every unit which it sold at $4.00. Its direct expenses, as stated, are $3.00 a unit and if it accepted the order for 1,000 units, it would be producing at the rate of 20,000 units a year, which would make its fixed costs $2.00 a unit — a total unit cost of $5.00. If then the firm sold 1,000 units at $4.00 each, we should naturally expect to find its net income diminished by $1,000. But strange to say, this would not be the result. Instead of being decreased by $1,000, the net income would be *increased* by that amount! The explanation of this paradox — that an enterprise can make more money by selling at a loss than by not taking the order — is to be found in the fixed costs, which go on whether the sale is made or not. The only expenses which are increased by accepting the order are the direct costs, which are $3.00 a unit. The production of 1,000 additional units means an extra outlay, therefore, of $3,000. But these 1,000 units, selling at $4.00, bring an extra income of $4,000. Hence, the net addition to income achieved by selling 1,000 units at $1.00 below cost is $1,000! Here we see why supply tends to be inelastic in response to decreases in demand when an industry has large fixed costs and is producing at less than capacity. Because, under the circumstances, *any* price above direct costs is better than *no* price, enterprises are not likely to make large reductions in output as demand drops. The effect of fixed costs upon prices will be discussed in more detail in the next chapter and attention will be called to a number of reasons why concerns with idle capacity are often far less willing to cut prices than one might expect. It remains true, however, that fixed costs *tend* very strongly to make supply inelastic in response to decreases in demand.

Suppose now that demand, after having dropped substantially below the capacity of the industry, begins to increase. Until the industry is close to operating at capacity, the supply is likely to be exceedingly elastic in response to increases in demand. Again the explanation is to be found in fixed costs. Suppose that two competitors, A and B, each have a producing capacity of 100,000 units a year, fixed costs of $100,000 a year, and direct costs of $1.00 a unit. Let us further assume that each has been making 100,000 units a year and selling them for $2.00 each. At this price, each firm can break even as long as it can sell 100,-000 units. Suppose now that the demand suddenly drops so that, at $1.50 a unit, the two firms together are able to sell only 100,000 units. If the demand were distributed equally between them, each would have a unit cost of $3.00, so that, at $1.50 a unit, each firm is selling far below cost. Demand now begins slowly to increase. Each firm is naturally eager to raise its price. But notice the difficulty which each would encounter. Assume that, thanks to the recovery of demand, each enterprise is now selling at the rate of 60,000 units a year. If A, encouraged by the increase in demand, were to raise its price to $1.75, much of its trade would quickly go to B. A's sales, it is not unreasonable to suppose, might immediately drop to the rate of 25,000 a year and very soon would drop even lower. But an output of 25,000 units a year would mean a cost of $5.00 a unit — higher than ever above A's selling price. And, more than this, by enabling B to increase its sales from 60,000 to 85,000 units a year, A would reduce B's costs from $3.00 to $2.18 per unit. In other words, A would not only increase its own costs *but it would decrease those of its rival B*. If A persists in demanding $1.75 a

unit, B will soon have all of the business that its plant can handle.
B will not be making money even under these conditions, for its
unit costs are $2.00 even when operating at capacity, but B will
be substantially better off than A, which will have only the residue
of business that B's plant cannot handle. Were B instead of A
to take the initiative in raising the price, the situation would be
the same except that the position of the plants would be reversed.
Thus it is plain why heavy fixed costs make it so difficult for competing plants to raise their prices in response to increases in demand as long as the demand is substantially below the capacity
of the industry and why, therefore, supply under these circumstances tends to be elastic in response to increases in demand.

The general shape of the supply curve for an industry with
large fixed costs is shown in the following diagram:

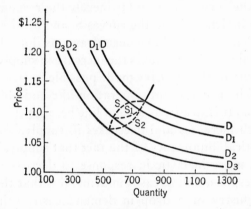

The initial demand is represented by the curve D. It is assumed
that the intersection of D and S represents the normal capacity of
the industry — the quantity which the industry is capable of producing without the use of overtime or bringing into operation
obsolete equipment. The reaction of supply to a gradual decrease
in demand from D to D_2 is indicated by the curve S. It will be observed that, when the demand is only slightly below the capacity
of the industry (down to about D_1, for example), supply is highly
elastic and drops rapidly in response to a small decrease in price.
But after substantial idle capacity has developed, the supply becomes highly inelastic — as the segment of S between D_1 and D_2
indicates. The response of supply to an increase in demand from
D_2 to D is indicated by the curve S_1. Until the demand has

reached D_1 and the capacity of the industry is fairly completely utilized, the supply is highly elastic — enterprises are willing to increase output in response to very slight price inducements. But after the demand approaches close to the capacity of the industry, producers begin to hold out for prices which are really remunerative and the supply becomes inelastic. Were the demand to drop below D (to D_3, for example) and then increase again to D, another curve S_2 is necessary to indicate the course of supply in response to the increase in demand. When the demand approximates the capacity of the industry, the supply curves S_2 and S_1 coincide. Most of the curve S_2, however, is substantially below S_1, because supply is highly elastic in response to an increase in the demand above D_3 until the capacity of the industry has almost been reached.

Because the curve S represents merely the response of supply to a decrease in demand and the curves S_1 and S_2, the response to increases in demand, they have been drawn as dotted lines. The supply curve above D represents the increase in supply beyond the normal capacity of the industry made possible by operating plants overtime and by bringing into operation idle and obsolete plants and machines. It is drawn as a solid line because this curve holds good for both increases and decreases in supply.

The practical importance of the fact that supply, below a certain point, is more inelastic in response to decreases in demand than it is in response to increases in demand is that the overbuilding of an industry or a drop in demand easily brings about a severe drop in prices to an unprofitable level and that, as long as competition is present, the industry is likely to find great difficulty in extricating itself from this situation.

VII. The Effect of Price Movements upon the Level of Supply and Demand

Thus far in discussing the stability of prices, we have assumed that the quantity of any commodity which would be demanded at a high price is less than the quantity which would be demanded at a low price and that the quantity which would be supplied at a high price would be greater than that which would be supplied at a low price. These assumptions seem to be beyond question. From them the conclusion naturally follows that price is a fairly perfect instrument for promptly restoring equilibrium whenever the quantity of goods offered for sale exceeds or falls short of the quantity demanded. Let the quantity offered for sale exceed the quantity demanded and the price will promptly fall until the demand equals the supply. Or let the quantity demanded exceed the quantity offered and the price will promptly rise until the two are equal. The natural inference is that demand and supply can never remain long out of equilibrium and that the maintenance of equilibrium in modern economic society is not much of a problem. As a matter of fact, however, price movements often do not seem to have the corrective influence which is ascribed to them by some economists. Instead of bringing about stability, price movements often aggravate a situation which is already unstable. Furthermore, it often happens that the demand for a good is greater at high prices than at low ones. This fact appears to be in conflict with the assumption upon which we have based our explanation of the determination of prices — namely that smaller quantities of goods will be demanded at high prices than at low ones.

In analyzing the conditions which make for stability or instability of prices, it is important to understand why price movements often fail to bring supply and demand promptly into equilibrium. The reason is to be found in the fact that price movements often produce changes in *the general level* of supply and demand. A change in price is likely to change *the willingness* of persons to buy or sell, making them ready to purchase more or to sell less at a high price today than at a low one yesterday. People often judge future prices by the price movements of the immediate past. A rise in price, for example, by creating the expectation of a further advance, may cause buyers to purchase in anticipation of it and may thus temporarily increase demand. It is true that a greater quantity of the commodity is demanded at a high price than at a low one, but this does not contradict the assumption which we have made in explaining prices that *at any given instant of time* a smaller quantity will be demanded at a high price than at a low one. The quantity demanded at the high price is greater than at the low one because *during an interval of time* the rise in the price has caused the general level of demand to increase. Price movements also affect the level of supply. The expectation of a higher price may make a good less, instead of more, plentiful by causing it to be speculatively hoarded. A fall in price, on the other hand, by creating the expectation of a further decline, may cause demand to drop and supply to increase.

The effects of price movements upon the levels of supply and demand can be represented graphically as follows:

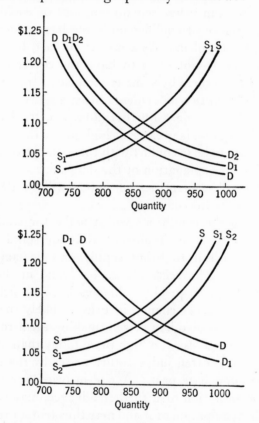

In each diagram, the curve D represents the original state of demand and the curve S the original state of supply. The first diagram shows a case of increasing demand and decreasing supply, the second a case of increasing supply and decreasing demand. In the first case, demand increases from D to D_1. The resulting rise in the price, by creating the expectation of a still further advance, causes supply to decrease from S to S_1 and demand to increase from D_1 to D_2. In the second case, the supply first increases from S to S_1. The resulting fall in price, however, causes demand to drop to D_1 because buyers expect the price to go still lower, and this causes supply to increase to S_2 because sellers are anxious to get rid of their goods before the price drops further.

The tendency for increases in price to produce increases in demand and decreases in supply, and for decreases in price to produce increases in supply and decreases in demand, is of great significance because it goes far toward explaining the instability of the whole price structure, which is the cause of so many important economic problems. As long, for example, as a rising price stimulates demand and restricts supply, the price will continue to advance. But since the large demand and the small supply are mainly the results of the rising price, it is evident that a day of reckoning is ahead. The rise in price will not continue forever and, when it ceases, a large part of the demand will disappear and the hoarded supplies will be dumped on the market with a precipitous fall in price as the result. The fall is made more severe by the fact that, for a time, it causes demand to decrease and supply to increase. This means that the drop must go far before equilibrium is established. In the meantime many enterprises which purchased at high prices have perhaps become insolvent. In our study of the business cycle, we shall recur to this problem of establishing equilibrium between supply and demand. Suffice it now to reiterate that equilibrium is far less promptly and easily established than has been sometimes assumed.

REFERENCES

Killough, H. B., " What Makes the Price of Oats? " U. S. Department of Agriculture, *Bulletin No. 1351*, September, 1925.

Schultz, Henry, *Statistical Laws of Demand and Supply with Special Application to Sugar*, 1928.

Smith, B. B., " Factors Affecting the Price of Cotton," U. S. Department of Agriculture, *Technical Bulletin No. 50*, January, 1928.

Warren, G. F., and Pearson, F. A., " Interrelationships of Supply and Price," Cornell Agricultural Experiment Station, *Bulletin No. 466*, March, 1928.

Warren, G. F., and Pearson, F. A., *The Agricultural Situation*, 1924. Ch. IV.

Working, Holbrook, " Factors Affecting the Price of Minnesota Potatoes," Minnesota Agricultural Experiment Station, *Technical Bulletin No. 29*, October, 1925.

CHAPTER XIV

COST OF PRODUCTION AND COMPETITIVE PRICE

I. THE LONG-RUN RELATIONSHIP BETWEEN COST OF PRODUCTION AND PRICE.   II. WHY SOME ENTERPRISES DO BUSINESS AT A LOSS. III. WHY ENTERPRISES ARE SLOW TO WITHDRAW FROM INDUSTRIES IN WHICH THERE IS EXCESSIVE PRODUCTIVE CAPACITY.   IV. SOME CAUSES FOR THE OVERDEVELOPMENT OF INDUSTRIES.   V. THE DETERMINATION OF PRICE WHEN GOODS ARE PRODUCED AT JOINT COST.   VI. HOW FIXED COSTS AFFECT PRICES.

I. The Long-run Relationship Between Cost of Production and Price

Competition tends to fix price, we have seen, at the point where supply and demand are equal. But at what point are they equal? Is it not possible to be more definite about this?

As far as short periods are concerned, this appears to be impossible because demand and supply at any moment are largely the products of special influences which change from day to day. A new style or fad, a change in the weather, or a special event causes the demand for some things to shoot up and for others as rapidly to drop. Strikes, fires, floods, crop failures, transportation tie-ups create temporary shortages in supply. On the other hand, liquidation to meet maturing indebtedness, to wind up the affairs of a bankrupt, or to settle an estate may throw substantial quantities of goods on the market for what they will bring. A drought on the cattle ranges produces first a great increase in the supply of cattle and later a shortage. In September, 1926, a heavy storm caused fruit raisers in central New York to advertise windfallen peaches for practically any price that buyers would name. The severe heat spell which covered the Middle West and the East in September, 1927, sent the price of lemons in Madison, Wisconsin, where they had been selling at three for 10 cents, to 15 cents apiece on September 17th. Influences such as these make it impossible to define for short periods the point at which demand and supply are in equilibrium.

If we consider longer periods, however, it becomes possible to be more definite concerning the determination of most prices — that is, concerning the prices of reproducible commodities. In the long run, the supply (and hence the price) of a reproducible good is determined by the expenses of production, including the return necessary to attract capital into the industry. This statement must not be misunderstood. It does not mean that sellers refuse to sell at any price which is less than their costs. Once goods have been made, there is nothing to do but to sell them, sooner or later, for what they will bring and this price may not cover the cost of production. *In the long run,* however, prices gravitate toward the cost of production, including, as was stated, the return necessary to attract capital into the industry.

At once the objection arises: "No two producers have the same cost of production. How then can it be said that prices are determined by cost of production? *Whose* cost of production is meant?" The answer is: The cost of no producer in particular. What is meant by saying that price is determined by cost of production simply is that the amount of capital which is devoted to producing each commodity depends upon the relationship between prices and costs. It is easy to see why this is so. Assume that the output of a commodity is so large and the price so low that much of the supply must be sold at a loss. Under these circumstances, some plants would shut down and others would shift to the production of other commodities. New capital would be discouraged from entering the industry. The losses of capacity due to shut-downs and shifts would exceed the gains from new construction, the output of the industry would diminish, and the price of the commodity would rise. This would continue until the return on new capital invested in the industry was no less attractive than the return on new capital invested in other industries. Assume, on the other hand, that the output of a commodity is so small and the price so high that additional quantities could be produced at a large profit. Under these circumstances, the industry would be an attractive field for investment, its productive capacity would expand, and the resulting increase in output would cause the price of the commodity to fall. The fall would go on until new capital invested in the industry yielded no more attractive return than new capital invested in other industries.

II. WHY SOME ENTERPRISES DO BUSINESS AT A LOSS

The fact that prices tend to be determined by the expenses of production (including the return necessary to attract capital) does not mean that prices are ordinarily high enough for every enterprise in every industry to meet its cost of production and to earn the current return on its capital. Possibly existing enterprises are immensely profitable; or possibly most of them are losing money. All that can be said is that when there are no hindrances to the investment of capital, the supply (and consequently the price) of each reproducible good tends to be such that *new* capital can command an equally attractive rate of return in all industries. (An equally attractive rate, of course, is not necessarily the *same* rate because there are differences in the financial risks in different industries.) The fact that *newly invested* capital can command a certain rate of return does not necessarily mean that *old* capital can command the same rate. Technical improvements, shifts in population, new centers of labor supply, new sources of raw materials, and new routes of communication are constantly making it possible to build new plants which can undersell many old ones. Consequently, a price which yields a comfortable profit to new enterprises and which attracts much new capital into the industry may leave no profit to many old enterprises.[1] Thus we see that the existence of more plants than can be operated at a profit is *a normal and constant condition in any dynamic society* in which industrial technique is improving, population shifting, and new routes or methods of communica-

---

[1] The returns for the corporate income tax indicate that in most years nearly half of the corporations earn no net income — as net income is defined for purposes of taxation. The proportion reporting net income is usually between 55 and 60 per cent out of the total. Of course many corporations which report net income do not earn enough to pay the rate of return to the owners which the investors of new capital expect. On the other hand, the fact that nearly half of the corporations ordinarily earn no profits, does not mean that nearly half of all business is done at a loss. The same conditions which prevent enterprises from making profits keep them small. Consequently, the concerns which make no money are for the most part small ones. About four-fifths of all corporate business appears to be done at some profit. See Crum, W. L., *Corporate Earning Power*, p. 270.

tion being created.[2] The cotton cloth and the coal industries
have both been notorious for the fact that an unusually large
number of enterprises in them have been losing money. And yet
each industry has attracted large amounts of new capital.   In
fact, it is *because* these industries have been so successful in attracting new capital, that so many old enterprises in them have
been losing money. The low operating costs of the mines in the
newly developed West Virginia and Kentucky fields have led the
coal industry to expand rapidly in those states despite the fact
that many mines in other states could not make profits. And
cheap labor and waterpower and the proximity of raw materials make it profitable to build new cotton mills in the Carolinas
and Georgia even when the more or less out-of-date mills of New
England are losing money. The acute distress of many wheat
growers and cotton raisers, of which much has been heard during
the last ten years, is due in large measure to the fact that it has
been profitable to expand production on the high plains at prices
which were below the costs of farmers in the older sections. Between 1918 and 1928, for example, the cotton acreage in South
Carolina and Georgia decreased from 8,342,000 to 6,285,000, or
nearly 25 per cent, but the acreage in Texas and Oklahoma increased over 56 per cent — from 14,231,000 to 22,261,000.[3]

III. WHY ENTERPRISES ARE SLOW TO WITHDRAW FROM INDUSTRIES IN WHICH THERE IS EXCESSIVE PRODUCTIVE CAPACITY

It is easy to understand why changes in technique, shifts of
population, or discoveries of raw material should prevent some
concerns from making money. But this does not entirely explain
why it is a normal and constant condition for industries to have
more plants than can operate at a profit. When this condition
exists, why is it not quickly corrected by some enterprises' dropping out or shifting to the production of other commodities?
Why do they remain in operation for years when they are losing

---

[2] But the existence of obsolete plants which are no longer making money does
not necessarily mean that the owners miscalculated when they made their investment.
A plant cannot be expected to be as profitable when it is old as when it was new. In
judging whether or not an investment is profitable, the average return *for its whole
life* must be taken into account. We shall learn presently why, when a plant has
ceased to make money, it is often more profitable to operate it than to scrap it.

[3] Nourse, E. G., "Agriculture," *Recent Economic Changes*, v. II, p. 572.

money? Are they not worse off every moment that they continue to operate at a loss?

Of course, the fact that a firm is losing money now does not mean that it has no chance of making profits in the future. And to its owners, the outlook often seems brighter than it really is. It is difficult for them to abandon the hope that their venture will ultimately succeed. Hence they often carry on as long as their resources permit, hoping for an improvement in demand or a drop in the cost of labor and supplies and endeavoring to reduce expenses by improving methods of operation.

But this does not explain why business establishments are *able* to operate for long periods at a loss. The explanation is to be found in the nature of modern industrial costs, which not only make it possible for firms to operate at a loss for a long time *but often make this course more economical than shutting down or shifting to the production of other things.*

Some costs, such as wages and salaries, raw materials, rent, freight, express, postage, and light, must be met promptly. A concern which could not pay them would be forced to shut down. But there are other expenses which need not be paid at once.[4] Suppose, for example, that a firm purchases a piece of land for $100,000. The interest on this investment must be included in the cost of the product and, if the firm fails to earn the interest, it is doing business at a loss. But failure to earn interest on the cost of the land is no reason for shutting down. That would not enable the enterprise to earn any more. By continuing to operate, however, it may succeed in earning *something* on its investment — possibly $2,000 or $3,000.

The situation presented by the purchase of buildings, machinery, and other semi-permanent equipment is similar. Interest on the cost of the building and equipment is, of course, part of the cost of production and must be earned before the business can be regarded as making expenses. In the case of buildings and equipment, however, there are two expenses which are usually not present in the case of land — depreciation and insur-

---

[4] The distinction between costs which must be met at once and those which can be paid later should not be confused with the distinction which we have already made between direct and fixed costs. All direct costs must be paid at once and all costs which can be paid later are fixed expenses. But there are *some* fixed costs, such as taxes, salaries, and rent, which must be paid promptly.

ance.[5] But failure to earn depreciation or insurance is not a reason for shutting down. Buildings and equipment become obsolete and to some extent deteriorate physically whether they are used or not. Hence it is usually advantageous to operate even though depreciation and insurance charges are not being earned.

But between failure to earn depreciation and insurance charges and failure to earn interest on the investment there is one vital difference. An establishment can go on *indefinitely* failing to earn interest on the funds invested in its buildings or equipment. Of course, if the property was obtained with borrowed money, failure to pay the interest may cause control of the enterprise to pass in whole or in part to its creditors. But they have no more reason than the original owners for shutting down the plant simply because it does not earn the interest on its debts. Their concern, like that of the original owners, is for the enterprise to earn as much as possible toward the full interest charges.

On the other hand, failure to earn depreciation or insurance is bound sooner or later to cause more serious trouble. Eventually machines and buildings wear out, become obsolete, or are destroyed. But if neither depreciation nor insurance has been earned, there are no funds with which to buy new buildings or equipment. A brief respite may be gained by employing working capital to make the replacements. But this use of working capital compels the firm to contract its scale of operations, to borrow more heavily from banks, or to buy more largely upon credit. If it contracts its operations, it reduces its income; if it borrows from banks, it loads itself with interest charges which must be met without fail; and if it purchases upon credit, its expenses are increased by the loss of cash discounts. As more and more buildings and equipment wear out, become obsolete, or are destroyed, the situation of the firm becomes increasingly desperate. Ultimately the enterprise is unable to raise the funds needed to replace equipment and is forced into a belated shutdown.

But granting that modern industrial costs make it financially *possible* for concerns to do business at a loss for a considerable period, would it not be more *profitable* — or *less unprofitable* — for losing ventures either to dismantle their plants and sell their

[5] But in the case of farm land, depreciation should often be charged.

equipment and buildings or to convert their plants to other uses? Undoubtedly either course would often be more advantageous than continuing to operate. But this does not necessarily mean that the plant will be dismantled or converted to other uses. The optimistic belief that better times are ahead and reluctance to confess failure deter owners from either course, and their unfamiliarity with other lines of business is an additional reason why they are slow to adopt the second alternative.

In many instances, however, it is more advantageous to operate at a loss than to dismantle the plant or to convert it to other uses. Second-hand tools and machines usually sell for so little that a plant which earns only a small fraction of the proper depreciation charges may yield more than could be obtained by selling the equipment. And the specialized apparatus in modern industry makes it difficult to change a plant from one use to another without discarding much old and purchasing much new machinery.

IV. Some Causes for the Overdevelopment of Industries

Although the existence of more plants than can earn profits must be regarded as a normal and constant condition in any dynamic society, it is not uncommon for industries to become so greatly overdeveloped that a very large proportion of the enterprises in them operate for years at a loss. These cases are important because they indicate how great are the difficulties of adjusting the supply of productive capacity to the demand for it.

Excessive capacity may be created through a sudden shrinkage in the demand for a commodity or through a rapid expansion in the producing power of the industry. Sudden and pronounced decreases in the demand may be caused by changes in fashions, the invention of competing commodities, greater durability of the article, substantial changes in the distribution of wealth, the creation of new tariff barriers. When lace and carpets passed out of vogue, the lace and carpet industries found themselves with a great excess of men and equipment; the development of composition roofing has left the wooden shingle industry with an excess of capacity; the invention of artificial silk, which can be sold for little more than cotton, has created surplus capacity in the cotton cloth industry; and the spread of electric refrigeration threatens to do the same thing to the ice industry. Improvements in automobile tires which make them wear longer have added to the surplus capacity of the tire industry. The territorial changes following the European war created many tariff barriers which deprived industries of their markets. When the Austro-Hungarian Empire was divided among eight states, the industries of Vienna found themselves separated from over three-fourths of their former customers by tariff walls. The new boundary between France and Germany transferred large quantities of iron ore to France and left the German coal mines without an adequate market for their coal.

Equally numerous are the ways in which the producing power of industries may be increased quite out of proportion to the demand for the product. To some extent the overdevelopment of industries is simply the result of planning for the future. It is often more economical to provide for expected increases in demand when a plant is first built than to enlarge the plant later. The sellers of equipment are sometimes responsible for the overdevelopment of industries. Their well-trained salesmen often persuade producers to buy more equipment than the market can keep busy at profitable prices. This is a serious complaint in the printing industry. There are many thousands of printing plants. Few managers have accurate knowledge of the relationship between the capacity of the industry and the demand for printing. Most managers, however, are optimistic about their ability to obtain more business for themselves. Consequently, it is relatively easy for the salesmen of printing presses and other machines to persuade printers to buy more equipment than they need. Good salesmanship plus the ignorance and optimism of many printers leads to the overdevelopment of the industry.

Any sudden increase in the demand for a commodity is likely to bring into existence a great surplus of productive capacity, especially when new plants take some time to build. The sudden increase in demand causes the price of the commodity to advance and this encourages speculative buying — that is, it causes the article to be purchased in advance of the need for it. Sellers are unable to fill all orders promptly and completely. This leads some buyers to order more than they really wish or to place duplicate orders with several enterprises with the intention of cancelling the orders which are not promptly filled. Speculative buying and the duplication of orders make the more or less normal and permanent demand difficult to estimate, and producers enlarge their plants or build new ones on the assumption that the demand will remain as large or almost as large as it is at the height of speculative buying.

Of course, if supply could be increased as promptly as demand expands, there would probably be no substantial rise in the price of the commodity and no overexpansion of the industry. But the longer the time needed to create additional productive capacity, the greater is likely to be the overdevelopment of the industry. The rise in the price of the commodity causes old plants to be enlarged and new ones to be built. But before the first new capacity comes into operation and affects supply and prices, the high price stimulates still other business men, unaware of how much the industry is being expanded, to initiate more new enterprises or to expand existing ones. Thus productive capacity is increased far beyond that which can be profitably operated. Many illustrations might be given. The European war, by diminishing the output of beet sugar in France and Germany, greatly stimulated the cane sugar industry in Cuba. But the clearing of forests for plantations and the building of roads and railways to move the cane to the mills take considerable time. Consequently Cuban production was still increasing long after the war was over and the European beet sugar industry had substantially recovered.

An interesting case of overdevelopment following a rapid increase in demand is provided by the California raisin industry. In 1912, when prices were unremunerative and growers in debt, the California Raisin Growers' Association was formed. It standardized the product, packed it in distinctive boxes, and advertised it extensively. As a result of these activities and of the general rise in prices, the price of raisins in California rose from 6 cents a pound in 1912 to nearly 19 cents in 1920. The grape growers became prosperous, their lands advanced in value to about $1,000 an acre, and Fresno, the chief city in the raisin district, boasted more wealth *per capita* than any other city in the country. This very prosperity, however, led to a doubling in

the production of grapes between 1912 and 1920. Many vine‑
yards planted during the period of high prices did not come into
bearing until a general depression had seized the country in 1921.
The increase in output at this particular time caused the price
to drop from nearly 19 cents a pound in 1920 to less than 11
cents in 1922. Furthermore, the plantings which had been made
during the period of high prices and which in 1923 had not yet
come into bearing, gave promise that within five years the pro‑
duction would rise from about 250,000 tons a year to over 400,‑
000 tons. So in 1923, as before in 1912, the raisin growers were
confronted with the problem of overproduction.

The formation of a monopoly often results in the overdevel‑
opment of an industry. When the sugar‑trust was formed, the re‑
fining facilities of the country were greater than could be profit‑
ably operated. The trust restricted output, raised prices, and
made refining highly lucrative. Independent refineries promptly
sprang up to reap some of the large profits. The trust, in self‑
protection, bought several of these plants at high prices and this
encouraged the building of still more refineries. The existence of
excess capacity in the whiskey industry led to cutthroat competi‑
tion and to the formation of pools for the purpose of keeping
prices at a profitable level. But the pools aggravated rather than
alleviated the situation because, by raising prices, they stimulated
the building of more distilleries and, when the pools broke up, as
they all did sooner or later, the industry found itself more over‑
developed than before. The glucose monopoly and the wire‑nail
pool appear to have produced similar effects. The Federal
Trade Commission, in ordering the American Photo‑Engravers'
Association to cease issuing a standard scale of prices which
tended to eliminate competition in price, said that the standard
scale had "resulted in bringing into the industry many new plants
of which a large proportion are managed by men ill‑equipped
by experience and capital. Hence, so many shops have entered
the trade that the capacity to produce engraving products much
exceeds the demand, thus increasing the loss due to idle labor
time and increasing the costs of production." [6]

Technical innovations frequently lead to the overexpansion of
industries. A new method or machine which greatly reduces

[6] *The American Photo-Engraver*, March, 1928, v. XX, p. 327.

operating costs must be adopted by every firm which expects to remain in the industry. And yet if the new method greatly increases the capacity of the plants using it, its general adoption is almost certain to create excess productive capacity — particularly if the demand for the product is inelastic. Business men may perceive this, but, unless willing to abandon the industry, must use the invention. Most of them, knowing the industry in which they are engaged better than any other and having trade connections in it, prefer to adopt the invention rather than take up another business, hoping to be fortunate enough to survive in the impending struggle for existence. The cigarette-making machine, invented in the late eighties, and the wire-nail machine, invented in the nineties, both illustrate how the general adoption of a new device, far more efficient than old methods, may create excess productive capacity. More recently still, technical innovations in agriculture, particularly the motorization of farms, have contributed heavily to the serious overdevelopment of many branches of farming and to the chronic depression which has prevailed in many of the agricultural industries since 1920. It is exceedingly significant that most of this period of agricultural depression has been one of great prosperity for the farm implement industry. Between 1918 and 1929, for example, the number of tractors on farms in the United States increased from 80,100 to 853,000 and in the same period the number of horses and mules on farms declined by nearly 7,000,000 — almost 27 per cent.[7] By substituting gasoline for horses and mules, not only did farmers obtain larger output per acre at a lower cost of production, but they also released between 15,000,000 and 18,000,000 acres of hay and pasture land for the raising of other crops.

Not only do technical innovations lead to the overdevelopment of industries, but the overdevelopment of industries encourages the invention and the adoption of methods and appliances which further increase the output and cut the costs of production. Indeed, as will be explained in a subsequent chapter, falling profits are often a more powerful stimulant of managerial efficiency than rising profits. If the efforts of managers to increase output and to reduce costs are widely successful and if the demand for the product of the industry is inelastic, the very efforts of managers

[7] Nourse, E. G., " Agriculture," in *Recent Economic Changes*, v. II, pp. 558–559.

to extricate themselves from their situation may cause matters to go from bad to worse. It is extremely easy for industries to get into a vicious circle in which a state of overdevelopment and depression prolongs itself by stimulating greater productivity. The current depression in many branches of agriculture appears to be an illustration. The depression has driven hundreds of thousands of men out of agriculture and it has caused a slight shrinkage in the acreage devoted to crop raising, but these have been insufficient to offset the tendency of technical progress to increase agricultural output.

When integration is created by building new plants, it may result in surplus producing capacity. An enterprise that builds a plant in which to produce its own raw material, may bring about an overdevelopment of that industry. In addition, the makers of the raw material, finding their market slipping away, may embark on the manufacture of the finished article, creating surplus facilities in that industry. Leather tanning furnishes an illustration of overdevelopment which has been accentuated by integration. The instability in the price of hides and leather led some packing plants to tan their own hides and some shoe manufacturers to make their own leather. The United States Steel Corporation was formed to prevent overdevelopment of the steel industry by the spread of integration. The National Tube Company, a producer of steel tubes which had purchased much of its steel from the Carnegie Steel Company, decided to make its own steel. The Carnegie Company, foreseeing the loss of an important customer and fearing that others might follow the example of the Tube Company, announced its intention of building an immense tube mill at Conneaut, Ohio. Had each concern executed its plans, a great excess of steel and tube mills would have resulted and a severe price war would have been inevitable. The struggle was averted by forming the United States Steel Corporation to control the National Tube Company, the Carnegie Steel Company, and other makers of steel and its products. In other words, overexpansion was prevented by substituting integration by combination for integration by the construction of new plants.

War is almost certain to leave an aftermath of many overdeveloped industries, not only because it creates an abnormal demand for some products but also because it temporarily destroys trade channels and causes industries to spring up in regions where they never before were able to get started. The overexpansion of the British coal industry has been accentuated by the fact that the German occupation of northern France compelled the rest of France to depend largely upon Great Britain for coal. The necessity of making heavy reparation payments in kind may accentuate the overdevelopment. The obligation of Germany to make large payments to France and Italy in coal has stimulated the expansion of the German coal industry at a time when the coal industry of Europe, as a result of the war, is already overdeveloped.[8]

V. The Determination of Price When Goods Are Produced at Joint Cost

A gas company buys coal and from it makes gas and coke. The expenditure for the coal is obviously part of the cost of both the gas and the coke. But there is no way of deciding how much of the price of the coal should properly be charged to the gas and how much to the coke and hence no way of ascertaining precisely how much it costs to produce either.

This example illustrates an important aspect of modern industry — the production of commodities at joint cost. A packing company purchases cattle. From them it produces many things — meat, hides, fertilizer, oleomargarine, soap, stock feeds, pharmaceutical supplies. The cost of the cattle is part of the expense of making each of these. From the same crude oil, a refining company produces gasoline, kerosene, paraffin, vaseline, lubricating oil, and other products. The farmer who grows cotton is producing two things — cotton fibre and cottonseed; and the cottonseed itself yields several products — cottonseed oil and cotton-meal cake, a stock feed. Wool and mutton are derived from the same sheep, sugar and molasses from the same sugar cane, the shipments carried by a railroad company are carried at joint expense, a street car is the means of furnishing not only transportation but advertising space, cutting timber produces not only logs but cut-over land.

---

[8] Germany might be regarded as paying reparations in the form of work and the British coal miners in the form of unemployment.

Thus far, in discussing the relationship between costs and prices, we have assumed that the expense of production is a definitely ascertainable amount. How, otherwise, could we assert that price tends to gravitate toward a point determined by the expense of production? But if it is impossible to ascertain the expense of producing a commodity which is made at joint cost, must not the assertion that price gravitates toward a point determined by the expense of production be confined to commodities which are not produced at joint cost?

Some modification of the statement is necessary but, strangely enough, it is possible to trace a fairly definite relationship between the prices of joint products and the cost of producing them. The minimum price of each joint product is set by the separable expenses of making it. Some labor and equipment, for example, are employed exclusively in manufacturing bacon, some exclusively in the production of hams, and some exclusively in the production of lard. The expenses which are directly and solely attributable to each by-product determine *the lowest* price at which the enterprise can afford to supply it. Rather than accept less, it would pay the firm to cease making the by-product. In addition, the total cost of producing all of several joint products (including the necessary return to the business owners) limits the supply and thus affects their prices in the same manner as does the expense of making a single commodity. Whenever the total receipts from the joint products yield more than the rate of profit necessary to attract capital into the industry, there is a tendency, such as we have already described, for output to be increased by the expansion of plants. Likewise when receipts fail to yield sufficient profits, output tends to be diminished by an exodus of capital from the industry.

When two goods are jointly produced, there is no assurance that the relative amounts of the two will be in proportion to the relative intensity of the demand for them. For example, at the same price per pound, the public might demand three times as much of A as of B. But the two goods might be produced in the proportion of two pounds of A for one of B. Obviously, in this case, the price of A would be higher than the price of B. The difference in the prices of several joint products is likely to be especially large when the less desired commodity happens to be produced in greater abundance. The choice cuts of beef, for example, the loin and the ribs, constitute only about 25 per cent of the total dressed weight. On the other hand, the "chuck," or shoulder part of the forequarter, and the round each amount to about 24 per cent of the total weight. Possibly the retailer pays 18 cents a pound for a whole side of beef but charges 50 cents a pound or more for the porterhouse. If the packer cuts up the side of beef, he gets only about one-third as much for the "chuck" as he does for the loin.

Naturally business men endeavor to change the proportions in which joint products are made, so that there will be a larger supply of the good which is in greater demand and a smaller supply of the one which is in less demand. The efforts of refiners to increase the proportion of gasoline yielded by crude oil are an illustration. But sometimes the relative quantities of joint products are beyond human control, as when copper, zinc, and lead are found in the same ore. When the proportions of joint products are naturally fixed, business men are likely to make a special effort to stimulate the demand for the product which is in less demand. The case of fancy meats is an example. By fancy meats is meant such things as sweetbreads, livers, tongues, brains, and oxtails. Only since 1910, has the trade in these products become important. By advertising, by inventing and publishing recipes, by teaching retailers how to display and sell, and by putting up meat such as oxtails and pork feet in special boxes, the packers have succeeded in greatly increasing the demand for these products.[9]

The distinction between joint products which are produced in proportions fixed by nature and those which can be turned out in variable proportions according to the will of business men is important in analyzing the effect of changes in demand upon the prices of the goods. When the relative amounts of two joint products are naturally fixed, a rise in the demand for one — the demand for the second remaining unchanged — brings about an increase in the supply of both and a decrease, therefore, in the price of the second. Thus new uses for copper, by encouraging the mining of ore containing copper, zinc, and lead, have tended to keep down the prices of zinc and lead. But when the propor-

[9] Swift and Co., *Year Book*, 1923, pp. 30–31.

tions of two joint products can be controlled, an increase in demand for one may cause more of it and less of the other to be made. As a result, there may occur the strange phenomenon of the good which is in *greater* demand *decreasing* in price and of the good which is *unchanged* in demand *rising* in price.

It is possible, of course, that the demand for one of two joint products may grow so much that it cannot be satisfied simply by changing the proportions in which the two are made. In this event, the total supply of the second commodity may be increased instead of decreased and its price may fall instead of advancing. This is illustrated by gasoline and kerosene. Before the development of the automobile, gasoline was a drug on the market. At one time, refineries dumped their surplus supply into the sea. Kerosene was the most important good obtained from petroleum, and refiners concentrated their attention upon making petroleum yield a larger percentage of kerosene and a smaller proportion of gasoline and other products. The automobile changed all of this. So much has the output of gasoline grown in response to the automobile demand that, despite new refining methods which greatly increase the proportion of gasoline, the production of kerosene is far greater than ten or twenty years ago. Kerosene is now difficult to dispose of. To get rid of it, the Standard Oil Company has given away millions of inexpensive lamps in China and has developed a kerosene stove. Kerosene has been unsatisfactory for heat because of its red or yellowish flame which gives light but little heat. To create a market, the company has developed a stove in which kerosene burns with a blue, heat-producing flame.

VI. How Fixed Costs Affect Prices

Machinery and large business units, as has been pointed out several times, have made fixed costs extraordinarily important in modern industry. This is of great significance because fixed costs are responsible for several of the outstanding price policies of modern business enterprises. It has been pointed out in the preceding chapter that, on account of fixed costs, business concerns can often make more by getting an order at anything above direct costs than by not getting it at all. Naturally they are under a strong temptation to cut prices down almost to direct costs. But, in the long run, enterprises cannot remain in operation unless they are able to meet both their fixed and their direct costs. Consequently, if competition compels establishments to sell their goods for a price which scarcely covers direct expenses, it is merely a question of time before they will be forced out of business or compelled to limit competition among themselves — that is, compelled to create some form of monopoly. In other words, we are confronted with the question of whether long-continued competition is possible in industries characterized by heavy fixed costs. To fixed costs also are attributable the phenomenon known as "dumping" — that is, the sale of goods in remote markets for less than in near-by ones — and a tendency to sell to different customers at widely varying prices.

Many — in fact, probably most — of the industries in which fixed expenses are heavy do not appear to be characterized by cutthroat competition. How is this to be explained? Let us begin by asking under precisely what circumstances heavy fixed expenses create a tendency to sell below cost. It will be recalled that in the preceding chapter a hypothetical case was given of an enterprise with direct costs of $3.00 per unit, fixed costs of $40,000 per year, a capacity of 25,000 units a year, and an actual output of 19,000 units. This concern, by accepting an order for 1,000 at $4.00 per unit, or $1.00 below cost, could increase its profits by $1,000. In other words, it made more by selling below cost than by not accepting the order. But why was it profitable for the concern to sell at less than cost? Clearly because it possessed idle productive capacity. It could make 25,000 units a year; it was operating only at the rate of 19,000 a year. Had it possessed all the orders that it could fill in the immediate future, it obviously would not have offered to supply 1,000 units at less than cost. In fact, if it had possessed orders which occupied *nearly* all of its productive capacity, it would probably have refused to sell below cost. The reason for this will be explained presently. *Idle productive capacity,* then, is necessary to make enterprises willing to sell below cost, and the eagerness with which they seek additional business at prices below cost depends upon the amount of their idle capacity.

The principal reason why heavy fixed costs do not more often lead to cutthroat competition probably is that, during much of the time, the capacity of the *more efficient* plants does not greatly exceed their orders. And the reason why it does not is simply that capitalists do not invest their funds unless they see — or think they see — an opportunity to get a return on them. During slack seasons and slack years, of course, the producing power of many plants far exceeds their orders and, if fixed expenses are heavy, prices may sink very low. In most industries, however, these times are balanced by other periods when orders closely approximate or exceed the capacity of the plants and when many enterprises are working overtime. It then becomes possible to get prices which enable the more efficient plants to make up for the failure to earn fixed costs during slack periods.

But even idle producing capacity does not necessarily cause concerns with heavy fixed expenses to sell below cost. One reason is that all concerns have many fixed costs — such as rent, interest on indebtedness, salaries of executives and clerks, and the wages of workers who do not directly work upon the product — *which recur frequently and must be paid without delay*. None of these expenses, be it noted, are direct costs, for they do not fluctuate closely with small changes in the volume of business. Yet they must be met promptly every week, every month, or every quarter if the concern is to avoid insolvency. In other words, to keep in operation at all, an enterprise must have coming in more or less regularly an income *which considerably exceeds its direct expenses*. This immediate necessity of earning substantially more than direct costs leads business men to feel that between a price that covers only direct costs and no sale there is little choice. Either means that the enterprise must soon shut down. Consequently, managers are led to gamble on getting a price which enables them to survive or not getting the order at all.

Another important reason why business men are reluctant to cut prices is the fact that a reduction to one customer must sooner or later be extended to all customers. Suppose that a concern is operating at half capacity. The sales manager is considering the advisability of offering a 10 per cent cut to obtain a certain order. He knows that the firm can continue to operate at half capacity without making the cut. He knows also that even if the reduction is made secretly, news of it will soon leak out and that other customers will insist upon the same treatment. To get this one order, is it worth while to risk bringing about a 10 per cent reduction in the price of the entire output of the firm?

Of course, if the sales manager could be certain that the reduction in price would bring a substantial increase in business, he might be quite willing to make it. But what expectation can he have that there will be an increase? For a short time, the firm may gain business from its competitors, but they are bound promptly to reduce their prices enough to hold their customers. The price cut may even cause the concern to lose customers. Buyers who purchased shortly before the reduction and who, because of the cut, are compelled to sell at a loss may, out of resentment, transfer their business elsewhere. So serious sometimes is the loss of good will which follows price cuts that manufacturers often shut down for several weeks immediately before a reduction, thus giving dealers a chance to dispose of their stock at old prices.[10] And finally, it is not certain that a lower price will immediately increase sales. The first effect of a price cut, we have seen, is often a *decrease* rather than an increase in demand. Buyers regard the reduction as presaging further cuts and hold off as long as possible; when they do buy, they purchase only for their immediate needs. Eventually, after buyers cease to look for further reductions, the lower price may increase demand. Especially in slack times, however, sellers are interested in an immediate increase in sales. Naturally they are reluctant to stimulate, even temporarily, the tendency for demand to decline. For these reasons, they often delay reducing prices in the face of diminishing demand, hoping that market conditions will soon change.

Some enterprises endeavor to stabilize their trade by not charging old customers as much as the market permits during boom times. The expectation is that those who are accom-

[10] The Armstrong Cork Company goes so far as to protect its jobbers against price reductions to the extent of 85 per cent of the difference between the old price and the new. The protection applies to the goods purchased by the jobbers from the company within ninety days of the cut. Palmer, J. L., "Sales Policies of the Armstrong Cork Company," *Journal of Business of the University of Chicago*, January, 1928, v. I, p. 123.

When the Grigsby-Grunow Company, makers of Majestic radios, cut $20 from the price of a certain model, it asked its dealers to report the number of that model which they had on hand. Each dealer received a check from the company covering his loss on the price cut. *Printer's Ink*, July 11, 1929, v. CXLVIII, No. 2, p. 157.

modated in this manner will continue to buy from the seller during slack times when goods could be obtained from other firms for less. Other concerns pursue the policy of asking all that they can get in times of boom and of ruthlessly cutting prices in order to obtain more business during times of depression. Consequently it often happens that a commodity is sold in the same market at widely divergent prices. But strictly speaking, *it is not the same commodity*. The enterprise which in a dull year charges more than its competitors is selling not merely so many tons or gallons or yards but also the willingness to supply its regular customers during busy times at less than boom prices.

Finally, the reluctance of managers to cut prices is affected by the strong sentiment which has grown up in the business world that it is unbusinesslike and even unethical to sell below cost in the domestic market in order to get more business. The very fact that, when demand is low, fixed costs per unit of output are large, is regarded as all the more reason why a good price should be realized on the quantity which is sold. This policy of standing pat in the face of falling demand and of making only moderate price concessions has received powerful support from trade associations, trade journals, and national business leaders.[11] The average business man, like the average man in other occupations, wishes to be " regular " and orthodox, to do the approved and accepted thing. In face of the powerful sentiment that has been built up against aggressive price cutting, a business head often needs unusual courage and independence in order to be willing to start a vigorous price-slashing campaign.[12]

---

[11] An interesting attempt to prevent price-cutting in the face of falling demand and an uncertain future was recently made by a group of eighty-four manufacturers of fabric woolens for men's wear. These eighty-four manufacturers, on December 11, 1929, authorized the Wool Institute to announce a list of mills which intended to maintain listed prices on all re-orders and new business for the spring, 1930, season. Prior to the action of the Institute, many manufacturers were delaying purchases due to lack of confidence in prices. With quotations on an assured level, it was believed that many manufacturers would take immediate steps to obtain the remainder of their spring requirements. *Journal of Commerce and Commercial*, December 12, 1929, p. 1. On December 13th, the original list of eighty-four was supplemented by ninety-one additional mills. This brought the total number declaring their intention of maintaining list prices up to 175. *Ibid.*, December 13, 1929, pp. 1 and 13.

[12] The following quotation from the official publication of the National Association of Building Trades Employers illustrates the effort to create sentiment against price cutting:

Despite the many considerations which make business men reluctant to cut prices, the possibility of getting work for idle machines creates a temptation difficult to resist. Consequently, price wars do occur and, once started, they are difficult to end. The reason was explained in the preceding chapter. When one of several competitors with idle capacity attempts to end a price war by raising prices, the enterprise simply makes its own condition worse than ever. It decreases its own sales and increases those of its competitors. This means that it increases its own unit costs and lowers the costs of its competitors. There appear to be only two ways by which the cutthroat competition produced by modern industrial costs can be ended. One is by an increase in demand so large that the rival enterprises can obtain, at remunerative prices, as much business as they can handle. The other is by an agreement between the competitors to raise prices simultaneously — in other words, by their creating a monopoly *at least temporarily*. Because it is not always easy for competitors to agree to raise prices and because increases in demand are frequently slow in coming, prices in some industries remain below the costs of most firms for years at a time.

Because fixed costs encourage business establishments to cut prices whenever they have unutilized capacity, firms which have ample funds or high credit standing are able to make substantial savings by buying for future requirements at times of general slackness. Hence fixed costs give an advantage to those enter-

---

"When contractors, either in small or large groups, get together the question of cut-throat competition is inevitably bound to come up for discussion. . . . During the past few years we have been witnessing an unprecedented period of activity in the building industry. Each contractor, from the small house builder to the largest of the general contracting firms, has been busy. There has been plenty of work for everyone, yet the utter disregard for legitimate profits in many instances would indicate just the reverse.

"Every contractor, large or small, should adopt a hard and fast rule to the effect that he is entitled to a reasonable profit on every operation. The rule once made should be adhered to in every instance. There is no glory in work done at a loss and there is certainly no financial gain.

"One of the distinct services that every trade association in the country can render to its constituents is to keep continually and everlastingly hammering away on this one all-important theme, *profit*." National Association of Building Trade Employers, *National Bulletin*, Nov. 10, 1925, v. III, p. 1.

For an excellent account of the attempts of a trade association to limit price cutting, see Brown, Emily C., "Price Competition in the Printing Industry of Chicago," *Journal of Political Economy*, April, 1930, v. XXXVIII, pp. 194–212.

prises in the strongest financial position. They also enhance the advantages of large firms over small ones. If all costs varied directly with output, large establishments could purchase for no less than small concerns. Fixed expenses, however, make it advantageous for a firm with idle productive capacity to quote a lower price per unit for an order of 25,000 than for an order of 5,000. For the same reason, the loss of a large customer is far more serious than the loss of a small one. Hence, firms which purchase in large quantities are usually able to obtain goods at substantially less than smaller buyers. Fixed costs, then, help explain why a favorite dictum of economists, that there can be only one price in one market at one time, is not true. Instead of one price, we often find several prices, each depending upon the size of the order and the bargaining position of the buyer.

We have seen that an important check to the tendency of enterprises to cut prices in order to obtain more business is the fear that a cut to one customer will spread to other customers. But sometimes a concern can make a special price to certain classes of customers or in certain markets without danger of being compelled to reduce prices to other classes of customers or in other markets. When this can be done, we find fixed costs exerting perhaps their most conspicuous effects upon price policies. Telegraph companies, for example, charge lower rates for night messages, telephone companies for night long-distance calls. Railroads sell commutation tickets at one-third to one-half the regular passenger fares. About half the tonnage handled by American railroads is carried under what are known as " commodity rates " — that is, especially low rates for heavy and bulky goods which would not be shipped under the regular classified rates. A long-standing dispute in the railroad business relates to the differences in rates to different cities. Not uncommonly the charge for a long haul has been less than for short hauls over the same line. For many years, freight has been carried from New York to San Francisco for less than from New York to Ogden, although Ogden is an intermediate point on the most direct route from New York to San Francisco. One of the most discussed problems of international commercial policy is the control of

" dumping." By dumping is meant selling abroad for less than in the home market. American steel manufacturers, for example, have often sold rails in Mexico for less than here. The dumping tactics of the German dye industry have been notorious — indeed, they were largely responsible for the first attempt of Congress to regulate dumping.[13] Dumping has been so widespread and so disadvantageous to the manufacturers and middlemen of the countries in which the goods are sold that most countries have made some effort to restrict it.

The explanation of these price differentials is to be found in fixed costs. Obviously, if all costs were direct, an enterprise could not afford to sell to some customers for less than to others — unless the regular price were exorbitant. But why does it pay a concern to make a special price to certain classes of customers or in certain markets? If a given price can be obtained from some customers or in some markets, why sell to other customers or in other markets for less? Clearly there is no reason unless the special price enables the enterprise to get business which would not otherwise be obtained and unless the enterprise has idle productive capacity which would not otherwise be used. A large proportion of night telephone calls would never be made at the day rates; railroads would have few commuters at the regular passenger fares; most of the tonnage hauled at commodity rates would not move at all at the regular class rates; the exceptionally low freight charges to San Francisco enable the railroads to obtain shipments which would otherwise go by boat; most of the goods which are dumped in foreign countries at low prices could not be sold there at all at higher prices. And in all of these cases, also, the firms have productive capacity which would otherwise be idle. The wires of the telegraph and telephone companies could carry many more messages during the night, railroads are almost always able to handle more freight, dumping abroad occurs only when the domestic demand fails to keep factories busy. Under these circumstances, enterprises find it advantageous to make special prices in order to gain additional business, provided: (1) the prices are large enough to cover the costs attributable to the additional output;[14]

---

[13] Fish, G. M., and Pierce, P. S., *International Commercial Policies*, p. 99.
[14] This is not precisely the same thing as saying that the price must be high enough

and (2) the special prices do not seriously diminish the volume of sales at regular prices.

REFERENCES

Basset, W. R., *Taking the Guesswork Out of Business*, 1924.   Ch. XI.

Clark, J. M., *The Economics of Overhead Costs*, 1923.

Engberg, R. C., *Industrial Prosperity and the Farmer*, 1927.   Ch. VI.

Hamilton, W. H., and Wright, H. R., *The Case of Bituminous Coal*, 1925.

Ripley, W. Z., *Railroads: Rates and Regulation*, 1913.   Ch. II–VII, XI, and XII.

Rufener, L. A., *Principles of Economics*, 1927.   Ch. VIII, IX, XI, XIII, and XIV.

---

to cover direct costs, because the additional output may produce some effect upon fixed costs.   For example, the additional traffic created by a commodity rate may compel the railroad to purchase additional cars and locomotives.   In this case, the commodity rate should be high enough to cover interest, depreciation, insurance, and taxes on the additional equipment.

CHAPTER XV

CHANGES IN DEMAND AND COMPETITIVE PRICE

I. THE COST OF PRODUCTION DEPENDS UPON THE VOLUME OF OUTPUT. II. PRODUCTION AT INCREASING COST. III. THE LAW OF THE PROPORTION OF FACTORS. IV. SOME CONSEQUENCES OF PRODUCTION AT INCREASING COST. V. HOW AN INCREASE IN DEMAND MAY REDUCE COSTS AND PRICES. VI. COMPETITIVE PRICES AND THE DISTRIBUTION OF RESOURCES AMONG DIFFERENT INDUSTRIES.

I. THE COST OF PRODUCTION DEPENDS UPON THE VOLUME OF OUTPUT

The immediate effect of an increase in demand, we saw in Chapter XII, is likely to be an advance in price, and of a decrease in demand, a drop in price. But, *in the long run,* this is not necessarily so. It was pointed out in Chapter XIV that *in the long run* the supply (and hence the price) of any reproducible good is determined by the expenses of production, including the return necessary to attract capital into the industry. From this it follows that the way in which changes in demand affect the price of a reproducible good depends in the long run upon how they affect the cost of production. If an increase in demand raises the cost of making a good, it tends to raise the price; if, on the other hand, it lowers the cost of production, it tends to lower the price of the commodity.

In analyzing the effect of changes in demand upon the cost of production, it is necessary to take account of two conflicting tendencies. In the first place, it is usually true that, after a given output has been reached, each successive unit of any given supply tends to cost more to produce than the preceding one. This means that the supply curve, after a given point, tends to rise to the right because additional units of supply will be forthcoming only at higher and higher prices. In the second place, it is also true that the cost of producing each and every unit of the supply depends upon the volume of production. Often an industry can make goods at a lower cost per unit when it produces a large volume than when it produces a small volume. Consequently an increase in demand, by making possible the economies of large scale production, may cause the general level of the supply curve to drop. When an increase in the volume of output makes possible a lower unit cost of production, the net effect of a change in demand upon price depends upon whether or not the tendency for successive units of output to cost more and more is so pronounced as to counteract the saving in costs made possible by an increase in the volume of production.

To illustrate the relationship between volume of output and costs, let us suppose that the demand for a commodity and the supply of it are as follows:

Original demand	Price	Original supply
1,000,000	$1.00	800,000
950,000	1.05	850,000
900,000	1.10	900,000
850,000	1.15	950,000
800,000	1.20	1,000,000

Plainly the price will be $1.10. Assume now that the demand increases so that at each price 300,000 more units are demanded. In response to the increase in demand, the enterprises in the industry install more specialized and more automatic machinery and subdivide the work more minutely. As a result, they so reduce their costs that at any given price they are willing to supply 400,000 more units than before. The changes in demand and supply are indicated in the following table:

Later demand	Price	Later supply
1,300,000	$1.00	1,200,000
1,250,000	1.05	1,250,000
1,200,000	1.10	1,300,000
1,150,000	1.15	1,350,000
1,100,000	1.20	1,400,000

It still remains true that each successive unit of supply costs more to produce than the preceding units. But because production on a larger scale lowers the general level of costs so substantially, the increase in demand has the net effect of lowering the price.

Inspection of the table indicates that, after the increase in demand, the price is \$1.05 instead of \$1.10. If the increase in the scale of output had had a smaller effect upon the general level of costs, the increase in demand would have raised, instead of lowering, the price.

II. Production at Increasing Cost

Let us first inquire why there is a tendency for each additional unit of supply to cost more than the preceding ones. Suppose that a country consumes 100,000,000 tons of coal each year. Naturally the coal mined will be that which can be marketed most cheaply — from relatively thick veins, near the surface, and not a great distance from the market. Assume now that the country's coal consumption increases to 102,000,000 tons a year. To obtain 2,000,000 more tons a year, it will be necessary to mine supplies which are remote from the market, to take out thinner veins, or to sink shafts deeper and to mine deeper-lying coal. If the consumption of coal still further increases, it will be necessary to draw on still more remote deposits and still thinner and deeper-lying veins. Thus we see that there is a tendency for each additional ton of coal to cost more to produce than the preceding tons — the 20,000,000th ton tends to cost more than the 10,000,000th, the 50,000,000th more than the 20,000,000th, the 100,000,000th more than the 50,000,000th. *When each successive addition to the supply of a good costs more than the preceding units to produce,* the good is said to be produced at increasing cost.

It is important to notice that production at increasing cost does *not* mean that the expense of producing a commodity is rising day by day. The expense of making it may be going down from day to day and yet the article may be produced at increasing cost. What is meant is simply that *at any given time* each successive addition to the supply costs more than the preceding unit to produce. For example, it undoubtedly costs less to produce a ton of bituminous coal today than it did fifty years ago. Pneumatic drills, undercutting machines, electric mine locomotives, larger cars, the belt loader, more efficient pumping and ventilating equipment have all contributed to this result. Nevertheless, coal is produced at increasing cost because successive tons tend to cost more to mine.

The tendency for successive increments of product to cost more and more is most pronounced in the so-called extractive industries; that is, in agriculture, mining, lumbering, fishing, hydraulic power, and the production of natural gas and crude oil. In each case, the expense of production is determined to an exceptional degree by the quality and accessibility of natural resources. The resources first utilized tend, of course, to be those from which goods can be produced most cheaply. As demand increases, resources which are less rich, less easily worked, or less favorably situated are developed. When a new region is settled, the land first cultivated is usually that which, all things considered, will produce at the least expense. This does not necessarily mean the land which is the most fertile and which will yield the most bushels per acre. The most fertile land may require draining or clearing or it may be so remote from markets that it is more economical to cultivate poor land which is less productive but more accessible. *All things considered,* however, the land first cultivated tends to be that from which the commodity can be put on the market at the least expense. As population grows, and with it the demand for agricultural products, land which yields goods only at a higher and higher outlay is utilized.[1] Likewise, the first timber cut is that which, because of its proximity to markets and streams and because of the size of the trees, can be manufactured with least outlay. As demand expands, more remote tracts are cut, logs are hauled farther to streams, or brought by rail or team all the way to the mills, and trees of less desirable size are taken. In the development of water power, the tendency has been to use first the dam sites from which power can be obtained most cheaply and, as more power is needed, to develop more remote or less favorable sites.

Although the extractive industries offer the most conspicuous

---

[1] Changes in the order in which different pieces of land are utilized are produced by improvements in transportation which lower the cost of producing goods on land that is remote from the market more than they lower it on near-by land. Hence, as transportation rates go down, it may pay to abandon poor land near markets and to cultivate more fertile but more distant land. For example, the cultivated area in New York and other eastern states is less now than it was sixty or seventy years ago. Lower freight rates have made it possible to put crops grown on more fertile, western farms into eastern and European markets for less than the crops raised on the poorer eastern land.

illustrations of production at increasing cost, the tendency for additional increments of supply to cost more and more is universal. In all industries, the best sites are, as a rule, used first. In manufacturing, in marketing, and, to a less extent, in transportation, there are so many good locations that new enterprises can usually obtain sites which are little, if any, inferior to those already in use. Often, indeed, a new enterprise can obtain a better location than most old concerns possess, because changes in the distribution of population or in the methods or routes of transportation and the exhaustion of some supplies of raw materials may cause locations which were once highly desirable to become undesirable. Nevertheless, differences in the desirability of locations create a slight tendency for additions to the supply to cost more and more. There are always some men who can be obtained for certain work at compensation which is low relative to their efficiency. As the demand for the commodity increases, it becomes necessary to use men for whom the work has less attraction or who are less well adapted to it and who, in consequence, cannot be hired on such favorable terms. Likewise, some capital can usually be obtained at an exceptionally low rate of interest but, as larger and larger amounts are required, it is necessary to offer a larger and larger return in order to get them.

When a commodity is produced at increasing cost, the ultimate effect of an expansion in demand is to raise price, and of a shrinkage in demand to lower it. In order to explain this, let us revert to our example of coal. Assume that the cost of producing different additions to the annual output of coal — including the necessary return to business owners — is as follows:

80,000,000th ton	$2.50
90,000,000th "	2.75
100,000,000th "	3.00
110,000,000th "	3.25
120,000,000th "	3.50
130,000,000th "	3.75

If a supply of 100,000,000 tons a year can be obtained only by mining some coal at an expense of $3.00 a ton, the public must be willing to pay about that much in order to get 100,000,000 tons produced year after year. It is, of course, true that most of the 100,000,000 tons cost much less than $3.00 to produce. At first thought, it may seem strange that the price must be as high as $3.00 when 99,999,999 of the 100,000,000 tons can be produced for less than this — many of them for much less. But obviously the fact that operators can sell some coal for much more than cost does not make them willing to sell other coal below cost. Consequently, 100,000,000 tons will not be produced year after year indefinitely unless the price is $3.00 or more a ton. If consumers were content with only 80,000,000 tons a year, they could get it for $2.50 a ton, for this is the cost of producing the 80,000,000th ton — including the return to the business owners. But if they wish 110,000,000 or 120,000,000 tons, they must be willing to pay the expense of producing a 110,000,000th or a 120,000,000th ton — that is, $3.25 or $3.50.

Let us inquire somewhat more closely what is meant by saying that an 80,000,000th ton of coal costs $2.50 to produce or a 100,-000,000th ton $3.00. It is obvious that a large part of the cost of coal is fixed costs — those connected with the investment in land, shafts, hoists, entries, track, cars, drills, pumps, ventilating apparatus, and many other articles of mine equipment. These costs are not, of course, associated with any single ton of coal. How, then, can a definite cost of $2.75 or $3.00 be ascribed to any specific ton?

It is clear, however, that the volume of investment in land, shafts, entries, and mine equipment, though not affected by small changes in the output of coal, must be affected by large changes in the productive capacity of the industry. To provide a capacity of 100,000,000 tons a year, for example, would require a substantially greater investment than to provide a capacity of 80,-000,000 tons. Quite probably, indeed, a more than proportionate increase in capital would be necessary. But obviously the funds to provide a capacity of 100,000,000 tons would not be forthcoming unless capitalists believed that 100,000,000 tons could be sold at a price which would make the investment worth while. Consequently, when we speak of the 100,000,000th ton's costing $3.00, we mean that a price of $3.00 is necessary (1) to cover direct costs of producing coal when it is being produced at the rate of 100,000,000 tons a year and (2) to cover the fixed costs on the investment necessary to give the industry a capacity of 100,000,000 tons a year.[2]

[2] Part of the supply of all or nearly all commodities, we have seen, is ordinarily produced at a loss. If, therefore, $3.00 is sufficient to cover the direct costs and the fixed costs entailed by an output of 100,000,000 tons a year, it would probably be

But, although $3.00 is sufficient to cover both the fixed and the direct expenses of producing 100,000,000 tons of coal a year, it does not follow that this price is sufficient to cover both the direct and the fixed expenses of *every* ton of coal which it pays to mine when the price is $3.00. We already know that it may pay to produce and sell a good at any price above direct cost rather than not to sell it at all. Assume, for example, that a mine has fixed costs of $200,000 a year and that its annual output is 400,-000 tons, making fixed costs 50 cents a ton. If coal is selling for $3.00, would this mine limit its output to coal which could be mined at a *direct* cost of less than $2.50? Clearly not. As long as coal sells for $3.00, it would even pay the enterprise to mine coal at a direct cost of $2.99, provided the additional production entailed no additions to fixed costs. A large part of the 100,000,000 tons which are produced when the price is $3.00 are mined at a direct cost very little less than the selling price.

III. The Law of the Proportion of Factors

To some extent the necessity of employing poorer natural resources, less favorable sites, or more expensive labor or capital can be avoided by changing the proportions in which the factors of production are combined; that is, by using some factors more intensively. For example, the supply of wheat might be increased either by cultivating more land, which would involve resorting to inferior land, or by applying more labor, fertilizer, and machinery to the best land. Or, if additional men could be attracted into a certain occupation only at a considerable increase in wages, labor might be economized by the use of more machines.

Although changing the proportions of the factors of production may diminish the tendency for successive units of output to cost more and more, it does not eliminate this tendency entirely. Suppose that the output of farm land is increased by hiring additional laborers. Presumably the first men employed by the farmers were the most efficient workers available. Consequently, the additional men are likely to be inferior. The farmer who

---

sufficient to induce a production of somewhat more than 100,000,000 tons a year. For the sake of simplicity, however, we may ignore that part of the output which is produced at a loss.

wishes to increase his output has the choice of using inferior men or using inferior land.[3]

But even if the additional laborers are not inferior to the original ones, the addition of successive workers will sooner or later yield smaller and smaller additions to product. Or, put in more general terms, additions to *any* instrument of production, the others remaining constant, will, after a given point, yield diminishing increments of product. Two men cultivating 320 acres may produce 8,000 bushels of wheat, but the addition of a third man would not necessarily increase the product by 50 per cent. Possibly he would increase it to only 10,000 bushels. Obviously in this case the labor cost of each of the last 2,000 bushels would be greater than the labor cost of the first 8,000.

The tendency for successive additions of any factor of production to result in less than proportionate increases in product is known as *the law of the proportion of factors*. Its nature can be made clearer by several examples. Let us take the case of a small factory and notice how the output is affected, first, when the number of laborers is increased but capital remains constant, and, then, when the number of laborers remains constant and capital is increased:[4]

VARIABLE FACTOR, LABOR

Capital	Laborers	Output	Output added by one additional laborer
$20,000	1	2,000	2,000
20,000	2	5,000	3,000
20,000	3	6,600	1,600
20,000	4	8,000	1,400
20,000	5	9,200	1,200
20,000	6	10,200	1,000

[3] This does not apply directly to use of additional machines. But if more machines are demanded, they can be made only by employing additional, and, presumably, less efficient workers. Consequently, there will be a *tendency* for additional machines to cost more and more. It must be borne in mind that we are speaking of tendencies only and that there are counteracting tendencies also. For example, the use of additional workers up to a certain point will make it possible to realize important gains from greater subdivision of labor.

[4] In constructing these tables, it has been assumed that there is some advantage in size, due to the possibility of specializing men and equipment. Thus, whereas the output of $20,000 of capital and two laborers is assumed to be 5,000 units, the output of $30,000 of capital and three laborers is assumed to be, not 7,500 units, but 8,300 units. Although the output of $10,000 of capital and three laborers is assumed to be 4,200 units, the output of $20,000 of capital and six laborers is assumed to be more than twice 4,200 or 10,200 units.

VARIABLE FACTOR, CAPITAL

Capital	Laborers	Output	Output added by $5,000 additional capital
$5,000	3	2,000	2,000
10,000	3	4,200	2,200
15,000	3	5,500	1,300
20,000	3	6,600	1,100
25,000	3	7,500	900
30,000	3	8,300	800

It will be observed that, in each instance, one agent of production increases but the others remain constant. It will be noted also that the output increases but that after a given point the increments become less and less. In the first case, this occurs when the working force passes two; in the second, when the capital exceeds $10,000. It is evident that when increases in a factor of production yield smaller and smaller additions to output, each successive unit of product will have a higher cost.

It is easy to believe that this is *frequently* true, but why must it *always* be true? The reason is simple. The output of a factory, farm, or mine is not solely the product of nature, labor, or artificial capital, but the *joint* product of them all. If only *one* of the factors is increased, a proportional increase in output is not to be expected. The productive power of a farm or factory is not necessarily doubled if only one out of the many productive factors is doubled. Only if *all* are doubled, may we expect the yield of the enterprise to double.

There is another way of viewing the matter. Each instrument of production may be regarded as producing with the help of the others. Labor produces with the assistance of capital; capital with the assistance of labor. Naturally the yield of each agent depends upon how much aid each receives from the other. The amount of assistance which each worker, for example, receives from capital depends upon whether laborers are numerous in relation to capital. When there is one man to every 100 acres of land and every $10,000 of machinery, the output per man is likely to be higher than where there are two men to every 100 acres and every $10,000 of machinery. But this is merely another way of saying that doubling the number of laborers, the other factors remaining constant, is not likely to double the output.

IV. Some Consequences of Production at Increasing Cost

From the fact that successive increments to the supply of many things cost more and more, important results follow.

One is that substantial reductions in the prices of some goods might be achieved by transferring the control of certain industries from capitalists to consumers or the government.[5] It is often assumed that the way to assure the lowest possible prices is to preserve competition. But when a good is produced at increasing cost and when the industry is controlled by either private capitalists or wage earners, a cause for an unnecessarily high price exists which competition is powerless to affect.

The coal industry illustrates the point. It was stated above that if the country is to have a given quantity of coal — say 100,-000,000 tons — year after year, the price must be high enough to cover the cost of producing the 100,000,000th ton. Let us assume that 100,000,000 tons are demanded at $3.00 a ton and that the cost of producing the 100,000,000th ton is $3.00. If competition prevails, the selling price will tend to be $3.00. But since the 100,000,000th ton costs more than any of the others to produce, the average cost of producing 100,000,000 tons would be less than $3.00. Assume that it is $2.00. This would mean that the organization which controlled the industry could offer 100,000,000 tons of coal at $2.00 a ton and still break even.[6]

Neither capitalists nor wage earners, of course, would be will-

[5] No assertion is made that such transfer would or would not be desirable. This would depend upon many things of which the effect upon price is only one. Possibly consumer or government control would involve some causes for high prices which would not exist under capitalistic or " laboristic " control. Nor is it to be taken for granted that the lowest possible price is the most desirable one. In the case of certain more or less limited natural resources, there is much to be said against permitting the price to become too low.

[6] The Sankey Commission found that among 458 collieries the cost of getting a ton of coal varied from 12s. 6d. to 48s. a ton. Tawney, R. H., *The British Labor Movement*, p. 73. Among these 458 mines, 8 per cent of the output was produced at a loss, another 8 per cent at a profit of less than one shilling a ton, more than one-half at a profit of more than 3 shillings a ton, and 27 per cent at a profit of 10 to 16 shillings. *Ibid.*, 74. Tawney refers to the action of the coal controller in raising the price of coal by 2s. 6d., per ton in January, 1918. It was done because 13 per cent of the output was being produced at a loss. In order to get approximately £10,000,000 to make a small part of the industry remunerative, it was necessary to take about £25,000,000 from the consumers.. *Ibid.*, p. 74.

ing to do this, but an organization of consumers or the government might do something very similar. It would not be practicable, however, for either the government or an organization of consumers to sell the coal for as little as $2.00. At this price, only 100,000,000 tons could be sold without suffering a loss on the total sales. But since 100,000,000 tons are demanded at $3.00, the demand at $2.00 would be much greater. Consequently, if only 100,000,000 tons were offered at $2.00, many prospective buyers would be unable to obtain coal and those in control of the industry would be confronted with the extremely difficult, if not impossible, task of rationing the coal and of preventing speculators from buying it up and reselling it at a higher price. To avoid these difficulties, the price might be fixed so that (1) demand would equal supply and (2) price would be no less than the average cost of producing each ton in a given supply. Let us assume that the average cost of producing certain amounts and the quantities which would be demanded at given prices are as follows:

Demand	Price or average cost	Supply
120,000,000	$2.00	100,000,000
115,000,000	2.10	105,000,000
110,000,000	2.20	110,000,000
105,000,000	2.30	115,000,000

If the price were set at $2.20, the total cost of production — including, of course, the return on the capital invested — would be met and it would be unnecessary either to ration the supply or to control speculators.[7]

It is a time-honored assumption of the theory of free enterprise that competition between business enterprises will stimulate

[7] If it were necessary for the government to purchase the mines from private owners, it might not be possible for the government to reduce the price of coal without suffering loss. The owners of the low-cost mines would scarcely be willing to sell to the government at a price which did not fully reflect the lower operating costs of their mines. Consequently the government would be compelled to charge enough for coal to pay interest on its heavy investment in low-cost mines. But if the present prices of low-cost mines did not fully reflect future increases in the demand for coal, the government might be able, at some more or less distant date, to sell coal for less than competition would set the price.

It is important to notice that attempts to lower the price to the consumer may involve great waste of labor and materials and may result in consumers' wants being less, instead of more, completely satisfied. In fact, if the prices which buyers are will-

efficiency among them and eliminate the business men who are least able to make profits. It is interesting to notice that when a commodity is made at increasing cost, competition performs each of these functions less effectively. Suppose, for example, that the demand for wheat increases. As the price rises to meet the cost of production on poorer land, the owners of the better land and the holders of it under long-term leases find themselves in easier circumstances. Less careful planning and economizing are necessary to make both ends meet. Under these conditions, it is natural for many farmers on the better land to become less efficient. In addition, the least competent farmers, who were on the verge of being forced out of business before the price went up, are able to make expenses. These incompetents can attribute their survival to the fact that additional supplies of wheat could be produced only at greater and greater cost, because otherwise the increase in demand would not have raised the price. Thus the tendency for successive units of certain goods to cost more and more retards the tendency for the resources of the community to become concentrated under the control of the men most competent to use them for their own profit. We have already discovered that large fixed costs enable poorly managed enterprises to operate for long periods at a loss. All of this suggests that our reliance upon competition as a selective agency may be overdone

---

ing to pay were an accurate measure of the satisfaction yielded by goods and if pecuniary costs accurately reflected the sacrifices involved in production, it could be asserted without hesitation that the sale, at cost, of goods produced at increasing cost is socially wasteful. In our hypothetical case, the cost of producing a 100,000,000th ton of coal is $3.00. When price is fixed so that demand and supply are equal and total receipts are equal to total costs, the quantity produced and sold is 110,000,000 tons. The cost of producing a 110,000,000th ton must be greater than $3.00. Let us put it at $3.25. Now if the $2.20 paid for this coal really represents the satisfaction or benefit yielded by it and if the $3.25 paid to get it produced really represents the sacrifice involved in producing it, it is evident that the 110,000,000th ton of coal was not worth mining. In fact, even if its production entailed *no sacrifice whatever*, its production might be wasteful. Labor and capital must be paid $3.25 to produce the coal because they could obtain this much for producing other things. If the public's willingness to pay for labor and capital accurately measures the satisfaction which they yield, then the fact that labor and capital could get $3.25 at other employment indicates that in other industries they could produce a satisfaction measured by $3.25. But if, in mining a 110,000,000th ton of coal, labor and capital produce a satisfaction measured by $2.20, it is clearly wasteful to mine so much coal. Of course, in a society in which wealth is unevenly distributed, as in our own, willingness to pay for things does not accurately reflect the satisfaction likely to be derived from them. Nevertheless, the danger is great that schemes to save money for consumers will prevent labor and capital from being used in the most economical manner.

and that it may be necessary to invent new ways of assuring that the resources of the community are directed by the ablest managers.

If we could increase our supply of all goods at no advance in unit costs, the question of how large a population we should have would probably not exist. But because additional supplies of crops, fuel, minerals, timber, power, and fish tend to cost more and more, we are compelled to choose between a larger population and a higher standard of living. The more rapidly population increases, the less rapidly the standard of living can rise. Up to a certain point, it is true, a greater population makes possible certain economies, such as minute specialization or large-scale production, which counteract the increasing cost of some goods. But after a given point, the disadvantages of larger plants or business units outweigh their advantages. Consequently, after population reaches a given point, further growth no longer brings about increases in *per capita* productivity. Undoubtedly many parts of the United States would be better off if they were more densely populated, but, taking the country as a whole, the present population of 120,000,000 appears to give us the principal economies of large-scale production. Further increase in numbers tends to make us nationally richer and more powerful but individually poorer. Hence we face the problem of whether to protect our standard of living by keeping our population at about its present size or to permit our numbers to increase at the expense of our standard of living.[8]

V. How an Increase in Demand May Reduce Costs and Prices

It is important to remember that the influences which tend to make additional increments of supply cost more and more apply

---

[8] One reason why European countries have a smaller *per capita* income than the United States is because they must support a denser population. This means that they are compelled to use poorer land, mines, quarries, and forests than are used in the United States. It also means that each workman has a smaller quantity of natural resources to help him produce — in other words, less help from nature. Hence their workmen produce less. Annual *per capita* income at the outbreak of the war has been estimated by the National Bureau of Economic Research as $146 for Germany, $243 for the United Kingdom, and $335 for the United States. These estimates are in terms of the 1914 price level and, if translated into present prices, would be substantially higher. It is interesting to note that Australia, with fewer people in relation to its resources and less necessity of using poor land and mines, had in 1914 a *per capita* income of $263 — higher than either Germany or the United Kingdom.

to *all* industries. But attention has been directed to the fact that, in some industries, an increase in the volume of production often makes possible a decrease in the cost of producing *each* unit of the supply. This second tendency is especially pronounced in the fields of manufacturing, marketing, and transportation. It still remains true that the price tends to approximate the cost of sup‹ plying the most expensive unit that is needed in order to satisfy the demand but, because of the economies of output on a larger scale, this unit may now cost less to make than it formerly did. To put the matter in figures: when 1,000,000 units a year are pro‹ duced, the 1,000,000th unit costs more to make than the 500,‹ 000th but, because of the economies of production on a larger scale, a 1,000,000th unit may cost less than did a 500,000th *when only 500,000 were produced*. In this event, an increase in consumption from 500,000 to 1,000,000 a year will ultimately bring about a decrease instead of an increase in price. The automobile is the most conspicuous commodity which is cheap because the demand is large. Only because millions of cars are bought each year is it possible to sell such a complicated mechanism for about 25 cents a pound in the case of the Ford and about 40 cents in the case of the Buick — or, as some one has said, for less than half of the cost of good candy.

The economies of large-scale production must not be confused with the economies of operating the equipment of industry more nearly to capacity. The immediate effect of an increase in the demand for a product may be that some plants operate more nearly to capacity and thus reduce their fixed costs per unit of output. But if the larger demand continues, the productive capacity of the industry is likely to be increased in proportion to the growth in demand so that eventually the equipment is utilized no more completely than before. The ultimate effect of an increase in demand, therefore, is simply to bring about the production of the commodity either in more specialized plants or in larger plants or both. Of course, the savings thus achieved are not confined to the plants which make the finished article. A greater demand for automobiles, for example, means a greater demand for steel plates, tires, electrical goods, plate glass, bodies, horns, carburetors, and makes it possible to produce all of these things in large plants and at lower cost.

In Chapter VI it was pointed out why some commodities can be made more economically in highly specialized plants, and in Chapter VII it was explained why many commodities can be made in large plants for less than in small ones. But why should an increase in demand result either in more specialized or in larger plants? Does not competition concentrate production in plants of the optimum degree of specialization and of the optimum size? Why does not an increase in demand simply produce more plants rather than more specialized ones or larger ones? If, for example, 500,000 units a year were demanded and factories with an annual capacity of 50,000 units could produce at the lowest cost, we might expect production to be concentrated in ten plants, each capable of producing 50,000 units a year. Suppose then that the demand increased to 1,000,000 a year. Would not the result simply be twenty plants producing 50,000 units each and no change in either costs or prices?

The error in this analysis consists in the assumption that there is a certain sized plant which is *always* most economical regardless of how large the demand for the product may be. It is extremely important to notice that *the size which is most economical varies with the demand for the product.* When 500,000 units of an article are demanded each year, possibly a 50,000-unit factory may be most economical, but, if the demand were to increase to 750,000, a 60,000-unit factory might be most advantageous. The explanation is to be found largely in the cost of marketing the product. Possibly a 50,000-unit plant could place a commodity in the freight cars ready for shipment at a cost of $1.00 per unit, and a 60,000-unit plant for 95 cents. Suppose, however, that demand was so sparsely distributed that any 60,000-unit factory would be compelled, in order to dispose of its output, to ship 10,000 units to remote markets at a transportation cost of 35 cents per unit. The additional cost of selling 60,000 units would be $3,500. The saving in the cost of manufacturing would be $3,000. Clearly, under these circumstances, 60,000-unit establishments would not be built. If, however, demand were to increase so that 60,000-unit plants could dispose of their output close at hand, it would be profitable to enlarge the 50,000-unit factories, and competition among them would force down the price of the commodity.

Other marketing expenses besides the cost of transportation

restrict the size of plants. A limited number of people can be persuaded to buy without great effort, but, *after a given point,* each additional sale requires more labor on the part of the salesman and a greater expenditure for advertising. Furthermore, the firm must accept poorer credit risks, extend credit more liberally, spend more money collecting debts, and suffer greater losses through bad debts and cancellations. Consequently, it might cost $10,000 to sell 50,000 units but $15,000 to sell 60,000. If the increase in the size of the plant reduced manufacturing costs only 5 cents per unit, the smaller plant would plainly be the more economical. A growth in demand, by pushing up the point at which selling costs began to increase more rapidly than the volume of sales, would increase the size of the plant which is most economical.

For many other reasons, an increase in demand may make possible larger plants, lower costs, and, therefore, lower prices. The plain fact of the matter is that competition does not concentrate production into plants of the most economical size for the existing volume of demand. There are several reasons why it does not. One of the principal is the fact that modern industrial costs often make it unprofitable for an enterprise to attempt to gain business from competitors by the method of price cutting. Suppose that a firm, by increasing its capacity from 50,000 to 60,000 units a year, could reduce its unit cost from $1.00 to 95 cents. It might at first appear to be a simple matter to enlarge the plant and to gain the additional business by cutting prices. Rival concerns, with smaller plants and higher costs, would have difficulty, it would seem, in competing at the lower prices.

But would this be the result? We have already learned that modern industrial costs make it more advantageous to run an enterprise at a substantial loss rather than to shut it down. More than this, they make it *possible* to run at a loss, because the payment of some costs can be long postponed. This means that any concern which seeks to take away business from its competitors must probably cut prices far below its own costs before it reaches a price which its rivals are unable or unwilling to meet. Often the possible gain does not appear to be worth the risk and cost of a long price war.[9]

[9] We have learned that when enterprises have considerable unused capacity, heavy fixed costs may produce cutthroat competition. But when unused capacity is

Some plants may be prevented from growing to the most economical size by smaller plants which, for one reason or another, are able to undersell them. Not all of the expenses of production are affected by the size of the plant. Costs of raw materials, marketing, and labor are, in large measure, independent of it. Small plants near the source of raw materials or the market, located on advantageous water powers or in cheap labor markets may survive and thrive though lacking the advantages of largeness. Efficiency of management has much to do with costs. Many small enterprises hold their own because they are operated unusually well, because the executives watch expenses with more care, purchase more skillfully, handle labor more wisely, extend credit more discriminatingly than the managements of larger competitors.

The concentration of production into larger and more economical establishments is greatly hindered by the inability of owners and managers to perceive the advantages of greater size and to assume the risks of expanding. It must be remembered that in any given case the advantages of greater size are more or less conjectural. Whether or not they exist must be found out by experience. The precise technical improvements which could be made if the plant were enlarged by a given amount are somewhat indefinite. Even more so are the savings which specific improvements might yield. The only way to discover precisely the economy of a larger plant is to enlarge the present one and get enough orders to operate it at approximately its new capacity. Undoubtedly there are at this moment thousands of managers who have a very inadequate appreciation of what savings could be achieved by operating on a larger scale and who will not discover them until the knowledge is literally thrust upon them by an increase in demand which compels them to expand their enterprises. Most uncertain of all is the elasticity of the demand. Suppose that a manufacturer decides after careful investigation

---

not great, fixed costs may *lessen* rather than increase the severity of competition, for, by making it more difficult to eliminate competitors, they discourage attempts to do so. From this it follows that heavy fixed costs may impair the efficacy of competition both as a device for keeping down prices to the consumer and as an agency for eliminating inefficient managers and enterprises. High-cost enterprises may have a better chance of surviving when fixed costs are proportionately large because it does not pay to drive them out of business. But, by surviving, they limit the ability of other firms to achieve the savings of quantity production.

that, by increasing his output one-third, he could reduce his unit costs one-fourth. But how much must he reduce prices in order to increase his sales by one-third? He is reasonably certain that his competitors will meet any cuts in his price. Expansion of sales must be achieved, therefore, by inducing the public to increase its consumption. Possibly a reduction of one-sixth in the selling price would easily enable him to increase his sales by one-third. But he has no way of knowing this. Consequently, he refrains from cutting his price, and his plant remains too small, simply because he does not know the elasticity of the demand for his product.

It must be remembered that competition is often more than a matter of price and quality, and that it may be extremely difficult for enterprises to grow merely by offering better quality for the same price. By attaching a trade name to an article and marketing it in a distinctive package, a manufacturer may endow his brand with a more or less specious individuality which causes thousands of consumers to demand it and it alone. Rival manufacturers do the same thing with the same results. Under these circumstances, plants are likely to have difficulty in growing to the most economical size. They cannot do so by offering better quality or a lower price, because consumers are not purchasing primarily on the basis of either quality or price. Of course, the growth might be achieved if an enterprise were fortunate enough to hit upon a peculiarly effective advertising appeal. But a more usual situation is for the market to be divided among as many manufacturers as have been reasonably successful in convincing the public that their wares possess peculiar virtues. This is likely to mean that the production is divided up among many more plants than are desirable from the standpoint of economical operation.

In view of the many obstacles hindering the growth of plants, it seems certain that a large proportion of existing establishments are too small for the greatest economy. A substantial and permanent increase in demand may reduce production costs and prices simply by making it easier for plants to grow and thus to attain a more economical size.

VI. Competitive Prices and the Distribution of Resources among Different Industries

Before we leave the analysis of prices under competition, it is desirable to inquire whether or not prices determined by competition produce a desirable distribution of capital and labor among industries. When there are no hindrances to the movement of capital and labor, the supply, and hence the price, of every reproducible good tends to be such that all industries offer an equally attractive return to additional capital and additional workers (of the same degree of skill). This obviously follows from the fact that each capitalist and wage earner seeks the most attractive return that he can find. If industry A offers a more attractive return than industry B, capital and labor flow into A in preference to B until there is no further choice between the two industries. Obviously this distribution of resources is most advantageous to those who have new capital to invest or labor to sell. Is it also the most advantageous to the community?

An affirmative answer would imply the assumptions that the money costs of production are in proportion to the human costs and that the prices which goods command in the market are in proportion to their ability to render satisfaction. Neither of these assumptions would be warranted. Some of the many reasons why money costs of production are not necessarily proportionate to the human costs will be discussed in Chapter XXV on The Labor Bargain and in Chapter XXVI on The Accumulation and the Reward of Capital. It is evident, however, that the prices which men charge for working are not necessarily proportionate to the human costs of doing the work. It is likewise evident that the ability of men to pay for goods does not necessarily correspond to their ability to derive satisfaction from them. Consequently, the sum-total of satisfaction may be increased when the state furnishes some goods free or at less than cost — as it does in the case of roads, parks, playgrounds, schooling, some forms of medical aid, and many other goods. But quite aside from the inaccuracy in assuming that the money costs of production are proportionate to human costs and that the demand for goods corresponds to the satisfaction which they render, there are several other reasons why unregulated competition does not produce an ideal distribution of resources.

One reason is to be found in the fact that in some cases *additional* capital or wage earners may increase the productivity of many of the units of capital and labor which are *already* employed. A simple illustration is furnished by the advantages of the specialization of labor. Because of the advantages of more minute specialization, one hundred men may turn out more than twice as much as fifty. To some extent, the gains of specialization apply to capital — although the advantages of more minutely specializing machines which have already been constructed are limited by the fact that the machines themselves cannot be altered without expense. When additional workers or capital increase the productivity of capital and labor already in use, unregulated competition does not produce the ideal distribution of resources among industries. The reason is that competition tends to drive prices down to the cost of production. Consequently, the savings in costs which the new additional capital and wage earners make possible tend to be passed on in large degree to the public in the form of lower prices. They do not accrue to those who supply the additional capital and labor. To this extent, of course, they do not cause additional capital and labor to enter the industry. For this reason, unregulated competition fails to induce as much capital and labor to enter some industries as would be advantageous from the standpoint of the community. If it were possible, as unfortunately it is not, to determine accurately which industries fail to attract enough labor and capital because the savings which are made possible by the additional labor and capital are passed on to the consumers, it might be desirable for the state to encourage the use of more labor and capital in those industries by the offer of a subsidy.

Another reason why unregulated competition does not produce an ideal distribution of resources among industries is that the investment of new capital in some industries may largely have the effect of forcing old capital out of use and thus not add greatly to the total output; in other industries, the investment of new capital may in the main add to the product. Suppose, for example, that the investment of $1,000,000 of capital in a new industry A would make possible the output of 100,000 units of a new commodity which would sell at $6 a unit and produce a net return for the capital of $60,000. In order to obtain labor for the new industry, it would be necessary to draw men from other industries. Assume that this would reduce the output of the other industries by 50,000 units which have been selling at $6 each. Suppose also that an old industry, industry B, has an investment of $1,000,000 and is producing 80,000 units of product which sell at a price of $7 each. The investment of $1,000,000 in new and more modern equipment for industry B would force out of use $500,000 of the old equipment. Because the productivity of the new capital would be greater than that of the old, the total output of the industry would be increased from 80,000 to 100,000. The price would fall from $7 to $6. This, by assumption, would be sufficient to yield the same rate of return on the new capital in industry B as the investors could obtain in industry A. The expansion of industry B could be accomplished without drawing labor from other industries and reducing their output. The new plants could be manned by workers who have jobs in the old plants which would be compelled to shut down.

From the standpoint of the community, it is plainly more desirable that most of the new capital should go into industry A rather than industry B. A million dollars invested in A produces 100,000 units of a commodity for which the public is willing to pay $6. The cost of these 100,000 units is the loss of 50,000 units of other commodities for which the public is also willing to pay $6. The net gain, therefore, is 50,000 units which are worth $6 each. On the other hand, if $1,000,000 is invested in industry B, the net gain to the public is 20,000 units which are valued at $6 each. From the standpoint of investors, however, there is no choice between industries A and B — $1,000,000 additional in each industry will yield precisely the same rate of return. Consequently, under a regime of unregulated competition, there is every reason to expect that new capital will be invested in about equal amounts in the two industries, instead of predominantly in industry A. If control could be intelligently and effectively applied, it would be to the interest of the community to retard the flow of capital into industries where the principal effect of new investments is to force existing capital out of use.

REFERENCES

Edgeworth, F. Y., " The Laws of Increasing and Diminishing Return," *Papers Relating to Political Economy*, 1926. Pp. 61–99.

Marshall, Alfred, *Principles of Economics* (eighth edition), 1920. Bk. V, ch. XI.

Pigou, A. C., *The Economics of Welfare* (third edition), 1929. Pt. II, ch. XI.

Rufener, L. A., *Principles of Economics*, 1927. Ch. VIII, IX, XI, XIII, and XIV.

Taussig, F. W., *Principles of Economics* (third edition), 1923. Ch. XII, XIII, XIV.

CHAPTER XVI

MONOPOLY AND CUSTOM AS DETERMINANTS OF PRICE

I. THE MEANING OF MONOPOLY. II. FORMS OF MONOPOLY. III. THE EXTENT OF MONOPOLY IN THE UNITED STATES. IV. THE DETERMINATION OF PRICE UNDER MONOPOLISTIC CONDITIONS. V. DOUBLE-SIDED OR BI-LATERAL MONOPOLY. VI. IS MONOPOLY PRICE NECESSARILY A HIGH PRICE? VII. MONOPOLIES AND THE DISTRIBUTION OF RESOURCES. VIII. MONOPOLY PRICE AND THE DISTRIBUTION OF INCOME. IX. THE INFLUENCE OF CUSTOM UPON PRICES.

I. THE MEANING OF MONOPOLY

More prices are probably fixed by competition among buyers and sellers than in any other way. But next to this, the most common situation is for a monopoly to exist among either buyers or sellers. How is price determined in such instances?

To draw the line between the independent action that constitutes competition and the concerted action which constitutes monopoly is exceedingly difficult, because each rarely exists in a pure form. A perfect monopoly exists only when a single person or enterprise or a combination of persons or enterprises controls the entire demand for or the entire supply of an article. If the control relates to demand, the monopoly is a buyers' monopoly; if to supply, a sellers' monopoly. But most monopolies are not perfect; that is, they do not control the *entire* supply of a good or the *entire* demand for it. This raises the question of the difference between a state of incomplete monopoly and a state of competition. An enterprise which produces 90 per cent of a commodity is substantially a monopoly, and one which makes only 10 per cent does not approach being a monopoly; but where and how are we to draw the line which distinguishes a state of monopoly from one of competition? What concentration of control must exist before competition becomes monopoly?

Light is thrown upon this question by inquiring just what peculiar or distinctive power a monopoly possesses. A buyers' monopoly cannot compel sellers to accept a price which they are unwilling to take nor can a sellers' monopoly compel buyers to pay a price which they are unwilling to give. A buyers' monopoly influences price through its control of demand — through its ability to withhold demand if the price is too high. Likewise a sellers' monopoly affects price through its control over supply — through its ability to withhold supply if the price is too low. But *any* buyer or seller can, by refusing to buy above or sell below a certain price, affect the point at which supply and demand come to equilibrium and, therefore, the price of the commodity. In fact, *every* enterprise *constantly* restricts demand and supply by limiting its purchases to the amounts which it can profitably buy and its sales to the quantities upon which it can at least realize its direct costs. What then distinguishes monopolies from other enterprises? This can perhaps be best explained by an illustration.

Suppose that a firm controls 20 per cent of the output of a commodity. By producing at half instead of full capacity, it could limit supply and thus bring about an advance in the price. The rise, however, would be small, because, at the very most, the total output of the commodity would be reduced by only one-tenth. The resulting increase in price would scarcely compensate the enterprise for the loss of half of its business. If, however, the firm controlled 80 per cent of the output, a decrease of one-fourth in its production would diminish the supply of the commodity by one-fifth. This would undoubtedly cause a substantial advance in the price. The rise might be so great that the enterprise would make more by producing at three-quarter's than at full capacity. If so, the firm would clearly be a monopoly. In short, effective competition exists when it pays each enterprise to produce as much as it can sell at the existing market price. A *sellers'* monopoly exists when it pays an enterprise — or a combination of enterprises — to restrict its output in order to raise the price or to prevent the price from falling. A *buyers'* monopoly exists when it pays an enterprise — or a combination — to restrict its purchasing in order to force down the market price or to prevent the price from rising.[1]

---

[1] Competition in selling is sometimes described as the situation where each enterprise produces without regard to the effect of its output upon price; monopoly, as

II. Forms of Monopoly

The control over supply or demand, which is the essence of monopoly, may be established in many ways. It may rest upon a legal foundation, as in the case of monopolies based on patents, copyrights, and franchises; one enterprise may buy or lease the plants of its rivals or purchase enough stock to control them; the competing firms may enter into formal agreements as to the prices which they will give or take or the quantities of goods which they will buy or sell; competitors may reach informal and somewhat indefinite understandings by regularly meeting for dinner or golf; the trade may accept an outstanding enterprise as a bellwether and adjust prices to those set by it.

In the eighties and nineties of the last century, combinations known as pools were numerous. The term " pool " is ordinarily used when concerns enter into formal written agreements regulating competition among themselves. Some pools simply set a minimum price below which their members agree not to sell. Others seek to control prices indirectly, by limiting the output of each member. This method was employed in the steel rail and the anthracite pools. Still other pools allot each member certain territory in which the other members agree not to sell. The cast-iron pipe pool used this plan. Another scheme, also employed by the cast-iron pipe pool, is for the members to agree that each contract will go to the member offering to pay the pool the highest price for it. At the end of the year, the money paid to the pool

---

a situation where output is restricted for the purpose of influencing price. But this definition is not satisfactory. Suppose that there are fifty firms in an industry. Each does 2 per cent of the business. Each has heavy overhead costs. Business falls off. No one of the fifty firms is willing to start a price war by cutting its price in order to sell more goods. There is no concert of action but there is identical action. Each enterprise limits output to the amount which can be sold at the price which prevailed before the drop in demand. Does this situation represent monopoly? Clearly there is restriction of production for the purpose of affecting price. But at the prevailing price, there is intense competition for business among the fifty competitors. Furthermore, although each of the fifty restricts output for the purpose of avoiding a *cut* in price, at no time is it conceivable that any one of the fifty would find it profitable to restrict output for the purpose of *raising* the price.

It should be noticed that the limitation of output which is characteristic of sellers' monopolies need not necessarily take the form of incomplete utilization of existing productive capacity. By operating at capacity, a monopoly might earn a return of 10 per cent on the investment. By enlarging its plant a given amount, it might reduce the rate of return to 9 per cent. Under these circumstances, the firm might well refrain from adding to its plant.

for contracts is divided among the members in prearranged proportions. Patents may be made the basis of pools. Thus certain manufacturers of enameled ironware combined to permit the use of their patents only upon the payment of a royalty and the execution of a license agreement which set the prices at which the licensee might sell.

Pools were unstable because they were based upon agreements which the courts refused to enforce on the ground that they were in restraint of trade.[2] Consequently it was difficult for enterprises to resist the temptation to cut prices in order to obtain or retain business. Especially was this true when the market was depressed or when independents were attracted into the business by the large profits of the monopoly. The frequent breakdown of pools led to a new form of combination — the merger of competing concerns, accomplished either by the outright purchase of the physical plants or by acquisition of stock control. The merger movement reached its height immediately before and after the turn of the century. The eagerness of the public to pay extravagant prices for the stock of combinations led to the formation of hundreds of them. Most of the combinations were not monopolies, but some were. Many of them proved less profitable than had been anticipated. Then came a decision of the Supreme Court holding that the Northern Securities Company, a company formed to control several competing railroads in the Northwest, violated the Sherman Act against the formation of monopolies, and the movement to create formal combinations subsided.

During the last two decades, informal understandings — gentlemen's agreements — appear to have been the favorite form of monopoly. No one, of course, knows precisely to what extent definite agreements, such as the pools of the eighties and nineties, still exist. The general impression, however, is that business men prefer to have no written evidence of their violation of the anti-monopoly laws. The informal understandings of today are created in various ways. The dinners which Mr. Gary once gave for the steel manufacturers have become famous. Until stopped by government suit, the retail lumbermen of St. Louis

[2] It is a rule of common law that the courts will not enforce certain types of contracts which are in restraint of trade.

met regularly at luncheon and discussed prices. The retail lumber dealers of Kansas City ceased holding similar luncheons when the St. Louis dealers got into trouble. The leading manufacturers of certain types of chain played golf once a month for the purpose of discussing prices. It is striking evidence of the changed sentiment among business men toward price cutting that informal understandings reached around the dinner table now command more allegiance than the written pooling agreements of a generation ago. In the eighties, the modern factory with its machinery and heavy fixed costs was a new thing in most industries, and business men had not learned what selling and financial policies were required by the new technology. It is not surprising that a generation and more was required for managers to learn. Trade associations sometimes act as monopolistic organizations. A hardwood lumber dealers' association was recently held by the Supreme Court to be violating the Sherman Act because its " market letters " advised its members to curtail production and to wait for higher prices.[3]

Most commonly, however, monopolies are not the result of patents, mergers, or concerted action. In the vast majority of cases, they are the result of special situations which bring about absence of competition. These situations are so numerous and so various that classification of them is scarcely worth while. An enterprise is established in which one man or a group of men have a controlling interest. The concern probably does not go into the open market and hire the best possible managers at the lowest necessary salaries. Undoubtedly the dominant man makes himself president at a salary which he fixes, or the dominant group select themselves as the principal executives at salaries which they themselves determine. Despite the fact that there are plenty of men available, the enterprise is confronted with a sellers' monopoly — the sellers of executive services in this case. In the South, it is common for retailers to create a monopoly situation by extending credit to impecunious tenant farmers. Should the debtors fail to purchase all their supplies from the retailer — at his own price — he presses for payment of the

---

[3] *American Column and Lumber Company, et al.,* v. *United States,* 257 U. S. 377 (1921). But see also *Maple Flooring Manufacturers' Association, et al.* v. *United States,* 268 U. S. 586 (1925).

debts. If one enterprise in an industry is substantially larger and more powerful than its competitors, it may compel them to adhere to its prices by threatening a price war against any concerns which sell below its prices. In Mexico and parts of eastern Europe, large landowners have used indebtedness as a device to hold laborers at far lower wages than competition would establish.

III. THE EXTENT OF MONOPOLY IN THE UNITED STATES

Because monopolies in the United States do not advertise their existence and usually take pains to conceal it, the precise extent of monopoly is difficult to estimate.[4] The discussion of the forms of monopoly, however, has suggested that it is more prevalent than many persons suspect. Incandescent lamps, shoe machinery, aluminum, cash registers, raisins, anthracite coal, cameras, optical goods, plumbing goods, and many steel products are all more or less completely monopolized. Many branches of the building industry in New York and Chicago were shown in recent public investigations to be controlled by rings of material men or contractors, aided often by trade unions.[5] Some contractors' associations have a rule that, after one member has been awarded the contract for a building, no other member will accept work on the building. This does not eliminate competition for the original contract, but it means that if there is extra work, the successful bidder has an opportunity to do it at his own price. Recent reports of the Federal Trade Commission direct attention to pools or other forms of monopoly among manufacturers of

[4] In Germany, where monopolistic combinations are not illegal, industrial combination has proceeded farther than anywhere else. The most prevalent form of organization in Germany is the cartel, which is similar to the pool but more highly centralized and possessed of greater control over the members. In 1911, there were about 600 cartels in Germany, and in 1925 about 3,000. There are also a number of international cartels, the most noteworthy of which is the recent steel combination formed between Germany, Belgium, France, Luxembourg, and the Saar. Basic production is estimated at both normal and maximum figures, and percentage quotas assigned to each of the five producing regions at both the normal and the maximum figure. The restriction of production is enforced by penalties. For each ton of crude steel produced, $1 is paid into the treasury. For each ton of production in excess of the quota, $4 is paid. When a country produces less than its quota (up to 10 per cent), it receives from the cartel $2 per ton of deficit. In addition to the steel cartel, there are international pools controlling pig iron, rolled wire, pipe, coffee, glue, benzine, bottles, incandescent lamps, enameled ware, rails, and other commodities.

[5] An excellent account of monopolies in the Chicago building trades will be found in R. E. Montgomery's *Industrial Relations in the Chicago Building Trades*, pp. 187–208.

washing machines, vacuum cleaners, sewing machines, refrigerators, brooms, aluminum cooking utensils, and household furniture. The Federal Trade Commission recently ordered 231 members of the American Photo-Engravers' Association to cease using a scale of standard prices. It also prohibited the officers of the Association from using " clause 10 " in the agreements between local branches of the Association and the photo-engravers' union to compel photo-engraving concerns to observe set prices or to desist from cutting prices. " Clause 10 " stipulated that union members would work only for members of the local branch of the Association. This permitted the branch to deprive any price cutter of his labor supply simply by expelling him.[6] During the spring and summer of 1930 the Cotton Textile Institute succeeded in getting most of the mills in the South to restrict the hours of operation to fifty-five a week for the day shift and fifty a week for the night shift. Most ambitious of all were the unsuccessful efforts of the Federal Farm Board in the spring of 1930 to induce the millions of wheat and cotton raisers to behave as if they were monopolists. The Board sought to induce the wheat growers to cut their acreage by at least 10 per cent and the cotton growers from 46,000,000 to less than 40,000,000.

Trade unions, of course, are monopolies, or at least attempts to create monopolies. Just as combinations of manufacturers or merchants establish prices below which their members agree not to sell, so unions establish scales of wages and standards of working conditions below which their members will not work. Not all members of trade unions are in a monopolistic position, but a large proportion of them are. Over 98 per cent of the actors on the legitimate stage, 90 per cent of the photoengravers, 86 per cent of the stereotypers and electrotypers, 69 per cent of the stone-cutters, and 54 per cent of the railway brakemen are organized. And even where the degree of organization is less, the unionists may possess monopolistic power. A union which embraces only a small percentage of the craft in the nation often includes all or nearly all of the occupation in many places. Thus the bricklayers' union contains but a minority of the bricklayers, but in many cities practically all belong to it.

[6] *United States Daily*, February 16, 1928, p. 10.

The Amalgamated Association of Street and Electric Railway Employees is far from including all of the street railway motormen and conductors in the country, but in Chicago every one of the eleven thousand motormen and conductors employed on the surface and elevated lines is a member and, as a result, is able to obtain wages far above the competitive level. Indeed, to obtain monopolistic benefits for its members, a union need not even be dominant in the city. If it has enough members *in a single plant* so that the employer could not easily replace them in case of a strike, it can usually obtain a wage distinctly above the rate in unorganized plants.

Exclusive information about business opportunities, the large capital required to take advantage of many of them, and the habit — quite pronounced among the more powerful business men of most communities — of not competing for an opportunity which other large interests are seeking to exploit, all create monopolistic situations. It is, of course, far from true that great business interests never compete with each other for opportunities. Rivalry among them is often acute, especially when a certain plant, patent, or piece of land is peculiarly important to several enterprises. But in the absence of special reasons, it is customary, once a powerful interest has begun negotiations for a business opportunity, for other large financial groups to hold off and not to bid competitively for it. This custom, it is true, is not without a selfish basis, for if several powerful capitalists were to compete strenuously for an opportunity, they would destroy its exceptional attractiveness. Furthermore, an interest which sought to cut out another would be making a formidable enemy which at some future time might retaliate.

The custom of marketing stocks and bonds, not by soliciting bids from several investment bankers, but by offering the securities only to one house which acts regularly as fiscal agent of the issuing company, puts the banking house in a monopolistic position and enables it to get the securities for less than it would otherwise have to pay. In a recent case before the Interstate Commerce Commission, it was charged that the Chicago, Milwaukee, and St. Paul Railway had sold equipment trust certificates to its fiscal agent for less than another banker was willing

to pay. In a vigorous dissenting opinion, Commissioner Eastman expressed the conviction that the railroad should have asked
for competitive bids on the securities, just as it did on the equipment which was purchased with the proceeds of their sale.
The Commission did not agree with Mr. Eastman, but it did
order the bankers to pay the road more than it had agreed
to accept.[7]

The price offered by the fiscal agent may be affected by the
fact that if the offer were too low, the corporation might seek
bids from other bankers. Not infrequently, however, the banking house either controls the corporation or has substantial
influence in the board of directors. Solicitation of bids from
other bankers might antagonize the fiscal agent and even
lead it to attempt to oust the management. Most officials do
not desire the enmity of an influential banking firm. Finally,
if the fiscal agent is exceptionally powerful and able to injure seriously any house which seeks to outbid it, the corporation might experience difficulty in finding other bidders for its
securities.

Many other examples might be cited to show the pervasiveness of monopoly and especially to show that it is to be found on
a local scale in every community. It is important to notice that
there is often, in fact *usually,* a *degree* of monopoly in competitive situations. Eminent actors or singers furnish examples.
They compete with one another and with less renowned artists,
and this undoubtedly affects the prices which they command. But
there was only one Caruso and there is only one Ethel Barry-
more, not to mention Al Jolson or Will Rogers. The ability of a
famous actor or musician to command a high income, therefore, rests largely upon the fact that there is no one else ex-

[7] Recently the method of marketing securities by competitive bids from bankers
was used by the Chicago and North Western Railway in selling $2,745,000 of equip-
ment trust certificates. Bids were invited from thirty-eight banks and bond houses.
Thirteen bids, representing twenty-three houses, were received. *United States Daily*,
February 23, 1928, p. 10.

For services rendered in reorganizing the Missouri-Kansas-Texas Railroad, the
bankers asked a fee of $1,614,249, and the counsel for the bankers $750,000. These
amounts were contested before the Interstate Commerce Commission and the Commission reduced them to $900,000 and $600,000 respectively. Commissioners Eastman
and McManamy dissented on the ground that even these allowances were excessive.
Interstate Commerce Commission, *Missouri-Kansas-Texas Reorganization, Finance
Docket No. 1250.*

actly like him — in other words, that he is in some sense a monopolist.

A mixture of monopoly and competition is found also in the case of many commodities. To the extent that a seller can convince buyers that his article has characteristics which its rivals lack, he is in a monopolistic position and can charge a monopoly price for the real or supposed unique qualities of his product. *Notice that charging a monopoly price for the peculiar characteristics which a brand possesses is not the same thing as simply charging a higher price.* When *several* brands of a commodity possess the same superiority, the extra price which they command over brands which lack the superior feature tends to be no greater than the cost of producing the superiority. But when *one* and only one brand has a certain desirable feature, the seller may be able to charge a differential over the prices of other makes, far greater than the expense of creating the superiority and of convincing the public that it exists. National advertising consists very largely of attempts to persuade the public that certain brands have qualities which no others possess; in other words, attempts to create monopolies. It is probably true that in many cases the attempt to put individual brands in a monopoly position fails, either because the unique characteristics are little or no more important than the unique characteristics of competing brands or because the advertising is not effective. It is doubtful, for example, whether the money spent to convince the public that certain makes of automobiles or automobile tires possess unique advantages has enabled the makers to obtain a monopoly price. Of course, the mere fact that an advertised article sells for more than an unadvertised one is not conclusive evidence that a monopoly price is being collected. The higher price may simply represent the additional cost of advertising. But often the brands upon which special selling and advertising efforts have been concentrated sell for so much more than unadvertised goods as to make it reasonably certain that a monopoly price is being charged. This conclusion is confirmed by the profits of some producers of trade-marked goods. It is estimated, for example, that the Lambert Company, the manufacturers of " Listerine," makes 181 per cent profit on its investment; Coty, Inc., producers of cosmetics, 60 per cent; Canada Dry Ginger Ale Company, 58 per cent; Maytag Company, producers of " Maytag " washing machines, 57 per cent.[8]

Often the monopoly element in a good is based upon prestige. If one desires the satisfaction of going to the most fashionable and pretentious hotel in town, there is probably one and only one hotel which can give it. One store may be looked upon as the most fashionable of its kind in the city. Such an enterprise is to some extent in a monopolistic position, because it is able to confer a feeling of self-satisfaction upon some customers which none of its rivals can do. On this account, the firm can often obtain prices which contain a considerable monopoly element; that is, which exceed the charges of its rivals by considerably more than the extra cost of maintaining its prestige.[9]

But although it is undoubtedly true that monopolies are far more prevalent than has been generally supposed, it is also true that many monopolies are remarkably ephemeral. This was especially true of the monopolies which were formed by pools. But many other monopolies have been destroyed. Large monopoly profits encourage the establishment of new enterprises which, if permitted to grow, would end the monopoly's control of the market. Naturally the monopoly seeks to destroy them. One method is to sell below cost in the markets of the independents. In regions where competition is not serious, the price, of course, is not cut. The high prices charged in these places help the monopoly to maintain low prices in competitive territory. These tactics are often successful but they are not invariably so — particularly when the independents have efficient plants and ample financial resources. The monopoly of the American Sugar Refining Company, for example, was quickly destroyed by the growth of new plants. High monopoly profits also encourage the invention of new processes of production and of substitute commodities. Japan's monopoly of camphor was destroyed by the synthetic product. Perhaps the most notable instances of

---

[8] Sloan, L. H., *Corporation Profits*, p. 152; cited by Epstein, R. C., in " Statistical Light on Profits," *Quarterly Journal of Economics*, February, 1930, v. XLIV, p. 341.

[9] Not only is it possible for these enterprises to charge more but it may be *necessary* for them to do it, because their prestige depends, among other things, upon their high prices.

monopolies which have been destroyed are the tobacco and petroleum monopolies. The relatively complete control of the old American Tobacco Company and the Standard Oil Company of New Jersey in these industries has been replaced by intense competition. The tobacco monopoly was destroyed in the main by the application of the Sherman Anti-Trust Law. By order of the courts, the American Tobacco Company was divided into four large competing concerns. The petroleum monopoly was destroyed in part by the application of the Sherman Act but in the main by the growth of large independent petroleum companies.

IV. The Determination of Price under Monopolistic Conditions

At what point will a monopoly fix price? Let us first consider the case of a buyers' monopoly. It is, of course, possible for the monopoly, by refusing to buy at higher prices, to force the price down very far. By so doing, however, it will lessen the quantity of the commodity which can be profitably produced and which, therefore, will be supplied. The monopoly must make a choice of paying a high price and obtaining a large quantity of goods or of paying a low price and obtaining only a small quantity. It may meet this difficulty by not making all of its purchases at any one price, but by buying from those producers who are willing to sell for the least, and at the lowest price which it can induce each to accept. Suppose, for example, that the monopoly is willing to pay $6.00 each for 1,000 units of product, $5.00 for a second 1,000 units, $4.00 for a third 1,000 units, and $3.00 for a fourth 1,000 units. Above $6.00 it is unwilling to go. Sellers are willing to supply the article as follows: A, 1,000 units at $1.00; B, 1,000 at $2.00; C, 1,000 at $3.00; and D, 1,000 at $4.00. If the monopoly knows the prices which each is willing, if necessary, to take, it can purchase 1,000 units each from A, B, C, and D at the lowest price which each will accept, namely, $1.00, $2.00, $3.00, and $4.00, respectively.

The monopoly, however, is unlikely to discover the lowest price which each producer will accept. It may suspect that A for some reason — possibly because his costs are known to be exceptionally low or his need for funds unusually pressing — will take a very low price. But if A is a clever bargainer, he may convince the monopoly that he will accept no less than $1.50, and it may pay him that price. Likewise B, instead of selling for $2.00, may succeed in getting $2.50; C may obtain $3.50 instead of $3.00; and D, $4.50 instead of $4.00.

But even if the monopoly knows which producers are most willing to sell, it may fear the antagonism which it would arouse by beating each down to his lowest price. For this reason, or because it cannot discover which sellers will sell for less than the others, it may purchase at a uniform price. In this event, it must choose between getting a small amount for a low price or a large amount for a higher price. It will compare the cost and the worth to it of different quantities of the commodity and will purchase the quantity which yields it the maximum excess of worth over cost. In the following case, the monopoly would purchase 2,000 units at $2.00 each:

Supply	Price	Total cost	Worth to the monopoly	Excess of worth over cost
1,000	$1	$1,000	$6,000	$5,000
2,000	2	4,000	11,000	7,000
3,000	3	9,000	15,000	6,000
4,000	4	16,000	18,000	2,000

Sellers' monopolies act in essentially the same way as buyers' monopolies. If the monopoly knows the approximate price which each customer is willing to pay and is not afraid of public opinion, it will ask of each buyer the maximum price which he is willing to give. But usually the impracticability of negotiating a separate price for each sale compels the monopoly to charge one price, or possibly several prices, only. In this case it will endeavor to select the price or prices which will yield it the largest net return. Just as a buyers' monopoly must decide whether to purchase a small quantity at a low price or to pay more in order to obtain a larger quantity, so a sellers' monopoly must decide between selling a small amount at a high price or a large amount at a low price. Since unit cost often decreases as output increases, the monopoly may make more by selling a large quantity at a low price. In the following instance, for example, the maximum profit would be obtained by selling at $1.20:

Quantity	Unit cost	Total cost	Selling price	Gross income	Net profits
1,000,000	$1.00	$1,000,000	$2.00	$2,000,000	$1,000,000
2,000,000	.90	1,800,000	1.60	3,200,000	1,400,000
3,000,000	.70	2,100,000	1.20	3,600,000	1,500,000
4,000,000	.60	2,400,000	.80	3,200,000	800,000

In deciding what to charge, the monopoly must take account of the fact that the price which yields the largest net return immediately, may not do so in the long run. An extremely high price may cause new enterprises to enter the industry, encourage the invention of substitutes for the monopolized product, or stir up the government to regulate or to dissolve the monopoly.[10] On the other hand, a low price may assist the monopoly to build up a large demand for its product. After the public has discovered the merits of the article and has acquired the habit of using it, the monopoly may be able to raise the price without serious loss of sales.

When it is said that sellers' monopolies tend to charge the price which yields the largest net profit, it must not be assumed that this price is usually closely approximated. So scanty and unreliable is the information concerning the elasticity of the demand for most commodities that few monopolies are able to determine what price would be most profitable. Consequently the monopolist must make a guess. The temptation is to collect a high price and it is probable that in most cases the price is too high even to yield the maximum profits to the monopoly. Consider, for illustration, the case of the Chilean iodine monopoly. Iodine is a by-product of nitrate in Chile and its output is controlled by the Chilean Iodine Producers' Association. Not more than about 10 per cent of the iodine content of the nitrate is extracted — the rest is allowed to go to waste. For several years preceding 1930, the monopoly fixed the price at $2.89 a pound, a price which yielded the producers, according to Dr. Julius

[10] How a high price may encourage the development of a substitute is illustrated by the experience of the Japanese camphor monopoly. The high price which the Japanese charged for crude camphor encouraged the German chemists to develop a synthetic camphor which, by reason of its uniform quality and lower price, has taken away a large part of the American trade. In 1922, 237 pounds of natural camphor for one pound of synthetic came into the United States; but in the first nine months of 1926, the imports of synthetic equalled those of crude and refined camphor.

Klein, a profit of about 500 per cent.[11]   Would it be more profitable for the monopoly to charge less and sell more pounds?   Dr.
Klein suspects that it would.   Much of the demand for iodine is
highly inelastic but Dr. Klein thinks that industrial uses might
expand greatly if the price were substantially lower.   But
whether or not this result would follow, no one knows.   It is
interesting to observe that the American Telephone and Telegraph Company has apparently concluded that it could make
more money at lower rates on some kinds of business.   In a three
year period, the company reduced the charge for New York-San
Francisco calls from $15.60 to $9.00 and New York-Chicago
calls from $4.65 to $3.00.

In analyzing the influences which affect the charges of sellers'
monopolies, it must be remembered that the owners have funds
to invest.   The more profitable the monopoly, the larger these
funds are likely to be.   By investing in other industries, the
owners would receive only the competitive rate of return.   If
their money is used to expand the capacity of the monopoly, it
may be necessary to sell the product for less in order to dispose
of the output of the enlarged plant, thus possibly reducing the
rate of profit upon the entire investment.   This, however, may
be more advantageous to the owners than investing their capital
where it would yield only the competitive return.   It should also
be remembered that the reinvestment of profits is often controlled
by the management rather than by the owners and that the managers may desire to reinvest income even when this gives the
owners less return than they might otherwise obtain.   Were the
owners aware that the reinvestment of earnings is reducing their
profits, they would, of course, object, but they may not know it.
For these two reasons the investment of additional capital in
sellers' monopolies may impose a substantial check upon the
tendency for their prices to be high.

V. Double-sided or Bi-Lateral Monopoly

A situation which is far from uncommon is for a sellers'
monopoly to deal with a buyers' monopoly.   Many negotiations
for business property are of this character.   An enterprise wishes
to purchase land.   A particular site, adjoining its present hold-

---

[11] Klein, Julius, *Frontiers of Trade*, p. 109.

ings, is likely to be more valuable to it than any other. Likewise that site is likely to be more valuable to the particular concern than to any other enterprise. Or a concern with plants in a certain territory may wish to expand by purchasing a plant in another territory. A certain plant in the other territory is far more valuable to it than any other plant and furthermore this plant may be more valuable to the enterprise than to any of its competitors. Here again is a double-sided monopoly — a unique piece of property with a unique value to one prospective buyer.[12] The negotiations between trade unions and employers often represent double-sided monopolies. The unions have a monopoly of a particular kind of labor and the employer (or the association of employers) is the sole buyer of that type of labor in the city. In a number of communities, the milk producers and the milk dealers are organized to bargain with each other as units over the price of milk.

[12] An illustration of a double-sided monopoly situation is provided by the recent purchase of the Buffalo and Susquehanna Railroad by the Baltimore and Ohio. Between the beginning of 1926 and August, 1929, the common stock of the Buffalo and Susquehanna had not sold above $65 a share. Yet in August, 1929, the Baltimore and Ohio offered to pay $90 a share. The Buffalo and Susquehanna appears to have had a greater value to the Baltimore and Ohio than it would have had to any other railroad. In approving the offer of $90 a share, the Interstate Commerce Commission pointed out the several reasons for this unique value of the Buffalo and Susquehanna to the Baltimore and Ohio:

> The operations of the Buffalo and Susquehanna in the coal territory near the Sagemore terminus have been conducted from Du Bois as a base, a distance of forty-four miles. This has involved considerable expense for overtime of train crews. Control by the Baltimore and Ohio would permit these operations to be conducted from Punxsutawney, a point on the Buffalo, Rochester and Pittsburgh (also controlled by the Baltimore and Ohio), at a saving of about $256.00 a day, or $75,000 a year.
> Routing of traffic originating on the southern portion of the Buffalo and Susquehanna over the lines of the Buffalo, Rochester and Pittsburgh to the north, use of a proposed new route to Williamsport, and use of the Punxsutawney yard for concentration of traffic interchanges would result in saving an out-of-pocket expense of $1,000 per day and would release equipment for more effective service elsewhere. These economies would reduce expenses about $375,000 a year without taking into account any saving through reduction in car days and ton miles.
> Part of the line of the Buffalo and Susquehanna would be valuable to the Baltimore and Ohio because it would provide a fifty-five mile link in a new short line between New York and Chicago which would be about eighty-three miles shorter than the present route of the Baltimore and Ohio, and which would cross the Alleghenies at about 700 feet lower. Diversion of traffic to the new route would obviate, to a large extent, the necessity of improving the present main line of the Baltimore and Ohio just west of Pittsburgh. It would also relieve the line through Baltimore which at times is overburdened. *United States Daily,* May 22, 1930, p. 12.

When a buyers' monopoly deals with a sellers' monopoly, at what point is the price fixed? Each monopoly naturally strives to fix the price at the point of greatest advantage to it. The sellers' monopoly knows that the more it asks the less it can sell. It endeavors to fix a price that will yield the largest net profit. The buyers' monopoly knows that the less it pays, the less it can buy. It endeavors to determine what supply at what price is most advantageous to it. The price which the buyers' monopoly offers is certain to be substantially less than the sellers' monopoly demands. In case it is the bricklayers' union dealing with the bricklaying and mason contractors, the contractors may offer $10 a day and the union may demand $12. No one can predict the outcome of the bargaining beyond saying that the price will not be less than $10 nor more than $12. If the union is represented by shrewd and resourceful business agents, if the outlook for the building industry is good, and if the union is well able to finance a strike, it may succeed in getting all, or nearly all, of its demand. On the other hand, if the outlook for building is poor, if the union treasury is empty, and if the contractors have able leadership, the rate may be set at $10 or close to it. But somewhere between the high price demanded by the sellers and the low price offered by the buyers, the actual price must be set, unless one or the other of the monopolies prefers not to deal at all rather than pay or accept a certain price. In some cases, it may be exceedingly difficult for the two parties to compromise because each is afraid that the other will interpret any concession as a sign of weakness and will stand out more firmly than ever for its original price. In such situations a mediator who commands the confidence of the two sides may be exceedingly useful in helping them arrive at a compromise. Or, the deadlock may be broken, as it frequently is in bargaining over wages or the price of milk, by referring the dispute to an arbitrator.

VI. Is Monopoly Price Necessarily a High Price?

In determining public policy toward sellers' monopolies, it is important to know whether or not their prices are necessarily high. It is usually taken for granted that they are. But this assumption is scarcely warranted.

Many sellers' monopolies do no more than prevent cutthroat competition among their members. The monopolies are composed of members who are in an extremely weak bargaining position, and the most which even a strong organization can do is to mitigate the severity of competition. The monopoly may succeed in raising the price and even in raising it substantially, but this does not necessarily mean that the price is unreasonably high. The best examples of monopolies which merely eliminate cutthroat competition are found among trade unions. There are many monopolies composed of business enterprises, however, which do little more than prevent the members from *losing* money. The American Photo-Engravers' Association was probably such a monopoly. Only a small amount of capital is required to enter the industry.[13] This resulted in the establishment of more plants than were really needed. Most of the master photo-engravers were former journeymen who understood the technique of making engravings but who were often lacking in business training and experience. Few of them had adequate cost accounting systems and consequently few of them knew whether they were selling above or below cost. The scarcity of skilled men made employers reluctant to lay off workers when business was slack. This converted wages into practically a fixed expense and created a strong tendency to cut prices. These were the general conditions which created cutthroat competition in the industry. The monopoly apparently did little more than end this competition.

Another monopoly which seems merely to have prevented cutthroat competition is the organization of malleable iron founders which several years ago was convicted of violating the Sherman Anti-Trust Law. Most malleable iron foundries are small enterprises with only limited resources. Many of their customers are large manufacturers with great buying power and, therefore, great bargaining power. The malleable iron founder cannot individualize his product because he does not determine what his product is; he simply makes castings according to patterns furnished by the customer. Consequently, competition among the founders is largely price competition and customers

---

[13] The amount required to establish a well-equipped plant is rapidly becoming larger.

are in an excellent position to play one founder against another by threatening to send their patterns elsewhere. Under these circumstances, cutthroat competition is almost inevitable unless the founders organize to prevent it.

But even if a sellers' monopoly succeeds in making large profits, its price may be less than would prevail under competition. Monopolies are often able to achieve substantial savings by concentrating production in large and more specialized plants, by operating more steadily, and by eliminating many of the expenses of competitive selling.[14] This, of course, is more likely to be true of monopolies created by merger than of those created by agreements among enterprises which retain their independence. The economies achieved by the monopoly make it *able* to sell for less than competing firms would have to charge. Whether or not it *will* sell for less depends largely upon whether the price which yields the largest net profit is above or below the cost of production under competition. This depends upon (1) whether the costs of the monopoly are largely fixed or largely direct; (2) whether the demand for the product is elastic or inelastic.

If the expenses of the monopoly are largely direct so that its unit costs do not rapidly decline as its output increases, a high

---

[14] Monopolies can afford to operate their plants more steadily than competing concerns. During a period of slack demand it is risky for one of many competing enterprises to produce large stocks of goods in anticipation of a subsequent increase in demand because there is no certainty how soon or how much demand will revive and, therefore, what price can later be obtained for the stored goods. A monopoly, however, because of its control over supply and price, escapes this risk in large degree. Consequently a monopoly can profitably economize capital and labor and obtain a relatively large output from a relatively small investment in plant by operating at capacity during the slack seasons of the year and piling up stocks of goods to meet the heavy demand of the busy season. In case the demand in the busy season does not attain the estimated volume, the monopoly can protect itself from serious loss simply by producing less than it otherwise would and selling off its accumulated stocks. The anthracite and bituminous coal industries illustrate how monopoly makes possible steadier operation. The anthracite industry is monopolized; the bituminous highly competitive. Anthracite is produced during the spring and summer months without much diminution and is held for fall sale. Bituminous coal is more difficult to store but, where special inducement exists, storage occurs. No one, however, cares to risk holding a product the price of which is competitively determined, unless the inducement is exceptionally strong. Consequently, during the period 1910 to 1918, the anthracite mines worked an average of 252 days each year out of a possible 308, while the bituminous mines worked an average of 223. Of late years, however, the anthracite industry has become more seasonal. The reason is that the demand is not sufficient to keep the mines busy the year round.

price is likely to be more profitable than a low one. This can be illustrated by assuming that the drop in unit costs which accompanies greater output is less rapid than was indicated in the last table. Although the conditions of demand are unchanged, the price which now yields the maximum profit is $1.60 instead of $1.20.

Quantity	Unit cost	Total cost	Selling price	Gross income	Net profits
1,000,000	$1.00	$1,000,000	$2.00	$2,000,000	$1,000,000
2,000,000	.95	1,900,000	1.60	3,200,000	1,300,000
3,000,000	.90	2,700,000	1.20	3,600,000	900,000
4,000,000	.85	3,400,000	.80	3,200,000	200,000

The point of maximum profit is affected also by the elasticity of demand. The less the quantity demanded falls as the price advances — in other words, the more inelastic the demand — the higher it pays the monopoly to raise its price. In the following table, the cost data are the same as in the original one but the demand is more inelastic:

Quantity	Unit cost	Total cost	Selling price	Gross income	Net profits
1,000,000	$1.00	$1,000,000	$2.00	$2,000,000	$1,000,000
2,000,000	.90	1,800,000	1.20	2,400,000	600,000
3,000,000	.70	2,100,000	.80	2,400,000	300,000
4,000,000	.60	2,400,000	.40	1,600,000	800,000

In this case the most profitable price is $2.00 or more — our data do not enable us to compare $2.00 with higher prices. Thus it appears that monopoly price is most likely to be far above competitive price when direct costs are relatively high and the demand inelastic. On the other hand, when direct costs are relatively low and demand highly elastic, the monopoly price may be little higher than the competitive one; in fact, if the cost of production is less than it would be under competition, the monopoly price may be less than competition would set.

VII. Monopolies and the Distribution of Resources

The man in the street is inclined to judge the desirability of monopolies by their effect on prices. A sellers' monopoly in most instances collects a higher price than would prevail under competition. For that reason and to that extent, therefore, sellers' monopolies impress the man in the street as undesirable.

But this view of monopolies tends to exaggerate their undesirability. Although sellers' monopolies do raise the prices of some goods, they indirectly lower the prices of others. The explanation is simple. Sellers' monopolies raise prices by restricting output. When they restrict output, they necessarily limit the amount of capital and labor which is absorbed by the monopolized industries. This means that more labor and capital must seek employment in non-monopoly industries. The output of these industries is greater than it otherwise would be, the rate of profit is less, and the prices of the products are less. Although buyers must pay more for monopolized products, they are able to purchase all other goods at somewhat lower prices.

This, however, does not mean that buyers are not injured by the monopoly. The higher price which they must pay for the monopolized article is offset *in part* by the lower prices at which they can obtain other goods. But it is not *entirely* offset. Proof of this is found in the fact that, if there were no monopoly, commodities would be produced in slightly different proportions. The good which is now monopolized would be produced in larger quantities and other goods in smaller quantities. The only reason why men would buy more of the good which is now monopolized and less of other goods simply is that they could get more satisfaction for their money by so doing. The immediate evil of a monopoly, therefore, is that it compels capital and labor to be so distributed among industries that they do not yield the maximum possible satisfaction, and the measure of the evil is the amount by which the satisfaction which consumers derive from their expenditures for all goods when the monopoly exists falls short of the satisfaction which they would derive from their total expenditures if the monopoly did not exist.[15] In order to illustrate this point, let us suppose that a community spends $3,000,-000 a year — $1,500,000 for 1,000,000 units of commodity A at a price of $1.50 per unit and $1,500,000 for commodity B at a

[15] It is interesting to notice that the essential evil of a protective tariff is the same as that of a monopoly; the tariff also prevents the most advantageous distribution of capital and labor because it causes more capital and labor to be used in the protected industries and less in the unprotected ones than would be the case if the distribution were determined solely by the relative demand for different goods.

price of $1.50 per unit. Assume now that the producers of commodity A form a monopoly and reduce production from 1,000,-000 to 900,000 units per year. This enables them to command a price of $1.778 per unit. But the laborers that the monopoly has dismissed must find employment in producing B, and new savings must in the main be used in the production of B. As a result, the output of B rises from 1,000,000 to 1,100,000 units and the price drops from $1.50 to $1.273. What is the loss inflicted by this monopoly upon the community? Evidently the monopoly is responsible for the community's having 100,000 units a year less of commodity A and 100,000 units more of commodity B. But if we may measure the importance of the commodities by the willingness of the community to pay for them, the 100,000 units of commodity A had an importance of not less than $150,000 because the community was willing to pay $1.50 when 1,000,000 were produced. The additional 100,000 of commodity B have an importance of $127,300 because, when there is a supply of 1,100,000, each unit is worth only $1.273. The net loss inflicted upon the community, therefore, is represented by the difference between $150,000 and $127,300. The monopoly deprives the community of $150,000 of product A and gives it $127,300 more of product B.

Monopolies are prevented from causing a wasteful distribution of resources when they are prevented by public price-fixing bodies from charging more than a competitive price. Herein is the principal value of bodies which regulate the prices of monopolies. The profit in restricting output comes, of course, from the fact that restriction enables the monopoly to charge a high price. To the extent that public regulating bodies remove the profit from restriction of output by preventing monopolies from earning more than the competitive rate of profit, such bodies discourage the uneconomical distribution of capital and labor.

When a monopoly is able to eliminate so many costs of competition that it finds it profitable to sell for less than competing enterprises, the consumers are, of course, able to obtain more satisfaction for their money than under a state of competition. But, even under these circumstances, regulation of the monopoly price may produce a still more advantageous distribution of resources and still further enhance the return which consumers obtain for their expenditures. Even though a monopoly may find it profitable to charge less than competitors could charge, it is able, by restricting output, to reap more than the competitive rate of return. In so doing, however, it compels labor and capital to enter other industries where they are used to produce goods which are less in demand and which, in most cases, probably yield less satisfaction to the buyers. Regulation of the monopoly is needed in order to prevent this.

VIII. Monopoly Price and the Distribution of Income

Another major objection to monopolies is that they result in unfair distribution of income. The high prices which a sellers' monopoly is able to charge, for example, might be expected to yield the owners (or at least the *original* owners) a higher return than most investors can obtain on their capital.[16] Furthermore, by restricting production and forcing new savings to be invested almost entirely in non-monopolized industries, the monopoly depresses the return which investors in general can obtain on their funds.

But the effect of monopolies upon the distribution of income must not be exaggerated. For, strange to say, ability to collect a high price does not *invariably* permit a monopoly to obtain more than the ordinary rate of return. It all depends upon whether the monopoly can control the number of persons who enter the business or occupation. The largest grocers of a town may meet regularly and agree on the prices at which they will sell and the other grocers may accept the prices fixed by the leaders. But although the principal dealers may be able to set the prices of groceries, they cannot prevent the establishment of new stores. Indeed, the large profits which the monopoly creates will probably encourage the starting of new stores and the number is likely to increase as long as the grocery business yields larger profits than pursuits requiring similar ability and involving no greater risks. In other words, the monopoly has raised prices above the competitive level, but, owing to its inability to limit the number of enterprises, it has only temporarily enabled its members to obtain

[16] Investors who purchase shares in a monopolized industry may obtain only the current rate of return on their investments because the price which they must pay for their shares reflects the large profits of the monopoly.

more than the ordinary rate of return. Instead of producing large profits, the high prices have simply attracted into the industry more persons and capital than are needed. Trade unions are the best example of monopolies which can raise prices but cannot control the number of persons who enter the industry or occupation. Though able to advance the wages of their members above the competitive level, they are often unable to prevent men from entering the trade. Because the high union scale attracts men into the occupation, the work is sometimes divided among more men than are really needed, unemployment is increased, and the *annual* earnings of the laborers may be reduced to little above the level in unorganized trades.[17]

IX. THE INFLUENCE OF CUSTOM UPON PRICES

In the wheat pit, the slightest indication of an increase in demand or a shortage in supply will cause the price to rise. If one goes to the drug store on a hot day to buy ice cream, one may find the supply about to give out. But, despite the great demand, the druggist does not raise the price. He charges no more than he did the day before when demand was normal. The demand for credit fluctuates considerably from year to year and with the seasons of the year. In large cities, the price of loans responds promptly to changes in demand. The charges of many country banks, however, remain substantially the same, year in and year out. Many country banks in central New York, for example, have for years charged regular customers 6 per cent, despite the fact that interest rates in large cities have fluctuated considerably. Here we see the influence of custom upon prices. The druggist, having set a certain price on his ice cream, continues to charge it, irrespective of daily changes in demand. Six per cent having become established as the interest rate in a country town,

---

[17] We have stated that the distinctive feature of sellers' monopolies is ability to exercise sufficient control over supply to make it profitable to restrict output and to raise the price. Now we are apparently denying that control of supply is an essential characteristic of a monopoly. But careful reading of the above paragraph will reveal that the control of sellers' monopolies over supply is not denied. It is simply stated that they may be unable to control the *productive capacity* of the trade or industry; that is, the number of workers or the amount of capital entering it. This is quite different from the *output* of the trade or industry. Regardless of the capacity of the industry, only as much may be produced as can be sold at the price fixed by the monopoly.

the banks continue to ask it as a matter of course, regardless of changes in the money market. The bankers probably give no thought to the possibility of altering their charge for loans. They know that their customers are used to paying a certain rate, expect to pay it, would resent being charged more, and would be surprised at being asked less.

The influence of custom extends to a vast variety of prices. The war caused the prices of wheat, flour, and labor to rise rapidly. The public, however, had become used to paying 5 and 10 cents a loaf for bread and resented so keenly being asked more that bakers found great difficulty in raising the price. No baker wished to incur public hostility by being the first to advance his price and many grocers preferred to sell bread at no profit rather than to risk the loss of trade by asking more. The price of common labor, street car rides, breakfast foods, retail tobacco, shoe shines, collars, shaves, hair cuts, soft drinks, confections, physicians' services, newspapers, soaps, hotel rooms are all influenced in large degree by custom.[18]

What makes some prices customary and other prices not? Why should the prices of breakfast foods, collars, or bread be customary, but not the prices of butter, eggs, vegetables, fish, or furniture?

A price is more likely to become customary, when the good is so standardized that the consumer purchases substantially the same thing each time he buys it. This is one reason why the price of collars is customary in greater degree than that of shirts, the price of shoe polish in greater degree than the price of shoes. It is also necessary that the supply of the good be fairly subject to human control and, if the product is a seasonal one, that

[18] The method and amount of the mark-up by retailers are frequently matters of custom. There are two principal methods in the retail coal industry. One is to add a flat amount per ton to the cost, the other to add a percentage of the selling price. The University of Nebraska College of Business Administration found that only two firms in Lincoln used the percentage rate, one adding 20 per cent of the selling price, the other 30 per cent. Seventeen dealers added a flat amount per ton, but the amount of the mark-up varied. Four were still using the " government " margins which were put into effect by the State Fuel Commissioner in 1918. The investigation was made in 1922. One dealer was marking up slightly less than the " government " margins and two slightly more. One used these margins plus 50 cents per ton. " Trade Practices and Costs of the Retail Coal Business in Lincoln, Nebraska, in 1922," *Nebraska Studies in Business, Bulletin No. 7,* p. 12.

storage be relatively inexpensive. Agricultural products are bound to fluctuate violently because the supply is so largely dependent upon the weather and because most of them can be stored only at considerable expense.

The more frequently a price is paid, the more likely it is to become customary. By paying the price often, consumers become used to it and regard it as fair. Goods which have customary prices — newspapers, street car fares, tobacco, shines, shaves, labor, gas and electricity, use of rooms or dwellings — are usually purchased at frequent intervals. Things which are bought less frequently — hardware, suits, gloves, furniture — are less affected by custom.

Customary prices are almost invariably retail prices. One reason is that, in selling at retail, the good will of the customer is of great importance, whereas, in wholesale markets, relations are on a more purely business basis. The importance which retailers attach to consumer good will makes them reluctant to ask more than the usual prices in the face of rising costs or of a sudden shortage in supply or increase in demand. This is especially true when only a small part of the retailer's income is derived from the sale of the article. Raising a price which has become customary may lose the dealer the entire trade of many buyers. Rather than risk this, he may prefer to sell the good for cost or less.

Another reason why custom influences retail prices far more than wholesale is that in wholesale markets both buyers and sellers are more or less familiar with the present and prospective state of supply and demand. If an increase in supply is impending, sellers cut prices in order to reduce their stocks before a greater drop in prices occurs and buyers reduce their orders to a bare minimum in hopes of obtaining lower prices later. When higher prices are likely, there is a general tendency to stock up before the rise goes very far. This adjustment of buying and selling to market prospects keeps wholesale prices in a constant state of change. The ultimate consumer, on the other hand, knows little or nothing about market trends or price movements and his purchasing is little influenced by them. It is governed primarily by his immediate needs and by his ability to pay. Consequently, the ultimate consumer does not produce price fluctuations, now by buying speculatively in anticipation of higher prices and now by waiting for prices to fall.

Customary prices, because of the very fact that they are customary, are poor regulators of economic activity. They fail to do the essential thing which prices are expected to do — namely, to reflect changes in demand and supply. A customary price which fails to rise when the demand for a good increases, obviously fails to stimulate an increase in production to meet the increase in demand. Because the price of the good is controlled by custom, part of the increased demand must go unsatisfied. Likewise, a price which does not fall when the supply of a good rises relative to the demand, fails to discourage the production of the good and to prevent the piling up of unsold supplies. Of course, the production soon is discouraged by the very inability of producers to sell all that they make.

But it must not be supposed that customary prices never change. The very failure of a customary price to keep supply and demand in equilibrium causes higher or lower prices to be asked or offered. If, for example, the demand exceeds the supply, a few buyers are likely to offer more than the customary price in order to be sure of obtaining a supply. Gradually more and more business is done above the customary price and eventually a new price will become recognized as the standard one. But because customary prices change more slowly than other prices, persons who derive their incomes through them are constantly experiencing undeserved gains and losses. Discussion of the problems created by the unequal movement of prices can be advantageously reserved to Chapter XXI, in which the general problem of changes in the price level will be analyzed. Suffice for the moment to say that movements in the general price level, such as the general downward trend from 1865 to 1896 and the upward trend from 1896 to 1920, may cause many buyers and sellers at customary prices to receive unearned income or to suffer undeserved losses for the greater part of their lives.

Several important problems, such as the labor problem and the public utility problem, are complicated by the effect of custom upon prices and particularly by its effect upon popular conceptions of what prices are fair. The tendency for wage rates to become customary is one reason why their adjustment to changes in the price level generates so much friction. It is characteristic of customary prices that they soon come to be regarded as fair. After employers become used to paying certain wages, they consider higher rates exorbitant; and likewise wage earners regard attempts to reduce the established scales as wicked. Regardless of whether an advance or reduction of wages is proposed, it is bound to arouse extraordinarily stubborn opposition. In a similar manner, the adjustment of public utility rates, such as street railway fares, to a rising price level is affected by the feeling of the public that the customary charges measure the fair value of the service. The intensity of this feeling, particularly when it is carefully stimulated by politicians, renders it exceedingly difficult for regulating bodies to decide requests for rate increases strictly upon their merits.

REFERENCES

Carver, T. N., *Essays in Social Justice*, 1922. Ch. XIII.
Jones, Eliot, *The Trust Problem in the United States*, 1921.
Keezer, D. M., Cutler, A. T., and Garfield, F. R., *Problem Economics*, 1928. Ch. XI.
Leifmann, Robert, *International Cartels, Combines, and Trusts*, 1927.
Marshall, Alfred, *Industry and Trade*, 1919. Bk. III, ch. I and II.
Pigou, A. C., *The Economics of Welfare* (third edition), 1929. Pt. II, ch. XIV–XIX.
Sherman, John H., " Observations on Custom in Price Phenomena," *American Economic Review*, December, 1928, v. XVIII, pp. 663–670.
Watkins, M. W., *Industrial Combinations and Trusts*, 1927.

CHAPTER XVII

PUBLIC AUTHORITY AS A DETERMINANT OF PRICE—
THE PROBLEM IN GENERAL

I. THE EXTENT OF PRICE-FIXING BY PUBLIC AUTHORITY. II. THE
ENFORCEMENT OF PRICES FIXED BY PUBLIC AUTHORITY. III. IS IT
DESIRABLE FOR THE GOVERNMENT TO FIX PRICES?

I. THE EXTENT OF PRICE-FIXING BY PUBLIC AUTHORITY

To an extent seldom appreciated, the prices we pay are fixed
directly or indirectly by the government. Sometimes the government sets the price because it operates the enterprise, as in the
case of the post office, the Panama Canal, the Alaskan Government Railroad, and municipal street railway systems, gas, electric,
or water plants. More frequently it regulates the charges of
private enterprises, as in the case of most public utilities — railroad, express, electric light and power, gas, telephone, telegraph,
water, street car, and taxi companies.[1] The Interstate Commerce
Commission has recently been given power to determine the
minimum prices at which common carriers may sell their securities. Some state public service commissions possess similar authority over the utilities under their jurisdiction. Many states
control the rates charged by insurance companies and some regulate the charges for small loans.

For products which are sold by public service enterprises at
government-controlled prices, we spend over $12,245,000,000 a
year. This amount is divided among the different industries as
follows:

Railroads, 1929 .... $6,486,175,000 [2]
Electric light and power (private com-
    panies only), 1927 .... 1,841,227,000 [3]
Telephone companies, 1929 [4] ...... 1,172,863,000 [5]

[1] For a definition of public utility see footnote 1 on page 389.
[2] Interstate Commerce Commission, *Statistics of Railways*, 1929, p. lx.
[3] *Statistical Abstract of the United States*, 1930, p. 369.
[4] Includes only companies reporting to the Interstate Commerce Commission.
[5] *Statistics of Railways*, 1929, p. xxii.

Electric railways, 1927	927,774,000 [6]
Manufactured gas (private companies only), 1927	446,245,000 [7]
Natural gas, 1929	419,000,000 [8]
Express, 1929	291,327,000 [9]
Pipe lines, 1929	251,410,000 [10]
Telegraph and cable, 1929	188,574,000 [11]
Water carriers, 1929 [4]	138,460,000 [12]
Pullman Company, 1929	82,384,000 [13]

Not every rate charged by every public service company is regulated. One state, Delaware, has no commission to fix the charges of public service companies, and the commissions in some other states do not have jurisdiction over all of the utilities in the state. But the fact that not all the utilities included in the table are regulated is compensated by the omission of figures for a number of things which are often sold at publicly set prices — insurance, securities, water, taxi service, and the services of the smaller telephone companies. In the year ending June 30, 1929, the people of the United States spent $696,900,000 for postal service and in 1927 over $122,400,000 for electricity produced by municipally owned plants.[14] If we add these amounts to the sales of public service enterprises, it appears that the total value of the goods purchased by the public at prices set by the government exceeds $13,000,000,000 a year. The National Bureau of Economic Research has estimated that the privately owned public utilities produce over 8 per cent of the national income.[15] The estimates of the Bureau of the Census indicate that public price-fixing regulates the return from over 12 per cent of the wealth which yields pecuniary income.[16]

[6] *Statistical Abstract*, 1930, p. 422.

[7] *Ibid.*, p. 776.

[8] *Ibid.*, p. 778.

[9] *Statistics of Railways*, 1929, p. xxiii.

[10] *Ibid.*, p. xxiii.

[11] *Ibid.*, p. xxiii.

[12] *Ibid.*, p. xxii.

[13] *Ibid.*, p. xxii.

[14] *Statistical Abstract*, 1930, pp. 352 and 369.

[15] Copeland, M. A., " The National Income and its Distribution," *Recent Economic Changes*, v. II, p. 799. Professor Copeland estimates that about 8.2 per cent of the national income was produced by private public utilities in 1926. But his estimate does not include gas companies, waterworks, or pipe lines.

[16] The Bureau of the Census estimated that the total wealth of the United States in 1922 was $320,804,000,000. But many forms of property — clothing, personal ornaments, and furniture — do not ordinarily yield pecuniary income. The Bureau

A number of countries regulate wages by law. The pioneer attempts were made in New Zealand and Australia. Wage rates in most industries in Australasia are now determined by government boards. Every province in Canada has established legal minimum wage rates for women and children in certain occupations. In 1909, Great Britain established four minimum wage boards. By 1925, there were sixty-three boards determining minimum rates for about 3,000,000 workers. Recently there has been a disposition in the United States to experiment with the government regulation of wages. Nine states, as we said in Chapter III, now have minimum wage laws for women and children in some occupations. Kansas, in 1920, established a Court of Industrial Relations to set wages in certain industries — food, fuel, and public utilities — when the parties could not agree. Later this law was repealed. In 1920 also, Congress established the Railroad Labor Board to fix wages on the railroads when the men and the employers were deadlocked. The parties were compelled to submit their disputes to the Board, but were not obliged to obey the Board's decisions. In 1926, the Railroad Labor Board was replaced by the United States Board of Mediation. Although the Board first attempts to mediate in disputes, it is expected to use its influence to bring about arbitration in case mediation fails. The railroads and their employees are not obliged to submit their disputes to arbitration, but in case they do submit them, they are obliged to abide by the board's decision for a year.

In addition to fixing prices directly, governments regulate many prices indirectly. Chile undertakes to raise the price of nitrates to foreigners by an export tax; Egypt levies an export tax on cotton. For several years the Straits Settlements limited the amount of rubber which might be exported. Brazil has endeavored to keep up the price of coffee by building warehouses in the interior for its storage, by limiting the amount of coffee which the railroads are permitted to bring down to the ports daily, and by restricting the entry of vessels into the coffee-

of the Census estimated that these forms of wealth were worth $39,816,000,000. The forms of wealth which usually yield pecuniary income totaled $280,988,000,000. Railroads and their equipment and other public service enterprises (street railways, telegraph, telephone, pipe lines, electric light and power stations, and private shipping) were estimated at $33,919,000,000.

exporting ports.[17]   Cuba recently engaged in an unsuccessful attempt to raise the price of sugar by imposing a fine of $20 for every bag produced in excess of the allowance for the mill and by requiring that the crop be exported only through a corporation established for that purpose.

A common method of checking the fall of a price is for the government, or an organization created or sponsored by it, to buy up and hold surplus stocks of a commodity, as in the case of the Bawra organization for dealing with Australian wool during the war, the Bandeong tin pool created by the governments of the Straits Settlements and the Dutch East Indies in 1921, or the coffee valorization schemes of the Brazilian and São Paulo governments. On October 9th, 1926, following a sensational drop of one-third in the price of cotton, President Coolidge appointed a committee composed of the Managing Director of the War Finance Corporation, the Secretary of Agriculture, the Secretary of Commerce, the Secretary of the Treasury, the Chairman of the Federal Farm Loan Board, and a member of the Federal Reserve Board to assist in raising the price. The committee held meetings in cotton states at which steps were taken to form organizations for financing a withdrawal of 25 per cent of the crop from the market for eighteen to twenty months.[18]   In the summer of 1929, after years of agitation, Congress established machinery by which it is hoped to reduce the fluctuations in the prices of some agricultural commodities. The principal features of the plan are a Federal Farm Board of nine members with $500,000,000 of working capital supplied by the government and with authority to establish and finance " stabilization corporations." When an exceptional season results in an abnormally large crop, the proper stabilization corporation, acting under the guidance of the Farm Board, is expected to diminish the drop in price by purchasing part of the so-called crop " surplus." It is expected that the surplus will be sold abroad or held until a year of shortage.[19]

Undoubtedly the most significant and ambitious attempt to

---

[17] For an excellent discussion of some of these attempts to regulate prices, see Wallace, Benjamin B., and Edminster, Lynn R., *International Control of Raw Materials*.

[18] *Federal Reserve Bulletin*, November, 1926, v. XII, p. 761.

[19] The operations of the Federal Farm Board are analyzed in Chapter XIX.

regulate prices indirectly in the United States is represented by the Federal Reserve Board and Banks, which, through rediscount rates and open market operations, undertake to control, within somewhat wide limits, the price, and therefore the volume, of short-time credit. But between the volume of credit and the general level of prices, there is an intimate relationship. The more liberally the banks supply borrowers with credit dollars, the greater, in terms of dollars, will be the demand for goods and, unless production grows in proportion, the higher will be the general price level. On the other hand, the fewer the credit dollars which the banks supply, the smaller will be the demand for goods and, unless output declines in proportion, the lower the level of prices. Many persons believe that the Federal Reserve authorities should confine their attention to controlling the volume of credit and should make no effort to influence general price movements. This, however, is an impossible demand, for, in deciding whether to permit an expansion of credit or to compel a contraction, one of the major questions which the authorities must decide is whether or not the effect upon prices will be desirable. The Federal Reserve authorities, therefore, cannot escape assuming some responsibility for price movements. Nothing indicates more emphatically how far we have departed from the principle of free enterprise than the fact that we have given a small group of public officials such power and responsibility that they cannot perform their duty without considering whether they are producing desirable or undesirable effects upon almost every price which the public pays.[20]

II. The Enforcement of Prices Fixed by Public Authority

Suppose that a public board sets the legal minimum wage in an industry at $17 a week. What is to prevent a job seeker, unable to obtain employment at that price, from offering to work for $15? Or what is to prevent a railroad company, to

---

[20] This is simply another way of saying that we have placed in the hands of the Federal Reserve system far-reaching control over private property. The authority of Congress and the legislatures over property has been distinctly limited by the interpretations which the Courts have placed upon the Fifth and Fourteenth Amendments, which stipulate that no person shall be deprived of property without due process of law. The Reserve Banks, on the other hand, by their power to regulate interest rates are able to transfer hundreds of millions of dollars from some individuals and business enterprises to others.

avoid losing a shipment, from agreeing to carry it below the rate approved by the Interstate Commerce Commission?

The problem raised by these questions may be put in general terms as follows: A price-fixing body sets the price of a commodity either above or below the point where the quantities supplied and demanded are equal. If the price is above the point of equilibrium, more of the commodity will be offered for sale than buyers are willing to purchase. This means that some producers will be unable to sell all that they are willing to supply at the market price. Are not some of them likely to sell secretly below the legal price rather than not sell at all? On the other hand, if the government fixes the price below the point of equilibrium, a greater quantity will be demanded than producers are willing to supply. Under these circumstances, are not some buyers likely to offer more in order to obtain goods? In other words, when secret agreements to buy or sell above or below the legally fixed price are so easy to make and so difficult to discover, can the state enforce any other price than the one at which the quantities demanded and supplied are equal? This, however, is the point at which competition would set price. But if the only price which the government can enforce is identical with the one which would prevail anyway, what is the use of price-fixing by public authority?

At the very outset it should be noted that in many instances the government regulates prices because there is a monopoly in the industry. In these cases, the purpose of the government may be to fix the price at the point where capital in the industry will receive about the same return as capital in other industries — in other words, to enforce the price which, in the long run, competition would tend to create.[21] In some cases, however, as when the government attempts to regulate wages, insurance rates, and many railroad rates, it deliberately seeks to impose upon competitors a price which differs from the equilibrium price. Can it hope to be successful?

It must be conceded that the problem of enforcing a minimum price that is above or a maximum one that is below the point

[21] The existence of a monopoly, however, may introduce operating economies which make it possible for capital to gain the current return from a lower price than would be necessary under competition.

of equilibrium may prove extremely difficult. But the difficulty is likely to be less, for example, than that of suppressing traffic in drugs or intoxicants. The reason is that some persons have a pecuniary interest in the enforcement of the price which the government fixes and they are willing, therefore, to assist in detecting violations. This is more true when the government is attempting to enforce a minimum price that is above the point of equilibrium than when it is attempting to enforce a maximum price that is below the point of equilibrium. Suppose, for example, that a railroad gives a rebate to a large shipper. The competitors of the shipper suffer because they are unable to ship their goods for as little as he pays and the competitors of the railroad suffer because they lose the business of the shipper. The competitors both of the concern which sells and of the concern which buys below the legally fixed price are interested in helping the authorities detect violations of the law.[22]

The difficulty of enforcing a government-fixed price depends partly upon whether the difference between the legal price and the equilibrium one is large or small. In some cases, the very fact that the government has set a price appears to affect the point at which supply and demand are in equilibrium. Experience with minimum wage legislation, for example, indicates that this method of setting wages results in a higher equilibrium point than is set by competition. Higher compensation for the most poorly paid workers increases their output and, therefore, the employers' demand for them. Not only do men tend to work with better spirit when better paid, but the very fact that they must be paid more encourages managers to make them worth the higher wage by training and supervising them more carefully and by providing them with better equipment. This does not necessarily mean that the equilibrium point is raised to the legal wage, but it does mean that the difference between the two is reduced and that the problem of enforcing the minimum wage is simplified. There is evidence also that the existence of public price regulation diminishes the disposition

---

[22] The government is likely to receive less help in enforcing a price which is *below* the point of equilibrium, because no seller is likely to report a buyer who offers to pay more than the legal price in order to obtain goods. Nevertheless, some buyers may report other buyers who are cornering the supply by paying more than the legal price.

of enterprises with large fixed costs, such as railroads, to grant rebates and special prices to large customers. Willingness to grant such rebates is intensified by the fear that competitors will grant them. When public rate regulation reduces this fear, each enterprise becomes less willing to cut prices. Thus the very existence of a law against rebates makes its enforcement easier.

The problem of enforcing a legally fixed price varies greatly with the commodity, and the fact that enforcement is fairly satisfactory in some cases does not mean that it will be equally so in others. The principal instances of direct regulation of prices in the United States are the rates of railroads and of municipal utilities. It happens, however, that in these cases a government-fixed price is unusually easy to enforce. In the first place, there are relatively few producers to supervise. In many cities there is only one gas company, electric company, or street railway. Nearly all of the railroad mileage of the country is comprised in several score large systems. In the second place, not everyone who desires may start a railroad, an electric plant, or a gas plant.[23] A public franchise is necessary. This restriction prevents embarrassment from overproduction in case the public authorities set the rates so high that they yield more than the usual return on the capital invested. In the third place, the expenses of railroads and municipal utilities are in large degree fixed costs. Even if the regulating agency sets a price so low that it yields no return on the capital in the industry, the enterprises lose less by selling at a loss than by not selling at all — provided, of course, that the price exceeds direct costs. Consequently, rates must be substantially below costs before they cause a drop in the supply of railroad service, gas, or electricity. Finally, the services of railroads and municipal utilities cannot

[23] In most states the law requires that a new public service enterprise or an established company which seeks to extend its service into new sections must obtain from the public service commission a " certificate of convenience and necessity." If the commission finds that the public is adequately served by the existing agencies, it refuses to grant the certificate. Even in the states where the law does not require a certificate of convenience and necessity, the government is able to control the entrance of new companies into the industry and the extension of old companies because municipal utilities require franchises in order to use city streets, and railroads and power companies require the right of eminent domain in order to obtain land for the right of way.

be stored and they are all delivered directly from the producer to the consumer. In case rates are so low that the quantity demanded exceeds the supply, there is no opportunity for speculators to hoard the services and to re-sell them above the legal prices.[24] For all of these reasons, the problem of regulating the rates of railroads and municipal utilities is far simpler than would be the task of enforcing a price for coal or wheat or cotton.

III. Is It Desirable for the Government to Fix Prices?

Governments regulate prices sometimes in order to prevent them from going too high, at other times to prevent them from going too low, at others to prevent them from fluctuating too violently. But is it desirable for the government to attempt to enforce a price which is either above or below that which competition would set? Suppose that supply and demand are as follows:

Demand	Price	Supply
4,800	$1.10	5,300
5,000	1.00	5,000
5,200	.90	4,700

Suppose also that the government enforces a price of either $1.10 or 90 cents. At $1.10, only 4,800 units of the commodity would be purchased. If more were produced, they could not be sold. At 90 cents, only 4,700 units would be supplied and, of course, only that quantity could be purchased. The effect of the government price-fixing in either case is to prevent consumers from buying as much of the commodity as they would buy if competition were permitted to set the price, and to compel them to spend more money for things that they desire less. Apparently public price-fixing prevents consumers from getting the maximum possible return from their expenditures. If this be

[24] On September 1, 1917, the government fixed the price of wheat at $2.17 a bushel in order to keep down the cost to our allies. But the crop in 1917 was small and both wheat and flour were scarce. A low price for wheat under these circumstances meant abnormally large profits for the millers. Consequently the government felt compelled to regulate the price of flour. This meant large profits for the bakers. When the Fuel Administration in 1917 reduced the price of coal sold by the mines, it was necessary to control the profits of jobbers and retailers. Difficulties of this nature are escaped in regulating the rates of railroads and of municipal utilities.

true, is it not uneconomical for the government to enforce any other price than that which competition would set?

But this is not all. Assume that competition sets the price of a necessity so high that the less well-to-do are able to purchase only inadequate quantities and that the government, in order to relieve distress, fixes a maximum price below the one established by competition. The *immediate* effect may be to relieve in some degree the distress of the less well-to-do, but the shortage of the commodity which lies at the bottom of the difficulty is likely to be prolonged because producers have less incentive to expand their output. Or suppose that an industry becomes so overdeveloped that most producers make little, if any, profit and that the government seeks to remedy the situation by setting a minimum price above the competitive one. The effect may be to retard the withdrawal of capital from the industry and the adjustment of the productive capacity to the volume of demand.[25] In other words, high prices and low prices, although they impose hardships upon parts of the community, perform the important function of regulating the output of goods to correspond with changes in the demand. A high price indicates that more output is demanded and tends to attract capital and labor into the industry; a low price indicates that the commodity is in less demand and tends to check the flow of labor and capital into the industry. To the extent that the government prevents prices from rising or falling as much as they would under free competition, does it not prevent them from performing the important function of regulating production?

It does not follow, however, that all public price-fixing is uneconomical. The occasion for much public regulation of prices in the United States, it has been pointed out, is the existence of monopoly. This is the reason for the regulation of electric, gas, street railway, telephone, and water rates, and, to a less extent, for the regulation of railroad rates. Unregulated monopolies, as we have seen, tend to produce an uneconomical distribu-

[25] Nevertheless, if the demand for the commodity is elastic, the higher price may accelerate the withdrawal of the excess capital from the industry. The advance in price may so reduce the volume of sales that producers will suffer greater losses under the higher price fixed by the government than under the lower one fixed by competition.

tion of resources by forcing too much capital and labor to enter the non-monopolized industries and by permitting too little to enter the monopolized industries.[26] Regulation of the charges of monopolies, by diminishing or removing the profit from restriction of output, discourages monopolies from limiting production and thus tends to bring about a more advantageous distribution of resources between the monopolized and non-monopolized industries. In other words, when monopolies exist, not only is public price-fixing not uneconomical, but it is *needed* in order to prevent the uneconomical distribution of resources.

But competition itself does not invariably produce satisfactory prices. If fixed costs are large, it is likely, as we have seen, to produce discriminatory charges.[27] The regulation of railroad rates, the most highly developed form of price control in the United States, was instituted because heavy fixed costs led railroads to make preferential rates to competitive points and to grant rebates to important shippers.[28] Heavy fixed costs are also likely to force prices uneconomically low. The regulation of insurance rates, for example, has been necessary because cutthroat competition rendered the companies insolvent and the public found itself deprived of the protection for which it had paid.

When the supply of a good is not closely subject to control and when the demand is relatively inelastic, as is true of many agricultural commodities, competition is likely to produce violent fluctuations in price. The efforts of governments to diminish these fluctuations do not *necessarily* interfere with the guidance of production by prices, provided the *average* annual return on capital in the industry is not changed, because the power of an industry to attract capital (and, therefore, its output) depends in the long run upon the average return rather than upon the profits or losses of any particular year.

Sometimes, as we have seen in the case of the minimum wage, the fixing of a price by public authority may change the point of equilibrium between supply and demand and the change may be a desirable one.[29] The change, of course, may not be sufficient

---

[26] See pp. 367–370.
[27] See pp. 317–325.
[28] Ripley, W. Z., *Railroads: Rates and Regulation*, pp. 443–446.
[29] See p. 382.

to make the point of equilibrium and the legal price identical and this may create difficult administrative problems.

In case a serious shortage threatens to send the price of a necessity beyond the reach of the poorest part of the population, the government may find it desirable to set a maximum price that is substantially below the one which competition would set. It is true that a price which causes the quantity demanded to exceed that supplied is likely to compel the government to ration the supply. Nevertheless, the authorities may feel compelled to keep the prices of necessities within reach of the poor. It is also true that, in controlling the price, the government may discourage producers from increasing their output and thus prolong the shortage. But an immediate opportunity for the less well-to-do to purchase may be more important than a later increase in the output of the commodity.

Under some circumstances, the government may attempt to improve upon competitively determined prices as guides to production. In time of war, for example, the prices of some war necessities may be raised by law above the equilibrium point in order to stimulate production of the goods.

Finally, there are the cases where one country is almost the sole source of supply for a good — as the Straits Settlements are for tin, as Brazil is for coffee, and as Chile once was for nitrates. To gain the benefit of its monopoly position, the country may set a minimum price at which the product may be sold abroad, or it may restrict exports. From the standpoint of the world, these restrictions may be injurious, but they may benefit the country imposing them.

All of this indicates that there are many occasions when government price control may be advantageous. But it is also clear that it is not necessarily desirable for the government to intervene whenever a price is so low that few producers can make money or so high that it is a hardship to many consumers. The real trouble is likely to lie deeper — in the conditions of supply or demand — and the remedy is likely to be regulation of output rather than regulation of prices.

The experiments in price-fixing which are of greatest importance in the United States are: (1) the control of the Federal Reserve Board and Banks over the price of credit and over the general price levels; (2) the establishment of legal minimum wage rates for women and children in some occupations; (3) the regulation of the charges of railroads and other public utilities by the Interstate Commerce Commission and the state public service commissions; and (4) the efforts of the Federal Farm Board to stabilize the prices of agricultural commodities. The influence of the Federal Reserve authorities upon prices can best be discussed in connection with our analysis of the business cycle and of long-time movements in the price level; and the efforts to regulate wages, in connection with our inquiry into the wage bargain. In the next chapter we shall confine our attention to the efforts of the government to regulate the rates of public utilities. In the following chapter we shall examine the efforts of the Federal Farm Board to stabilize the prices of agricultural commodities, particularly wheat and cotton.

REFERENCES

Clark, J. M., *Social Control of Business,* 1926. Ch. XX, XXI, XXII, and XXVI.

Pigou, A. C., *The Economics of Welfare* (third edition), 1929. Pt. II, ch. XII, XIII, and XXI, and pt. III, ch. XII and XIX.

Taussig, F. W., " Price Fixing as Seen by a Price-Fixer," *Quarterly Journal of Economics,* February, 1919, v. XXXIII, pp. 205–241.

Wallace, B., and Edminster, L. R., *International Control of Raw Materials,* 1930.

CHAPTER XVIII

PUBLIC AUTHORITY AS A DETERMINANT OF PRICE — PUBLIC UTILITY RATES

I. The Determination of Rate Differentials

Railroad rates have been regulated far more minutely, carefully, and effectively than the rates of other public utilities. The following discussion of the problem of fixing public utility rates will run largely, though not entirely, in terms of the problem of setting railroad rates.[1] In regulating the charges of railroads

[1] Public utilities, or public service companies, as they are sometimes called, include a great variety of enterprises — inns, roads, wharves, ferries, bridges, warehouses, stockyards, waterworks (including irrigation works), railroads, gas companies, street railways, electric light and power companies, telegraph companies, telephone companies, pipe lines, and others. But what *is* a public utility? What common characteristics distinguish it from other enterprises? Legally a public utility is distinguished from private enterprises by certain peculiar legal duties. (1) It may not select its customers as may a groceryman or a factory owner; it is under a legal duty to render reasonably adequate service to all who apply. (2) It may not charge any price which it sees fit; its charges must be reasonable. (3) A purely private enterprise may charge one price to one customer and another price to a second customer for the same service at the same time. A public utility, however, may not discriminate arbitrarily between customers. (4) It may not retire from business or withdraw service unless properly authorized to do so.

But what economic difference underlies the legal distinction between industries which are public utilities and those which are not? It cannot be said that, in passing on the legal status of industries, the courts have classified as a public utility every industry which possesses certain economic characteristics. No doubt some industries which should be classified as public utilities have not been so classified. The basis

and other public utilities, there are involved two groups of problems: determining what are reasonable *differentials* between the rates charged to different classes of customers or for different classes of service, and determining what general *level* of rates is reasonable. The first group of problems includes such questions as: What differences, if any, should exist between night telephone rates and day; should electricity be sold for heating at less than for lighting or to large users for less than to small; should gas be sold for industrial consumption at less than for domestic use; is it reasonable to charge no higher freight rate from Boston to San Francisco than from Chicago to San Francisco; how should the charge for carrying a ton of wheat a given distance compare with the charge for carrying a ton of coal or a ton of cement? The determination of what is a reasonable level of rates involves: (1) ascertaining the operating income and expenses of the enterprise or enterprises; (2) ascertaining the investment upon which the owners are entitled to a return; (3) determining what is a reasonable rate of return. We shall discuss first the problems of fixing rate differentials and then the problems of determining rate levels.

The tremendous importance of rate differentials is inadequately appreciated by the general public. Upon the differentials in railroad rates, for example, often depends the prosperity of whole regions. The ability of Western lumber to compete with Southern in the great Middle Western market, and of California oranges to compete with Florida oranges is largely a matter of railroad rates. Whether the meat-packing industry is located close to the source of raw material or close to the centers of consumption depends upon the relationship between the rates on cattle and those on dressed meat. Shall the wheat of Kansas, Nebraska, and the Dakotas be exported through Galveston, New York, or Montreal? Shall the Northwest be kept warm by coal

---

of the distinction appears to be either the fact that in some situations it is in the public interest to have a monopoly in the industry rather than competition or the fact that, in the particular industry, competition is notoriously ineffective as a regulator of prices and the quality of service. In other words, an industry is held to be a public utility either when competition is not present or when competition does not function satisfactorily. The regulation to which public utilities are subject is a substitute for competition.

transported by an all-rail haul from Illinois or by coal from West Virginia, Ohio, and western Pennsylvania moving by rail to the lower lake ports and by vessel to Duluth, Manitowoc, and other upper lake cities? Can the mines in western Pennsylvania and Ohio hold their own in competition with the mines in Kentucky and West Virginia? The answers to these questions all depend upon railroad rates. The Interstate Commerce Commission, as arbiter in these struggles for markets, holds in its hands the economic fate of whole regions and industries. Scarcely the Supreme Court itself is shouldered with greater responsibility.

If all costs were direct, there would be no problem of establishing differentials between different classes of service. Only one procedure would be possible: to base the charge for each class upon the cost of rendering the service. It would not be possible to charge some customers less than cost without either charging other customers more than cost or inflicting a deficit upon the public utility. The problem of determining rate differentials exists because the several classes of service are largely produced by the same labor and equipment. The same wires carry both day and night telephone messages; the electricity used for lighting is produced by the same power plant as the electricity used for heating; coal, wheat, and hundreds of other commodities are carried over the same roadbed in the same train. Under these circumstances, we have seen, enterprises with idle productive capacity may seek to gain business by selling to some customers at much less than to others, provided, of course, that the sales at low prices do not seriously diminish the sales at high prices.

There are two rival theories of rate-making — *cost of service* and *value of service*. According to the *cost of service* theory, rates should be based upon the cost of rendering the service. This would make 1,000 kilowatt hours of electricity cost the same regardless of whether it was used for power, heat, or light and would make the rate of transporting 100 pounds of freight the same, regardless of whether it was 100 pounds of gloves or 100 pounds of sand. Of course, in cases of commodities such as cattle or fresh strawberries which require special equipment, unusually expeditious movement, or special attention such as watering or icing, the extra costs would be reflected in higher rates.[2] The *value of service* theory, on the other hand, may result in different rates to different groups of customers or on different classes of service, even though it costs precisely the same amount to produce the several classes of service or to supply the several groups of customers. In fact, the value of service theory may result in a lower rate on one class of service and a higher rate on the second class even when it costs more to produce the first class than the second. According to the value of service theory, rates should be based upon the value of service to the user or, in other words, upon what the traffic will bear. A high rate will produce a large profit per unit of output but a small volume of sales, a low rate will produce a small profit per unit of output but a large volume of sales. According to the value of service theory, the rate should be fixed at the point which yields the maximum total return in excess of the direct costs of performing the service. Night telephone rates are then less than day rates, and relatively light and valuable commodities, such as clothing or shoes, pay higher rates than steel or lumber.

The cost of service and the value of service theories both have merits, but neither is acceptable as a sole guide in rate-fixing. To the cost of service theory there are four principal objections. In the first place, it is often impracticable to apply the theory. For example, there are obvious technical difficulties in the way of

---

[2] It is often assumed that the cost of service theory requires that each unit of output should bear the same proportion of the overhead charges of the enterprise. This is usually true, but it is not invariably so. To illustrate, let us take the case of day and night telephone rates. If rates were based on the cost of service, night rates might be expected to be higher than day rates because of the fact that night labor usually costs more than day labor. But this result does not necessarily follow. Let us assume that calls per hour during the daytime are double those during the night. The night business, therefore, requires only half as many wires as the day service. Let us assume also that the day business requires ten wires and the night business five and that each wire imposes fixed costs of $6,000, making a total of $60,000. If each message bore the same share of the overhead, one-third of the $60,000, or $20,000, would be borne by the night business. But it would be erroneous to charge the night service with any of the overhead on the five wires which it does not require. The *entire* fixed costs on these wires should be carried by the day messages. On the other five wires, the overhead should be divided between the day and the night service in proportion to use. This would mean that the night messages would bear half, or $15,000. In other words, the night messages, which are *one-third* of the total business, would bear only *one-fourth* of the fixed costs associated with the wires. Consequently night rates, even when based upon cost of service, would probably be lower than day rates.

charging an especially high rate on all electricity or gas sold during the hours of peak demand because the consumption of many
customers is too small to warrant the expense of two meters — one
to measure the consumption at the peak and one consumption at
other times.[3]   In the second place, the cost of service theory
would result in a higher level of rates than is necessary.   One
reason is that the rigid application of the theory would prevent
the utility from cutting rates on certain classes of service in order
to increase the excess of its total revenues over direct costs and
thus to reduce the amount of overhead costs that must be borne
by other classes of service.   When night telephone rates, for
example, are set in accordance with the value of service principle,
they will yield the maximum total return over direct costs.   Consequently, it is unnecessary for the day service to bear such a
large part of the overhead expense and it is possible, therefore,
to set the day rates lower than would otherwise be necessary.
Another reason is that strict adherence to the cost of service
theory may prevent the utility from operating a plant of the most
economical size.   Suppose, for example, that an output of
100,000 units a year can be produced for $150,000 and an
output of 150,000 units for $200,000.   Possibly there is a de-
mand for 100,000 units at $1.50 a unit.   But possibly the utility
can develop a demand for 50,000 additional units among a special
group of consumers by making a rate to them of $1.15 per unit.
In this event, it would obviously be advantageous for the utility
to enlarge its plant and to establish the special rate.   It might
also be advantageous to the consumers who have been paying
$1.50 because they might be permitted to share in the economies
of the larger plant.   A third objection to the cost of service
principle is the fact that, in extreme instances, it would prevent
a utility from meeting expenses.   In these cases the service cannot be supplied at all unless rates are based upon the value of
service.   For example, it may be profitable to build a railroad into
a sparsely settled region provided the road is permitted to charge
substantially lower rates for hauling out pulpwood than for
carrying the settlers' crops.   If the same high rates were charged
for both pulpwood and crops, the pulpwood would not be shipped

---

[3] To the service rendered during the peak period should be charged *all* of the
overhead costs attributable to the equipment that is used only during that period.

and the road could not pay expenses. Likewise if the low rates on pulpwood were applied to the crops, the income of the road would be insufficient. The road can pay expenses only by charging a high rate on the crops and a low rate on pulpwood. Unless this can be done, the road will not be built and the region will not have railroad service. Finally, strict application of the cost of service principle to railroad rates would greatly raise the rates on many necessaries, such as wheat, coal, lumber, and steel, which are heavy and bulky in proportion to their value and which now, under the value of service principle, move at relatively low rates. It would mean also a reduction in the charges on many luxuries which are light in proportion to their value and which can afford to pay high rates. The result would be relatively large increases in the prices paid by consumers for many necessities and relatively small decreases in the prices paid for many luxuries. It cannot be postulated as a *general* and *necessary* result that application of the cost of service principle would raise the price of necessities and lower the price of luxuries. Yet where this result would occur, most people would probably agree that the cost of service principle should not be inflexibly applied.

The preceding analysis shows that, to a considerable extent, rates *must* be based upon the value of service. Nevertheless, rigid and universal application of this principle would yield undesirable results. In many cases it would produce unreasonably high charges. If freight rates, for example, were in every instance set at the point of greatest net return, the earnings of most railroads would be intolerably high. The reason is that the rates on light but valuable commodities, such as clothing, fine cloth, china, or rugs, would be far higher than they now are. A suit of clothes which sells for $50 or $75 is now transported several hundred miles for a few cents. Without appreciably affecting the demand for suits and therefore without greatly affecting the shipments of suits, the existing charges could be increased many times. In fact, if regulating bodies were to base every rate upon the value of service, rate regulation would cease to be a protection to the public. For to exact for each service the price which would yield the maximum net return is precisely what an uncontrolled monopoly would do.

The strict application of the value of service principle also leads to many forms of waste. This is especially true in the case of railroad rates. One of the most obvious wastes is the circuitous routing of goods. When rates are based on what the traffic will bear, the longer routes between two points charge no more than the shortest. This leads some of the traffic to move over the longer routes.[4] Some circuitous routing, of course, is inevitable if competition is to exist, and it may be desirable in order to avoid the necessity of double-tracking the most direct line.[5] But there can be little justification for sending freight from northern Illinois to Maine via Cincinnati, or from San Francisco to Omaha via Winnipeg, or from Chicago to San Francisco via New Orleans.[6] And yet this is the result actually produced by charging what the traffic will bear. Naturally the *very* longest routes have difficulty in competing with the very shortest even when the rates are the same, because the time of transportation by the longest routes is greater. The strict application of the value of service theory would result in *lower* rates by the longer routes in order to compensate shippers for the longer time of transit, and a few such differentials actually exist.

The value of service principle may also lead to the use of uneconomical methods of transportation. To carry freight from Seattle or San Francisco to the Atlantic seaboard by vessel may entail a smaller consumption of labor and material than to transport it overland by rail. Unless the saving in time is important, it is wasteful to send the freight by train instead of by boat. Yet under the value of service principle, rates are so adjusted as to enable the railroads to capture a large share of the business.

Railroad rates, of course, should be fixed to permit competition between plants in different cities, but this does not mean that it is economical to arrange them so that every plant can com-

---

[4] The shortest route, of course, does not always have the lowest costs, because it may have heavier grades and sharper curves. In this case we are using the term "circuitous routing" to mean any routing by other than the most economical road. The cost of switching makes the route which is most economical vary for different plants in the same city.

[5] It may be desirable also in order to equalize the movement of tonnage in opposite directions.

[6] Ripley, W. Z., *Railroads: Rates and Regulations*, pp. 284, 287, and 288.

pete in every part of the country with every other plant — even though that might be profitable to the railroads. To put the matter more specifically, it would be wasteful to adjust the rates on cement so that the Kansas mills could compete in the Lehigh valley and the Lehigh valley mills in Kansas. And yet basing rates on the value of service makes possible such uneconomical overlapping of markets on a large scale. Charging only what the traffic will bear also tends to foster an uneconomical distribution of plants and to counteract the natural advantages which some locations have over others. Suppose, for example, that paper can be made at some points in the South for less than it can be made in Wisconsin and New York, where the forests have been more or less seriously exhausted. Should the growth of the Southern industry be prevented by low rates on paper pulp from Canada to the New York and Wisconsin mills? Rates based upon the value of service principle may easily become a subsidy by which poorly located plants are kept in business.

Finally, rates based on value of service may encourage the wasteful overdevelopment of industries. Every railroad which has coal deposits within its territory wishes the growth of the coal industry to occur along its lines rather than along competing railroads. Consequently, it tends to make rates which encourage the opening of new mines along its lines. The result is that the industry is stimulated to expand despite the fact that it already has far more mines than are needed.

The upshot of this discussion clearly is that neither the cost of service nor the value of service theory provides an adequate basis for fixing individual rates. The universal application of either would result in an unnecessarily high level of rates, and the value of service theory would, in addition, produce many forms of waste. The direct costs of supplying a class of service and the fixed costs for which that service is clearly responsible mark, of course, *the lowest rate* which it is economical to charge, and the value of service principle indicates, with a few exceptions, the *maximum* price which is economical.[7] In many cases, as we have

[7] It has been pointed out on the preceding page that in some instances the value of service principle results in rates which are uneconomically low. Hence it is not invariably true that the value of service principle indicates the maximum rate that is economical.

seen, the latter is a lower price than would be set if, according to the cost of service theory, each unit of physical output bore its proportionate share of the overhead. Nevertheless the value of service principle, if *universally* applied, would produce an unreasonably high rate level because, as has been said, it would lead to the rates which a monopoly would charge. But between the minimum rate indicated by costs and the maximum rate indicated by the value of service principle, there may be a wide range of choice. In fixing the rate, the public authorities must be guided by the fact that the owners are entitled to a reasonable return, but no more than a reasonable return, upon their property, and by the additional fact that under some circumstances basing rates upon the value of service results in waste.

II. The Control of Accounts

The determination of the rate level involves, as we have pointed out, three major problems: (1) ascertaining the operating income and expenses of the public utility; (2) determining the amount upon which the investors are entitled to a return; and (3) ascertaining what rate of return is reasonable.

In order to prevent public utilities from concealing their profits by charging capital expenditures as operating expenses or by allowing excessive rates of depreciation, the regulating body must prescribe with precision and in detail just how thousands of items of income and expense shall be recorded. This means that it must prescribe a complete system of accounts and that its accounting experts must render many decisions defining the meaning of the accounting classifications and determining how specific items shall be classified. It also means that the regulating body must from time to time check up the accounting practices of the utilities in order to ascertain that its rules are being observed. Unfortunately the importance of effective control of accounts is inadequately appreciated, and in many states this aspect of rate regulation is gravely neglected. In 1930, seven states did not authorize their commissions to supervise the accounting of public utilities and in Oklahoma and South Carolina the commission's authority over accounts was inadequate.[8] Mere authority to determine the accounting classifications is of little use, of course,

---

[8] Mosher, W. E., and others, *Electrical Utilities*, pp. 28–29.

unless the commission actually checks up the accounting practices of the utilities in order to ascertain whether the rules are being observed. Because of inadequate funds or because of indifference, state commissions do not audit the books of the utilities except in special cases. It is obvious, however, that the effectiveness of the whole scheme of regulation depends upon whether or not the accounts of utilities tell the truth. If they do not yield accurate information, the commission cannot really know whether an advance in rates is needed or a decrease is justified.

III. FIXING THE ORIGINAL RATE-BASE — MARKET VALUE AS A MEASURE

The determination of the amount upon which investors are entitled to a return, or of the rate-base as it is called, has three principal divisions : (1) the problem of setting a fair value *for the first time* upon the investment made prior to the establishment of rules of valuation; (2) the problem of *revising* from time to time the valuation of this investment; (3) the problem of how to treat the investments which may be made in the future.

The problem of determining a fair value for past investments arises because these investments were not made with the expectation that one rather than another rule of valuation would be followed. Many of them, indeed, were made before the beginning of government price-fixing and without even the expectation that the government would control prices. And, since regulation started, opinions concerning what is a proper rate-base have been so divergent that no investment can be assumed to have been made with any definite expectation as to which rule of appraisal would prevail. The problem, therefore, is one of working out rules of equity which can with fairness be applied *retroactively.*

Three principal rules for valuing past investments have been suggested : (1) market value; (2) reproduction cost; (3) original cost. Let us examine them one by one.

At least one test, *market value,* may be rejected without hesitation. This test is fair, it is said, because investors in other industries tend to receive the current return upon the market value of their property. If the owners of public utilities were given a return upon a smaller amount, they would receive less than the owners of unregulated firms and this, it is said, would be unfair.

The difficulty with this reasoning is that the market value of a business is largely the result of its present and prospective net income. The reason why an enterprise has value at all, why any one is willing to give anything for it, is because it either pays or has prospects of paying some return over expenses. Its value in the market depends upon (1) the amount which the enterprise is earning (or is soon likely to earn) and (2) the current rate of return upon investments of similar risk. If the enterprise nets about $6,000 a year and is not likely to earn more or less, and if the current return on investments of similar risk is 6 per cent, the enterprise is worth $100,000. The net income of a business, however, depends, among other things, upon the prices which it charges. This means that its market value also depends upon the prices which it charges. Consequently, barring a few exceptional cases, its charges are never higher than enough to yield the current return upon its market value. If the rates are high, earnings, and, therefore, market value will be high; if rates are low, earnings and market value will be low. Even low rates yield the current return upon the market value. *In other words, the market value test of fair value would justify almost any rates no matter how high or how low.* To use market value as a test of fair value, therefore, is simply to let existing rates justify themselves.

IV. Fixing the Original Rate-Base — Reproduction Cost as a Measure

The *reproduction cost* test of fair value is based upon the same principle of equity as the market value test, namely, that the owners of regulated enterprises should fare no better and no worse than the investors in unregulated competitive industries. The value of any piece of property tends to correspond, it is said, to the cost of reproducing it. The fact that a plant may have cost $100,000 does not mean that it is worth $100,000. If it can be reproduced for $50,000, no one would be willing to pay more than $50,000 for it. If it cannot be reproduced for less than $200,000, it may command as much as $200,000. Thus, when the cost of reproducing a plant in an unregulated industry goes up, its owners receive an unearned increase in wealth, and when the cost goes down, they suffer an undeserved loss. Equity requires that the owners of public utilities have the same opportunities for gain and that they be exposed to the same risks as all other property owners. This is assured, it is said, by valuing the property of public utilities in the same way that other property is appraised — by its cost of reproduction.

There are several objections to this theory. In the first place, it is based upon an erroneous theory of value. *Sometimes* the value of goods tends to correspond to the cost of reproducing them, *but not always*. The principal determinant of the value of industrial plants is not the cost of reproducing them, but the cost of producing the commodity in new plants having the latest technical improvements. If up-to-date plants can produce the commodity for less than the prevailing price, they will be built, supply will increase, and the price will decline until it is no longer above the cost of adding to the supply — including in cost, of course, the necessary profits for the business owners. As the price falls, the earnings of the old plants decrease and the plants themselves become less valuable. Thus important technical improvements often cause the value of old plants to fall far below the cost of reproducing them. If, on the other hand, the cost of building new plants should rise and if the demand for commodities should increase, the value of existing plants would tend to advance. But the value of a plant would not ordinarily exceed the cost of reproducing it because buyers would not be willing to give more than they would have to pay for a new plant like it. Reproduction cost then tends to set the *maximum* value of plants but not their *usual* value. Such a measure of fair value scarcely seems just from the standpoint of consumers. Possibly it may be accepted as indicating the highest amount at which the rate-base might equitably be fixed, but beyond that it seems to possess no validity as a test of fair value.

The proposal to measure fair value by reproduction cost rests upon the assumption that this would give investors in regulated enterprises substantially the same return as investors in unregulated, competitive industries. Since this result does not follow, there is apparently no need to discuss reproduction cost further.

Nevertheless, there are other objections to the use of reproduction cost and it is perhaps not amiss to call attention to them.

The concept of reproduction cost is extremely conjectural
and hazy. This makes it difficult to apply and complicates the
process of rate-fixing by giving both the utilities and the consumers opportunities to press extravagant claims. For example,
in estimating the cost of reproducing a plant, is it to be assumed
that conditions are as they now are or as they were when the
plant was built? Gas mains were laid before a street was paved.
In estimating the cost of reproducing the mains, is the expense
of cutting through and replacing the pavement to be included?
The New York Central Railroad acquired its right-of-way in
New York when the city was relatively small. In computing the
cost of reproducing the road, is it to be assumed that the city
is built up as it now is, and that the railroad must purchase land
and the hypothetical buildings on it and then demolish the buildings? Or suppose that a plant is so old that the machinery in
it is no longer found on the market and can be made only at great
extra expense. Should the very fact that the machinery is out-
of-date and expensive to reproduce make the plant more valuable?
Nor can the difficulty be avoided simply by substituting, for the
cost of reproducing the original plant, the cost of building a
modern plant of equal capacity. The modern plant might cost
more but it might be able to produce for less, because it contains
more labor-saving and material-saving devices. Suppose, for
example, that an obsolete plant could be reproduced for $500,000
and a modern one of equal capacity could be built for $700,000.
The operating expenses of a modern plant, however, might be
$40,000 a year less than those of the existing obsolete plant.
Obviously it would be unfair to require the public to pay the
high operating expenses of the existing plant and *in addition* a
return upon the greater cost of an up-to-date plant. Problems
such as these make reproduction cost an exceedingly cumbersome
and uncertain concept and create many opportunities for public
utilities to obtain inflated valuations.[9]

[9] No general rule has been adopted as to whether original or present conditions are to be assumed in estimating the cost of constructing plants. The expense of
cutting through and replacing pavements is ordinarily excluded where streets were
not paved at the time that the utility was constructed. Likewise the Interstate
Commerce Commission has refused to assume that the railroads must gain entrance to

Reproduction cost is an unsatisfactory measure of fair value because it is an ever-changing amount, rising and falling with the undulation of prices. If a utility were appraised at a time of depression, when prices were low, reproduction cost would give a low value; if the valuation occurred in a boom period when prices were high, the value would be high. It is equitable neither to the public nor to the utility that the rate-base should depend upon the accident of whether prices are high or low when the appraisal is made. To some extent this objection can be avoided by basing the cost of reproduction upon the average of prices over a period of five years or even longer. In most instances this procedure would eliminate the influence of the short-time ups and downs in business but it would not always do so. The five years ending with 1897, for example, were years of depression, and the five years ending in 1920 were almost entirely years of boom. In addition, it must be remembered that prices may have an upward or downward trend for a generation or more.

A final objection to reproduction cost is that it often cannot be applied in periods of falling prices without disastrous results. It is sometimes said that reproduction cost is a satisfactory measure of fair value because, when prices are rising, it gives to the owners of the enterprise the same speculative gains which other investors obtain, and when prices are falling, it subjects the owners to the same speculative losses which other investors suffer. As a matter of fact, it is often impracticable to apply the reproduction cost test when prices have substantially decreased. Most public utilities raise a large part of their funds by issuing bonds and notes. For example, a group of gas and electric companies in Wisconsin, comprising all of the larger companies, had at the end of 1924 a long-term debt of over $147,000,000, preferred stock of over $52,000,000, and common stock of about $38,500,-

---

cities by purchasing land which is built up as is the land which adjoins the right-of-way. But the Commission has assumed that other railroads exist as they now do and that they might be used to haul construction material, thus making it possible to carry on the hypothetical reconstruction of a railroad from several points and shortening the time of construction. In the Minnesota Rate Case, the Supreme Court adopted a compromise solution of the railroad land problem. It held that the railroad lands should be valued at the present value of adjoining farm land. This is much more than the railroads originally paid for the land but much less than it would cost the roads to acquire the land by court proceedings today.

ooo.[10] Over 60 per cent of the securities represented borrowed money and over 20 per cent were preferred stock. If a public service company has constructed its plant largely with borrowed funds and if, between the time of construction and the date of valuation, prices have fallen, basing rates on the cost of reproduction might prevent the company from earning more than barely enough to meet interest charges. Under these circumstances, no one would care to purchase stock in the enterprise and investors would be unwilling to lend to it except at high rates. Hence, the company would have extreme difficulty in obtaining funds to enlarge its plant as population grew. In an effort to increase the surplus of earnings over interest charges and thus to facilitate borrowing, the management would probably economize at the expense of good service. Wages would be kept low, the quality of the working force would deteriorate and with it the quality of the service, the replacement of out-of-date equipment would be postponed as long as possible. In short, even when it would be practicable to apply the reproduction cost test in periods of falling prices — which would not always be the case — consumers would pay for lower rates by being compelled to accept less adequate facilities and poorer service. Hence, it is inaccurate to say that the reproduction test of fair value works both ways, in favor of the utility when the cost of reproduction is rising and in favor of the public when the cost is falling. It works against the public always in the first case and often in the second.

V. Fixing the Original Rate-Base — Original Cost as a Measure

The third test of fair value is *original cost;* that is, the amount of money actually invested in the enterprise. This test is based upon the theory that the owners of utilities should be paid in proportion to the service which they perform. Their service is the provision of capital, and the amount of service is measured by the quantity of capital which they supply.

Of the three theories of fair value, the original cost or, as it might be called, the quantity of service theory, seems on the

[10] Mathews, George C., " Undepreciated Investment as a Utility Rate Base," *Journal of Land and Public Utility Economics,* July, 1925, v. I, p. 261.

whole the most satisfactory. The reason why the owners are entitled to a return at all is because they furnish capital. It therefore seems reasonable that the amount of their return should depend upon the amount of capital which they supply. And original cost possesses the important merit of being, on the whole and under most circumstances, the most definite and the least conjectural measure of fair value — a characteristic which makes it the easiest to administer.[11] This does not mean that original cost is easy to discover, because in many instances the records which would reveal it are incomplete. In these cases, the records must be supplemented by estimates. But this is usually a less conjectural procedure than guessing what it would cost to reconstruct the existing plant under hypothetical conditions. For these reasons, the original cost theory — or some modification of it — has commanded far more support among economists than the reproduction cost theory. But the latter theory, despite the objections which impress the economist as serious, has received considerable support from the courts.

It must not be assumed that the original cost of an enterprise is completely represented by the cost of its physical property. Every concern has certain organization expenses. During construction, before the enterprise is earning any income, it must pay interest on funds borrowed to meet the cost of the plant. This interest, of course, is part of the cost of producing the plant. Business is often worked up by supplying service for several years at a loss — as when a street railway company builds an extension or a gas company lays mains in an undeveloped part of town. Deficits incurred in creating business may be regarded as an investment upon which the owners of the utility are entitled to a return.

Original cost should not be rigidly and blindly applied as a measure of fair value. Incompetency or dishonesty in constructing or designing the plant may have made the cost excessive. The plant may be far larger than the public demands or is likely

---

[11] On this point a leading valuation engineer dissents as follows: "Doubtless as many opportunities exist for the distortion of the investment or historic cost as the most alert and partisan mind may conclude is to be found in the other measure — reproduction cost." In illustration of the conjectural nature of original cost is cited the problem of determining, in the case of outlays for major renewals, the proper allocation between operating expenses and investment.

to demand in the near future — larger than a prudent business man would build to serve the particular market. In these cases it would be unfair to expect the public to pay the current return upon the entire original cost. In other cases the cost of the existing plant may be too low to be a fair rate-base. For example, the San Pedro, Los Angeles and Salt Lake Railway was washed out over long distances three times before a location safe from floods was discovered. The cost of building the present line is far less than has actually been spent on the road. Yet if the three washouts were not due to incompetent engineering, if the proper location could not have been discovered in advance and had to be learned by experience, there is strong reason for allowing a return, not only upon the cost of the present line, but also upon the cost of the ones which were washed out. Indeed, it is easy to interpret cost of production so that the expense of building the washed-out lines would be a part of the cost of building the existing one.

Changes in the price level raise difficult problems in the application of the original cost theory of fair value. Assume that a plant cost $100,000 and that 6 per cent is the current rate of return for ventures of similar risk. Between the date when the plant was constructed and the date when it is first valued for rate-making, prices have doubled. This means that the purchasing power of the dollar has fallen in half. If the owners continue to receive only $6,000 a year, they obtain *in purchasing power* only 3 per cent on their original investment. On the other hand, if prices had fallen by half and the owners been permitted to earn 6 per cent on their original investment, they would be receiving a return *in purchasing power* of 12 per cent. Should the utility be appraised at original cost, modified to correspond with changes in the purchasing power of money, so that, regardless of fluctuations in the value of the dollar, investors will get the same return in terms of purchasing power? Or should it be appraised at unmodified original cost and the investors left to gain or lose as the value of money rises or falls?

As far as *future* investments are concerned, no question of fairness is involved, provided only that capitalists are informed which rule is to be followed *before* they invest. But our discussion relates to the original appraisal of the utility — to the appraisal of capital which in large part was invested before the beginning of regulation. The weight of the argument seems to be against modifying original cost to allow for changes in the value of the dollar. It is true that the use of unmodified original cost causes the utility owners to lose when prices in general have risen since the construction of the plant. This is a loss which they probably would not have suffered under unregulated competition because, as prices in general advanced, the cost of building new plants would probably have increased also and the old enterprises, in consequence, would have been able to raise the price of their products. But the losses which unmodified original cost inflicts upon utility owners when prices rise are compensated by the gains which it confers when prices fall. Under unregulated competition, a general decline in prices compels established firms to reduce their prices because it reduces the cost of constructing new plants. Unmodified original cost, however, permits utilities to earn the same return in dollars despite the drop in prices.

A more effective argument in favor of correcting original cost for changes in price between the construction of the plant and the date of valuation is based upon the undesirability of both speculative gains and speculative losses and the fact that correction of original cost for changes in the value of the dollar eliminates both. This is a persuasive argument, but it would be more persuasive if the utility owners proposed to do as they ask to be done by. Although they ask that their return be increased when the purchasing power of the dollar falls, they do not propose under the same circumstances to pay more to their bondholders or preferred stockholders.

A serious objection to correcting original cost for changes in the price level is the probability that it would be impracticable to use this procedure during periods of falling prices. Were the rate-base reduced accordingly, the earnings of the utility might be insufficient to cover interest on the bonded indebtedness. The fairness of a rule which works mainly against the public is doubtful.

VI. FIXING THE ORIGINAL RATE-BASE — THE DEPRECIATION PROBLEM

A new machine is generally regarded as more valuable than an old one. This is so even though machines are of the same design and constructed of the same materials and even though one renders as satisfactory service as the other. In fact, an old machine may render even *better* service than a new one and still be less valuable. The reason is that the old machine represents a smaller *store* of service-rendering power. A machine (or building or any other piece of durable equipment) may be conceived as embodying a certain capacity to render service. Because an old machine is nearer the end of its usefulness, because it represents a smaller quantity of unconsumed service-rendering capacity, it is less valuable than when it was new. Furthermore, as it nears the end of its life, the cost of keeping it in repair is likely to grow. The machine may run as well as ever, but only at an ever-increasing expense for repairs. In fact, the rising cost of repairs, rather than the absolute impossibility of getting additional use out of equipment, is likely to be decisive in causing it to be discarded. If the average cost of repairing a machine throughout its life is $100 a year and if, during the last half of its life, the cost averages $200 a year, it is evident that for this reason also the old machine is less valuable than a new one. Finally, as the arts advance, it constantly becomes possible to construct new machines, buildings, and tools, which render superior service at less expense. The better and cheaper the new devices, the less valuable, of course, become the old ones.

The decline in the value of a good because of the decrease in its store of service-rendering capacity, because of the increase in the costs of keeping it in repair, and because of the possibility of obtaining new articles of superior quality is, we have learned, known as *depreciation*.[12] The prices paid for industrial plants in private sales are, of course, affected by the amount of their depreciation. In fact, it is usual for prospective purchasers, before making an offer, to employ engineers to report on the condition of the property. In appraising utilities for rate-setting, should a deduction also be made for depreciation? Should a new

[12] Pp. 24–25.

and up-to-date plant which cost $100,000 and an old and obsolete plant which also cost $100,000 both be valued for purposes of rate-setting at the same amount? A deduction for depreciation would, in most cases, diminish the rate-base by from 20 to 40 per cent. Whether or not such a deduction should be made is one of the most controversial problems of valuation.

The question must be considered in the light of what measure of fair value is being applied. If reproduction cost is being used, a deduction for depreciation should be made. This inevitably follows from the theory of fair value upon which the reproduction cost test is based. This theory, it will be recalled, asserts that the owners of public service companies should fare no better and no worse than the owners of unregulated enterprises in competitive industries. It is assumed, somewhat erroneously we have seen, that, under competition, the market value of industrial plants tends to correspond to the cost of reproducing them. Consequently, it is said that equal treatment of public utilities requires that fair value be based upon cost of reproduction. Be this as it may, it is evident that the value of unregulated industrial plants is affected by their state of depreciation. Hence, if public utilities should be valued so that the owners fare no better and no worse than the owners of other enterprises, a deduction for depreciation should be made.

A deduction for depreciation tends to make reproduction cost a more satisfactory measure of fair value. It has been pointed out that no one would think of reproducing many public utility plants, for the simple reason that they are obsolete. If competition prevailed, the lower operating costs of the up-to-date plants would result in lower prices to the public and in smaller profits to the owners of the obsolete plants. If a utility is valued at cost of reproduction without deduction for depreciation, the policy of treating it and its customers as they would fare under competition is not followed. But the possibility of producing with improved equipment at lower cost — the cost which under competition tends to fix the price of the product — is reflected in the deduction for depreciation. If the deduction is not made, the customers do not benefit from improved equipment, as they would under competition, and the owners do not suffer the losses which, under competition, technical progress would inflict upon them.

Suppose, however, that original cost is being used as the measure of fair value. In this case, apparently no deduction should be made for depreciation. This test of fair value, it will be recalled, is based upon the theory that public utility owners should be compensated for the service which they perform and that this service is measured by the amount of capital which they provide. The fact that the buildings and equipment into which they have put their money have become less valuable does not diminish the amount of service which investors render as providers of funds. Their compensation, therefore, it would seem, should continue at the same rate regardless of depreciation.

But the case against a deduction for depreciation when original cost is used as the rate-base is not so conclusive as might at first appear. The decline in the value of the assets of an enterprise represented by depreciation is regarded by many accountants and business men as one of the costs of producing goods. In order to avoid selling below cost, the enterprise must charge sufficient for its wares to enable it to purchase enough new assets to offset the depreciation in the value of its old ones. If, for example, depreciation on the buildings and equipment of a firm during a year was $50,000, the concern should invest $50,000 of its income in new assets so that the value of its property at the end of the year would be no less than at the beginning.

Suppose that a public service company has fixed its rates so that they yield enough to cover all costs, including depreciation, and, in addition, to pay the current rate of return on the funds invested in the plant. Each year the company sets aside enough to offset the depreciation of its property. The depreciation reserve may be invested in high-grade securities readily convertible into cash or, if the firm is rapidly expanding and badly needs new equipment, the money may be put back into the business.[13] Let us assume that the money is put into the business. The depreciation reserve now takes the form of land, buildings, equipment, and

---

[13] If the reserve is invested in the extensions of plant, it ceases, of course, to be a liquid asset which can be readily converted into cash when funds for the renewal of equipment are needed. It simply becomes an asset which can be mortgaged in order to obtain cash by borrowing.

other parts of its plant. If an appraisal of the utility is made in order to ascertain the original cost of its property, the things purchased out of the depreciation reserve will be included. But the theory that original cost measures fair value is based upon the fundamental assumption that the compensation of the utility owners should depend upon the capital which they supply. *The money used to maintain the value of the company's assets, however, did not come from the utility owners.* The utility charged its customers high enough rates to enable it to build up the depreciation reserve. Obviously it would be unfair to permit the owners to receive the current return upon their investment and, *in addition,* a return upon capital which the consumers themselves furnished to create a depreciation reserve. Since the property purchased to offset depreciation is included in the estimates of the original cost, the owners should receive the current rate of return, not upon the total original cost, but upon original cost minus depreciation. In this way the investors obtain a return only upon the amount of property which they actually supply.

The situation is essentially the same if the assets purchased to offset depreciation are securities instead of additions to the plant. In either case the money comes from the consumers rather than the investors and in neither case, therefore, are the investors entitled to a return on it. The income from the securities purchased to offset depreciation, however, forms part of the income of the company. But it would not be fair to permit the enterprise to receive the current rate of return upon the *undepreciated* value of its plant, and to appropriate also the income from the securities in the depreciation reserve. Either the rates should be set so that the operating income of the company and *the income from the depreciation reserve* together yield a fair return upon the original cost of the property without deduction for depreciation or, what amounts to the same thing, the company should be permitted to appropriate the income from the depreciation reserve, but should be permitted to collect from the consumers only enough to yield it a fair return upon the original cost of its property less allowance for depreciation.

All of this would appear to indicate that a deduction should be made for depreciation when original cost is used as the rate-base. But notice that this conclusion is based upon the assumption that depreciation reserves actually have been accumulated. That practice, however, has been far from universal. Many business men and accountants reject the view that the depreciation reserve should be large enough to prevent shrinkage in the value of the assets of an enterprise. An alternative conception has been that the purpose of the depreciation reserve is merely to equalize the burden of replacing worn-out property. Such a reserve is more properly designated a *replacement reserve*. If the same amount of property were replaced each year, no reserve would be necessary — the cost of renewals could be treated as an ordinary operating expense. But usually the cost varies more or less from year to year. It is small in years when no large items of property wear out; it is large when expensive buildings or machines must be renewed. The smaller the enterprise, the greater, of course, are the relative annual fluctuations in replacement costs. If no provision is made for equalizing the burden of renewals, a firm may, in years of small replacements, disburse more in dividends than it has really earned. On the other hand, in years of heavy renewals the enterprise may be compelled to reduce or suspend dividends or even to borrow money. These difficulties are avoided by setting aside enough each year to provide a reserve fund which can be drawn upon in years when replacements are exceptionally large. But the replacement reserve need not be large enough to offset the decrease in the value of the firm's assets because of depreciation. For example, the property of an enterprise may have depreciated $100,000 and yet a reserve of $25,000 may be ample to equalize the annual cost of replacements. And if the enterprise is large, and if the stockholders do not object to some fluctuations in the dividend rate, no replacement reserve whatever is needed.

This brings us to the heart of the depreciation problem. If all public service companies had set up depreciation reserves, a deduction from original cost for depreciation should undoubtedly be made — in order to relieve consumers from the necessity of paying interest on money which they themselves had provided. But many companies, before the days of regulation, did not set up depreciation reserves — some merely set up small reserves to equalize the burden of replacements, and many accumulated no reserves whatever. They were justified in not accumulating depreciation reserves, we have seen, by the fact that such reserves are not absolutely necessary. *All that is essential is that the enterprise be able to replace equipment when it is worn out.* A reserve may be convenient in order to equalize the burden of replacements from year to year, but, as we have learned, it may be considerably smaller than the actual degree of depreciation.

Would it be fair to make a deduction from original cost for depreciation in cases where no reserve was established or where only a small reserve for replacements was created? Some economists say, "Yes," on the ground that the utilities which did not establish reserves had so much more to disburse to their stockholders. But is it not unjust to apply retroactively standards of business practice which even today are far from universally accepted? Consequently, when original cost is used as the rate-base, no deduction should be made for depreciation which occurred prior to the inception of regulation, provided that no depreciation reserve was actually accumulated. No doubt some public service companies, by not establishing depreciation reserves, were able to pay their stockholders higher dividends — possibly far higher than the current rate of return on capital. But prior to regulation it was the right of every utility to take all that the consumers were willing to pay and to do with the money as it saw fit.[14] If the consumers chose to accept the charges of the company as reasonable, the money which it collected became its property. It might pay it out as dividends or use it to set up depreciation reserves. It is now too late to insist that depreciation reserves should have been established and to make a deduction from original cost as if this actually had been done.

But some enterprises did set up reserves. Should not a deduction from original cost for depreciation be made at least in these cases? Again the answer is "No," because a deduction for depreciation would impose a penalty upon the concerns which happened to set up reserves. It would be arbitrary and inequitable to single out these companies and only in these in-

---

[14] Consumers could have contested, if they had desired, the reasonableness of the utility's charges, but if they paid the charges without protest there seems no doubt that the money became the property of the utility to do with as it chose.

stances to require that a deduction for depreciation be made in applying the original cost measure of fair value. The depreciation problem illustrates clearly how important it is in working out the principles of fair value to distinguish between what is equitable when applied retroactively and what is equitable when applied prospectively.

VII. The Problem of Revising the Original Rate-Base

Thus far our discussion has related to the problem of making the *initial* determination of the rate-base. But as the general price level, the cost of reproducing the plant, or other conditions change, may not a new determination of fair value be necessary? Notice that we are not here discussing the principles which should be followed in appraising *additional* investments which have been made since the first valuation. The question which we are raising is simply the one of *revising* from time to time the value placed upon specific items of property. Once a piece of property is appraised at a certain sum, should its value remain at that amount as long as the property is in use or should there be reappraisals from time to time? The fair value of a machine is set at its reproduction cost, which is estimated at $5,000. Ten years later its reproduction cost is estimated at $3,000. Disregarding allowance for depreciation, should this machine in the second appraisal be valued at $5,000 or $3,000? A piece of land in the original appraisal was valued at $2,000 because it had cost that amount. In the meantime, land values in the community have increased about 25 per cent. Should the land now be valued at $2,500? A machine was first valued at its original cost, which was $5,000. The price level has doubled so that $10,000 buys no more than $5,000 formerly did. Should the machine now be appraised at $5,000 or $10,000? A machine was appraised immediately after its purchase at $5,000. After ten years it is half worn out. Should it now be appraised at only $2,500?

Let us take up these cases one by one. The first example raises the question: In case reproduction cost is used as the measure of fair value, should this amount, as estimated in the original appraisal, determine the fair value of an item of property as long as it remains in service, or should its fair value be revised from time to time as the estimated cost of reproduction changes?

From the standpoint of administrative expediency, it is desirable to let the original valuation stand unaltered except as corrected for changing depreciation. If value were revised to meet the changing cost of reproduction, expensive and time-consuming reappraisals by both the utility and the regulating body would be necessary. These appraisals would inevitably yield conflicting results. Extended hearings and perhaps appeals to several courts would be necessary to settle the matter. The side which expected to lose by the revision of the original appraisal would introduce every possible delay into the proceedings. All of this would make the process of readjusting rates expensive to both the utility and the public and, more important, would prevent rate changes from being made promptly.[15] Unless serious injustice would be done to either the consumers or the

---

[15] This is a disadvantage principally to the utility because when a petition to reduce rates is involved it is usually possible to provide for a refund on payments made between the time when the case is started and the time when the decision is rendered. Regulating commissions, however, are rarely willing to permit utilities to raise their rates first and attempt to prove the justice of the increase afterward.

The importance of prompt adjustment of government-fixed prices to changes in the business situation has been clearly pointed out by Professor G. F. Warren. Describing the recent movements of freight rates and their effect on the agricultural situation, he said: " Freight rates were held down to practically the pre-war basis until July, 1918. This greatly stimulated the shipment of goods that would not ordinarily have been shipped. But wages and materials that the railroad had to buy rose, so that new equipment was not purchased. This process of wearing out the railroad system continued. In the fall of 1920, three months after prices began to drop, freight rates were given their last and most striking advance. If freight rates had advanced along with prices, the railroad equipment could have been kept in repair and a large amount of unnecessary shipment and travel would have been checked. If rates had fallen with prices, the burden of the panic would have been less severe. The holding down of freight rates when prices were rapidly rising resulted in stimulating the production and shipment of hay and other farm products from distant points. When prices fell and freight rates rose, these regions suffered severely. For example, in a case in which hay on farms was worth $5, the freight rate $5, handling charges $5, and the city price $15, when the city price doubled and handling charges doubled, but freight rates were held down, there would be deducted from the $30 price $10 for handling and $5 for freight. This would allow a $15 farm price, which would stimulate shipment. When the city price dropped to $20 and handling charges remained at $10 and freight was increased to $10, there remained nothing for a farm price. Some western regions had these experiences. The agriculture of the West was first artificially stimulated by holding down freight rates, and then artificially depressed by raising rates when prices were falling." Cornell University Agricultural Experiment Station, " Prices of Farm Products in New York," *Bulletin 416.*

utility, the original valuation should not be changed as the cost of reproduction changes.

But justice does not appear to demand such revision of the rate-base. Revision is not necessarily demanded by the theory that the owners of public service companies should fare no better and no worse than the owners of unregulated enterprises because, as we have seen, it is not invariably true that under competition the value of plants fluctuates with the cost of reproducing them. Rather it fluctuates with the expense of production in new and up-to-date plants, which may be going down when the cost of reproducing old plants is going up. And while it is true that failure to revise the rate-base with changes in the cost of reproduction causes the owners to lose when prices rise, it permits them to gain when prices fall.

If the rate-base is revised as reproduction cost changes, it is important that changes in the fair value of the utility be treated as current income or losses in determining whether the utility is earning a fair return. Suppose that a utility is appraised at its reproduction cost, which is found to be $500,000, and that five years later it is again appraised at its reproduction cost which is now found to be $600,000. The increment of $100,000 in the value of the enterprise is a form of income for its owners. If a fair return is 6 per cent, the enterprise should not be permitted to earn this amount and, *in addition,* to have the value of its property increased as cost of reproduction advances. The increase in value should be taken into consideration in computing the return to which the utility is entitled. On the other hand, if reproduction cost decreases, the utility is entitled to earn not only 6 per cent but enough to make up for the shrinkage in the value of its property.

Our second example raises the question of whether or not the land of a public utility should be reappraised because land values in the community have been changed. This, however, is really a special form of the general question raised by the first example — whether or not the rate-base should be revised because of changes in the cost of reproduction. Changes in land values represent changes in the cost of acquiring land. There is no more reason why the rate-base should be altered because of changes in the price of land than because of changes in the price of any other part of the utility's property.

Our third example raises the problem of whether the original rate-base should be modified when changes occur in the purchasing power of money. Our discussion of whether, in fixing the original rate-base, allowance should be made for changes in the value of money between the date of construction and the date of appraisal sheds some light on the present question. *In principle,* periodic revision of the rate-base to allow for changes in the value of money is highly desirable because it would tend to prevent both the utility owners and the consumers from obtaining unearned gains or suffering undeserved losses when the price level changes. The main objection to such revisions is a practical one — they can be made in periods of rising prices when they work against consumers, but the fixed charges of utilities prevent substantial reductions in the rate-base when the price level falls. This objection, however, is not an insurmountable one. As existing bond and note issues mature, they might be replaced with securities paying a definite amount of *purchasing power* rather than a definite number of dollars. It might even be possible to induce present bond and note holders, and even preferred stockholders, to exchange their holdings for new securities which pay definite quantities of purchasing power. Once a large part of the dollar fixed charges had been converted into purchasing-power fixed charges, there would be no financial obstacle in the way of basing fair value upon corrected original cost.

Our last example raises the question of whether the rate-base should be revised to allow for changes in the depreciation of the property. If the regulating body does not require the utility to create a depreciation reserve and does not adjust rates to permit the accumulation of a reserve, the rate-base should not be revised to allow for depreciation. But if, on the other hand, the utility is required to create a reserve out of earnings, either to maintain the value of its assets or to equalize the burden of replacements, the consumers should clearly not be required to pay interest upon the funds which they contribute to the reserve. In order to protect them from doing this, it may be necessary to make a deduction from the rate-base corresponding to the amount which has been added to the depreciation or replacement reserve since the inception of regulation. Whether or not this is necessary depends upon the method used in accumulating the reserve. There are two principal methods — the straight-line and the sinking-fund.

Suppose, for example, that an enterprise has a machine costing $10,000 and that it wishes to provide a fund to pay for the renewal of this machine at the end of ten years. It might set aside $1,000 a year for ten years. This plan is known as the straight-line method. If it is used, a deduction for depreciation should be made. But annual payments of $1,000 are more than are absolutely necessary to build up a fund of $10,000 in ten years. If the money is invested to yield interest, the annual payments which at compound interest would equal $10,000 in ten years are much smaller than $1,000. This plan of providing for replacements is known as the sinking-fund method. If it is used, no deduction should be made for depreciation.

Why should a deduction for depreciation be made if the reserve is accumulated by the straight-line method but not by the sinking-fund method? When the straight-line method is used, the interest earned by the depreciation reserve goes into the general funds of the company and may be distributed to the owners as dividends. Since the consumers, not the utility owners, provided the depreciation reserve, the owners are scarcely entitled to *both* interest from the reserve and the current rate of return upon the original rate-base. They are entitled to a return from operations, which, when added to the interest from the depreciation reserve, will yield the current rate of return upon the original rate-base. Put in a different way, they are entitled to the current rate of return upon the original rate-base minus the depreciation reserve and, in addition, to the interest yielded by the reserve. But when the sinking-fund method of accumulating a reserve is used, the situation is entirely different. In this case, the interest earned by the reserve does not go to the owners of the enterprise, but is added to the reserve. The reason for making a deduction for depreciation which exists when the straight-line method is used is no longer present and no such deduction should be made.

VIII. The Treatment of New Investments

In a few years the property of public service companies will be largely the result of investments which have not now been made. By far the most important part of the rate-base problem, therefore, is how to treat future investments of capital. And yet this question has received little attention — indeed, in most discussions of the rate-base it has been ignored. The fixing of a rate-base has been conceived essentially as a matter of appraising property which is already in use, the assumption apparently being that whatever principles are applied to past investments will hold also for future ones. As a matter of fact, the controversies over the rate-base — whether it shall be determined by original cost or reproduction cost — *have no application to the future investments* because these controversies relate to the problem of what rule it is fair to apply *retroactively*. Whatever may be the method of appraising past investments, no one can object to the principle that future investors shall simply be paid a return on the amount which they actually invest. Indeed, it would be ridiculous to complicate the problem of rate setting by allowing future investors a return on any amount other than that which they actually invest. Whoever dislikes the terms offered need not invest. This makes the problem of the treatment of future investors simply a problem of determining what rate of return is fair.[16]

[16] The Interstate Commerce Commission has never been given a definite rule for valuing the railroads either by Congress or by the courts. On January 24, 1930, the Commission, in a letter to the Senate Committee on Interstate Commerce, asked Congress for " definite directions " as to " how we should exercise reasonable care in arriving at ' fair value ' and ' fair return.' " In addition, the Commission suggested a basis for valuation which distinguished between investments made prior to 1914, when Congress authorized the Commission to make a valuation of the railroads, and investments made subsequent to that date. The Commission proposed that " up-to-date " valuations at any time be determined by taking the cost of reproduction new at the 1914 unit prices of the property existing at that date, plus the then value of the land, adding or subtracting the subsequent net increase or decrease in the property investment account as shown by the accounts when correctly kept, adding further a proper allowance for working capital and deducting the balance standing in the depreciation reserve.

The Commission called attention to the danger in a rate-base which is dependent upon and varies with current costs of reproduction. It pointed out the dangers to

IX. The Determination of the Rate of Return

Not only is it just but it is also a sound economic principle that public utilities should be permitted to earn the same rate of return as is received, on the average, by investors in other industries where the prospects for profit and the risk of loss are similar. Were the rate received by investors in utilities lower than that received by investors in other industries, the utilities would have difficulty in raising capital and the public would not receive adequate service. But it would also be undesirable to permit utilities to charge prices which would yield a higher rate of profit than investors can obtain in other industries because this would bring about the same uneconomical distribution of capital between industries as exists when there is an unregulated monopoly. Because their high charges would limit the demand for their output, the utilities would need less capital and labor than they would require if their charges were lower. Consequently, capital and labor which would yield a larger return both in terms of money and in terms of goods when invested in the public utility would be forced to seek employment in other industries.

But although investors in public utilities should be permitted to earn the same return as that received by investors in other industries of *comparable* prospects and risks, it is probable that the return to investors in many public utilities should be lower than is current in most unregulated industries. In the first place, the public supervision of the accounts and finances (where effective) reduces the risk to investors by making it more difficult for officers or other insiders to exploit the corporation. In the second place, the risks of competition are either removed or

---

the owners of the railroads in a fluctuating rate-base and called attention to the fact that this danger is enhanced by the large part of the investment which is represented by fixed-income securities. The Commission also directed attention to the need for a rate-base capable of ready ascertainment in order to reduce the cost and the delay of litigation. The Commission said that the proposed rate-base " allows full increment in value of lands over original cost up to the original valuation date, including all parcels, of which there are a multitude, which were originally donated to the carriers by governments, communities, or individuals " and " includes full allowance for all property, of which there is much, charged by the carriers in the past to operating expenses or acquired out of surplus earnings after the payment of generous dividends to stockholders." The Commission pointed out that its proposal " would tremendously simplify the task of bringing valuation down to date by reducing it practically to an accounting process." *United States Daily*, January 25, 1930, pp. 1 and 10.

much reduced.   Municipal utilities, as a rule, are protected from all *direct* competition — though this, of course, does not protect street railways from the competition of automobiles.   Railroads compete among themselves, but public regulation prevents their rivalry from taking the form of extreme price cutting.   In the third place, the sales of all public service companies decline less in times of depression than do those of most businesses.

Thus far the problem of what is a fair rate of return has received little careful study either by public service commissions or by the courts.   The commissions have not collected statistics on the rate of return of capital in other branches of industry or the rate of return (measured by the ratio between the value of shares of common stock and the earnings per share of common stock) which investors in the common stock of public service companies expect.   The practice of both the commissions and the courts appears to be to allow a more or less conventional rate of return. It has been the custom of the New York commission, for example, to allow a return of 8 per cent.   This was the rate in thirty out of forty-two cases decided between April, 1921, and November, 1926.   In several cases where the credit position of the company was unusually strong, the commission allowed a return of only 7 per cent; in several others, the company was limited to a lower rate because its property was overdeveloped relative to the demand for the service; and, in several street railway cases, a still lower limit was allowed because it was felt that the traffic could not be made to yield a higher return.[17]

Until there is available adequate statistical information concerning the return obtained by investors in common stocks throughout industry, it is impossible to judge what is a reasonable return to allow public service companies.   It has been a conventional rule in estimating the proper selling prices of common stocks that a stock should sell at about ten times its annual earnings.   The rule, of course, is merely a rough and ready one, because each security must be judged by the peculiar position of the company and particularly by the outlook for future earnings. Using this ten to one ratio as a basis for judgment, it might ap-

[17] New York State Commission on Revision of the Public Service Commission Law, *Report of Commissioners Frank P. Walsh, James C. Bonbright, David C. Adie,* pp. 131–132.

pear that a return of only 7 or 8 per cent is too low. Such a conclusion would be misleading, however, because the return of 7 or 8 per cent applies to the *entire* valuation allowed by the commission. A large part of the capitalization of most public service companies consists of bonds and notes upon which the companies pay substantially less than 7 or 8 per cent. Consequently, a return of 7 or 8 per cent on the entire valuation is likely to yield about 10 per cent on the common stockholder's equity. But it must be stressed that the question of what is a fair rate of return is largely an unsolved problem.

If an attempt is to be made by public service commissions to stimulate managerial efficiency in the operation of public utilities, the best way to do so is probably to allow a slightly higher rate of return to the most efficiently managed companies. This would require the establishment of statistical tests for measuring the efficiency of management — a task of great difficulty. It may be objected that a greater return to the stockholders is not an economical way of encouraging efficiency in the management because the managers usually own only a small part of the stock and would receive, therefore, only a small part of the higher return. This is true. There are advantages, however, in having the stockholders keenly interested in the efficiency of the management and eager to have the efficiency improved. If it is desired to have the management stimulated by profit sharing or by bonus schemes, it is advantageous to permit these to be established by each enterprise to suit its own peculiar needs and conditions. If the stockholders receive a larger return when the management is unusually efficient, they are likely to see that the management is well provided with incentives to greater efficiency.

Thus far, few public service commissions have given much attention to the problem of encouraging more efficient management of public utilities. Possibly it is not of vital importance that the commissions should give attention to this problem, because the large holding companies which control chains of local utilities are giving such great attention to it. By comparing the performance of the local managers in different cities and promoting on the basis of this comparison, they put each manager under terrific pressure to do his best. Commissions could hardly add to the incentive which already exists in a great many cases.[18]

X. The Effect of Regulation upon the Charges of Public Service Companies

How has public price-fixing affected the charges of public service companies? Is there reason to believe that regulation has made the rates of railroads and of municipal utilities distinctly different from what they otherwise would have been?

Naturally a question of this sort cannot be answered with precision. We cannot know how different the rates of public service companies would have been if regulation had not existed. As far as railroad rates are concerned, there is reason to believe that the Interstate Commerce Commission has exercised a real influence both upon the rate level and upon the relationships between individual rates. The influence of the Commission was probably greater during the period of rising prices from 1906, when the Commission first acquired effective authority over rates, until 1918, when the government took over the railroads for wartime operation, than it has been during the period of falling prices since 1920. It is highly probable that, in the absence of the Commission, railroad rates would have risen far more rapidly between 1906 and 1918. The railroads would have advanced them in order to offset the effect of rising prices upon operating costs. The Interstate Commerce Commission recognized that most of the roads were entitled to more net income but it steadfastly refused to permit substantial advances in rates. The Commission held that in many respects the roads were inefficiently operated and that the needed additions to income could be obtained by reducing costs instead of raising rates.[19] Since

---

[18] Thanks to the inefficiency and ineffectiveness of regulation, no serious results have followed from the failure of the commissions to create incentives for managerial efficiency. This may appear to be a paradoxical statement. The truth of the matter is that regulating bodies have been so tardy in reducing rates when utilities have succeeded in cutting costs that the savings have gone to the companies for some years before the public has shared in them. Consequently, managements have had almost as much of an incentive to be efficient as if no regulation had existed. But if regulation ever becomes efficient and rate adjustments are made promptly when the production costs are reduced, it will become increasingly important to provide managements with special incentives to improve their efficiency.

[19] The substantial economies which the railroads have accomplished since 1920 indicate that the Commission was right.

the downward trend of prices began in 1920, the influence of the Commission upon rates has been less, because the railroads have not, for the most part, sought increases. It is possible that the Commission has slightly accelerated the drop in rates.

It is also true that the state commissions which regulate the charges of municipal utilities had far more effect upon rates when prices were rising, up until 1920, than during the subsequent period of falling prices. During the period of rising prices, many utilities sought rate increases. In many instances, the increases were urgently needed. But the increases were also unpopular and the state commissioners were exceedingly reluctant to grant them. There can be no doubt that the state commissions delayed and moderated the advance in public utility rates during the period of rising prices prior to 1920. But since 1920 the influence of the commissions has been much less. The fall in the general price level and rapid technical progress have made rate increases unnecessary for most utilities. Many companies, particularly in the electric light and power industry and in the gas industry, have made such drastic cuts in costs that substantially lower rates would be possible. But the public asks for rate reductions less readily than the companies ask for increases and most of the commissions do not initiate proceedings as to the reasonableness of established rates. Indeed, many commissions lack the legal authority to do so. The result has been that, since 1920, commissions have had little influence upon the rates of most municipal utilities. The great savings in costs which many utilities have effected have gone to raise the prices of their securities rather than to reduce rates to consumers. Indeed, the spectacular rise in the securities of many utilities, though partly attributable to the drop in interest rates which lasted until 1928 and to the nation-wide speculation in securities, may be accepted in no small degree as a measure of the ineffectiveness of the state public utility commissions. So large have been the reductions in costs which many public service companies have achieved and so great has been the inertia of the commissions, that many companies have found it profitable voluntarily to reduce rates.

Many specific reasons can be cited why the commissions have

exercised little control over rates during the period of falling prices. Underlying these specific reasons, however, is a fundamental cause — the indifference of the public toward utility rates. It is this indifference which tolerates the persistence of the specific conditions which are responsible for the ineffectiveness of the commissions. The principal of these conditions are: the personnel of many commissions is weak; the technical staffs of nearly all of the commissions are too small and many are lacking in men of ability; the legal authority of most commissions over the utilities is seriously inadequate; and, finally, the work of the commissions has been hampered by the intervention of the courts, which do not understand the problems of regulating utilities and which have imposed upon the commissions many rules, particularly rules of valuation, which are administratively unworkable.

The difficulty in getting satisfactory men on the commissions arises from a number of causes. In twenty out of the forty-seven states which have public service commissions, the commissioners are elected.[20] It is difficult to induce men of the most desirable type to become candidates. In many states, the term of office is too short to be attractive. The average term is about six years, but in some states, Arkansas and South Carolina, for example, it is only two years.[21] The salaries of public utility commissioners are far too low to attract men of ability. The average salary is about $5,000 and some states pay as little as $2,000 a year.[22] Because of the indifference of the public to the type of men on the commissions, governors have not felt compelled to appoint the best men available. In fact, during the summer of 1927, Governor Small of Illinois appointed to the public service commission Dan Jackson, a notorious gambler known as " King of the Gamblers," but the action appears to have raised no public outcry.[23] Almost no state commissions now possess a large enough technical staff and, despite some exceptions, in most cases the competency of the staff is mediocre. The staffs, of course, reflect in large measure the quality of the commissions. But the quality of the staffs is also affected by inadequate appropriations,

---

[20] Mosher, W. E., and others, *Electrical Utilities*, p. 8.
[21] *Ibid.*, p. 9.
[22] Ruggles, C. O., " Regulation of Electric Light and Power Utilities," *American Economic Review, Supplement*, March, 1929, v. XIX, p. 185.
[23] New York *Times*, August 28, 1928, p. 10.

and by the fact that as many as thirty-nine states, even at this late date, possess no civil service laws! [24] With salaries small and security of employment uncertain, the commissions cannot compete with the public utilities for the best accountants, engineers, and statisticians.

Many commissions are seriously handicapped by lack of adequate legal authority. In seven states, for example, the public service commissions have no control over electric light and power companies. In eight additional states, the jurisdiction of the commissions over electric companies is seriously limited by the jurisdiction of the municipal governments.[25] Most commissions possess no jurisdiction until a plant begins operating. This substantially increases the difficulty of preventing the padding of the cost of construction figures. In nearly all states, the commission may not begin rate proceedings on its own initiative; it may only adjudicate cases brought by others.[26] But a rate proceeding is expensive. The New York Edison Company, for example, has recently spent $5,000,000 fighting an attempt to reduce the electric rates to small consumers. Obviously the individual consumer cannot afford to attack the existing rates, and even the governments of many small villages and cities find it burdensome to bring cases. Moreover, some states do not even permit municipalities to initiate proceedings except under very special circumstances.[27] The logical body to question existing rates is the commission itself, which has authority to call upon the companies for the information that sheds light on the reasonableness of rates and which has a technical staff to work up the case. And yet even some commissions, such as the one in New York, which possess the authority to initiate proceedings, refrain very largely from doing so.[28] Few of the commissions possess authority to regulate the holding companies which control and manage most of the local utility companies. The holding companies charge the local utilities for managerial and engineering services and

[24] National Civil Service Reform League, *Good Government*, September, 1929, v. XLVI, p. 80.

[25] Mosher, W. E., and others, *Electrical Utilities*, p. 6.

[26] *Ibid.*, p. 19.

[27] *Ibid.*, p. 19.

[28] See New York State Commission on Revision of the Public Service Commissions Law, *Report of Commissioners Frank P. Walsh, James C. Bonbright, David C. Adie*, pp. 68–70.

for supervising new construction. No one, except the holding companies themselves, knows how much it costs to render the services for which they charge the local companies or what contributions they make for the money which they receive, and the state commissions have no authority to inquire into the books of the holding companies and discover the cost of rendering their managerial services. There is, however, great variation in the charges of the holding companies. The Electric Bond and Share Company charges a service fee of 1.6 to 2 per cent of gross revenue; Stone and Webster $3,000 per annum plus 2.35 per cent of gross revenue; the Northwestern Public Service Company in 1926 was paying the Electric Management and Engineering Corporation a management fee of 5 per cent of its gross earnings; the Buffalo, Niagara and Eastern Power Corporation collects a management fee of 5 per cent of gross revenues.[29] The variation in the fees may simply represent differences in the managerial supervision rendered. But a contract for managerial services between a local utility and a holding company which controls the local company is a patent means of holding up the public. All such contracts are naturally suspect. Commissions will not be in a position to determine the real profits of public service companies and thus to regulate rates effectively until they are able to determine from the books of the holding companies the cost of rendering managerial supervision.

The courts have hindered effective regulation in numerous ways. Although the commissions have not reduced rates as fast as operating costs have fallen and in some instances as fast as the public utilities themselves have found it profitable to do, the courts have vetoed many of the rate reductions that the commissions have made.[30] In addition, the courts have made exceedingly slow progress in providing the commissions with definite and administratively practicable rules to guide them in determin-

[29] Mosher, W. E., and others, *Electrical Utilities*, p. 110.

[30] How do the courts possess authority to intervene in rate proceedings? Both the Fifth Amendment, which applies to the federal government, and the Fourteenth Amendment, which applies to the state governments, provide that no person shall be deprived of property without due process of law. The peculiar (and probably unwarranted) meaning which the courts in the United States have placed upon the phrase " due process of law " enables them to hold that orders of public service commissions which do not permit a utility to earn a " reasonable " return on the " fair value " of the property devoted by it to the public service are unconstitutional and void.

ing the value upon which utilities should be permitted to earn a return. The problems presented to the courts by the regulation of public utility rates are multitudinous and extremely technical and it is to be expected that the courts would require some years to solve them. Nevertheless, it is a fair criticism that the courts have shown little appreciation of the administrative problems of regulation. As a result, rate controversies have provoked an enormous amount of expensive and long drawn out litigation. It commonly takes several years and the expenditure of hundreds of thousands or even millions of dollars to determine whether or not an important rate change should be made. In times of rising prices, when most cases involve the question of increases in rates, the law's delay works to the advantage of the public; in periods of falling prices, when the issue is usually a decrease in rates, it works against the public.

REFERENCES

Bauer, John, *Effective Regulation of Public Utilities*, 1925.
Clark, J. M., *Social Control of Business*, 1926. Ch. XX–XXVI.
Glaeser, M. G., *Outlines of Public Utility Economics*, 1927.
Morgan, C. S., *Regulation and Management of Public Utilities*, 1923.
Pigou, A. C., *The Economics of Welfare* (third edition), 1929. Pt. II, ch. XII, XVII, XX, and XXI.
Ripley, W. Z., *Railroads: Rates and Regulation* (second edition), 1913.
Ripley, W. Z., *Railroads: Finance and Organization*, 1915.

CHAPTER XIX

PUBLIC AUTHORITY AS A DETERMINANT OF PRICE— THE STABILIZATION OPERATIONS OF THE FEDERAL FARM BOARD

I. THE MACHINERY FOR STABILIZATION OPERATIONS. II. THE STABILIZATION OPERATIONS IN WHEAT. III. THE STABILIZATION OPERATION IN COTTON. IV. ARE STABILIZATION OPERATIONS ADVISABLE?

I. The Machinery for Stabilization Operations

Possibly the most interesting attempts to control prices by a government agency in the United States today have been several recent operations of the Federal Farm Board. The Farm Board has many duties. Among them is the duty of preventing " undue and excessive " fluctuations in the prices of agricultural products. Violent fluctuations in farm prices occur (1) because the output of farm products in any given year is largely controlled by the weather rather than by man, and (2) because the demand for many agricultural commodities, particularly staples, is inelastic — at least in the United States and in the richer countries of Europe. The fluctuations in prices are often so violent as to produce substantial fluctuations in the incomes (and consequently the buying power) of farmers. This is obviously a disadvantage to the farmers, but it is also a disadvantage to all who sell to them.

The problem of the Farm Board, in seeking to stabilize the prices of farm products, is very different from the problems of the Interstate Commerce Commission and of the state public service commissions. The Farm Board has no authority to fix prices. It must influence them solely through affecting the flow of farm products to market. And it has no control over the number of persons who are engaged in agriculture or the number of acres that are cultivated, nor authority to forbid an expansion of farm acreage, as the Interstate Commerce Commission may forbid the construction of new railroads, or the state public service commissions the establishment of new and competing gas companies or electric light and power companies.[1]

There are two types of fluctuation in the prices of farm products — *intra*-seasonal and *inter*-seasonal. *Intra*-seasonal fluctuations result from the fact that the flow of products is often ill adjusted to the current demand and to the storage space available at the central distributing points. Consequently, during the crop marketing season, the price may be unduly low in relation to the price later. *Inter*-seasonal fluctuations are produced by the great variations in the annual yield of crops. The Farm Board has been in existence only since the summer of 1929. Nevertheless, during this brief period, it has undertaken three major stabilizing operations — two in wheat and one in cotton. It is desirable to examine these operations in order to learn what light they throw upon the feasibility of attempting to stabilize agricultural prices through the medium of such a body.

The theory upon which the Farm Board operates is that fluctuations in the prices of agricultural commodities can be reduced by controlling the rate at which the commodities are marketed. The Board has been provided by Congress with a revolving fund of $500,000,000 to be used, among other purposes, for financing the temporary withholding of farm products from the market. The machinery by which the Board seeks to reduce intra-seasonal fluctuations, however, is somewhat different from that by which it seeks to reduce inter-seasonal fluctuations.

As a means of accomplishing various improvements in the marketing of agricultural commodities, the Board is seeking to assist the development of coöperative marketing associations. In particular, it has sought to establish, for each principal agricultural commodity, a national sales agency or coöperative organization. The stock in the national coöperatives is subscribed by regional, state, and local coöperatives and, nominally

---

[1] The Federal Farm Board is expected by many of its supporters to influence the long-time level of some agricultural prices by encouraging farmers to reduce the acreage devoted to crops which are now badly overproduced. But this part of the Farm Board's work is distinct from its stabilization operations. Its stabilization operations, however, may affect the success of its efforts to persuade farmers to reduce the acreage of certain crops.

at least, the national coöperatives are controlled by locals. Nevertheless, the Farm Board stipulates that as long as a coöperative borrows from the Board's revolving fund, its management and policies must be satisfactory to the Board. During the first year of its existence, the Board brought about the establishment of seven national coöperative selling organizations, one each for grain, cotton, wool, beans, live stock, pecans, and sugar beets.[2] The coöperatives are the agencies through which it is hoped to control the rate at which commodities are marketed and thus to reduce intra-seasonal fluctuations in prices.[3] If it seems desirable to hold back part of a crop for several months in order to avoid depressing the price too low, this can be done by the coöperative. But if the coöperative delays selling a substantial part of its holdings, it must also delay making final payment to its members for their crop.[4] By borrowing upon the crop in storage, the coöperative is able to make a partial advance to its members at once. But ordinarily coöperatives can borrow only from 60 to 65 per cent of the value of staple commodities, such as wheat or cotton. Consequently the members must wait for a substantial part of their return and this may render many farmers unwilling to join the coöperative. In order to enable coöperatives to hold back part of the crop and to make larger advances to their members, the Federal Farm Board is authorized to make them loans from its revolving fund.[5] The practice has been for the Board to lend to the national coöperative, if one has been established for the commodity, and otherwise to local coöperatives. The nationals, in turn, make loans to their affiliated locals, which are the bodies that deal directly with the

[2] These organizations are: Farmers' National Grain Corporation, American Cotton Coöperative Association, National Wool Marketing Corporation, National Bean Marketing Association, National Livestock Marketing Association, National Pecan Marketing Association, and National Beet Growers' Association.

[3] Some members of the Farm Board apparently believe that in some branches of agriculture coöperatives may be able to exert substantial influence upon the acreage devoted to crops and, therefore, upon the long-time average price of the product. Federal Farm Board, *First Annual Report*, pp. 4 and 25.

[4] Some coöperatives (the wheat coöperatives, for example) permit the farmer, if he desires, to sell his crop at once in the local market at the prevailing competitive price. The more usual practice, however, is to pool the supply of all members and to pay each his proportionate share of the amount received for the total supply. Allowance is, of course, made for the grade of product delivered by each member.

[5] It is not intended to imply that this is the only purpose for which the Board is authorized to lend to the coöperatives. There are many others.

individual farmers. The loans of the Board are usually in addition to the loans which the coöperatives have obtained from other sources. For this reason they are often known as "supplemental loans." [6]

To some extent, coöperatives may also engage in inter-seasonal stabilization operations.[7] But these operations are likely to require that a substantial stock of a commodity be held off the market for several years. The members of the coöperatives cannot be expected to wait so long for the final payment on their crops. Consequently, if an inter-seasonal stabilization operation is undertaken, a special organization is needed to buy part of the crop in years of extraordinarily large output and to hold it until a short crop occurs or until there is a favorable opportunity for selling it abroad. In order to provide for inter-seasonal stabilization operations, the Farm Board is authorized to encourage the establishment of stabilization corporations.

The stock of each stabilization corporation must be owned by the coöperative associations handling the commodity. It is not expected, however, that the capital of stabilization corporations will come primarily from the coöperatives. It is expected that it will be provided by the Farm Board in the form of loans from its revolving fund. During its first year, the Board sponsored the establishment of two stabilization corporations — one for wheat and one for cotton.

II. The Stabilization Operations in Wheat

Within a few months of its establishment, the Federal Farm Board was led by circumstances to undertake two stabilization operations of great magnitude and importance. The newly created Board found itself confronted with an exceedingly diffi-

[6] The Farm Board does not lend to coöperatives merely for the purpose of helping them to stabilize the price of the commodity by withholding part of a large crop. The Board is interested in strengthening the coöperatives, and the supplemental loans are one way of doing this. It has been explained above (p. 430) that coöperatives have always been handicapped by their inability to advance as large a proportion of the value of the produce as can a private dealer who buys for cash. Consequently many farmers prefer to sell through commercial dealers. By enabling coöperatives to make substantially larger immediate advances to their members, the Farm Board assists them to acquire and to retain members.

[7] The Farm Board recognizes this possibility. See Federal Farm Board, *First Annual Report*, p. 25.

cult situation in the wheat market and with the demand that it
" do something " at once.   Largely as a result of the enormous
world crop of 1928, the 1929–1930 crop year began in the United
States with record-breaking stocks of wheat on hand.[8]   The new
crop of 1929 moved to market early and rapidly.   For this the
combine-harvester method of harvesting was partly responsible.
This method, which has spread rapidly during the last decade,
has shortened the period of harvest and tended, therefore, to concentrate the movement of wheat from the farms to the terminal
markets into a shorter period.   Ordinarily, exports of wheat are
heavy in August and reach a peak in September.   In 1929, however, the exports of the United States during August and September were substantially less than the average of the immediately preceding years.   One reason was that the European crop
in 1929 was large; another was that the European demand
was satisfied in substantial degree by exports from Argentina as
a result of a bumper crop in the preceding winter.   The large
carry-over, the rapid movement of the new crop to the terminal
markets, and the smaller exports resulted in a serious congestion
at the terminal centers, which in turn produced an unusually high
carrying charge, or price for storage, and depressed the price of
cash wheat in relation to the price of futures.   This situation was
one of the first problems with which the Federal Farm Board was
called upon to wrestle.   On August 3, 1929, after the flood of
wheat pouring into Galveston had led to an embargo against
further shipments, the Board issued a statement urging farmers
to hold their wheat on the farms and to avoid depressing the cash
price unduly in relation to the future price by overtaxing the
storage facilities in the terminal markets.[9]

[8] The visible supply of wheat on June 29, 1929, was 116,000,000 bushels, compared with 53,000,000 the year before and an average of 29,000,000 for the five
preceding years.   U. S. Bureau of Agricultural Economics, *The Disparity between
Wheat Prices in Canada and in the United States and the Grain Storage Situation*, p. 1.

[9] The statement of the Board in part was as follows: " This excessive crowding
of wheat on the market has created a far wider spread between cash wheat prices and
prices of wheat sold for future delivery than usually exists.

" The Federal Farm Board has made no statement or forecast whatsoever concerning a proper price for wheat for this market year, nor does it propose to do so, but
under conditions which exist this season, when all reports agree on a substantial reduction in world supply as compared with last year, it seems unfortunate to crowd
wheat onto the market faster than existing facilities can handle it, resulting in cash
prices which are much lower than contract prices for future delivery."   New York
Times, August 4, 1929, Part I, p. 1.

Possibly the advice of the Board helped to arrest the sharp drop in wheat prices which occurred during the first week of August. Early in September, the Board undertook to lend to coöperatives on the basis of 10 cents a bushel on unsold wheat and on the basis of 90 per cent of the value of wheat on which a price had been fixed by sale or hedging. From the middle of September, the price of wheat drifted downward. During the second half of October, concurrently with the decline in the stock market, the price dropped about 15 cents. The practice of the Board, as has been explained, had been to assist the coöperatives to borrow up to 90 per cent of the value of their wheat. After urging farmers to hold wheat, the Board no doubt felt under a peculiar obligation to support the market. However that may be, it abandoned its policy of limiting its advances to 90 per cent of the market value of wheat. The formation of the Farmers' National Grain Corporation on October 25th, an organization for advancing credit to local grain growers' coöperatives and for handling their grain, was closely followed on October 26th by an emergency policy of fixed-loan values on wheat. The Board stated that it believed the price of wheat to be too low and that it was prepared to make loans to coöperatives sufficient to bring the amount borrowed per bushel up to a fixed schedule which practically represented the current market price. For example, the Board announced that it was ready to lend up to $1.18 a bushel on No. 1 Hard Winter wheat in Chicago and $1.25 on No. 1 Northern at Minneapolis. After this action, the price of wheat recovered somewhat. It fell to a new low at the time of the second crash in the stock market on November 13th, but during the remainder of the year the trend of the price was upward.

When the Farm Board encouraged the coöperatives to hold wheat at the prices fixed in its loan schedule of October 26th, the Board no doubt felt that it would be possible for the coöperatives to sell their wheat before the end of the crop year at the schedule prices or better. It was probably the purpose of the Board simply to prevent a very temporary dip in the price. In other words, the stabilization operation which the Board initiated was intended to be an *intra*-seasonal rather than an *inter*-seasonal operation. In fact, it would obviously have been bad policy to hold wheat at that particular time with the intention of carrying it over until the next season. In the first place, both the world crop and the crop in the United States were smaller than in any year since 1925. In the second place, the carry-over from the preceding crop year was unusually large both in the United States and in the world as a whole. Indeed, the carry-over had been climbing for several years. On July 1, 1929, the wheat in storage throughout the world was estimated at 614 million bushels as against 275 million on July 1, 1926, 346 million on July 1, 1927, and 424 million on July 1, 1928.[10] Obviously it would be unfortunate, in a year when the crop was not large, to add to a carry-over which already was abnormally large.

But although it is now plain that conditions in the fall of 1929 did not warrant an *inter*-seasonal stabilization operation, most experts, in October, 1929, would probably have agreed that an *intra*-seasonal operation was justified and that the prices at which the Board sought to support the market were not too high. It is true that the carry-over from the bumper crop of 1928 was large. Nevertheless, the 1929 crop in Canada had been small—about half the average for the preceding five years — and the Argentine crop was expected to be small. For the world as a whole, the outlook was for a crop of more than 10 per cent below 1928. Not only did the Farm Board conclude that the price of wheat was too low, but the Canadian wheat pool, which controlled about 55 per cent of the grain from the prairie provinces, acted on the same assumption and held back its wheat for prices which Europeans were not prepared to pay. The policy of holding was also adopted by powerful grain and elevator firms which controlled most of the remainder of the Canadian crop.

The fact that the Canadians were holding their wheat greatly improved the prospect that the Farm Board's policy of supporting the market would succeed. But the policy did not succeed. It was the general expectation that Europe would exhaust other sources of supply by about January 1st and would then be compelled to purchase American and Canadian wheat. But Europe showed unexpected ability to get along without American and Canadian supplies. Europe was greatly aided by the fact that,

[10] U. S. Bureau of Agricultural Economics, *Foreign News on Wheat*, April 16, 1930, p. 3.

although the *world* crop in 1929 was less than in 1928, the *European* crop was about 100,000,000 bushels larger. Moreover, other crops in Europe, such as potatoes, corn, and others, were larger than in 1928. Argentina had an immense carry-over from its crop of 1928. This source of supply proved larger than most experts had estimated and the exports from Argentina did not end with the beginning of the year as had been predicted. Finally, a number of European countries discouraged the importation of wheat — some by raising their import duties and some by requiring that local mill grindings must contain a definite percentage of domestic wheat.[11]

The failure of the European demand to equal expectations led to a sharp drop in the price. The slump began late in January. By the first week in February, the price of wheat had sunk below the loan values established by the Farm Board in October. By this time it was fairly probable that, unless the 1930 winter wheat crop suffered severe damage during the winter, the wheat held by the coöperatives could not be sold during the 1929–1930 crop year at prices sufficient to cover the loan values established by the Board in October, 1929. Thus the Board found itself financing a carry-over of wheat from a small crop year in the face of stocks which were already large. But the Board considered it essential to protect the coöperatives, their members, and even independent farmers from loss. Consequently, in spite of the decline in the price of wheat, the Farmers' National Grain Corporation, the national sales agency organized in October, 1929, continued to lend to the coöperatives at the October, 1929, loan prices, and the coöperatives continued to advance these amounts on wheat received from their members. In order to help farmers who were not members of coöperatives, the Farmers' National Grain Corporation purchased from them country-run wheat at the loan values. Early in February, the Farm Board considered it advisable to protect the coöperatives by organizing the Grain Stabilization Corporation to purchase the holdings of the coöperatives and the Farmers' National Grain Corporation at the loan-value prices. It also continued for a brief period the policy of the Farmers' National Grain Corpora-

---

[11] On the other hand, some European exporters of wheat reduced their export duties on wheat.

tion in paying the loan-value prices to farmers for country-run wheat. It was found that others than farmers were taking advantage of this buying, and the Stabilization Corporation soon restricted its purchasing to coöperatives and their members.[12]

The market price at times during February was nearly 20 cents below the price which the coöperatives received from the Stabilization Corporation. For probably the first time in its history, the country witnessed the strange spectacle of two prices for identical grades of wheat at the same time. But since the Farm Board agencies were willing to buy only country-run wheat or wheat owned by coöperatives, only farmers could obtain the higher price offered by the Farmers' National Grain Corporation and the Grain Stabilization Corporation. Naturally the Board received a flood of telegrams from private speculators asking that it take their wheat off their hands. In addition to buying cash wheat at the loan base prices, the Stabilization Corporation began to support the market by purchasing May futures. On March 1st, the Corporation discontinued the policy of buying wheat at the loan values established by the Farm Board in October. It continued, however, to support the market by buying cash wheat at market prices and by buying May futures. Late in March, this support became unnecessary and ceased. Lending on the established loan bases was discontinued on April 30. Recovery in wheat prices during the spring enabled the Grain Stabilization Corporation to dispose of a substantial part of its holdings, but on June 30, 1930, it held over 60,000,000 bushels.[13]

What had begun as an *intra*-seasonal stabilization operation, intended to protect farmers from " purely temporary factors unconnected with the demand and supply situation for the year as a whole," [14] was transformed by the course of events into an

[12] Mr. Legge, chairman of the Farm Board, declared on February 24th that the Board was not operating to help the grain trade. " If we went into the wheat market and tried to lift the whole price level now in order to help the farmer," Mr. Legge explained, " four dollars out of five of the benefit would go to somebody else." *Journal of Commerce* (New York), February 25, 1930, p. 1. But several days later Mr. Legge admitted that, although the policy of the Stabilization Corporation was to purchase only the wheat of farmers, actually it was getting more than that. " Some of the roll-top desk farmers are selling us some wheat," said Mr. Legge. New York *Times*, February 28, 1930, p. 14.

[13] Federal Farm Board, *First Annual Report*, p. 32.

[14] *Ibid.*, p. 27.

inter-seasonal operation of great magnitude. The smaller crop in 1929 — over 100,000,000 bushels less than in 1928 and the smallest since 1925 — should have enabled the wheat industry to attain a much improved statistical position. But the reverse occurred. The world as a whole reduced its carry-over by more than 100,000,000 bushels — from about 614,000,000 in July, 1929, to about 500,000,000 on July 1, 1930 — but the carry-over in the United States, which had been rising for several years, continued to increase from 245,000,000 bushels on July 1, 1929, to the record-breaking total of 256,000,000 on July 1, 1930. With the prospects for a growth in the output of wheat in Russia, on the great plains of the United States, and in other countries, there is small chance that this wheat will be sold for as much as it would have brought in the crop year of 1929–1930.[15] At the end of the crop year, the Stabilization Corporation still held about 60,000,000 bushels. What the Corporation shall do with this wheat is likely to become an important political issue. The Farm Board made it clear that its holdings would not be sold in competition with the 1930 crop.[16] But will they be sold in competition with the crop of any subsequent year? The millions of voters who raise wheat would most certainly punish any administration which dared to keep down the price by permitting the Stabilization Corporation to sell its holdings. Unless there is a crop so small in the United States as to make our tariff on wheat effective, it is probable that most of the Corporation's holdings will never be sold.

During the summer of 1930, when most classes of wheat were selling most of the time for less than 90 cents, there was some demand that the Board again support the wheat market. But for several months it refused to act. World stocks of wheat were large and those in the United States were at record levels. Naturally the Board was reluctant to add to them. In November, 1930, however, there occurred a severe break in the price of wheat. The price at Winnipeg reached an all-time

[15] In July, 1930, the price of wheat was about 35 per cent below that of July, 1929.

[16] The actual announcement of the Board was that wheat held by the Stabilization Corporation would not be sold during the current season *for less than its purchase price.*

low and the price at Liverpool touched the lowest point since 1894. The break was due partly to unexpectedly large exports from Russia but in the main to the prospects for bumper crops in the Argentine and Australia. With the large carry-over from 1929, the world supply of wheat was estimated at little short of the record supply in 1928–1929. The drop continued through December and, by the end of the month, wheat in Liverpool was selling at the lowest price in over three hundred years.

When the break occurred in November, the situation, in the judgment of the Farm Board, represented a national emergency.[17] The Grain Stabilization Corporation supported the December future at about 73 cents and the May future at about 80 cents. The July future was not supported. As a result, the May future in Chicago on December 31, 1930, was 27 cents above the Winnipeg May future and 19 cents above the Liverpool — although normally the Chicago price is below the Liverpool price.[18] The support of the Stabilization Corporation continued throughout the winter. As a result, its holdings of wheat increased enormously — to over 200,000,000 bushels by April, 1931.

III. The Stabilization Operation in Cotton

The stabilization operation in cotton was on a somewhat smaller scale than the operation in wheat but in broad outline it was about the same. As in the case of wheat, the rapid marketing of cotton (the result apparently of open weather in the South) had produced weakness in spot prices. The price declined during the first half of October, 1929, and more acute weakness developed after the first crash in the stock market. The statistical position of cotton was somewhat better than that of wheat. On October 21, the Board expressed the opinion that the price of cotton was too low and announced that it was prepared to lend to the coöperatives sums sufficient to bring the total amount borrowed up to 16 cents per pound on graded and classed cotton, basis middling, and ⅞ inch staple, less freight to port concentra-

---

[17] Davis, J. S., "The Program of the Federal Farm Board," *American Economic Review, Supplement,* March, 1931, v. XXI, p. 112.

[18] Stanford University, *Wheat Studies of the Food Research Institute,* January, 1931, v. VII, p. 217. The fact that the July future was not supported created a difficult problem for the millers because it meant that they were compelled to adjust their business to the prospect of a rapid drop in the price of wheat during the late spring and early summer of 1931.

tion points. At this time, cotton was selling at approximately 18 cents a pound. The Board's announcement caused a strengthening of demand and for a few weeks there was a slight recovery in the price.

It is not probable that the Board expected that its schedule of fixed-loan values would compel it to carry over cotton into the 1930 crop year. In view of the fact that, ever since the record-breaking crop of 1926, the world carry-over of cotton had been large, it would not have been wise for the Board deliberately to use its resources to increase the carry-over.[19] But the industrial depression which became acute immediately after the drop in the stock market diminished the purchasing power of many important consumers of cotton in the tropics and the Far East. The buying power of Central and South America was reduced by the precipitous drop in the prices of sugar and coffee, and that of New Zealand and Australia by short wheat crops and low prices for butter and wool. The sharp fall in the price of silver was disastrous to China, the principal country on the silver standard. The drop in the purchasing power of these countries was several months in making itself fully felt, but, on January 30, 1930, the price of cotton broke through the loan value of 16 cents a pound. Up to this time, there had been no national sales agency in cotton, through which the Board might make advances to the coöperatives. The Board had dealt with the coöperatives directly. Early in February, 1930, a national coöperative, the American Cotton Coöperative Association, was created under the sponsorship of the Board to handle the cotton of the state coöperatives. In order to enable mills to meet their special requirements, it was necessary for the coöperatives to sell cotton, but each sale was matched by the purchase of a future upon which delivery was accepted. Thus the coöperatives, in spite of their sales, were constantly holding a substantial amount of cotton off the market. Nevertheless, the price throughout the spring remained below the loan price of 16 cents. In order to protect the coöperatives from loss, the Cotton Stabilization Corporation

---

[19] In 1926, the world carry-over of cotton was 10,600,000 bales, of which 7,800,-000 were American bales. The American carry-over had been reduced to approximately 4,500,000 bales on July 31, 1929, but the world carry-over was 9,300,000 bales. U. S. Department of Agriculture, "The Agricultural Outlook for 1930," *Miscellaneous Publication No. 73*, February, 1930, p. 13.

was formed on June 5, 1930. With funds advanced by the Board, it took over the holdings of the coöperatives — about 1,300,000 bales. This, of course, simply transferred the loss from the coöperatives to the Stabilization Corporation. Just as in the case of wheat, events beyond the ability of the Farm Board to foresee or to control had converted what was intended as an intra-seasonal stabilization operation into an inter-seasonal operation. At the beginning of the new crop year, on July 31, 1930, carry-over of old cotton in the United States was about 6,000,000 bales — 1,500,000 more than the year before.

IV. Are Stabilization Operations Advisable?

The ideal of reducing the violent fluctuations in agricultural prices sufficiently to give farmers a more or less steady income is attractive. The procedure also *seems* simple and practicable. Of course, holding over a part of the supply after a large crop has always been done on a fairly extensive scale by farmers and other business men. Studies of the Food Research Institute at Stanford University, covering the thirty years from 1896–1897 to 1926–1927, indicate that, in thirteen years of large crops when production was on the average 80.3 million bushels above normal, stocks at the end of the crop year were 38.1 million bushels above normal; in seventeen years, when the crops averaged 63.6 million bushels below normal, stocks at the end of the crop year were 29.3 million bushels below normal.[20] Furthermore, there is no conclusive evidence that the annual fluctuations in the net incomes of farmers are greater than the annual fluctuations in incomes of other parts of the population.[21] Nevertheless it is true that farmers' incomes do fluctuate violently from year to year. Consequently, it might be desirable for the government to help stabilize prices by financing the withholding of part of the supply in years of abundance.

In considering whether it would be desirable, the first ques-

[20] Stanford University, "Disposition of American Wheat since 1896," *Wheat Studies of the Food Research Institute*, February, 1928, v. IV, p. 173. "Normal" is a ten-year moving average. The rest of the variation from normal was largely absorbed by changes in the volume of exports, rather than in changes in consumption.

[21] It is probable that the agitation for stabilization is the result of the fact that the incomes of farmers are lower than formerly rather than a result of the fact that they fluctuate. Some advocates of stabilization appear to seek a leveling up of prices in years of large crops but not a leveling down in years of small crops.

tion which arises is: Would more stable prices, as a matter of fact, produce more stable net incomes? The answer depends largely upon the relationship between the output of crops and their prices, and this is not the same for all farm products. Such data as are available indicate, for example, that large cotton crops sell for less than small ones. The case of wheat is complicated by the fact that the output of the United States is only a small fraction of the world supply. Apparently, large wheat crops usually yield somewhat more than small ones.[22] These facts are of the greatest importance from the standpoint of the problem of stabilizing farmers' net incomes. The incomes of cotton growers would evidently be stabilized by holding part of the crop in years of large output and selling out in years of small output. In the case of wheat, however, this procedure would apparently accentuate the fluctuations in incomes. In order to stabilize the income of wheat farmers, it would be necessary for the government to withdraw part of the crop in years of *small* output and sell it in years of large crops. It is fairly obvious that neither farmers nor consumers would tolerate such procedure. And since withholding wheat in years of large crops and selling it in years of small crops would accentuate fluctuations in the net income from wheat, the wise policy would appear to be for the government to refrain altogether from inter-seasonal stabilization operations in wheat — except possibly in periods of greater emergency, such as occurred in the fall of 1930.

But would it be desirable for the government to attempt stabilization operations even in the case of commodities such as cotton, where greater stability of prices would apparently mean greater stability of income? If the government advances funds to stabilize prices, will not capital be diverted from some more useful employment? Is it not reasonable to suppose that as much capital is already devoted to holding agricultural commodities from years of low prices to years of high prices as the profit and risks of the operation warrant? Is not capital now employed in this way until a better return can be gained by employing it in other ways?

---

[22] An excellent discussion of the relationships between the yield of various crops and farmers' net income will be found in Black, J. D., *Agricultural Reform in the United States*, pp. 95–151.

Probably it is true that as much capital is now employed in holding crops as is warranted, in view of the profit to be had in alternative and less risky employments. Consequently, it is to be expected that funds advanced by the government will yield less than the current rate of return — possibly (or even probably, as will be explained presently) no return whatever. And yet it does not follow that it would be uneconomical for the government to advance the funds. The reason is that the benefits of more stable prices (so long as more stable prices mean more stable incomes) accrue to the farmers and those who sell to them, rather than to those who advance the funds that are used to hold crops. Stabilization operations, therefore, may be worth while from the standpoint of the community even though they would not yield the current rate of return on the capital invested in them. Here we encounter another case where a useful service must be performed largely by the government because private capital cannot appropriate enough of the benefits.

There are three principal objections to government stabilization operations. One is that they interfere with the market's usefulness for hedging purposes.[23] If the cash price is supported but the future prices are not, the cash price is thrown out of line with futures. If one future (say, the May) is supported but not the July or December, that future is thrown out of line. The change in the spread between the cash price and future prices, or between future prices, diminishes the protection afforded by hedging and is a hardship upon processers and middlemen who are accustomed to use this method of protection. In other words, although stabilization operations may increase the security of farmers, they diminish the security of processers and middlemen.[24]

A second objection arises from the great difficulty in determining when to undertake a stabilization operation and at what price to support the market. Purchases at the wrong time or in too large quantities may accentuate rather than diminish the fluctuations in prices. The brief experience of the Federal Farm Board indicates plainly how difficult is the technical problem of deciding when to undertake stabilization operations and how easy

[23] For a discussion of hedging, see Chapter X, pp. 219–221.
[24] The Federal Farm Board discusses this problem briefly in its *First Annual Report*, p. 33. Another discussion will be found in *Wheat Studies of the Food Research Institute*, January, 1931, v. VII, pp. 217–218.

it is for highly competent men to make an erroneous decision. The Farm Board is composed of men of ability and has had the assistance of a competent technical staff. It is true that the rush of events and the pressure of politicians have compelled the Board to arrive at enormously difficult decisions in an exceedingly brief time, but these are disadvantages which are always likely to be present. It is reasonable to infer, however, that the Board felt that it was safe in undertaking to support the wheat and the cotton markets at the fixed-loan prices which it announced in October, 1929. And yet it is now clear that in both cases the Board attempted to keep the price too high. The problem of when to hold back part of the supply and how much to hold back is complicated by the fact that the course of the business cycle affects the demand for commodities. We are not yet able to forecast with accuracy either the duration or the intensity of the cyclical movements of business. The Farm Board now has large quantities of wheat and cotton on its hands partly because it could not foresee the severity of the depression which followed the crash in the stock market.

The third objection to government stabilization operations is the probability that they will become subsidies to some branches of agriculture. This conclusion is based upon the belief that stabilization operations are almost certain to result in losses to the government. It is true that the past records of crop yields reveal occasions when part of a large crop could have been held over for a year or two without a loss. These records, however, are misleading because, when prices are fixed by uncontrolled supply and demand, an extraordinarily large crop in one year is likely to induce a reduction in acreage for the next year or two.[25] This, of course, may result in a much smaller crop. Opportunities to stabilize prices without incurring losses appear to have existed *only because stabilization was not attempted.* But suppose that stabilization had been attempted on a substantial scale. The very fact that the price was supported by the withdrawal of a great part of the supply in years of large crops would have destroyed the incentive for farmers to reduce the acreage devoted to the commodity. But if the acreage had not been reduced,

[25] The record-breaking cotton crop in 1926, for example, resulted in a reduction in cotton acreage harvested, from 47,100,000 in 1926 to 40,100,000 in 1927.

would it have been possible to hold back part of the large crops and subsequently sell this surplus for as much as was paid for it? It is highly probable that a large number of stabilization operations, probably a majority if they are on a large scale, will result in a loss to the stabilizing body.

But if stabilization operations result in a loss and if the loss is incurred, not by the farmers themselves, but by a government agency such as the Farm Board, it is obvious that agriculture is being subsidized. If, for example, the Board pays $100,000,000 to the farmers' coöperatives for cotton which it sells a year or two later for $70,000,000, it is practically giving a subsidy of $30,000,000 to the growers of cotton. Possibly some branches of agriculture need to be subsidized; possibly the community would be better off if it offered a subsidy to encourage capital and labor to enter certain branches of farming. But if a subsidy is desirable, it obviously should be given only to those particular branches which need to be expanded and only in the amounts that are needed. There is no reason to believe that the subsidy which the Farm Board would give, by buying part of a crop for more than the price at which it is later able to sell its holdings, would encourage the proper crops or that it would be large enough without being too large. As a matter of fact, it would be sheer accident if the losses of the Farm Board happened to subsidize the proper branches of agriculture in approximately the proper amounts.[26] For example, it happens that up to this time the two outstanding stabilization operations of the Farm Board have been in wheat and cotton. By supporting the market during the fall of 1929 and the winter of 1930, the Board saved the wheat and cotton raisers from losses (or at least reduced their losses) and thereby, of course, encouraged them to continue raising wheat and cotton. And yet it happens that the Farm Board believes that farmers are already devoting too much acreage to wheat and cotton. At the same time that the Board, by supporting the market, has been discouraging them from reducing their acreage, it has been making a valiant effort, through the speeches of its members

[26] In reply, it may be urged that the subsidies which a Farm Board might give would be no more arbitrary and ill adapted to the interests of the community than those which have been imposed by the protective tariff for many years. This is doubtless true, but it scarcely justifies a bad method of subsidizing to point out that other bad methods of subsidizing are in operation.

and through press releases, to induce cotton- and wheat-raisers to make substantial cuts in their acreage.

Thus far we have assumed that it would at least be possible for the Farm Board to sell the holdings of agricultural commodities which it might acquire as a result of stabilizing operations. But would the Board be permitted to sell its holdings? The brief experience of the Farm Board indicates that this is likely to be an important issue. In the event of a serious crop failure, the Board would undoubtedly have no difficulty in selling at least part of its holdings. But it could not, of course, count on every bumper crop's being followed within several years by a crop failure. And barring an extreme shortage of a commodity, would the Board be permitted to sell? Even if the crop happened to be below the average and the price fairly high, the farmers would not welcome the competition of the Board's supply. When the growers have so many votes as have the raisers of wheat and cotton, it is highly probable that the Board would not be permitted to sell in the domestic market. Could it sell abroad? In the case of cotton, which is not raised by many other countries, the Board would probably have little difficulty in finding foreign countries which would be glad to take its holdings, provided the price were low enough. In other words, the dumping of cotton would not arouse opposition in other cotton manufacturing countries. But even if the price in the domestic market were protected by a tariff, the Board's sales abroad would arouse intense opposition among American cotton growers, who export about half of their crop, and American cotton manufacturers would, of course, object if American cotton could be purchased abroad for less than here. The Board's sales of its wheat holdings would also arouse strong opposition, but from somewhat different sources. Our high tariff on wheat (42 cents a bushel) would probably prevent most of our wheat raisers from objecting to dumping abroad. But many countries which are large consumers of wheat are also large wheat raisers. In contrast to cotton, the dumping of wheat would arouse intense opposition abroad and would lead to the prompt application of anti-dumping laws which nearly every country now has.

When part of a crop is withdrawn from the market by the Board and not sold, it is as good as destroyed. In fact, it would be better to destroy it and save the cost of storing it. But are we willing to sacrifice a substantial part of the output of agriculture every few years in order to stabilize the incomes of farmers? Is the benefit worth the cost? Stabilization of agricultural income must yield benefits of great magnitude in order to justify the permanent withdrawal or destruction of a large part of the agricultural output at frequent intervals. There is danger that the attempt to stabilize agricultural prices will degenerate into a process by which, on the one hand, certain branches of agriculture are encouraged to increase output and, on the other hand, a large part of the increased output is prevented from ever reaching the market.

Because any attempt on the part of the government to assist in the stabilization of agricultural prices by financing the carry-over of a substantial part of large crops to years of small crops is almost certain to result in a subsidy to agriculture — a subsidy which does not necessarily represent the needs of either agriculture or the consumers — and because there is no assurance that the government would ever be permitted to sell the commodities which it purchased, it appears to be unwise for the government, as a normal policy, to finance inter-seasonal stabilization operations. If such operations are attempted, they should be performed by the national coöperatives and financed with their own capital and such funds as they are able to borrow from commercial sources.[27] But although it would be wise for the government to refrain from financing inter-seasonal stabilization operations, this does not mean that the Federal Farm Board should cease helping coöperatives, by the device of supplemental loans, to make larger immediate advances to their members.[28] Nor does it mean that on rare occasions of great emergency, such as the fall of 1930, it may not be wise for the Board to protect the farmers and business

---

[27] But it should be frankly recognized that if the government gives financial assistance to the coöperatives and if a coöperative undertakes to support the price by a stabilization operation, it will be exceedingly difficult for the government to avoid becoming a participant — particularly if the coöperative has a large membership. The experience of Canada on this point is instructive. The Canadian wheat pool financed the holding of wheat in 1929, not with government funds, but with money obtained from the banks. Nevertheless, in the winter of 1930, the three prairie provinces jointly guaranteed the advances made by the banks to the wheat pool in order to prevent the banks from calling their loans and thus compelling the pool to sell its wheat.

[28] But advances up to 90 per cent of the market value are undoubtedly too large.

interests from great losses. When one contemplates the probable results to the business of the country had wheat, in the fall of 1930, been permitted to drop to 55 or 60 cents, one must conclude that the money used by the Board in supporting the market was well spent. This is true even if the wheat is never sold and the money is completely lost. But occasions which warrant action of this sort are rare.

REFERENCES

Black, J. D., *Agricultural Reform in the United States*, 1929.
Boyle, J. E., *Farm Relief*, 1928.
Davis, J. S., " The Program of the Federal Farm Board," *American Economic Review, Supplement*, March, 1931, v. XXI, pp. 104–113.
Estey, J. A., " Stabilizing Agricultural Prices," *Journal of Political Economy*, February, 1925, v. XXXIII, pp. 81–93.
Federal Farm Board, *Annual Reports*.
Stanford University, *Wheat Studies of the Food Research Institute*.
Stokdyk, E. A., and West, Charles H., *The Farm Board*, 1930.

CHAPTER XX

THE BUSINESS CYCLE

I. WHAT IS MEANT BY THE BUSINESS CYCLE. II. THE GENERAL CHARACTERISTICS OF BUSINESS CYCLES. III. THE BUSINESS CYCLE AS A SOURCE OF WASTE. IV. THE BUSINESS CYCLE AND THE LABOR PROBLEM. V. HOW WAVES IN BUSINESS ARE PRODUCED. VI. THE CONTROL OF THE BUSINESS CYCLE — STEPS WHICH SHOULD BE TAKEN DURING BOOM PERIODS. VII. THE CONTROL OF THE BUSINESS CYCLE — STEPS WHICH SHOULD BE TAKEN AT THE TIME OF THREATENED CRISIS. VIII. THE CONTROL OF THE BUSINESS CYCLE — STEPS WHICH SHOULD BE TAKEN DURING DEPRESSION.

I. What is Meant by the Business Cycle

We have said that getting a living in modern economic society is largely a process of buying and selling. But buying and selling do not proceed at an even and steady pace. On the contrary, they move in waves of boom and depression. There is no such thing as a normal state of supply and demand if by *normal* is understood *usual*. In some years, demand is brisk, jobs are plentiful, men are scarce, and prices usually are rising. Factories have orders for months ahead and are working overtime and employing night shifts. Buyers frequently must wait months for deliveries. But prosperity does not continue indefinitely. Demand declines, prices drop, men are laid off, and many weak enterprises are forced out of business. Other firms operate with greatly reduced forces and many of them only part time. But the depression does not last indefinitely. Sooner or later, demand revives, forces are enlarged, working hours are increased to full time, and prosperity returns. This constant ebb and flow of business activity, this never-ending succession of prosperity and depression, is known as the *business cycle*. From it arise many of our most important economic problems. The relations between wage earners and employers are put to severe strain, and

448

great waste is introduced into the conduct of industry. Most remarkable of all, we have the strange spectacle of men almost starving in the midst of plenty, of millions of men who lack the necessities of life walking the streets in search of work, while all about them are thousands of machines which they know how to run and which could produce the goods which they need.

It may be questioned whether we should speak of *a* business cycle for all industry or of *a multitude* of business cycles in different industries. Certainly the movements of demand, production, prices, and profits in the construction industry are very different from the movements in the banking business. And the cycles of production in agriculture differ widely from those in manufacturing. In fact, within agriculture there are many distinct commodity cycles — the cycles of hog production and prices do not have the same amplitudes as the cycles of cattle production and prices. The justification of the conception of *a* business cycle for all industry arises from the fact that most of the individual commodity cycles are partly the products of common general causes or partly produced — or at least accentuated — by each other, so that they tend to synchronize. To this generalization, however, there is an important exception. Because the output of agricultural products cannot be promptly increased or decreased, and because the period of production is determined by nature rather than by man, agricultural cycles are quite distinct both from the cycles in other branches of industry and from each other. Agriculture, no less than other branches of industry, is subject to cyclical movements, but the concept of a *general* business cycle does not fit the biological industries. We shall center our attention primarily upon the general business cycles which cause more or less simultaneous movements of demand, production, and prices in most non-agricultural industries.

II. The General Characteristics of Business Cycles

All business cycles represent a rhythmical change in the relation between supply and demand, accompanied, as a rule, by a rhythmical rise and fall in prices, and, to a less extent, by a rhythmical rise and fall in the volume of physical production. But in their detailed characteristics, business cycles vary considerably. They differ in amplitude, in intensity, and in the events which convert prosperity into depression or depression into prosperity. There is a distinction of some importance between business cycles that are accompanied by more or less violent speculation in commodities, real estate, or stocks and those in which there is relatively little speculation. The length of business cycles appears to be from two to about five years. The studies of Professor Persons show that the intervals between troughs in the curve for commodity prices from 1892 to 1914 varied from twenty-six to forty-four months, indicating that the cycle in the United States is from two to four years in length. This result is confirmed by the studies of the National Bureau of Economic Research, which found thirty-two cycles in the United States during the 127 years from 1796 to 1923 — an average length of not quite four years.[1] In other countries, the business cycle appears to be somewhat longer. In England, the Bureau found twenty-two cycles between 1793 and 1920, an average length of five and three-quarters years; in France, the average duration of fifteen cycles between 1838 and 1920 was five and a half years; in Germany, the average of fifteen cycles from 1847 to 1920 was five years.[2]

III. The Business Cycle as a Source of Waste

That the business cycle is a potent cause of waste there can be no doubt, but the amount of this waste cannot be accurately measured. It is well known, for example, that the fear of unemployment causes workmen to restrict production. But if the unemployment caused by the business cycle were substantially eliminated, would not the unemployment due to seasonal fluctuations in demand cause wage earners to restrict production almost as much as they now do? And in the case of pieceworkers, is not the tendency to hold back through fear of unemployment counteracted by the fact that during boom periods prices rise more rapidly than wage rates and that, consequently, pieceworkers apply themselves more in order to keep up with the rising cost of living? To what extent does the unemployment caused by depression more or less permanently impair the earning capacity of workmen and their families? During periods of

[1] Thorp, W. L., *Business Annals*, p. 43.   [2] *Ibid.*, pp. 45–46.

depression, many working-class families are less adequately clothed, fed, and housed than normally. Sickness is iikely to be more prevalent and to receive less adequate treatment. Lack of proper food, particularly lack of milk, permanently injures the health of many thousands of children. Wives seek work in order to supplement the meagre and uncertain earnings of husbands. This means that the children are less well cared for and often that they are exposed to bad influences. Sometimes older children must be taken from school in order to care for the younger ones because the mother is working. Often the older children leave school to work themselves. All of these things influence the immediate or future productivity of the worker and his family, but it is obviously impossible to measure their effects.

The most obvious way in which the business cycle causes waste is through the idleness of men and equipment which characterizes periods of depression. The depression of 1921, for example, is estimated by Dr. W. I. King to have caused a diminution of approximately one-sixth in the total of employment in the United States.[3] During depressions, many men work only part time. An inquiry of the Bureau of Labor Statistics during the depression of 1915 showed that, of the 647,394 workers covered, 16.1 per cent were under-employed and 11.5 per cent were totally unemployed.[4] In December, 1921, the New York State Department of Labor found that, among 300,000 workers in over 1,300 factories, 24.1 per cent were employed part time.[5]

But how much production is lost by industrial depression? If we measure the loss by the output of factories, mines, and railroads, it appears to be substantial. An average of Day's and Stewart's index numbers for the physical production of mines, factories, and railroads shows that output in 1908 was 87 per cent of that in 1907 and in 1914 was 92.8 per cent of that in 1913.[6] Dr. Stewart's index shows that production of mines, factories, and railroads in 1894 was 92.2 per cent of that in 1892.[7] In 1921, the Federal Reserve Board's index of indus-

[3] Mitchell, W. C., and others, *Business Cycles and Unemployment*, p. 6.
[4] U. S. Bureau of Labor Statistics, *Bulletin No. 195*, p. 6.
[5] New York Department of Labor, *The Industrial Bulletin*, January and February, 1922, v. I, p. 67.
[6] Computed from data given in *Business Cycles and Unemployment*, p. 36.
[7] *Ibid.*, p. 35.

trial production (which covers the output of factories and mines only) was about 23 per cent below 1920. In 1930, it was nearly 19 per cent below 1929. But if we measure the results of industrial depression by the variations in the total national income, the effect appears to be less pronounced. The following table shows the variations in industrial production and in the national income for the period 1920 to 1928:

Year	National income [8]	Industrial production
1919	100	100
1920	98	105
1921	96	81
1922	107	102
1923	120	122
1924	124	115
1925	128	125
1926	129	130
1927	141	128
1928	144	134

It will be observed that, although industrial production in 1921 was 19 per cent below 1919, the national income was only 4 per cent below. The mild depression in 1924 produced a drop of nearly 6 per cent in industrial output but no drop at all in the national income. Another mild depression in 1927 caused industrial production to drop by nearly 2 per cent, but the national income increased by 10 per cent over 1926. It is apparent that the business cycle causes a substantial loss in the output of factories and mines but that many other elements in the national income are little affected. It is important to notice, however, that the loss of production is probably greater than the statistics indicate because the drop in output during depression is largely a drop in the output of capital goods rather than in articles for consumption. Consequently the loss of output is not confined to

[8] The indexes of the national income are computed from the estimates of W. I. King in *The National Income and Its Purchasing Power*, p. 77. The national income includes goods and services of *all* kinds — the products of factories and mines and, in addition, the output of farms, railroads, and, of course, the intangible services rendered by lawyers, physicians, government employees, and others. In his estimates of the national income Dr. King includes a class of income which he designates " imputed income." It includes the services that are rendered by durable consumption goods, such as automobiles and houses. It represents the consumption of goods rather than the production of goods. For the purposes of the present comparison, it should obviously be excluded and it has been excluded in computing the indexes of national income in the table above.

the depression. Because less capital was produced during the depression, the output of industry in *all subsequent years* is less than it otherwise would have been.

The business cycle also creates waste by causing goods to be produced by inefficient methods or under disadvantageous conditions. During boom times, when demand is intense and prices are high, all plants tend to be more or less inefficient. Time is too important and costs are too unimportant, in periods of urgent demand, for adequate attention to be paid to costs. The quick rather than the most economical way is likely to be used. The rising prices and large demand of boom periods also permit many inefficient enterprises to survive longer than they otherwise would — in fact, rising prices are a subsidy to inefficiency. The high prices and large demand of boom periods also make it possible to operate old and obsolete plants which can only produce at a high cost and which would not be needed if demand were more steady.[9]

Finally, the business cycle prevents the attainment of the highest operating efficiency because it makes business success depend only to a limited extent upon low costs and to a large extent upon skill in buying, selling, and extending credit, upon abundance of capital, and upon financial connections. The enterprise which stocks up when prices are low and sells before they drop, which extends credit liberally enough to make large sales but not so liberally as to acquire bad debts, which has enough capital to avoid forced sales when prices are low — such an enterprise is likely to survive and prosper in competition with concerns which have lower costs but less skillfully managed purchasing, sales, and credit departments, and smaller financial resources. On the other hand, a firm with low operating costs may be destroyed because it extends credit unwisely, purchases too heavily at high prices, or, through lack of capital or of financial connections, cannot obtain funds with which to meet its obligations during the periods of liquidation. And because so much

[9] The question may be asked, " But if there are enough laborers to operate these plants, why should they not be operated? If they were not operated, not only the old plants but also many workers would be idle and the community would have less goods."

There is some merit in this argument, for old and obsolete plants sometimes do give employment to men who could not otherwise obtain it. To a substantial extent, however, they merely take away part of the labor supply from the better equipped plants and thus prevent men from working under the most advantageous conditions.

is gained or lost by purchasing, selling, extending credit, or borrowing wisely or unwisely, business heads are compelled to concentrate attention upon these matters, often to the neglect of production problems, and to hire many able and expensive men to supervise sales, purchases, credit, and finance — men who, under more stable conditions, might be available to study problems of reducing the costs of production.

IV. THE BUSINESS CYCLE AND THE LABOR PROBLEM

If the severity of the business cycle could be substantially diminished, one of the greatest obstacles to amicable relations between wage earners and employers would be removed. The business cycle generates friction in several ways. It disturbs the relative bargaining power of capital and labor. In boom periods, when good men are scarce, labor takes advantage of its bargaining position and compels employers to grant demands which they consider unfair. This arouses their resentment and they wait for the first opportunity to retaliate. When depression comes, they organize open-shop campaigns and seek to destroy unionism. They go to extremes, as did the unions in periods of prosperity, and, like the unions, they arouse intense bitterness and antagonism.

When depression occurs, wholesale prices decline far more than the cost of living. But many of the large fixed costs of business enterprises go on without change. This combination of circumstances inevitably subjects industrial relations to intense strain. Suppose that the price at which an enterprise sells its product drops from $1.00 to 70 cents, the annual volume of sales from 1,000,000 to 850,000 units, and fixed costs from $500,000 to $450,000. The balance of income over and above fixed costs decreases more than two-thirds — from $500,000 a year to $145,000. Naturally the management feels that drastic wage cuts are needed. But because the cost of living remains little changed and because employment is slack, the wage earner sees no justice in wage cuts. The conflict of interests is especially acute when some plants in an industry are unionized and others are not. In times of depression, the non-union concerns have a great advantage in the struggle for business. They can cut wages at once, but union plants are bound by trade agreements which run for a stipulated period. When these agreements expire in periods of depression, the employers may feel compelled to insist on drastic cuts. It is noteworthy that the great coal strike of 1922 was due to the refusal of the coal operators of western Pennsylvania and southern Ohio to meet the union officials and negotiate a new agreement. These operators, hard hit by the competition of the near-by non-union mines in West Virginia and Kentucky, felt that substantial wage cuts were essential. They feared that the operators of Indiana and Illinois, who were less affected by the non-union competition, would not insist on sufficient reduction. Hence, in violation of the terms of the agreement which expired on March 31, 1922, the western Pennsylvania and southern Ohio operators refused to attend an interstate conference to negotiate a new agreement.

V. How Waves in Business Are Produced

In accounting for the existence of business cycles, it is important to keep very clearly in mind precisely what we have to explain. *It is an oscillating relationship between supply and demand.* For a time, demand is large relative to supply and prices tend to rise. Sooner or later, the situation changes; supply grows relative to demand, and prices fall.

Since the business cycle represents an oscillating relationship between supply and demand, it can occur on a comprehensive scale only in a society where buying and selling constitute a central feature of economic activity. But in an exchange system such as ours, where most men gain their living by buying and selling, the rate of production depends, within certain physical limits, upon how rapidly men spend money and upon how much they have to spend. Any conjunction of events which creates widespread optimism accelerates spending and consequently production — particularly in view of the fact that the credit system permits men to obtain additional dollars in great volume almost overnight. On the contrary, any conjunction of events which creates widespread pessimism or even uncertainty or caution slows up the rate of spending and produces a drop in production, which in turn produces a still further drop in the rate of spending. In other words, when the rate of production depends so largely upon the rate at which men spend money, it is inevitable

that there will be pronounced fluctuations in industrial activity —
boom periods, when for one reason or another both business
enterprises and consumers are willing to spend freely, and depressions, when for various other reasons business enterprises
are cautious about making commitments and consumers are inclined to conserve their cash.   Precisely because there are so
many ways in which spending may be encouraged or discouraged,
it is exceedingly difficult (and probably misleading) to formulate
a theory of the business cycle — that is, a theory which attributes
the waves in business to one particular cause to the exclusion
of others.

But although *any* changes in the flow of events which produce
variations in the willingness to spend money are bound to produce booms and depressions in an exchange economy, there are
several specific types of economic behavior which cause rhythmical fluctuations in production and prices.   In addition, there are
certain characteristics in our economic system which tend to make
an increase or a decrease in the volume of spending cumulative for
a time, but also self-limiting.   Because of these limiting factors,
each movement tends eventually to produce its opposite — an acceleration of spending tends to produce conditions which later
diminish spending, and vice versa.   It is apparently these limiting
factors in the economic system which explain why cycles rarely
exceed five years in length.   Did limiting factors not exist, business cycles would undoubtedly be far more variable in length —
a boom might continue for ten or fifteen years and be followed
by a depression equally long.   Let us first examine two of the
types of behavior which produce rhythmical fluctuations in output and prices.   Then we shall endeavor to follow in some detail
the course of the business cycle in order to understand what conditions limit both the expansion and the contraction of business
activity.

Rhythmical fluctuations in production and prices are bound
to result when producers are guided in expanding and contracting
output by *present* prices and profits rather than *prospective* prices
and profits (or by too short a view of prospective prices and
profits).   Under these circumstances, producers invariably over-
step themselves in adjusting output to changes in demand.   Sup-

pose, for example, that automobile tires are selling at $20 apiece and that this is exactly enough to pay the current rate of return on capital in the industry. The demand then increases beyond the capacity of existing plants. Naturally the price rises and tire manufacturing becomes unusually profitable. New plants are built and old ones are enlarged. But it takes some months to create the additional productive capacity. Consequently the price of tires does not immediately drop. This gives other business men an opportunity to decide that it would be profitable to enter the tire business. *If the adjustment of output to the increase in demand only takes long enough,* the capacity of the industry is bound to be increased so much that the output cannot be sold at $20. The reason simply is that business men, *according to hypothesis,* are being guided in building plants by *present* prices and profits rather than *prospective* prices and profits. Consequently, as long as the price remains above $20, the construction of new plants will be *started.* By the time the last new plant is *completed,* the price will have fallen below $20. As long as the price remains below $20, new plants will not be built and old ones will not be enlarged. But the price will not remain below $20 indefinitely. As the number of automobiles increases, the demand for tires will steadily grow. Eventually the price will rise, first to $20 and finally to more than $20. Then the cycle of new construction and over-development will begin anew.

Rhythmical fluctuations in production and prices may be created also by a tendency to engage in speculative buying and selling. Suppose that the price of a commodity advances. Business men may assume that, because the price has advanced a little, it will advance still more. In order to avoid paying the higher price or in order to make a profit from the increase in price, they purchase beyond their immediate needs or purchase for the purpose of selling when the price has risen. The expansion in demand causes the price to continue rising and stimulates more speculative buying. The increase in the demand means: (1) that eventually demand is likely to *decrease* because some business men have purchased today the goods which they otherwise would have purchased tomorrow, and (2) that eventually supply is likely to *increase* because some purchasers have been buying only for the purpose of making speculative sales.

Sooner or later, therefore, the price is likely to drop and, when it does, it will drop below the original point because the demand for the commodity will be unusually small and the supply will be unusually large. After the enterprises which purchased in advance of their immediate needs have exhausted their surplus stocks and after speculators have sold their supplies, the price will begin to rise and, as it does, it will set in motion again the speculative purchasing which will first raise the price and later cause it to fall.

The severity of business cycles is greatly accentuated by certain features of our modern economy, particularly the credit system and the nature of modern industrial costs. It is probable, however, that business cycles are, in the main, merely somewhat complicated manifestations of the two rather simple causes of rhythmical price fluctuations that we have just discussed: (1) a tendency of producers to be guided by present prices and profits or by too short a view of prospective prices and profits, coupled with inability to adjust supply immediately to changes in demand, and (2) a tendency to engage in speculative buying and selling.

Every business cycle is more or less unique. The conjunction of events which creates optimism and stimulates spending is never precisely the same. Neither is the combination of circumstances which causes a breakdown of prosperity. The boom which culminated in 1920, for example, was characterized by extraordinarily heavy speculation in inventories. The heavy inventories were in large degree responsible for the severity of the subsequent depression. Recovery from the depression of 1920 and 1921 was accelerated by the revival of the demand for building, which had not kept pace with needs during the war period, and by the demand for automobiles. To a large extent, the expansion in demand was made possible by the spread of installment buying. The depression of 1924 was arrested in the United States by a sudden improvement in the purchasing power of American farmers due to the fact that we had a large wheat crop in a year of a small world crop. The boom which culminated in 1929 was marked by almost no speculative accumulation of inventories. The drop in the demand for housing and automobiles, however, was in large degree responsible for the end of the boom. Although there was no widespread speculation for a rise in commodity prices, the stocks of some raw materials, such as wheat, sugar, cotton, coffee, and rubber, which had been greatly overproduced, were large, and the depression, when it came, was greatly intensified by the sharp drop in the prices of these and other goods. The boom period was also characterized by enormous speculation in securities. The spending of paper profits made in stock speculation undoubtedly accentuated the boom, and the crash in security prices, which followed the recession in business, accentuated the depression.

But despite the fact that no two cycles are precisely alike, it is possible to trace in rather broad outline the process by which depression becomes prosperity and by which prosperity in turn becomes depression. With the warning that the sequence of events is never precisely the same, let us examine the course of the business cycle and attempt to understand why depression sooner or later develops into prosperity and why prosperity sooner or later develops into depression.

We shall begin by asking how depression becomes prosperity. The essential features of a depression are that large quantities of goods are offered for sale at low prices but that, even at these prices, demand is not large. This means that the production of goods is relatively small, that business concerns are operating at only part capacity, and that thousands of men are unemployed. The principal reason for the general eagerness to sell and the reluctance to buy is the fact that most commodity prices are falling. The explanation of why they started to fall must be postponed until we analyze how prosperity changes to depression. Once prices start falling, however, sellers become anxious to sell their goods before prices drop lower and buyers become disposed to delay purchasing as long as possible.

But falling prices are not the only reason for the general eagerness to sell and reluctance to buy. It often happens that during the periods of prosperity many enterprises seek to profit from the advancing prices by buying in anticipation of their immediate needs. The beginning of the depression, therefore, is likely to find jobbers and retailers with unusually large stocks of finished goods, and manufacturers with large supplies of raw materials.[10]   These large stocks of commodities increase the intensity of the depression by increasing the supply of goods offered for sale and by diminishing the demand for goods. Retailers who stocked up heavily are eager to sell to consumers but do not need to buy from jobbers; and jobbers who stocked up heavily are anxious to sell to retailers but do not need to purchase from manufacturers.

The speculative purchasing of goods during times of rising prices is largely done with borrowed money, and the necessity of repaying this money increases the eagerness to sell.   But the indebtedness incurred during prosperity also diminishes the demand for goods.   It does this in two ways.   In the first place, the drop in prices and sales causes many enterprises to experience difficulty in meeting their debts when due.   In order to escape bankruptcy, they must apply every dollar which they can obtain in paying their obligations.   This in many cases means postponing much-needed repairs and replacements and hence diminishes the demand for labor and materials.   In the second place, the payment of the debts contracted during the boom period tends to diminish the demand for goods by reducing the amount of money in active circulation.   The money was borrowed in the main from banks and, when the debts are paid, the money goes back to the banks.   If it were immediately lent again, it would help purchase goods and thus sustain demand.   Despite low interest rates, however, the banks cannot lend all of the money which they receive. Business establishments are producing on too small a scale to need all the money that the banks can lend.   Some of it is invested by the banks in bonds, but part of it remains idle and buys no goods.

If all expenses were direct, prices could remain below costs only until the existing stocks of goods were exhausted.   But we have already learned that enterprises which have large fixed costs are likely to cut prices whenever they have idle producing capacity.   During the depression, however, idle producing capacity is almost universal.   For this reason, prices may remain below

---

[10] It is one of the characteristics of the business cycle that it plays tricks with our vision.   In boom periods, inventories do not seem excessive although, when considered in relation to demand over a period of years, they may be far too large; in depression, on the other hand, inventories seem more excessive than they really are.   Particularly at the beginning of depression do they seem discouragingly large.

costs long after existing stocks of goods have been sold. The prolonged and drastic price cutting for which fixed costs are partly responsible keeps down profits, discourages enterprise, and accentuates the severity of the depression.

The drop in the demand for goods means that the demand for labor is less and that many workers are laid off or receive only part-time employment. An unemployed man, however, is a poor customer. He spends his money more slowly and thus diminishes the total volume of spending and the demand for goods by reducing the times each dollar is spent in the course of a year. The larger the number of men who are laid off, the smaller the demand for goods and the greater, in turn, the number of men who lose their jobs. The existence of severe unemployment also affects men who have not lost their jobs, for they fear that they too may soon be without work. Consequently, they do not spend their money so freely as formerly but save part of it against a possible period of unemployment.[11]

What puts an end to this seemingly hopeless situation, in which everyone wishes to sell but is reluctant or unable to buy? The postponement of purchasing does not continue indefinitely. Many persons have reduced their expenditures drastically

[11] But what do they do with their money when they save it? Some of them hoard it, which means that it is temporarily withdrawn from circulation. Others who have checking accounts — and not a few workmen now have — deposit it in commercial banks where in many cases it lies idle because the bank has more money than it can lend. During every period of depression, the commercial banks gain large quantities of cash which, as long as business remains slack, they are unable to lend. Or the bank may invest the money in bonds. But, in this event, is the total demand for goods diminished by the saving of the money? Will not the company which issued the bonds use the proceeds to demand goods? Is not the essential effect simply that the money is spent by the firm which sold the bonds rather than by the workman who earned it? In other words, is not the total demand for goods unaffected?

In many cases it will be true that the money which the workman saved is used to buy new equipment by the company which sold the bonds. But there are also many cases in which the savings banks purchase, not new issues which are being offered to enable some enterprise to purchase new equipment, but old issues which are being sold by investors who incurred heavy debts when prices were rising and who are now forced to sell their bonds in order to meet their debts. Especially during periods of depression — when few enterprises are expanding their plants and when there are not many new bond issues, but when many debtors are selling their high-grade securities in order to meet their obligations — are the savings banks likely to purchase old instead of new security issues. And this means that the savings of the workman may be used, not to increase the present demand for goods, but to pay some one's debts.

for a time because they have feared unemployment or cuts in the dividends on their investments. But as time goes on, it becomes necessary to replace shoes, clothing, and automobiles. Likewise business enterprises find it impossible to delay longer in making many replacements — railroads can postpone replacing ties and rails for a year or two, but not indefinitely, factories find that certain machines must at last be scrapped, many concerns discover that it would be wasteful to delay longer about repairing or re-painting buildings and equipment. All of this expenditure for repairs and replacements increases the demand for commodities and labor. Many firms would have made repairs and replace-ments sooner, had it not been necessary to apply every available dollar to paying large debts which they incurred during the boom period.

Most business enterprises are more or less constantly study-ing how to improve their products and their methods of produc-tion. This, of course, is necessary in order to keep abreast with competition. But under modern methods of machine production a change in the product or in the methods of operation is likely to be expensive. It often involves discarding expensive dies, jigs, fixtures, and templets, the making of new ones, changing the location of some machines, and possibly the purchase of some new equipment. All of this is not only costly in itself but it interferes temporarily with production. And after the changes have been made, several weeks or months must elapse before the plant is again running smoothly. For all of these reasons it does not usually pay to introduce each improvement in product or proc-esses as soon as it is discovered. It is more profitable to permit the discoveries to accumulate for a year or two and then to apply a number of them simultaneously. How long it pays to delay depends largely upon the competitive situation. If a plant is so busy that it is having a hard time to fill its orders promptly, not only are changes in the product or in methods of operation un-necessary for the time being but they are likely to be disadvan-tageous because they would make it more difficult to fill orders promptly. Consequently, boom periods are times when enter-prises are likely to accumulate a large number of unapplied ideas (more or less completely worked out) for improving their wares and operating practices. When depression comes, managers have time and opportunity to put these ideas into practice without interfering too much with the filling of current orders. Moreover, business conditions make it imperative that everything possible be done to give buyers a better commodity at a lower price. Most enterprises are not likely to go to great expense to redesign their products and to change their methods of operation until they have substantially reduced the heavy floating indebtedness with which they usually enter a period of depression. But after debts have been reduced, managers feel safe in spending some money on new dies, jigs, fixtures, templets, and machines and making changes in their plants to cut the cost of operation. This increases the demand for labor and materials and assists in producing a revival in business.

Of particular importance is the exhaustion of the large stocks which retailers, jobbers, and manufacturers often accumulate during prosperity. When the retailer's stock is nearly exhausted, he can no longer postpone ordering from the jobber; when the jobber's stock is low, he can no longer postpone ordering from the manufacturer; and when the manufacturer has nearly consumed his supply of raw materials, he can no longer delay ordering from the producers of raw materials.

All of these sources of greater demand mean that more men are being put to work and this, of course, means a further increase in demand, for employed men spend more than unemployed. As enterprises cease laying off labor and begin slowly to increase their forces and to restore part-time men to full time, the workers feel less need of hoarding or of saving money to provide against unemployment. In fact, they begin to spend some of the money which they hoarded or saved earlier in the depression. Eventually, demand is likely to be reënforced by a revival of new construction. Conditions are exceptionally favorable for economical building. Raw materials and labor are cheap, contractors have the pick of the most efficient workers, the small demand for capital makes it possible to borrow at exceptionally low rates of interest. These conditions lead some concerns, especially those which possess good credit and which occupy a secure position in the market, to build in advance of their immediate needs.

Once the recovery from depression gets well under way, it is likely to develop rapidly into prosperity, for every increase in demand means more profits for investors and more employment for wage earners, and these in turn mean a further increase in demand.[12] There are, however, several influences in the development of prosperity which deserve special mention. One is the tendency of enterprises to increase their stocks of raw materials and repair parts. As long as prices are falling or unsteady, many concerns, in order to avoid losses from a drop in prices, endeavor to get along with inventories which are inconveniently small from the standpoint of operating efficiency. As soon as the danger of a drop in prices appears to be over, these concerns increase their supplies of raw materials and replacement parts. *This increase is not to be confused with the speculative accumulation of inventories which often occurs later in the business cycle.* It is merely an increase based on considerations of operating efficiency, but it brings about a perceptible expansion in the demand for goods. Another important influence in the development of prosperity is the growing demand for equipment. We are familiar with the fact that fixed costs cause small changes in output to produce large changes in profits. As the output of business establishments gradually grows, their profits mount rapidly. This sends a feeling of optimism throughout the business world. Many enterprises prepare to handle a larger demand. The construction of new plants or the enlargement of old ones is stimulated.

If the expansion of business continues long enough without interruption, prices will eventually rise. It is *possible,* however, for a boom to occur and to run its course on falling prices. Dr. W. M. Persons has called attention to two such instances — the periods 1886–1892 and 1925–1926.[13] The essential thing

---

[12] The development of prosperity may be accelerated by various events. It is hastened by anything that gives business men confidence in the future and makes them ready to buy in anticipation of future orders or to enlarge their plants. A pronounced bull market on the stock exchange may help because the stock market is regarded — possibly somewhat superstitiously — as a barometer of business. And a bull market may occur just when it will do the most good — early in the period of revival — for the banks have plenty of money which they are willing to lend at very low rates, and business men have paid the debts which they incurred during the last period of prosperity and have got over the fears which obsessed them during the early phases of the depression when falling prices threatened everyone with insolvency.

[13] *Review of Economic Statistics,* January, 1928, v. IX, pp. 27–28.

is that profits increase, and this may be made possible, despite falling prices, by technical progress and the expansion of physical output. In most instances, however, the boom is accompanied by a rise in prices. It might be expected that this rise would begin when the orders in sight closely approximate industry's capacity to produce. It might be expected that the heavy fixed costs of modern industry would prevent the rise from beginning earlier. As a matter of fact, however, the rise apparently does begin even when industry has much idle productive capacity. The immediate movement of prices appears to depend less upon the relationship between demand and productive capacity of industry than it does *upon the relationship between orders received and the stock of raw material on hand.* When, as a result of the revival of business, orders increase with unexpected rapidity, enterprises suddenly find their stocks of raw materials inadequate, and raw materials must be replenished quickly or the delivery of orders will be delayed and the good will of customers impaired. Possibly accounts will be lost. To avoid these results, enterprises pay premiums for prompt delivery of raw materials. When the underestimation of demand has occurred on a wide scale and many concerns in a variety of industries are bidding actively for goods, there begins a general rise in prices. Of course, if business men had judged the future more accurately, the revival of business would have started more promptly and without producing a rise in prices — or, at least, without producing so much of a rise. The rise which starts speculative buying and the exaggerated optimism of the boom is made possible by the unduly pessimistic judgments of business men during depression.

When the increase in prices becomes general, the demand for goods is likely to be heavily reënforced from two sources. The construction of new plants may increase more rapidly than ever and business men, eager to meet their future need for goods before prices advance further, are likely to place orders far beyond their immediate needs. They are able to do this, we have learned, largely because the banks are able to create millions of credit dollars for them overnight. Once speculative buying gets well started, it is sustained for some time by its own momentum, every increase in price encouraging business enterprises to buy heavily in anticipation of further increases, and this heavy buying itself producing the expected increases in prices.

What brings the boom to an end? Why does it not continue indefinitely? What essentially happens is that the demand for goods decreases, relative to the supply of them, but the precise process by which this occurs varies considerably.

One of the earliest causes for an increase in the supply of goods is the output of the new plants which began to be constructed on a substantial scale when demand began to outrun the existing capacity of industry. Six months to several years are required to complete most plants. When new plants come into operation in large numbers, the rate at which prices increase is likely to be moderated.

Simultaneously with the increase in the power of industry to supply goods, there occur a number of changes which affect the demand for goods. Mounting costs of production gradually narrow the margin of profits. The expense of selling, it is true, may diminish somewhat in boom periods and thus help for a time to preserve the margin between costs and prices. Most costs, however, increase. For this there are several reasons. As long as enterprises had idle capacity, an increase in output meant substantial reductions in fixed costs per unit of product and, therefore, in total unit costs. But after the capacity of the plant has been reached, little or no net gain is achieved by still greater production. To obtain additional output, it may be necessary to work men overtime at high overtime rates, to have some operations done outside the plant at a high cost, or to crowd in additional machines at points where they would not normally be placed and where they more or less disturb the flow of work through the shop. About the time that the decrease in fixed costs stops, direct costs begin to rise. In the early phases of prosperity, wages were more or less stationary, for there were still many men unemployed. But when labor becomes fairly well employed, wages begin to rise and the efficiency of men who are not paid by the piece to fall. This is partly because workers know that jobs are easy to obtain and partly because this knowledge greatly increases the turnover of labor, which in itself reduces the efficiency of the workers.

Other operating expenses go up also. The cost of borrowing money advances. The higher level of prices and the large physical volume of business increase the demand for loans. At the same time, the higher prices and the increase in borrowing cause the banks to lose cash to the rest of the country and thus diminish their reserves. Consider, for example, the effect on the banks when an enterprise borrows $15,000, instead of $10,000, to meet its payroll. The money is possibly withdrawn from the bank on Friday morning. The men receive it in their pay envelopes Friday night. They (or their wives) spend it at the stores and the stores deposit it again in the banks. By Tuesday afternoon most of the $15,000 may be back in the banks. In the meantime, however, the banks have been without $15,000 instead of $10,-000 and their power to lend has been just so much less. With the demand for credit increasing and their supply of cash decreasing, naturally the banks raise their discount rates. More important than the greater cost of loans are the rising prices of raw materials, which usually advance more than do finished products. The explanation of this is partly found in speculative buying. Suppose that the customers of a manufacturer buy 10 per cent beyond their immediate needs and that the manufacturer, in turn, buys raw material 10 per cent beyond his immediate needs. Then, instead of selling at the rate of 100 and purchasing raw material at the rate of 100, he will sell at the rate of 110 and buy raw material at the rate of 121. Under these conditions it is to be expected that raw materials will advance in price more rapidly than finished commodities. Finally, costs rise because, when enterprises have more orders than they can fill promptly, they deliberately sacrifice economy to speed. The situation is aggravated by the necessity of stopping work on the orders of small and unimportant customers in order to placate large buyers who threaten to withdraw their business unless given immediate delivery. This disorganization of production increases the expense of filling both the large and the small orders.

What is the effect of rising costs and the narrowing margin of profits on the demand for goods? For one thing, it discourages the building of new productive capacity because, even though the demand for goods is strong and profits are still large, many business men hesitate to enlarge their plants after the rate of profit shows a tendency to drop. New construction is also discouraged by the high prices of labor and material and the high interest rates on capital. It is easy to see why the demand for buildings and equipment should be greatly affected by high construction costs and high interest rates. Suppose that, because of the high cost of labor and material, a building will cost $100,-000 instead of $80,000, and that the money will cost 7 per cent instead of 6. Assuming that the building has a life of twenty years, the annual depreciation charge will be $5,000 instead of $4,000 and the annual interest charge $7,000 instead of $4,800, making a total for the two of $12,000 instead of $8,800. In other words, an increase of one-fourth in the cost of construction and of one-sixth in the rate of interest increases annual depreciation and interest charges *by over one-third*. If this increase were only for a year or two, it might not be serious, *but the extra cost lasts for the life of the building.* Some enterprises, it is true, seek to avoid committing themselves to the payment of high interest rates over long periods by issuing short-term notes to meet their financial needs when interest rates are high. It is expected that, when interest rates are lower, the notes will be refunded by an issue of long-term bonds. This procedure, however, is a risky one for concerns which do not possess excellent credit standing because, at the time when the short-term notes mature, market conditions may make it difficult to float new loans.

Rising costs and declining profits also affect speculative buying which, we have seen, often characterizes boom periods. This buying is a product of optimism, which, in turn, is largely the product of rising prices and large profits. As prices advance more gradually and as profits tend to fall, the optimism of business men is tempered. They do not necessarily cease buying in advance of their needs, but they purchase more cautiously and on a more moderate scale. If the speculative piling up of inventories is not checked by the caution of business men, it will sooner or later be checked by their inability to obtain additional credit from the banks. Notice, however, that a decrease in the extent of forward buying — say from 10 per cent above immediate requirements to 5 per cent — *means an absolute decrease in demand.*

These four conditions — the increase in supply as new productive capacity comes into operation, the tempering of optimism as rising costs catch up with selling prices, the decline in new construction, and the check to speculative buying — all pave the way for the end of prosperity. But the end may be precipitated by an accidental event. Since the demand for goods rests largely upon the expectation that prices will go higher, anything which destroys this confidence will bring about a collapse in the demand for goods, a more or less precipitous drop in prices, and general business stagnation. A crop failure, an election which is regarded unfavorably by business men, the outbreak of a war, may shatter confidence in the immediate future of business. The effect is to check the increase in demand and to cause a rush to sell the accumulated stocks of goods before prices fall — with the result that there is a sudden and precipitous drop in prices.

The collapse of the boom may be precipitated by a slump in the stock market. Such a slump is likely to occur at this stage of the business cycle. The value of a stock depends upon the profits of the enterprise and the current rate of interest. When the current rate of interest is 5 per cent, a security which has the prospect of paying five dollars a year is worth $100, but if the prevailing rate of interest rises to 6 per cent, then a security which pays five dollars becomes worth only $83.33. We have already learned that, late in the period of prosperity, interest rates are rising and rising costs are lowering the profits of business enterprises. Both of these changes tend to diminish the value of stocks. In addition, the speculative demand for securities tends to be checked by rising interest rates.[14]

How does a drop in stock prices tend to bring about a collapse of prosperity? For one thing, stock prices are commonly regarded as a barometer of business. A sudden and substantial drop may shatter the confidence of business men and start the liquidation of inventories. More than this, however, a slump

[14] It is interesting to notice, however, that the slackening of business in 1927 was not forecast by the stock market. On the contrary, there occurred the remarkable spectacle of a boom in stocks at a time when business profits were declining. The monthly average of 337 industrial stocks was 17.6 per cent above 1926, but profits, as measured by the returns of 574 industrials, were nearly 8 per cent below 1926. New York Federal Reserve Bank, *Monthly Review*, April, 1929, p. 29. Stock prices, however, reflect expected future profits as well as present profits, and in 1928 the profits of these 574 industrials were 15 per cent above 1926.

in stock prices diminishes the demand for goods because it inflicts heavy losses upon thousands of speculators who have been carrying stocks on margin and who are compelled to sell at a loss. Speculators who sold " short " just before or during the decline profit from the drop, but the gains of the " bears " are usually a small fraction of the losses of the " bulls." The result is that thousands of persons, who were planning to buy new automobiles, homes, or what not and who *would* have bought these things if stock prices had not fallen, do not do so and industry finds the demand for goods restricted.[15]

But if prosperity is not terminated by an untoward event, such as a crop failure, an unfavorable election, or a slump in the stock market, an end is bound to come simply as a result of the natural development of the business situation itself. As large quantities of goods are thrown on the market by newly constructed plants, as narrowing profit margins diminish demand by discouraging new construction and speculative buying, and as banks become more cautious in extending credit, some prices rise at a slower rate and others begin to fall. Business men begin to suspect that the peak of prices is close at hand. Speculative buying ceases, many enterprises begin to dispose of their accumulated stocks, and the fall in prices spreads to more and more commodities.

Once started, the general fall in prices continues of its own momentum because the expectation that commodity prices will be lower tomorrow causes buyers to postpone purchasing and makes sellers eager to dispose of their goods at once. The conversion of goods into cash may go on gradually without a violent drop in prices or it may develop into a mad stampede to sell at any amount — a *crisis,* as it is called. In either case, the general drop in prices is bound to result in general industrial stagnation,

---

[15] It may be replied, however, that if a stock drops from $150 to $100, the person who is able to buy it at $100 instead of $150 has just so much more to spend for other things. The seller, of course, has less to spend but his loss is counteracted by the buyer's saving. Hence, it may be argued that there is no *net* shrinkage in industry's market at all. This reasoning would be sound if all securities were purchased out of income. To a large extent, however, stocks are purchased with borrowed money. This is especially true of those purchased by speculators. A drop in the prices of stocks, therefore, means, not that the purchasers have more to spend for other things, but that they borrow less heavily from the banks. It means, in other words, that the banks are being called upon to create fewer of the credit dollars with which the general demand for goods is financed.

for, when every prospective buyer is waiting for prices to fall, business concerns have few orders and thousands of men are thrown out of work, reducing the purchasing power of the community, and accentuating the depression. Thus we find ourselves back at the point where we began, with prices falling, everyone eager to sell and reluctant to buy, thousands of men walking the streets in search of work, and business enterprises having difficulty to make enough money to pay their indebtedness as it falls due.

VI. The Control of the Business Cycle — Steps Which Should Be Taken during Boom Periods

At our present stage of economic knowledge, we can scarcely hope to manage industry so as entirely to avoid recurring periods of depression. But it may be possible to diminish greatly the intensity of depressions and to reduce the number of crises, which frequently mark the collapse of prosperity — possibly to eliminate crises altogether. In discussing ways and means, it is convenient to distinguish what can be done during periods of prosperity, what at times of threatening crisis, and what during depression.

The most important preventive steps must be taken during prosperity, when business enterprises have plenty of orders and when no one is worrying about hard times. This is one reason why crises and depressions are so difficult to prevent — because the principal steps must be taken so far in advance. During the boom period, two principal things should be done: (1) business men should be discouraged from bidding up the prices of goods higher than the demand for them warrants or from producing more than can be sold at profitable prices; (2) enterprises should be discouraged from building up large stocks of goods — large inventories, the business man calls them — with the intention of selling them later when prices have advanced.

Our analysis of the course of the business cycle makes it plain why these two steps would reduce the intensity of depressions. If production is adjusted to the long-run trend in demand and if prices are not bid up too high, a temporary recession in demand for any cause will not bring such a precipitous drop in prices. If the fall in prices is less precipitous, the postponement of buying, which is so largely responsible for crises and for general business stagnation, will be diminished. Fewer men will be laid off, the incomes of business concerns will decline less, and the willingness and ability of both wage earners and business owners to demand goods will be less seriously impaired. Furthermore, as most goods are bought with borrowed money, checking the rise of prices during prosperity means that a smaller volume of indebtedness must be paid off during depression. This, combined with the fact that the drop in prices is less, means that enterprises can pay their debts more easily and need not, therefore, reduce their demand for labor and material by postponing repairs and replacements which should be promptly made.

Checking the speculative accumulation of goods during boom periods also diminishes the intensity of the subsequent depression because it means that, when prices begin to fall, enterprises have a smaller supply of goods to sell. And having smaller debts to pay off, they are under less necessity of selling at once for any price and of skimping on repairs and maintenance. Finally, the duration of the depression is shortened because, the smaller the hoards of goods in the warehouses when the depression begins, the sooner must men be put back to work in order to meet the current demand for goods.[16]

In checking the rise in prices and the speculative accumulation of inventories, reliance should not be placed upon any

[16] The reader may wonder whether the *net* gain from checking the accumulation of inventories during boom periods will not be slight. If enterprises build up smaller inventories during prosperity, will there not be a smaller production of goods then, smaller demand for labor, and consequently less employment? By reducing the speculative hoarding of goods during prosperity, are we not merely transferring unemployment from one part of the business cycle to another? It must be confessed that to some extent this result may occur. But it is a gain for both business concerns and wage earners, instead of working overtime one year and only half time the next, to have demand spread out more or less evenly from year to year. And it is quite certain that if there is a decrease in the employment of men and machines during prosperity, it will be much less than the gain in employment during depression. The reason is not hard to understand. One effect of the accumulation of inventories, we have seen, is to raise prices. But the higher the prices of goods, the smaller the quantities which consumers are able to buy. To the extent that checking the hoarding of goods also checks the tendency for prices to rise, it enables purchasers to buy more goods and thus creates a demand for labor. Limiting the accumulation of inventories means that men and machines may be less employed in making goods which will be stored away in warehouses and on retailers' shelves, but it means that they will be more employed in making goods for immediate use.

single method. The methods which are likely to be most useful are: (1) the publication of more adequate market statistics; (2) the use of indexes of general business conditions — business barometers, as they are sometimes called; (3) the warnings of banks; (4) the wider use of trade acceptances instead of promissory notes in the extension of credit; (5) the influence of the Federal Reserve system.

The tendency of business men to judge the immediate future by the immediate past and to assume that, because sales and profits have been growing, they will continue to grow, and the willingness of business men to bid up prices higher than the demand warrants and to accumulate dangerously large stocks of goods are partly attributable to the lack of easily available and readily understandable market information. If they knew definitely the rate of production in the industry, the amount of productive capacity under construction, the supply of goods in the possession of retailers, wholesalers, and manufacturers, the volume of unfilled orders, and the rate of consumption, many business men would hesitate to bid up prices as high as they do or to build up such large inventories. It has been pointed out that the Federal Reserve Banks, the Department of Commerce, and many trade associations are gathering and distributing statistics on the market situation in many industries, but the information needs to be made more complete and accurate and additional industries need to be covered. The figures on the stocks of goods on hand, for example, are seriously incomplete. A grave lack is the absence of satisfactory figures on the rate of ultimate consumption. Of considerable value would be more complete and prompt reports of business profits. Many enterprises publish their profits only once a year and many others only twice a year. Reports should be issued not less than four times a year, and monthly reports, such as the railroads make to the Interstate Commerce Commission, would be highly desirable. Frequent reports of profits are needed, not only to indicate the trend of business, but also to prevent the prices of securities from getting out of line with the earnings of business enterprises. The losses which speculators suffer when the market collapses at the end of a boom period tend to intensify the subsequent depression. Up-to·

date information concerning profits will not necessarily prevent security prices from rising too high or falling too low, but speculative excesses are likely to be less pronounced when trading is based upon reliable information.

The figures which relate to specific industries — statistics on stocks of goods, output, productive capacity under construction — throw light in the main upon the prospective *supply* of goods. The *demand* for goods depends largely upon the general business situation. Furthermore, it is not always possible to obtain complete and accurate information concerning the volume of production, the size of inventories, and the amount of unfilled orders in different industries. Even when this information can be obtained, it is several months old before it is published and usually it cannot be gathered more frequently than once a month. Consequently, it is helpful for business men to have figures which throw light upon the *general* business situation — especially figures which can be gathered and distributed promptly and at weekly intervals. Such statistics are represented by freight car loadings, debits to checking accounts, electric power consumption.[17] Several attempts have recently been made to construct averages of highly sensitive prices, the assumption being that changes in these averages will forecast changes in the general price level. It is still too early to estimate the value of these averages.

The collection and the interpretation of data which throw

[17] The Department of Commerce, in its *Weekly Supplement of the Survey of Current Business*, publishes a compilation of the most significant business indicators for which weekly figures are available. Among the items included are: Fisher's index of sensitive prices, debits to individual accounts, freight car loadings, steel plant operations, building contracts, bituminous coal production, lumber production, bank loans and discounts, interest rates (call money), interest rates (time money), stock prices, bond prices, composite index of iron and steel prices, price of No. 2 wheat, price of middling cotton, business failures.

Among the monthly indexes published in the United States which shed light on the general business situation are: the level of wholesale prices, the volume of industrial production, the volume of factory employment, the volume of factory payrolls, the volume of wholesale trade, the volume of retail sales, stocks of agricultural and non-agricultural commodities, the volume of unfilled orders. These indexes are computed by various organizations — the United States Bureau of Labor Statistics, the Federal Reserve Board, the Department of Commerce, and the New York Federal Reserve Bank. They are all published monthly in the *Survey of Current Business*, issued by the Department of Commerce. Some of them also appear in the *Federal Reserve Bulletin*, issued by the Federal Reserve Board.

light on the general business situation are difficult and time-consuming. Often the figures are misleading. For example, freight car loadings may be increasing long after the demand for goods has begun to diminish, because old orders are being shipped. Or debits to individual accounts may increase, not because more goods are being purchased, but because debts are being paid. In interpreting the data, it is easy to be misled by merely seasonal fluctuations in business activity. Some large enterprises have their own economists or statisticians who gather and interpret information concerning the business outlook, and recently there have sprung up a number of forecasting services which gather data and issue forecasts. Business forecasting is a newer art than weather forecasting, and erroneous predictions are probably more frequent now than they will be later. In fact, the errors of the forecasters during the last few years have been so serious that there is probably less confidence in our ability to foresee business developments today than there was ten years ago. The factors which determine the trend of business are so numerous and their relative importance is so difficult to estimate that forecasting will probably never attain a really high degree of accuracy. Nevertheless, forecasting services are likely to improve and, as they do so, they may eventually become important in mitigating the severity of the business cycle, especially by discouraging excessive speculation and expansion in boom periods.

A majority of business men are unlikely to subscribe to business forecasting services or to pay much attention to statistics which throw light on the business outlook. Their attention is absorbed in the detailed problems of producing and selling goods. Consequently, when they have been making money and are in an optimistic mood, they are likely to bid up prices and to build up large inventories despite the fact that danger signals are in the air.

The best way to influence such men is through their bankers. Whether or not the head of an enterprise pays any attention to information on the business outlook, whether or not he subscribes to a forecasting service, he borrows money from a bank. The more competent bankers study the general business situation carefully. It is true that in the past many banks have not given much weight to business prospects in determining the amount of credit which customers could be safely allowed, but it must be remembered that the existence of more or less regularly recurring cycles of prosperity and depression has been widely realized for less than two decades. As the importance of considering general economic conditions in granting credit is more generally appreciated, we may expect bankers to assist in controlling the business cycle, both by warning customers against stocking up too heavily at high prices and by being more cautious under some circumstances in making loans.

But the restraining influence of banks upon reckless buying will always be limited by competition among them and by fear of losing the accounts of customers who would resent being refused the amount of credit which they request. Then there will always be bankers of narrow vision who, in determining how much to lend, do not look beyond the momentary financial condition of the borrower.[18] It is desirable, therefore, to have some more automatic devices than the advice and the lending policies of banks to check the disposition of business men to bid up prices too high or to build up dangerously large inventories. Among such devices are trade acceptances.

The two principal methods of granting short-term credit in the United States are the open book account and the promissory note. When an enterprise borrows from a bank, the promissory note is ordinarily used, but when one concern buys on credit from another, the open book account is used — that is, the seller simply records on his books that the buyer owes a certain amount. Each

[18] There are other limits upon the influence of the banks. For one thing, business men often seek money only after they have embarked on a project and have made commitments. The bank is confronted with an accomplished fact. The customer *must* have credit or suffer serious loss. If the customer is a good risk, the bank can scarcely refuse a loan on the general ground that, in the country at large, speculative buying is going too far. Of particular importance in diminishing the influence of banks over the expansion of credit is the development of the *line of credit loan*. This is an arrangement by which a business enterprise each year submits its financial statements to a bank and arranges for a " line " of credit — that is, an amount which the bank agrees to lend the enterprise at any time during the year. For example, a bank may decide to allow a merchant a " line " of $10,000, which means that at any time during the year the bank stands ready to advance the merchant $10,000. Once a line of credit has been granted, the bank is obviously not in a position to limit the loans to the enterprise on the ground that the expansion of credit is being generally overdone.

of these methods encourages extravagant buying. A concern which has purchased more goods than it should and has trouble in paying its note at the bank when due, can usually persuade the bank to accept a new note in payment of the old one, because the bank wishes the future business of the enterprise. The situation is similar when one concern buys on credit from another and the open book account is used. An understanding may exist that the account will be paid at a certain date, but such understandings are often not observed. Buyers, knowing that sellers wish to retain their patronage, do not hesitate to ask for more time. It is estimated that less than 50 per cent of open accounts are paid when due or within fifteen or twenty days from the due date.[19] When extensions of time are easy to obtain, enterprises are naturally willing to carry larger inventories than they would otherwise dare.

We already know why trade acceptances discourage extravagant buying.[20] When a business man accepts a bill of exchange, he knows that he must pay it on the date of maturity. A request for more time will do no good. The creditor will probably have sold the bill and it will be presented for payment by some one who has no interest in obtaining or retaining the acceptor's patronage. Realizing the necessity of paying his debts promptly, the merchant is careful to buy no more goods than he is sure of selling before the maturity of the debt.

Most goods, we know, are purchased with borrowed money. This suggests that the Federal Reserve Banks, simply by making credit more difficult to obtain, might check the tendency for business men to bid prices too high or to build up excessive inventories. But can the Reserve Banks compel the member banks to raise their interest rates as soon as the expansion of credit needs to be checked? And even if the Reserve Banks succeed in this, are higher interest charges likely to check the voracious appetite of business men for more credit, once prices are rising rapidly? In other words, how elastic is the demand for short-term loans when business men are optimistic?

The first question arises because the point at which the ex-

---

[19] American Acceptance Council, *Should the Buyer Accept?* p. 3.
[20] See Chapter XI, pp. 232–233.

pansion of credit needs to be checked is when the increase in loans begins to outrun the increase in physical output — in other words, when the credit dollars which the banks create are being used, not merely to increase production, but to bid up prices. This point, however, is likely to be reached long before the member banks have lent all that their reserves permit and when it is unnecessary for them to rediscount with the Reserve Banks in order to expand their loans. Under these circumstances, will higher rediscount rates induce most member banks to charge more for credit?

We have already learned that the Reserve Banks can reduce the reserves of the member banks by the sale of securities. But can the Reserve Banks reduce the reserves of the member banks so much that the banks must rediscount paper in order to expand their loans? This obviously depends upon the size of the surplus reserves of the member banks and the volume of securities which the Reserve Banks can offer for sale. *Sooner or later,* of course, the growth of business will reduce the reserves of the member banks so far that the Reserve Banks will be able to force up interest charges, but in the meantime the continued expansion of credit, making possible speculative buying on a large scale and the reckless bidding up of prices, may create a dangerous situation.[21] It is, of course, possible that the member banks, even though pos-

[21] In order for the advance in the rediscount rate to be effective, there must be no other sources from which banks can increase their reserves at less than it would cost them to borrow from the Reserve Banks. There are five sources from which the banks might gain funds: (1) a flow of money from general circulation into the banks as a result of the public's depositing more than it withdraws; (2) a flow of gold from abroad resulting from an excess of exports over imports; (3) newly mined gold; (4) loans from foreign banks; and (5) the United States Treasury. Of these five, the first two are not likely to be available at the precise periods when overexpansion of credit threatens; the third is not likely to supply sufficient cash to make possible a great expansion of credit and the amounts derived from it are likely to be least when the danger of credit expansion is greatest; and the fourth is not likely to be sufficient to make possible a large expansion of credit without an increase in interest rates.

The times when overexpansion of credit threatens are usually periods of boom when prices are higher and business more active than usual. They are precisely the times, however, when banks are least likely to gain cash from the general public, because the rising price level and the growing volume of buying and selling enhance the need of the public for money. Periods of high prices and brisk business are also the very times when exports are least likely to exceed imports. The high prices and the slow deliveries — the latter a result of the large volume of orders — discourage foreign buyers from purchasing here and encourage domestic buyers to place orders abroad. Thus, in boom times, the balance of trade is likely to cause exports rather than imports of gold. It should be observed, however, that the prosperity

sessing substantial surplus reserves, will voluntarily raise their interest charges when the rediscount rate is advanced. In many instances, they would make as much profit, possibly even more, at higher rates. Furthermore, a growing number of bankers appreciate the desirability of controlling the business cycle and realize that stability is probably more profitable to most enterprises than intense prosperity followed by profound depression. But just how banks with surplus reserves will respond to changes in rediscount rates, experience alone can tell.[22]

---

of domestic industry may attract foreign investors in such large numbers that the tendency for gold to leave the country is counteracted. In fact, foreigners may invest in domestic industry on such a large scale that gold flows into the country — as it did in the case of the United States in 1928 and during most of 1929.

The coinage of newly mined gold tends, of course, to increase the funds at the disposal of the banks. The gain from this course, however, is negligible. Only once has the total annual gold production of the United States and Alaska exceeded $100,000,000, and by 1929 it had fallen to $45,651,000. As the cash reserves of the Federal Reserve Banks in 1930 exceeded $3,100,000,000, it is evident that the coinage of the entire annual production would make possible only a relatively small expansion of loans. Allowance, however, must be made for the gold used in the arts. This fluctuates from year to year but it is far more than half as large as the new production of the United States. Finally, this source of cash is likely to be least important during periods of prosperity and high prices. Because the price of gold does not rise when other prices increase, articles made of gold are relatively cheap in times of high prices. This causes more gold to be used in the arts and less to be brought to the mint for coinage. Gold articles, being largely luxuries, are in greatest demand during prosperous times. This still further increases the industrial consumption of gold during boom periods and reduces the quantity available for coinage.

The most likely source from which the banks might gain additional funds without resorting to the Reserve Banks is the United States Treasury. It is important to notice that, when the nation is reducing its debt, the Treasury can negative a restrictive policy of the Federal Reserve authorities by putting money into circulation through the purchase of government securities. The party in power may desire a boom period to continue unchecked until after elections and, at the same time that the Reserve Banks are *selling* government obligations and bankers' acceptances in order to make money scarce, the Treasury may buy bonds or short-term government notes.

[22] Notice that all member banks need not be willing to respond to the higher rediscount rate. If a substantial proportion of them do, the other banks will find themselves losing cash to those which are charging more and lending less. Consequently, the other banks too will soon be compelled either to rediscount or to cease expanding loans.

The Federal Reserve system is a new piece of machinery and it has been necessary to learn how to operate it. The process of learning is still going on. The experience of the European central banks has been a valuable guide but also a misleading one. Not only are European conditions different but the purposes of the European central banks have been less ambitious than controlling the business cycle. These banks have been primarily interested in protecting their reserves. At first, the Federal Reserve authorities relied chiefly upon the rediscount rate to control

Suppose that rediscount rates are advanced and that, as a result, the banks charge more for loans. How is this likely to affect the expansion of credit? Is not interest on short-term loans too small a cost to affect seriously the demand for credit when prices are rising and business men are optimistic? It is no answer to say that, if a given advance in the rediscount rate fails to check credit expansion, the rate can be raised still more. Practically there are limits to the ability of the Reserve Banks to raise rediscount rates. Business men have become accustomed to a certain range which they regard as fair. The Reserve Banks dare not outrage the community's sense of justice by charging what business men regard as exorbitant rates, permissible only in periods of crisis, at a time when industry is prosperous and the reserve ratios of the Reserve Banks are high. The plea that the increase in rates is necessary to nip a tendency toward speculative buying would scarcely satisfy business men. The Reserve Banks must be able to prevent over-expansion *by relatively slight advances* in their rediscount rates — increases which still leave the rates within the range regarded as reasonable by the business community.

An advance in the cost of short-term loans will scarcely deter men from borrowing to take advantage of opportunities which appear to promise substantial profits. To a large extent, enterprises borrow money in order to sell goods to other enterprises on credit. When fixed costs are heavy, as they are in many lines of business, it is obvious that no concern can afford to diminish its sales, and hence its borrowings from banks, simply because short-term loans cost one or two per cent more. But a higher discount rate does, of course, add to the cost of carrying goods. Consequently, although a higher interest rate is not likely to cause enterprises to curtail the volume of production, it may lead some concerns to reduce their inventories. Particularly in businesses where the turnover is large relative to fixed capital and the profit margins are small, higher interest rates make a substantial dif-

---

credit. After a somewhat unsatisfactory experience with this device in 1920, the authorities placed their main reliance upon open-market operations. But an unsatisfactory experience with this method in the spring of 1928 has diminished faith in its efficacy. It seems clear that the method employed must depend upon the specific situation which is to be controlled and that in many cases the rediscount rate and open-market operations must be employed simultaneously.

ference in profits. Some branches of wholesaling are of this sort. Especially after the boom has reached the point where costs are overtaking income, are business men reluctant to bear the burden of higher interest rates and they seek to protect their profits by reducing their working capital, which means cutting down their inventories. Most important of all, the charges for short-term loans cannot rise without affecting rates for long-term loans. The banks in particular are induced by the higher short-term rates to reduce their holdings of bonds and to increase their short-term loans. This tends to depress the price of bonds and to make it impossible for enterprises to sell issues on such favorable terms. We have already learned why the demand for long-term credit is so sensitive to changes in interest rates. Rather than pay half a per cent more over a period of ten or twenty years for the money needed to construct a building or to purchase additional equipment, many concerns prefer to postpone erecting the building or buying the equipment. Hence a rise in the rates on short-term loans, by affecting the rates on long-term loans, is likely to check the demand for goods and thus to restrict the expansion of business.

Last of all, a word should be said concerning the possible effects of a higher rediscount rate upon business sentiment. It is possible that the better informed, more intelligent, and more farsighted business men may accept the rise in the rediscount rate as fairly satisfactory evidence that expansion of business and speculative buying have gone far enough and that the time has come to liquidate stocks and to get goods into the hands of the ultimate users. Consequently, these business men may cease buying in advance of their immediate needs and quietly begin to realize on the goods in their possession. Other business men, noticing the tendency for demand to decline, supply to increase, and prices to weaken, buy more cautiously, and begin to reduce their stocks. Thus, in a cumulative manner, demand falls off, inventories are cut down, and the danger of inflation and a subsequent severe period of liquidation is avoided.

Just how much weight enterprisers are likely to attach to the rediscount rate as a barometer of business is highly conjectural, for our experience is still brief. Unfortunately the history of 1919, 1928, and 1929 indicates that, when restraint on speculation and business expansion are most needed, the influence of the Reserve Board and the Reserve Banks upon business sentiment is likely to be least. It is true that, in 1919, the Reserve Banks were prevented from resorting to increases in rediscount rates by the desire of the Treasury to maintain easy credit conditions in order to facilitate the floating of the Victory Loan. Nevertheless, the Reserve Board issued several warnings in which it pointed out the dangers in the excessive speculation. Despite these warnings, the loans of all member banks increased about 25 per cent between March and November, 1919.[23] Finally, in November, 1919, and again in January, 1920, the New York Reserve Bank raised its rediscount rate, but these advances appear to have had little effect in checking the expansion of credit. It may also be argued that the history of 1928 and 1929 does not provide a fair test of what the Reserve system might do to control the business cycle, because the Reserve system was not sufficiently prompt or vigorous in raising rediscount rates to check the expansion of credit.[24] In addition, the willingness of the public to purchase securities at high prices put the supply of funds largely beyond the control of the Reserve Banks.[25] Nevertheless, several advances in the rediscount rate were made, and, on February 6 and March 4, 1929, the Reserve Board issued plain-spoken warnings against the excessive speculation. Consequently, the position of the Reserve Board was well known. But, except for the fact that some bankers, brokers, congressmen, and business men vigorously criticized the Board's action, the community apparently paid little heed to the Board's warnings. After the experience of 1919 and 1929, it is difficult to resist the conclusion that the Federal Reserve system is likely to be most useful in checking relatively mild booms and to have little

[23] Goldenweiser, E. A., *The Federal Reserve System in Operation*, p. 40.

[24] The responsibility must rest in the main upon the Reserve *Board* rather than upon the Reserve *Banks*, because in the spring of 1929 the Board refused the request of several of the Reserve Banks to advance their rediscount rates to 6 per cent.

[25] The Reserve Board asked the member banks to coöperate in checking the growth of speculative credit and the banks responded. But the boom in the stock market enabled corporations and investment trusts to sell their own securities at high prices and to lend the proceeds in the stock market at attractive interest rates to finance further speculation in securities. Corporations and investment trusts did not have the same sense of responsibility for the general credit situation which the commercial banks possessed and were not sensitive to the warnings of the Reserve Board.

influence when the boom becomes intense and the country is caught by a speculative mania.[26]

VII. The Control of the Business Cycle — Steps Which Should Be Taken at the Time of Threatened Crisis

Crises are the result of an acute fear that a violent drop in prices impends — a fear which causes enterprises to dump huge quantities of goods on the market for what they will bring. Business men are most easily alarmed over a possible price drop when they have large debts which must be paid in the near future. And naturally, the more rapid the fall in prices after a boom, the greater the fear that it arouses. All of this makes it plain that the most important steps in preventing crises must be taken far in advance — during the boom period. The short-term indebtedness of business establishments must be kept down and the danger of a rapid fall in prices must be guarded against *during the boom period* by granting credit wisely and by discouraging the bidding up of prices and the speculative hoarding of goods.

But suppose that the period of prosperity is past and that a crisis is threatening. Is there no last-moment step which may avert it? In our study of credit we learned that at a time of possible crisis it is extremely important that the banks be able to expand credit, because one reason why enterprises seek to sell at almost any price is the fact that they have debts which must be paid at once. If these concerns can borrow to meet their immediate obligations, they need not cut prices so drastically, the fall in prices will be retarded, and the danger of a stampede to sell will be diminished.

But the extent to which the banks dare give aid depends in part upon how successfully during the boom period the advance in prices and the speculative accumulation of inventories were checked. Suppose that they were checked very little. When prices begin to fall, hundreds of concerns which purchased large quantities of goods at high prices ask the banks for extensions

---

[26] Early in 1923, for example, when there were signs that the business boom might stimulate dangerous speculation and overexpansion in some industries, the Federal Reserve system had better success in controlling the situation. Several Reserve Banks advanced their rediscount rates from 4 to $4\frac{1}{2}$ per cent and the Reserve Banks sold securities in the open market. No doubt the experience of 1920–1921 made business men more sensitive to warnings from the Reserve authorities.

of existing loans or for new loans with which to pay their debts. How much credit dare the banks give these concerns? Because the general business situation makes a large drop in prices probable, it is unlikely that the banks will lend the enterprises enough to meet their large indebtedness. Only when an extremely large drop in prices is unlikely and when the short-term indebtedness of business firms is not too great — in other words, only when something has been done to check the rise in prices and speculative buying during the boom — can the banks be expected to give enough aid to avert a crisis.

VIII. The Control of the Business Cycle — Steps Which Should Be Taken during Depression

When depression finally comes, as it must in our present state of knowledge, what steps can be taken to diminish its intensity and to hasten the return of prosperity? The essential difficulty at times of depression is, of course, the small demand for goods. The small demand is partly due to the fact that men spend their dollars more slowly because they are waiting for prices to fall still further and it is partly due to the fact that there are fewer dollars to be spent because enterprises are borrowing on a smaller scale from the banks. What can be done to increase the volume of spending?

One step is for the Federal Reserve Banks to lower their rediscount rates. This encourages the member banks to reduce their interest rates. Lower interest rates help to diminish the severity of the depression in several ways. The banks, finding their earnings reduced by lower interest rates in the short-term money market, invest a larger part of their funds in bonds. This, of course, increases the demand for bonds, helps investment bankers reduce their stocks of unsold bonds, makes them willing to bring out new issues more rapidly, and, most important of all, tends to raise the price of bonds. The improvement in the bond market is of substantial help in relieving the depression. It enables enterprises, which, during the period of prosperity and high interest rates, met their needs for permanent equipment by selling short-term notes, to refund these notes on advantageous terms. This, of course, helps them to reduce their costs by reducing their interest charges. And what is more important, the retirement of the short-term notes improves the financial position of these concerns. As long as an enterprise has a large floating indebtedness which is represented by permanent equipment rather than by goods which can be easily converted into cash, the concern is not likely to be able to obtain funds for additions and improvements to its plants on favorable terms. A pronounced revival in business is not likely to occur until enterprises have put their financial houses in order by funding the floating debts which they incurred for permanent equipment during the boom period. Finally, the favorable terms on which concerns can sell their bonds encourage them to make improvements and enlargements to their plants — improvements not immediately needed but ones which managers find it worth while to make when money can be obtained on exceptionally favorable terms. The improvement in the bond market is likely to be aided by the Federal Reserve Banks' increasing their purchases of government securities. The favorable opportunity to sell government securities encourages the member banks to reduce their holdings of these issues and to place more of their money in high grade private bonds.[27]

It has been frequently suggested that demand during periods of depression might be increased by concentrating public construction as far as possible into these periods. As a matter of fact, public construction is often unusually large during the early stages of the depression and thus tends for a time to reduce the severity of the depression. Voters are naturally most ready to authorize large public expenditures during boom periods — when every one is prosperous. But the time required to prepare plans and let contracts often delays the actual construction until many months after it was authorized. This is why public construction may be large early in the depression. Depression itself, however,

[27] Improvement in the bond market is important, but too much must not be expected of it because it is likely to be of little help to the vast number of enterprises which are not in a strong competitive position. Even if they could sell bonds in a period of depression, these concerns are not likely at that time to expand their capacity or to make expensive renewals. Some of them would be glad to borrow for the purpose of replacing short-term notes with bonds. But a period of depression is a time when investment bankers hesitate to bring out bond issues that are not of the first grade. Consequently, many concerns which would gladly borrow if they could are compelled to wait until the business horizon brightens and investors are less cautious.

discourages the initiation of new public works and thus, during the latter months of a business recession, there is likely to be a substantial drop in public construction. This drop may continue into the period of business revival itself and no doubt often delays the revival.

It has been estimated that in 1928 about $3,599,000,000 was expended on public construction in the United States and that about 800,000 men were directly employed on it. It is now about 35 to 40 per cent of all construction.[28] But although the volume of public building is no doubt large, it is only a small part of the total national output in all fields. In fact, the 800,000 persons directly employed on public works are only a tiny fraction of the 49,000,000 persons gainfully employed in 1930. Consequently, it would be foolish to expect that, by timing of public construction, depression could be largely eliminated. Nevertheless, some good can be done and the device must not be scorned simply because it will not do everything that one might wish. Furthermore, it must be remembered that the expansion of public works may have an exceedingly wholesome effect upon business sentiment and may diminish the drop in the demand for goods by preventing many business enterprises from cutting their expenditures as much as they otherwise would.

But if the government spends more for public construction during periods of depression, may not the rest of the community have just so much less to spend and may not the total demand for goods remain unchanged? Suppose, for example, that the government takes the money by taxation. Evidently the taxpayers have less to spend and the government more, but there are no more dollars being offered for goods.

The matter, however, is not so simple as this. An increase in the *appropriations* of the government does not necessarily involve an increase in the *receipts*. It may simply involve a decrease of the balance in the public treasury. In this case, of course, an increase in appropriations would represent a net increase in the demand for goods. The government may provide itself during the period of prosperity with the funds needed to finance an expansion of construction during the period of depres-

[28] Wolman, Leo, *Planning and Control of Public Works*, pp. 108–115.

sion. In this case, by withdrawing dollars from circulation during the boom period, it would tend to diminish demand at the time when demand was outrunning supply, and, by spending these dollars during the period of depression, it would increase demand at that time. In other words, the government would be doing essentially the same thing as the Reserve Banks when they sell securities during the boom and buy them during the depression. Finally, the government may finance public construction through the sale of bonds. In this case, there is some net gain in demand — though less than the receipts from the bonds. In so far as people spend their money for bonds instead of something else, there is, of course, no increase in the demand for goods. But some persons *borrow* the money with which to buy bonds, and some bonds are bought by banks which have idle funds and which are ready to buy government securities but which, at a time of depression, are unwilling to invest a larger part of their funds in other securities. In short, the expansion of public works during times of depression does not automatically and inevitably increase the total demand for goods, but it may do so *provided it is properly financed*.

How can public construction be concentrated to some extent into periods of depression? One method might be to postpone commencing some projects until a period of depression exists. But this method is not likely to be satisfactory because most projects cannot be postponed without inconvenience or loss to the public. A second method is to accelerate the construction of works which have already been authorized. This is perhaps the simplest method. There is usually an opportunity to put many thousands of men at work more promptly by speeding up the preparation of plans and specifications and the letting of contracts. It is obvious, however, that the method of acceleration, if carried too far, may result in poorly planned or located structures and great waste of public money. This brings us to the third and most important, but also the most difficult method of concentrating public construction more largely into periods of depression — the forward planning of public works. If a city or a state adopts a plan of public improvements to be made during the next five years and has plans and specifications prepared for the structures in the plan, it obviously becomes possible to concentrate public construction in certain periods by authorizing some projects to be started ahead of schedule. If, for example, a depression should occur in 1933, the city or the state might authorize that certain items on the 1934 program be commenced in 1933. The essence of the scheme, it is obvious, is the adoption of a plan covering the needs of the community for a number of years ahead and the preparation of detailed plans and specifications. This means that work on any part of the plan will not be delayed by controversies over the relative merits of different locations for a building, bridge, street, or park or over the relative merits of different types of construction, nor by the fact that plans and specifications have not been made. Everything must be in readiness so that bids for any part of the plan can be requested as soon as funds for construction are voted.

When a period of business depression sets in, it is made worse because many enterprises curtail expenditures in every way possible and thus reduce the demand for goods. Repairs, replacements, and improvements to the plant are often cut down to the minimum and new construction is postponed. For many concerns, this retrenchment is imperative; they have trouble in getting enough money to pay their indebtedness as it falls due. But some enterprises undoubtedly cut expenditures farther than is necessary for their own safety and thus unnecessarily accentuate the severity of the depression. Furthermore, by delaying repairs, replacements, and improvements too long, they may raise their own operating expenses. During the depression of 1929–1930, an exceedingly interesting and important attempt was made to stimulate the demand for goods by inducing business enterprises to avoid extreme and unnecessary curtailment of expenditures. The attempt was made under the general leadership of the National Business Survey Conference — a conference organized by the United States Chamber of Commerce for this express purpose. The conference sought to encourage enterprises to make as many repairs, replacements, and improvements as they conservatively could and to avoid curtailing new construction more than was necessary. The conference enlisted the coöperation of many trade associations and chambers of commerce. The National Electrical Manufacturers' Association and the International Association of Electragists created a joint committee to encourage manufacturers of electrical machinery and motor specialists to repair worn machines and to supplant those which were obsolete; the Wool Institute, the National Tool Builders' Association, the American Face Brick Association, the Writing Paper Manufacturers' Association, and others all sought to stimulate the repair and replacement of equipment among their members. The National Association of Building Owners and Managers encouraged its members to keep up their customary expenditures on maintenance.

How much was accomplished under the leadership of the National Business Survey Conference no one can say. Many of the expenditures which have been made for repairs and equipment would doubtless have been made any way. But probably some of them would not and, to this extent, money that would have been lying idle in the banks has been used to purchase goods. It is an open question, however, whether the efforts of the Conference did not do more harm than good. The reason is, not that there is anything inherently unsound in the methods of the Conference, but that the Conference acted on the assumption that the depression would not last beyond the spring or summer of 1930. Business enterprises, of course, have only limited ability to make expenditures which bring no immediate return. When business failed to revive by the summer of 1930, many concerns found it necessary or desirable to reduce their expenditures on repairs and replacements. The experience of the railroads in 1930 is illuminating. Partly at the instance of President Hoover, they did not at first curtail their expenditures on plant and equipment when the depression of 1929–1930 set in. During the first quarter of 1930, their outlays for equipment and their expenditures on roadway and structures were far above the first quarter of 1929. But when business failed to revive in the late spring and the summer of 1930, the railroads were unable to continue their large outlays. Other concerns also appear to have found it necessary to curtail their expenditures. This general reduction of expenditures by enterprises in the late spring and the summer, in conjunction with other circumstances, brought about a secondary reaction. A reaction which occurs when business is already poor is likely to be doubly bad because the business community is so easily alarmed and so easily driven to make drastic retrenchments. Probably the greatest lesson to be learned from the depression of 1930 is the fact that efforts to support markets in times of depression must be based upon accurate estimates of the duration of the depression and must be so timed that business concerns will not find it necessary to reduce their spending before a revival of business sets in. At present, however, we are not able to forecast accurately the duration of depressions.

Some economists believe that depressions are intensified by the failure of wages to fall as rapidly as other prices. This, it is argued, reduces the profits (or increases the losses) of business concerns, makes it more difficult for enterprises to fund the large short-term debts which many of them incurred during the boom period or retards the rate at which they can liquidate these debts, intensifies the spirit of caution and pessimism, and thus, by rendering business men less willing to make expenditures for replacements, repairs, or extensions, diminishes employment. These economists believe that depressions would be shorter and less severe if enterprises were to cut wages more drastically and promptly. An opposing line of reasoning is that wage cuts would simply intensify the downward spiral in prices and thus make it more difficult for business concerns to pay their debts; that they would increase the number of business failures and intensify the fear and the reluctance to buy which are the essential characteristics of depressions.

What men expect will happen to prices is scarcely less important than what actually does happen to them. It does little good to maintain wages if business men expect them to fall and postpone buying until they do fall. Likewise it does little good to cut wages, if one cut simply arouses the expectation of other cuts and thus produces postponement of buying. When the choice is between a cut and the failure of an enterprise, the cut should usually be made, because every failure intensifies the general reluctance to buy. Probably the most accurate generalization that can be made is that wages should be cut where cuts would increase the volume of wage payments and should be maintained where cuts would reduce the volume of wage payments. In other words, wages should be cut where the demand for labor is elastic and maintained where the demand for labor is inelastic.[29] This generalization is based upon the assumption that, since the essential difficulty in the time of depression is a general reluctance to buy, the most helpful course is to make such cuts in prices (whether prices of labor or of other goods) as will increase the general volume of spending. Cuts which reduce the general volume of spending simply do harm, not only because a reduction in the volume of spending is itself harmful, but also because a lower price level increases the burden of debts and makes it more difficult for enterprises to make profits and to borrow in order to expand or to improve their plants.

REFERENCES

Hansen, A. H., *Business-Cycle Theory*, 1927.
Hardy, C. O., and Cox, G., *Forecasting Business Conditions*, 1927.
Hawtrey, R. G., *Trade and Credit*, 1928.
Mitchell, W. C., *Business Cycles. The Problem and Its Setting*, 1927.
Pigou, A. C., *Industrial Fluctuations*, 1927.
Reed, H. L., *Federal Reserve Policy, 1921–1930*, 1930.
Snyder, Carl, *Business Cycles and Business Measurements*, 1927.
Wagemann, Ernest, *Economic Rhythm*, 1930.
Wolman, Leo, *Planning and Control of Public Works*, 1930.

[29] Obviously, if a 5 per cent wage cut causes the volume of employment to be 10 per cent greater than it would be in the event of no cut (demand elastic), the reduction in wages produces a 4.5 per cent increase in wage disbursements. But if a 5 per cent cut produced only a 3 per cent increase in employment, it would decrease wage disbursements by 2.15 per cent.

CHAPTER XXI

THE DETERMINATION OF THE PRICE LEVEL

I. THE SIGNIFICANCE OF CHANGES IN THE PRICE LEVEL. II. THE
MEASUREMENT OF CHANGES IN THE PRICE LEVEL. III. THE RE-
LATION BETWEEN THE QUANTITY OF MONEY AND PRICES. IV. GOV-
ERNMENT FINANCES AND THE PRICE LEVEL. V. THE INTERDE-
PENDENCE OF PRICE LEVELS IN DIFFERENT COUNTRIES. VI. HOW
FAR IS IT DESIRABLE TO STABILIZE THE PRICE LEVEL? VII. THE
PLAN OF "THE STABILIZED DOLLAR." VIII. CONTROLLING THE
PRICE LEVEL BY REGULATING GOLD OUTPUT. IX. A "MANAGED
CURRENCY." X. LONG-TERM CONTRACTS WHICH RUN IN TERMS
OF PURCHASING POWER.

I. THE SIGNIFICANCE OF CHANGES IN THE PRICE LEVEL

Suppose, Professor Fisher has suggested, that in 1896 you
had put $100 into the savings bank and that you had allowed it to
accumulate at 3 per cent compound interest until 1920. You
would then have had a little more than $200. You withdrew the
money to spend it. Things cost at retail about three times as
much as in 1896. When you spent your money, you found that
you could not obtain as much for it as you could have obtained
for your $100 back in 1896. You had waited twenty-five years.
You had carefully saved the interest on your money during all
that time. And finally, due to the rise in the price level, you
found that you had less than when you started out.

Our whole economic life is based upon contracts which run
in terms of dollars. Every day millions of exchanges are made
in which dollars are given or promised in return for goods. We
are so used to expressing the values of specific commodities in
terms of money and so unaccustomed to expressing the value of
money in terms of goods, that when prices change, we think of
goods rather than *dollars* as changing in value. When eggs go
up from 25 to 60 cents a dozen, pork chops from 20 to 45 cents

a pound, milk from 6 to 12 cents a quart, we think of these things as rising but of the dollar as stable. A dollar, we are accustomed to think, never changes in value. It is always worth a dollar.

Despite its prevalence, the notion that the value of the dollar never changes is false. It is, of course, true that a dollar will always bring one hundred cents just as it is true that a quart is always equal to two pints. But the value of an article is its purchasing power, its ability to command other goods, and the purchasing power of the dollar is constantly changing. The following diagram showing the course of wholesale prices in the United States during the last ninety years gives an idea of how great have been the fluctuations in the dollar's buying power.

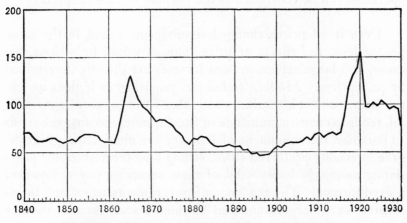

WHOLESALE PRICES IN THE UNITED STATES, 1840–1930.
1926 = 100

It will be observed that during each of our two great wars — the Civil War, and the World War — prices rose rapidly and that shortly after each war they dropped precipitously. During the thirty years immediately following the Civil War, the trend of prices was downward. From 1865 to 1896, for example, the purchasing power of the dollar in the wholesale markets doubled. From 1896 to the outbreak of the World War, on the other hand, the value of the wholesale dollar fell about one-third and from 1914 to 1920 over one-half. Between 1920 and 1930 its value nearly doubled.

Retail prices fluctuate less than wholesale prices, but their changes are substantial. In 1913, for example, it required nearly a dollar and a half to buy at retail the food which one dollar purchased in 1900; and in 1920, over two dollars to buy the food which one dollar purchased in 1913. Between 1920 and 1922, retail food prices fell 30 per cent.[1] The recent paper-money regimes in some European countries caused prices to reach astronomical figures. In Germany, for example, prices went to three trillion times their pre-war level. The pronounced tendency for prices in general to move upward or downward together suggests that there are comprehensive influences affecting the entire price level and causing it to rise and fall. To discuss what these forces are, what effects they produce, and how their operation can be controlled is the purpose of this chapter.

Even if all prices changed simultaneously and in the same proportions, the effects of price changes would be serious, because, to a large extent, present incomes are directly determined by past prices. Modern technique, requiring as it does an immense investment in machines and other forms of permanent capital, tends to create a multitude of fixed incomes, because the funds to purchase the equipment of industry are obtained in great degree by issuing preferred stock, selling long-term notes, or negotiating mortgage loans. All of these securities pay the owners a fixed income. The tendency of governments to engage in expensive wars, largely financed by bond issues, creates another important group of fixed incomes, and the demands for better roads, streets, and school buildings give rise to additional public bond issues and many more fixed-money incomes. Real estate is often rented on long-term contracts. Between 1870 and 1929, the amount of life insurance in force in the United States increased from about $2,300,000,000 to nearly $100,000,000,-000.[2] The number of dollars to which the policy holders are entitled remains the same, regardless of whether dollars become more or less valuable. Many persons depend upon savings accounts for income or for support in old age. In 1929, the volume of savings deposits in the United States was $28,218,000,000.[3]

---

[1] *Statistical Abstract of the United States,* 1929, p. 329.   [3] *Ibid.,* p. 273.
[2] *Ibid.,* pp. 163 and 304.

Finally, there are thousands of persons receiving fixed incomes in the form of annuities, pensions, compensation under accident insurance policies, and awards under workmen's compensation acts.

But all prices do not move upward or downward at precisely the same time or in precisely the same degree. Some are more responsive than others to the causes which produce general price movements. Wholesale prices, as a whole, are more sensitive than retail. For example, between 1914 and 1920 the wholesale prices of foods in the United States increased on the average 112 per cent but the retail prices 99 per cent. Between 1920 and 1929, the wholesale prices of foods decreased an average of 27 per cent and the retail prices 23 per cent.[4] Rents are one of the most sluggish prices. Between 1913 and December, 1920, when wholesale prices advanced 126 per cent and the cost of living about 100 per cent, rents rose only 51 per cent. And although prices in general began to decline in 1920, rents did not drop until 1925.[5] Wages are sluggish in their movements both upward and downward. Between 1914 and 1918, the hourly earnings of factory workers increased about 56 per cent,[6] in comparison with an increase of over 65 per cent in retail food prices and of nearly 80 per cent in non-agricultural wholesale prices. Between 1920 and 1922, the hourly earnings of factory workers decreased about 13 per cent [7] but non-agricultural wholesale prices fell about 30 per cent. Salaries respond to general price movements even more slowly than wages, and the salaries of government employees are less responsive than salaries in general. In 1919, for example, salaries of federal employees in the District of Columbia were only 17 per cent above the average for 1909, 1911, and 1913.[8] In the meantime, the cost of living had nearly doubled. The differences in the recent movements of several important price groups is shown in the following table:[9]

[4] *Ibid.*, pp. 322 and 329.

[5] *Handbook of Labor Statistics*, 1924–1926, p. 112.

[6] Douglas, P. H., *Real Wages in the United States, 1890–1926*, pp. 60 and 108. Wage *rates* probably decreased slightly more than hourly *earnings*, possibly as much as 20 per cent.

[7] *Ibid.*, p. 108.

[8] *Monthly Labor Review*, June, 1920, v. X, p. 1327.

[9] The indexes of wholesale food prices and retail food prices are based on the

	Wholesale food prices	Retail food prices	Cost of living	Wages in manufacturing
1914	100	100	100	100
1918	184	165	157	156
1920	212	199	206	231
1922	136	139	165	200
1926	158	158	174	225
1929	154	154	170	236

Because some prices move upward or downward more rapidly than others and because many incomes and the amounts of many claims are limited by contract to a fixed number of dollars, every change in the general price level produces stupendous shifts in the distribution of purchasing power throughout the community. For example, Dr. W. I. King has estimated that the rise in prices and the decline in the purchasing power of the dollar between 1914 and 1920 had the effect of confiscating some $16,000,000,000 (at 1914 prices) of the $30,000,000,000 of debts owed by individuals and corporations to others than banks, and transferring it to debtors as a gift.[10] " When one considers the furore created when burglars now and then succeed in appropriating the contents of a single safe, it seems strange," says Dr. King, " that the legal filching of a sum amounting to thousands of dollars from each of millions of families has been accomplished with relatively little protest." When prices in general rise, many persons, especially business men, find a welcome margin opening up between their expenditures and their incomes. The prices at which they sell rise but some of their costs, such as interest on indebtedness and rent, remain stationary or rise more slowly. But the enterprises which sell at publicly fixed prices may find themselves being gradually crushed between rising costs and incomes which increase slowly or not at all. Wage earners and salaried workers find prices rising faster than their earnings. " The high cost of living " becomes a topic of universal discussion. Wage earners seek the help of unions in raising wages,

---

indexes of the United States Bureau of Labor Statistics. The index of the cost of living and of factory wages are those of Professor Douglas (see his *Real Wages in the United States, 1890–1926*, pp. 60 and 108) down to 1926. The series have been extended to 1929 by using the cost of living index of the U. S. Bureau of Labor Statistics and the factory wage index of the National Industrial Conference Board.

[10] King, W. I., " Circulating Credit: Its Nature and Relation to Public Welfare," *American Economic Review*, December, 1920, v. X, p. 746.

union membership increases rapidly and so does the number of strikes. Creditors, bondholders, mortgage owners, landlords, pensioners, and preferred stockholders find that *practically* the terms of the contracts under which they receive their income have been altered and that they are receiving an ever-diminishing amount of purchasing power. Hospitals, universities, churches, and other endowed institutions find their endowments steadily shrinking.

In periods of falling prices, the benefits and detriments are reversed. Most business men find their incomes dropping because selling prices decrease more rapidly than costs. Wage earners and salaried employees gain because the cost of living usually falls more rapidly than wages and salaries. In case the decline in prices is rapid, however, the tendency to postpone buying may cause the workers to lose through unemployment as much as they gain through lower living costs. The greatest gainers from a decrease in prices are the receivers of fixed incomes and the greatest losers are the debtors, who, no matter how low prices drop, must still pay the same number of dollars in interest on their debts and who must repay the same amount of principal. This is why periods of falling prices have created great political unrest among farmers. Farmers must often go heavily into debt to acquire a farm from which a relatively small income can be obtained. Even a slight drop in prices diminishes seriously the small surplus yielded by the farm after interest, taxes, and operating expenses have been paid.

It is, of course, true that the injustices inflicted by rising and falling prices are mitigated by the fact that the gains do not all accrue to some persons nor the burdens all fall on others. Many persons are both debtors and creditors and what they lose in one capacity they gain in the other. The salaried man, whose income lags behind both upward and downward price movements, is likely to be a tenant or to be paying for a house. When prices advance, he is compensated in part for the failure of his salary to rise promptly, by the failure of his rent to increase as rapidly as other prices, or by the fact that the interest and principal on his debt remain unchanged. When prices fall, he gains by the tendency of his salary to remain stable and he loses by the slowness of his rent in dropping and by the fact that his debts do not decrease at all. The tendency of the cost of living to rise and fall more rapidly than wages is counteracted in part by the fact that rising prices stimulate business and hence employment and that falling prices create unemployment by causing postponement of buying.

But the fact that the results of changes in the price level to some extent cancel one another should not blind us to the seriousness of these changes. The unpredictable shifts in the distribution of purchasing power for causes over which individually we have little control make speculators of us all. When, within a six-year period, a rise of prices may transfer $16,000,000,000 from creditors to debtors, how idle it is to think of our economic system as distributing wealth according to merit! Luck must play a leading part in the fortune of every one of us. Men who struggled and saved in their youth and prime to provide against old age may find, when the time of need arrives, that their savings have been cut in half by a sudden rise in prices. No one today really knows how much life insurance he is carrying because he does not know what will be the purchasing power of the dollar when he dies. The problem of how to invest money safely is almost impossible of solution because *all* securities are speculative. Even government bonds are highly speculative, more speculative probably than conservative common stocks. The owner of a government bond is gambling that the dollar will not fall in value, and if it does, he loses. The common stockholder is protected to some extent, however, because the same increase in prices which diminishes the value of the dollar increases the profits of most enterprises and enables them to pay higher dividends. To make our economic system one in which there is a reasonably close relationship between merit and reward and to reduce luck and accident to secondary importance, we must find a way of preventing violent changes in the price level.

II. The Measurement of Changes in the Price Level

Before we proceed farther with the discussion of the changing value of the dollar, it is desirable to touch briefly upon the problem of measuring changes in the dollar's purchasing power. Since all prices do not change in the same degree or even in the same direction, the only way in which we can compare the value of the dollar at different times is by finding out how much prices have changed *on the average.* This might appear to be a simple problem. As a matter of fact, however, it has many difficulties. It is impossible to analyze them exhaustively in this brief discussion but it is desirable to point out some of the principal ways of measuring changes in the purchasing power of money and to indicate some of their limitations.

One of the simplest methods is to compare the amounts needed to purchase selected commodities at two different times. The commodities selected naturally depend upon the kind of purchasing power which one desires to measure — whether the ability of wage earners to buy food, of farmers to purchase all of the things which they customarily use, or of some other class in the community to satisfy a certain class of needs. For example, if we were studying the retail price of food, we might find that the prices of certain articles in the consumer's budget at different dates were as follows:

	First date	*Second date*
Bread, per loaf	$.10	$.12
Butter, per pound	.60	.50
Coffee, per pound	.35	.50
Eggs, per dozen	.48	.60
Milk, per quart	.08	.16
Steak, per pound	.32	.40
Sugar, per pound	.06	.04
Total	$1.99	$2.32

The quantities $1.99 and $2.32 indicate the change in the power of money to purchase specified amounts of selected commodities. Quantities such as these which vary with other quantities or aggregates of quantities and which, therefore, *indicate* the variations in the other quantities or aggregates are known as *index numbers.* This particular type of index number is known as the *simple aggregative type,* because it is a total of actual quantities. For convenience, it may be desirable to reduce the aggregates to percentages. If we represent the cost of the budget on the first date at 100, the index number for the second date becomes 116.5.

Another way of measuring changes in prices is to reduce the prices of each commodity at different dates to percentages and then to obtain an average of these percentages. This type of index number is known as an *average of relative prices*. In the case of the retail prices of the selected food items, this index would be as follows:

	First date	Second date
Bread, per loaf	100	120
Butter, per pound	100	83
Coffee, per pound	100	144
Eggs, per dozen	100	125
Milk, per quart	100	200
Steak, per pound	100	125
Sugar, per pound	100	67
Arithmetic average	100	123.4

In averaging the relatives it will be noticed that a simple arithmetic average was used. This is an obvious procedure and yet it is not a desirable one, because the arithmetic average of relatives has the serious defect of possessing an upward bias. This results from the fact that increases in percentages can be infinite but decreases, of course, cannot be more than 100. The existence of the upward bias in the arithmetic average of relatives can be easily demonstrated by reversing the dates upon which the relatives are based. If the price level doubled between any two dates, then obviously the price level of the first date would be only half the price level of the second date. In other words, when the bases are reversed, the index for the price level of the first date should be the reciprocal of the original index for the second date. This means that one multiplied by the other should equal unity.[11] The bias of the arithmetic average of relatives is indicated by the fact that, when the bases are

[11] In the case of the price level's doubling between two dates, the index of the second date in terms of the first becomes 2 and of the first in terms of the second becomes $\frac{1}{2}$. The product of the two is, of course, unity.

The upward bias may be so great that the index number shows a rise in prices no matter which date is taken as the base! For example, suppose that two commodities changed in price as follows:

	First date	Second date
Milk, per quart	$.10	$.20
Bread, per loaf	.10	.04

When the prices are reduced to relatives and averaged, with the *first* date as the base, the average for the second date is 120, showing an increase of 20 per cent. But when the *second* date is taken as the base, the average for the first becomes 150! The price level at each date is represented as higher than at the other!

reversed, the product of the two indexes is more than unity. In the case of the selected food items, for example, if the second year is made the base, the index for the first year becomes 90.4 per cent. But 1.234 × .904 is not unity but 1.115.[12]

This bias is not present in the case of simple aggregative indexes. It can be eliminated from averages of relatives by using the geometric instead of the arithmetic average. The geometric average is the *nth* root of the product of *n* relatives.[13] Thus, in the case of our budget items, the geometric average would be

$$\sqrt[7]{120 \times 83 \times 144 \times 125 \times 200 \times 125 \times 67} \text{ or } 117.0.$$

The geometric average of relatives has no bias either upward or downward. When the bases are reversed, the resulting index numbers are reciprocals. In addition, the geometric mean has the characteristic, which is often desirable, of giving less weight than does the arithmetic average to extremely small and extremely large items.

The reader has undoubtedly noted a serious defect in the indexes in our examples. The weights which have been given the commodities have been arbitrary. In the case of the simple aggregative index, the weights depend upon the units in which the prices happen to be quoted. The fact that the price of a pound of coffee is far greater than the price of a quart of milk causes the rise of 44 per cent in the price of coffee to affect the index far more than the rise of 100 per cent in the price of milk — although the change in the price of milk is undoubtedly far more important to the consumer than the change in the price of coffee. Nor is the difficulty avoided by reducing the actual prices to percentages. This method causes a 20 per cent change in one price to affect

---

[12] The relatives are as follows:

	First date	Second date
Bread, per loaf	83	100
Butter, per pound	120	100
Coffee, per pound	70	100
Eggs, per dozen	80	100
Milk, per quart	50	100
Steak, per pound	80	100
Sugar, per pound	150	100
Average	90.4	100

[13] It is, of course, computed with logarithms.

the index the same as a 20 per cent change in any other price, regardless of the importance of the commodities in the consumer's budget.

Obviously the commodities should be weighted in accordance with their importance. If the purpose is to ascertain changes in the consumer's cost of living, then the commodities should be weighted in accordance with the amounts spent for them. This can be done in constructing the simple aggregative index by multiplying the prices paid for a unit of each commodity by the number of units purchased during a given period — the price of a loaf of bread by the number of loaves purchased, the price of a quart of milk by the number of quarts purchased. It can be done in constructing averages of relatives by multiplying the relatives for each commodity by a weight which is proportionate to the expenditures for the commodity and by dividing the result by the sum of the weights.[14] In computing a weighted geometric average, each item is repeated a number of times, that number being determined by the weights (that is, the weights become exponents of the items), the results are multiplied, and a root, corresponding to the sum of the weights, is extracted.[15]

The problem of weighting the various items in constructing index numbers raises many questions. In determining how to weight the several items in a budget, for example, one encounters the fact that the relative amounts spent for various commodities differ from year to year. In one year, a workman may spend 3 per cent of his income for coal; in another year, 5 per cent. In determining what weight to give the price of coal, which year

---

[14] To illustrate, let the weights be as indicated:

	First date	Second date	Weight	Weight × the relatives
Bread, per loaf	100	120	12	1440
Butter, per pound	100	83	15	1245
Coffee, per pound	100	144	5	720
Eggs, per dozen	100	125	10	1250
Milk, per quart	100	200	5	1000
Steak, per pound	100	125	10	1250
Sugar, per pound	100	67	1	67

The sum of the weights is 58 and the sum of the weights × the relatives is 6,972. Dividing the latter by the former gives a weighted arithmetic average of 120.2.

[15] Using the figures in the preceding footnote, the weighted geometric average is

$$\sqrt[58]{120^{12} \times 83^{15} \times 144^{5} \times 125^{10} \times 200^{5} \times 125^{10} \times 67} \text{ or } 116.3$$

should be used? Should it be determined by expenditures in the first year or by expenditures in the second? Or should the price in the first year be weighted in accordance with expenditures in that year and the price in the second year by expenditures in that year? Or should the weight be determined by the average of the expenditures in the two years or over a period of time?

These are technical questions which may be more appropriately discussed in a book of statistics. They are raised here merely to indicate the nature of the problems that are encountered in attempts to measure changes in the price level. The weights that are used should depend upon the purpose of the index. If it is desired to show how changes in prices affect the cost of a given budget, then the weights should be constant for all years. The weights should ordinarily represent the importance of the commodities today rather than at some distant date in the past. But it may be desired to show how the price level is affected by a shift in the buying from some commodities to others. For example, a change might occur in the average of the prices actually paid even though there were no change in the price of any commodity. This change might be produced by consumers' shifting from the purchase of expensive commodities to the purchase of cheap ones. Such a change in the average of actual prices would not be reflected if the index were based on constant weights, but it would be reflected if the weights were adjusted in accordance with the importance of expenditures each year.

Weighting introduces bias into index numbers. This bias may be upward or downward depending upon the system of weighting that is used. The problem of bias introduced by weighting will not be discussed here. It should be stated, however, that the bias introduced by weighting is not usually serious and that it is nearly always more desirable to have *planned* weighting, with the bias which may go with it, than to be content with the more or less arbitrary weighting of the so-called " unweighted " indexes. Furthermore, by constructing more elaborate index numbers which involve additional computations, it is possible to eliminate the bias which goes with weighting.[16]

[16] One of the several formulae which eliminate the bias introduced by weighting has, by reason of its relative ease of computation, been called by Professor Irving Fisher the " ideal index." This index is the geometric average of two weighted aggregative indexes — one in which the weights are derived from the base year and the

III. The Relation between the Quantity of Money and Prices

Before discussing the possibility of controlling the price level, we must analyze the causes for changes in the level of prices. We shall begin with a discussion of a famous and widely accepted explanation — the so-called *quantity theory* of the value of money.

Suppose that the currency of a country consists of fifty million cash dollars and fifty million credit dollars and that each dollar is spent an average of fifty times a year. The total amount spent in the course of a year is obviously $5,000,000,000. If the quantity of goods sold is 10,000,000,000 units, it is clear that the average price per unit is 50 cents. Assume now that, other things remaining the same, the number of cash and credit dollars is doubled. Since by hypothesis each dollar is still spent an average of fifty times a year, the total annual expenditures must be $10,000,000,000. Twice as much money being offered for the same quantity of goods, the price level must also double. If, on the other hand, the number of dollars is decreased by half and each dollar is still spent fifty times a year, the total expenditure must fall to $2,500,000,000 and, if the quantity of goods exchanged remains the same, the average price must fall to 25 cents. Or suppose that the original number of dollars remains unchanged but that each dollar is spent one hundred times a year. Again the annual expenditures are $10,000,000,000 and the average selling price per unit is $1.00. Finally, assume that sales of goods fall from 10,000,000,000 to 5,000,000,000 units. If expenditures remain at $5,000,000,000, the average price again goes up from 50 cents to $1.00.

---

other in which the weights are derived from any given year that it is desired to compare with the base year. The formula for the ideal index is:

$$\sqrt{\frac{\Sigma p_1 \, q_0}{\Sigma p_0 \, q_0} \times \frac{\Sigma p_1 \, q_1}{\Sigma p_0 \, q_1}} \text{ in which}$$

p_0 = the price in the base year
p_1 = the price in the given year
q_0 = the quantity purchased (or sold) in the base year
q_1 = the quantity purchased (or sold) in the given year

It should be noted that when the "ideal" formula is used to derive indexes for a series of years (say, ten years), the indexes are valid only for a comparison between the base year and the given year. The indexes for two years *which do not include the base year* do not accurately indicate the change in price between those two years.

The relationship between the quantity of money and credit, the rates at which money and credit are spent (often called the *velocity of circulation*), the volume of goods sold, and the price level is represented by an equation known as the *equation of exchange*:

$$MV + M_1V_1 = PT, \text{ in which}$$

$P =$ the average price at which goods are sold during a given period.

$M =$ the amount of cash in circulation during the same period.

$M_1 =$ the amount of credit in circulation, that is, the volume of deposits subject to check.

$V =$ the average number of times each cash dollar is spent for goods during the period — the velocity of circulation of cash.

$V_1 =$ the average number of times each credit dollar is spent for goods.

$T =$ the total quantity of goods sold.

The obvious arithmetic relationship between these factors furnishes the basis for the quantity theory. The theory asserts that the price level — and, therefore, the value of money — is the result of the relationship between the quantity of money and credit spent $(MV + M_1V_1)$ and the quantity of goods sold. It asserts furthermore that changes in the price level occur in the main because of changes in the quantity of either money or credit $(M$ and $M_1)$, or because of changes in the volume of goods sold. The price level tends to vary, therefore, it is said, directly with changes in the quantity of money and credit and inversely with the total volume of goods sold.

The theory, it will be observed, makes three major assumptions: First, it assumes that the rates at which money and credit are spent $(V$ and $V_1)$ are more or less constant and, therefore, of little significance in explaining changes in the price level. Second, it assumes that fluctuations in the quantity of money and credit and in the volume of goods sold produce effects primarily upon prices rather than upon each other. For example, it is conceivable that an increase in M or M_1 might result primarily in an increase in the total volume of trade, leaving prices substantially unchanged. Finally, the theory regards the price level as largely passive — determined by, rather than determining, the quantity of money and credit and the volume of trade. As far as the equation of exchange is concerned, price changes might be either *causes* or *results* of changes in the other factors in the equation. The quantity theory asserts that they are primarily results.[17]

Prices, of course, are dependent upon the number of dollars which people offer for goods, and the number of dollars which buyers offer depends partly upon how many dollars they have. To this extent, plainly, the quantity theory is true. It is easy to find cases where prices have risen because the quantity of money and credit have increased more rapidly than the physical volume of trade, and other cases where prices have fallen because the physical volume of trade increased more rapidly than the quantity of money and credit. During the latter part of the nineteenth and the early part of the twentieth century, physical production was apparently growing at an average rate of roughly 2½ to 3 per cent a year. During this period, an annual increase of the same percentage in currency was needed in order to prevent prices from falling. From about 1860 to 1885, the world's annual output of gold was slowly decreasing. At the same time, the adoption of gold as standard money — in place of the bimetallic gold and silver standard — in France, the new German Empire, and other countries, greatly increased the monetary demand for gold. It is not surprising that, between 1865, the height of Civil War inflation, and 1896, the index of wholesale prices in the United States declined nearly two-thirds.

About 1890, the cyanide process of refining gold was invented and several years later large gold discoveries were made in South Africa and the Klondike. As a result, between the early nineties and the outbreak of the World War, the annual gold production of the world nearly trebled and the monetary stock of the United States more than doubled. At the same time, the volume of credit greatly expanded. The decline in wholesale prices continued for several years after gold production began to increase, reaching its low point in 1896, but from that date until 1913, wholesale prices advanced by approximately 50 per cent. The year 1913 saw the creation of the Federal Reserve system which, by changing the reserve requirements, greatly increased the ability of the banks to extend credit.

---

[17] Professor Irving Fisher concludes that the price level is " normally " " the one absolutely passive element in the equation of exchange." *The Purchasing Power of Money*, p. 172. But on p. 169, Professor Fisher qualifies his position.

War sales and loans to European belligerents caused our stock of gold to double between 1914 and 1920, and credit increased in proportion. Consequently, it is not surprising that wholesale prices in 1920 were more than twice the level of 1913 — 226 as compared with 100.

That the price level should rise when gold and credit increase more rapidly than commodity output and fall when they increase less rapidly seems obvious. As a matter of fact, the relationship between the quantity of gold and credit on the one hand and the price level on the other is more complicated than one might suspect. Before we examine the limitations of the quantity theory, it is desirable for us to analyze more closely the precise relationship between gold supply and prices. The usual form of currency, we have seen, is credit. The volume of credit which a banking system can supply depends, among other things, upon its gold reserves. Consequently, it is to be expected that the rate of gold production would affect the price level by affecting the supply of credit. During a period when gold output lags behind commodity output, credit might be expected to be scarce and interest rates high; during a period when the gold output is outrunning commodity output, credit might be expected to be plentiful and interest rates low.

But this theory of the relationship between gold and prices does not appear to fit the facts. Periods of falling prices are not characteristically times of tight credit and high interest rates, and periods of rising prices are not characteristically times of abundant credit and low interest rates. Between 1865 and 1896, for example, when the price level was falling, the trend of interest rates (as indicated by the yield of high-grade bonds) was downward; and from 1900 to 1920, a period of rising prices, the trend of interest rates was upward. The theory that a shortage of gold produces a drop in prices primarily because it produces a shortage of credit overlooks the existence of the business cycle. *The rate of gold production affects the long-time trend of prices through its effect upon the cyclical movement of business.* A low rate of gold production, for example, affects the trend of prices by prolonging the periods of depression and shortening the periods of boom; a high rate of gold production, on the other hand, affects the trend of prices by prolonging the boom periods and shortening the depressions. During periods of depression, short-time credit is likely to be abundant and interest rates low, and during periods of boom, credit is likely to be scarce and interest rates high. This is why a period of falling prices, when booms are short and depressions long, may have, on the average, lower interest rates than a period of rising prices, when booms are long and depressions short.

But how does the rate of gold production affect the duration of booms and depressions? The explanation is fairly simple. The trouble in a period of depression is that not enough dollars are being offered for goods. If the money of the country is increased by a large output of gold, the demand for goods is increased and the revival of business is accelerated. Likewise, large additions to the money supply, as a result of the rapid production of gold, prolong the boom phase of the business cycle by adding to reserves of the banks and thus postponing the time when the banks are compelled to adopt a restrictive credit policy. For these reasons, periods of large gold output are characteristically periods of short depressions and of long booms. On the other hand, when the production of gold is small, depressions are prolonged by the fact that the demand for goods is not increased by large additions to the money supply, and booms are shortened by the fact that the slow increase in reserves compels the banks soon to adopt a restrictive credit policy.

As a *partial* explanation of changes in the price level, the quantity theory is valuable. But the fact that changes in the relationship between the quantity of currency and the volume of trade often produce changes in the price level does not prove that changes in the price level are always or even *usually* due to changes in the relations between currency and trade.[18] May there not be important increases or decreases in the price level without corresponding increases or decreases in money and credit relative to trade, and may there not be increases or decreases in money and credit relative to trade without corresponding increases or decreases in prices? And may not changes in prices

---

[18] For the sake of brevity, we shall use currency to refer to any variety of circulating medium, whether money or credit.

be the *cause* of as well as the *result* of changes in the relationship between currency and trade?

As a matter of fact, each of the three major assumptions of the quantity theory exposes it to serious criticism. Fluctuations in the velocity of circulation are more important than the theory assumes; so also are the interactions between changes in quantity of money or credit and in the quantity of goods sold; and prices are by no means simply the result of the other factors in the equation of exchange.

How changes in the velocity of circulation affect prices is well illustrated by an extreme case. For centuries, the West has been sending gold and silver to India with little effect upon the price level there. Between 1900 and 1919, India imported about $800,000,000 in gold; in 1924 the imports were about $146,000,000 and in 1925 about $200,000,000. The reason why these huge receipts of cash have affected prices so little is because the money has been hoarded instead of spent — *in other words, the increase in M has decreased V instead of increasing P*. So strong is the grip of customary standards of living in India that merely having more does not lead the Indians to spend more. And so few and so little trusted are the banks and so restricted are the habits of buying securities or life insurance, that when the money is saved it is not put into savings accounts, securities, insurance policies — and thus transferred to others to spend — but it is hoarded, thus bringing down the average velocity of circulation.

The rate of circulation is naturally sensitive to prospective price changes. Rising prices mean more profits, put business men in an optimistic mood, and render them more willing to spend. Furthermore, the very fact that prices are rising induces enterprises to convert their money promptly into goods in anticipation of still higher prices. To a less extent, consumers are influenced in the same way. Falling prices, of course, have the opposite effect. The relationship between prospective price changes and the rate of circulation is shown in an exaggerated degree by European experience with inflated currencies. As long as the people expected their money to depreciate rapidly, they rushed to spend it as soon as they got it. Thus in Austria, from

January, 1920, to September, 1922, prices advanced approximately twice as much as the volume of currency — largely because of more rapid velocity of circulation. Following stabilization, however, the volume of currency increased from 1,701,000 millions of crowns on September 15, 1922, to 7,126,000 millions on December 31, 1923, while the cost of living declined 205 points from its high level of 14,153 in September, 1922.[19] Restoration of confidence in the currency caused people to spend it so much more slowly that even a great increase in the amount of currency did not raise prices.[20]

The recent experience of the United States also illustrates the influence of the velocity of circulation upon prices. Between November, 1920, and June, 1921, for example, when the volume of trade was diminishing, deposits subject to check in the United States fell about 6 per cent and money in circulation about 10 per cent.[21] This, according to the quantity theory, would lead us to expect little or no change in prices. In fact, if the drop in the volume of trade exceeded 8 per cent, we should expect prices actually to have *increased*. Nevertheless, prices *fell* about 45 per cent. Evidently the rate of spending greatly decreased. The very fact that prices had started to fall and that money was becoming more valuable made it profitable to hold money rather than spend it. In addition, business enterprises were selling less rapidly. Consequently, it was more difficult for them to accumulate enough money to pay their debts. Many of them were compelled to set aside every dollar which could be spared in order to have enough by the time their debts came due.

In the four years ending in 1924, the United States imported about $1,500,000,000 in gold. But, surprising to say, this did not produce a great inflation of prices. One reason was that in 1921 the member banks were heavily indebted to the Federal Reserve Banks. The imports of gold were largely used to reduce this indebtedness rather than to increase the reserves (and the lending power) of the member banks. Consequently, the gold

[19] De Bordes, J. v. W., *The Austrian Crown*, pp. 49, 50, 83, and 152.

[20] When confidence in domestic currency has been lost, foreign currency is used in many transactions. This explains in part why, during a period of extreme inflation, prices rise more rapidly than the volume of domestic money. When confidence in the domestic currency is restored, the foreign currency leaves the country. Hence prices may fall even while domestic currency is increasing.

[21] Hawtrey, R. G., *Monetary Reconstruction*, p. 119.

imports came under the control of the Reserve Banks, which had no interest in encouraging an expansion of credit. In other words, the gold was hoarded, but the hoarding was done, not by individuals, as in India, but by the Reserve Banks.

The second assumption of the quantity theory, that changes in the quantity of money or credit, on the one hand, and in the volume of trading, on the other, act primarily upon prices rather than upon each other, is also unjustified. In order to make goods, it is necessary to buy labor, raw materials, machines, and many other things. An increase in the quantity of money — and, therefore, in the number of dollars being spent — may lead to an expansion in output rather than to an advance in prices. It is possible, of course, that the money might be invested in gold mines, in which case it would tend to increase the quantity of money offered for the same volume of goods and thus raise prices. Or it might be used by business men in various ways to restrict the volume of production and thus might tend to raise prices. Usually, however, money invested in business *sooner or later* increases the output of goods. To the extent that this is true, the greater expenditure of dollars does not permanently raise the price level. And it follows also that a shrinkage in the volume of money or credit does not necessarily produce a proportionate drop in prices. For if dollars — either cash or credit — are used to make goods, a decrease in the number of dollars will reduce the output of goods.[22]

Sometimes an expansion of credit brings about a decrease instead of an increase in the volume of trade. Ordinarily money is borrowed for the purpose of purchasing goods. But we have learned that, in times of small demand and falling prices, it may be borrowed *in order to avoid selling goods*. An enterprise may have taxes, interest, payrolls or other obligations which must be met at a certain time. To raise cash by dumping goods on a weak market might cause a disastrous drop in prices. To avoid this, the firm may borrow money to meet its obligations

[22] The commodities *offered for sale* may temporarily increase or at least not decrease, because a drop in prices causes accumulated stocks to be hastily thrown on the market. Likewise it causes, as we have seen, a decrease in the velocity of circulation. Consequently, the first effects of a decrease in the quantity of money may be a precipitous drop in prices.

and sell its goods more gradually. In this case, the increase in credit undoubtedly affects prices by checking their fall, but it does so by first affecting the volume of trading.

Finally, it is a mistake to regard the quantities of money and credit, the velocity of circulation, and the volume of trading as primarily causes and the price level as primarily an effect. Prices are not simply passive things. The prices of today, by their influence upon the quantities of money and credit, the velocity of circulation, and the volume of trading, help create the price level of tomorrow. Rising prices, by causing men to spend money more rapidly in expectation of a further rise, tend to produce a further advance; falling prices, by making buyers hold off, tend to produce a further decrease. The kind of credit that is represented in the equation of exchange (that is, the volume of deposits subject to check) is primarily a result of the price level, because deposits subject to check represent, in the main, borrowed money and the amount which business establishments need to borrow for working capital depends on the price level. It is true that credit has much to do with prices but it is a *very different kind of credit* from that symbolized in the equation of exchange by M_1. The kind of credit which affects prices is the *ability* of enterprises to borrow. Of course, this in itself is partly a result of the price level. On the basis of its ability to borrow, an enterprise contracts to buy goods at certain prices. Possibly weeks later, the manager goes to the bank and borrows the funds to pay for the goods. It is ability to borrow, not deposits subject to check, which affects the demand for goods and hence prices.[23] Not only do prices affect the amount which enterprises borrow but they also affect the ability of the banks to lend. When prices rise, stores need more till money and consumers more pocket money. Consequently, the banking system tends to lose cash to the rest of the country. Thus its cash reserves and hence its capacity to lend are diminished.

The quantity of money, no less than the quantity of credit, is affected by the price level. Rising prices encourage imports

---

[23] Ability to borrow is itself partly a result of the price level and of price movements because it depends largely upon the value of the assets of the firm which, of course, depends on the price level and upon the profits of the firm which are greatly affected by price movements.

and discourage exports, and thus tend to decrease the supply of money by causing gold to be exported. As prices mount, the increasing expense of mining diminishes the output of gold by making the high-cost mines unprofitable. The war-time drop in the purchasing power of gold caused a substantial decrease in gold production. In 1922, the world's gold output was about one-third less than in 1913.[24] When commodity prices rise, gold becomes relatively cheap in countries where it is the standard money, because in such countries the price of gold does not change. As long as the government is willing to coin bullion in unlimited quantities and without charge, the maximum quantity of money which buyers are willing to pay for a given quantity of gold bullion and the minimum amount of money which the sellers of bullion are willing to accept remain substantially the same, despite changes in other prices.[25] This means that articles made of gold tend to rise in price less than other commodities and that their consumption is encouraged. Consequently, a larger proportion of the gold output is used in the arts. These things tend, of course, to limit the country's monetary stock and hence to check the rise in prices. When prices drop, imports are discouraged, exports are encouraged, and gold tends to flow into the country; mining becomes more profitable and the output of mines increases; articles made of gold become relatively more expensive, the quantity of them demanded falls off, a smaller proportion of the gold output is used in the arts, and a larger part of it is coined.

[24] But it may be questioned whether a rise in prices diminishes gold output *in the long run*. The decreased purchasing power of gold stimulates economies and improvements in mining and refining. Several years may be required for these economies to be developed, but they come. Consequently, it is possible that a rise in prices primarily accelerates the development of gold-mining technique rather than diminishes the output of gold. In fact, a rise in the price level, by accelerating the advance of mining and refining technique, may be responsible for still further increases in prices. The volume of low-grade ores is so great that every improvement which reduces the cost of production is likely to cause a great increase in output.

[25] The price of gold, like the price of anything else, is simply the number of dollars for which a given quantity of it can be sold. As long as the government stands ready to exchange coins for their pure gold content in bullion, the owners of bullion, of course, are unwilling to sell their bullion to any one for less. And since the owners of money can obtain bullion by melting coins, they are willing to pay only slightly more for bullion than its weight in money. They may be willing to pay a little more because coins become light through use. A bank, especially a central bank, which wishes to increase its reserves may pay a small premium for gold in order to avoid the expense of importing it.

What then are our conclusions concerning the determination of the price level? The relationship between the quantities of money and credit and the volume of trading undoubtedly has much to do with fixing the price level. But it is far from the *sole* determinant. Every factor in the equation of exchange, *including the price level itself,* is a determinant of the price level of to-morrow. All react upon each other, and often a factor reacts upon itself — as when a greater velocity of circulation, by caus-ing prices to rise, creates a still more rapid circulation, or when an advance in prices, by making possible large profits and an accumulation of capital, causes prices to decline again. Any attempt to single out certain factors which are of dominant im-portance seems futile. Some of the most conspicuous movements in the price level, such as the downward trend from 1865 to 1896, the upward trend from 1896 to 1913, and the extreme inflation of the war period, have been associated very plainly with changes in the quantity of money and credit, and it seems clear that these changes had much to do with these price movements. But in view of the complicated fashion in which the different factors in the equation of exchange react upon each other, it is impossible to assert positively that these price movements were primarily the products of changes in the quantity of currency. It is only safe to say that, through the ever-shifting interaction of the quantity of money and credit, of the velocity of circulation, of the volume of trade, and of prices, present and anticipated, upon each other and upon themselves, the price level of tomorrow is in constant process of making.

IV. Government Finances and the Price Level

The most violent price changes of recent years have been caused by the financial policies of governments. It is, therefore, desirable for us to examine the relationship between government finances and prices.

The basic cause for the inflation which the governments have produced has been the necessity of greatly increasing the purchas-ing power of the state upon extremely short notice. War and the aftermath of war have created this necessity. War invariably means inflation of prices because modern warfare is a race. That side is likely to win which equips men and puts them into the field the more rapidly. It is impossible, however, for the government to obtain funds fast enough to meet its heavy war expenses either by taxes or by bond sales. There are obvious political difficulties in the way of suddenly compelling people to pay greatly increased taxes or to purchase huge quantities of government bonds. There are also financial difficulties — many people and enterprises do not have the ready cash and are not in a position to borrow. Finally, there are administrative difficulties — it takes time for the legislature to pass a tax law and it takes even more time to create tax-collecting machinery. Meanwhile, the government must pay its bills and pay them promptly, for munitions manufacturers cannot operate unless they can pay for raw materials and labor.

The government might meet the emergency by issuing paper money and by making it legal tender. This was one of the methods employed by both sides in financing the Civil War. During the World War, all the belligerents in Europe issued paper money. The result of this method is, of course, a rapid rise in prices with all of the attendant evils. The government, however, achieves its essential purpose of quickly acquiring a vast amount of purchasing power.

But financing war by the sale of bonds also brings inflation. It is not easy to sell huge quantities of government securities on short notice. A few months before our entrance into the World War, notes secured by government obligations were made eligible for rediscount by the Federal Reserve Banks. During the War, the Reserve Banks, at the suggestion of the Reserve Board, established preferential rates in favor of loans secured by government obligations. This encouraged the banks to lend money on government bonds as collateral. But when one purchases a bond from the government and then takes it to the bank and borrows on it as collateral, the quantity of currency is plainly being increased — for the government obtains the dollars which the buyer paid for the bond and the buyer obtains from his bank a deposit account to replace the dollars which he gave to the government. The banks themselves purchased bonds in large quantities and then replenished their reserves by using the bonds to obtain loans from the Reserve Banks. Whenever a war is financed by borrowing, inflation is unescapable because the government obligations are bound to be used as the basis of private borrowing from the banks.[26]

Any situation which prevents governments from balancing their budgets is likely to lead to inflation. The war left many European countries burdened with enormous interest payments on war debts and heavy outlays for reconstruction. Their revenues, however, were diminished by the industrial disorganization which reduced receipts from income taxes and customs duties. Unable to make both ends meet or to sell bonds at home or abroad, they issued paper money. This, of course, caused prices to rise and the expenses of the government to mount. It also caused the income of the government to increase, but the rising revenue did not keep pace with the mounting expenses.[27] The result was a vicious circle in which inability to balance the budget led to inflation and inflation led to inability to balance the budget. How to break this vicious circle and to stabilize the currency and at what value to stabilize the currency — whether to raise it to the pre-war value or to stabilize it at a much lower level — were problems of great difficulty and importance. If the currency were stabilized at too low a value, many creditors would lose most of their property. If it were stabilized at too high a value, many debtors would be unable to meet their obligations and would lose their property. Few nations were able to stabilize their currencies without help from other countries. For this reason, the problems of how and at what value to stabilize a depreciating currency can advantageously be discussed in connection with the analysis of international financial and monetary policies in Chapter XXX.

[26] A pronounced inflation of prices naturally causes gold to leave the country because it will buy more abroad where prices have not risen. But in times of war, when governments are borrowing heavily, it is vital that the banks be in a position to grant large credits. If gold were to be exported, the reserves of the banks would be depleted and the banks would be compelled to reduce their loans. Consequently, governments which permit an inflation of prices find it necessary to impose an embargo on gold exports. Such a law, of course, is not easy to enforce. It is necessary, therefore, to restrict the internal circulation of gold. This is done by forbidding the banks to pay gold to their customers. The demand for cash is met by bank notes or government paper money. Such a law is easy to enforce because the banks naturally prefer to keep their gold.

[27] The reasons for the lag of revenues behind expenses will be discussed in more detail in Chapter XXX.

V. The Interdependence of Price Levels in Different Countries

The levels of prices in different countries are not the same, but they are closely interdependent. Suppose that the prices in the United States became high in relation to prices abroad. Buyers would find it advantageous to purchase abroad but sellers would find difficulty, because of their high costs, in selling abroad. Soon we should be exporting gold to pay for our excess of imports. The decrease in the quantity of gold would reduce the reserves of the banks and compel them to curtail loans. The decrease in the number of both money and credit dollars would diminish domestic demand for goods and cause prices to fall. Much of the gold sent abroad would be added to the reserves of the foreign banks and would become the basis of an expansion of credit. The result would be a tendency for prices abroad to rise. As prices decreased in the United States and advanced in other countries, domestic buyers would find less advantage in purchasing abroad and domestic sellers would find it easier to sell abroad. Consequently, our imports would gradually decrease and our exports would increase. Eventually the price level here would be brought into equilibrium with the price levels of other countries and the exportation of gold would cease. If prices in the United States were to fall too low in relation to prices elsewhere, the process which we have described would be reversed — our exports would increase, our imports would decline, gold would flow in, the volume of credit here would increase, prices would rise here and decline abroad, exports would diminish and imports would expand, until finally equilibrium would again be established.

This general statement of the relationship between the price levels in different countries must be amplified and qualified in order to avoid misunderstandings. To begin with, it should be noted that the price level in the United States does not necessarily tend to be the *same* as price levels in other countries, because tariffs, the cost of transportation, and the impossibility of exporting or importing many articles or services prevent that. But the relationship between prices here and prices abroad tends to be such that gold is neither exported nor imported. Moreover, it must not be supposed that a state of equilibrium between price levels *usually* prevails and that periods of gold imports or exports are exceptional. As a matter of fact, it is *the state of equilibrium* which is exceptional; it is constantly being *approached,* but, before it is attained, conditions often change, and the price level which was *below* the point of equilibrium is now *above* it.

In determining the movement of gold from one country to another, all prices are not equally important. In fact, the prices of the vast majority of commodities have little or no effect upon gold movements. The prices which affect gold movements are the prices of the relatively few commodities which enter into international trade. Most goods and services, for one reason or another, do not enter into international trade on a large scale. It is when the prices of the few commodities which are exported become relatively low, that a country gains gold. The effect of the gold is expended, of course, upon all the prices of all commodities in the community. Some time may elapse before it produces a marked effect in the costs of producing the exported commodities and thus tends to bring exports into equilibrium with imports. Consequently, a country with marked advantages over the rest of the world in certain export industries may draw gold for many years. This is particularly true if the country is making faster technical progress in these industries than are other countries. In that event, it may attract such a large part of the world's gold supply that it causes a serious drop in prices abroad. In a small degree, some such effect has apparently been produced during recent years by the rapid technical advance in the United States. The fact that gold movements are determined by the prices of a relatively few commodities means gold may be entering a country where the general price level is already substantially above the price level of most other countries.

The relations between the price levels in different countries cannot be explained solely in terms of gold movements. In some degree, these relations must be explained in terms of the policies of the central banks; and in even greater degree they must be explained in terms of security and capital movements.

Over short periods of time, the movement of gold is substantially affected by the policies of central banks. Indeed, the influence of central banks is greater today than ever before. The gold held by each central bank constitutes the ultimate reserve for the credit extended by all banks in the country and the central bank may be exceedingly reluctant to lose it in large quantities. When the balance of trade causes large gold exports, the central bank may attempt to check them. Suppose, for example, that a substantial drop in the price of raw cotton were to cause a large drop in the value of exports from the United States and to start an outflow of gold to pay for our imports. If the Federal Reserve Banks wished to hold their gold, they might do so by several methods. To prevent the loss of gold due to a purely temporary cause, such as a slump in the price of cotton, the banks might sell some of their holdings of bills on foreign money centers. But if the unfavorable balance of trade were likely to continue for some time, a rise in the rediscount rate might be necessary. This would raise interest rates and attract funds from abroad. The movement of balances from abroad tends, of course, to counteract the effect of the excess of imports and to check the export of gold.[28] But it might do more than this. By increasing the cost of credit, it would discourage borrowing, and thus tend to lower the price level. This would encourage exports and discourage imports and thus tend to end the outflow of gold. The effect upon the price level in the end would be about the same as that which would be produced by export of gold, except that the exportation of gold on a large scale would not actually occur.

Not only may the central banks control, to some extent, the movement of gold but, in large degree, they may counteract the effect of gold movements upon domestic credit conditions and, therefore, upon domestic prices. This, of course, may cause a given movement of gold to persist longer than it otherwise would. For example, the normal effect of large importations of gold, we have seen, is to raise the domestic price level. A central bank can postpone or reduce this effect to a substantial

[28] It is possible, however, that the *first* effect of an increase in the rediscount rate would be to accentuate the export of gold. If foreigners were speculating on a large scale in the domestic stock market and if the rise in the rediscount rate precipitated a general liquidation of securities, foreign speculators might sell their holdings and transfer their funds abroad. After the foreign funds employed in stock speculation had left the country, the higher rediscount rate would tend to check the export of gold.

extent by selling securities in the open market. The sale of securities enables the bank to increase its cash holdings and thus tends to prevent the gold receipts from lowering interest rates and stimulating an expansion of credit. The normal effect of gold exports, on the other hand, is to produce a scarcity of domestic credit and to lower the domestic price level. The central bank can counteract this effect by buying securities in the open market. At various times in recent years (the fall of 1927, for example) the Federal Reserve Banks have purchased paper in the open market to balance the effect of an exportation of gold. The Reserve Banks were able to do this because of their enormous surplus reserves and they were willing to do so, partly in order to save the domestic market from disturbance and partly to encourage the exportation of gold to countries which were returning to the gold standard and which needed to build up their reserves.

Differences in exports and imports may be settled by security movements instead of gold movements. Indeed security movements are today probably more important in settling balances between nations than gold movements. By preventing the movement of gold, or at least postponing it for many years, security movements tend to prevent an excess of imports or exports from affecting price levels in different countries. Suppose, for example, that a country which has relatively low production costs and which can sell at low prices has, in consequence, a substantial excess of exports over imports. It may not, for many years at least, attract gold. It may take payment for its excess of exports in foreign securities instead of gold. In fact, an excess of exports over imports and large investments abroad are likely to go together. The large export surplus of the United States during post-war years has been made possible in large degree by the ability and willingness of the United States to finance foreign buyers. If the ability of a concern to sell in foreign markets depends upon the ability of foreign buyers to obtain capital with which to buy, the enterprise may help foreign buyers float capital issues in the domestic market. It may even form a subsidiary holding company which sells its own stock to domestic investors and, with the funds thus obtained, buys stock or bonds in foreign companies. Eventually, of course, the continuous investment of capital abroad will cause annual interest and dividend payments to domestic investors to exceed new investments and gold may begin slowly to enter the country. In the meantime, however, the purchase of foreign securities may prevent the excess of exports from producing much effect upon the domestic price level.

Security movements also explain why a country with a high general price level and with an excess of imports over exports may not necessarily be losing gold. If capital in the country is relatively scarce, so that interest rates and profits are relatively high, foreign investors may be buying into the domestic industries. The excess of imports over exports may be paid for, therefore, not by exporting gold but by selling to foreign investors stocks and bonds in domestic corporations. As a result, the excess of imports may have little effect upon the domestic price level and the price level may remain high relative to prices abroad for many years.

The interdependence between the price levels of different countries sheds light on the oft-repeated statement: "Trade is necessarily reciprocal." That is, a country cannot sell to others unless it buys from them. To test the truth of this statement, let us make the extreme supposition that costs of production in one country were so low that it sold goods to other countries but bought nothing from them. It would then be paid in gold. The reserves in its banks would increase, and those in foreign banks would decrease. Interest rates would drop at home and rise abroad, the volume of credit and prices would rise at home and drop abroad. As prices declined abroad and increased at home, the country would experience more and more difficulty in selling to other countries. At the same time, it would find it more advantageous to buy from them. Eventually it would begin to import and its imports would gradually increase and its exports decrease until ultimately the influx of gold would cease. For reasons which have been indicated in the preceding discussion, exports may not be *immediately* responsive to a change in imports and imports may not be immediately responsive to a change in exports. In the long run, however, it is true that trade tends to be reciprocal.[29]

All of this helps us to understand the economic effects of customs duties. Protective tariffs are said to protect home industries. But many home industries are injured by a tariff, and the protective effect of a tariff may be nullified in large degree by the higher prices which it often brings. A tariff, of course, tends to diminish imports. But if foreigners sell less to us, they must pay for part of their purchases from us in cash instead of goods. The influx of gold tends to raise domestic prices. Naturally this diminishes the protective effect of the tariff because it increases the operating expenses of all domestic producers. In addition, those industries which have been doing an export business find themselves positively injured instead of protected by the tariff. As the domestic price level advances, their costs advance, but the prices which they can obtain abroad for their goods are presumably about the same — perhaps a little less because the export of gold from foreign countries tends to lower prices abroad. As prices at home advance, it becomes more and more profitable, despite the tariff, to purchase abroad. The diminishing exports and growing imports which result from higher domestic prices eventually cause the importation of gold to end. Domestic prices no longer rise, exports cease declining, imports cease decreasing. The net effect of the tariff has been to reduce both imports and exports and to raise domestic prices.

[29] It must not be imagined, however, that the interdependence of prices in different countries renders it impossible for a country to have for an indefinite period an *apparent* excess of exports over imports or of imports over exports. Great Britain, for example, has had for many years an excess of imports over exports. The United States, on the other hand, for a long time has exported more than it has imported. The explanation of these cases is to be found partly in the security movements which have been explained above and partly in so-called *invisible exports* and *invisible imports*, which do not enter into the usual statements of exports and imports but which do affect the balance of payments no less than the so-called " visible " items. Great Britain, for example, can go on year after year importing more than she exports because she has large investments abroad upon which she is being paid interest and dividends and because she has a large merchant marine for the services of which she receives payments from many countries. We in the United States can go on exporting more than we import because we are investing capital abroad, repaying loans made to us by foreign investors, paying interest and dividends on foreign capital invested here, and buying the services of foreign vessels and insurance companies; because American tourists are spending money abroad; and because immigrants here are sending money to relatives and friends.

Although there is a tendency *in the long run* for equilibrium between exports and imports to be reëstablished by gold movements, a country may not feel able to permit the balance in its trade to be restored in this slow and possibly painful manner. Suppose that a country experiences a sudden drop in its exports relative to its imports. Gold leaves and domestic prices fall. To permit this to occur without restraint may impose a crushing burden on debtors. If the public debt is large, it may seriously increase the burden of taxation. Worst of all, so much gold may leave the country before exports again balance imports that the maintenance of the gold standard is threatened. The recent experience of Australia is illuminating. Heavy borrowing from abroad had created an annual interest claim of approximately $150,000,000. The severe drop in the price of wool and wheat during the depression of 1929–1930 reduced Australia's exports by approximately $250,000,000. Obviously the government could not stand by and permit the adverse balance of trade to drain the country of gold. Consequently, in April, 1930, the government adopted the policy of drastically restricting imports. Prohibitive tariff rates were placed on certain luxuries and on some manufactured ware, an embargo was imposed on other commodities, and the importation of still other goods was limited by the establishment of import quotas.

VI. How Far Is It Desirable to Stabilize the Price Level?

The problem of how to stabilize the price level is here conceived as the problem of checking the long-time movements of prices, such as the drop between 1865 and 1896 and the rise between 1896 and 1920, rather than the problem of controlling the shorter, wave-like movements of prices that accompany the business cycle. The problem of controlling the long-time movements of the price level has aroused many violent political controversies. During the last third of the nineteenth century, for example, when gold was becoming relatively scarce, it was proposed to check the decline in prices by making debts payable in silver as well as in gold — that is, by making the dollar consist of *either* silver or gold.[30] Such a plan is known as *bimetallism*.

---

[30] The present silver dollars are not really dollars. They are simply tokens which circulate as dollars because they are exchangeable for gold dollars. The silver

Bimetallism was discredited because its popular advocates proposed to put so little silver in the dollar that its value would have been greatly reduced. This would have permitted debtors to pay their obligations in depreciated currency. As luck would have it, the discovery of the cyanide process and the gold strikes in the Klondike and South Africa gave debtors the chance to pay in depreciated *gold* dollars, and popular interest in bimetallism died out. Because of the specific form in which it was advocated, bimetallism remains associated in the popular mind with inflation. But, carefully worked out, it might possibly provide a more stable money than gold.

The violent upheavals of prices produced by the war have renewed interest in the problem of stabilizing the price level. Before examining the principal proposals for stabilizing prices, let us examine briefly the question how much stabilization of the price level would be desirable. Would it be desirable, even if possible, to stabilize the price level *completely* — in the sense, that whatever changes might occur in the prices of individual commodities, the average of all prices would remain unchanged? Or would it be desirable to permit some upward or downward movement in the price level? If the answer to the second question is "Yes," how much movement should be permitted and under what conditions?

Everyone will doubtless agree that such violent movements in the price level as occurred between 1865 and 1896, 1896 and 1920, and 1920 and 1930 are undesirable. Under certain conditions it might be wise to permit a very moderate, long-time advance in the price level. Those occasions, however, are exceedingly rare and may be ignored in this discussion. But the case of a falling price level is different. Suppose that, as a result of technical progress, the costs of production steadily fall. Would it be desirable under the circumstances to prevent the drop in prices? The effect of complete stabilization would be to prevent all owners of fixed incomes (pensioners, bondholders, mortgage holders, owners of preferred stocks, and the lessors of real estate) and all holders of contracts payable in a fixed number of dollars (insurance, for example) from participating in the

---

dollar does not contain a dollar's worth of silver. A dollar is a certain quantity of *gold* — 23.22 grains of pure gold.

gains of technical progress. The rest of the community would be sharing in the gains but to the extent that anyone was the recipient of a fixed-income security or the owner of a contract payable in a fixed number of dollars, he would not participate. Would it be fair thus to discriminate against one class in the community? The answer is obvious.

But the drop in the price level might not be entirely due to the technical progress of industry. It might be due in part to the growth in population and capital. Suppose, for example, that during a given period the technique of industry remained absolutely static with no improvements of any kind. Assume also that, because of the increase in the population of the country, the output of industry increased more rapidly than the supply of money and that the price level fell. Would it be desirable for a stabilizing agency to prevent this drop in the price level? The answer is obviously "Yes." No improvements have occurred to make prices fall. Simply the number of producers has increased. If the fall in prices is not checked, the recipients of fixed incomes will profit from the decreases in prices at the expense of the rest of the community. Plainly this would be just as unfair as to exclude them from participating in the benefits of technical progress.

These two hypothetical situations indicate how far it would be desirable to prevent a drop in prices. To the extent that a drop is attributable to improvements in productive methods, it should not be checked. To the extent that it is attributable to a mere increase in the number of producers and in the amount of productive equipment, it should be checked. As a practical matter, of course, there is no way of distinguishing between the effects of these several causes. Technical improvements are constantly occurring, the number of gainfully employed workers and the volume of industrial equipment are constantly increasing. Possibly the best rough and ready rule for a stabilizing body to follow would be to assume that increases in production per gainfully employed person are attributable to technical improvements. This part of the total increase in output should be permitted to produce a drop in prices. But steps should be taken to prevent the mere growth in the number of producers from affecting the price level.

Two amplifications of the above rule are desirable. There is good reason to believe that *slowly* falling prices accelerate technical development. They do not destroy the hope of profits but they make large profits slightly more difficult to achieve. They impose small inventory losses upon enterprises and they expose established concerns to slightly more formidable competition from new plants constructed at a lower price level. For these reasons slowly falling prices cause managements to be somewhat more alert, enterprising, and persistent in searching for ways to reduce operating costs.[31] In order to accelerate technical progress, it may seem wise on some occasions to permit prices to fall somewhat more rapidly than technical progress alone might cause them to fall — to permit the mere increase in the number of producers to have some effect upon the price level.

On other occasions, however, it might be wise to pursue a different policy. Very rapid technical change may produce acute distress among large groups in the community who must suddenly find new ways of making a living. There is such a thing as the cost of progress (or of change) being too great. In this event, it may be desirable to reduce the rate of change by preventing technical progress from producing its full effect upon the price level. Possibly it would even be desirable to inflate prices temporarily. A rise in prices is, of course, a subsidy to every old enterprise because it raises the cost of constructing new and more efficient competing plants. The effect of a rise in prices (or of a retarded fall in prices) is to slow up the shift of production from old plants to new and from some regions to other regions and thus to diminish the pains of too rapid change. During periods of too rapid industrial change, moderate inflation may be a wise social policy.

VII. The Plan of "the Stabilized Dollar"

The foregoing discussion has taken for granted that the price level can be subjected to rather complete control. Is that assumption justified? Three principal proposals for stabilizing prices have been made: (1) the plan of "the stabilized dollar," of which Professor Irving Fisher is the leading advocate; (2) the control

---

[31] Let it be emphasized that reference here is only to *slowly* falling prices. *Rapidly* falling prices, which interrupt production by causing postponement of buying, present an entirely different case.

of prices by the regulation of gold output; and (3) a "managed currency," with which the name of Mr. J. M. Keynes is prominently associated. Let us examine these proposals one by one.

The plan of "the stabilized dollar" is extremely simple. At present the dollar consists of a given quantity of gold — 23.22 grains of pure gold. Because the dollar consists of an unchanging amount of gold, it naturally fluctuates in value as gold becomes worth more or less, just as a bushel of potatoes changes in value as potatoes become worth more or less. Professor Fisher proposes to keep the dollar fixed in value by making it variable in weight. When gold became worth less, the dollar would be kept from falling in value by putting more gold into it; when gold became worth more, the dollar would be kept from rising in value by reducing its gold content. Since credit dollars are redeemable in gold dollars, their value depends upon that of the gold dollars. Consequently, if gold dollars were kept at constant value, credit dollars too would be worth an unchanging amount.

In order to determine when to change the weight of the dollar, it would be necessary to construct an extremely accurate index number of the general price level. It would be necessary also to authorize a board to supervise the collection of data for the index number and to determine how much the weight of the dollar should be changed. Professor Fisher has proposed that the weight should not be changed more frequently than every two months and that no single adjustment should alter the weight by more than one per cent.[32]

---

[32] To protect the government against loss from speculation in gold, Professor Fisher proposes that the price at which the government buys gold shall be one per cent less than that at which it sells it. At present the government buys and sells gold at the same price — $20.67 an ounce. Assume that the plan of the stabilized dollar were in operation and that the government bought and sold gold at the same price. Suppose also that prices were falling, making it quite certain that, at the next adjustment date, the weight of the dollar would be decreased or, in other words, that the government would advance the price at which it would buy and sell gold. It would then be possible for speculators to buy gold of the government at today's price and sell it back tomorrow at a higher price — for one per cent more in case the weight of the dollar were decreased by this amount. If, however, the price which the government paid for gold were always one per cent less than the price which it charged, there would ordinarily be no profit in buying gold from the government in order to sell it back after the maximum adjustment of one per cent had been made. It is true that the possibility of speculation would not be

But how would it be possible to change the weight of millions of gold coins in the hands of millions of persons scattered over the whole country? Obviously the plan would require that gold coins be withdrawn from circulation and that they be replaced with certificates which would entitle the holder to a stipulated number of gold dollars. This would not be a radical change, because, except in the Pacific states, it is gold certificates which usually circulate rather than gold itself. The government would hold the actual gold, just as it now does, in coins or bars and it would give gold, just as it now does, to any one presenting certificates for payment. But, instead of paying a *constant* weight of gold for every dollar of certificates presented, it would pay an amount which would vary as the weight of the dollar changed. Likewise, in exchanging dollars for bullion, the government, instead of giving a constant price of $20.67 an ounce, would pay more or less, depending upon whether the dollar had been made lighter or heavier.

The plan of the stabilized dollar would encounter powerful political opposition. The greatest opposition would probably come from exporters and importers. As long as the weight of the dollar remains constant and the government imposes no embargoes on the export of gold, exporters and importers can tell within narrow limits the future worth of the dollar in terms of the money of other gold standard countries which also permit the free exportation of gold. Under these circumstances, the price of dollars in London cannot be much *more* than the number of pounds sterling containing an equal amount of gold *plus* the cost of shipping bullion to America.[33] Nor can it be *less* than the number of pounds containing an equal amount of gold *minus* the cost of importing bullion from America. It would pay to export bullion rather than pay more than the former price for

---

entirely eliminated. Prices might fall so much that it would appear reasonably certain that the government would have to make *several* successive one per cent reductions in the weight of the dollar. In such a case, speculators might buy the gold today, hold it over several adjustment dates, and eventually sell it back for one or two per cent more than they paid for it.

[33] The cost of shipping includes, of course, the loss of interest during transit. Shipment takes time. Consequently some buyers who must have balances abroad immediately may bid up the price of exchange above the gold content of the foreign coins plus the cost of shipping.

dollar exchange and it would be more profitable to import bullion than to accept less than the latter price for bills on New York.

Were the plan of the stabilized dollar in operation, there would be no definite limits to the price which the dollar might command in the currencies of other countries. Its price would depend fundamentally — as it does now — upon its gold content, but its gold content would not be constant. It might change by several per cent within four or five months. In international trade, where credits are for longer terms than in domestic trade, the possibility of a change of one or two per cent in the weight of the dollar would be highly distasteful to both importers and exporters. The exporter wishes to know how many dollars he is going to receive, the importer how many he is going to pay. Yet if the weight of the dollar were increased, an exporter who sold goods to an English firm for £1,000 would receive fewer dollars for his wares; if the weight were decreased, an importer who had agreed to pay £1,000 for a shipment of goods, would be compelled to pay more dollars.

It may be replied that, although the exporter receives fewer dollars, he gets the same amount of purchasing power, and, although the importer pays more dollars, he gives no more purchasing power. We may grant that no grave injustice would be done, but this would scarcely satisfy the exporters and importers. The exporter expects to receive, not a certain amount of purchasing power, but a certain number of dollars. To produce the goods costs him a definite amount. After this expense has been paid, it is not altered by subsequent changes in the weight of the dollar. On the basis of this cost he quotes a price. Later he finds that the changed weight of the dollar prevents him from receiving all that he expected to obtain. Naturally he is not pleased with the stabilized dollar. The importer expects to pay a certain number of dollars. On the basis of that expectation, he may have sold part of the goods before they even arrived. The terms of those contracts are fixed and are not altered by changes in the weight of the dollar. If the weight of the dollar is decreased because of falling prices, the importer is compelled to pay more dollars for the goods. Naturally he, no less than the exporter in periods of rising prices, is not pleased with the stabilized dollar. This opposition on the part of exporters and importers may appear unreasonable because what they gain or lose when the price trend is downward they lose or gain when it is upward. It must be remembered, however, that the general movement of prices may be upward or downward for a generation or more.

The difficulty is enhanced by the fact that foreign exchange rates tend to anticipate changes in the domestic purchasing power of money. If exchange rates were to anticipate changes in the weight of the dollar, exporters would find, when the price trend was upward, that the dollar had appreciated abroad in anticipation of expected increases in its weight. They would find themselves compelled to accept fewer dollars for goods sold abroad *before* adjustments in the weight of the dollar enabled them to buy more with each dollar here. When the price trend was downward, importers would find the dollar worth less in terms of foreign currency before decreases were made in its weight. They would be compelled to pay more dollars for goods purchased abroad *before* decreases in the weight of the dollar enabled them to sell the goods for more dollars here. Under some circumstances, the situation of some exporters and importers might be much worse than we have just depicted. Suppose, for example, that in a period of generally rising prices, the price of the commodity sold by some exporters is decreasing. They would, therefore, be receiving fewer marks, pounds, or francs for it. But if the weight of the dollar were being increased because of the general trend of the price level, the income of these exporters would be still further diminished. Not only would they receive less in foreign currency but each pound or mark or franc which they did receive would purchase fewer dollars.

The inconveniences which the stabilized dollar would impose upon exporters and importers are trivial in comparison with the injuries which the present unstable dollar now inflicts upon the community as a whole. The effects of "the stabilized dollar" upon exporters and importers are not, therefore, a serious *economic* objection to the plan.[34] They are significant because they indicate why the scheme is bound to arouse great *political* oppo-

[34] In a country such as Great Britain which is highly dependent upon foreign trade, these objections would be far more important than in the case of the United States.

sition. There are, however, several important questions in regard to the economic effects of the plan.

Professor J. H. Rogers has pointed out that the stabilized dollar, unless skillfully administered, might accentuate the ups and downs of the business cycle by encouraging imports of gold during periods of rising prices and exports during periods of falling prices. Let us suppose that the plan were in operation and that, following a collapse of prosperity, prices in this country were falling rapidly. Since the weight of the dollar could not be reduced by more than one per cent every two months, there would soon be an accumulated deficit in the index number of prices, making it practically certain that further decreases in the weight of the dollar would be made at the end of the immediately succeeding two-month intervals. Under such circumstances, foreign banks would almost certainly begin to borrow extensively in New York (interest there, under falling prices, would probably be low), convert their loans into gold, and ship it abroad, where the funds thus secured would be loaned at the prevailing rates of interest. Later, when the dollar had been lightened by say, 5 per cent, the gold would be returned and reconverted into a number of dollars 4 per cent greater than the original sum. The speculating bankers would thereby make 4 per cent from the government in addition to interest at the rates prevailing abroad. The drain of gold would tend to raise interest rates and check the expansion of credit in the United States. But the critical period which follows a collapse of prosperity is precisely the time when it is important that the banks be able to help enterprises by granting them credit at low rates. Should the stabilized dollar, by causing gold exports, prevent the banks from giving credit liberally and at low rates, it would accentuate the severity of the depression. In periods of boom, a reverse evil might occur. If rising prices created an accumulated surplus in the index number of prices, making it certain that the weight of the dollar would be substantially increased, gold would flow to this country, bank reserves would increase, credit would become extremely cheap, and speculative buying would be stimulated.[35]

[35] This account follows closely the testimony of Professor Rogers before the House Committee on Banking and Currency. " Hearings before the Committee on Banking and Currency of the House of Representatives on H. R. 11788," 67th Congress, 4th Session, pp. 30-31.

The criticism of Professor Rogers is significant because it indicates that the smooth operation of the stabilized dollar would require the coöperation of the Federal Reserve Banks. By using their resources to check the upward and downward movements of prices, the Reserve Banks could possibly prevent the development of any significant accumulated " deficits " or " surpluses " in the index number of prices and therefore prevent the exports and imports of gold which Professor Rogers fears.

The plan of " the stabilized dollar " would probably have been of use in preventing the downward trend of prices between 1865 and 1896 and the upward trend between 1896 and 1917 — the date of our entrance into the war. But it could scarcely have been used to prevent the tremendous upheaval of prices that accompanied the war. Indeed, it would be necessary to *suspend* the operation of the plan during a major war. Modern warfare, we have said, is a race in which the combatants must spend money faster than they can raise it by taxation. This means that inflation is an inevitable accompaniment of war under modern conditions, for it is the only way by which money can be raised fast enough. Inflation, however, means rising prices, and rising prices under the plan of the stabilized dollar would mean increasing the gold content of the dollar. The larger the gold content of the dollar, however, the less adequate would be the gold reserve behind the gold certificates. If the gold content of the dollar were sufficiently increased, the reserve might become so inadequate that public confidence in the certificates would be impaired and they might circulate at a discount. When the war was over and deflation and a fall in prices seemed imminent, there would undoubtedly be a rush to obtain gold for the certificates — a demand which the government could not meet. Consequently, it is probable that the plan would have to be suspended during a large war. But this does not mean that the plan might not be desirable at other times.

VIII. Controlling the Price Level by Regulating Gold Output

Another proposal for stabilizing prices is that control be established over the world's output of gold. It has been proposed that an international commission buy up the gold mines of the world and operate them in the social interest, providing more gold when gold becomes too scarce, and restricting the output of gold if gold should become too abundant.

The plan could accomplish its purpose only in so far as price changes are the direct or indirect results of changes in the quantity of gold currency. It would not prevent increases in prices caused by the issuance of paper currency or by improvements in the credit system which enable a dollar of gold to support a larger volume of credit. The effect of such changes could, of course, be counteracted in some degree by reducing the production of gold.

The output of gold could be limited in periods of rising prices by licenses or taxation, and stimulated in periods of falling prices by subsidies. To be effective, the plan would have to be adopted internationally and administered by an international body. Besides the usual difficulties of establishing international coöperation, there would be an additional one in this case because South Africa, Australia, and Canada, in which gold mining is a leading industry, would scarcely permit an international body to throw hundreds of miners out of work and to impose depression upon the entire country because an excessive output of gold was raising price levels throughout the world. These countries would be eager, of course, to have their mines subsidized during times of falling prices. This, however, is a wasteful way of providing an adequate monetary supply of gold. It would be simpler and more economical to discourage the use of gold in the arts by taxing articles containing a large amount of gold.

IX. A "MANAGED CURRENCY"

Professor Fisher conceives the problem of stabilizing the value of money as one of keeping the metal coinage at constant value. But the vast majority of our dollars are credit dollars. It is true that the amount of gold in the metal dollar regulates the value of the credit dollars, but it is also true that the number of credit dollars affects the value of gold and of both gold and credit dollars. We have seen that, under the conditions prevailing in western countries, when currency increases more rapidly than the production of goods in general, prices tend to rise, and that when it increases less rapidly than production, they tend to fall. Consequently, it has been proposed to regulate the value of the dollar by regulating the quantity of currency. When prices rise, it is proposed to check the increase in the quantity of currency by raising the rediscount rate and by open market operations of the central banks — in the United States, the Federal Reserve Banks. These are devices with which we are familiar. When prices fall, it is proposed to stimulate an increase in currency by lower rediscount rates.

There is no reason to doubt the ability of the leading central banks of the world *in coöperation* to check a large output of gold from producing a rise in the price level. All that would be necessary would be for the central banks to hoard gold—that is, to acquire gold through the sale of securities and to charge sufficiently high rediscount rates to maintain large surplus reserves. The operation might be somewhat expensive to the banks, because, although they would receive higher interest rates, a large part of their assets would earn no interest whatever. But one central bank, *acting alone,* would have great difficulty in preventing a rise in the domestic price level in the face of a rise in world prices. Suppose, for example, that the central bank of a country attempted to keep the domestic price level from rising in conformity with a rise in the price level abroad. By maintaining a high rediscount rate and hoarding gold, the central bank would check the rise in domestic prices. Consequently these prices would become low relative to prices abroad. Naturally exports would increase, imports would diminish, gold would tend to flow into the country. In addition, the high short-term interest rates would attract foreign funds into the domestic market and this would accentuate the influx of gold.[36] By selling securities in the open market, the bank might acquire the control of the addi-

---

[36] It is impossible to predict how the attempt to hold down the domestic price level would affect the movement of funds seeking long-term investment. No doubt the high short-term rates in the domestic market would tend to affect long-term rates in the domestic market also, because some funds would leave the long-term market and enter the short-term. This would tend to keep long-term funds from going abroad and would also tend to attract funds from abroad. An offsetting influence, however, would be the fact that stable prices at home would tend to keep down the profits of domestic enterprises and rising prices abroad would tend to enhance the profits of foreign enterprises. Capital seeking investment in stocks rather than in bonds would tend to go abroad. The movement of long-term funds would depend upon which influence was the stronger — higher interest rates at home or higher profits abroad.

tional gold and prevent a rise in the domestic price level. This would cause more gold to enter the country. Sooner or later, the ability of the central bank to absorb gold by the sale of securities would be exhausted.

Could a central bank, through the device of a low rediscount rate, prevent the fall in the price level when gold output lagged behind production in general? With considerable confidence it can be said that a bank acting alone could do little, because it would soon find its reserves dangerously depleted. If the central bank succeeded by an easy credit policy in checking the drop in the domestic prices, those prices would be high relative to prices abroad, exports would shrink, imports would rise, and a large part of the bank's gold reserve would be sent abroad to pay for the excess of imports over exports. The loss of gold would soon compel the bank to abandon its easy credit policy. If the country were cut off from the rest of the world by a high tariff, the increase in imports might be very small and the bank might succeed in maintaining low interest rates for some time before its reserves became dangerously low. The general conclusion, however, must be that the possibility of checking downward movements of prices through an easy credit policy, must depend upon coöperation among the central banks in the principal countries.

But can coöperative action by central banks check a long-time downward trend in prices? Time alone will tell. There are two principal reasons for skepticism. The first arises from the business cycle. When gold output lags behind production in general, depressions tend to be long, it has been pointed out, because demand is not revived by large additions to the monetary stock from the mines. It is proposed to counteract the effect of the small gold output by lending money at low rates. But will very low interest rates be effective in increasing the money in circulation during the periods of depression and, therefore, in shortening the periods of depression? In order for low interest rates to increase the volume of money in circulation, some one must be willing to borrow. But in the midst of depressions, with prices falling, with confidence at low ebb, and with business men reluctant to make commitments, will the volume of borrowing be substantially affected by lower interest rates?[37] If low interest rates

[37] On March 14, 1930, the New York Reserve Bank reduced its discount rate

are not effective in increasing the volume of borrowing (and, therefore, of spending) during periods of depression, they are not likely to have much effect in shortening the long depressions which are characteristic of periods when the long-time trend of prices is downward. But it is the drop of prices during the long periods of depression which produces the long-time downward trend in prices — for during boom periods the movement of prices is usually upward. If low interest rates have little effect upon the volume of spending during periods of depression, their efficacy in preventing a downward trend in the price level is likely to be small.

A second reason for doubting the possibility of checking the downward movement of prices by low interest rates arises from the effect of low interest rates upon the use of capital. Low short-time interest rates would tend to produce low long-time rates. This would encourage a wider use of machines and other labor-saving devices [38] which in turn would accelerate the increase in the general output of industry. But the basic difficulty is that the output of goods is increasing faster than the supply of currency. Thus, although lower interest rates may increase the volume of money in circulation, their net effect upon prices may be very slight.

But one thing at least seems clear — whatever can be accomplished by central banks in controlling either upward or downward movements of prices must be achieved, in the main, by international coöperation. The prospects and methods of international coöperation to stabilize prices will be discussed in Chapter XXX.

X. Long-Term Contracts which Run in Terms of Purchasing Power

The extreme difficulty of devising a plan for controlling the price level which is both economically sound and politically

---

to 3½ per cent for the first time since the second half of 1927. It might have been expected that this important step in easing money would lead to the stabilization of commodity prices. In fact, this result was predicted in the weekly letter of the Harvard Economic Society for March 15, 1930. On May 2, 1930, the rediscount rate of the New York bank was reduced to 3 per cent, on June 20, to 2½ per cent, and on December 24, to 2 per cent, but prices continued to fall throughout the year.

[38] The reason for this is explained in Chapter XXIII, pp. 613–615.

feasible has led to the suggestion that the parties to long-term contracts protect themselves against movement in the price level by making their contracts run in terms of *purchasing power* instead of a fixed number of dollars. Thus a 5 per cent bond which, if the principal is $1,000, now pays interest at $50 a year regardless of changes in prices could be made to pay whatever amount is equivalent in *purchasing power* to $50 at the time of issue. Thus, if prices on the average doubled, the bond would pay $100 a year and if prices dropped one half, it would pay only $25. A multitude of contracts — insurance, leases, royalties, savings bank accounts, annuities, bonds, preferred stocks, mortgages, salaries — could be made to run in terms of purchasing power.

Some trouble might be experienced in obtaining a satisfactory measure of changes in purchasing power. This difficulty, however, is not an insurmountable one, particularly since index numbers are constantly being improved. Although the plan would not give complete protection against the injustice caused by price movements, it has the great advantage of not requiring political action to be put into effect. It would not be necessary to overcome the political opposition which, because of ignorance, prejudice, fear, and selfishness, is bound to exist against even the best plan. Any enterprise desiring to appeal to investors by making it unnecessary for them to speculate in gold whenever they buy bonds or preferred stock, any life or accident insurance company which wishes to attract policyholders by relieving them of the necessity of gambling in gold, could adopt the plan. The best way to introduce it would be for the government to offer to its bondholders the opportunity to exchange their present holdings for bonds payable in fixed amounts of purchasing power. Whoever buys a government bond now is gambling in gold just as he would be gambling in wheat or copper or cotton if the bond were payable in those commodities. The government might well lead the way by offering the public a security which is a real investment, which a man might buy, with the knowledge that he was thereby providing his dependents with a fixed amount of purchasing power. If the national government took the initiative, many states, municipalities, and private corporations would undoubtedly follow.

REFERENCES

Anderson, B. M., Jr., *The Fallacy of the Stabilized Dollar*, 1920.

Anderson, B. M., Jr., " The Gold Standard versus a Managed Currency," *The Chase Economic Bulletin*, March 23, 1925, v. V, No. 1.

Angell, J. W., *The Theory of International Prices*, 1926.   Ch. V, VI, VII, XV, and XVI.

Fisher, I., *The Purchasing Power of Money*, 1915.

Hawtrey, R. G., *Currency and Credit* (second edition), 1923.

Keynes, J. M., *A Treatise on Money*, 1930.

Mitchell, W. C., *Business Cycles. The Problem and Its Setting*, 1927.   Pp. 128–139; 116–128.

Warren, G. F., and Pearson, F. A., *The Agricultural Situation*, 1924.   Ch. IV, V, and XXIV.

CHAPTER XXII

THE POSITION OF THE CONSUMER

I. THE CONSUMER GUIDES PRODUCTION. II. BUYING IS LARGELY DONE BY AMATEURS. III. SOME CONSEQUENCES OF THE CONSUMER'S IGNORANCE. IV. THE ATTEMPTS OF BUSINESS ENTERPRISES TO CONTROL DEMAND. V. THE PROTECTION OF THE CONSUMER.

I. THE CONSUMER GUIDES PRODUCTION

Free private enterprise has been described as the only economic system "under which the consumer can ever stand a chance," "the only one under which the consumer can be perfectly sure of obtaining the article he wants rather than having forced on him the article which somebody else thinks he ought to want." [1] In modern economic society, production, as we have seen, is not controlled by any central authority which studies the needs of the community and arranges to have industry satisfy these needs. It is guided in the main by the choices of consumers. By willingness or unwillingness to spend money for this or that, each consumer participates in determining what is produced and in what relative quantities. If ugly, flimsy, or harmful things are made, it is only because consumers buy them. In a sense, ours is a democratic method of guiding production. "Every human being," as Foster and Catchings say, " has a vote every time he makes a purchase. No one is disfranchised on account of age, sex, race, religion, education, length of residence, or failure to register. Every day is election day. . . . Moreover, minorities count." [2] And it should be added that no one need possess any qualities which peculiarly fit him to decide what industry should make, and that, instead of everyone's having one vote only, each person has as many votes as he has dollars.

In order to understand the operation of modern industry, it

---

[1] Benn, E. J. P., *The Confessions of a Capitalist*, pp. 133–134.
[2] *Profits*, p. 191.

is important for us to learn how this method of guiding production works. Is it true that free private enterprise is the only economic system under which the consumer " stands a chance "? Are consumers in a favorable position to assume the responsibility of determining what shall be produced? Are their decisions informed decisions; are they the result of investigation and reflection or of habit, prejudice, and impulse? It is often said that each person knows his preferences better than anyone else can possibly know them. But how many persons really know *goods?* And is it not as important to know *goods* as it is to know *preferences?* Might not many persons gain more satisfaction from their money if more of their expenditures were made for them by representatives or agents? Of course it is true even now that substantial sums are spent by organizations which buy on behalf of their members — the various government units, trade unions, fraternal organizations, churches, coöperative societies, and innumerable clubs. Might the expenditures of the community possibly produce more satisfaction if choice-making were in still greater degree transferred from the market place to the legislative hall or the club meeting?

We have said that in modern economic society the choices of consumers guide production. But what determines the choices of consumers? During the last hundred years, the methods of selling goods have undergone a revolution scarcely less profound than the methods of making them. Business concerns no longer wait for buyers to come to them. Through marketing campaigns that often are planned as carefully and as ingeniously as military campaigns, enterprises endeavor to stimulate demand for their wares. In other words, industry is not simply engaged in satisfying men's desires — it is also engaged in creating desires to be satisfied. How then shall we describe the existing situation? Is industry the servant of the consumer, producing the things which he desires and doing its best to satisfy his desires? Or is it the master of the consumer, dominating instead of serving him? Does the consumer determine what industry makes, or does industry determine what the consumer uses? And in so far as industry does affect the choices of consumers, what is the nature of its influence? Does it encourage consumers to seek information and to compare alternatives or does it encourage them to act upon impulse, whim, or prejudice? To what extent do business establishments seek to make consumption intensely competitive with the result that a large part of every increase in income goes into competitive expenditures and adds relatively little to human happiness?

In considering these questions, it is essential to remember that the wise spending of money is no less important than the avoidance of wasteful methods of production, because no labor or capital is more completely wasted than that which is used to produce something that satisfies no desire. It has well been said that " as buyers make good or bad choices in spending their money, so they raise or lower the standards of living of the entire nation." No matter how efficient may be our mines and farms and factories, we cannot regard our economic system as efficient if it induces consumers to spend a large part of their income for goods which yield little or no satisfaction.

II. Buying Is Largely Done by Amateurs

The outstanding fact about most spending of money in modern economic society is that it is done in spare moments by amateurs. Despite the fact that the attainment of the maximum excess of satisfaction over sacrifice depends as much upon skill in buying goods as upon skill in making them, specialization, which is the very foundation of skill, has scarcely entered the field of consumer buying. Of course, when a large business enterprise or a government department buys goods, it usually acts through an expert purchasing agent who spends his entire time finding where the best goods can be obtained at the lowest prices. The purchasing agent is not influenced by the attractiveness of the package, by pictures of pretty girls in the advertising, by slogans or catchwords. He endeavors to ascertain the quality of the products of different sellers and he selects the quality which best suits the needs of his principal, or else he buys on specification from the seller who offers goods of the required quality at the lowest price. But the ordinary consumer uses too little to warrant hiring an expert shopper. Furthermore, the consumer often does not know his (or her) own desires with sufficient definiteness to describe them to another person. Frequently he does not know what he wishes until he has seen what is offered for sale. He makes his choice by going to market and looking over the goods displayed. And finally, there is the fact that, to most persons under most circumstances, spending money is itself a pleasure, a form of consumption, if you will. By hiring a shopper, the consumer might obtain better goods at lower prices, but he would lose the pleasure of making the choices and spending the money himself.

III. Some Consequences of the Consumer's Ignorance

The fact that consumer buying is largely done by amateurs is undoubtedly the greatest source of industrial waste today. It means that the ultimate guidance of industry is largely in the hands of people who act on the basis of extremely inadequate information and even no information at all. Specifically what are the results of this incompetent guidance of industry?

To begin with, the ignorance of the consumer prevents him from buying where he can obtain the most for his money. So ill informed are many consumers concerning prices in different stores that a retailer does not find it essential to quote the same prices as his competitors. A brand of crackers was regularly sold by one chain store for 18 cents a box and by a second chain store a block away at 19 cents. A brand of soap flakes, however, was sold by the second store for 23 cents a package and by the first for 25 cents. Neither store gave credit nor made deliveries. A grocery store sold a brand of Camembert cheese at 55 cents a package. Another store, two blocks away, sold the same brand for 60 cents. Both of these stores gave credit and made deliveries. None of these price differences were temporary — all persisted for months. A stationery store sold a scrap book for $1.50; a competitor in the next block asked $1.75 for exactly the same book. The cash price of a certain model Simmons bed in three competing furniture stores was $8.55, $9.00, and $10.45.

The ignorance of the consumer makes it possible to deceive him concerning the quantity which he receives for a given price. The essential requirement of a storage battery for radio use is its ampere hour capacity, not its size, its weight, or the number of plates. Because many buyers do not realize this, batteries are often unmarked as to capacity and so designed that the buyer overestimates it. A common deception has been to put batteries in oversized boxes or jars. In some cases, manufacturers mis-brand the capacity of the batteries. The New York Better Business Bureau purchased a battery branded as 120 ampere hours which was found to have an actual rating of 75 ampere hours. A battery advertised as 140 ampere hours was found to have a capacity of 80. A prominent Chicago store advertised tomatoes at 49 cents a basket containing " about five pounds." In many cases the baskets were found to contain less than four pounds. The price was made to appear about 10 cents a pound when actually it was about 14 cents. Diversity in the weight of loaves of bread makes it difficult for consumers to compare the price of bread in different stores. Among 3,000 loaves gathered in 67 cities, there were 105 different weights.[3] Some butchers require their clerks to make their salaries by short-weighing and overcharging. The Department of Agriculture describes the method as follows : " To facilitate short-weighing and overcharging, prices are made to include fractions of cents. The clerk places the meat on the scales and quickly announces a total price but not the weight."[4] The investigators of the Department found that customers were being overcharged from a few cents up to seventy-five cents on a purchase. They advise consumers to avoid meat markets where prices are quoted in fractions of cents per pound.[5] Short-weighing is a serious abuse in the retail coal business. The Chicago Better Business Bureau, which has conducted a campaign against short-weighing of coal, reported after the campaign was several months old : " Short weight has not disappeared. The Bureau is satisfied that systematic short-weighing practiced by some dealers still exists to a considerable extent. . . ."[6]

[3] Chase, Stuart, and Schlink, F. J., *Your Money's Worth*, p. 115.

[4] Davis, W. C., " Methods and Processes of Retailing Meat," U. S. Department of Agriculture, *Department Bulletin No. 1441*, p. 15.

[5] *Monthly Labor Review*, July, 1925, v. XXI, p. 49.

[6] Chicago Better Business Bureau, *Special Coal Bulletin*, May, 1928, p. 2. The wagon driver carries a receipt for the buyer of the coal to sign. The ordinance of the city of Chicago requires that the receipt show the weight of the coal delivered and permits the buyer to have the weight checked on the public scales. Some dealers make a practice of issuing the driver two receipts — one shows the correct weight of the load and the other an inflated weight. The driver is instructed not to present the receipt to the consumer for signing until *after* the coal has been put in the cellar — when it would be too late to check the weight. In case no check on the weight was asked, the driver presents the receipt with the inflated weight. But if a check on the weight was made, the customer is asked to sign the receipt with the correct weight.

In a large proportion of cases, the consumer does not know the quality of what he buys. Consequently he purchases many things which are useless or even harmful. The numerous medical nostrums which have found a ready market for years are an example. The influenza epidemic during the winter of 1928 caused many articles suddenly to be advertised as preventives or cures for the disease. This caused Mr. W. G. Campbell of the Drug and Insecticide Division of the Department of Agriculture to warn the public against misleading advertising. He called attention to the fact that the Federal Pure Food and Drug Act does not refer to false advertising appearing in the press or in any advertising medium not included with the package or the preparation itself. It merely forbids unwarranted claims from being made on the labels or on or in the packages. The interest of the public in vitamins has led to the production of many cod liver oil extracts, preparations, and tablets which are alleged to give the vitamins in cod liver oil in a palatable form. A report of the Food, Drug, and Insecticide Administration on these preparations stated: " During 1927 the Department of Agriculture conducted an extensive survey of extracts of cod liver oil and various products alleged to contain vitamins of cod liver oil found in interstate commerce. A biological examination for the vitamins A and D in these products showed practically all of the extracts and concentrates examined to be virtually devoid of vitamin A and that few contained any material amount of vitamin D."[7]

The ignorance or indifference of the average consumer frequently leads him to purchase goods which he would not be willing to buy at all or at least would be willing to buy only at a much lower price if he knew their real quality. For example, consumers are often unable to distinguish between " firsts " and " seconds." Consequently " seconds " or goods of poor quality are often sold at the same price as " firsts." When the butcher purchases meat from the packer, he pays a price which depends upon the grade, but when steak is sold to the consumer, grades are not distinguished. And yet " a prime sirloin steak differs

[7] *United States Daily*, December 28, 1927, v. II, pp. 1–3.

from a common sirloin just as much as a piece of fine linen differs from a coarse cotton cloth." [8] Butter is sold by score in the wholesale market but not in the retail market.

The inability of the public to distinguish imperfect and irregular hosiery led the National Better Business Bureau [9] to call a meeting in May, 1926, of manufacturers, jobbers, and retailers, to consider the problem of marking seconds. Manufacturers of about 75 per cent of the output of women's full fashioned hosiery and more than 50 per cent of circular knit hosiery, pledged themselves to mark all hose other than firsts with the term " imperfect " or " irregular." [10]

Only a small part of the fur sold in the United States is marketed under its true name. Rabbit is marketed under as many as seventy-five different names, according to David C. Mills, General Director of the National Association of the Fur Industry. [11] It appears as " Russian leopard," " French beaver," " French sable," " squirreline," " moline," " nutriette," " seal," " musquash," and many others. Hudson seal is merely a trade name. Few consumers know the relative durability of the different pelts.

The misrepresentation of fabrics is extremely common. Scores of instances discovered by the Better Business Bureaus might be cited. Women's hose, described as silk and wool, were priced at " two pairs for one dollar " and found to be rayon and cotton; " silk and wool union suits," offered at two suits for one dollar, were found to be cotton with a small rayon stripe and without any perceptible percentage of silk or wool. A nationwide survey by the Better Business Bureaus indicated that the label " part wool " as applied to blankets is in most instances used to mislead the public. The majority of blankets labeled

[8] Armour's Livestock Bureau, *Monthly Letter to Animal Husbandmen*, October, 1929, v. X, No. 7, p. 1.

[9] An account of the work of the National Better Business Bureau and of the affiliated local Better Business Bureaus is given in a subsequent section of this chapter.

[10] National Better Business Bureau, *Better Business News*, February, 1927, v. II, No. 2, p. 1. The Cincinnati Better Business Bureau reports: " An effort was made some time ago to obtain the co-operation of manufacturers to label all seconds of hosiery as such. Some of the manufacturers have followed the suggestion, but others have refused to comply. Their excuse has been that retailers do not want the hosiery so stamped." Cincinnati Better Business Bureau, *Better Business*, April, 1928, v. I, No. 4, p. 4.

[11] New York *Times*, September 16, 1927, p. 23.

"part wool" were found to contain from 5 to 7 per cent wool.[12] A questionnaire sent to the public asking an opinion of the wool content of "part wool" blankets showed that 68 per cent of the consumers believe that a part wool blanket is more than one-fourth wool.[13]   Blanket manufacturers have been asked by the National Better Business Bureau to mark blankets properly so that the percentage of wool will be accurately given.   But the Cincinnati Better Business Bureau reports that the "manufacturers as a whole have been hesitant about agreeing to the proposal."[14]   The word "jersey" is described in standard and textile dictionaries as a "fine, choice wool combed from the rest of the wool" and as a "very fine woolen yarn."   Yet occasionally the word is found in advertisements to describe dresses which are made entirely of cotton.   Three such cases are cited by the Chicago Better Business Bureau in a recent information bulletin. The value of silk depends, among other things, upon its weight. A mineral salt bath is often used to convert a pound of silk into several pounds of silk cloth.   The bath, however, diminishes the fibre strength and life of the silk.[15]

Physicians recommend silk and wool shirts for young babies. A Better Business Bureau recently analyzed eight shirts which had been advertised and sold as "silk and wool" by eight different stores in the city.   Not one of these shirts was accurately represented.   One shirt had no wool thread; four were entirely rayon and cotton; one was rayon and cotton with one wool thread running between rows of rayon threads; still another had one wool thread in four and the rest cotton; the last was rayon, cotton, and wool.[16]

The inability of consumers to recognize woods has long caused furniture manufacturers and dealers to misrepresent their wares and has led to the creation of many misleading trade names.   In 1926, the Federal Trade Commission succeeded in getting 861 concerns to subscribe to a code of honest labeling and cataloguing.   The National Retail Furniture Association first ap-

[12] Cincinnati Better Business Bureau, *Better Business*, April, 1928, v. I, No. 4, p. 4.
[13] *Ibid.*, p. 4.
[14] *Ibid.*, p. 4.
[15] Chase, Stuart, and Schlink, F. J., *Your Money's Worth*, p. 108.
[16] National Better Business Bureau, *Better Business News*, February, 1927, v. II, No. 2, p. 3.

proved the rules but later withdrew its approval after the Grand Rapids manufacturers decided not to accept them.[17]

Spring lamb is defined by the United States Bureau of Agricultural Economics as having been born since November 15th last. Three stores which advertised "legs of lamb and finest meat the market affords" were found to be selling goat legs and common mutton legs.[18] In investigating meat advertised as spring lamb at 19 cents a pound, a shopper was sold a seven and one-half pound leg which was submitted to the United States Bureau of Agricultural Economics for inspection. The leg was graded as mutton of common grade from a ewe three to four years old, weighing 90 to 100 pounds. The Department of Agriculture finds that misleading practices in the retail meat trade form " an important retarding factor in the development of the industry although such practices appear to involve only a small proportion of the retailers." The unscrupulous dealers are active and persistent advertisers, and they influence the activities of other dealers who would prefer to deal honestly. To the trade, the unscrupulous dealers are known as " clean-up men." In their advertising they stress the excellent quality of their meats but they limit their purchases to the most inferior quality. "Prime native steer beef," "genuine spring lamb," "milk fed veal," and "young pig pork" are the terms used to describe meats offered at very low prices. Sometimes the prices quoted for these preferred cuts were less than the cost of the live animals. For example, "lamb legs" were found advertised from 12½ to 17½ cents per pound at a time when live lambs were worth 13 to 15 cents and their dressed carcasses were offered at 26 cents wholesale. When live hogs were costing about 14 cents, "pork sausage" was offered at two pounds for 25 cents and, in at least two cities, three pounds for 25 cents. This sausage was made from beef suet, beef fat, tripe, and cereal. Common and medium grades of steer beef, cow beef, or bull beef are offered as prime beef; mutton of low quality or cut is offered for lamb; heavy carcasses from grass calves offered as milk fed veal; cuts from stags and old sows as young pig pork.[19]

---

[17] Chase, Stuart, and Schlink, F. J., *Your Money's Worth,* p. 98.

[18] *Monthly Labor Review,* July, 1925, v. XXI, p. 49.

[19] Davis, W. C., " Methods and Processes of Retailing Meat," U. S. Department of Agriculture, *Department Bulletin No. 1441,* p. 14.

Illustrations of misrepresentation could be extended almost indefinitely. Among the best sources of information are the reports of the Better Business Bureaus. Goods advertised as linoleum were found to have a felt base instead of a burlap base as is standard with linoleum; a five-piece walnut dining room suite was found to be veneered on gumwood instead of solid walnut; "leather" purses were found to be imitation leather. A prominent soap manufacturer has sold "white naphtha soap chips" although the soap contains less than one-half of one per cent petroleum distillate by weight, and although the Federal Trade Commission has found that less than one per cent petroleum distillate is too small to be effective as a cleansing ingredient.

Even when the consumer is reasonably certain that one article is better than another, he or she rarely knows whether or not it is *enough* better to justify a given difference in price. Suppose that a housewife wishes to buy a broom. One grade costs one-third more than the other, but how is she to know whether the more expensive broom is worth the extra money? Possibly the better broom will last twice as long as the inferior one, possibly only one-fourth longer.

Again and again the consumer finds himself in a situation similar to that of the housewife who must decide between two brooms. In the first place, there is the difficulty of learning just how several articles differ in materials, construction, and workmanship, and, in the second place, there is the difficulty of discovering how these differences affect the service rendered by the article. Suppose that the consumer is purchasing a refrigerator. Some are much better insulated than others. But just how much is better insulation worth? It has been estimated that an extra inch of cork board insulation, adding about $20.00 to the price of the 100 pound capacity box, saves six pounds of ice a day.[20] How many consumers possess accurate information on this point? Six-ply tires cost more than four-ply, high test gasoline costs more than low test, but which is the more economical to purchase? Which of two chairs has the more durable upholstery, what difference is there in the nutritive value of different brands

[20] Chase, Stuart, and Schlink, F. J., *Your Money's Worth*, pp. 82–83.

of flour, which of the several thousand paint formulae in current use gives the most satisfactory out-of-door paint? Rarely does the ordinary consumer know enough about goods to get the most for his money.

Because so many consumers do not know either quality or the prices usually charged for many articles, dealers are able to stimulate sales by creating the impression that bargain prices are being offered when, as a matter of fact, this is not the case. A store advertised tarpaulin at half price. Investigation showed that the prices quoted were regular. The store was asked by the Better Business Bureau to change its copy, and complied. Other advertisements read "regular $1.50 men's silk hose, two pairs for $1.00." These hose were not only rayon with no silk, but many were sub-standards and menders. The comparative price was grossly exaggerated. The store agreed to discontinue the exaggerated comparative prices and to use accurate descriptions. Bags were advertised at $4.95 with the added statement: "would sell regularly at ten to twelve dollars." The Better Business Bureau investigated and found that the same bags could be bought at three other stores for $5.00 regularly. A Chicago store advertised ladies' fitted cases at $55 value. The cases were priced at $27.50. One of the cases was submitted to four authorities on leather goods for their opinion of its value. They estimated the case's regular sale price at $35 or $36. The Chicago Better Business Bureau states that many oriental rug merchants admit that their advertisements contain exaggerated comparative prices. For example, a Kandahar rug was advertised at $460. The regular price was quoted at $925. Investigation showed that rugs of this kind and size usually retail at about $500. Some of the oriental rug merchants sought the help of the Better Business Bureau in eliminating exaggerated comparative price statements from advertising.

The great profit in "sales" consists largely in the fact that the ordinary consumer does not know values and is, therefore, easily convinced that he is obtaining a bargain. A store found that children's summer underwear was going slowly at 59 cents a suit. On "dollar day" it was marked up to two for $1.30 at which price it sold rapidly. A prominent New York department store advertised a sacrifice sale of floor lamps for the low price of $4.94. It was announced that the former price had been $9.94. The lamps were not the regular $9.94 grade but $1.98 lamps which had been painted up to resemble the $9.94 ones. "The Factory Store" offered hand bags during the Christmas buying season "values to ten dollars at $1.89, and $25 steer-hide purses at $9.95." The advertisement described this as a "factory sale, values less than wholesale." The Better Business Bureau which investigated this case reported that the merchandise was of a value "comparable with the selling price, though not with the comparative price." The store owner agreed not to continue the misleading comparative prices in his advertisements.

It is usual for women's wear stores to have fur sales during August, and to advertise that the prices of furs will advance on September first. The Cincinnati Better Business Bureau made a study of fur prices during the August sales and again late in September. Thirty-seven coats were "shopped" by bureau representatives during August and identified again in September. Only twenty-two of the thirty-seven were marked up in September. In 1927, the bureau made a similar survey and found even worse conditions.[21] The Better Business Bureau of Indianapolis investigated several "no-profit day" sales of an Indianapolis department store. They were far from being "no-profit" sales. Boys' caps, listed at 79 cents, were found to cost at wholesale approximately $7.00 a dozen; men's union suits, listed at 89 cents, about $8.00 a dozen; overalls, selling for $1.29, $11.87½ a dozen. A lot of men's socks, advertised as silk and wool of 50 cent value and offered for 19 cents, were found by chemical test to consist of practically all cotton. Another no-profit day sale offered "women's 29 cent grade lisle hose strictly first quality" at 15 cents. The bureau's shoppers who were sent to the store for these hose were sold irregulars instead of first quality as advertised. "Women's $1.00 grade pure silk hose," offered at 73 cents, when submitted to a chemical test, were found to contain less than 19 per cent silk.[22] A well-informed writer on advertising and marketing has this to say concerning fire and

[21] Cincinnati Better Business Bureau, *Better Business*, v. I, No. 9, p. 3.
[22] Indianapolis Better Business Bureau, *Bulletin*, June, 1927, pp. 4 and 5.

bankruptcy sales: "There are so few genuine fire sales and so few genuine bankruptcy sales that the average buyer will do well to consider them all fakes. Goods of inferior quality are bought for such sales, second hand goods are renovated, and all the practices of illegitimate merchandising are brought into play to victimize the credulous." [23]

Because the consumer does not know quality, he often judges it by price. But prices of articles are not a reliable index of quality. Tests of the warp and filling strength of five Turkish towels indicated that a 25-cent towel was clearly a better buy than a 50-cent towel and that a $1.00 towel was far superior to a $1.50 one.[24] In a test of five other towels, it was found that the most expensive ranked fourth in quality.[25] Tests of six suits of men's woven cotton underwear, selling at from $1.50 to $3.00 a garment, indicated that, in strength of the warp, the three suits selling at $1.50 were superior to those selling at $2.25 and $3.00. In the filling strengths there was less difference but the weakest filling was used in one of the $3.00 suits.[26] Difficulties in buying canned goods are illustrated by the experience of Mr. F. M. Shook, field secretary of the Tri-Packers Association, in purchasing twenty-four cans of corn to be used in a school of grading. The cans were graded by a carefully selected committee, the chairman of which was a licensed grader under the Federal Warehouse Act. Of the twenty-four cans, one was judged U. S. Grade A, or "fancy," (that is, according to the scoring system used, above 89 points); fourteen graded U. S. Grade B, or "extra standard" (75 to 89 points); and nine, U. S. Grade C, or "standard" (60 to 74 points). How did the prices compare with the grades? The one can which graded fancy cost 17 cents; the fourteen which graded extra standard cost from $8\frac{1}{3}$ to 25 cents; the nine which graded standard had exactly the same price range as the fourteen grading extra standard, namely, $8\frac{1}{3}$ to 25 cents. The average price of the Grade B cans was 14.85 cents, the average price of the Grade C cans was 16.92 cents. The poorest grade cost, on the average, more than the medium and

[23] Moriarty, W. D., *The Economics of Marketing and Advertising*, p. 569.
[24] Johnson, G. H., *Textile Fabrics*, p. 115.
[25] *Ibid.*, p. 116.
[26] *Ibid.*, pp. 159–160.

almost as much as the one can of fancy. The labels of seven cans contained statements concerning the quality of the contents. Two of the cans which graded standard and four of the cans which graded extra standard were labeled fancy. Only two of the seven cans were properly labeled, one extra standard and one fancy.[27]

Dealers, of course, know that the consumer often judges quality by price and they take advantage of it to dispose of inferior grades at high prices. Not infrequently it is easier to sell an article at a high price than at a low one. In marketing a four ounce bottle of toilet water, which could have been sold at a profit for 25 cents, such a price was not considered. The question was whether 50 cents or $1.00 would be the more profitable price. A test was made by offering the toilet water in some stores at 50 cents and in others at $1.00. Over twice as many bottles were sold at $1.00 as at 50 cents. Consequently $1.00 was made the standard price.[28] When a prominent tooth paste was ready to be marketed, the makers decided that consumers might not believe in its superiority if it were sold for 25 cents a tube. Consequently it was offered for 50 cents, despite the fact that 25 cents would have left a good profit.[29]

But the effects of the consumer's ignorance are more far-reaching than is at first apparent. Not only does it cause the consumer to pay high prices for poor quality and often for short measure, but it also tends to reduce the output of the community.

The fact that many consumers do not buy where they can obtain goods on the best terms retards the concentration of production in the hands of enterprises with the lowest operating costs and enables many poorly managed, poorly equipped, and poorly located concerns to survive. In other words, *consumer ignorance acts as a subsidy to inefficient plants.* The result is that much labor and capital are employed where they are less productive than they might easily be.

The ignorance of consumers also reduces the output of industry because it hinders the growth of large plants where they are

[27] Shook, F. M., " Distributing Canned Goods," *The Canner,* January 10, 1931, v. LXXII, No. 4, pp. 44 and 46.

[28] Moriarty, W. D., *The Economics of Marketing and Advertising,* p. 272.

[29] *Ibid.,* p. 271.

more economical than small ones. Because most consumers know little about the quality of goods, it is relatively easy for each producer to persuade some consumers that his particular brand is "different" and is superior to most other brands. If consumers really knew quality and purchased on the basis of grades instead of sales talk, it is scarcely conceivable that there would be 10,000 brands of wheat flour, 4,500 brands of canned corn, 1,000 brands of canned peaches, 1,000 brands of canned salmon, 1,000 brands of peas, 500 brands of mustard, and 300 brands of pineapple.[30]

Finally, the ignorance of consumers reduces the output of industry by tying up unnecessarily large amounts of capital and labor in distributing goods. Consider the enormous waste of capital represented by the multitude of brands which wholesalers and retailers must carry. If purchases were made on the basis of *quality* instead of *brand,* every drug store and every grocery store could substantially reduce its inventory. Many of the persons now engaged in advertising and selling would be released for other work, because much of the present selling activities would be pointless if addressed to persons who knew the quality of goods.

IV. The Attempts of Business Enterprises to Control Demand

The Industrial Revolution, it has been pointed out, has been a revolution in selling as well as in making things. The essence of the revolution in selling consists in the development of extremely aggressive efforts on the part of business establishments to control the choices of buyers. Several generations ago, manufacturers and wholesalers sold unbranded ware, which meant that they made no special efforts to influence consumer demand. The influencing of consumers was left largely to retailers and they were not notably aggressive in their efforts. Advertising, for example, which today employs half a million people and on which the business concerns of the country spend a billion and a half a year, was not respectable — solid, substantial, and dignified enterprises did not use it. The first advertising agency in the United States was not established until 1864.[31]

---

[30] Mr. George K. Burgess, director of the Bureau of Standards, is authority for the estimates of the number of brands. See *United States Daily,* June 13, 1928, p. 5.

[31] Veblen, T., *Absentee Ownership,* p. 314.

Business enterprises have abandoned their relatively passive attitude toward consumer demand. It is estimated that the advertising bill of the General Motors Corporation in 1928 was over $20,000,000 and of the American Tobacco Company in 1929 about $12,000,000.[32] Thousands of manufacturers and wholesalers now sell their goods under brand names. By a vast variety of methods — by advertisements in newspapers, magazines, subways, street cars, and theatre programs, by billboard, direct mail, movie, and radio advertising, by house to house canvassing, by demonstrations at fairs, in stores, or before clubs, and by the distribution of samples or instruction or recipe books — these manufacturers and wholesalers endeavor to influence consumer demand. Salesmen in many cases are given special instruction in selling the product to retailers and they are also taught how to assist retailers to sell it to consumers. On the basis of some index of the purchasing power of each community — such as the income tax payments or the number of automobiles or telephones per 1,000 of population — a quota is set for the territory of each salesman and he is expected to sell no less than this amount. Often he is further stimulated by a house organ, by sales contests, and by an annual convention of the entire selling force. Some manufacturers and wholesalers also employ dealer-service men. These men do no selling to retailers; their sole duty is to help dealers in selling to consumers.

Retailers have been equally aggressive in seeking to influence consumer demand. The clerks in many chain stores, department stores, and larger specialty shops are carefully trained in the art of selling; a record is kept of the sales of each clerk, and salaries depend upon the volume of sales. The display of goods in windows and on counters has become a highly developed art. All manner of special sales — fall openings, spring openings, anniversary sales, post-holiday sales, midsummer sales, one-cent sales, "mystery package" sales, "dollar days" — are used to capture trade.

Illustrative of the elaborate selling methods of modern business are those of the California Fruit Growers' Exchange. They were recently described as follows:

[32] Presbrey, Frank, *The History and Development of Advertising*, pp. 593-594.

"Among the special pieces of advertising matter distributed during the year were: 1,546,427 copies of Sunkist bulletins to domestic science teachers; 140,640 dietetic bulletins to nurses' training schools and hospitals; 12,923 bulletins of recipes, menus and merchandising information to tea rooms, cafeterias, etc.; 19,692 colored posters to elementary schools for use in art and health classes; 16,741 educational wall charts to commercial geography classes; 15,000 copies of a new text book and syllabus on California's citrous industry to elementary grade teachers; and 10,102 Sunkist recipe file cabinets were sold to girls in home making classes in high schools. Twenty-three permanent dealer-service men and ten temporary men were employed in aiding retailers develop a demand for Sunkist fruit; personal calls were made on 51,391 dealers in fresh fruit, 29,991 window displays were installed, 5,889 fountain displays were arranged, 261,645 pieces of advertising matter were distributed, and 7,100 fruit juice extractors were sold." [33]

What are the effects of industry's intense and persistent efforts to make us want more goods? Do these efforts greatly influence demand? Does industry really control the consumer?

[33] U. S. Department of Agriculture, *Agricultural Coöperation*, November 26, 1927, v. I, p. 458.

Equally elaborate and carefully planned are the marketing methods of the Armstrong Cork Company, makers of linoleum. An excellent account of these methods by Mr. J. L. Palmer appeared in the *Journal of Business of the University of Chicago* for January, 1928. The company distributes its product through jobbers, but it spends about $2,000,000 a year on advertising, and its own salesmen call on the retail trade. The salesmen are young college men. Before starting on the road, they receive a training course of five to six months at the factory in Lancaster, Pennsylvania. During this time they work through the manufacturing departments. Twice a year all salesmen are brought to Lancaster to discuss marketing problems with the sales executives. The company also does educational work among its jobbers, the salesmen of the jobbers, and retailers, architects, and builders. Each year it holds a three-day convention of its jobbers. At six-month intervals, conferences of jobbers' salesmen are held at Lancaster. The company pays half of the expenses of one salesman from each jobber at these conventions. Classes for retail salesmen are also held frequently. Both at Lancaster and at its sales branches, the company gives instruction in laying linoleum.

A statistical and planning section in the sales department conducts an annual survey of retail dealers to secure detailed data on every dealer of over $10,000 rating in all towns of over 5,000. Once a year each salesman submits a complete report on every dealer with a credit rating of over $10,000 — what lines of linoleum the dealer is not handling, the competitive situation of the dealer, the weak points in his methods, who is the key man in his organization. The statistical and planning section also receives daily reports of linoleum shipped by each jobber to dealers — the dealer's name and the amount and kind of linoleum purchased. It also receives monthly reports from jobbers showing the amount of linoleum on hand.

The data gathered by the statistical and planning section indicate by states and by counties the number of square yards of Armstrong linoleum sold per 100 of population and enable the market analysis division of the sales department to follow up dealers whose sales have declined and to give them special assistance in increasing their sales. The head of the market analysis division is sent into any trading area where sales are low to analyze conditions and to assist the branch manager in the solution of his problem.

Is he induced in the main to desire the things that business enterprises find it profitable for him to desire and is he prevented from desiring the things that it is not profitable for business to have him desire? Do modern selling methods compel the producer to be more careful about the quality of his ware? Do they make possible large scale production and thus bring goods to the consumer at a lower price? Or do they so increase the margin between the manufacturing cost and the retail price that the consumer pays more? Do they give the consumer a wider acquaintance with the alternative ways of spending his money and a better knowledge of goods? In short, do they make him a better informed and a more competent buyer?

It seems reasonably certain that present marketing methods influence demand less fundamentally than either their defenders or their critics usually assume. Marketing technique seems to influence the *brands* which people buy far more than the *products;* it appears to *accelerate* changes in consumption rather than to *initiate* them. By far the most effective advertisement of many new products is the new product itself and what is said about it by its users. What salesmen and advertisements say is relatively unimportant in comparison with what people learn by actual experience, by observation, or by asking the man who owns one. Not primarily because of expert salesmanship or of advertisements in the *Saturday Evening Post* are the roads of America congested with automobiles. The actual cars on the road have been by far the most effective automobile advertisements. Salesmanship has induced owners to discard their old cars more rapidly and it has increased the number of families owning two cars, but most automobile salesmen do not begin to talk to a prospect until he has already decided to purchase *some* make of car. Nor do advertising and salesmanship appear to be *primarily* responsible for the rapidly growing purchases of cigarettes, radios, rayon, milk, vacuum cleaners, electric irons, electric refrigerators, canned foods, and baker's bread. Doubtless these changes too have been *accelerated* by modern selling methods, but they would all have come anyway. Efficient marketing is generally credited with making us eat more oranges, but it is remarkable that the consumption of spinach and bananas, which have been little advertised, has increased substantially as much. Salesmanship undoubtedly accentuated the speed with which the country took up Mah Jong but it could not sustain public interest after people tired of the new game. And all the arts of modern marketing have not kept women using sapolio or wearing corsets or petti-coats, nor have they prevented a drop in the sale of Victrolas, men's shoes, cigars, or bicycles.

All of this makes it fairly clear that the consumer is not the plastic clay that he is sometimes pictured. And yet it is easy to cite cases where modern marketing methods have really created a demand for a *product,* not merely a brand. Raisins and cranber-ries are examples.[34] Listerine could scarcely have taken the country by storm — despite the declarations of medical authori-ties that its claims are grossly exaggerated — without the help of advertising. Life insurance, unlike the automobile, is not a good which advertises itself effectively. Were it not for thousands of skilled salesmen, we should undoubtedly not be insured (in 1929) for practically $100,000,000,000.

[34] When the national advertising of raisins started in 1914, the annual per capita consumption was 1.66 pounds. By 1919 this had increased to 3.41 pounds. *Judicious Advertising,* September, 1922, v. XX, p. 59. In 1916, the production of cranberries in the United States was about 545,000 barrels. Output had increased nearly 200,000 barrels since 1906, the cost of production had been rising, and the price was insufficient to yield a profit to most producers. As an experiment, $23,000 was appropriated for a coöperative advertising campaign in Chicago. New methods of serving cranberries in an appetizing manner were suggested. On account of a sugar shortage, ways of cooking cranberries with less sugar were explained. By the close of the season, the Chicago sales were 47 per cent greater than in 1915. In 1917, no advertising was done because the crop had been cut in half by a September freeze. In 1918, however, the first national advertising of cranberries was attempted. Begin-ning about October 15th, $54,000 was spent in advertising for thirty days. The mild fall and winter were detrimental to the consumption of cranberries and the sugar regulation was still in effect. The trade believed that cranberries would be a drug on the market, but, to the surprise of everyone, they sold in larger quantities than ever before, and by January were bringing the record price of $22 per barrel. Those in charge of the campaign estimated that had no advertising been done the crop would have netted the growers no more than $6 per barrel. Through advertising, an aver-age of $8.89 was realized. *Printers' Ink,* October 13, 1921, v. CXVII, No. 2, pp. 89–96.

Advertising undoubtedly increased the *demand* for raisins or cranberries but did it increase the consumption? Once produced, the raisins or cranberries would be offered at almost any price necessary to dispose of them. Was not the effect of advertising, therefore, to raise the price rather than to increase the consumption? The answer to this is that the production *in the long run* is influenced by the price, and advertising, by raising the price, tends to increase production. But, of course, if more labor and capital are used in growing raisins or cranberries, less is available for producing other goods. Consequently, in increasing the production of some goods, advertising may decrease the production of others.

Between 1880 and 1910, the total number of gainfully employed persons in the United States increased by 119 per cent. The number engaged in certain strictly selling occupations (commercial travelers, salesmen and saleswomen, agents, hucksters and peddlers, retailers, and wholesalers) increased 300 per cent. Between 1910 and 1920, the total number of gainfully employed increased by 9 per cent but the number engaged in trade increased 35 per cent. Such figures as these are often cited as proof that modern marketing is wasteful and that it absorbs an unnecessarily large number of men.

The figures in themselves, however, prove nothing about the wastefulness of marketing, because conditions of production and consumption have greatly changed since 1880. Territorial specialization and the production of goods in large plants have steadily developed. Both of these changes tend to increase the distance between producers and most consumers and create the need for a more elaborate marketing organization. In addition, a much larger part of the national production now consists of manufactured goods which are luxuries or semi-luxuries; families are smaller; and a larger part of the population now lives in cities, and not only in cities but in small apartments. These changes all tend to increase the labor needed in marketing goods.

But the critics of modern marketing assert that it employs an excessive number of persons because the work of each person is largely directed to counteracting the work of the others. If a manufacturer or a wholesaler has his salesmen call on the trade once a month instead of once in two months, his competitors must do likewise. If he doubles his advertising space, his competitors must double theirs. Modern selling methods are comparable, it is said, to the competitive building of armaments. Each enterprise increases its expenditures on selling in an effort to outdo its rivals but in the end they are in the same relative position as at the beginning. The community, however, is worse off because there are fewer persons available for other work.[35] In the case

[35] Dr. A. E. Taylor of the Food Research Institute has raised some pertinent questions concerning the efforts to increase the consumption of various kinds of food. He points out that though the demand for individual foodstuffs is elastic, the demand for calories is inelastic. Yet the stock raisers and meat packers are attempting to increase the per capita annual meat consumption of the country from 155 to 179 pounds, the flour millers to raise the consumption of flour from 200 to 220 pounds, the milk producers are asking the public to drink a quart of milk a day,

of advertising, it is undoubtedly true that expenditures are uneconomically large. The reason is that advertising agencies are paid on the basis of the amount of advertising used in the campaign. If $500,000 is used, the agency receives more than if $300,000 is used. Consequently the agencies have a strong incentive to do whatever they can to persuade enterprises to purchase large amounts of advertising space.

The defenders of modern marketing reply that strenuous sales promotion methods help to concentrate demand in the hands of a few large enterprises and thus to make possible the economies of production in large plants. By facilitating more minute subdivision of labor and greater use of machines, modern marketing is said to save more labor than it absorbs.

This argument is of doubtful validity. Unquestionably some enterprises, by skillful selling or by hitting upon peculiarly effective advertising appeals, have succeeded in capturing much of the trade of their rivals and have thus achieved the savings of mass production. But such a result presupposes that the marketing department of one concern is vastly superior to the departments of most rival concerns and that the successful methods cannot be imitated. This situation is not typical. Furthermore, in some ways modern marketing methods tend to retard the development of large plants. In the first place, the rapid style changes for which modern selling methods are at least partly responsible discourage mass production. In the second place, high pressure sales methods sometimes make it possible to induce a limited number of persons to pay such a high price for a product that it is more profitable for the seller to adopt the policy of a high price and limited sales than of a low price and mass production. Vacuum cleaners appear to be an illustration.[36] Finally, the marketing experts of each enterprise use all their skill to diminish the intensity of price competition by convincing the con-

---

the canners are endeavoring to raise the demand for fruits and vegetables. Taylor, A. E., "Consumption, Merchandising and Advertising of Foods," *Harvard Business Review*, April, 1924, v. II, p. 291. The money spent on these selling campaigns may be amply justified by the information which is spread concerning the merits of various foods. But one thing is quite certain. Not all of these efforts to induce us to eat more can succeed. If we purchase more of some foods, we are certain to use less of others.

[36] Cf. Borsodi, Ralph, *The Distribution Age*, p. 140.

sumers that the product of the particular concern is different. No doubt the individuality claimed for most brands is more or less specious. Nevertheless, many consumers come to have a definite preference for a certain brand and are not easily persuaded to take another. Under these circumstances, the ability of one enterprise to produce for less than the others does not enable it to gain much business by underselling them. In other words, the marketing experts, by creating a preference for each brand among part of the public, check the tendency for competition to concentrate output in a few low cost plants.[37]

Do modern selling methods give consumers better or poorer goods? Do skillful salesmanship and advertising take the place of good materials and workmanship? Or is it folly to spend much money attempting to sell an article which is poorly made?

No general answer to these questions is possible. Unquestionably it often pays to spend large sums selling worthless goods, especially if repeat sales are not expected or if it is difficult for consumers to judge the service rendered by an article. But in the somewhat limited number of cases where the consumer is able to judge the performance of goods, the current practice of marketing goods under brand names probably makes for better quality. Skillful salesmanship or a well written advertisement may induce a customer to buy a certain brand once but he will not buy it again unless it has given satisfaction. And expensive national marketing campaigns are not likely to pay unless they lead to repeat sales.

[37] The proprietary medicine industry illustrates how success in establishing the individuality of products creates a multitude of small plants. From the standpoint of technology, there is no reason why medicines should not be mixed and bottled in a few immense plants. The products are well adapted to production by automatic machines. As a matter of fact, however, the proprietary medicine industry exhibits the very reverse of mass production. According to the 1927 Census of Manufactures, there were no less than 1,282 plants making proprietary medicines. The average number of employees was 19 and the average annual gross sales were only $217,000.

But the economies of large scale production may be achieved *in spite of* advertising provided the several firms are willing to market a common product under different names and to have the product made in one plant. An example is an arrangement, made in 1930, between the General Electric Company, the Westinghouse Electric and Manufacturing Company, General Motors Corporation and the Radio Corporation of America. It provides for the Radio Corporation of America to manufacture radio equipment which the other three companies distribute under their names. Substantially the same product, therefore, is sold under three trade names.

But retailers, as well as manufacturers and wholesalers, are interested in repeat sales. Back in the days before nationally advertised brands, some retailers took care to see that the consumer received satisfactory quality. Is the consumer then really any better off?

To this question there are two replies. In the first place, the marketing of advertised brands does not necessarily destroy the protection, meagre though it may be, which the retailer has always given the consumer, but it may make the manufacturer or wholesaler more interested in supplying satisfactory goods. In the second place, the articles which manufacturers and wholesalers sell under brand names are exposed to criticism from the whole nation or at least from a large section of it. Goods which satisfy the most critical part of the national market must be better than goods which would satisfy many local markets.

Do modern marketing methods assist the consumer to spend his income more advantageously? Do they make him a better informed and a more discriminating buyer? Do they help him to obtain more satisfaction for his money?

These also are questions which cannot be answered definitely. Modern marketing methods are used to persuade the consumer to buy almost everything under heaven. On the one hand, he is asked to buy worthless stocks, radium ore bars, electric belts, hair restorers, anti-fat remedies, radiotized water, alleged cures for bad breath, cures for incurable diseases, books which will make him a brilliant conversationalist; on the other hand, he is urged to guard his health by a physical examination once a year, to purchase five feet of literary classics, to protect his family with life and accident insurance, to start a savings account, to make a trip to Europe. Nevertheless, it is possible to make a few generalizations concerning the kind of guidance which modern selling methods give the consumer.

No doubt the aggressive selling efforts of business enterprises provide consumers with much important information — facts about what goods are available, where, and at what prices. Especially is this true of much advertising of retail stores in the daily newspapers. So many are the ways of spending money that the consumer is bound to overlook most of them in making his decisions. Undoubtedly he is often helped in gaining the maximum return from his dollars by having the various ways of spending money brought vividly to his attention. Of course, the goods which advertise themselves are pushed no less (often even more) vigorously than other goods, but the net effect of selling efforts is probably to increase the alternatives which most persons consider before spending their money and thus to increase the satisfaction which they obtain.

But despite the multitude of articles which modern marketing brings to the attention of the consumer, he cannot be said to receive a well balanced guidance in spending his money. Business enterprises invariably urge the consumer to buy, never not to buy. The custom of going without hats, for example, must make headway without support from the business world. Through skillful salesmanship, the consumer is persuaded to buy new shoes and to buy them frequently. But no one helps him visualize the comfort of old shoes. With a little encouragement from a few pages in the *Saturday Evening Post,* many of us might gladly postpone the purchase of shoes. The stores organize " dress up and look prosperous " campaigns. If the consumer is to make a balanced decision, should not someone present the case for wearing old clothes and being care free? The money and skill of business are invariably devoted to persuading him to buy the new, regardless of whether or not he would gain more satisfaction by using the old a little longer.

Some desires are more profitably stimulated than others, but not always to the advantage of the consumer. For example, it is more profitable to stimulate a demand for newness rather than for durability, because, if consumers prefer durable things, the frequency with which each person can be sold will be diminished. But may not the consumer get more satisfaction for his money if, for example, he pays one-third more for a car that will last nine years instead of five?

The home industries lose out in competition with the factory because there is no one to say a word on their behalf. The Buffalo bakers recently began a coöperative advertising campaign to enlarge the cake market. Although about 90 per cent of the bread is now commercially baked, housewives still make about

80 per cent of the sweet goods.[38]   But who is to finance a rebuttal in favor of home baking?   And if there is no rebuttal, may not the housewife decide to buy her cakes simply because she does not fully realize the advantages of making them?

All industries are not equally able to spend large sums on influencing demand.   The inability of some industries to advertise their products means that those goods tend to escape the attention of the consumer and he perhaps fails to buy them despite the fact that they would yield him more pleasure than some things which he does buy.   Honey loses out in competition for the consumer's dollar because the individual beekeeper cannot afford to do much advertising and because the industry has no coöperative organization which might standardize honey and advertise it. Goods made in large plants can be more economically advertised than goods made in small plants.   In other words, advertising is a result of mass production, far more than mass production is a result of advertising.   Large automobile companies, for example, can afford to purchase double spreads in the *Saturday Evening Post,* and to issue elaborate brochures with expensive half-tones printed on costly glazed paper.   But most men do not know how much pleasure they would derive from horseback riding. If they did know, they might use horses more and automobiles less.   The facilities for marketing horseback riding are inferior to those for marketing automobiles.   Its pleasures are not advertised in the *Saturday Evening Post.*   Of course, smaller plants may jointly support an advertising campaign.   This was done by the Jantzen Knitting Mills, manufacturers of bathing suits; the Roberts Filter Manufacturing Company, producers of filters and re-circulating equipment; Wallace and Tiernan, makers of chlorine control apparatus; and the Graver Corporation, filter manufacturers, which financed a campaign to advertise swimming.[39]

Despite the fact that modern marketing presents the consumer with immense amounts of information which he would not otherwise have, one kind of information he is rarely given — that is, information about the quality of goods.   Of course, every

[38] *Printers' Ink,* August 2, 1928, v. CXLIV, No. 5, p. 25.
[39] *Ibid.,* August 2, 1928, v. CXLIV, No. 5, p. 57.

salesman and every advertisement have much to say about quality, but not, as a rule, anything which can be regarded as *information*. All of the many millions that have been spent advertising tooth pastes, gasoline, and automobile tires, for example, shed no light whatever on which tooth paste, if any, cleans teeth effectively, which gasoline gives the most power, which tire wears the longest. Every advertisement abounds in emphatic declarations of superiority but the consumer can read every one without gaining an iota of help in deciding what tooth paste, gasoline, or tire to purchase. That modern marketing fails to inform consumers about quality is undoubtedly one of the gravest indictments to be brought against it.

But we should overlook much of the significance of modern marketing methods if we regarded them solely as ways of informing consumers about opportunities to spend money. Marketing is an attempt to mold the consumer's valuations, to influence the importance which he attaches to things — in other words, to do the very thing that religion and education endeavor to do. By their influence upon the valuations of millions of men, marketing experts help mold the very philosophy of the age. Indeed, they are doing more than this, for since men are largely what their desires make them, marketing experts are engaged in nothing less momentous than the molding of human character on a gigantic scale. Well may we ask whether it is wise to permit our valuations, our philosophy, our very desires to be molded by men who are guided by no higher aim than to make a profit for themselves or for their employers.[40]

In no way is the danger of the control of our valuations and of our desires by business more clearly shown than in the endeavors of enterprises to stimulate competitive consumption. Man appears to be a competitive animal — at least most men derive satisfaction from feeling superior to their fellows. Among all peoples and in all ages, among primitive tribes as well as among industrialized people, we find this competitive disposition manifesting itself in innumerable forms. Men gain satisfaction from being better born than their fellows, more humble, more

[40] For a brief but excellent discussion of the social significance of advertising, see Copeland, M. A., *American Economic Review, Supplement,* March, 1925, v. XV, pp. 38–41.

virtuous, more wicked, more daring, more learned, more orthodox, more unorthodox, more patriotic, more beautiful, even more
ugly, more skillful at some game or craft, more wealthy, from
living in a better house, driving a better car, wearing more stylish
or more expensive clothes. Marketing experts intensify demand
by appealing to men's competitive dispositions and by stimulating
rivalry in consumption. From the standpoint of the satisfaction
which men derive from their incomes, the stimulation of competitive consumption by skillfully planned and abundantly financed marketing campaigns is a serious form of industrial
waste.

Two principal devices are used by business concerns to extend competition in consumption. One is fostering the belief
that only a certain style is " correct " for a certain occasion. For
example, on November 15, 1921, the American Association of
Wholesale Opticians authorized the appointment of a committee
to urge on the public the wearing of eye-glasses suitable for the
occasion on which they were worn. It was the sense of the committee, for example, that shell-rims are not proper for evening
or street wear.[41] Following this action, appeared advertisements
headed " Style says: Different glasses for work, dress and play ";
" To be ' well-dressed ' includes appropriate glasses." [42] The annual convention of the National Retail Shoe Dealers' Association in July, 1927, decided to raise $4,000,000 for a four-year
national campaign to persuade men to buy more shoes. The
advertising began appearing in the autumn of 1928 and sought
to persuade the public that different types and colors of clothing
require different types and colors of shoes — so much so that
the well dressed man needs no less than six pairs.[43]

The other device for spreading competition in consumption
is to accelerate changes in styles. Style changes, in fact, may
be regarded as a device for destroying the value of goods by
rendering them obsolete. No better description of this function
can be asked than that given by the chairman of the style com-

---

[41] A report of the meeting and of the action taken will be found in the New
York *Times*, November 16, 1921, p. 5.

[42] Cf., for example, the advertisements of the Shur-On Optical Company in the
Atlantic Monthly for May and July, 1922.

[43] The campaign is described in *Printers' Ink*, May 23, 1929, v. CXLVII, No. 8,
p. 133.

mittee of an association of retail clothiers. He is quoted as follows:

" It is a well-known fact that in women's clothing styles change three or four times a season and that the wardrobes of women throughout the country are filled with good clothing they do not wear for the reason that it is out of style. There is no good reason why we cannot fill the men's wardrobes of the country with the same method as is pursued by the women's wear houses." [44]

New styles, of course, are planned to be conspicuously different from the old in order that old goods cannot easily be altered to conform to the new styles. Sometimes, of course, consumers may resist the new styles but good salesmanship may possibly overcome this resistance. For example, we find the New York *Times* making the following report on changes in dress styles for the fall of 1929:

" Special merchandising . . . should be placed on longer skirt lengths and the normal or nearly normal waistline in dresses, according to the latest market report of the Merchandise and Research Bureau. Pointing out that the new silhouette applies chiefly to afternoon wear, the report says that possible consumer resistance to the longer skirt can be overcome by proper salesmanship by retailers." [45]

Increasing the variety of styles and accelerating the rate of style change are wasteful because they compel many consumers to spend a large part of their incomes for things that they do not really desire — to spend money not to gain satisfaction but to avoid dissatisfaction. And for all but the well-to-do, every additional dollar spent on competitive consumption means one less dollar for other expenditures. In order to escape the pain of *seeming* poor, many consumers are compelled to suffer the discomforts of *actual* poverty.

In many instances, modern sales methods raise the price of goods to consumers. It was estimated that the advertising of cranberries in 1918 enabled the raisers to realize nearly three dollars more a barrel.[46] The Simcoe Poultry Farms of Ontario report that advertising enabled them to sell eggs — " good, fresh, heavy and clean but no more so than hundreds of other poultry farms around us were producing " — at an average of

[44] Copeland, M. T., *Problems in Marketing* (second edition), p. 9.
[45] New York *Times*, August 4, 1929, Section 2, p. 8.
[46] *Printers' Ink*, October 13, 1921, v. CXVII, No. 2, p. 90.

20 cents a dozen above the ordinary price.[47]   Mr. J. W. Young,
vice-president of the J. Walter Thompson Company, cites another illustration: " One association with which I am familiar is
engaged in marketing a by-product of its members' principal line
of business.   The total volume of this by-product cannot be increased from year to year due to the nature of the parent industry.   The total output of the by-product is being sold but it is
probable that a greater conviction about its value among users
would enable it to fetch a higher price.   Advertising is being used
to create that conviction." [48]

But although the *immediate* effect of an increase in the demand for any good is an increase in price, it is not necessarily the
ultimate effect.   If the good is one which is produced at less cost
when made in large quantities, the increase in demand may eventually decrease the price.   No doubt this may be the result in
some cases.[49]   And yet the savings made possible by mass production are not necessarily passed on to the consumer.   In the
first place, they may be more than offset by the cost of creating
the additional demand.   In the second place, the supposition
that savings in costs will be passed on to the consumer rests upon
the assumption that the concern can make more money by selling
a larger quantity at a lower price.   But the marketing experts of
the enterprise may have succeeded in creating such an inelastic
demand for its brand that a cut in price cannot be expected to
produce a large increase in sales.   Under these circumstances
a cut may not pay.[50]

[47] *Printers' Ink Monthly*, May, 1929, v. XVIII, pp. 45, 108, and 111.

[48] *J. Walter Thompson News Bulletin*, November, 1926, p. 4.

To some extent the consumer may be compensated for the higher prices which
he is induced to pay for some things by his ability to obtain others for less.   He has
a limited number of dollars to spend.   If he is induced by high pressure sales methods
to pay more for some things, he has less to spend for others.   The demand for the
other goods is less and their price falls.   Whether or not the permanent effect is a
rise or a fall in the price of other goods depends upon whether a permanent decrease
in the volume of output raises or lowers their cost of production.

[49] There are a few cases in which high pressure sales methods have diminished
the seasonal slump in industries.   This, of course, tends to reduce overhead costs per
unit of output.   The Grigsby-Grunow Company, makers of Majestic radios, by concentrated advertising, is said to have largely overcome the summer slump in its sales.
Printers' Ink, June 27, 1929, v. CXLVII, No. 13, p. 17.   For other cases see Feld-
man, H., *The Regularization of Employment*, pp. 176–179.

[50] This is simply one way of saying that the marketing department may have
been so successful in eliminating competition in price that it has created a monopoly.
The commodity may be only one of many makes of shaving cream or tooth paste between which there is intense competition.   Nevertheless, if the maker of a brand is so

To the evidence that high pressure selling often raises prices, the defenders of modern marketing reply that the consumer has no legitimate complaint if he is induced to pay $10 instead of $5 for an article, because the very fact that he is willing to pay $10 instead of $5 proves that high pressure selling has intensified his desire for the good. Although the article itself has not been changed, its desirability and its power to yield satisfaction have been increased. The consumer pays $10 instead of $5 but he obtains $10 instead of only $5 worth of satisfaction.

The above reply is an accurate description of the facts in some cases and, for such cases, it is an unanswerable reply to the complaint that modern marketing compels the consumer to pay more. *Satisfaction*, not pounds or yards of goods, is the essential thing which the consumer buys. If his satisfaction increases in proportion to his expenditures, he has no complaint even though the pounds or yards of physical goods which he buys actually decrease. In other words, modern marketing can be defended on the ground that it increases the want-satisfying efficiency of goods so that one yard or pound yields more satisfaction than before.

Unfortunately, however, the fact that a consumer pays a high price instead of a low one does not always mean that he gains a correspondingly greater return from his purchase. The satisfaction yielded by goods is often not connected with the price paid for them. A mattress is not more comfortable, a furnace does not heat any better, a shaving soap does not soften the beard more effectively, paint does not wear any longer because bought at a high price instead of a low one.[51] In some cases, the con-

successful in spreading the conviction that his brand is unique that he finds it profitable to limit sales in order to keep up the price, he has created a monopoly. The point at which it is profitable for the monopoly to set its price depends upon the elasticity of the demand. It is the purpose of marketing departments to create an inelastic demand and thus to make a high price most profitable.

But in so far as the marketing departments of several rival enterprises succeed in persuading the public that *each* brand is meritorious, they make the demand for *all* brands elastic because they make the buyers of each brand more willing to buy another if the price of the preferred brand is raised. In other words, the work of the marketing department of each enterprise has two effects: (1) it tends to create an inelastic demand for the brand which it is pushing; and (2) it tends to create an elastic demand for all other brands.

[51] But so great is the power of suggestion that a person who *thinks* that he has purchased a superior mattress or shaving soap may actually believe that the expensive mattress is softer or that the more expensive shaving cream gives an easier shave.

sumer may pay a high price simply because he is temporarily convinced by clever salesmanship that he has an intense desire for something which, on sober second thought, he finds he does not wish at all. And finally, he may be induced to buy an expensive grade of a commodity by being persuaded that this grade is usually purchased. If, as a matter of fact, it is a more expensive grade than that usually bought, there is no reason to suppose that his satisfaction is correspondingly greater. The point is made clearer by the methods used on an occasion by Marshall Field and Company to induce customers to pay more for hand bags. The bags were on display in a case and were marked from $5 up to $65 and $70. The purpose of the expensive bags in the display was described by an official of the store as follows:

". . . a man will come in here to buy a bag for his wife, or she will come herself, for that matter, and have in mind paying five or ten dollars. But when they look over the assortment and see that, while they can get a fine looking bag for that money, there are others on up to several times that sum, it simply lifts their conception of what constitutes a desirable shopping bag, and they end up by paying $25 or $30. The more expensive bags haven't sold, and yet they have earned half their cost on that one transaction — at least one of them has. Then that woman goes out with her fine bag and sets a new standard for her friends, and they come in with $20 ideas and end up with $40 purchases." [52]

It would be ridiculous to assume that a person who was led by such a display to purchase a $20 bag instead of a $10 one would necessarily gain double the satisfaction from the $20 bag. The only safe assumption is that the buyer paid more in order to be sure that her bag was as good (or as expensive) as those which other women were carrying.

The great advantage of free private enterprise is that the individual, being free to make his own choices, is more likely to get the things which satisfy his desires. But may not modern high pressure sales methods frequently lead consumers to purchase goods which they do not really desire or which they cannot afford? Unfortunately it is difficult to obtain objective evidence concerning whether consumers are satisfied with their choices. The percentage of goods returned to department stores, which permit (and even encourage) the practice of returning unsatisfactory

[52] Warren, Waldo P., "Getting People to Pay More," *Printers' Ink*, December 28, 1911, v. LXXVII, p. 36.

articles, is usually small.[53] But there are cases where high pressure selling leads a large proportion of buyers to purchase goods which, on second thought, they apparently do not desire or at least do not consider worth the price. Industrial insurance is an example. In Massachusetts, for instance, the number of weekly premium policies that were permitted to lapse during 1928 was 59.6 per cent of the number of new policies issued.[54] These are the policies issued by industrial insurance companies such as the Metropolitan, the John Hancock Mutual, and others. The savings banks of Massachusetts are also permitted to sell industrial insurance but they are not permitted to employ salesmen or agents to solicit business. This prohibition is designed to keep down the cost of savings bank insurance by preventing the growth of expensive marketing organization. In other words, those who buy policies from savings banks must go to the bank themselves and *ask* for insurance — they are not persuaded to purchase by a salesman. It is significant that the number of savings banks policies which were permitted to lapse in 1928 was only one per cent of the number of new policies issued.[55]

V. The Protection of the Consumer

When the ordinary consumer knows so little about quality or prices, when he often cannot even tell quantities, and when he deals with experts who are eager to make him buy on impulse rather than after reflection, it is surprising that he obtains as much for his money as he does. But he is not without protection. One of his most important protections is " word-of-mouth advertising," which may be defined as what users of articles say about them to their friends. Even though a consumer cannot tell the quality of an article by inspection, he may be able to do so by using it for a short time. Word-of-mouth advertising is sometimes described as the most important kind of publicity

[53] A study of merchandise returns in department stores by the Bureau of Business Research of Ohio State University indicated that the rate in nineteen stores averaged 5.5 per cent of sales — 1.4 per cent in the case of cash sales and 6.3 per cent in the case of charge sales. Ohio State University, *Bulletin of Business Research*, July, 1928, v. III, No. 6, p. 20.

[54] Commonwealth of Massachusetts, *Annual Report of the Commissioner of Insurance*, 1928, Part II, pp. 46 and 48.

[55] *Ibid.*, pp. 36 and 48.

and in the case of most articles this is probably true. Of course, there are many articles, such as tires, tooth brushes, or medicines, which the consumer cannot accurately appraise even by using them. Furthermore, the buyer who has been fooled is sometimes ashamed to confess it to his friends. This reluctance is a god-send to the sellers of worthless stocks and real estate. Finally, some sellers fail to appreciate the importance of word-of-mouth advertising and therefore are not greatly influenced by it. Despite these limitations, however, word-of-mouth advertising must be accounted one of the most effective safe-guards of the consumer.[56]

Possibly an even greater protection is the desire of sellers for repeat sales. In order to make a small extra profit on one sale, it would often be foolish to risk losing the entire future business of the customer. So much importance do many retailers attach to repeat sales that they permit customers to return any article which is unsatisfactory. This policy is followed despite the fact that the return privilege is grossly abused.[57] Some stores, in order to protect themselves by protecting their customers, have found it desirable to establish testing laboratories. R. H. Macy & Company of New York City is one. Such a laboratory may discover "sun-fast" curtains which fade almost immediately; borax-powdered soap which contains no borax whatever; wash-

[56] Before buying an oil heater, a prospective purchaser is likely to inquire into the experience of his friends who have already bought one. The quality of service rendered by oil heaters is greatly affected by the nature of the installation. For this reason, the Williams Oil-O-Matic Heating Corporation requires every dealer to send a man to its training school for a five-day session on the installation of heaters. The expenses are borne by the dealer. Mr. R. D. Marshall, registrar of the school, says that the company estimates that about 23 per cent of its sales are produced, in the main, by advertising; 27 per cent by direct dealer effort; and 50 per cent by the influence of satisfied customers. *Printers' Ink*, August 9, 1928, v. CLXIV, No. 6, pp. 85–86.

[57] In Chicago the proportion of returned goods is unusually high largely because of the exceptionally liberal policy of Marshall Field and Company which has even advertised its willingness to accept returns without question. Among the department stores, the returns average about 18 per cent on gross sales. The returns are almost solely confined to credit purchases.

Buying goods without intending to keep them is a form of conspicuous consumption. Women, who are accompanied by friends, make purchases which they never intend to keep. Some people like to have the department store delivery truck drive up to their door. A purchase which is returned gives two drive-ups and costs nothing to the "customer." Some department stores take away the credit accounts of purchasers who return more than they keep.

able articles of all kinds which fade, stain, or shrink excessively during the laundering process.[58]

But even where the managers of an enterprise attach great importance to repeat business, the sales clerks may not. The clerks are frequently paid partly or wholly on a commission basis; many of them do not expect to remain with the house for long; and many of them fail to appreciate the importance of future sales. Nor does the desire for repeat sales protect the consumer in the numerous cases where he cannot accurately judge an article even by using it. And finally, it does not help when the dealer does not expect to sell twice to the same customer. The flagrant abuses in the sale of real estate and in the construction of houses are largely explained by the fact that many real estate operators and contractors are not looking for repeat business.

Because the amateur buyer is at a great disadvantage in purchasing hundreds of commodities with which he is only slightly familiar, the local, state, and national governments and some organizations of business men step in to protect him. Protection takes four principal forms — regulation of prices; of weights and measures; of quality; and of trade practices.

The public regulation of prices has been discussed in Chapters XVII and XVIII and need not detain us here. One of the oldest and simplest forms of protection is the definition by law of weights and measures and the inspection of scales and measures by government inspectors to see that the law is obeyed. Obviously it is easy to cheat customers by giving short measure or weight. But although the pound, yard, quart, gallon, and some other units have been standardized, many units have not. For example, nine states — Arizona, Colorado, Delaware, Georgia, Louisiana, North Dakota, Oklahoma, Tennessee, and Wyoming — have no laws standardizing vegetable or fruit containers. Other states have standardized at least one type of berry box, grape basket, apple barrel, hamper, round stave basket, splint or market basket.[59] In 1915, Congress established standard sizes

[58] Freedman, E., " The Testing of Merchandise by Department Stores," *Journal of Home Economics*, September, 1930, v. XXII, p. 733. A test for washability has been worked out which prescribes in definite terms the type of soap, the method of drying, the temperature, and the permissible limit of shrinkage.

[59] U. S. Department of Agriculture, *Marketing Activities*, August 31, 1927, v. VII, p. 215.

for fruit and vegetable barrels used in either interstate or intrastate commerce; in 1916, it established standard sizes for climax baskets for grapes, berry boxes, and till baskets and prohibited the use of other sizes in interstate commerce; and in 1928, it established standard sizes for hampers, round stave and straight side baskets, and splint or market baskets and prohibited the use of other sizes in either interstate or intrastate commerce.[60]

But much remains to be done in order that consumers may receive full measure or standard sizes. Many states do not test gasoline pumps, and standard sizes have not been established for garments. Some hosiery manufacturers board goods on boards that are a half size larger than the finished hose, thus allowing a half size for shrinkage during dyeing and finishing. Other manufacturers make no allowance.[61] Likewise there are no standard sizes in men's and women's suits. This encourages manufacturers to make sub-standard sizes and it leads shipping clerks, in their eagerness to earn bonuses for filling orders rapidly, to select the nearest sizes available and send them. As a result, merchants are unable to tell what sizes they have been selling and a consumer who buys one size in one store is likely not to obtain the same dimensions when he asks for this size in another store.[62] In many states, sizes of the loaf of bread have not been standardized. During the war, the National Food Administration prescribed the 16 ounce, or pound, loaf. When national regulation ceased, the weight of loaves immediately fell to anywhere from 11½ to 14 ounces. The New Jersey State Department of Weights and Measures says: " The acknowledged custom of bakers has been, when for any reason their overhead increased, to pinch off an ounce or two of dough from each individual loaf." [63] The dimensions of dressed lumber are not legally established. Consequently, by a nibbling process, the sizes have been becoming smaller and smaller. Mr. Edward Hines, the Chicago lumberman, when asked how small he in-

[60] U. S. Department of Agriculture, *Outline Showing Federal Standardization of Fruit and Vegetable Barrels and Baskets.*

[61] Johnson, George H., *Textile Fabrics,* p. 209.

[62] Ohio State University, *Bulletin of Business Research,* v. I, No. 2, p. 8.

[63] New Jersey State Department of Weights and Measures, *Brief Pertinent to Senate Bill No. 80.*

tended to make his 2 x 4's when the finished size was lowered from 1¾ x 3¾ to 1⅝ x 3⅝, is said to have replied: " Just as small as you will take them." [64]

The inability of the consumer to determine the quality of many articles by inspection has led the national and local governments to prohibit the sale of a few commodities, principally foods, which fail to meet certain minimum standards. The Federal Meat Inspection Act excludes from interstate commerce meats which fail to pass the federal inspectors, and the Pure Food and Drug Act excludes foods or drugs which are adulterated or misbranded. An article is adulterated when it is made wholly or in part from filthy or decomposed materials, when it has been cheapened by the substitution of some less valuable material, when some valuable component has been removed, or when a poisonous or deleterious substance has been added. An article is misbranded when the label or package contains either out and out misstatements or statements or illustrations which convey an erroneous impression. Many cities prohibit the sale of milk from herds which are not tuberculin tested. In North Dakota, all gasoline and kerosene and some foodstuffs must meet standards prescribed by the state government. Some states prohibit the sale of secondhand mattresses and require that mattresses be manufactured of new and clean material.

But in protecting the consumer against goods that are unfit for consumption, much remains to be done. The Federal Meat Inspection Act applies only to interstate commerce, and many states have no inspection of meat that is slaughtered and sold within the state. Only five states have a state-wide system of market milk inspection.[65] A law on the statute books means little

[64] From an address by Mr. N. M. Reis, Vice-President of the New York, New Haven and Hartford Railroad, " The Railroad Man's Interest in Forest Conservation," before the joint meeting of the American Forestry Association and the Connecticut Forestry Association.

[65] *American Journal of Public Health*, October, 1929, v. XIX, p. 1131. In general, public education on the subject of a pure milk supply lags far behind public appreciation of the importance of a pure water supply. In many parts of the country, milk is a far more important source of typhoid than water. From 1911 to 1928, inclusive, there were in Massachusetts alone, 1,468 cases of typhoid attributed to milk and only 369 cases attributed to water. During the same period, 1,147 cases of scarlet fever and 3,986 cases of septic sore throat in Massachusetts were attributed to milk. *Ibid.*, July, 1929, v. XIX, p. 784.

unless it is well administered.   The administration of the pure food laws in many states is inadequate, partly because the enforcement officers are too few, partly because most states and cities possess no civil service laws,[66] and partly because the responsibility for enforcing the laws often belongs to no one in particular but is an incidental duty of some busy public official.

But it is not sufficient merely to protect consumers from goods which are worthless or positively injurious.   Among the multitude of things which meet the requirements of the law, the consumer needs to know which are superior and which are inferior. Business enterprises and governmental bodies commonly purchase goods on the basis of standards or specifications.   It would obviously be of immense advantage for consumers if they could do likewise.   It is one of the ironies of modern business that advertising space itself is now purchased on the basis of definite information.   Mr. Paul T. Cherington, director of research of the J. Walter Thompson Company, describes the progress in this respect as follows:

" The Audit Bureau of Circulations (founded in 1914) has put circulation statements on an entirely new footing.   Comparative figures sworn to and presented in a form suited to the needs of the advertiser were substituted for the intangible and glowing generalities of many of the earlier publishers.   This advance alone would have made the quarter century a notable one in the advertising business." [67]

The ordinary consumer, however, must still buy on the basis of " intangible and glowing generalities."

During the last few years, there has been a pronounced movement to market products on the basis of standards and specifications.   Progress has been unusually rapid in the case of agricultural products.   The federal government and many state governments have established official grades.   Federal grades have been established for small grains, cotton, wool, tobacco, meat, butter, and eggs.   As of June 30, 1930, federal standards

---

[66] A recent survey covering thirty-four states shows that nine require a civil service examination for dairy and milk inspectors and twenty-five do not.   *American Journal of Public Health*, October, 1929, v. XIX, p. 1131.   Effective administration can scarcely be expected until appointments are made on the basis of merit after competitive examination.

[67] Cherington, Paul T., *The Consumer Looks at Advertising*, pp. 98–99.

had been established for forty-six fruits and vegetables.[68] Recently Congress amended the Federal Food and Drug Act to require the Secretary of Agriculture to establish reasonable standards of quality and of fill for canned foods and to designate how canned foods shall be labeled when they fail to meet the standards. The labeling of sub-standard products as such is compulsory, provided they are sold in interstate commerce.[69]

The use of grades or standards may be obligatory or voluntary. The grain standards established by the Grain Standard Act of 1916 are mandatory in all transactions in interstate and foreign commerce except those by sample. Under this Act, grades have been established for shell corn, wheat, oats, rye, feed oats, mixed feed oats, and barley. The Cotton Futures Act requires that all cotton intended for delivery on future contracts shall be classified by federal inspectors. The use of federal apple grades is compulsory in New York, Virginia, Maryland, North Carolina, and South Carolina. Six other states — West Virginia, Pennsylvania, Delaware, Illinois, New Hampshire, and Maine — also require the use of apple grades. The first five require that either the state or the United States grades be used. Maine makes the use of its own state grades compulsory.[70] Pennsylvania and New York require the marking of all closed packages of grapes in conformance with the United States grape grades.[71] Oregon has made potato grading compulsory.[72] In 1927, the state of New York established retail grades and standards for eggs. The statute makes it a misdemeanor punishable by fine to sell or offer for sale any egg unfit for human consumption; places certain restrictions on the use of " fresh " or words of similar import, such as " new laid," " day old," when applied to eggs; and establishes five grades — "nearby fancy," " grade A," " grade B," and "grade C," and "unclassified." Retailers are

---

[68] U. S. Department of Agriculture, *Report of the Chief of the Bureau of Agricultural Economics*, 1930, p. 32.

[69] It is important to notice that sub-standard products may be wholesome and edible. They are simply less palatable and attractive than the standard grade. It is also important to notice that the amendment does not require the Secretary of Agriculture to establish grades for canned goods *above* the standard.

[70] U. S. Department of Agriculture, *Marketing Activities*, September 21, 1927, v. VII, p. 233.

[71] *Ibid.*, May 1, 1929, v. IX, p. 105.

[72] *Ibid.*, February 12, 1930, v. X, p. 41.

required to notify purchasers, by a placard, of the grade of eggs sold and to stamp the grade on the carton or bag. Formerly, for all practical purposes, any edible egg could be sold as fresh, provided it had not been held in cold storage. Freshness is now determined by internal quality and candling and only eggs which meet the requirements for " nearby fancy " grades or for " grade A" may be offered as fresh. All eggs offered or sold to retailers or consumers, except eggs which are the vendor's own products, must be offered on the basis of grades. But farmers selling their own eggs are not exempt from the provision regarding the sale of bad eggs, or regarding the use of such terms as " fresh," " strictly fresh." [73]

The use of most grades and standards, however, is voluntary. This, of course, is true of nearly all grades established by private bodies such as the American Standards Association and of many official standards established by the state and federal governments. For example, the federal government does not require that its grades for wool, tobacco, butter, fruits, vegetables, and meat be used in interstate commerce. Nevertheless, once a grade is established, the preference of buyers for graded goods tends to spread its use. Mr. Nils A. Olsen, Chief of the Bureau of Agricultural Economics, estimated at the end of 1928 that not less that 60 per cent of wholesale trading in fruits and vegetables was then done on the basis of national standard grades. [74]

In order to encourage the use of grades and standards, the federal government provides an inspection and certification service for many agricultural commodities. The service is supported by the inspection fees. During the year ending June 30, 1930, the government inspectors examined more than 288,000 cars of produce. [75] The service extends to forty-one states. The United

[73] *Ibid.*, October 12, 1927, v. VII, p. 251. Concerning the administrative problems created by the law, Dr. A. E. Albrecht, Director of the New York office of the New York Department of Agriculture and Markets, writes as follows: " As no additional appropriation has been made for the enforcement of this law, it has been necessary to attempt it with the regular inspectional force. Accordingly, its enforcement has been somewhat troublesome. However, the candling of eggs has been considerably improved in the last few years, but substantial shrinkage in eggs occurs in retail stores. I believe that jobbers and especially retailers must make several very important changes in the handling and distribution of eggs before the consumer gets much better egg quality, on account of the large shrinkage that takes place in retail stores."

[74] *Ibid.*, December 19, 1928, v. VIII, p. 311.

[75] *Ibid.*, September 3, 1930, v. X, p. 210.

States Department of Agriculture also maintains a certificate service for eggs and butter. Certificates of quality for eggs are issued only when a federal inspector supervises the packing of the eggs. Certificates of quality are given for butter that is graded by a butter grader of the Department of Agriculture, and which scores 93 points or better. At the proposal of the Better Beef Association, formed by cattle breeders for the purpose of popularizing the higher grades of beef, a class or grade stamp for a carcass or a wholesale cut of beef was created by the Department of Agriculture. In 1930, official beef graders were grading and stamping beef in eight cities. The service is paid for by the party who requests it. To label the beef, the class and grade are stamped with a roller which is run the length of the carcass so that there is a printed label on all the major retail cuts. In 1930, only two classes of beef (steer and heifer) and four grades (prime, choice, good, and medium) were stamped. The service is of most importance to the government (which buys one-third of the graded beef), and to hotels, dining-cars, and other large buyers of beef, but an increasing number of retailers are buying and selling graded and stamped beef. Some chain stores in the East are selling stamped beef and have used large advertisements to bring this to the attention of consumers. Beef possesses an unusually wide range of quality, but to the average person all grades look much alike.[76]

Although official grades or standards have been established for many commodities, these form only a small proportion of the multitude of articles which consumers purchase. Most of the official grades and standards apply to agricultural products and relatively few to manufactured goods. The federal government purchases an immense variety of commodities, most of them on the basis of specifications. The specifications which are satisfactory to the government are not necessarily so to the ordinary consumer. Nevertheless, in some cases it would be advantageous to the buyer to know whether or not the article which he purchases meets the specifications of the government.

[76] U. S. Department of Agriculture, "Beef Grading and Stamping Service," *Leaflet No. 67*, and *Report of the Chief of the Bureau of Agricultural Economics*, 1930, p. 40.

It would also be advantageous for the government to have its specifications widely demanded, because this would mean that a larger number of producers would be prepared to furnish goods of the grades which the government uses. During recent years, the Bureau of Standards has developed a certification and labeling plan under which the Bureau compiles and issues a list of manufacturers who are willing to certify that their goods comply with government specifications. In January, 1929, about 2,000 manufacturers were on the " willing-to-certify " list.[77] Unfortunately the government has made no provision for assuring that goods offered to the public as meeting official specifications actually do so.

But of what use are grades or specifications to the *ordinary consumer?* Even if the wholesaler or retailer buys on the basis of official grades, it does not follow that the ultimate consumer can do so, because the goods may not be sold by the retailer from the original package that contains the grade mark. And of course, the ordinary consumer does not write to the Bureau of Standards for a "willing-to-certify" list and request the manufacturer or retailer to furnish goods which meet government specifications. Usually the consumer does not know that official grades or specifications exist.

But even if he is totally ignorant of the existence of grades or specifications, he gains something from them. Official grades help producers to obtain a premium for superior quality from wholesalers and retailers and this encourages them to improve the quality of their output and to turn out a larger proportion of the better grades. Furthermore, the low prices paid for the lower grades tend to keep them off the market altogether. For example, as long as fruit is not graded, it pays the growers to market the poorest as well as the best, for every bushel brings the same price. But when the fruit is sold by grade, the low price received for the poorest grade may not cover the cost of packing and shipping.

In some cases, the use of grades is compulsory in retail trade. This is true of the Oregon potato grades and, as we have seen,

[77] U. S. Bureau of Standards, *Monthly News Bulletin of the Commercial Standards Group*, January 15, 1929, p. 8.

of the New York egg grades.   And even when retailers are not required to sell by grade, goods may be marked so that the consumer can ascertain the grade.   The federal meat graders, for example, run a roller stamp the length of the carcass so that every cut bears evidence of the official grading.   Turkeys which meet the specifications of United States prime are so stamped on their backs and, in addition, they have attached to the wing a tag giving the grade.   The certificates of quality issued by the federal butter inspectors are often placed in the pound cartons which the consumer purchases.   The state of Iowa has adopted a trade mark for butter manufactured within the state.   It may be placed on the package if the butter is manufactured in a creamery that meets the state sanitary code, if it scores not less than 93, and if it complies with other state standards.[78]   The United States Department of Agriculture has started a grading service on Wisconsin cheese whereby inspection and certification will be carried through to the consumer by stamping the paraffined cheese with the grade.[79]   Canned foods which fail to meet the federal standard are so labeled on the can.   A few trade associations, such as the American Gas Association, have a label which the members are permitted to use on that part of their product which meets certain specifications.   A few manufacturers advertise that their goods meet specifications used by the government in its own purchasing.[80]   But, on the whole, only a tiny fraction of the

[78] U. S. Department of Agriculture, *Marketing Activities*, October 13, 1926, v. VI, p. 404.

[79] *Ibid.*, April 30, 1930, v. X, p. 104.

[80] A maker of sheets, for example, certifies that each sheet " fulfills all requirements of United States Government master specifications No. 304 for high-count cotton sheets and No. 305 for high-count cotton pillow cases "; a maker of varnishes states on the labels of his cans that his goods conform to the specifications issued by the United States Bureau of Standards.   McAllister, A. S., " Certification Plan and Labeling System," *Annals of the American Academy of Political and Social Science*, May, 1928, v. CXXXVII, p. 245.

It is important to notice, however, that retail advertising may misuse, as well as use, government specifications.   Consumers' Research, Inc. (an organization which is described below), in its May, 1930, *Bulletin*, calls attention to the misuse of specifications in the advertising of a prominent mail order house.   For example, sheeting was advertised to excel federal specifications for thread count.   But thread count is only one of the important items which determine quality of sheets.   The statement in the advertising that " laboratory tests prove long wear superior to federal specification 304 for medium thread count " leaves out the most important item, namely tensile strength, which is, of course, included in the federal specifications.   Another advertisement reads: " Rigid laboratory tests prove that the denim used in Pioneer Overalls is better than U. S. Government specifications in weight, thread count, and shrinkage."   But again tensile strength, the most important single item, is missing.

goods that enter retail trade bear official grade marks. During the year ending June 30, 1930, only 30,000,000 pounds of butter and 50,000 cases of eggs were marketed with federal certificates of quality. This was less than one-fifth of the total butter and one-seventh of the eggs graded by federal inspectors and a far smaller fraction of the total retail sales of butter and eggs.[81]

It is difficult to exaggerate the possibilities of the work which the government and a few trade associations are doing in establishing grades and standards. If the government establishes official grades for tobacco, wool, cotton, wheat, meat, fruits, and vegetables, why should it not do so for shoes, gloves, clothing, furniture, paints, gasoline, lubricating oil, tires, and scores of other articles? If the consumer is permitted to know what he receives for his money when he purchases butter or meat, why should he be kept in ignorance when he buys soap or gasoline? No doubt many manufacturers and retailers will bitterly object to the extension of government grading because they profit from the consumer's ignorance. Nevertheless, the establishment of official grades for more and more commodities and the labeling of more and more goods to indicate their grade or their conformity with government specifications is inevitable because the consumer, docile and ignorant though he is, is eventually bound to insist upon knowing what he is getting for his money. And when an article is made to conform to an official standard or to a government specification, both manufacturers and retailers are bound sooner or later to use this fact as a selling point. In this way, consumers will be slowly trained to demand goods which meet certain grades or specifications.

No single change would do more to reduce industrial waste, because undoubtedly the greatest waste in industry today is the spending of money for things which fail to give the return expected of them. Standards and specifications would not, of course, eliminate mistakes in spending, but they would at least give the consumer a chance to know what he is getting. In addition, the widespread use of standards and specifications, more than anything else, would make possible the economies of mass production by helping the low-cost plants to capture the business

[81] U. S. Department of Agriculture, *Report of the Chief of the Bureau of Agricultural Economics*, 1930, p. 50.

of high-cost plants which now succeed in surviving by persuading the public that their brands are " different." And finally, the use of standards and specifications would accelerate technical progress by putting competition among plants upon a price basis. The more successfully each producer makes sales by asserting that his product is unique and superior, the less necessary it is for him to cut prices in order to obtain business. But if the use of standards or specifications makes it evident that the rival brands are of substantially the same quality, business must be sought through price-cutting. In order to cut prices, however, enterprises must reduce their costs. Hence the practice of purchasing by grade or specification will compel managements to strive more strenuously to discover ways of cutting costs.[82] Or possibly the effect may be to stimulate managements to improve the product — to give it unique characteristics and to make it superior to goods which merely correspond to a given standard or specification. In either case, the use of standards or specifications accelerates technical progress.[83]

Very inadequate are the efforts to protect consumers (and honest business enterprises) against dishonest trade practices. Over twenty states have passed the bill, sponsored by *Printers' Ink,* against misleading advertisements. Most cities have ordinances dealing with unscrupulous selling methods — false advertising, stuffed flats, lottery schemes, failure to mark seconds, jewelry auctions, and endless-chain selling. These laws are for the most part, dead letters. By far the most important work in policing the selling methods of business is done by the Better Business Bureaus and the Federal Trade Commission.

The origin of the Better Business Bureaus may be traced to a discussion of "What is the matter with advertising?" at the 1910 meeting of the Associated Advertising Clubs of the World. The conclusion was that not enough people believed advertise-

---

[82] Price competition may lead enterprises to combine for the purpose of regulating prices. Consequently the government, by establishing standards, may create for itself the problem of regulating monopolies.

[83] As the products change, it is necessary to revise the prevailing standards or specifications. It must not for a moment be assumed that standards or specifications can be set once for all. They need to be constantly altered and improved. As a matter of fact, the specifications used by the United States in its purchasing are subject to constant revision.

ments. The discussion led to the formation in 1911 of the
National Vigilance Committee which endeavored to create confidence in advertising by promoting truth and accuracy in advertisements and selling. Local organizations, performing the same
function, were established. They were known as Better Business Bureaus. There are now about fifty of these organizations.
Recently the National Vigilance Committee has been superseded
by the National Better Business Bureau. The work of the Better
Business Bureaus has gradually broadened so that now they are
concerned in promoting, not merely accuracy in advertising, but
honesty and fairness in all selling practices. The Chicago Better
Business Bureau describes itself as follows:

" It is a non-profitable organization, established and supported by the legitimate business interests of Chicago. Its purpose is to maintain and increase public
confidence in advertising, selling of merchandise and sound business methods in
general; to protect legitimate business enterprises from unfair and deceptive trade
practices; to guard the public against unscrupulous and fraudulent operators; and
to secure and make available to the public sufficient facts and information upon
which they can decide whether the proposition offered is honestly conceived,
truthfully presented and economically sound." [84]

The Better Business Bureaus fight questionable merchandising methods and shady business enterprises of all sorts. Through
their monthly news sheets, advertising in newspapers, posters on
the bulletin boards of factories and stores, slips enclosed in pay
envelopes, and radio talks, the bureaus warn the public against
fake stocks, " tipster " sheets, " stuffed flats," dishonest aviation
schools, fraudulent home work schemes, the " gyp " methods of
some mail order clothing firms. The Cleveland bureau estimates
that during 1928 its fight on the selling of worthless stocks saved
the public $1,000,000.[85] The Cincinnati and the Chicago
bureaus have coöperated with retail coal dealers in checking
the weights of coal. The Chicago bureau signed contracts with
107 coal dealers by which the bureau representatives are authorized to stop and check the trucks of the signer. Dealers
who refused to coöperate were checked by arranging with home
owners to permit a representative of the bureau to check the
coal delivered to them.[86] Of special interest is the check which

[84] Chicago Better Business Bureau, *Buying with Safety in a Complex Market,*
p. 7.
[85] Cleveland Better Business Bureau, *Monthly Bulletin,* January, 1929, p. 1.
[86] Chicago Better Business Bureau, *Special Coal Bulletin,* May, 1928.

the Better Business Bureaus make of advertising and selling methods. The bureaus act upon specific complaints of customers who have been misled or of competitors whose trade is being injured. For example, during 1928 the merchandising and advertising department of the Cleveland Better Business Bureau received 6,903 complaints and inquiries concerning advertising and selling practices.[87] But the bureaus do not necessarily wait for some one to complain. They read all advertising in the local papers and "shop" suspicious cases. During 1928 the Cleveland bureau investigated 2,265 cases of advertising suspected of being inaccurate. Slightly more than half (51.1 per cent) of the advertisements were found to be accurate.[88] During May, 1927, the Chicago bureau investigated 414 cases of advertising, of which 144 were found to be accurate and 270 inaccurate. In February, 1928, the Cincinnati Better Business Bureau investigated 176 cases, of which 63 were found to be inaccurate and 113 accurate. When an advertisement is found to be inaccurate, a representative of the bureau calls on the firm and endeavors to convince the management that in the long run misleading advertising does not pay. In cases of persistent inaccuracy, the bureau may prosecute under the honest advertising statute, if there is one. Or it may induce the newspapers, which usually are members of the bureau, to refuse the advertising. It may even issue a special bulletin calling attention to the inaccuracies in the advertising of a certain firm. The Chicago bureau recently published a list of thirty-three super-claims in the advertising of a prominent clothing firm, the Maurice L. Rothschild Company, during a three months' period. The bureau then stated:

" We leave it to our readers — what will be the effect on Confidence in Advertising if puffery, and unrestrained superlatives of the type illustrated above continue? The Advertising Braggart and Egotist tends to jeopardize the dignity of advertising even to the point of ludicrousness." [89]

The National Better Business Bureau, assisted by the local bureaus, has conducted a number of notable campaigns to improve the accuracy of advertising. Commercial correspondence schools of the more conservative type found the response to their advertisements dwindling as the claims and offers of less scrupulous ad-

---

[87] Cleveland Better Business Bureau, *Monthly Bulletin*, January, 1929, p. 2.

[88] *Ibid.*, January, 1929, p. 2.

[89] *Report of the Chicago Better Business Bureau*, February 18, 1929, v. I, No. 25, p. 3.

vertisers grew more and more vociferous. On July 8, 1928, at a meeting sponsored by the national bureau, the representatives of thirty commercial schools adopted a code of advertising and selling standards. The misleading description of furniture led the National Better Business Bureau to start a " Name-the-Woods " campaign. A code governing the advertising of furniture was agreed to by over 90 per cent of the furniture manufacturers and received the approval of the Federal Trade Commission, Some manufacturers refuse to accept the code because they object to describing veneered funiture as such. The national bureau has also conducted a " Name-the-Pelt " campaign in the fur trade. Hosiery manufacturers found their product suffer- ing from competition of " seconds." The " seconds " were of- fered at low prices but the fact that they were seconds was not indicated. At a meeting of hosiery manufacturers called by the bureau it was agreed to stamp imperfect hose so as to prevent their sale as " firsts." Not all of the trade, however, has been willing to follow this practice. Complaints from pur- chasers of infants' underwear that the so-called " silk and wool " garments were largely cotton and rayon and the " all wool " garments largely cotton led the national bureau to arrange a meeting of the leading manufacturers at which it presented a code to govern all advertising and printed matter and also all verbal statements of salesmen. Manufacturers of 85 per cent of the infants' wear have accepted the code.[90] An investigation of the wool content of blankets advertised as " part-wool " dis- closed that the average was from 5 to 7 per cent and led the national bureau to recommend to blanket manufacturers that the labels on " part-wool " blankets state the actual percentage of wool. In October, 1928, the bureau was asked by the periodical publishers to assist them to eliminate fraudulent advertising from their magazines. Early in 1929, the bureau started a campaign against the so-called " tainted " testimonial — that is, the testi- monial purchased from a person of prominence.

Undoubtedly the Better Business Bureaus have lessened the worst inaccuracies in advertising — especially the local news- paper advertising of stores. The Philadelphia bureau reports: " A marked improvement in the general accuracy of the advertis- ing of Philadelphia's stores is apparent since the Bureau began

---

[90] National Better Business Bureau, *Bulletin 0007*, June, 1927.

to work." [91]   The Chicago Better Business Bureau says: " No longer than a year ago, it was not unusual to find sub-standard quality, seconds and even menders advertised as ' firsts.' Some advertisers forgot to say that the tops and feet were lisle although usually remembering to mention that they were silk when such was the case. . . .   More recently the Bureau has noticed a decided movement toward accuracy in hosiery descriptions.   This is believed to be the result of the constant reminders forwarded to advertisers from the Bureau explaining the inconsistency in their copy." [92]   The same Better Business Bureau in discussing accuracy in silk advertising said: " Careful checking of advertising no longer discloses the former careless and faulty description which confused the mind of the average buyer." [93]   But much as the Better Business Bureaus are doing, there is need to do an enormous amount more.   Recently the National Better Business Bureau, in checking 438 advertisements in four prominent magazines, found 131 claims that were open to serious question as to the facts.[94]   Indeed, some well-informed advertising men believe that advertising is becoming less, instead of more, reliable.   Mr. C. B. Larrabel, of the editorial staff of *Printers' Ink,* the leading journal of the advertising profession, writes:

"Today a number of men within and without the advertising business are worried.   They see an alarming growth of deception in advertising, deception which cannot be reached by any law but which, all the same, is unethical.   The tainted testimonial, pseudo-science, exaggerated claims and other phases of super advertising are, they feel, attacking the credibility of advertising." [95]

Even more outspoken is Mr. John F. Hurst of the advertising agency of Henri, Hurst, and McDonald, Inc.   He begins an article on the current needs of advertising as follows:

"Advertising today, in my opinion, is less truthful than it was ten years ago. If not less truthful, it at least is more deceptive.   And it is just as bad to imply a falsehood or an exaggeration as directly to state it.   The result is that there is a constantly growing distrust of advertising — of all advertising." [96]

[91] Philadelphia Better Business Bureau, *Annual Report,* January, 1928, p. 1.

[92] Chicago Better Business Bureau, *Merchandise Department Information,* January 30, 1928, p. 1.

[93] *Ibid.,* March 3, 1928.

[94] National Better Business Bureau, *Annual Report of Commercial and Medicinal Departments,* 1929–1930.

[95] " Advertising Reform Must Come from Advertising Men," *Printers' Ink Monthly,* July, 1929, v. XIX, No. 1, p. 85.

[96] *Ibid.,* June, 1929, v. XVIII, No. 6, p. 29.

Of course, from the standpoint of the consumer it is undoubtedly better that advertising be so bad that it is not believed than that it be good enough to command confidence which it does not deserve. *A half-way reform of advertising would be worse than none at all.*

The Federal Trade Commission is given the duty, among other things, of preventing unfair methods of competition in interstate commerce. Although the Commission acts to protect the enterprises which are injured by the unfair competitive methods, it incidentally protects the consumer, because unscrupulous selling methods are often held to be a form of unfair competition. For example, the Commission has ordered the Calumet Baking Powder Company to desist from using the so-called " water glass test " which the company has employed for twenty years to demonstrate the alleged superiority of its product. The Commission found that the difference in the peculiar reactions of the Calumet powder to the test was due to "a minute quantity of dried white of egg or dried albumen " which did not affect the leavening efficiency of the powder. Consequently the Commission held that the test does not indicate differences in the powders as leavening agents.[97] The Commission has prohibited the use of the label " U. S. Army " on shoes which are not built under the specifications of the government and under government contract.[98] In determining what is misrepresentation, the Commission has had to determine what is a permissible use of many terms, such as merino wool, silk, Sheffield plate, rebuilt typewriters, and many others. A favorite method of creating the impression that the prices of a firm are unusually low is to advertise " Direct from factory to you " or to use the word " mills " or " factories " in the name of the enterprise. The

[97] *Printers' Ink*, June 27, 1929, v. CXLVII, No. 13, p. 145.

In Docket No. 1133, the Federal Trade Commission ordered a well known mattress company to desist from using as a trade mark the picture of a mattress with one end open so as to disclose the extended layers of compressed cotton. The picture indicated an expansion of thirty-five inches or more. Actually the expansion was from three to six inches. The United States Circuit Court of Appeals overruled the order of the Commission on the ground that pictorial exaggeration of the quality of articles cannot be deemed misrepresentation or an unfair method of competition. It is simply an instance of the " time honored custom of puffing."

[98] *United States Daily*, February 4, 1928, p. 4.

Commission has held that the use of " mills " or " factories "
as part of a trade name is unlawful unless the firm actually
operates or directly controls a mill or factory where its merchandise is made.   On February 7, 1928, the Union Woolen
Mills of Racine, Wisconsin, and the Woolen Mills of Jackson,
Michigan, were ordered to discontinue the use of the word
" mill " in their corporate titles until they owned, controlled, or
operated a mill for the manufacture of the cloth from which their
wares were made.[99]

In order that business enterprises may know in advance which
are fair and which are unfair methods of competition, the Commission has adopted the policy of holding trade practice confer-
ences with representatives of industry for the purpose of drawing
up rules of fair practice.   If a conference succeeds in agreeing
upon rules and they are subsequently approved by the Commission, they become the recognized rules of fair competition.
For example, the Commission on March 6, 1928, approved the
rules for the proper naming of furs adopted at a trade practice
conference held at New York in February, 1928.   Among other
things, the rules provide that in describing furs the correct name
of the fur must be the last word of the description.   When a dye
or blend is used to simulate another fur, the word " dyed " or
" blended " must be inserted signifying the fur that is simulated.
When the name of any country or region is used, it must be the
actual country of origin of the fur.[100]   The Commission, of course,
may refuse to approve rules recommended by the trade.   For
example, the soap manufacturers recommended that the Commission permit the use of the word " castile," when qualified,
upon soaps containing other fatty matters than olive oil.   The
Commission, however, held that " castile " should be applied only
to the pure olive oil soap, that is, soap made of olive oil with
no admixture of other fats.[101]

In view of the helplessness of the individual consumer and
the failure of the government to provide more effective protection, it might be expected that consumers would organize to pro-

[99] *Ibid.*, February 8, 1928, p. 5.

[100] *Ibid.*, March 7, 1928, pp. 1 and 9.

[101] National Better Business Bureau, *Better Business News,* June, 1926, v. I, No.
7, p. 3.

tect themselves. But consumers are the great unorganized interest in the United States. As manufacturers, farmers, wholesalers, retailers, and, to a less extent, as wage earners, we are organized; as consumers, we are not. In many countries, consumers have established their own coöperative stores but in the United States, as we know, the coöperative movement has not prospered. A small but a rapidly growing and important organization devoted to the interests of the consumer is Consumers' Research, Inc., of New York City. It is a non-commercial organization for the purpose of supplying consumers with unbiased information concerning the hundreds of articles bought by the ordinary consumer. The organization issues an annual bulletin in which over 1,000 products are listed by brand name as either recommended or not recommended. The listings are based upon the best technical information which the organization can obtain, supplemented by its own tests and investigations. Consumers' Research also issues periodical bulletins which contain detailed discussions of selected items. Early in 1930, the organization had 2,500 members and was not self-supporting. A year later, it had 15,000 members and was nearly self-supporting. Its importance, however, is far greater than its size indicates, because it represents an organized and systematic attempt to arouse "consumer consciousness," to make consumers aware of how grossly they are being exploited by high-pressure marketing methods, and to give the consumer, in place of the biased and exaggerated claims of advertisements and salesmen, the kind of information which he must have in order to spend his money intelligently.

In order to improve the protection which the laws give to the consumer, it would be desirable to create a National Consumers' Council composed of representatives of such organizations as the American Home Economic Association, the American Public Health Association, the Consumers' League, Consumers' Research, the Federation of Women's Clubs, the National League of Women Voters, and others. In addition, state and municipal councils should be established. The members of the councils should receive no salary, but the expenses of their meetings should be borne by the government. The government should also provide them with funds for an executive secretary and for a small secretarial staff.

What would the councils do? They should possess no authority. They should be advisory and contact bodies only. An important part of their work would be to assist the Better Business Bureaus in their fight on unscrupulous selling practices. Another part of their work would be to keep in close touch with the work of the government bureaus and departments in whose work the consumer has an interest and to improve the enforcement of the laws that are intended to protect the consumer. In some cases, it is possible to make laws almost self-enforcing, simply by publishing the results of inspections or tests. This is true, for example, of sanitary inspection laws and of milk testing laws. But publicity is an enforcement device which has been strangely neglected in an age which pays so much attention to publicity. The reason apparently is that, with consumers unorganized, the law enforcement officers do not care to antagonize powerful business interests by publishing the results of inspections and tests. With stronger support from consumers, officials might be expected to display far more initiative, efficiency, and courage in enforcing the laws.

It has been pointed out that there are now wide gaps in the protection which the law gives to consumers. This is particularly true of state and municipal legislation. An important duty of the councils would be to point out the need for additional legislation, to assist in drafting new laws, and to arouse support for them among consumers.

One of the greatest needs of the consumer, we have seen, is the extension of the use of official grades from wholesaling into retailing. This is not likely to occur rapidly unless consumers demand it and it is not likely to do much good when it does occur unless consumers familiarize themselves with the meaning of the official grades. The Consumers' Councils would be proper organizations to conduct an educational campaign among consumers concerning the value of grading and the meaning of the different grades. It has been pointed out that thus far the use of official grades has been confined, almost entirely, to staple agricultural products. The application of official grades to manufactured goods is far more difficult. Yet it is needed and, to a substantial extent, it can be accomplished. The Consumers' Councils would be useful in bringing about the extension of grades to manufactured goods.

Perhaps the best way to describe the usefulness of Consumers' Councils is to say that they would furnish the consumer with eyes, ears, and voice. The consumer, being unorganized, is not able to hear or see most of the things which affect his interests and he is not able to express himself concerning his interests, as is the business man through his trade association, the laborer through his trade union, and the farmer through his farm bureau or grange. The consumer badly needs eyes, ears, and voice.

REFERENCES

Annals of the American Academy of Political and Social Science, May, 1928, v. CXXXVII, No. 226, "Standards in Industry," especially the papers by R. M. Conner, L. S. Tenny, Alice L. Edwards, F. J. Schlink, Robert A. Brady, and H. E. Agnew.

Borsodi, Ralph, *The Distribution Age,* 1927.

Chase, Stuart, and Schlink, F. J., *Your Money's Worth,* 1927.

Cherington, Paul T., *The Consumer Looks at Advertising,* 1928.

Hoyt, E. E., *The Consumption of Wealth,* 1928.

Mitchell, W. C., "The Backward Art of Spending Money," *American Economic Review,* June, 1912, v. II, pp. 269–281.

Ross, E. A., *Social Psychology,* 1908. Ch. VI, VII, IX, X, and XI.

Vaughan, Floyd L., *Marketing and Advertising,* 1928.

Waite, W. C., *Economics of Consumption,* 1928.

CHAPTER XXIII

THE LABOR BARGAIN — WAGES AS AN INCENTIVE

I. THE IMPORTANCE OF THE LABOR BARGAIN. II. SOME PROBLEMS OF MEASURING PERFORMANCE. III. PROBLEMS IN THE ADMINISTRATION OF INCENTIVE SYSTEMS.

I. The Importance of the Labor Bargain

The equipment of modern industry is so expensive that it must be operated in the main by persons who do not own it. Of the 45,400,000 gainfully employed persons in the United States in 1927, approximately 9,800,000, or slightly more than one-fifth, were employers or in business for themselves and approximately 35,600,000, or nearly four-fifths, worked for wages or salary. About 8,300,000 were salary workers and nearly 27,300,000 were wage earners.[1]

In examining how the institution of working for hire operates, we are concerned with three principal things — with wages as an incentive, with wages as a source of income, and with the labor bargain as a device for controlling the conditions of work. From the standpoint of consumers and employers, wages are a device for making men willing to work for others. Naturally the question arises: How effective are wages as an incentive, as a method of stimulating men to do good work?

From the standpoint of the worker, wages, of course, are a source of income, usually his principal source. Dr. W. I. King has estimated that during the period 1909 to 1928, wages and salaries constituted from 50.3 to 58.2 per cent of the total national income.[2] In manufacturing, mining, and transportation,

---

[1] King, W. I., *The National Income and Its Purchasing Power*, pp. 50, 56, 60, 62. A salary, of course, is simply a form of wage. The economist, in discussing wages, usually does not distinguish between salaries and wages in the narrower sense.

[2] *Ibid.*, pp. 124–125. The figures include a small amount received as pensions and as compensation under workmen's compensation acts.

The Federal Trade Commission has estimated that approximately 55 per cent of the pecuniary income of the nation is received as wages or salaries and 45 per cent

a substantially larger proportion of the net product goes to pay wages and salaries — in 1925, according to Dr. King's estimate, 87.8 per cent in manufacturing, 71.8 per cent in mining, and 75.6 per cent in transportation. Much of the income received as profits by the independent business men, such as farmers and retailers, must be regarded as payment for their services. It is safe to conclude that over two-thirds of the national income is received as compensation for human services. It is important to discover how the compensation of labor is determined, why it is higher in the United States than in other countries, and how it might be made still higher.

But the worker's income is not all that is at stake when the labor bargain is made. The labor bargain is, we have seen, the principal way in which wage earners affect the conditions of work in industry — the nature of jobs, managerial policies, and physical conditions in the shop. When a Polish molding-machine operator accepts or rejects a position in a foundry, the conditions which shall exist in that foundry are in process of determination. If enough men are willing to accept and retain jobs under existing conditions, those conditions are not likely to improve. But if the number of satisfactory applicants is too small, then wages or working conditions or both are likely to be made more attractive. What kinds of jobs and working conditions does this method of controlling industry produce? Does it give effective representation to the interests of wage earners? Or is there anything in the bargaining situation which makes it peculiarly difficult for wage earners to influence the conditions of work?

In this chapter, we shall discuss wages as an incentive; in the next chapter, the determination of wages; and in the following chapter, the labor bargain as a method of controlling work and working conditions.

II. Some Problems of Measuring Performance

It is not unusual to hear employers complain that workmen are not interested in doing their best. Instead of coöperating with managements to increase production and to reduce costs,

---

as profits and income on property. " The Nation's Wealth and Income," *69th Congress, 5th Session, Senate Document 126*, p. 229.

workmen are said deliberately to restrict output. The thought and ingenuity which they might use to improve methods of work are expended upon concealing how far actual production falls short of possible production. The output of many shops is the result of a contest in which the management attempts to get as much as possible and the men to give no more than is necessary. In some cases, undoubtedly, the employer expects too much but in others the workmen do far less than they easily could. In the latter cases, it is probable that something is wrong with wages as an incentive. What determines whether or not wages work well as a stimulant of efficiency?

It is elementary that wages can be an effective incentive only when the compensation of each employee depends upon his performance. This, of course, presupposes that the management can measure what each worker does. The performance of workers includes more than is usually supposed. The quantity and quality of output are the two most important elements. In addition to these, however, performance includes many other things — such as how economical each worker is of materials, power, and light, the amount of spoiled work for which he is responsible, his breakage of equipment, the rate at which he wears out equipment, his ability and willingness to suggest improvements in methods and products, his regularity of attendance, and the number of jobs which he is capable of doing.

The measurement of these elements of efficiency is often extremely difficult or positively impracticable. The volume of output is usually the easiest to measure but even it cannot always be easily ascertained. In the case of non-repetitive work, for example, such as special order and repair work, output often cannot be measured because there is no common unit of performance.[3] In other cases, measurement is impossible because the contributions of individual workmen become indistinguishably merged in a common result. This is illustrated by many

[3] Sometimes work which seems to be non-repetitive can be reduced to elements which occur again and again. This is true, for example, of composition and also of the making of women's garments. From data showing the time required for each element under different conditions, a fairly close estimate can be made of the time required to do any job. So great, however, is the cost of getting data on element times and so heavy is the expense of an estimating department, that this method of measuring output is of limited applicability.

assembling operations, by construction work, maintenance of railway track, and the work of yard gangs.

The quality of the work done by, say, a factory hand can be measured, to a limited extent, by the proportion of pieces which fail to pass inspection. But not infrequently it is even impossible to apply this test of quality. The work of several men may be thrown together before reaching the inspector; there may be doubt whether a defect is the result of workmanship or of materials; or several men may have handled a piece and it may be impossible to discover who was at fault. When the quality of a man's work is judged by the proportion of pieces which fails to pass inspection, he has an incentive only to get his work accepted by the inspector. Often, however, it is desirable to have the quality as perfect as possible. But to induce the best possible work requires that the compensation of each man be based upon the *average* quality of his output. This necessitates that at irregular intervals a large number of pieces be individually measured and the average computed. This is likely to be prohibitively expensive. Even more difficult is the measurement of the quality of the work done by repairmen, such as the employees in railroad shops or garages.

Responsibility for the breakage of equipment is easily ascertained as long as only one man uses each piece. But when several men use the same equipment, as in the case of buildings, locomotives, railroad cars, and in the case of machines when the work is not minutely subdivided or when there is more than one shift, responsibility for out-of-order equipment often cannot be assigned. Still more difficult to determine is the wear and tear which does not result in definite breakdown but which affects the depreciation rate. Nevertheless, the influence of the operator upon the life of an expensive machine is of great importance. Each worker's consumption of light and power can ordinarily be ascertained if the management cares to undergo the expense, but the cost is usually prohibitive. This is also true of materials, but occasionally, as in the case of cutters in the shoe and clothing industries, measurement is feasible and a bonus is paid for saving material.

The difficulty in measuring efficiency compels managements to pay many men on the basis of the time worked — that is, by the hour, week, or month. Among 220,536 wage earners in 175 manufacturing establishments, 113,526, or 51.5 per cent, were paid on a time basis.[4] In other branches of industry, the proportion is even greater. The Wisconsin Industrial Commission found that the proportion of manual workers paid on a time basis in the public utility and transportation industries was 61.7 per cent; in personal and professional service, 83.2; in retail stores, 85.5; and in the construction industry, 99.3.[5] Time work, of course, rewards men for working slowly and creates the problem of controlling, through means other than wages, the rate at which they work.

III. Problems in the Administration of Incentive Systems

Where measurement of performance is feasible, wages are likely to be based upon individual efficiency. As volume of output is the aspect of efficiency which is most easily measured, payment by output is the most common form of payment by results. The simplest and most usual method of paying for output is piecework — so much for every piece upon which the employee performs his operation. About one out of three factory workers is paid by the piece.[6] In other branches of industry, the proportion is much less. The Wisconsin Industrial Commission found that the proportion was 0.7 per cent in the construction industry, 1.7 in retail stores, and 0.1 in public utilities and transportation.[7] The incentive created by piecework is tremendous because the reward for efficiency and the penalty for inefficiency are both certain and immediate. Every additional piece means just so much more in the worker's next pay envelope, and every one that he fails to make means just so much less. Pieceworkers, in consequence, can usually be counted on to produce at least

---

[4] *American Economic Review, Supplement*, March, 1925, v. XV, No. 1, pp. 94–95.

[5] Industrial Commission of Wisconsin, *Wisconsin Labor Statistics*, November, 1924, v. II, No. 11, p. 8.

[6] Out of 220,536 manual workers in 175 factories, 78,837, or 35.8 per cent, were pieceworkers. *American Economic Review, Supplement*, March, 1925, v. XV, No. 1, pp. 94–95. The Wisconsin Industrial Commission found that, among 108,360 manual workers in 706 factories, 64,653, or 31.2 per cent, were paid by the piece. *Wisconsin Labor Statistics*, November, 1924, v. II, 11, p. 8.

[7] *Ibid.*, November, 1924, v. II, No. 11, p. 8.

one-fourth more than time workers. Often they produce twice as much.

Many employers have found that it is unnecessary to pay such large rewards as piecework gives to induce men to do their best. This has led them to devise bonus systems under which workers earn more, *but not proportionately more,* as their production increases. There are innumerable types of bonus schemes but they are nearly all alike in that the reward for additional output is less than it would be under piecework. A much used type of bonus plan is the following: A standard time is fixed for each operation. Let us assume that the time for a certain task is four hours. For performing the operation, the worker is given four hours' pay at his regular hourly rate — no matter how long he actually takes. (Of course, a man who regularly took more than four hours would soon be replaced.) If he does the task in less than the standard period, the time saved is divided between him and the company. The proportion in which the time is shared varies, but an even division is typical. This means that if the man does a four-hour job in two hours, he is paid for four hours plus half the time he saves, or for five hours in all.

It will be observed that, as the man produces more, the average amount he receives per unit of output becomes less and less. In other words, the rate per piece is automatically cut. Suppose that the worker is paid 60 cents an hour. Were he to make two pieces in eight hours, he would receive 8 × 60 cents or $4.80 for his day's work. Suppose, however, he makes four pieces. Under piecework, he would receive twice as much as when he makes two, or $9.60. But not under the bonus plan. In addition to his regular pay for eight hours, he is paid for only half the time that he saves. He has saved eight hours which means that he receives a bonus of four hours' pay. Consequently he receives twelve hours' pay in all, or $7.20 instead of $9.60. When his production went up from two to four pieces a day, his compensation per piece went down from $2.40 to $1.80. Because bonus plans are devices for automatically cutting piece rates as output goes up, almost all trade unions, even those which willingly accept piecework, vigorously oppose bonus plans.

It is extremely important to notice that a wage system which rewards one kind of efficiency, such as large quantity of output, may penalize another kind, such as accurate workmanship, simply because the man who takes time to do exceedingly accurate work cannot produce so much. If extremely accurate work is desired but the quality of work cannot be easily measured, the management may be compelled to refrain from offering an incentive for large output. In repairing locomotives, for example, good workmanship is of great importance but it is not easy to keep track of how well each man does each job. Consequently, many roads do not use piecework in their repair shops — although the output of each worker can be measured.

When the difficulty in controlling the quality of work makes piecework or a bonus system impracticable, it may be feasible to use standards of production. Several hourly rates of pay — usually three to five — are established. All workers who maintain a given average hourly output during a given period — usually two to four weeks — receive a given hourly or weekly rate of pay. Those who maintain a lower output receive a lower rate. The fact that a worker has a small output on a certain day or even during a week or more does not necessarily reduce his earnings. No change in his rate of compensation is made unless his average hourly or daily production for the whole period falls below a given amount. For this reason, standards of production may be the best form of wage when it is desired to give some incentive to produce but not one so powerful as to encourage careless work. Standards of production are also preferred by many workers who resent the terrific incentives which are imposed by piecework and bonus plans. They dislike being compelled to feel that they are letting pennies slip through their fingers every time they slow up or take a rest. And undoubtedly it is often morally injurious for men to be placed in a position where money depends upon every quickening or slackening of their movements.

In the case of some operations, such as the assembling of machines or the loading of vessels, it may be impossible to keep track of what each member of the assembling gang does but it may be easy to measure the performance of the gang as a whole or of a whole department. In such cases, group piecework or a **group** bonus may be used — that is, the whole gang may be paid so much for each machine assembled or each ton loaded and the money divided among the members according to a predetermined ratio. Each member of the group, of course, watches every other member to see that no one slacks. The incentive created by group piecework or a group bonus is often more powerful than that created by individual piecework or bonuses. In addition, it creates an incentive for team work within the group — something which individual piecework or bonuses do not do.

Despite the fact that piecework automatically and immediately rewards the worker for every additional piece that he turns out, it has failed in many cases to stimulate men to produce as much as they can. In fact, it is not unusual to find pieceworkers carefully restricting their output. Such a practice (among pieceworkers) seems incredible and yet the explanation is simple. When a foreman or a rate setter fixes a piece rate, he bases it upon two things: the amount which he believes that the worker should earn in a day and the number of pieces that he believes the worker should make in a day. But it is extremely difficult to judge how many pieces a man can make in a given time. For one thing, the employee is likely to slow down while being timed. But aside from this, it is difficult to judge how much a man can do. After he has worked at a job for a few days or weeks, he acquires a swing which accelerates his transition from one part of the operation to another. Furthermore, he discovers short cuts. Soon he is able to do much more than either he himself or anyone else would have believed possible and his piecework earnings are far above the usual wages of men of similar experience and skill. Under the circumstances, it is difficult for the management to resist the temptation to cut the piece rate. But if the employee believes that the rate will be reduced if his earnings exceed a certain amount, he is likely to restrict his output. Thus the incentive of piecework is in large degree destroyed.

The situation is quite different if there is a union in the shop which is strong enough to prevent arbitrary rate cuts. Then, of course, the workers are not afraid to do their best. The employer may lose because high piece rates mean high labor costs, but the community gains because labor is more productive than it would be if there were no union to prevent rate cuts.[8]

In order to preserve the piecework incentive, many managements have established the rule that every rate will be permitted to stand unchanged for at least a year. In most plants, however, this rule has done little to eliminate restriction of output. Some enterprises endeavor to conceal rate cuts by making changes in the operation or in working conditions which necessitate a new piece price. The new price is invariably much lower than the old one. But this scheme also does not deceive many workmen. Of great importance in eliminating rate cutting, and thus in eliminating restriction of output, has been the invention of time and motion study. This is a method of determining how long a worker needs in order to perform a given operation. The operation is divided up into parts, usually called elements. With a stopwatch, a time is obtained for each element. The worker is observed long enough to obtain several times for each element. If he is deliberately restricting his speed, he will take much longer to do some elements on some cycles of performance than on others. Likewise if the operation is a new one and he has not established a rhythm, he will take much longer at some times than others. The method may be illustrated as follows:

Cycle	Element times in hundredths of a minute				
	A	B	C	D	E
1	.25	.41	.33	(.38)	.60
2	.23	.42	.33	.14	.61
3	.26	(.98)	.32	.13	.62
4	(.72)	.40	.35	.14	.59
5	.24	.43	(.80)	.15	.60

The hypothetical operation has been divided into five elements, and five cycles have been observed — that is, the workman has been timed five times. As a rule each part of the operation took about as long to do one time as another, but in four instances, (indicated by the parentheses) the element times were abnormally long. In some cases, the worker may have deliberately slowed up; in others, he may have had trouble because of the newness of the

---

[8] In some cases, however, unions seek to prevent rate cuts by setting a limit to the amount which any member may earn in a day. But if the employer can give adequate assurance that he will not reduce rates because of large earnings, the union may remove the limit on production.

operation; in still others, the delay may have been due to causes which would hinder even experienced operatives. The time study man must decide what is the reason for each abnormal time. In case he concludes that the cause is deliberate slowing up or inexperience, he rejects the abnormal time in estimating the time needed for the operation, but if the cause is one which would delay even an experienced operative, he counts the abnormal time.[9] The theory of time study is that a summation of the average element times, after the elimination of the abnormally high times which are due to either slowing up or inexperience, will indicate how rapidly the worker will be able to do the operation after he has become used to it. To this time is usually added an additional allowance to cover waiting for materials, personal needs, fatigue, and other causes beyond the worker's control.

When rates are set by competent time study men, the proportion of cases in which workmen are able to " run away with the rate " is extremely small. Under these circumstances, managements find it profitable to guarantee that *no* rates will be cut under *any* circumstances. The small amount which is lost by paying a few unnecessarily high rates is more than offset by the gains from unrestricted production. Of course, in the absence of a union, the promise not to cut rates depends simply upon the good faith of the management, and some workmen naturally have difficulty in believing that rates will never be cut.

Restriction of output is less often found in connection with bonus plans, because managements are not inclined to reduce the standard time fixed for an operation when some workers earn unexpectedly large amounts. Such a reduction would, of course, be the equivalent of rate cutting. The temptation to cut the standard time, however, is less than the temptation to cut piece rates because, as we have seen, when a workman increases his production, his compensation per piece is automatically reduced.

In examining wages as an incentive, it is desirable to consider the effect of wage payment systems upon managements as well as upon workers. Here we encounter the important fact that, al-

[9] Naturally there are great differences among time study men in interpreting element times. Some men are inclined to decide doubtful cases against the workers and acquire the reputation of being " tight " timers. Others are more lenient and become known as rather " loose " timers.

though piecework tends to make workmen efficient, it tends to make managements inefficient. The reason is obvious. Suppose that a pieceworker reports that his machine is out of order or that he is being handicapped by poor material or by having to wait for material. Why should the management go to great trouble to have the machine fixed at once, or to discover why the worker is not kept supplied with material or why poor material is being supplied? The management knows that the man is accustomed to earning a certain amount and that, rather than fall below it, he will work a little harder in order to overcome his handicap. It knows also that if he fails to produce the usual amount, the labor costs of the company will be so much less, because pieceworkers are paid only for what they produce. Consequently, in piecework shops, managements are often lax about planning the work so that every employee always has something to do, about keeping tools and equipment in excellent condition, and about providing raw material of proper quality. These administrative inefficiencies become a live issue in case the workers are organized. The efforts of unions of pieceworkers to protect their members against managerial inefficiency are reflected in the terms of trade agreements. These agreements often stipulate that employees shall receive their average hourly earnings when kept waiting for work and that when work is spoiled because of poor materials or for any causes beyond the control of the employee, he shall be paid for it at the regular piece rate. It is a safe generalization that the efficiency of the management in most piecework shops would be improved by the presence of a strong union among the employees.

The impossibility of measuring many aspects of workers' performance means that wages are an imperfect device for stimulating efficiency. Business men, of course, know this. As long as immigration was abundant, many employers sought to supplement wage incentives by various drive methods. During recent years, managers have become aware, more vividly than ever, of the limitations of wage incentives. The cessation of immigration in 1914, the great inefficiency of labor during the war boom, and the sudden need for making drastic reductions in labor costs when the price level fell in 1920 led many managers to reëxamine the problem of labor efficiency. As a result, they became profoundly impressed by the fact that the efficiency of most workers is largely beyond the direct control of the management and that it depends more than has been supposed upon the willingness of men to do their best. Managers also have been impressed by the fact that many workers deliberately withhold production and use great ingenuity to conceal how little they are doing, because they fear that more output will mean less employment. Consequently, managers have endeavored to make their forces more efficient by making employment more steady and by gaining the good will of their employees. The methods which have been used are too numerous to describe here, but there is abundant evidence that substantial results have been accomplished. As the art of management develops, non-financial incentives are likely to become increasingly important.

REFERENCES

Diemer, H., *Wage-payment Plans that Reduced Production Costs,* 1930.
Hobson, J. A., *Work and Wealth,* 1914. Ch. XIII.
Hoxie, R. F., *Scientific Management and Labor,* 1915.
Taylor, F. W., *Principles of Scientific Management,* 1911.
Tead, Ordway, and Metcalfe, H. C., *Principles of Personnel Administration* (revised edition), 1927.

CHAPTER XXIV

THE LABOR BARGAIN — THE DETERMINATION
OF WAGES

I. WHY THERE IS INTENSE CONFLICT BETWEEN CAPITAL AND LABOR

It is well known that there is often great hostility between the buyers and sellers of labor. A similar antagonism is frequently found between other classes of buyers and sellers but rarely is the hostility so intense as between wage earners and employers. Before analyzing what determines the rate of wages, it is desirable to ask why the labor bargain should generate more heat and conflict than other bargains.

One reason is found in the extraordinary importance to the wage earner of the price at which he sells his labor. His entire income for a considerable period depends upon this one price. Most business enterprises sell several products. Even when they make but one, they sell to many customers and at prices which apply only to the particular order and not to all orders from all the customers over a considerable period. The workman, however, has nothing but his labor to sell, and his wage, once fixed, continues for some time. His position is analogous to that of a manufacturer who sells to a single customer his entire output at a price which holds for months. When price is of such peculiar importance, naturally the wage earner struggles stubbornly for an extra cent or two per hour.

Another reason why the labor bargain frequently generates antagonism is the peculiar relationship which exists between the earnings of the manual worker and his needs. It will be observed that it is usually the bargain between manual workers and employers rather than the one between salary workers and employers which causes trouble. One distinctive thing about the workers in the executive class is that they can increase their income by winning promotion. Not until his fiftieth year or later does the business executive or the technical expert usually reach the peak of his earning capacity. As his family increases and as his children become older, his expenses grow but so also does his income. The great mass of manual laborers find it impossible to obtain promotion as their needs for cash grow. Most of these workers reach their maximum earning capacity at the age of thirty or earlier. Their need for money, however, continues to grow long after their wages have become practically stationary. The man who had a comfortable margin over expenses when he married finds himself ten years later with only slightly greater income and substantially greater needs. As his needs continue to increase, he can satisfy them only by demanding more pay for the same work. It is among this class of workers that acute conflict with employers develops.

II. The Demand for Labor — How Much Can Employers Afford to Pay?

Investigations of the International Labor Office indicate that the *real* wages — that is, the purchasing power of money wages — in the United States are roughly four-fifths greater than in Great Britain, nearly three times as much as in Germany, and nearly four times as much as in Italy or Austria.[1] They are many times higher than in China or India. Skilled craftsmen are usually paid from 50 to 100 per cent more than common laborers,

---

[1] *International Labour Review*, January, 1927, v. XV, p. 130. The results are based on wages and the cost of living in selected large cities and consequently represent only roughly the wage levels of the different countries.

and executives receive many times more than even skilled manual workers. Why are wages so much higher in the United States than elsewhere? And why are some occupations so much better paid than others?

Wages are a price and are determined, of course, in accordance with the same general principles which apply to all prices. In the United States, they are generally determined by competition among the buyers and the sellers of labor. If, at a given price, the quantity of labor offered for sale exceeds the demand, wages fall, and they continue to fall until the supply and the demand are equal. On the other hand, if the supply is less than the quantity demanded, wages rise until supply and demand are equal.[2] High wages, then, occur where the demand for labor is large relative to the supply; low wages where the supply is large relative to the demand. But what determines the demand for labor and what the supply of it?

Let us first analyze the demand for labor. Labor is simply *one form* of producing power — one form of productive capacity. Let us begin our analysis by asking what determines the demand of business establishments for producing capacity in *any* form.

The reason why enterprises buy producing power — in the form of machines, tools, raw material, or human services — is, of course, because it yields a product which in turn yields an income. Naturally it pays business concerns to expand their capacity as long as by doing so they increase their net profits. Subject to a qualification which will be explained presently, it pays an enterprise to add to its productive capacity as long as the additional capacity adds to the income of the concern more than its cost. The more of a commodity that is produced, the lower, of course, is the price at which it can be sold. Furthermore, additional units of productive capacity can be obtained only at a higher

---

[2] This does not mean that wages are always adjusted so that every job seeker can promptly find a place. The fact that a man is hunting for a job does not necessarily mean that he is willing to accept work at the prevailing rates. He may look for several weeks before he finally becomes willing to accept the current wages. Although he is a job seeker, he is not necessarily part of the supply of labor that is available at prevailing rates. And the tendency for wages to fall when the supply at a given price exceeds the demand at that price may be a very tardy one because employers are often reluctant to make wage cuts. Some of the reasons for this reluctance will be explained presently.

and higher outlay, because additional wage earners can be obtained only by offering higher and higher wages and additional supplies of capital only by offering higher and higher interest rates. Sooner or later, therefore, the point is reached where the income yielded by additional productive capacity does not exceed the cost of that capacity, and expansion ceases.

But what determines the maximum price which business establishments are willing to pay for a unit of productive capacity? Naturally this price is closely related to the amount by which the unit is expected to increase the income of the concern. This amount sets the *maximum* price which enterprises are willing to pay for the instruments that produce it. If there is competition for the instruments of production, the price of the instruments is likely to be bid up close to the limit that enterprises can afford to pay — that is, just below the value of the income attributable to the instrument. Assume, for example, that the income which a concern could obtain by the use of different amounts of producing capacity were as follows:

Units of producing capacity	Annual output	Price of product per unit	Gross annual income
10	1,000	$1,000	$1,000,000
11	1,100	950	1,045,000
12	1,200	900	1,080,000
13	1,300	850	1,105,000

The enterprise would obviously be willing, if necessary, to pay up to $35,000 more a year to keep its capacity at twelve units rather than at eleven, because twelve units produce $35,000 more income than eleven. But since the loss of *any one* of the twelve units would not reduce the income by more than $35,000, the enterprise would be willing to pay only $35,000 a year for each and every one of the twelve units. And since a thirteenth unit would add $25,000 to the income, the concern would be willing, if necessary, to pay up to $25,000 a year in order to obtain a thirteenth unit.

Producing power, as has been said, may take the form either of labor or of capital. Every enterprise uses some of each. But what determines whether the demand for productive capacity takes the form of a demand for labor rather than a demand for capital? The answer is fairly obvious. Capital and labor tend to be combined in those proportions which give the lowest cost of production. The proportions in which it is *possible* to combine labor and capital vary tremendously because there are many operations which can be performed either by hand (with the assistance of a relatively small amount of equipment) or by automatic or semi-automatic machines. It is not intended to suggest that enterprises are always successful in discovering the relative amounts of capital and labor which give the lowest cost of production. As a matter of fact, by a process of experimentation enterprises are constantly testing whether it would be economical to use more labor here or more capital there. If a concern finds it can cut costs by using more labor and less capital, it does so; if it finds it can save by using more capital and less labor, it does so. The demand for labor tends to be determined by the proportions in which it is most economical to combine labor and capital, because these proportions determine the number of men that it pays employers to hire at a given price.

Another way of describing the determination of the demand for labor is that enterprises tend to hire men as long as the output of the additional men is worth more than the cost of producing it. In other words, the number of men which a concern will hire at a given price is limited by how much additional men will increase the income of the enterprise. Or, to state it still differently, the wages which enterprises offer to obtain a given number of men are limited by the income which would be lost by the loss of any one man. Assume, for example, that with the indicated number of men an enterprise can obtain the following amounts of income:

Size of force	Annual income	Amount added by an additional man
50	$100,000	. . . .
51	101,800	$1,800
52	103,500	1,700
53	105,100	1,600

At just below $1,700 a year, the concern would demand fifty-two men because a fifty-second man would add $1,700 a year to its income. Should labor be obtainable at slightly less than $1,600, the enterprise would hire fifty-three men, for a fifty-third man would add $1,600 a year to its income. Suppose now that the efficiency of labor increased 10 per cent so that a given number of men produced 10 per cent more from a given quantity of equipment. The income of the enterprise would then be:

Size of force	Annual income	Amount added by an additional man
50	$110,000	....
51	111,980	$1,980
52	113,850	1,870
53	115,610	1,760

The price which the concern would bid for a given number of men would now be raised 10 per cent. A fifty-third man would now add $1,760 instead of $1,600 to the annual income; consequently the concern would now be willing to take fifty-three men at any price below $1,760. Likewise it would be willing to take fifty-two at any price below $1,870.

It must be conceded that this is a somewhat unrealistic description of the determination of the demand for labor because employers do not ordinarily think in terms of adding a particular kind of productive agent, such as labor. Employers think in terms of costs of production and of income — they consider how much it would cost to produce so and so much more output and whether the additional output could be marketed at a price which would cover costs. Nevertheless, it is obvious that if enterprises add productive capacity as long as it pays for itself and if they combine the various agents of production so as to produce the given volume of output at the lowest cost per unit, they are in fact adding each of the several agents of production up to the point where the last unit of each produces barely enough additional output to pay for itself. If employers were told that this is what they are doing, they would undoubtedly be surprised, because they are consciously addressing themselves only to two interdependent problems: (1) how much output does it pay to produce, and (2) how can the unit costs of producing this amount be kept at a minimum.

In the immediately preceding numerical illustrations, it is assumed that an increase of a given per cent in the total number of men employed resulted in a less than proportionate increase in the income of the plant. Is the assumption justified? This is a question of considerable importance because, when successive increases in the force result in more than proportionate increases in income, the enterprise obviously cannot afford to pay each man as much as its income would be decreased by the loss of one man. Suppose, for example, that a force of 99 men turned out a product of $98,000 a year, and a force of 100, a product of $100,000. By adding a hundredth man, the concern gains $2,000, but it could not afford to offer $2,000 a year to obtain 100 men because this would make the annual wage bill $200,000.

If cases of this sort were numerous, they would invalidate the principle that the demand for labor is determined by the income which additional men would produce. But these cases are exceptional and are not likely to exist except for short periods. There are two conditions under which increasing the force might yield more than proportionate increments of income. One is where natural resources and artificial capital have been combined in the wrong proportions — that is, too much natural resources or artificial capital and too little labor have been used. The other is where the advantages of more minute specialization of labor, which a larger force makes possible, are unusually large. Neither of these conditions is likely to persist long. The first would cease as soon as enterprises found that they could increase their output and lower their costs by using less capital. The second would not persist because, as soon as it was discovered that larger enterprises using more minute subdivision of labor could undersell smaller concerns, business would be concentrated (as a result of either competition or combination) into fewer and larger plants. This process would continue until additional men no longer added increasing rather than decreasing increments of income.

The explanation of why additions to the force normally result in smaller and smaller increments of income is to be found in the law of the proportion of factors. This law, it will be recalled, states that after a given point the addition of successive increments of one factor of production to constant quantities of other factors yields smaller and smaller additions to income.[3] The reason is that the output of an establishment is not solely the

[3] Pp. 333–335.

product of any one agent of production but the joint product of them all. Consequently, when one agent is increased, the others remaining constant, there is not a proportionate increase in the producing power of the plant.

It must not be imagined that managers can tell easily and with precision just how many men it is profitable to hire. Often the number is conjectural in the extreme and yet *some* decision must be made. How many " red caps " does it pay a railroad to provide at a railroad station? Will an extra one pay? Some one must decide the exact number and that means that some one must make a guess as to whether an additional " red cap " would sufficiently improve the service to earn his wages. Someone must also decide whether the railroad could not dispense with some of the " red caps." Or consider the case of an industrial development department of a railroad. The purpose of such a department is to induce new industries to locate on the lines. A certain road now spends about $20,000 a year on this department. The new plants which have located along the lines of the company during an eight-year period provide about $12,000,000 worth of freight a year. Does the industrial development department pay? The president of the railroad admits that he does not know how many new plants would have come if the department had not been in existence. And yet he must somehow decide whether or not it pays to spend this $20,000. A retailer installed an itemized stock-control system which diminished by about 50 per cent the number of cases in which his store was " out " of articles which customers requested. How much is such a stock-control system worth? How much does a store lose when it is unable to fill an order? No doubt it loses the profit on the sale and something besides, because its overhead costs go on whether or not the sale is made. In addition, there is a loss of prestige and good will. But obviously it is not easy for the dealer to estimate the loss.

III. Some Conditions That Affect the Proportions in Which Labor and Capital Are Used

It has been said that the quantity of labor which will be demanded depends, among other things, upon the proportions in which it is most economical to combine labor and capital. What determines these proportions? They depend upon (1) the relative productivity of men and capital and (2) the prices at which labor and capital can be obtained.

The greater the productivity of labor, the greater, of course, the extent to which it pays to use men instead of capital in making goods and the larger the number of men that it pays employers to hire at a given price. But is this reasoning sound? Suppose that the efficiency of every workman in the country suddenly increased by one-fourth? Would the demand for labor increase or decrease? Eighty men could now do the work formerly done by 100. Assuming that the amount of *labor-power* demanded by employers at any given price is the same as before, would not the number of *men* demanded be less? Might not the gain in labor efficiency possibly *diminish* the number of men that employers would demand and thus lower wages?

It is possible that an increase in the efficiency of labor might diminish the demand for men *in some occupations* and thus lower wages *in those occupations* until the supply of labor had redistributed itself. It is extremely unlikely, however, that *a general increase* in efficiency would diminish the number of men demanded. The explanation is found in the nature of the demand for labor. Men's desires for goods are so far from satiated that the community is *willing,* if able, to purchase many times the existing production. Under these circumstances, it ought not to be necessary for business establishments to reduce their forces when labor becomes more efficient. With labor 25 per cent more efficient, enterprises can turn out 25 per cent more goods. Assuming that wages and the other disbursements of business concerns remain the same, the public has the same amount of money with which to buy the output of industry. This means that prices must be reduced 20 per cent in order to enable the public to buy 25 per cent more output. If competition prevails, enterprises may be expected to make the reduction in prices. Such a reduction will not diminish profits, because 25 per cent more output sold at 20 per cent less per unit yields the original amount of income. On the other hand, if enterprises do not cut prices by 20 per cent, they will have idle productive capacity, because the gain in the efficiency of labor has increased the productive capacity of industry by one-fourth. The net result is that output increases

25 per cent, prices (other than wages) diminish 20 per cent, the income, the disbursements, and the profits of business concerns remain unchanged, money wages remain unchanged, and *real* wages rise one-fourth — by exactly the amount of the gain in the efficiency of labor. In other words, the demand for labor has increased so that employers are willing to hire the same number of men at wages which, in purchasing power, are 25 per cent above the old wages.[4]

At a low rate of wages and a high rate of interest, it pays establishments to use a large proportion of labor and a small proportion of capital; at a high rate of wages and a low rate of interest, to use a small proportion of labor and a large proportion of capital. Assume, for example, that capital is obtainable at 6 per cent. If, then, labor is obtainable at $8 a day, a concern might find it most economical to hire fifty-five men. But if men were obtainable at $7 a day, it would be advantageous to use more men and less capital. At $7 a day, therefore, it would hire more than fifty-five men — let us say sixty. At $6 a day, it would hire still more men — say sixty-five.

If capital were available at 5 per cent instead of 6, it would pay the enterprise to use more capital and fewer men. At $8 a day, it might hire only fifty men; at $7, fifty-five; at $6, sixty. But if capital cost 7 per cent a year, it would be economical to use less capital and more labor. At $8 a day, the number of men demanded might be sixty; at $7, sixty-five; at $6, seventy. These figures may be put in the form of a table showing the number of men that would be demanded at different wages and different interest rates:

	Number of men demanded when the interest rate (price of capital) is:		
Wage	*5 per cent*	*6 per cent*	*7 per cent*
$6	60	65	70
7	55	60	65
8	50	55	60

The table could, of course, be extended to show the number of men who would be demanded at still other interest rates

[4] The relationship between the productivity of labor and real wages is discussed in more detail in Section XII of this chapter and it is explained why advances in productivity do not invariably raise real wages.

and at still other wage rates. The conclusion is that the number of wage earners that business establishments are willing to hire at different prices depends upon the prices at which different quantities of capital can be obtained. Conversely, it follows that the amounts of capital which are demanded at different prices depend upon the wages at which labor can be obtained.[5]

It must not, of course, be assumed that even establishments in the same industry find it advantageous to combine the instruments of production in the same proportions. A concern with exceptionally good credit may borrow at 5 per cent while its competitors must pay 6 or 6½ per cent. The prices of raw material, power, and labor are different in different cities. So also is the price of space — one of the most important instruments of production. These differences naturally affect the proportions in which different enterprises combine the factors of production. For example, manufacturers of women's garments in Cleveland have expressed astonishment at the small amount of space in which their New York competitors conduct operations. The high cost of space in New York has compelled employers to economize it in ways that are extraordinary to other employers. The process of adjusting the factors of production so as to get the lowest possible cost is, of course, going on constantly. Technical changes and price movements are constantly altering the proportions which are most advantageous. Interesting evidence of the tendency of employers to use less labor as wages become relatively higher is furnished by the change in horsepower per wage earner in manufacturing during the period 1914 to 1927:

---

[5] Because buildings, machines, and other articles of equipment are all made by labor, it may be objected that it is misleading to assert that the demand for men depends upon the prices at which labor and capital can be obtained. A demand for more buildings and machines is simply an *indirect* way of demanding labor. A shift from hand methods to machine methods, therefore, does not mean a change in the total demand for labor. It simply means a shift in the *kind* of labor that is demanded.

It is true that most kinds of capital are man-made, but it is not true that all of the costs connected with the use of capital are labor costs. Hence a shift from hand methods to machine methods does *not* mean that enterprises are simply spending their money on one kind of labor rather than another. The cost of using capital depends upon the rate of interest, the cost of insurance, the cost of depreciation, and the rate of taxation. None of these costs are in the main labor costs. As they rise, it becomes economical to use less capital and more direct labor; as they fall, to use more capital and less direct labor.

	1914	*1919*	*1920*	*1925*	*1927*
Hourly earnings of factory workers [6]	100	184	231	225	229
Price of producers' goods [7]	100	195	234	146	132
Long run interest rates [8]	100	110	122	103	98
Primary horsepower per wage earner [9]	3.2	3.3		4.3	4.7

Between 1914 and 1920, wages and the prices of producers' goods (that is, goods used in the production of other goods) increased in roughly the same proportion and the rate at which money could be borrowed rose. Consequently, the amount of capital per worker, as measured by installed horsepower per factory worker, increased very little. Between 1920 and 1927, however, the cost of labor relative to the cost of producers' goods increased about 76 per cent and the cost of funds diminished about one-fifth. It is not surprising, therefore, to find manufacturers shifting to the use of more capital and less labor. Between 1919 and 1927, the number of factory workers diminished by about 8 per cent but the horsepower per worker increased nearly one-third.

Suppose that the quantity of capital available at a given rate of interest increases. Will wages rise or fall? Let us assume that the prices at which labor and capital are available have led industry to use labor and capital in the ratio of one man to every $5,000 of capital and to pay $5 a day for labor and 6 per cent for capital. At these rates, let us assume that the number of men employed is 1,000,000 and the total investment of capital $5,000,000,000. Suppose now that 20 per cent more capital becomes available without a rise in the interest rate. Will wages rise or fall?

They will rise, because the demand for labor will increase. But why will the demand for labor increase? Our assumption is

[6] Douglas, P. H., *Real Wages in the United States*, 1890–1926, p. 108. The index for 1927 is based upon the index of the National Industrial Conference Board in *Wages in the United States, 1914–1927*, p. 25.

[7] *Monthly Labor Review*, May, 1927, v. XXIV, pp. 250–253, and March, 1928, v. XXVI, p. 665.

[8] *Survey of Current Business*, February, 1928, No. 78, p. 127. The indexes represent the average yield of fifteen industrial bonds.

[9] Computed from data in the *Biennial Census of Manufactures*, 1925, p. 44; and 1927, p. 16.

that, with labor at $5 a day and capital at 6 per cent a year, the most economical combination is one man to every $5,000 of capital. With $6,000,000,000 instead of $5,000,000,000 of capital available, more men are needed to maintain the most economical ratio between labor and capital — 1,200,000 men instead of 1,000,000. Whereas it formerly paid industry to offer $5 a day in order to obtain 1,000,000 men, it now pays to offer $5 for 1,200,000. And there is a corresponding increase in the number of men which industry is willing to take at other prices. The increase in the demand raises the point at which demand and supply reach equilibrium and thus raises the general wage level.

The matter may be put in another way. A workman, we have seen, is worth to an employer as much as the employer would lose if he lost the man. If a reduction in the staff by one man would reduce the income of the enterprise by $6 a day, the employer would naturally be willing, if necessary, to pay anything up to $6 to avoid a decrease of one in the size of his force. An increase in the supply of capital tends to raise wages *because it tends to increase the amount by which the loss of any one man would reduce the income of the enterprise.* The explanation is found in the fact that each instrument of production produces with the help of others. Naturally the yield of each depends upon how much help it receives from the others. The amount of aid which each laborer receives from capital is greater when the supply of capital is large. Consequently, the loss of output that follows the loss of a worker increases as the amount of capital per worker increases.

This explanation of why a relatively large supply of capital makes for high wages throws light upon the differences in the wage levels of different countries. A principal reason for high wages in the United States, for example, is the large supply of natural resources and other capital per worker.

IV. Other Determinants of the Demand for Labor

Although business establishments *tend* to demand productive capacity up to the point where additional capacity barely pays for itself, this general tendency is subject to important limitations. Strange to say, it is not always profitable to hire men as long as additional workers will increase the income of the concern by more than their wages. The reason grows out of the fact that enterprises are often able to obtain or hold a large number of men for less than they are worth. In this case it may not pay to offer more in order to obtain more men.

Why is it possible for business concerns to obtain men for less than they are worth? In the past an important source of supply has been newly arrived immigrants who were ignorant of the language, who did not know where to seek work, who were reduced in circumstances by the expenses of their long journey, and who were accustomed to substantially lower compensation than prevails in the United States. This source of supply is now far less important than before the war. Another important source of cheap labor is the flow of men from the farms to the cities — a flow made up largely of young, unmarried men, who, like the immigrants, are used to lower wage standards than prevail in most cities. Some cheap labor is supplied by men whose resources have been diminished by sickness, accident, family misfortune, or long unemployment and who need money so urgently that they are ready to accept work at almost any price rather than remain idle longer. Finally, there are the men who have reached the age when employment is difficult to obtain. They are often actually worth more than younger workers but the widespread prejudice against older men may compel them to accept less than they are really worth.

Even if a plant has hired its men at a wage which closely approximates what they are worth, their value is soon likely to rise above their wages. There are several reasons for this. Managements are constantly striving to make their men do more and better work. Just as long as the management does not demand too much at one time, just as long as it does not outrage too much the workers' sense of justice, most employees slowly submit to its demands. A few men may leave because the requirements of the management become too stiff, and under some market conditions many men may leave. Most of the force, however, will remain. Changing from one position to another is a gamble. The jobs which are most frequently vacated and which make up the majority of those waiting to be filled are naturally the less attractive ones — the ones which pay the least and which involve the heaviest and most disagreeable tasks.[10] Most workers know from experience the difficulties of finding a satisfactory job and this renders them reluctant to leave a reasonably good place without strong provocation. Furthermore, if a man has worked in a plant for several years, he usually feels that his service record has given him a certain standing. It makes the management more reluctant to discharge him and it protects him against lay-off. Should slack times arrive, he expects that the junior men will be laid off before him. Even if the management lays him off, he believes that it will give him back his job when business revives.

Most changes in standards of performance are put into effect during years of depression or during an off-season when the men are plentiful and jobs are scarce. Before the demand for labor becomes brisk, the workers have grown accustomed to the new standards and accept them as normal. But even in boom times, some firms succeed in speeding up their men, particularly the piece-workers. Rising prices, which are characteristic of boom periods, render the men eager to increase their earnings. This leads them to work faster and to hunt more carefully for short cuts. Thus the earnings of the men keep pace with the rising cost of living without piece rates' being raised. Some firms went through the entire war and post-war periods of inflation without raising more than a few scattered rates and few rates were increased by any firms in proportion to the rise in the price level. For these reasons, an enterprise which, at a given date, was paying its men the full worth of their services may soon be paying them distinctly less than their worth.

From time immemorial technical improvements and the increase in the supply of capital relative to the number of wage earners have been causing the value of labor to rise. This steady rise in the value of labor causes the wages of many workers to become less than the value of the men. Furthermore, the predominating movement of prices for hundreds of years has been

[10] That the vacant jobs are usually the least attractive ones is indicated by the high rate of turnover among newly hired men. Figures which I collected a few years ago indicate that from 60 to 80 per cent of the men hired by industrial establishments leave the newly accepted positions within a year. Slichter, S. H., *The Turnover of Factory Labor*, p. 50. That the typical employee does not leave the position so frequently is shown by the fact that in most plants from 50 to 90 per cent of the force have been in the service for two years or more. *Ibid.*, p. 49.

upward. Naturally, if the product which wage earners make increases in price, the workers become worth more to their employers.

Suppose now that an employer, because of any or all of the causes enumerated, finds that he is paying his men substantially less than they are worth to him. Will this lead him to go into the market and hire additional men as long as they can be obtained at wages which are less than the amount by which they would increase his income? By no means! If he must pay more than his present wages in order to obtain more men, he is likely to go without hiring them. There are serious managerial difficulties in paying some men more than others who do the same work and who are equally efficient. It is likely to injure morale, arouse discontent, provoke resignations among the lower paid men, and possibly cause a strike. This is particularly true if the highest paid men are newly hired employees. Consequently, if the enterprise were to hire new men at higher rates, it would soon be compelled to raise the wages of its entire present force. Rather than do this, it would not increase its force. This is shown by the following table:

Number of workers	Daily income of the enterprise	Contributions to income by any one man	Wages needed to attract given number of workers	Daily wage outlay	Surplus of income over wage outlay
12	$118.50	....	$3.40	$40.80	$77.70
13	127.00	$8.50	3.55	46.15	80.85
14	135.00	8.00	3.75	52.50	82.50
15	142.50	7.50	4.00	60.00	82.50
16	149.50	7.00	4.30	68.80	80.70
17	156.00	6.50	4.65	79.05	76.95
18	162.00	6.00	5.05	91.90	70.10
19	167.50	5.50	5.50	104.50	63.00
20	172.50	5.00	6.00	120.00	52.50

If the firm were to hire men as long as additional ones produced more than their wages, it would employ eighteen, because not until a nineteenth was added would wages equal the increase in the income. And, of course, if an eighteenth man could be added at $5.05 *without increasing the wages of the other men,* it would pay the enterprise to hire him. If, however, it is not practicable to pay some employees more than others in the same occupation and of the same efficiency, the concern would gain nothing by hiring more than fourteen men at $3.75 a day or fifteen men at $4.00, because at these points it would realize the maximum surplus of income over its labor costs. From this analysis, we deduce the extremely important principle that *the present level of wages is quite as real a determinant of the demand for labor as the value of additional men.* The existing wage level, if below the worth of labor, causes the demand for labor to respond only slowly and imperfectly to increases in the value of labor.

V. The Supply of Labor at a Given Time

It is often assumed that the supply of labor is in the main independent of wage rates and that it depends almost exclusively upon the population of the country. Most men, it is reasoned, must work for their living regardless of whether wages are high or low. And because men *must* work in order to live, the number who seek employment must be about the same regardless of whether wages are high or low.

But this reasoning is inaccurate. To begin with, a substantial number of men are able to decide between working for wages and becoming independent business men — storekeepers, farmers, and even small manufacturers. A still larger number are able to decide between working or not working. Youths decide whether to continue in school or to enter industry, men whether to retire now or to work a few years longer, women whether to marry or to hold their jobs, housewives whether or not to supplement the family income by industrial employment. During the last several generations there has been a rapid tendency for young people to remain in school longer and to enter industry at a later age. For example, between 1920 and 1928, when the population of the country increased 14 per cent, the enrollment in secondary schools and colleges increased about 77 per cent.[11] There is still room for considerable further postponement of the age of entering industry. In 1920, only 8.5 per cent of the children between ten and fifteen years of age in the United States were employed gainfully, but in Mississippi the percentage was 25.9, in South Carolina 24.4, in Alabama 24.1, in Georgia 20.8, in Arkansas 18.5, and in North Carolina 16.6.[12] At present, only about 30

[11] *Statistical Abstract of the United States,* 1930, pp. 107–108.
[12] *Fourteenth Census of the United States,* v. IV, " Occupations," 1920, pp. 476 and 514.

per cent of the pupils reach the first year of high school and only 14 per cent finish high school.[13] About 40 per cent of the males 65 years of age or over are not gainfully employed.[14] Ill health or infirmity prevents some of these men from working, but many others have retired simply because they have saved enough so that they do not need to work. At a better salary or under better working conditions, they might continue to work for a few years longer. Postponing the age of entering industry and moving forward the age of retirement make a surprising difference in the supply of labor. If a man works from ten to seventy, his life yields sixty years of employment but if he works from sixteen to sixty-five it yields only forty-nine years — a drop of 18 per cent.

Particularly large are the variations in the proportion of the women who are gainfully employed. As a general rule, the proportion seems to be low where the wages of male workers are high. This is indicated by the great variation among different countries. As the proportion is affected by the importance of agriculture, it is necessary to compare countries in which approximately the same part of the gainfully employed population is engaged in agriculture.[15] Such a comparison indicates that where wages are high, as in the United States, a much smaller proportion of the women work for hire than in countries where wages are low. In the United States, the proportion of women and girls of ten years and over who were gainfully employed in 1920 was 16.5 per cent, in comparison with 54.0 per cent in Germany, 32.7 per cent in the Netherlands, and 48.0 per cent in Switzerland.[16]

In addition to the persons who are able to choose between working and not working for relatively long periods, there are

[13] U. S. Bureau of Education, *Biennial Survey of Education,* 1924–1926, p. 576.

[14] *Statistical Abstract of the United States,* 1930, p. 49.

[15] Where agriculture is important, a larger proportion of the women work at home and so are not counted as gainfully employed.

[16] League of Nations, Economic and Financial Section, *International Statistical Year-Book,* 1928, Tables 6 and 7. The proportion of gainfully employed population engaged in agriculture was: United States, 26.3 per cent; Germany, 30.5 per cent; Netherlands, 23.6 per cent; Switzerland, 25.9 per cent. In France, although 41.5 per cent of the gainfully employed population was engaged in agriculture, 48.8 per cent of the women and girls ten years and over were gainfully employed. In Italy, where 56.1 per cent of the working population was engaged in agriculture, 45.6 per cent of the women were gainfully employed.

There are some differences among the countries in the definition of a gainfully

many others who are able to abstain from work temporarily. A large proportion of wage earners have savings. In many families there are regular sources of income other than the earnings of the husband. An investigation of the United States Bureau of Labor Statistics during the years 1918 and 1919 showed that, among 12,096 working class families, 10.8 per cent of the income came from sources other than the earnings of the husband.[17] The importance of income not earned by the husband increased as the total family income increased. Among 1,594 families receiving between $1,800 and $2,100, 12.1 per cent of the income was not earned by the husband; among 353 families receiving $2,500 or over, 35.6 per cent. The Travelers Insurance Company in 1923 found that among the families of 2,000 recipients of benefits under its group accident and sickness policies, 810, or 40.5 per cent, had income in addition to the wages of the beneficiary. The average additional income in these 810 cases was $27.06 a week. This was slightly higher than the average weekly wage of the beneficiaries in these families, which was $24.70.[18]

The ability of wage earners to go short periods without employment is greatly enhanced by unemployment insurance. Comprehensive state schemes of unemployment insurance exist in several European countries — notably Great Britain and Germany. In the United States, all of the schemes are private. A few employers, such as the General Electric Company, the Eastman Kodak Company, the Dennison Manufacturing Company, and the Consolidated Water Power and Paper Company, provide unemployment insurance. So also do a few unions, such as some locals of the photo-engravers' union and the lithographers' union. In the Cleveland women's garment industry and the Chicago men's clothing industry, insurance schemes have been established under the joint control of the unions and the employers.

The fact that many workers can go for weeks or months without employment has important effects upon the labor supply. It tends to reduce the number who seek anything they can get at

employed person. An effort was made in compiling the figures to render them as comparable as possible.

[17] U. S. Bureau of Labor Statistics, *Handbook of Labor Statistics, 1924–1926,* p. 118.

[18] Bailey, W. B., " When Sickness Stops Wages, What? " *Industrial Management,* January, 1924, v. LXVII, pp. 32–33.

almost any wage and thus tends to keep the wages of common labor higher than they otherwise would be. It also prevents many men in seasonal trades from seeking jobs in other occupations during the slack period in their own industries. Because they can afford to remain idle temporarily, they prefer to wait for employment in their own industries to pick up. They fear that if they accept jobs elsewhere, they may lose an early opportunity to resume their regular occupations. Nevertheless, these workers are part of the labor supply available for other employment provided sufficiently attractive terms are offered.

The ability of wage earners to go without employment for short periods increases the frequency of resignations and the number of men who are idle because they are looking for better jobs. Studies of labor turnover and of unemployment indicate that idleness of this sort has an appreciable effect upon the supply of labor. Suppose that a man leaves a job at which he has been receiving $5 a day in order to hunt for one paying better wages. For possibly a week he will accept nothing less than $6. But six-dollar jobs do not happen to be available. As his funds diminish, his reservation price falls. After a week's idleness, he may be willing to take $5.50. After two weeks, he may be ready to accept, $5, and at that price he may promptly find work. For two weeks, however, he has been idle because his reservation price has been too high. Idleness of this sort is particularly prevalent during times of rising prices and prosperity.

But the labor supply does not depend merely upon the number of persons who are willing to work. It depends also upon how many days in the year and how many hours in the day men are willing to work and upon how intensely they are willing to apply themselves. It is a familiar fact that the more some men earn in a day, the fewer days in the week they show up for work. This is especially pronounced among Negroes, Mexicans, and most primitive peoples. Many workers seriously object to a seven-day week and expect higher compensation for work done on Sunday. The movement for a five-day week has already made substantial progress in the building trades. The attitude toward holiday work is similar to that toward Sunday work — some men are glad to work holidays at the ordinary rate of pay, but many (possibly most) men insist upon more than their regular wages. The labor supply is affected even more by the number of hours a day men are willing to work. Once the hours were from sun to sun. The ten-hour day began in the United States in the building trades during the decade of the thirties. By the Civil War, it was fairly general outside of agriculture. In the steel industry, however, the twelve-hour day persisted well into the twentieth century. The eight-hour day began in the building trades during the eighties. It became general in manufacturing, however, only during the World War, and a large proportion of factory employees still work nine or ten hours a day. With the working day as short as eight to ten hours, it is possible to expand the labor supply substantially by paying overtime rates — usually one-fourth or one-half more than the regular rates — and by working the force from two to four hours a day overtime. Finally, the labor supply depends upon the intensity with which men apply themselves, and for extra compensation they are often willing to work more intensely. Some managers insist upon an unusually fast pace but pay above the market rate in order to induce good men to work at this pace.

What light does the preceding analysis throw upon the relationship between the supply of labor and the rate of wages? Ordinarily the quantity of a commodity offered for sale is less at a low price than at a high one. Is this also true of labor?

The labor-supply curve for *any given industry or occupation* is similar to most supply curves. At a low wage only a few workers are willing to enter the industry or the occupation; at higher wages, many more persons are usually willing. But is it also true that the total number of people who are willing to work at existing wages rises as the wage level rises and falls as the wage level falls? The answer to this question is in doubt. At an *exceedingly low* wage level, a large number of persons would probably become criminals or independent business men. As wages rose, the number willing to work for hire would increase up to a certain point. It is probable, however, that the labor supply is less at an intermediate wage level than at a lower one. Possibly it is also smaller at a very high wage level than at an intermediate one, but this is much more doubtful. The shape of the curve is possibly as follows:

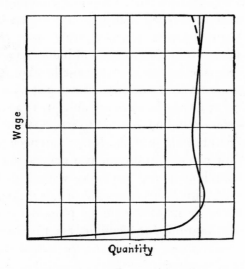

When the wage level is low, the supply of labor is large because nearly every one finds it necessary to work steadily and to lose no time unavoidably, children enter industry at an early age, wives endeavor to obtain jobs, employees in seasonal industries endeavor to find other employment to tide them over the slack season, and no one can afford to retire as long as he is able to hold a job. The effect of a high wage level is far more uncertain. High wages undoubtedly induce some children to enter industry earlier, some wives to work outside the home, and some men to postpone retiring. But they also lead many families to keep their children in school longer, many wives not to accept industrial employment, many men to retire earlier. The net effect is uncertain. The dotted line indicates the possibility that at very high wages fewer men may offer to work than at slightly lower wages.

An exceedingly important characteristic of the labor-supply curve is that the entire curve is a result of the wage level which actually exists. For example, the number of men who would offer to work at any given wage level, say $7 a day, might be

1,000,000 if the existing wage level is $6 a day, but it would un-
doubtedly be greater than 1,000,000 if the wage level were less
than $6 — say $5. A wage of $7 would seem more attractive to
persons who were used to $5 than it would to persons who were
used to $6. Consequently, it would draw more children from
school, more wives from the home, and induce more workers to
postpone retiring when it followed a wage level of $5 than when
it followed a wage level of $6. There are just as many possible
supplies of labor at $7 as there are possible prices of labor. Like-
wise fewer workers could be induced to work at low wages after
the wage level had been high than after it had been low. Rather
than accept a low compensation, many workers would prefer to
retire — and the higher the previous wages, the larger the
number who could afford to retire. All of this means that a separate supply curve for labor should be plotted for every price.
In the following diagram, for example, are three supply curves.
S represents the supply of labor when the actual wage is $4, S_1
when it is $5, and S_2 when it is $6.

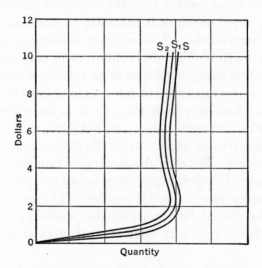

From the standpoint of the principles of wage determination,
the fact that the supply of labor depends upon the wage actually
established means that the door is open to the determination
of wages by bargaining. This is illustrated by the following
table:

Demand	Wage	Supply of labor assuming that the actual wage is	
		$6	$7
1,150,000	$4	950,000	850,000
1,100,000	5	1,000,000	900,000
1,050,000	6	1,050,000	950,000
1,000,000	7	1,100,000	1,000,000
950,000	8	1,150,000	1,050,000
900,000	9	1,200,000	1,100,000 ·

It will be observed that two wage rates are possible — $6 or $7. Suppose that the wage, to begin with, was $6. If the workers through a series of strikes forced it up to $7, the supply of labor would temporarily exceed the demand by 100,000 because, as long as the supply of labor was under the influence of the $6 wage rate, there would be 1,100,000 men willing to work at $7. At the beginning, therefore, the strikers would have to preserve their unity and to prevent the unemployed from undercutting the rate in order to hold the wage of $7. But a wage of $7, by accelerating the retirement of men, making it possible for wives to remain out of industry and for children to remain longer in school, would gradually reduce the number of job seekers. It might take months or years for the wage of $7 to produce the full effect. Nevertheless, if the workers can hold the wage long enough, the supply will fall to 1,000,000, which makes as stable an equilibrium as does a wage of $6. Conversely, the employers by unity of action might reduce the wage from $7 to $6 because the drop would eventually increase the supply of labor at $6 to 1,050,000 — enough to create a stable equilibrium. Important to notice is the fact that the purchasing power of a wage of $7 would not be one-sixth more than a wage of $6. The reason is that at $7, 50,000 fewer men would be employed — 1,000,000 instead of 1,050,000. Consequently, the output of industry would be slightly less and the prices of goods slightly higher.[19]

VI. The Long-Run Relationship Between Wages and the Supply of Labor

Thus far our discussion has related to the connection between the wage level and the supply of labor *at any particular time.*

[19] A brief but lucid analysis of the bargaining element in wages and of the relationship between the wage level and the supply curve of labor will be found in Maurice Dobb's *Wages*, pp. 94–108.

But wages may also react upon the supply of labor *in the long run.* If workmen, for example, receive higher wages than they have been accustomed to obtain, are they not likely to marry earlier and have more children? And if the wage-earning class is better clothed, housed, and fed, is not the death rate likely to diminish? Consequently, may not an advance in wages today increase the supply of labor a generation hence and thus cause wages to fall toward the level which prevailed before the advance?

It was an analysis of this sort which led most economists of a century ago to believe that wages could not permanently rise above the level of subsistence. The leading exponent of this view was Thomas R. Malthus, a British economist and clergyman. Malthus argued that population has an inevitable tendency to outrun the means of subsistence. Were there no checks to increase, population could easily double itself every twenty-five years. But one important instrument of production, natural resources, is limited in quantity. As population grew, each worker would have less help from nature in producing. The output of the community, therefore, would not long continue to increase as rapidly as the population.[20] Two checks, according to Malthus, a " positive check " and a " preventive check " limit the tendency of population to outrun the means of subsistence. By " positive checks," Malthus meant all causes which increase the death rate — disease, war, famine, and the effects of extreme poverty; by " preventive checks," causes which reduce the birth rate — the postponement of marriage, the desire to give children more advantages, the desire to avoid poverty.

It will be noted that the theory of Malthus does not assert that population *inevitably* increases whenever wages rise above the bare level of subsistence. In fact, in strict logic, the theory does not exclude the conclusion that a rise in income might result in a rise in the standard of living and no increase in population. Nevertheless, Malthus and most of his contemporaries believed

---

[20] Although Malthus stated that population has a tendency to outrun the means of subsistence, he did not explain *why* this is so. The use of the law of the proportion of factors (then called " the law of diminishing returns ") to explain why an increase in population would result in less product per capita, unless in the meantime methods of production improved sufficiently, was made by Ricardo, a contemporary of Malthus.

that *as a matter of fact* a rise in wages would, in the long run, mean more people instead of a better standard of living.

It is obvious that the tendency of population to outrun the means of subsistence does not apply to all classes in the community. Indeed, the average family among the well-to-do is *smaller* than among the poor. The fact that the " preventive checks " are so powerful among the well-to-do creates a presumption that they may be important among the less prosperous classes. As a matter of fact, experience indicates that it is impossible to predict in any particular case how a gain in income will affect the growth of population. The effect depends largely upon the influence of custom. Among custom-bound peoples, the habitual standard of living is likely to be little changed by a sudden increase in income and the principal result is likely to be more people rather than a better standard of life. The work of the British government in constructing irrigation works and railroads in India and Egypt has made no great improvement in the condition of the peasants. As rapidly as more people could be supported at the old standard, population has increased.[21] The introduction of the potato into Ireland during the seventeenth century produced a similar result. The standard of living remained about the same but the number of Irish increased. On the other hand, the agricultural revolution in England during the eighteenth century resulted in both a substantial improvement in the standard of living and a great growth of population. Most fatal to the conclusions of Malthus, however, has been the course of population during the nineteenth century.

During this century, the productivity of industry and the volume of income rose more rapidly than ever before. Population, as Malthus would have predicted, also grew at an unprecedented rate. Between 1800 and 1900, the inhabitants of Europe increased from about 175,000,000 to about 390,000,000. Nevertheless, the growth in population did not keep pace with the growth in production, and the lag was so great that the people

---

[21] And yet it is not entirely accurate to say that the condition of the population has not greatly improved. The increase in population occurred primarily because the death rate has diminished rather than because the birth rate has increased. And a decrease in the death rate must itself be regarded as an improvement in the condition of the population. Certainly it carries with it in most instances a great reduction in human anguish and misery.

had time to acquire new habits and standards of living. Most remarkable of all, however, the increase in population occurred in a way very different from that which Malthus would have predicted. Malthus would have expected an advance in real wages to be followed by a rise in the birth rate as well as a fall in the death rate. During the first three-quarters of the century, however, the birth rate throughout Europe was substantially stationary and during the last quarter, it was falling in most countries. In France, it began to fall about the end of the first quarter of the century. The spectacular increase in the population of Europe, therefore, occurred on a stationary or falling birth rate. The following table shows the changes in the birth and death rates of various European countries during the last eighty years.

CHANGES IN THE BIRTH AND DEATH RATES PER 1,000 OF POPULATION IN CERTAIN EUROPEAN COUNTRIES [22]

	1841–1845			1871–1875			1905–1909			1928		
	Births	Deaths	Excess of births	Births	Deaths	Excess of births	Births	Deaths	Excess of births	Births	Deaths	Excess of births
Hungary	....	....	....	44.3ª	36.6ª	7.7ª	37.2ᶜ	26.2ᶜ	11.0ᶜ	26.1	17.0	9.1
Austria	39.6	30.0	9.6	39.3	32.6	6.7	35.6ᶜ	24.2ᶜ	11.4ᶜ	17.5*	14.4	3.1*
Italy	....	....	....	36.9	30.5	6.4	32.6	21.7	10.9	26.1	15.6*	10.5
Germany	36.7	26.1	10.6	39.2ª	26.1ª	13.1ª	32.2	18.3	14.0	18.6	11.6	7.0
Spain	....	....	....	36.5ᵇ	30.9ᵇ	5.6	34.0	24.9	9.1	29.7	18.	11.3
Netherlands	34.4	23.9	10.5	36.1	25.5	10.6	30.0	14.7	15.3	23.3	9.	13.7
Belgium	32.9	23.5	9.4	32.6	23.4	9.2	25.1	16.2	8.9	18.4	13.	5.2
England and Wales	32.3	21.4	10.9	35.5	22.0	13.5	26.7	15.1	11.6	16.6ᵈ	12.3ᵈ	4.3ᵈ
Scotland	....	....	....	35.0	22.7	12.3	28.1	16.3	11.8	19.8ᵈ	13.5ᵈ	6.3ᵈ
Denmark	30.1	19.6	10.5	30.8	19.5	11.3	28.4	14.1	14.3	19.6	11.0	8.6
Switzerland	....	....	....	30.3	23.8	6.5	26.4	16.5	9.9	17.3	12.0	5.3
Norway	30.4	17.4	13.0	30.2	17.5	12.7	26.7	14.1	12.6	18.0	10.6	7.4
Sweden	31.3	20.2	11.1	30.7	18.3	12.4	25.6	14.6	11.0	16.1	12.0	4.1
France	28.1	22.7	5.4	25.3ª	22.4ª	2.9ª	20.1	19.5	.6	18.2	16.5	1.7

ª 1876–80.   ᵇ 1866–70.   ᶜ 1901–05.   ᵈ 1927.   * Provisional figures.

[22] Based upon: Republic of France, Ministry of Labor and Social Welfare, *Statistique International du Mouvement de la Population*, pp. 68–69; League of Nations, *International Statistical Year-Book*, 1928, p. 23, and 1929, p. 52; Webb, A. D., *The New Dictionary of Statistics*, p. 66.

For the United States, satisfactory figures are not available except for recent years. In the "registration area" of 1919, the birth rate was 22.3 and the death rate 13.0. In the same area in 1927, the birth rate was 20.6 and the death rate 11.4. *Statistical Abstract of the United States*, 1930, p. 85.

The (unweighted) average excess of births over deaths in the nine countries making reports during 1841–1845 was 10.1 per 1,000 inhabitants. In 1905–1909, however, despite the substantial drop in the birth rate, the average excess of births over deaths for these same countries was 11.1. The (unweighted) average excess of births over deaths in all fourteen countries was 9.3 during 1871–1875 and 10.9 during 1905–1909. It will be observed also that the countries with the highest birth rates do not necessarily have the highest excess of births over deaths. During 1871–1875, for example, the excess averaged 8.5 in the seven countries with the highest birth rates and 10.2 among the seven countries with the lowest birth rates. But if the decline of the birth rate continues long enough, the excess over deaths is bound, of course, to diminish and eventually to disappear because the death rate cannot fall to zero. By 1928, it will be noted, the excess of births over deaths had become smaller in nearly every country. In this year also, the average excess among the six countries with the highest birth rates was distinctly larger than among those with the lowest birth rate — 9.1 against 5.4.

The experience of the nineteenth and early twentieth centuries demonstrates that, among western peoples at least, the birth rate is far more subject to human volition than Malthus suspected. The rate may even drop rapidly at a time when wages are rising rapidly. This, of course, means that the supply of labor and the general wage level are also more subject to human control than Malthus believed. One generation, by restricting the size of families in order to live better, assists its children to obtain higher wages. The rise in the wage rate does not follow for a generation. Nevertheless, it is true that the standard of living is not merely a result of the wage level — it is also the determinant of the wage level of the next generation.[23]

[23] The facts that the birth rate has been falling during a period when wages have been rising and that families tend to be smaller among the well-to-do than among the poor have led some persons to suggest that high wages *cause* a decrease in the birth rate. Possibly there is some truth in this generalization. Nevertheless, evidence which would prove it has never been assembled and the drop in the birth rate during the last fifty years appears to be mainly explained by causes other than wage movements.

VII. The Importance of Higgling

Attention has already been called to the fact that the dependence of the supply of labor upon the wage actually in effect creates an opportunity for bargaining. Another opportunity is created by the facts that many jobs are distinctly unique and that no two men have precisely the same combination of abilities.

Consider, for example, the case of a foreman who has been in charge of a department for ten or fifteen years. No small part of his value to his employer consists in his familiarity with the work of his department — with the machines, jigs, and fixtures used in different operations — and in his intimate knowledge of the capacities, deficiencies, and idiosyncrasies of his men. For another man to acquire a comparable store of information would require several years. Because of his special knowledge and experience, the foreman is worth more to the firm in his particular position than another man of equal ability. And yet much of the foreman's knowledge and experience are of value only in the job that he holds. In another plant they would be of little use. The firm could possibly afford to pay the foreman $300 a month rather than let him go, but he could probably not obtain a job elsewhere for more than $200 a month. Between $200 and $300, therefore, there is a bargaining area. The bargaining skill of the foreman and the wage policy of the firm determine where, between $200 and $300, the foreman's salary is actually set.

The opportunity for bargaining is, of course, greatest in the case of executive and technical positions, because these possess the greatest degree of uniqueness and because experience at them gives the employee the most unique value to the enterprise.[24] To a less degree, however, the opportunity for bargaining extends throughout the force. A workman may be exceptionally accurate, speedy, and industrious but the only employers who know this are those for whom he has worked. He cannot leave his present job and obtain another at several cents above the prevailing rate because of his exceptional efficiency. And yet his

[24] The Associated Gas and Electric Company advertises that 77 per cent of its executives and department heads have served their respective properties five years; 58 per cent, ten years or more; 23 per cent, twenty years or more; and 14 per cent, twenty-five years or more. *The Nation's Business*, March, 1927, v. XV, p. 122.

employer could perhaps well afford to give him three or four cents an hour more than the standard rate rather than let him go. Whether or not he obtains an extra three or four cents depends upon his bargaining skill, the willingness of his foreman to recommend an increase, and the wage policy of the employer.

VIII. THE EFFECT OF INVENTIONS UPON WAGES

Does machinery raise or lower wages? Would wages be higher if we had no machines? Is not a machine, which enables a given number of workers (counting, of course, those employed in making and repairing it) to turn out a greater quantity of goods, equivalent to an increase in the supply of labor? An increase in the supply of labor would lower wages. Will not the invention of a new machine have the same effect?

This reasoning ignores the effect of machinery upon the demand for labor. Labor cannot produce without some sort of equipment to help it. All machines are aids to labor in production. To the extent that they enable men to turn out more goods and, therefore, make labor more valuable to employers, they increase the demand for labor and raise wages. Consequently the last two centuries, which have seen such an extraordinarily rapid development of machinery, have also seen an unprecedented increase in wages.

Many persons have difficulty in seeing why machinery should raise wages because new inventions often lower wages in the particular industry in which they are used. It does not follow, however, that they reduce the *general* level of real wages. Real wages depend, of course, upon how much men can buy with their money wages. By reducing the cost of production and thus the price of goods, an invention may raise the purchasing power of wages in general more than it diminishes the money wages of particular occupational groups. This, in fact, is the typical way in which machinery raises the wage level, for most machines have an adverse effect upon the earnings of particular occupational groups.

Although machines have been largely responsible for the rapid rise in wages during the last century, it must not be imagined that they *necessarily* increase wages. It is quite possible for them to have the opposite effect. The proportions in which it is most economical to combine labor and capital depend upon the state of industrial technique. Suppose now that a new invention greatly increases the amount of capital which enterprises find it advantageous to use. It might pay managers to offer such a high price in order to obtain more capital that even out of the increased output of industry there would be less left for labor. Assume that, before the new invention, labor and capital were combined in such proportions that 60 per cent of the output of industry went to pay labor and 40 per cent to pay capital. The new invention increases the product of industry by 10 per cent but increases the need for capital and diminishes the need for labor to such an extent that it pays managers to spend as much for capital as for labor. Under these circumstances, the purchasing power of wages would fall by one-twelfth. To begin with, a product of 100 was divided: 60 to labor and 40 to capital. After the change in technique, a product of 110 is divided: 55 to labor and 55 to capital. But although this result is possible, it is extremely improbable. The proportion of industry's output which goes to labor may be reduced, but the very fact that an invention increases the total output makes it unlikely that the absolute amount of labor's share will diminish also.

IX. THE EFFECT OF WAGES UPON THE PRODUCTIVITY OF LABOR

It has been pointed out that money wages are determined in the main by the pecuniary productivity of labor — that is, by the effect of labor upon the pecuniary income of business enterprises. The more additional laborers would increase the income of an enterprise, the more the concern will bid in order to obtain additional men. It is important to notice, however, that, *within limits,* the productivity of labor may be determined by wages. This is most likely to be true during periods of falling prices. When the price of a commodity falls and thus diminishes the pecuniary productivity of the men who make the commodity, managers may be unwilling to reduce wages by a corresponding amount. They may fear that drastic wage cuts will injure the morale, and hence the efficiency, of the force. Rather than cut wages, therefore, managers may strive assiduously to find ways and means of increasing the physical productivity of labor, so that even at the lower price level the workers will be worth their wages.

Something of this sort appears to have occurred in the years immediately following the precipitous drop in prices in 1920. The great fall in prices created an imperative necessity that enterprises quickly and drastically reduce costs. Managers cut wages, but, for various reasons, they were unwilling, in most instances, to reduce them in proportion to the drop in prices. Consequently, managers were compelled to search, as they had never searched before, for ways of obtaining more output from labor. In the fifteen years from 1899 to 1914, the physical output per factory worker in the United States increased only 8 per cent. Under the pressure of falling prices, however, it increased 23 per cent in the three years, 1920 to 1923. The relationship between non-agricultural wholesale prices and physical output per factory worker during recent years is shown in the following table. A column has been added showing the trend in the hourly earnings of factory workers.[25]

	Non-agricultural wholesale prices	Physical output per factory worker	Hourly earnings of factory workers
1920	100	100	100
1923	71	123	88
1925	69	134	92
1929	68	148	102

The experience of recent years appears to demonstrate: (1) that in modern industry, with its multitude of research laboratories and its large staffs of technical specialists, the physical output per worker is exceedingly flexible and, *under favorable conditions,* can be quickly and substantially increased; and (2) that a drop in commodity prices, instead of simply producing wage cuts, may be the underlying cause for an increase in physical output per worker. But the great difficulties of British employers in adjusting themselves to a lower price level remind us that it is not always possible to counteract a drop in prices by increasing output per worker.

[25] The index of the physical output per factory worker is based upon the estimates of Woodlief Thomas and of the Research Division of the Federal Reserve Board. See *Federal Reserve Bulletin,* January, 1931, v. XVII, p. 46. The index of the hourly earnings of factory workers is based on the reports of the National Industrial Conference Board.

X. The Influence of Unions on Wages

A much disputed question is whether or not trade unions can raise the income of the wage-earning class. That unions can often raise the *wages* of those of their members who are employed admits of no doubt. Instances could be cited by the score. Unions are simply more or less complete monopolies and possess the same ability to raise prices as does any sellers' monopoly. But, at a high wage rate, fewer men will be employed than at a low one. Consequently, it is by no means certain that unions can raise the *income* even of their own members.

The ways in which unions affect wages and the income of the working class are exceedingly numerous. In some respects, unions tend to raise the income of wage earners; in other respects, to lower it. Few of their effects can be definitely measured. Consequently, it is impossible to say whether the *net* result is an increase or a decrease in the income of wage earners as a whole. Nevertheless, it is important to analyze the various ways in which trade unions affect the income of workers.

It is sometimes argued that unions cannot raise the general level of real wages because whatever they gain for their own members is lost by the rest of the working class. About 14 per cent of the non-agricultural workers in the United States are organized. If the union men succeed in raising their wages, their employers will find it profitable to use fewer men. The displaced men will undoubtedly seek work in other industries or occupations and will tend to lower wage rates there. Possibly there is no positive reduction of wages in the non-unionized occupations but simply a retardation in the long-time upward trend — a trend which is produced by the more or less constantly increasing productivity of labor.[26]

---

[26] It may be argued, for example, that the employers of unorganized men would find it impracticable to lower wages immediately after the employers of union men had raised them. To do so might provoke strikes or lead the men to organize. Some employers of non-union men might even raise wages.

This objection does not affect the outcome of the argument. If the wages in unorganized plants remain stationary or increase following an increase of wages in union plants, the average wage level will, of course, be higher but unemployment will increase. If the demand for labor is elastic, the workers will lose more through unemployment than they gain through higher wages. The *money* income of the

It cannot be predicted in a given case whether the losses of the non-unionists will exactly equal the gains of the unionists or whether they will be greater or less than the gains. *Any* of these results are possible. What result occurs in any particular case depends upon the elasticity of the demand for men in the unionized and non-unionized occupations, upon the relative wage levels in the unionized and non-unionized trades, and upon the relative numbers of men in the two classes of occupations. If the demand for men in the unionized occupations were inelastic and in the non-unionized elastic, the unions would raise the income of the entire working class. Under these conditions, an increase in the wages of unionists would produce a relatively small displacement of men and these men would be absorbed by the unorganized occupations and industries without a proportionate drop in wages. The total income of both groups of workers, union and non-union, would be greater. On the other hand, if the demand for men in the union occupations were elastic and in the non-union inelastic, unions would be unable to increase the income of the working class. By raising wages in the occupations where the demand for men was elastic, unions would cause the displacement of a more than proportionate number of men who, by entering the occupations where the demand for labor was inelastic, would cause a more than proportionate drop in wages. The total earnings of both groups would be less. If the elasticity of the demand for labor were the same in both union and non-union occupations, the effect of unions upon the total earnings of the working class would be indeterminate. In general, however, the higher wages are in union occupations relative to wages in non-union, the greater the likelihood that unions, by forcing a wage increase, will increase the total income of the working class. The reason simply is that when wages are high, a given percentage in-

---

working class, therefore, will be less. But the fact that fewer men are employed means that the output of industry will be less and the price level higher. The *purchasing power* of the workers' income will drop even more than the income in dollars. If the demand for labor is inelastic, the working class will gain through higher wages more than it loses through unemployment. Nevertheless, there is still the possibility that the higher price level will make the purchasing power of its income less than before the wage increase.

Whether the demand for labor is elastic or inelastic is not definitely known. In view of the ease with which capital can be substituted for labor in most industries, the probability is that the demand for most kinds of labor is elastic.

crease means a larger absolute increase in income and when wages are low, a given percentage decrease means a small decrease in income.[27]

The foregoing analysis is faulty because it ignores the tendency for wages to remain below the amount by which additional men would increase the incomes of business enterprises. The reasons for this discrepancy were discussed above in Section IV. The essence of the matter is that when — because of technical progress, increases in the supply of capital, or a rise in prices — the value of labor increases, employers are reluctant to bid more for new men because, if they do so, they will be compelled to raise the wages of their old employees. Rather than do this, they fail to increase their forces to the point where an additional man would add no more than the amount of his wages to the income of the concern.

Unions may raise the general wage level by diminishing this lag in the movement of wages behind the increase in the value of labor. No statistical information is available concerning the size of the usual discrepancy between actual wages and the worth of labor, but it is reasonably certain that such a discrepancy exists. As the art of management advances, as new mechanical inventions are made, and as the accumulation of capital increases the amount of equipment per wage earner, the productivity of labor

---

[27] To illustrate this point, let us suppose that the demand for labor in union and non-union occupations is as follows:

| Union occupations | | Non-union occupations | |
Wage	Demand	Wage	Demand
$1.20	9,000	52 cents	49,000
1.00	10,000	50 cents	50,000

The elasticity of the demand is the same in each case — that is, an increase of a given per cent in the wage rate reduces the number of men demanded by half that percentage. Assume that union men have been receiving $1.00 an hour and the non-union men 52 cents an hour. The union raises the wage of its members to $1.20 an hour. One thousand union men are displaced and the wage rate of the non-unionists is reduced from 52 cents an hour to 50 cents. Before the change, the total hourly income of the working class was 10,000 × $1 + 49,000 × 52 cents, or $35,480. After the change, the income is 9,000 × $1.20 + 50,000 × 50 cents, or $35,800, a gain of $320. Suppose, however, that wages in non-union occupations are much higher — 93.6 cents an hour when 49,000 men are employed and 90 cents when 50,000 are employed. In this case, the union, by raising wages and compelling 1,000 men to seek employment in the non-union occupations, reduces the total hourly income of the non-union workers from 49,000 × 93.6 cents, or $45,864, to 50,000 × 90 cents, or $45,000. This is slightly more than sufficient to offset the increase of the income of the trade unionists from $10,000 to $10,800.

increases. The increase undoubtedly occurs more rapidly at some times than at others, but there is reason to believe that it is occurring more or less constantly. Wages, on the other hand, do not go up constantly. Their course is like the steps of a stairway — possibly a 5 per cent increase is made by a plant one year and another 5 per cent several years later. If we assume that on each occasion wages are increased as much as the productivity of labor warrants, then it is obvious that *during most of the time* wages are below the productivity of labor. This is indicated by the following diagram in which the shaded area between the line P (productivity of labor in terms of dollars) and the line W (wages) represents the amount by which wages fall short of labor's productivity and the amount, therefore, by which trade unions might raise wages without causing unemployment.

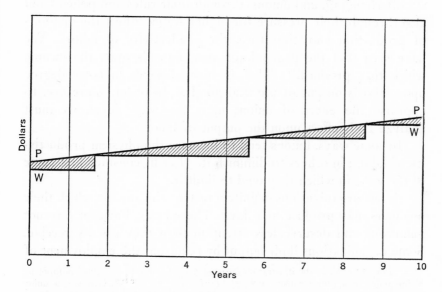

Important to notice is the fact that in so far as unions merely bring wages closer to the value of labor, they do not diminish the number of workers employed. *In fact, they may increase the number.* It will be recalled that a reason why employers may refuse to increase their forces up to the point where the output of an additional man would merely equal his wages is because to do so would require an increase in the compensation of the entire present force. But if the employees, through a union, raise their wages, the management may find it profitable to bid the same rate for additional men. If more men are willing to work at the higher rate, the wage earners achieve a twofold gain. Their money wages are higher and the purchasing power of each dollar is increased by the additional output of goods made possible by the greater volume of employment.[28]

Any attempt to analyze the influence of unions upon the wage level solely in terms of the demand for labor at a given time is unsatisfactory. When one assumes a given state of demand for labor, one necessarily assumes a given state of industrial technique, which in turn results in a certain productivity of labor and which makes it profitable for employers to hire a certain number of men at each wage. But the technique of production is constantly changing, and unions, through their rules and policies and also through their pressure for higher wages, affect the methods of production and, therefore, the productivity of labor. We have seen that the demand for men depends upon the income which they produce.[29] This, in turn, depends in large degree upon labor's output of physical goods. In order, therefore, to appraise the effect of unions upon the wage level, we must analyze their effect upon the output of labor.

In some ways, unions tend to increase the physical productivity of labor; in others to diminish it. Let us consider first some of the ways in which they tend to limit it.

A few organizations definitely restrict the amount which their members may produce in a day. These cases, however, are not numerous and deserve less attention than they usually receive. Some organizations limit output by requiring the employment of

[28] For example, in the illustration on page 619, the enterprise gained nothing by hiring more than fourteen men at $3.75 or fifteen at $4.00. If, however, a union were to increase the wage to $5.25, it would be profitable for this employer to increase his force to nineteen. It should be remarked that the difference between the actual wage and the value of labor is probably much less than was assumed in the example on page 619.

[29] Some economists have seriously misconceived the nature of the problem of whether or not trade unions can affect wages. They have regarded it simply as a static problem and have been content to explain why trade unions cannot raise wages above the point of equilibrium between supply and demand without causing unemployment. But this evades the question. The central problem is a dynamic one. The question is: Do trade unions affect the point of equilibrium between the supply of labor and the demand for labor? Do they tend to raise or lower this point?

more men on a machine or in a gang than the employer would use.[30] Many locals of the pressmen's union, for example, regulate the size of the crews on presses. Unions may limit output by opposing the use of labor-saving devices. This may take the form of excluding the device from union plants by threat of strikes or it may take the form of retarding the adoption of the device in various ways. For example, a union may insist upon exceptionally high piece rates for operations performed on a new machine (as the coal miners' union has done); it may limit the number of shifts a day during which the machine may be operated; it may require that a given number of hand workers be employed for each machine installed; it may insist that the machine be operated by expensive skilled labor when it might easily be handled by cheap, semi-skilled men. Unions may limit the productivity of their members by various make-work rules, such as the famous rule of the typographical union which requires that plate-matter be reset in each newspaper shop where it is used.[31] Probably the most important way in which unions restrict production is through their efforts to create security for their members by protecting them against discharge or lay-off. Some unions make it extremely difficult for employers to discharge the less competent men. They also prevent the lay-off of the less efficient workers during slack times by insisting that lay-offs occur according to juniority or by prohibiting lay-offs altogether and requiring that work be divided equally among the entire force. When men have little reason to fear that inefficiency will mean lay-off or discharge, one of the principal incentives for efficiency is destroyed.

But unions do not merely limit output. In many ways they tend to increase it. One way in which they do so is by their constant pressure for higher wages. Managements, of course, are never as efficient as they might be. They often do not use the

[30] It must not be assumed that the unions necessarily require the employment of an unreasonably large number of men, for the fact is that the employer, if given a free hand, would often use an unreasonably small number. The effect of the union's requirement, however, is in most cases to reduce the output per man. In a few instances, this may be compensated, to some extent, by the reduction in the number of accidents which the use of a larger crew makes possible.

[31] But even this famous rule has less effect upon output than is usually supposed, because a large part of the resetting is done in idle time. Hence the rule probably does not greatly increase the number of men employed in newspaper composing rooms.

method of production which would be most economical under the circumstances and frequently they do not strive as energetically and as persistently as they might to discover more economical methods. Competition between enterprises does not appear to be a sufficiently powerful stimulus to make managers do their best, and in many cases competition is not very intense. When a union succeeds in obtaining a wage increase, managers feel a special need of finding ways to get more work out of the force. In fact, the shock to managerial complacency which is produced by the success of the union in gaining a substantial wage increase may be precisely what is needed to jolt an administration out of a rut. An illustration of the effect of a wage increase upon managerial efficiency is furnished by the experience of a large western railroad which, on April 1, 1929, granted the union in its car repair department a wage advance of 8 per cent. In this instance, the management was an efficient and energetic one. Nevertheless, the wage increase was a spur to still greater efficiency. The car repair department is operated on a budget with a monthly allowance for labor determined at the beginning of the year. When the new wage rates took effect, the general superintendent of car equipment informed his shop superintendents that their allowance for labor would be increased by 8 per cent for the first month. The extra allowance, however, would be diminished one-sixth each month, which meant that he expected his superintendents to absorb the increase through greater efficiency and staff reductions within six months. So rapidly did the superintendents economize labor that four months after the increase took effect, the labor cost was nearly down to the original budget allowance.

Probably the greatest contribution of unions to increasing the productivity of labor occurs in piecework plants. When pieceworkers are unorganized, they often refuse, we have seen, to produce more than a certain amount for fear the employer will cut the piece rate. But when the men are protected by a union against arbitrary cuts in rates, they become willing to produce to the best of their ability. In unorganized plants, as was pointed out above, pieceworkers are ordinarily not paid for time spent in waiting for work nor are they paid for spoiled work, even if it has been spoiled through no fault of theirs. For these reasons, managements often fail to plan the work so that each worker is always busy, to provide satisfactory material, and to make repairs to equipment without delay. By insisting that the men be paid for waiting as well as for working, unions compel managers to improve the planning and scheduling of production; and by requiring that the management pay a man at the rate of his average hourly piecework earnings whenever it is responsible for his failure to earn the usual rate, unions compel managements to provide proper raw materials and to keep machines and other equipment in good repair.

In analyzing the effect of unions upon output, we must distinguish between productivity per *day* and productivity per *lifetime*. Some of the very methods which reduce productivity per day may increase productivity per lifetime. Suppose, for example, that a union succeeds in directly or indirectly enforcing a more moderate pace. One result may be 5 per cent less work each day. But another result may be an increase in the average working life of the men in industry. Unions also prolong working life by protecting the health of the men and by helping to reduce industrial accidents. Many locals of the granite cutters' union, for example, prohibit the use of hand surfacers known as "bumpers." It is impossible to provide suction to remove the dust created by the machine, and the operator must bend over in such a way that he is particularly exposed to dust. Undoubtedly the union, by prohibiting the use of the machine, reduces the daily output of the men, but the protection of their health and the prolonging of their working life must be counted as offsetting factors in estimating the net effect upon production. In many other ways, the granite cutters' union has fought against dust, the great hazard of the industry and the cause of the high tuberculosis rate among granite cutters. The photo-engravers' union has waged war against fumes. The rules of the union require that each chapel establish a committee on sanitation which is expected to make periodic reports to the local union on sanitary conditions in the shop. Perhaps the most important work of all has been done by the women's garment workers' union in New York City. For a number of years the union, together with the employers, supported a joint board of sanitary control. Shops were required to observe a code of rules governing ventilation, overcrowding, lighting, and other matters of sanitation. The board employed its own inspectors to visit the shops and to enforce the code. The sanction behind the orders of the inspectors was the refusal of the union members to work in shops which failed to observe the code.

Possibly the way in which unions exercise the greatest influence upon output per lifetime is through their restrictions against the arbitrary discharge and lay-off of men. When employers are free to " hire and fire " as they see fit, they are likely to select the older men for lay-off in times of slack business and replace them later with younger men. From the standpoint of the individual business enterprise, this is often advantageous, but from the standpoint of the community it is wasteful. Since most employers prefer to hire young men, the older men who have been displaced find it difficult to obtain steady work and are unemployed much of the time. This means that the community's labor supply is not completely utilized. When the older men do obtain work, they must often accept jobs for which they are not fitted by training and experience and at which they are less productive than at their customary occupation.[32] Unions, by prohibiting lay-offs altogether or requiring that the junior workers be laid off first, and by prohibiting discharges except for adequate cause, prevent employers from replacing older men with younger and increase the number of years at which men can obtain steady employment at their customary occupations.

Before leaving the topic, two possible long-run effects of unions upon wages should be mentioned — their effect upon standards of living and their effect upon the rate of saving.

[32] It may be argued that the waste is due to the unwillingness of the older men to accept sufficiently low rates of pay. If they are worth less than the younger men, they must expect to be paid less. And if they were willing to accept lower wages, they might obtain as steady employment as their younger competitors.

There is some merit to this argument, but in the main it is unsound. Many companies refuse to hire manual workers above the age of forty-five or fifty *at any wage.* A general rule of the company prevents the employment of such men. In explanation of this rule, it may be said that differentials in wages for the same work are always more or less unsatisfactory to administer and many managements prefer to avoid them altogether. Some managements, it is true, are willing to pay *more* than the standard rate to a few men of exceptional merit, but a differential *below* the standard rate is another matter. It may have an undesirable effect on morale, and managements avoid it by refusing to hire men above a certain age limit.

By raising the compensation of their own members, unions may raise the standard of living and hence, in the course of a generation, the wages of the entire working class. Standards of living spread by imitation from the well-to-do to the poor. It is probable, however, that the great bulk of the wage earners are influenced by the most prosperous wage earners far more than by the professional and business classes. For example, most workmen are probably little influenced by the use of automobiles by merchants or physicians. But as soon as bricklayers or plumbers or other better paid wage earners become car owners, they become intensely interested in acquiring cars. They look upon the bricklayer or the plumber as one of themselves and what he has, they expect to have also. It is probable, therefore, that unions, through raising the wages of a small aristocracy of the working class, raise the standard of living of the entire class, diminish the birth rate, reduce the future supply of labor, and thus raise wages a generation hence.

Labor organizations also influence wages through their influence upon savings. The savings of the community may be divided into three principal parts: those made by business concerns; those made by wealthy individuals; and those made by the less well-to-do. Business establishments and wealthy individuals naturally save a much larger proportion of their income than the less well-to-do. In so far as the pressure of unions for higher wages accelerates technical progress and increases the output of industry, it naturally increases the rate of saving. This increases the investment of capital in industry and tends to raise wages. In so far, however, as unions achieve higher wages at the expense of business enterprises or wealthy individuals, they tend to diminish the rate of saving, because the dollars received by wage earners are less likely to be saved than those received by business concerns or the well-to-do. The immediate effect upon wages will be extremely slight. Nevertheless, if each year slightly less capital is invested in industry, the time will eventually come when the amount of equipment per laborer and, in consequence, the pro-

---

But regardless of whether the waste is to be attributed to the labor policies of employers or to the unwillingness of older men to accept a sufficiently low wage, the fact remains that the waste exists and that it is reduced by the restrictions which unions place upon lay-offs and discharges.

ductivity and the wages of labor are less than they otherwise would be.[33]

XI. Can Wages Be Raised by Law?

Can wages be raised by law? In 1896, Victoria established boards to set minimum wage rates in a few poorly paid trades. So successful was the plan that it has been extended to scores of industries in Victoria and, in some form or another, to New South Wales, Tasmania, Queensland, West and South Australia, Great Britain, South Africa, every province of Canada, a number of states in the United States, and many other countries. In most instances, the minimum wage boards fix wages only in the so-called " sweated " trades. This is especially true of the United States, where the boards regulate only the wages of women and children. In Great Britain, however, the minimum rates apply to over 3,000,000 workers.

The experience of the minimum wage boards appears to indicate that *within certain limits* wages can be raised by government fiat. But have wages really been raised in the sense that the income of the working class has been increased? Money wages may be higher, but are not prices also higher than they would have been? And is not employment less than it would have been? May not the workers lose, through higher prices and less employment, as much as they gain through higher money wages?

Statistics of prices and employment do not enable us to answer these questions because we do not know what prices and employment would have been if the government had left wages alone. *Within limits,* however, it seems probable that the general wage level can be raised by law. The reasons for this conclusion are essentially the same as those for believing that unions are capable of increasing the general wage level. In the first place, within a dynamic society, wage rates tend to lag behind the rising value of labor to employers. This is probably more

---

[33] This must not be construed as meaning that it would be worth while for wage earners to accept lower wages now in order that their children or grandchildren may have higher wages. Whether or not it would be worth while, each individual must decide for himself in the light of his own criteria of value. And it should not be forgotten that, although wage earners by relaxing their pressure for higher compensation might accelerate the accumulation of capital, they would probably also diminish the rate of technical progress.

true of women, children, and unskilled workers, to whom minimum wage laws principally apply, than of the skilled craftsmen who make up the bulk of trade unionists. In so far as the minimum wage does not place the compensation of workers above their value to employers, it raises wages without increasing unemployment. In the second place, higher wages are likely to make labor worth more, either by causing the workers themselves to become more efficient or by improving the efficiency of the managements. A Washington employer is quoted as saying: " It (the minimum wage) has made the girls more efficient as they realize they have to make good and earn the wage or they will be discharged. It serves as an incentive better than anything we could have planned." [34] When labor is extremely cheap, as is the labor of unskilled workers, women, and children, little effort is made to keep down the rate of turnover; small care is taken to avoid creating grievances; efficient machinery for hearing and adjusting complaints is likely not to be provided; scant attention is paid to the amount of time that employees are kept waiting for work; and little is done to protect them from unnecessary discomfort or fatigue. In short, cheap labor, like cheap raw material, is likely to be used wastefully. But let labor become substantially more expensive, and managements become more concerned with how much they are getting for their money. Employment practices are improved in order to assure the selection of persons better adapted to the work; special attention is given to training new employees for their tasks; the work is more carefully routed and scheduled to avoid keeping employees idle; the reduction of labor turnover becomes a matter of real concern; a careful hunt is made for conditions which give rise to dissatisfaction; foremen are trained in handling men; workers who resign are interviewed in order to discover why each one is leaving; opportunities are created for enabling the men to bring complaints to the attention of the management; efforts are made to stabilize employment in order to avoid losing experienced employees during the slack season. The experience with minimum wage laws furnishes abundant evidence that higher wages tend to improve the management of labor. For example, the enforcement of time

[34] Bureau of Labor Statistics and Factory Inspection of the State of Washington, *Tenth Biennial Report*, 1915–1916, p. 273.

rates in the California fruit-canning industry led to better instruction of the women in the best and quickest ways of cutting and canning fruit.[35]   The canners' representatives reported to the California Industrial Welfare Commission that the minimum piece rates in the industry led to reduction of lost time and encouraged the standardization of the sizes of boxes of fruit and vegetables so that the cutters could produce more.

XII. The Relationship Between the Productivity of Labor and Real Wages

Up to this point, our analysis of the determination of wages has assumed that an increase in the productivity of labor means an increase in real wages — that is, in the quantity of goods which money wages will buy.   In general, this is true.   But great stress has been placed upon the fact that the kind of productivity which determines the demand of business concerns for labor is *pecuniary* productivity — that is, additions to the money income of enterprises.   Business establishments tend to enlarge their forces as long as the additional men increase the income of the concern by enough to cover the additional costs.   But the income of enterprises may be increased in a vast variety of ways.   Among them, it may be increased by selling the output at a higher price or by buying labor at a lower price.   A concern may hire men who, in various ways, help it to raise the price of its product or to keep down the prices which it pays for labor.   Obviously, from the standpoint of the enterprise, these employees are no less productive than those who work directly on the physical product.   And yet their effect upon real wages is precisely the opposite of the effect of the men who increase the physical output of a factory. Consequently, it is not strictly accurate to assume that a gain in the productivity of labor, resulting in an increase in the demand for labor and an advance in money wages, *necessarily* means a rise in real wages.   It may or it may not, depending upon the *kind* of productivity which has increased.

The number of men who make a living in ways which tend to reduce, rather than to increase real wages, is far from negligible. The proportion is especially large among the " white collar "

---

[35] Frankfurter, Felix, Dewson, M. W., and Commons, J. R., *State Minimum Wage Laws in Practice*, p. 50.

employees. Consider the large amount of labor employed to assist enterprises to obtain higher prices for their wares. If it is hoped to collect higher prices by obtaining a high tariff on an article, lobbyists and publicity experts must be hired to persuade Congress to enact the high duty and, later, to prevent Congress from lowering it. If a monopoly is formed to limit production and raise prices, labor must be used to devise a plan for controlling the market, to persuade the competing enterprises to accept the plan, to see that they live up to it, to persuade the public that no monopoly exists, to defend the monopoly against efforts to dissolve it or to regulate its profits, to harass competitors that spring up when it raises prices. If the charges of the monopoly are regulated by law, labor may be needed to persuade the price-fixing authorities to allow an excessive valuation on its property or to permit it to earn an excessive rate of return. In all of these cases, an increase in labor's productivity is likely to mean a decrease in real wages.

Many of the workers engaged in advertising and selling tend to lower rather than to raise real wages. Of course, in so far as salesmen arouse new desires or intensify old ones, they add to the satisfaction which consumers obtain from goods and thus tend to increase real wages. But we have seen that enterprises may attempt to increase their sales by reducing the usefulness of goods. Witness the efforts of the optical manufacturers to force the public to buy more glasses by seeking to create the convention that certain types of glasses are proper only on certain occasions.[36] Surely the men who wrote the advertising for this campaign were lowering rather than increasing real wages. To a substantial extent, goods are sold by creating pains or fears — the consumer who lacks the latest fad or frill is made to feel so uncomfortable that he or she buys in sheer self-defense. The persons engaged in creating such pains are no more raising real wages than would a man be who sought to create business for physicians by slashing passers-by. In large degree, salespeople are engaged less in arousing real desires for goods than in stimulating a momentary impulse to buy without much regard to alternatives or consequences. To the extent that they are skilled in inducing consumers to buy uncritically, they tend to reduce real wages.

[36] This attempt is discussed in Chapter XXII, p. 565.

Finally, there are the workers who are employed, in part at least, to keep down the wages of other employees — personnel experts who contrive how to keep men satisfied with meagre compensation; industrial spies hired to break up trade unions; propagandists employed to give unions a bad name; guards and special police to keep out union organizers; professional strike breakers; labor agents sent to Europe, Canada, and Mexico to stimulate a flow of cheap labor; lobbyists and publicity experts hired to oppose the restriction on immigration, to fight minimum wage laws and other labor legislation.

As more and more ways are discovered of making money by raising prices, by inducing the consumer to buy worthless goods, or at least goods which he does not desire, and by keeping down wages, real wages will tend to respond less consistently to changes in the pecuniary productivity of labor.

REFERENCES

Burns, E. M., *Wages and the State*, 1926.

Dobb, Maurice, *Wages*, 1928.

Hamilton, Walter, and May, Stacy, *The Control of Wages*, 1923.

Marshall, Alfred, *Principles of Economics* (eighth edition), 1920. Bk. VI, Ch. I, II, III, IV, and V.

Pigou, A. C., *The Economics of Welfare* (third edition), 1929. Pt. III, Ch. XII, XIV, XV, XVI, and XVII.

Rowe, J. W. T., *Wages in Theory and Practice*, 1928.

Valk, William L., *The Principles of Wages*, 1928.

CHAPTER XXV

THE LABOR BARGAIN — THE CONTROL OF WORK
AND WORKING CONDITIONS

I. SCIENCE IS MAKING THE CONTROL OF WORK AND WORKING
CONDITIONS OF GROWING IMPORTANCE.   II. INDIVIDUAL BARGAIN-
ING OVER WORK AND WORKING CONDITIONS.   III. COLLECTIVE
BARGAINING OVER WORK AND WORKING CONDITIONS.

I. SCIENCE IS MAKING THE CONTROL OF WORK AND WORKING
CONDITIONS OF GROWING IMPORTANCE

In 1925, the British Ministry of Labor investigated the qualifications of 3,331 boys and 2,701 girls of eighteen years or less
registered in the juvenile employment bureaus in all parts of
Great Britain.   Thirty-seven per cent of the boys and 25 per
cent of the girls were graded as fit to learn skilled occupations.
This superior group was designated "Class A."   Probably a
larger proportion would have been included in Class A had the
appraisal been made before the children had been subjected to
deteriorating employment.   The investigation revealed that only
59 per cent of the boys in Class A had been engaged in educative
employments.   Eighteen per cent had been in the lowest category
of jobs — in casual or seasonal work.   An investigation of the
jobs obtained by all of the boys in the sample showed that only
16.5 per cent were Class A — that is, vacancies suitable for boys
of the best type.[1]

These figures indicate an exceedingly grave situation because
they show that youths who are actually or potentially capable of
assuming responsibility and mastering skilled occupations are being converted by experience on lower grade work into lower grade
workmen.   Work is educational.   It molds the men who do it.
Consequently, it is vitally important that methods of production
shall be planned not only to turn out goods at low costs but to

[1] Davison, R. C., *The Unemployed*, pp. 184–187.

provide the kind of jobs which develop the desirable capacities of the workers. This is particularly true of the jobs held by youths from sixteen to twenty-one.

Not only is it important that jobs should help workmen develop desirable capacities, but it is also important that work should be enjoyable and that it should be done under pleasant conditions. Indeed, from the standpoint of making industry yield the maximum net satisfaction to the community, it is just as important to make work more pleasant and less onerous as it is to make farms and factories produce more commodities. Larger production that is achieved by robbing men of the opportunity to enjoy their work may be a loss instead of a gain to the community.

The principal way in which wage earners influence the nature of jobs and the conditions of work is through the labor bargain. Is this a satisfactory method? To be more specific, is it a satisfactory procedure to determine the conditions of work for common laborers in the mills of the United States Steel Corporation by the ability of the Corporation to obtain and hold men? Do the very nature of the bargaining process and the conditions under which bargaining occurs make it difficult for wage earners to put strong pressure upon employers to develop industrial technique and to organize production in such ways as to create the kind of jobs which men need? Is there a bias in our economic arrangements which makes it difficult for wage earners to give effective expression to their desire for the right kind of jobs, for pleasant working conditions, and for joy in work?

These questions are particularly pertinent today for two reasons. In the first place, science has accumulated many facts about the effects of jobs and working conditions upon men. As long as this information did not exist, there was no reason to ask whether a given method of controlling working conditions permitted the scientific knowledge of the time to be put into practice. Now, however, we cannot escape inquiring whether the labor bargain takes account of the available scientific information. In the second place, the development of industrial technique, which formerly occurred in a more or less accidental and haphazard manner, is now largely guided by the investigations of experts who devote their full time to searching for new methods of production. But when industrial change is the result of deliberate and systematic effort, it is pertinent to ask what part the interests of wage earners play in guiding the effort. If scientists endeavored to reduce the human costs of production as assiduously as they strive to reduce money costs, would they not achieve as remarkable progress in making jobs more attractive as they have achieved in making machinery more productive? But to what extent are processes deliberately modified in order to make jobs more attractive to wage earners? If such an extraordinarily efficient instrument as modern science is vigorously used to modify technique solely in the interest of more profits, regardless of the consequences to workmen and subject to little control by them, is it not true that man is a slave to industry rather than industry a servant to man?

II. Individual Bargaining Over Work and Working Conditions

There are several circumstances which hinder wage earners from exercising much control over working conditions through the medium of the labor bargain. Let us consider first the method of individual bargaining and then the method of collective bargaining.

The workers exercise their influence, it will be recalled, by discriminating in favor of the enterprises which offer the best conditions and against those which offer the worst. One of the important difficulties of wage earners is discovering which plant or which job offers the best working conditions. To make this clear, let us contrast the situation of the wage earner with that of the consumer buying articles from retailers. How does the consumer decide where he can obtain the best quality for his money? In the case of some commodities, such as automobiles, radios, vacuum cleaners, he often makes a trial of several brands before purchasing. Even when he must buy the article before using it, he can often make a thorough inspection of alternatives. He can try on B's brand of clothing without sacrificing the chance of purchasing A's brand. In many cases, he can buy a small quantity of the article and try it before deciding which brand to use. Even these methods, as we have already seen, do not give the consumer reliable information about the quality of goods, but he is far better off than the wage earner. A workman must ordinarily give up his old job before deciding in favor of a new one because most enterprises do not hire men who are already employed elsewhere. The practice of asking for references makes it difficult for an employee to hold one job while taking a day or two off to hunt for another. After a man has given up his old job, he cannot select a new one by trying out several and then taking the one which he likes best — as he can in buying a suit of clothes or a pair of shoes. He must be guided largely by what other workmen tell him about different plants. This is likely to be as inadequate a basis of choice in selecting jobs as it would be in selecting clothes or shoes.

Not only do job seekers find it practically impossible to obtain accurate information about jobs and working conditions in different plants, but even if information were available, most workmen would not appreciate its significance. Consider, for illustration, the matter of the fuel used on typesetting machines in the printing industry. In some cases, it is gas and in other cases electricity. Electricity is far superior from the standpoint of health, because imperfect combustion of gas releases carbon-monoxide gas, which, even in small quantities, produces chronic poisoning symptoms and digestive disturbances, headaches, and lassitude. But this is a hazard of which few workers are aware. Often they suspect lead poisoning when the real trouble is carbon-monoxide poisoning. Under the circumstances, the labor bargain cannot be expected to cause the substitution of electricity for gas. It is not surprising, therefore, to find nearly twice as many typesetting machines using gas as electricity. The survey of hygienic conditions in the printing trades by the Bureau of Labor Statistics disclosed 2,314 typesetting machines using gas and 1,262 using electricity.[2]

A second reason why wage earners find it difficult to control

[2] U. S. Bureau of Labor Statistics, " Survey of Hygienic Conditions in the Printing Trade," *Bulletin No. 392*, p. 228.

It may be suggested that wage earners are not interested in better working conditions and that they often show little appreciation of these conditions when they are provided. Numerous instances might be cited. But the things that men value are, in a large degree, those that they have received encouragement to value. No organized or systematic effort is being made to encourage wage earners to attach a high value to better working conditions. Consequently, the indifference of workmen to them does not necessarily indicate that better working conditions have no potential appeal. The very indifference of wage earners may itself be evidence of a bias in existing economic arrangements — a bias which tends to make the whole economic system operate with little regard for the human cost at which operations are conducted.

jobs and working conditions through individual bargaining is that this method gives relatively little influence to minorities. Again it is useful to compare the position of the wage earner with that of the consumer. The small minority of consumers who demand a better product and who are willing to pay for it usually have no trouble in obtaining it. It is more difficult for the minority of workers who wish better conditions, even at the cost of lower wages, to obtain them. A manufacturer who specializes upon the production of a superior quality ordinarily has no difficulty in getting his goods into the hands of consumers. But it is not so easy for the manufacturer who offers superior conditions and at a slightly lower wage to attract the workmen who are especially interested in better working conditions. The very fact that working conditions in different plants are not easily discovered and compared is one obstacle. Another is the fact that it is expensive and inconvenient for wage earners to travel. The failure of minorities to count in the labor market is important because the best informed and most critical part of the public, the part which sets the standards for tomorrow, is always a minority. The minority which demands something better in automobiles creates standards which the majority will expect tomorrow. Among wage earners there is a minority which is strongly interested in better working conditions because it has greater foresight than the majority and places a higher value upon future health. If it counted enough in the labor market to influence labor conditions in more plants, it could lead much of the working class to demand better conditions.

A third reason why wage earners find it difficult to influence working conditions through individual bargaining is that the labor market does not reflect changes in jobs or working conditions which result in small reductions in human cost — that is, an establishment which makes a small change which is beneficial to its employees is not able as a result to attract more men or more desirable men. For example, the fact that a job on such and such a milling machine has been made more attractive does not definitely and immediately enhance the power of the enterprise to attract labor. This means, of course, that small reductions in the human costs of production, small improvements in working conditions, do not pay the employer.

It is quite otherwise with changes which reduce the money costs of production. No matter how minute the saving, the profits of the concern are immediately increased by that amount. But changes in industrial technique typically consist of small improvements. Dramatic and revolutionary changes are the exception. Because these small changes count definitely when they make possible more output or lower money costs but are not translated into money savings for the enterprise when they produce savings in human costs, industrial research tends to focus rather exclusively upon the achievement of money savings.

But let us assume that a reduction in human costs is sufficiently large and definite to attract more desirable workmen. Is a business concern in a favorable position to take advantage of it? Can it afford to discharge old employees in order to make room for better men who might seek employment? As soon as it begins such a policy, it reduces the attractiveness of the jobs in its plant and thus tends to counteract the very things which it has done to make its jobs more desirable. One of the most important elements in the attractiveness of jobs is their permanency. As soon as the enterprise adopts an employment policy which makes its jobs less permanent, it makes them less attractive. Furthermore, the wholesale discharge of old employees in order to replace them with new men is likely to lower the morale and the efficiency of the whole force. Even though the improved conditions do attract more desirable workmen, it may not pay to discharge old employees in order to make room for new men. No similar obstacle prevents enterprises from accepting the customers who seek to purchase its wares.

Finally, individual bargaining is an unsatisfactory way of controlling work and working conditions, because employers who use methods which improve the labor supply are not sure of gaining as a result and employers who use methods which spoil the labor supply suffer no direct loss. It may not pay an employer to organize his work so as to create more jobs with educational value, because he cannot be sure of retaining the best workers developed in his shop. On the other hand, the employer who uses production methods and labor policies which spoil the labor supply does not suffer directly or immediately. In fact, he may positively gain by taking a boy who is a potential Class A workman and converting him, by the wrong kind of work, into a competent and satisfactory Class B or Class C worker who knows too little and who has too little self-confidence to resign and hunt up a better job elsewhere.[3] Frequent unemployment is likely to convert some men into unemployables. Obviously, there is a loss here, but it is spread thin over the entire community rather than concentrated upon those employers who fail to stabilize employment.

III. Collective Bargaining Over Work and Working Conditions

The sale of much labor — over 10 per cent of the supply in the United States — is governed by terms of collective bargains negotiated between trade unions and employers.[4] Do not trade unions, through their superior bargaining power, counteract the bargaining deficiencies of the individual wage earner and thus make the labor bargain a more satisfactory method for controlling the nature of jobs and of working conditions? To some extent they do. Many unions have done much to improve the educational value of jobs, to protect wage earners against demoralizing policies, and to improve working conditions. Unions raise the educational value of jobs by their rules governing the training of apprentices. These rules specify a minimum period of training, require that boys be moved from department to department and given an opportunity to acquire a broad foundation in the trade, and, in many cases, require that the employer send his apprentices to school for a specific number of hours each week. Organizations differ greatly in the care with which they super-

[3] Many employers will emphatically deny that a larger proportion of jobs of the educational type are needed. They stress the fact that really good men are scarce. This is why such constant efforts are being made to reduce the proportion of jobs which require good men. But employers view the labor supply as a whole. They do not compare the qualities of boys who are entering industry and the characteristics of the jobs for which these boys are hired. Many boys, it is true, prefer simple jobs at which they can earn fairly high wages at piecework rather than jobs which offer an opportunity to acquire useful knowledge and experience. It is also true, however, that a large proportion of the jobs offered boys and girls are either temporary or blind alley jobs. These are the most demoralizing kinds of employment and they are offered to boys and girls when their industrial habits are being formed. One reason, therefore, why employers find that good men are scarce is because of the kind of work which many boys do when they first enter industry.

[4] It was pointed out above (pp. 176–177) that approximately 14 per cent of the non-agricultural wage earners in the United States are organized. But not all trade unions have succeeded in negotiating trade agreements. It is probably safe to say that more than 10 per cent of the wage earners of the country work under trade agreements.

vise the training of apprentices, but ever since the restriction of immigration they have shown an increasing interest in apprentice training and have done much to improve it. Unions protect the quality of the labor supply by reducing the amount of intermittent and casual employment. Many organizations in seasonal trades enforce an equal-division-of-work rule which provides that during slack times no one shall be laid off but that work shall be divided equally among the force.[5] Finally, many unions have brought about substantial improvements in working conditions. On many railroads, for example, they have greatly improved ventilation, heating, and the general cleanliness of the shops; the granite cutters' union has put great pressure upon employers to control the dust hazard; the unions in the printing trades have worked hard to improve sanitary conditions in the shops.

On the whole, however, it is somewhat surprising that labor organizations have not done more to improve jobs and working conditions. In part, the explanation is found in the fact that the leaders themselves often do not possess the technical knowledge to appreciate what should be done and what easily could be done. In part, the explanation is found in the fact that unions are democratic organizations and their policies necessarily reflect the desires and the interests of their members. If the members (partly because of ignorance) are far more interested in wages and hours of work than in the educational value of jobs, in safety, or in sanitation, the leaders too are likely to concern themselves almost exclusively with wages and hours. Accomplishments which can be measured in those terms are what count in helping business agents gain reëlection.

To a substantial extent, however, the failure of unions to do more about work and working conditions is attributable to the fact that, with all their bargaining power, they are not in a strong position when it comes to dealing with relatively unimportant issues. Unions are able to inflict great loss upon employers but only at great cost to themselves. Hence the only demands upon which they can insist are ones of major importance. The strike, indeed, as an instrument of policy is comparable to war. It is suitable only

---

[5] Sometimes a distinction is made between permanent and temporary workers. The employer may be permitted to employ a limited number of temporary workers during the peak season. These must be laid off before the permanent staff is put on part time.

for settling issues when much is at stake — such issues as a general wage increase or a general reduction in hours. But the specific demands which unions might make for improvement of working conditions are rarely of sufficient importance to warrant a strike. Consider, for example, the efforts of two powerful unions, the locomotive engineers and the locomotive firemen, to obtain the vestibule cab. During recent years, the locomotive has undergone rapid development. The feedwater heater, the superheater, and the booster have been added to it; the three-cylinder locomotive has been placed in service on several roads; boiler pressures have been raised to 250 pounds. But despite the radical changes which have been made in locomotives, only a few roads — the Boston and Maine, the Canadian National, the Grand Trunk Western, the Pennsylvania, and the Union Pacific — operate some locomotives with fully enclosed cabs, and the engineers and firemen are still struggling to obtain this improvement. For a wage increase the unions can afford to strike, but not for the enclosed cab.

REFERENCES

Beveridge, W. H., *Unemployment, A Problem of Industry* (new edition), 1930.
Davison, R. C., *The Unemployed*, 1929.
Hapgood, William B., *An Experiment in Industrial Democracy*.
Hobson, J. A., *Work and Wealth*, 1914. Ch. IV, V, and XIV.

CHAPTER XXVI

THE ACCUMULATION AND THE REWARD OF CAPITAL

I. THE IMPORTANCE OF CAPITAL IN MODERN INDUSTRY

In large degree, the high per capita output of modern industry is due to the great use of capital. The best index of the use of capital is the horsepower of prime movers per wage earner. In 1849, for all industries in the United States it is estimated to have been 1.44; in 1923, 5.31, or nearly four times as much.[1] Because capital is important in production, it is also important as a source of income. Over one-fourth of the pecuniary income of the nation goes to property owners in payment for the use of their property.[2]

[1] U. S. Geological Survey, "Power Capacity and Production in the United States," *Water-Supply Paper 579*, p. 54. The figure for 1923 does not include the horsepower of pleasure automobiles.

[2] See the estimate by M. A. Copeland in *Recent Economic Changes*, v. II, pp. 766–768. The proportion of the national income that is paid for the use of capital is difficult to estimate because the owners of many unincorporated enterprises supply all or part of their capital from their own funds. The income which they obtain from their businesses, therefore, represents partly compensation for their own labor and partly a return upon their capital. Professor Copeland has estimated that about 23 per cent of the pecuniary national income is paid as interest, dividends, or rents. In addition, 20 per cent of the income is paid as profits to the owners of unincorporated enterprises. Part of this must be regarded as payment for the use of property. It is important to notice that Professor Copeland's definition of income tends to reduce his estimate of the share going to property owners for the use of their property, be-

What determines the amount of capital that is available for use by industry? What conditions are favorable to the rapid accumulation of capital and what are unfavorable? Are the methods by which capital is created economical or are they unnecessarily costly? Are they fair or unfair? What determines the rate of return received by the owners of capital? How does this return affect the rate at which capital is accumulated?

II. How Capital Becomes Available to Industry

Capital becomes available to industry in two principal ways: (1) by being discovered and (2) by being made. Discovery, of course, is the principal way in which natural resources, such as waterpowers, deposits of ore, oil, coal, or stands of timber, become available. Most forms of capital, however, — machines, buildings, bridges, railroads, vessels, — are made by men. Even farm land is in large degree a product of human effort, for it has usually been cleared and fenced, and often it has been drained and improved by fertilization.

The acquisition of capital by discovery introduces into our economy a fortuitous element of great importance. Although the application of science to prospecting is reducing chance in discovering natural resources, there is not, and probably never will be, an exceedingly close relationship between the amount of effort devoted to the discovery of natural resources and the quantity discovered. On the other hand, the amount of capital that is made depends largely upon the amount of capital and the number of men that are devoted to making it. What determines this? To some extent, business men make capital for themselves, as when a farmer spends part of his time improving his farm by clearing the land, putting in drainage, building barns, fences, roads. To the extent that he devotes himself to the improvement of his farm, he is adding to his capital. In an exchange economy such as ours, however, where making a living involves buying and selling, the additions to capital depend upon the proportion of the community's total expenditures devoted to making them rather than goods for immediate consumption. Suppose that a community spends $90,000,000,000 a year for

cause he does not count as income the undistributed profits of corporations. These profits, of course, belong to the shareholders.

consumption goods and $10,000,000,000 upon the discovery or creation of capital. It is probable that about nine-tenths of the resources of this community will be devoted to making consumption goods and about one-tenth to making additions to capital.

But what determines the proportion of the purchasing power of the community which is used for consumption goods and the proportion which is spent for the discovery or creation of capital? The money that is spent for the discovery or creation of capital comes from four principal sources: (1) the savings of individuals; (2) the savings of business enterprises; (3) taxes levied by the government; and (4) loans made by commercial banks. Not all of the funds from these sources are used to increase the community's supply of capital, for they are, of course, spent for many purposes. Nevertheless, it is from these four sources that the funds are obtained for the discovery and creation of capital. In order to explain the rate at which capital is discovered or accumulated, we must analyze the conditions which determine how many dollars each one of these sources contributes to the discovery and the creation of capital.

III. The Volume of Saving in the United States

Dr. W. I. King has estimated that during the decade 1910 to 1919 the national wealth of the United States increased nearly one-fourth. This is equivalent to an average annual gain equal to about one-seventh of the average annual income.[3] In making his estimate, Dr. King used a somewhat broader definition of saving than we are using in this chapter. He included in saving all acquisitions of durable consumption goods — automobiles, dwellings, furniture, and so forth. Nevertheless his figures may be accepted as a rough index of saving in the narrower sense of income not spent for consumption goods by the income recipient.

It is probable that today annual savings are greater than one-seventh of the national income. Between 1917 and 1926, the national income (measured in dollars of constant purchasing power) increased about 26 per cent, but the annual additions to saving and time deposits and the assets of life insurance and building and loan funds (also expressed in dollars of constant

[3] King, W. I., "The Net Volume of Saving in the United States," *Journal of the American Statistical Association*, December, 1922, v. XVIII, p. 463.

purchasing power) increased over one-third.[4] At the present time, the annual savings of the country are probably close to $15,000,000,000.

The volume of saving is widely variable from year to year — much more so than the volume of the national income. Dr. King's estimates for the period 1909 to 1917 are as follows:[5]

	National income (in millions of 1913 dollars)	Savings (in millions of 1913 dollars)	Percentage change in national income	Percentage change in savings
1909	$30,608	$5,231	–	–
1910	32,176	5,509	+5.1	+5.3
1911	31,397	4,289	−3.4	−23.3
1912	33,985	5,298	+7.6	+23.6
1913	35,436	4,880	+4.3	−7.9
1914	33,067	4,140	−6.7	−15.1
1915	35,150	7,381	+6.3	+78.4
1916	41,669	11,401	+18.6	+55.9
1917	42,377	7,162	+1.7	−37.2

It will be observed that the national income and the volume of savings fluctuate together in all years except two, but that the fluctuations in savings are substantially greater than those in the national income.

Most of the saving is done by individuals and by business enterprises. The savings of both individuals and business enterprises vary considerably from year to year and in some years one is substantially greater than the other. Over a period of time, however, they appear to be about equal. The following table, based on the estimates of Dr. King, is a rough comparison of the savings of business enterprises and all other non-governmental savings of the community for the period 1909 to 1916. Nearly all of the non-governmental and non-business savings are made by individuals. To some extent, however, additions to the national wealth are made possible by funds supplied by commercial banks. These amounts are included in the non-governmental and non-business savings. Consequently, the totals in this column are slightly larger than the savings of indi-

[4] Sprague, O. M. W., and Burgess, W. R., " Money and Credit and their Effect on Business," *Recent Economic Changes*, v. II, p. 674.

[5] *Journal of the American Statistical Association*, December, 1922, v. XVIII, p. 467.

viduals. For the entire period, business savings (expressed in dollars of 1913 purchasing power) were $23,201,000,000 and other non-governmental savings were $25,120,000,000. The savings of individuals were probably less than $24,000,000,000.[6]

	Non-governmental and non-business savings in 1913 dollars	Savings by business enterprises in 1913 dollars
1909	$2,823,000,000	$2,460,000,000
1910	2,669,000,000	2,840,000,000
1911	2,301,000,000	1,970,000,000
1912	2,595,000,000	2,710,000,000
1913	2,478,000,000	2,401,000,000
1914	2,766,000,000	1,410,000,000
1915	4,082,000,000	3,260,000,000
1916	5,406,000,000	6,150,000,000

The estimates for the individual years are admittedly very rough and are undoubtedly less accurate than the totals for the period. It should be noted also that the savings of many individuals take the form of the purchase of durable consumption goods such as houses and automobiles. Hence, although the savings of individuals are about as large as the savings of business enterprises and possibly slightly larger, business savings are undoubtedly more important than individual savings as a source of capital.

IV. Saving by Individuals

If we deduct from the national income the savings of business enterprises and the government and the non-pecuniary forms of income, such as the rental value of owned urban homes and interest on the value of other consumption goods, we have the

---

[6] The estimates of Dr. King were published in the *Journal of the American Statistical Association*, December, 1922, v. XVIII, pp. 455-470.

The savings of individuals are estimated by subtracting from Dr. King's estimate of the total savings his estimate of business savings and increasing or decreasing the resulting figure by the amount of the net debits or credits of the federal government. This takes no account of savings of the state and local governments. Dr. King's estimates of the national savings and of business savings cover the years 1917 and 1918 also. It is impossible to make even a rough approximation of individual savings for these years by deducting the business savings from the total savings and by adding the net debits of the government. The large debits of the government were made possible by borrowing but this borrowing did not entirely represent saving by individuals because the bonds of the government were purchased in large degree by business enterprises and because also they were purchased with funds which individuals borrowed from banks.

total amount of pecuniary income from which individuals might make savings. The estimates of Dr. W. I. King show that, during most of the period 1909 to 1916, individuals saved slightly less than 10 per cent of their pecuniary income. The estimates (expressed in dollars of 1913 purchasing power) are as follows:

	Income in millions of 1913 dollars (excluding business savings and non-pecuniary income) [7]	Non-business and non-governmental savings in millions	Per cent of income saved
1909	$26,599	$2,823	10.7
1910	27,581	2,669	9.7
1911	27,644	2,301	8.3
1912	29,483	2,595	8.8
1913	31,191	2,478	7.9
1914	29,907	2,766	9.2
1915	29,871	4,082	13.7
1916	32,359	5,406	16.7

It will be observed that, as a rule, slightly less than 10 per cent of the income was saved. It cannot be said that changes in the annual volume of savings correspond closely to changes in the total income, because in only two out of seven cases were the changes in the same direction. But the estimates are so rough that no significance should be attached to correspondence or lack of correspondence between the movements of income and the movements of savings.

What determines the volume of individual savings? A few persons have such large incomes that, after they have gratified all their desires for goods, they still have part of their incomes unspent. For example, in 1919 there were 521 persons in the United States who had incomes of $500,000 or over. Their total income was $536,000,000.[8] It is highly probable that most of this half billion dollars was saved because the recipients had completely satisfied their desires in so far as money could provide satisfaction and had nothing else to do with most of their

[7] The estimates for the national income are the revised estimates of the National Bureau of Economic Research given by Dr. W. I. King in the *Journal of the American Statistical Association*, December, 1922, v. XVIII, p. 467. The estimates of the non-pecuniary income (deducted from the total national income) are found in *Income in the United States*, v. II, p. 231.

[8] National Bureau of Economic Research, *Income in the United States*, v. I, p. 136.

dollars except to save them. But saving of this sort accounts for only a small part of the saving by individuals. Dr. King has made a rough estimate on the assumption that any one can spend $50,000 without completely satisfying his desire for goods.[9] In 1918, the total income of persons receiving more than $50,000 a year was about $2,730,000,000.[10] If $50,000 is deducted from the income of each of the persons receiving more than $50,000 in 1918, the remainder is $657,000,000. This is slightly more than one-seventh of the average annual non-business savings during the nine years 1909 to 1917.[11]

For more than 99 per cent of the population, however, it is safe to say, saving involves letting some immediate desires go unsatisfied. The estimates of the National Bureau of Economic Research indicate that, in 1926, 99 per cent of the income recipients received less than $8,309 a year, and 99.89 per cent less than $41,543.[12] For nearly all of these persons, it is probable that saving means going without goods which they would be glad to consume. But this must not be interpreted as meaning that saving involves sacrifice, because it is a reasonable inference that most of the persons who save gain more satisfaction by so doing than they would by spending all of their income at once.[13] Otherwise they presumably would not save. It does mean, however, that the amount invested by these persons of moderate or small incomes depends upon the satisfaction which they derive from the possession of investments in comparison with the gratification which they would obtain from the purchase of larger quantities of goods for immediate consumption. The fact that a man saves $500 instead of spending it for consumption goods indicates that (in so far as he compares alternatives in spending his money) he believes that an investment of $500 will yield him the greater satisfaction.

[9] *Journal of the American Statistical Association*, December, 1922, v. XVIII, p. 466.

[10] National Bureau of Economic Research, *Income in the United States*, v. I, p. 136.

[11] This proportion is computed by reducing to dollars of constant purchasing power both the figure $657,000,000 and the average annual savings exclusive of savings by business enterprises.

[12] King, W. I., *The National Income and Its Purchasing Power*, pp. 173–175.

[13] Some persons undoubtedly save out of habit who would be happier not saving so much or possibly not saving at all.

But what determines the amount of money which people prefer to invest rather than to spend for immediate consumption? One important determinant is the ability of men to visualize their future needs for money — their foresight. When a man saves to provide for his old age or to provide for his family in the event of his death, or simply because he considers it wise to be prepared against unforeseen and unforeseeable emergencies, his saving may be regarded as a manifestation of foresight. But there is a vast amount of saving which is not a result of foresight. In fact, in a few cases it may even reflect a lack of foresight, as when a man of small means saves to buy an automobile which he can ill afford. Among the wealthy, saving primarily reflects the fact that incomes are larger than the recipients can conveniently spend on consumers' goods. Among the less well-to-do, much saving reflects the desire for certain goods — a house, a farm, an automobile, a piano, a radio, a trip, an education for one's children — which are too expensive to be purchased out of current income.

The source of a man's income is likely to influence how much he saves. Suppose that two men each have an income of $6,000 a year. One derives his solely from property, the other receives his as a salary. Other things being equal, the second man is more likely to save than the first. The man who works for a salary must expect to retire some day. He must save enough to provide for himself and his family after his salary ceases. But the first man will continue to receive income from his property indefinitely. He feels no such urgent need to provide for his old age.

Undoubtedly the most important determinant of the volume of individual saving is the size of men's incomes. Many desires for consumable goods — desires for food, clothing, shelter, heat, and amusement — are exceedingly intense and urgent. Not until these desires are fairly adequately satisfied are most men willing to save a very large part of their incomes. This, of course, means that by far the largest part of the country's saving is done by the rich. Unfortunately we lack statistics showing the total amounts saved by persons in different income groups. The estimates of the National Bureau of Economic Research indicate that about one-fourth of the income recipients obtain

about one-half of the national income.[14]   In 1918, the highest
fourth of the income receivers had incomes of about $1,500 or
over.[15]   It is safe to say that these persons do nearly all of the
saving by individuals — probably nine-tenths.   In 1918, less
than 9 per cent of income receivers, all of whom had incomes of
$2,500 or more, had nearly one-third of the national income.
The estimates of Professor M. A. Copeland indicate that, in
1925 and 1926, it was still true that about one-tenth of the income recipients received about one-third of the national income.[16]

It is probable that the 10 per cent of the income recipients
who have about one-third of the national income do substantially
more than half of the saving by individuals.   In fact, if we assume that the proportion of their income saved by the 10 per cent
who have the largest incomes is three times the proportion saved
by the other 90 per cent — a conservative assumption — it follows that three-fifths of the saving by individuals is done by
one-tenth of the income receivers.   And if we assume that the
proportion of income saved by the one-tenth who have the
largest incomes is four times the proportion saved by the remaining nine-tenths, then the 10 per cent most well-to-do save two-
thirds of the amount saved by individuals.[17]

V. Saving by Business Enterprises

Saving by business enterprises, we have seen, probably exceeds saving by individuals.   But business savings are far more
variable from year to year than individual savings.   During the
period 1909 to 1916, for example, the low point of business savings (when expressed in dollars of constant purchasing power)

---

[14] *Income in the United States*, 1909–1919, v. I, pp. 134–135.

[15] Between 1918 and 1927, the per capita income of the country increased
about 17 per cent.   Consequently, it is probable that at the present time the highest
fourth of the income receivers begins somewhat above $1,500.

[16] " The National Income and its Distribution," *Recent Economic Changes*, v. II,
p. 836.

[17] If the volume of saving by individuals tends to vary with their incomes, it
might be expected that changes in the volume of individual saving from year to year
would correspond to changes in the volume of individual income from year to
year.   But, during the period 1909 to 1916, we have seen that such correspondence
existed in only two cases out of seven.   Attention has been called, however, to the
rough character of these estimates.   Consequently, no great significance should be
attached to the failure of changes in the volume of savings to correspond to changes
in the volume of income.   In the long run, it is safe to conclude that the volume of
savings tends to change with the volume of income.

was $1,410,000,000, or nearly $900,000,000 less than the low point of individual savings. The high point of business savings was $6,150,000,000, or nearly $750,000,000 more than the high point of savings by individuals. According to the estimates of Dr. King, business savings between 1909 and 1917 varied from scarcely one-third of all savings in 1914 to nearly three-fourths in 1917.[18] Business savings, however, appear to be more responsive than individual savings to changes in the national income. This is indicated by a later estimate of savings by corporations which Dr. King has made for the period 1909 to 1926. During this seventeen-year period, changes in corporate savings corresponded to changes in corporate profits in sixteen years and to changes in the total national income in eleven years.[19]

What proportion of their earnings do business enterprises save? No complete statistics are available, but Dr. King's estimate of corporate savings for the period 1909 to 1926 indicates that corporations saved 40.5 per cent of their profits.[20] This is no doubt a larger proportion than would hold true for all enterprises, because the available reports probably do not adequately represent the relatively unsuccessful concerns which save little or nothing.

The proportion of profits saved by business concerns varies tremendously from year to year. In 1921, a year of severe depression, there were no net savings — the dividends of corporations during that year were over five times their profits. In 1914, another year of depression, 23.3 per cent of the profits were saved; and in 1924, a year of mild depression, 34.6 per cent. On the other hand, in 1917, savings were 62.6 per cent of profits; in 1919, 61.7 per cent; and in three others (1915, 1916, and 1918) over 50 per cent.

Why do business enterprises save? There are two principal reasons — their need for more capital and the great fluctuations in their profits from year to year.

If a newly established concern is successful, it is almost cer-

---

[18] *Journal of the American Statistical Association*, December, 1922, v. XVIII, p. 470.

[19] King, W. I., *The National Income and Its Purchasing Power*, pp. 74, 278, 280, and 285.

[20] *Ibid.*, pp. 278, 280, and 285.

tain to find itself in need of more capital. Each additional order increases the need for working capital because, even if the customer pays cash, the enterprise must meet pay rolls and possibly pay for raw materials before the finished goods reach the customer. And, of course, some customers do not pay cash. If the concern expands very rapidly, it may be compelled to purchase additional equipment. But the very fact that an enterprise is new and has not demonstrated its earning power over a series of years may prevent it from obtaining additional capital on favorable terms. Reinvestment of earnings, therefore, may constitute the most economical way of raising funds. Or a concern may be able to obtain capital on reasonably favorable terms but the owners may prefer not to admit other capitalists into the business or they may prefer not to jeopardize their control by borrowing and thus creating fixed charges which may be difficult to meet in years of depression.

But old, established concerns, as well as new ones, are likely to find it necessary or desirable to supply their needs for capital by reinvesting part of their earnings. The need for more capital may come at a time when it is not easy to raise funds by selling stock or bonds. Furthermore, an enterprise cannot sell bonds on favorable terms unless its income, after the deduction of operating expenses and interest charges on previous bond issues, is substantially greater than the interest charges on the proposed bond issue. This means that the need for more capital must be satisfied in part by increases in the investment of the stockholders. The easiest way to increase the investment of the stockholders, however, is to reinvest part of the profits in the business. It is cheaper, quicker, and less trouble than to sell more stock to the public or even to the existing stockholders.[21]

But probably the most important reason why enterprises reinvest part of their earnings is because of the violent fluctuations

[21] During the last few years, a number of companies have followed the practice of paying no cash dividends on the common stock. Instead, common stockholders are paid in scrip which is convertible into additional shares of stock. The stockholder who wishes a cash return must sell his scrip or convert it into stock and sell the stock. In this way, the stockholders can obtain a cash return and the enterprise can reinvest all of the net earnings in the business.

in their earnings from year to year. These fluctuations are particularly large because of the business cycle and also because of the importance of fixed costs in most industries. But the stockholders expect a steady return upon their investment. Particularly do they object to decreases in the dividend rate. And, of course, an enterprise which has difficulty in maintaining its dividend rate has difficulty in selling its stock and this, in turn, handicaps it in selling its bonds. Consequently, in years of good business, the directors do not distribute all of the earnings in dividends. They put the dividend rate at about the amount which the concern will be able to pay in poor years and they reinvest the amount left over. And, as the net income of the enterprise rises, there is likely to be a delay in the increase in the dividend rate. The course of the net earnings and the dividend disbursements over a ten-year period may be somewhat as follows:

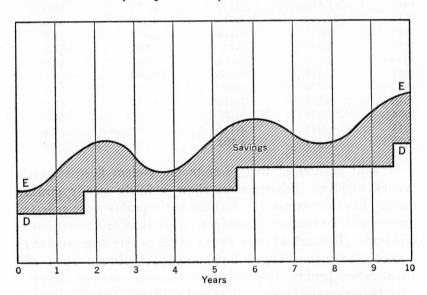

Curve E represents net earnings, curve D dividend disbursements, and the shaded area savings. If the directors had been willing to advance the dividend rate so rapidly that subsequent reductions were necessary, the savings of the enterprise would, of course, have been less, but its ability to raise capital would also have been less.

The policy of not raising dividends above the point at which it is expected that they can be permanently maintained is reflected in the annual dividend disbursements and the annual savings of business enterprises. In the following table are given Dr. King's estimates of the profits, dividend payments, and savings of corporations in the United States for the decade 1909 to 1926: [22]

	Profits (millions)	Dividends (millions)	Savings (millions)	Percentage of profits saved
1909	$2,887	$1,560	$1,317	45.6
1910	3,024	1,839	1,185	39.2
1911	2,600	1,881	719	27.7
1912	3,252	1,971	1,281	39.4
1913	3,630	2,187	1,443	39.8
1914	2,679	2,055	624	23.3
1915	4,248	2,074	2,174	51.2
1916	8,109	3,336	4,773	58.9
1917	10,101	3,774	6,327	62.6
1918	7,672	3,544	4,128	53.8
1919	8,416	3,226	5,190	61.7
1920	5,873	3,111	2,762	47.0
1921	458	2,958	−2,500	−546.1
1922	4,770	2,649	2,121	44.5
1923	6,308	3,346	2,962	47.0
1924	5,363	3,509	1,854	34.6
1925	7,621	4,158	3,463	45.4
1926	7,505	4,764	2,741	36.5

It will be noticed that, despite the violent fluctuations in profits, dividend disbursements show a fairly steady upward trend. In other words, the fluctuations in profits were reflected primarily in fluctuations in savings rather than in fluctuations in dividends. Between 1910 and 1911, when profits dropped $424,-000,000, savings dropped $466,000,000; between 1913 and 1914, when profits dropped $951,000,000, savings dropped $819,000,000; and between 1917 and 1918, when profits dropped $2,429,000,000, savings dropped $2,199,000,000. In the first case, the drop in savings absorbed all of the decrease in profits; in the second case, five-sixths of the decrease; and in the third case, over nine-tenths. Because of the policy of corporations' paying out only a part of their profits, dividend payments become close

[22] King, W. I., *The National Income and Its Purchasing Power*, pp. 278, 280, and 285.

to a fixed return — not fixed in the sense that there is an obligation to pay them, but fixed in the sense that the volume of dividend disbursements *for industry as a whole* is not likely to drop substantially even during periods of depression. In the disbursements of individual enterprises there is, of course, much greater variation.

VI. Saving by the Government

When the government invests part of its current income — that is, its income from taxation — in permanent improvements, such as roads, buildings, bridges, canals, levees, sewerage systems, irrigation works, it is saving just as an individual is saving when he invests part of his current income. In so far as public works are financed by borrowing, they do not, of course, represent saving by the government. The saving is done (subject possibly to a few exceptions) by the purchasers of the government bonds.[23] No satisfactory estimate of the amount of governmental saving exists. Some states — Wisconsin, for example — are not permitted by their constitutions to incur a public debt, and all of the public works constructed by the state itself are paid for out of income.

But suppose that a government raises funds for a public improvement through taxation. Is the net amount of saving in the community increased? If the public is taxed more, does it not save just so much less? Does saving by the government appreciably increase the total volume of saving in the community?

The answer depends upon the nature of the taxes and upon who pays them. If the money is raised by a sales tax which falls largely upon commodities that are elastic in demand, it may possibly diminish the volume of individual saving very little. But a tax on a commodity that is inelastic in demand is likely to diminish the volume of saving by individuals. The result will depend upon whether the demand for investments is more elastic than the demand for consumption goods. If it is, the amount invested will be reduced and the expenditures for consumption goods will remain about the same.

The result also depends upon who pays the taxes. In so far

[23] When the government reduces its indebtedness, it is, of course, saving.

as the taxes fall upon the very rich, there is likely to be a drop in individual savings by the amount of the taxes. The rich are likely to satiate their desires for consumption goods and save the remainder of their incomes. Higher taxes, therefore, do not cause the wealthy to spend less on consumption but do diminish the amount which they have left over to invest. If the taxes fall on the very poor, the result is likely to be much the same — except that the very poor do not save much. But they can so ill afford to cut their consumption, that a tax is likely to reduce greatly their small savings. Among the middle income groups, a tax is likely to diminish savings somewhat, but not by the amount of the tax. Persons in this class do not simply save what they have left after they have satisfied their desires for consumption goods quite completely. And much better than the poor can they afford to cut their consumption in order to maintain their savings. When the state raises money for permanent improvements by a tax that falls in the main upon the middle classes, the total amount of saving in the community is most likely to be increased.

VII. How Commercial Banks Help Create Capital

Some of the dollars used to create or to discover capital are not saved — they are supplied by commercial banks through loans. We have already discovered that the commercial banks do not have to have a dollar for every dollar that they lend. They are able to lend far more dollars than they possess. Hence most of the dollars which they supply to be used in creating or discovering capital are not saved by anyone. They are created by the commercial banks.[24]

How are the dollars lent by the commercial banks used to create capital? Perhaps the simplest case is that of a man who borrows $1,000 from the bank with which to buy a bond. The enterprise that sells the bond obtains money with which it can buy capital goods just as if the buyer had paid for the bond with money that he had saved. Or a syndicate of bankers may purchase a bond issue or stock issue with funds borrowed from com-

[24] For a more extended discussion of this topic see H. G. Moulton's paper: " Commercial Banks and Capital Formation," *Journal of Political Economy*, July, 1919, v. XXVII, pp. 590–600.

mercial banks. Some of the newly issued stock is likely to be purchased by speculators on the stock exchange. In this case, it is probably paid for largely with funds borrowed from commercial banks.[25] Finally, a business enterprise may itself borrow from a bank the funds with which to purchase a machine or a motor truck.

In all of these cases, however, the loans by the commercial banks are for a short period only and, when they mature, are they not repaid out of savings? The man who borrows from his bank in order to pay for a bond, for example, must soon repay the loan and, when he does so, he presumably repays it out of savings. In the last analysis, the bond is paid for with savings. Likewise, a business enterprise which borrows from a commercial bank in order to buy a machine must soon expect to be able to repay the loan out of earnings. This means that the concern is eventually paying for the machine out of savings from earnings. But if the money used to finance the creation or the discovery of capital eventually comes out of savings, is it correct to say that the creation or discovery of some capital is financed with funds supplied by commercial banks rather than out of savings?

In answer to this question, it should be noticed that in some cases the loans made by commercial banks may be repaid with other loans made by commercial banks. The investment in capital goods may be financed, therefore, by an indefinite succession of short-term loans. This is likely to be true when commercial loans are used to finance speculation in stock. The stock is purchased with borrowed money and sold by the first purchaser to another speculator who pays with borrowed money and who sells to a third speculator who likewise pays with borrowed money. In cases where the loans of commercial banks are repaid indefinitely with money supplied by other loans from commercial banks, it is clear that the creation and the discovery of capital is being financed, not by savings, but by dollars created by commercial banks.

Nor does it make any essential difference that many loans

---

[25] The borrowing is done by the broker instead of the speculator but this, of course, does not alter the fact that the stock is purchased largely with money supplied by a commercial bank. The speculator may advance his share of the price (his " margin ") out of savings or he may borrow it.

by commercial banks for the purchase of capital goods are repaid out of savings. As the old loans are repaid, the banks make new ones for the purchase of additional capital goods. The result is that a large number of credit dollars supplied by commercial banks are *constantly* invested in capital goods. But the *specific objects* in which the dollars are invested are constantly changing, as some loans are repaid out of savings and new loans are made for the purchase of additional capital goods.

During the last seven or eight years, there has been a pronounced tendency for commercial banks to play a more and more important rôle in financing the acquisition of capital goods. This is indicated by the rapid increase in loans on securities. It is not meant to imply that every loan on securities is used to finance the acquisition of capital. Nevertheless, it is probable that this is the purpose of most loans on securities and that the relative change in the volume of these loans indicates relative changes in the volume of credit advanced by the commercial banks for the purchase of capital goods. It was pointed out in Chapter XI that between December, 1921, and December, 1929, the loans on securities of about 700 large banks, which possess nearly half of the banking resources of the country, increased from $3,765,000,000 to $7,968,000,000, or 112 per cent. All other loans increased less than one-fourth.[26]

But even if the commercial banks supply a large number of dollars for the purchase of capital, do they actually increase the rate of capital accumulation? By creating more dollars to be used in the purchase of capital, do they not raise the general price level? This, of course, would mean that things in general, including capital goods, cost more. Although more dollars are being spent for capital, will they buy any greater physical quantities of equipment than could have been bought by the savings of the community, provided the commercial banks had not raised the price level by lending dollars for the purchase of capital?

It is, of course, true that when commercial banks lend money for the purchase of capital goods, they increase the total number of dollars in the community. If the total output of goods does

---

[26] See pp. 239–240.

not increase in proportion, then the average price level must rise. But it does not follow that the amount of capital goods purchased is no greater than it was at the lower price level. The reason is that *a larger proportion* of the community's expenditures are now for capital goods. This can be made clear by a simple illustration. Suppose that a community consists of 100,-000 wage earners each of whom receives $1,000 a year. Each worker spends $900 of his income on consumers' goods and invests $100. The total outlay for consumers' goods is, therefore, $90,000,000 a year and for capital $10,000,000. Presumably nine-tenths of the workers in the community are engaged in making consumers' goods and one-tenth are adding to the capital of society. Assume now that commercial credit is used to finance the acquisition of capital. Suppose that $10,000,000 a year is borrowed for this purpose. To keep our illustration as simple as possible, let us assume that the entire $10,000,000 is spent to hire more labor in the plants that produce capital goods. As the total number of workers in the community remains unchanged, a larger proportion of them are engaged in making capital goods and a smaller proportion in making consumers' goods. The total outlay for labor is now $110,000,000 a year instead of $100,000,000 and the annual wage of each worker is $1,100 instead of $1,000. But if a larger number of men are employed in making capital goods and a smaller number in making consumers' goods, the output of consumers' goods will decline and the prices of consumers' goods will rise even more rapidly than the rest of the price level. The higher prices of consumers' goods in relation to wages may compel some persons to reduce their savings. It is unlikely, however, that saving will fall sufficiently to offset the dollars which the banks are lending for the purchase of capital. Let us assume that the relatively high prices of consumers' goods cause the wage earners to reduce their savings from $100 to $50 a year. The total outlay of the community, therefore, is $95,000,000 for consumers' goods and $15,000,000 for capital — $5,000,000 from the savings of the workers and $10,000,000 supplied by the banks. Instead of nine-tenths of the workers being employed in making consumers' goods, only nineteen-twenty-seconds are so employed — instead of 90,000, only 86,363. The output of consumers' goods temporarily drops in proportion — by slightly more than 5 per cent. But the number of men engaged in making capital goods increases from 10,000 to 13,637 and the output of capital goods may be assumed to increase in proportion, or by over 36 per cent. Eventually, of course, the larger supply of capital raises the output of both capital and consumers' goods.

In judging the effect of commercial credit upon the rate of capital formation, it is important to observe that the volume of savings is likely to be sluggish in responding to an increase in the demand for capital. The demand for capital is likely to grow rather suddenly with a boom in business which creates the prospect of greater profits. The rate of saving, on the other hand, can increase only after income has been received. In the case of business enterprises, this means that saving can occur only after profits have been realized. In the case of individuals who receive a large part of their incomes through dividends, it means that an increase in the rate of saving must wait on advances in dividend rates. For these reasons, it is conceivable that an increase in the demand for capital might spend itself mainly in producing a rise in interest rates rather than an acceleration in the volume of capital accumulation. This result is prevented by the use of commercial credit in financing capital creation. Commercial credit provides a way by which dollars can be made immediately available to finance an increase in the output of capital goods and thus makes it unnecessary for an increase in capital to wait on the sluggish response of saving to the demand for more capital.

VIII. The Demand for Present Purchasing Power

What determines the reward of those who invest funds in industry? The reward is affected by whether the investor lends money to industry or whether he becomes an owner of industry. In the first case, it depends upon the rate of interest prevailing in the community. In the second, it depends *in large degree* upon the rate of interest, but also upon other factors which peculiarly affect the return of business owners. In this section, we shall analyze the determination of the rate of interest; in the next chapter, we shall analyze the peculiar conditions which affect the return received by business owners. The rate of interest, like other prices, is determined by supply and demand. We have analyzed some of the principal determinants of the supply of funds seeking investment. What determines the demand for loans?

When a man borrows $1,000 for one year at 6 per cent, at the end of the year he pays the lender $1,060. This may seem improvident, because the borrower is giving $1,060 for $1,000. The reason why it is not necessarily improvident is because the borrower receives the $1,000 *now* and pays the $1,060 *a year hence*. In other words, interest represents the premium which men are willing to pay for present purchasing power. There are many reasons why men are willing to pay this premium. One is that money is often more useful to them today than it is likely to be a year or so later. A farmer may need funds to support his family until his crops are harvested or sold; a laborer may need money to pay living expenses while he is incapacitated by sickness or accident or while he is unemployed because of industrial depression; a man may need money to buy legal aid or medical advice. In cases such as these, when the immediate need for funds is acute, a borrower may be willing, if necessary, to pay several hundred dollars a year hence in order to obtain a hundred dollars today.

In less urgent cases, men may be willing to pay a premium for present purchasing power simply in order to avoid waiting a year or two before buying an expensive commodity, such as an automobile, a radio, a piano, or a house. The interest which the borrower pays on his loan means in essence that he is paying so much more for the article. But he is willing to do this in order to have the article now. The rate of interest which he is willing to pay depends, of course, upon how strongly he objects to waiting for the automobile or radio or whatnot until he has saved the purchase price.

A substantial part of the demand for funds comes from the government. This demand is largest, of course, in time of war but even in times of peace the government borrows huge sums to pay for roads, buildings, various forms of public works, bonuses or " loans " to former soldiers, and even to cover deficits in the budget.

Except in time of war, by far the greatest demand for funds comes from business enterprises. The reason why business men are willing to pay a premium for present funds is because they see (or think that they see) opportunities for making profits by the use of money. If, for example, a business man believes that in the course of a year he can increase $1,000 to $1,100, he may be willing to pay $60 or even $99 for the use of $1,000 for one year. The amount that he is willing to pay depends (1) upon how much profit he expects to make and (2) upon what he believes to be his chances of making it. The total demand for funds from business enterprises depends, of course, upon how many opportunities of making profit by the use of more funds managers have succeeded in discovering.

The business demand for funds breaks up into several parts because money may be used to make a profit in a multitude of ways. It may be employed to raise the price of goods. This is the *monopoly use* of money. The funds may be used to obtain a patent, a franchise, a tariff, or to purchase control of competing plants. The creation of a more or less complete monopoly enables the producers to raise the price. Interest on the funds used in creating the monopoly is paid from the difference between the competitive price of the commodity and the monopoly price.

Money may be used to make a profit by anticipating the future price movements of commodities or securities and buying in anticipation of a rise. This may be called the *speculative use* of money. Closely related to it is the *working capital use* of money. A large part of the business of the community consists in buying goods from those who have them to sell and selling them to others who are willing to pay a higher price for them. But since the middleman must hold the goods some time before he finds a buyer for them, he must have funds. He can afford to pay interest for money as long as he can find buyers who are willing to pay him enough to cover the cost of the goods and the expenses of operating his business, including the interest on the borrowed funds. The output of a factory or a farm depends in part upon the amount of working capital which it has. One way of increasing the output of a factory, for example, is to introduce more minute subdivision of labor. In our analysis of specialization, it was pointed out that although the subdivision of labor enhances the productivity of labor and capital, it usually lengthens the productive process and increases the amount of partially fabricated material which the enterprise has in its possession.[27] Consequently, the achievement of the advantages of more minute subdivision of labor depends upon the possession of more working capital.

Finally, funds may be used to make a profit by increasing the equipment used in industry, by purchasing more machines or buildings. This may be called the *fixed capital use* for money.

Business men continue to demand funds as long as additional capital promises to yield enough additional income to pay the interest. The number of dollars on which they can afford to pay 5 per cent is, of course, greater than the number on which they can afford to pay 6 per cent. A few monopolies may be so profitable that business men could afford, if necessary, to pay 50 per cent or even 100 per cent a year for the money needed to create them. But other monopolies are less profitable and business men are not willing or able to pay such a high price for the funds to establish them. The gains from the subdivision of labor tend to become less and less, it has been pointed out, as the subdivision of labor becomes more and more minute.[28] Consequently, an enterprise could possibly afford to pay 8 per cent for the funds to establish a certain degree of division of labor but perhaps it could afford to pay only 6 per cent for the funds needed to carry the division of labor still further. Finally, the amount which business men can pay for funds with which to increase the equipment of industry is limited by the fact, with which we are already familiar, that additional quantities of one agent of production, when used in conjunction with constant quantities of other agents,

[27] See pp. 115–116.
[28] See pp. 134–135.

yield smaller and smaller increments of product.[29]   With the labor supply of the community constant, additions to the equipment of industry will tend to yield smaller and smaller increments of product.

In analyzing the demand of business enterprises for funds, it is extremely important to notice that more physical product does not *necessarily* mean more profits.   It depends upon whether the additional output can be sold for enough to pay for the capital that is consumed in producing it.   Consider, for example, the following two cases:

Capital	Life of capital in years	Annual depreciation	Physical output per year	Selling price per unit	Value of output per year
$100,000	10	$10,000	10,000	$2.00	$20,000
200,000	10	20,000	18,000	1.90	34,200
$100,000	10	$10,000	10,000	$2.00	$20,000
200,000	10	20,000	18,000	1.50	27,000

In each case, the investment of a second $100,000 increases the physical product by the same amount — from 10,000 units to 18,000 units a year.   But in the first case the capital is productive and in the second case it is not.   The explanation for the difference is to be found in the effect of the larger output upon the value of the product.   In the first case, it is assumed that an increase in the output from 10,000 units to 18,000 units causes the price to fall from $2.00 to $1.90 a unit.   Hence the increase in the investment from $100,000 to $200,000 causes the gross income of the firm to rise by $14,200.   In order to obtain this increase, the enterprise must consume $10,000 more of capital a year — it is assumed that the life of the capital is ten years. Hence there is a net gain of $4,200 which represents the productivity of the capital or the maximum sum which the concern could afford to pay as interest on the new capital.[30]   In the second case, however, it is assumed that the increase in output causes the

[29] See pp. 332–335.

[30] Other capital costs, such as taxes and insurance, have been disregarded for the sake of simplicity.

price to drop from \$2.00 to \$1.50 a unit so that the value of the total output increases only from \$20,000 to \$27,000 a year. But the cost of gaining this \$7,000 additional product is the consumption of \$10,000 more of capital a year. Evidently when productivity is measured in terms of dollars and cents, the additional capital is not productive. It would be entirely consumed before it had paid for itself. Only to the extent that capital produces more than its cost can business men afford to borrow funds with which to purchase it. And the amount which they can afford to pay in interest depends, of course, upon the amount by which the output of the capital exceeds the cost of the capital consumed in producing the output.

To summarize this brief survey of the demand for funds: funds may be demanded to finance consumption, wars, public works, monopolies, and speculation, to provide working capital, and to increase the equipment of industry. The division of the available funds among these uses depends upon the prices which borrowers are willing to pay. If a monopoly is able to outbid other enterprises for \$50,000,000, this amount may be used to finance the withholding of goods from sale rather than to finance an increase in production. The amount which is devoted to financing the creation of additional capital depends upon the profitableness of this use of money compared with other uses.

IX. The Determination of the Rate of Interest

The rate of interest tends to be fixed, of course, at the point where the quantity of money which lenders are willing to lend and the amount which borrowers are willing to borrow are equal. If the interest rate is 6 per cent, for example, it means that the demand is sufficient to take, at 6 per cent, all of the funds which men are willing to lend at this rate. The ability of business men to discover opportunities for profit — which determines the principal demand for funds — depends, in the last analysis, upon the amount of money that is being spent for consumers' goods. This is obvious, because it is from the prices paid by ultimate consumers that all costs of producing goods must be paid. It follows that a decrease in the proportion of incomes saved is likely to raise interest rates not only by diminishing the volume of money seeking investment but also by increasing the demand for consumers' goods and thus increasing the opportunities to invest funds at a profit. An increase in the proportion of incomes saved, on the other hand, is likely to reduce interest rates, both by increasing the volume of funds seeking investment and also by diminishing the demand for consumers' goods and, hence, the opportunities for investing funds at a profit. Were the community to spend too little for consumers' goods and to save too much, the demand for consumers' goods would be so small and the prices of such goods so low that savings could not be invested at a profit. Under these circumstances, the interest rate might fall close to zero — perhaps just enough above to cover the extra risk of investing money rather than hoarding it. Under some circumstances, it might be safer to invest than to hoard. In this event, men would undoubtedly be willing, if necessary, to lend some money for less than nothing — for *negative* interest. That is, lenders might be willing to pay borrowers — to let a borrower have $1,000 in return for the promise to pay back, let us say, $998 at the end of the year.[31] The interest rate is positive instead of negative because people, by spending most of their incomes for consumers' goods, create so many opportunities for business men to use money profitably and there are so many persons who wish to borrow in order to buy now rather than later or to meet emergencies, that demand and supply do not reach equilibrium until a positive rate of interest has been reached. In other words, the interest rate is positive, instead of negative, simply because more present purchasing power is demanded at a premium than would be supplied without a premium. This is illustrated by the following table:

[31] At first blush, this statement may seem ridiculous, but this is only because it is not necessary for lenders to pay negative interest and hence it is a little difficult to see why some of them might be willing to do so. The reason, however, is precisely the same as induces men to buy safes and strong boxes, to rent safe deposit vaults, and to purchase burglary and fire insurance. Rather than risk the loss of one's funds by fire or theft, it would be advantageous to lend them to financially responsible persons in return for the promise that the original sum, less a small fee for insurance, would be returned at a stipulated time.

Demand for loans	Price for use of $100 for one year	Supply of loanable funds
$200,000,000	$7	$350,000,000
250,000,000	6	325,000,000
300,000,000	5	300,000,000
350,000,000	4	250,000,000
375,000,000	3	175,000,000
400,000,000	2	125,000,000
450,000,000	1	115,000,000
550,000,000	0	105,000,000
700,000,000	−1	100,000,000
850,000,000	−2	10,000,000

In this case, the interest rate would be 5 per cent — $5 for $100 for one year. But if business men were to find such difficulty in discovering opportunities for profitable investment and if the demand for durable consumption goods were to become so small that the demand for present purchasing power even at a negative interest rate of one per cent did not exceed $100,000,000, then the interest rate would sink to minus one per cent.[32]

[32] It will be noticed in the supply schedule that there is a sharp drop from a supply of $100,000,000 at −1 per cent to $10,000,000 at −2 per cent. It is assumed that practically every one could purchase fire and burglary insurance or rent a safe deposit vault for slightly more than one per cent of his funds. Consequently, although many persons might be willing to lend at a rate of −1 per cent, in lieu of buying insurance, almost no one (except possibly a few very small savers) would be willing to lend at a loss of 2 per cent per year.

It will be noticed also that the supply of loanable funds drops rapidly between 4 and 2 per cent. This is because of the assumption that many commercial banks would find it unprofitable to do business at less than a 4 per cent return on their loans. Consequently, when interest rates sink below 4 per cent, there is a substantial shrinkage in the funds supplied by the commercial banks. But if the commercial banks lend less money, the community has fewer dollars to spend and the price level will be lower. This is reflected in the small increase in the funds demanded as the interest rate drops from 4 to 2 per cent. It is quite possible that, as a result of the lower price level at 2 per cent, the number of dollars demanded at that rate would be less than at 4 per cent.

Some economists have regarded an interest rate of zero or less than zero as inconceivable because, in their opinion, it would require that permanent sources of income, such as land, possess a value of infinity. The value of a durable good is conceived as the present value of the future services that the good is expected to render. If money in the future were not regarded as less desirable than money in the present, would not a good which is capable of rendering services indefinitely be infinitely valuable?

Very few goods, of course, are capable of rendering services indefinitely, but land, in some instances, may be regarded as a permanent source of income. What would be the value of land in the event that the interest rate were zero or negative? Would it be infinite? By no means. The assumption that it would is based upon an errone-

X. Different Interest Rates

Thus far we have been discussing the interest rate as if there were simply one universal rate. As a matter of fact, there are a vast variety of interest rates depending upon the nature of the loan. The principal things which differentiate loans are: (1) the duration; (2) the nature of the security; and (3) the relationship between borrower and lender. Some loans are made subject to termination any day at the call of the lender, others

---

ous inference made from the fact that the present value of any good which yields services forever (land, for example,) can be expressed as the value of an infinite series of future payments discounted at a certain rate. But this does not mean that as *a matter of fact* the purchasers of land actually are discounting the future income from the land at this particular rate. Indeed, it does not necessarily mean that the purchaser considers that money in the future is less desirable than money now. As a matter of actual preference, the purchaser may value money in the future above money today and, in buying a piece of land, he may be willing to pay a substantial premium in money today in order to acquire a reliable source of future income. Consider the case of a man with a life expectancy of twenty years who has $20,000 which he wishes to invest in order to provide himself with an income for the rest of his life. Assume that he is afraid to keep the money in cash or to put it in a bank. He finds a piece of land will yield him a rent of $800 a year and purchases it. This price can be expressed, if one cares to do so, as the present value of an infinite number of annual incomes discounted at 4 per cent. Actually it may be nothing of the sort. The purchaser is giving $20,000 for the probability of receiving $16,000 in annual installments spread over twenty years plus whatever satisfaction he may derive from bequeathing the property to relatives or friends. One may simplify the case, if one cares to, by assuming either that the right to bequeath the property is of no importance to the buyer or that the state imposes an inheritance tax of 100 per cent.

In a community in which there were a negative rate of interest, land would have a value determined by what men were willing to pay for it. This value could be expressed as the discounted value of an infinite number of increments of income. But this would not necessarily be inconsistent with the fact that rate of interest in the community was negative, and that men, in buying land, were paying a premium for an income in the future.

The only condition under which the rate of interest would be negative would probably be a state of general insecurity. Under such circumstances, most persons might be unable to protect their property from injury, destruction, or theft, except at great expense. Consequently, they might be willing to exchange most of their savings for claims to a smaller amount of property in the future. The value of claims to property in the future would depend, of course, upon the ability of the state to enforce such claims and one might question whether a state which could not protect property could enforce claims to titles in the future. It is possible, however, that claims could be enforced more certainly and effectively than physical property could be protected. The situation might be represented by a country exposed to raids from mountain or desert tribes. The state might be inefficient in preventing the raids and at the same time able to enforce claims against its own subjects. Under these circumstances, so many persons might prefer to exchange their savings for claims to future payments that the rate of interest would be negative.

may run for fifty or seventy-five years; some are secured by specific pieces of property such as real estate or collateral, others rest simply upon the general credit of the borrower; some loans are made by lenders to regular customers, others are made by selling obligations to pay in the open market. The following is a classification of the principal interest rates:

1. The call money rate, applying to loans terminable at any time upon the demand of the lender. These loans are used primarily by speculators in securities, grain, and cotton.

2. The commercial paper rate, applying to the short-term commercial paper that is bought and sold in the open market.

3. The banker's acceptance rate — the rate paid on banker's acceptances.

4. The customers' rate — the rate charged by commercial banks to their customers. This is the rate which applies to the great bulk of the loans made by the commercial banks.

5. The rate paid by commercial banks on deposits subject to check.

6. The rate paid by savings banks and commercial banks on time deposits.

7. The "personal character" loan rate — the rate charged by the Morris Plan banks and other so-called "industrial" banks on small personal loans.

8. The rediscount rates of the Federal Reserve Banks.

9. The interest rate on bonds.

10. The interest rate on mortgages.

Even this list is an undue simplification because, within many of the classes of loans, there are differences in rates. Every bond issue, of course, sells at its own rate and there are differences in the rates on commercial paper depending upon the quality and the maturity of the paper. Mortgages fall into two principal classes, first and second mortgages, and within these classes there are differences in rates.

Not only are the rates on these various classes of loans not the same, but often they are moving in opposite directions. This is most likely to be true of rates on the various classes of short-term loans and rates on long-term loans. In the long run, of course, short-term and long-term rates move together, because if one becomes too high relative to the other, funds move from one field into the other. During short periods, however, the rates may move in opposite directions. Much money which seeks investment in the short-term market can only be invested in that market — funds which commercial banks must have available again in a few months to meet the seasonal needs of their customers; funds which corporations expect to disburse in a short time as interest, dividends, or tax payments; free funds which corporations happen to have on hand but which they expect to need soon for working capital. All of this money will seek investment in the short-term market even though long-term interest rates are rising. If the demand for short-term funds at the particular moment is small, because it is between seasons in most industries or because speculation in stocks or grains is quiet, short-term rates may fall. On the other hand, the pronounced seasonal fluctuations in the demand for short-term funds, particularly the demand associated with the marketing of the crops in the fall, may cause short-term rates to rise even when long-term rates are declining, because the fact that high rates are temporarily obtainable in the short-term market does not draw much money that is seeking long-term investment.

Not only may the various rates move in opposite directions but some are far more variable than others. As a rule, the short-term rates are far more variable than the long-term.[33] The short-term needs for money are usually exceedingly imperative. When enterprises require money to finance current operations, they must have it at almost any price. Long-term funds, on the other hand, are used to finance permanent improvements which for the most part can be postponed. Furthermore, a rise in the short-term interest rate, if the rise is likely to be temporary, has only limited effectiveness in attracting funds from the long-term money market. The commercial banks, of course, are always ready to shift some money from bonds to the short-term market when short-term rates become high, but the ordinary investor,

---

[33] A rough comparison of the relative variability of the rates for long-term and short-term loans is made by O. M. W. Sprague and W. R. Burgess in their discussion of " Money and Credit and their Effect on Business " in *Recent Economic Changes*, v. II, p. 663. Their method was to compute the average per cent deviation of the monthly average rates from the twelve-month moving averages. This indicates by how much the monthly averages rise and fall above the long-time trend. For the period 1922 to 1928, the averages deviated from the twelve-month moving average as follows:

Corporation bond yield	0.62	per cent
Industrial stock yield	2.60	" "
Commercial paper	4.33	" "
Time money	6.12	" "
Call money	8.39	" "

who, as a rule, prefers long-term investments, is not willing to refrain from purchasing a security which seems attractive simply because it is possible for him to obtain an exceptionally high rate of return in the short-term money market for a few months.

Of all the short-term rates, the call rate is the most variable. The reason for this is the fact that both the demand for call money and the supply are inelastic, at least when short periods of time are involved. The demand is inelastic because speculators prefer to pay high call rates for a short time rather than sell securities which, it is believed, are soon likely to rise in price. The supply is inelastic because the funds in the call market are, in large degree, money for which banks and corporations have no use temporarily but which they will be needing shortly. When the need for the money comes, it is withdrawn even in the face of a very pronounced rise in call rates. Banks cannot afford to permit their regular customers to suffer from lack of credit in order to keep money in the call market even at a high rate. If the call market were not the place where temporarily unneeded funds are invested, a relatively small rise in call rates would be sufficient to check the outward flow of funds, and the rise in the interest rate would not go far.

XI. How Interest Rates Affect the Volume of Loanable Funds

In discussing why individuals save, it was pointed out that much of the saving of the well-to-do is simply a result of the fact that they have more income than they can conveniently spend on consumers' goods and that much of the saving of the less well-to-do reflects the desire for specific goods which are too expensive to be purchased out of current income. In these cases, obviously, the interest received on investments has little direct influence upon the volume of saving.

Is it true in general that the volume of loanable funds is affected by interest rates? Assume that the rate of interest rises. Some persons undoubtedly are led to increase their savings. But it is also true that an advance in the interest rate may diminish rather than increase the saving of many persons. This may seem strange but the reason is easily understood. Suppose that a man wishes to have a certain income in order to meet his living expenses when he retires. Suppose that he decides that he should have an auxiliary income of $1,000. If he can obtain 5 per cent for his money, he must save $20,000 in order to have an annual income of $1,000. But if he can obtain 6 per cent, he need save only $16,667. Hence a rise in the interest rate from 5 per cent to 6 per cent is likely to cause him to stop saving when he has accumulated $16,667 instead of $20,000. No doubt many savers are in the position of this man.[34]

But what is the *net* effect of a change in interest rates upon the volume of funds offered for loan? On the whole, it seems probable that an advance in interest rates increases the volume of loanable funds and a drop in interest rates decreases the volume. This is unquestionably true of the part of loanable funds that are supplied by commercial banks. The higher the rate of interest on commercial loans, the larger the volume of capital which enters commercial banking and the greater the volume of credit dollars supplied by the commercial banking system. On the other hand, if short-term interest rates dropped far enough, many commercial banks would be compelled to shut down because of inability to pay operating expenses. Among individual savers, the number who would be induced by higher interest rates to reduce their savings is probably a minority. Many persons save because they wish to have larger incomes in the future. They do not have in mind a definite and limited amount by which they wish to increase their incomes — they simply wish a larger income, the larger the better. The greater the return which they can obtain by investing part of their present incomes, the greater the degree to which they are inclined to use saving as a method of adding to them. To such persons a return of 10 per cent is a greater inducement to save than a return of 5 per cent. Furthermore, a high rate of interest means that the prices of durable goods such as houses or land, are low relative to other

[34] Another way of stating the question of whether a rise in the interest rate would increase or decrease saving is to ask whether the demand for annuities is elastic or inelastic. The man who invests money to obtain an income from it may be regarded as purchasing an annuity. If the demand for annuities is elastic, more money will be spent for them when the price is low (i.e., when the interest rate is high) than when the price is high. See a discussion of this by Professor G. R. Davies in "Factors Determining the Interest Rate," *Quarterly Journal of Economics*, May, 1920, XXXIV, pp. 451–452.

goods. For example, if the interest rate is 5 per cent, a farm that yields a net income of $1,000 a year is worth $20,000, but if the interest rate is 10 per cent, then a farm yielding $1,000 a year, is worth only $10,000. More men may be willing to save in order to gain their independence if they can buy it for $10,000 instead of $20,000.

But the most important effect of changes in interest rates upon the supply of loanable funds appears to be indirect. In the analysis of the supply of labor, attention was called to the fact that the *entire supply curve* for labor depends upon the wage rate which prevails. The same thing appears to be true of savings. Most of the saving is done by wealthy individuals and by business enterprises. One effect of a higher rate of interest is to increase the incomes of the rich, who draw most of their incomes from investments. But the very rich, as has been pointed out, tend to save what is left after they have rather completely satisfied their desires for consumers' goods. Consequently, a rise in interest rates, or anything else which increases their incomes, tends to increase saving. Saving by business enterprises appears to depend upon the size of profits. High interest rates mean that the return on capital is large, which, in turn, means that the profits of business concerns are large and that enterprises have more money to put back into their businesses.

XII. Does Saving Cause Business Cycles?

Is the process of saving responsible, in part at least, for business cycles? Many economists have thought so, and during the last fifty years the theory has been offered in many variations. Among economists today, those who explain business cycles most purely through the effects of savings are John A. Hobson in England and W. T. Foster and Waddill Catchings in the United States.[35] The theory that too much saving may explain the business cycle is exceedingly interesting because it suggests that we

[35] Hobson's theory is stated in his *The Economics of Unemployment* and that of Foster and Catchings in their *Profits* and also in their *The Dilemma of Thrift*. The belief that the process of capital creation in one way or another generates business cycles is widespread and forms the basis of many theories of the business cycle. Convenient summaries and descriptions of these theories will be found in Hansen, A. H., *Business-Cycle Theory*, pp. 11–119, and also in Mitchell, W. C., *Business Cycles. The Problem and Its Setting*, pp. 23–31.

might possibly save more *in the long run* and might, therefore, increase the equipment of industry more rapidly if we saved more gradually or possibly by a different process. Is it true, for example, that the very creation of additional productive capacity, by adding to the supply of goods and thus unsettling prices and causing postponement of buying, destroys, temporarily at least, the market which the additional productive capacity is designed to serve? Does a spurt in the building of productive capacity inevitably create depression and unemployment which cause us to lose much of the savings made during prosperity?

Hobson bases his explanation of business cycles upon the unequal distribution of wealth. The well-to-do are unable to consume most of their income, they invest it in capital, the output of industry increases, consumers are unable to buy the larger output of industry except at lower prices, prices collapse, and there is business depression. The depression brings, in addition to lower prices, smaller profits and hence smaller incomes for the well-to-do. The savings of the well-to-do diminish and consumption is able to catch up with production. But the very process of catching up brings an increase in profits, larger incomes for the well-to-do, larger savings, larger output, and, finally, another collapse of prices and depression.

Foster and Catchings agree with Hobson in attributing business depression to the failure of consumer demand to keep pace with the production of goods, but the difficulty, according to them, is more deep-seated than inequality in the distribution of wealth.[36] The difficulty, say Foster and Catchings, arises from two facts. In the first place, industry fails to disburse to consumers — that is, to wage earners and investors — an amount of money equal to the final sales price of its products. The reason for this is that part of the profits of industry are not paid out to investors as dividends but are used by industry to increase its equipment and hence its productive capacity. In the second place, wage earners and investors do not spend for consumers' goods even as much as they receive from industry in wages and dividends and interest. Consumers find it necessary to save.

---

[36] For several excellent criticisms of Foster and Catching's theory, see Souter, R. W., and others, *Pollak Prize Essays* and also Hansen, A. H., *Business-Cycle Theory*, Ch. VII.

Not all of their savings are used to increase the output of industry but most of them are invested in securities, either by the consumers themselves or by savings banks, and thus are used to enable business concerns to increase their productive capacity. In short, because of the saving by business enterprises and by consumers, some money is used *twice* for production before it is used for consumption. To the extent that money is used more frequently for production than for consumption, the supply of goods outruns the purchasing power of consumers. This is the reason why, according to Foster and Catchings, stocks of goods periodically pile up until there is a collapse of prices and a depression, during which consumers use up the accumulated stocks by buying them for less than the cost of producing them.

The problem of the relationship between saving and the business cycle is more complicated than the analyses of Hobson and Foster and Catchings indicate. To begin with, it seems necessary to reject the extreme conclusions of Foster and Catchings that there is a " dilemma of thrift," that, " as industry is now financed and corporate savings are now effected, the flow of money to consumers does not long keep pace with the flow of goods." [37] It is, of course, true that when the output of consumers' goods increases faster than the purchasing power of consumers, a fall in the prices of consumers' goods is inevitable. But such a fall does not necessarily reduce the profits of business enterprises, because the addition of better equipment to industry and the larger scale of production may lower operating expenses. Indeed the very fact that there is a demand for savings by business enterprises is itself evidence that managers think they see opportunities to use more capital in ways which will not diminish profits. Obviously, slowly falling prices which do not bring about a drop in profits do not necessarily bring about a business depression. In fact, we may go a step further and assert that even if the fall in prices does cause a slow drop in profits, a depression is not inevitable. Business owners must be content with smaller returns but this in itself does not necessarily bring about a destruction of confidence in the future and a curtailment or suspension of business operations.

[37] *Profits*, p. 339.

No doubt savings may be so invested that they lead to a great oversupply of some goods and to a disastrous drop in their prices which weakens business confidence, produces a drop in still other prices, and causes a general business depression. And no doubt it is also true that, when savings are used to increase capital, they are *very likely* to introduce cyclical fluctuations into business or at least to accentuate fluctuations which are created by other causes. The increase in capital means an increase in output and this is likely, sooner or later, to mean a drop in prices. If the drop in prices was not accurately foreseen and discounted, it may shatter business confidence and produce a depression. But it is obvious that the essential difficulty in this case is not with the process of saving itself *but with the unwise investment of savings.* No doubt the unwise investment of savings has been an important contributing cause of many depressions. But the question upon which we are seeking light is whether the process of saving itself *necessarily* produces business cycles.

In attempting to answer this question, a distinction must be drawn between the mere decision of individuals or enterprises to invest part of their income and the involuntary saving that is forced upon the community when commercial credit is used to finance additions to capital. When an individual decides to invest part of his income instead of spending it for consumers' goods or when an enterprise plows back part of its earnings instead of distributing them to the owners, the total number of dollars spent in the community is not thereby increased. Consequently, the mere process of saving does not produce a rise in prices which might in turn produce a speculative boom.

Very different is the effect when the purchase of additional capital is financed by an expansion of commercial credit. And in modern economic society, as we have seen, the accumulation of capital is to a large extent financed temporarily by an increase in short-term loans. This is likely to occur on an especially large scale, we have seen, during boom periods when the demand for capital increases faster than the saving of individuals and business enterprises. Consequently, the acquisition of capital may be financed, temporarily at least, by short-term loans. An enterprise which buys equipment may plan to pay for it eventually either out of profits or by a security issue, but it may purchase the equipment with funds borrowed for a short term at a commercial bank. If the concern issues stocks or bonds, they may be purchased by investment bankers with the proceeds of short-term loans. Finally, the investment bankers may sell the securities to investors who pay for them with borrowed money — money which the investors expect to repay out of income. In other words, although the equipment may be eventually paid for out of savings, the saving may occur six months or a year or more after the equipment was constructed.

The series of short-term loans by which the equipment has been financed during the interval have the effect of increasing the demand for goods, particularly consumers' goods, because the dollars which the banks supply are paid largely to persons (such as the employees and the owners of the enterprises which sell equipment) who spend them for consumers' goods.[38] If industry can easily and quickly increase its output of consumers' goods in response to the growth in demand, there may be little or no advance in prices. But if the financing of increases in capital by the expansion of commercial credit continues for an appreciable period, the prices of consumers' goods will eventually rise. The advance in prices may stimulate speculative increases in inventories and orders far in advance of needs and thus a price spiral may be started, each increase leading to a further increase. But when the new equipment, which was financed by the short-term loans that started the price spiral, comes into operation, the rise in prices tends to be checked. The expansion of business, however, may be occurring at such a rapid rate that the advance in prices does not immediately cease. On the contrary, the rise in profits, which advancing prices and expanding production make possible, may lead enterprises to expand their equipment still further. Commercial credit is likely to play an important part in financing this additional expansion. Eventually, the expansion of credit ceases. But the increase in the supply of goods may continue after credit is no longer increasing, because productive capacity which has been under construction is completed and brought into operation. The growing supply of goods, in conjunction

---

[38] Likewise, when investors borrow in order to buy securities, the dollars may form part of the gross income of investment bankers and may increase the demand for consumers' goods when spent by the employees or the owners of investment banking houses.

with the cessation in the expansion of credit, causes prices to drop and this may produce a severe business depression, especially if, during the rise in prices, large inventories were speculatively accumulated.

Our conclusion is that in so far as the process of accumulating capital involves an expansion of commercial credit, it is likely to produce a rise in prices and to start a speculative boom which is bound to result in a collapse and a depression. This analysis is far different from the theory that business cycles are caused, or at least accentuated, by too much *voluntary* saving. It points to the opposite conclusion — that business cycles are accentuated by the fact that during boom periods voluntary saving lags behind the sudden increase in the demand for capital, with the result that the acquisition of capital is financed, to a substantial extent, by an expansion of commercial credit. This expansion tends to produce a level of prices which cannot be maintained when the supply of goods is increased by output from the new capital and when the money in circulation is diminished by the liquidation of the short-term loans used in temporarily financing the acquisition of capital. Business cycles would probably be less severe if the use of commercial credit in financing the acquisition of capital were rendered less necessary by a more prompt response of voluntary saving to increases in the demand for capital — in other words, if voluntary saving occurred on a larger scale during boom periods.

In order to avoid any distorted view of the relationship between forced savings and the business cycle, however, it is important to call attention to the fact that, under a credit system such as ours, *any* increase in output, regardless of whether it be output of capital or of consumers' goods, is likely to introduce a cyclical movement into business. The reason, as has been explained, is that, under a credit system, *any* increase in output produces an increase in the supply of dollars before it produces an increase in the supply of salable goods. Consequently, the increase in output has the initial effect of producing a rise in prices. Later, when the increase in the supply of goods has occurred, the rise in prices is halted and eventually turned into a drop. If this drop has been accurately foreseen and allowed for by business men, it may not destroy confidence and may produce little retardation of industry. But if the drop has not been foreseen, it may cause a severe slowing up of industry. Because *any* increase in output is likely under a credit system to produce waves in business, it is erroneous to attribute business cycles to the process of saving itself. The cyclical movement of business, however, is likely to be more severe when short-term credit is used to finance the acquisition of capital than when it is merely used to finance the production of more consumers' goods, because the additions to capital, by increasing the capacity of industry, tend to accentuate the drop in prices which sooner or later occurs.

XIII. Do We Save Too Much or Too Little?

Spending and saving are two ways of deriving satisfaction from income. Saving, as we have seen, increases satisfaction by conferring a sense of security upon the savers, by giving them an income to fall back on when income from wages or salary drops or ceases, by enabling them to purchase expensive consumption goods such as houses or automobiles, which most persons could not buy without saving, and, finally, by enabling them to have larger incomes in the future. When the income of each person is so apportioned between spending for immediate consumption and saving that he derives from his income, in the course of a life time, the maximum surplus of satisfaction over sacrifice, both the total volume of saving and the distribution of saving among the members of the community may be said to be the optimum *for the particular distribution of income.* The qualification " for the particular distribution of income " is important because, by disturbing the distribution of income, it might be possible to obtain the same volume of saving at a smaller sacrifice. It is possible that if the very rich were compelled to save more and the very poor were relieved from the necessity of saving such a large part of their incomes (as when the government taxes the well-to-do in order to provide old age pensions for the poor) the total volume of satisfaction over sacrifice in the community might be increased. But obviously this would involve a redistribution of income. The desirability of changing the distribution of income by taxation does not at this point concern us. It is, however, important to inquire whether the prevailing methods of saving result in the optimum volume and distribution of saving for the existing distribution of income. Or do they result in too much or too little saving or an undesirable distribution of the burden of saving among different persons in the community?

In a large proportion of cases in modern economic society the actual decision to save is made by persons who do not do the real saving — who do not limit their consumption in order to make saving possible. If a corporation keeps down its dividend rate in order to invest part of its earnings in the business, the real saving, of course, is done by the stockholders, who, for the time being, receive less income from their shares; but the decision to save is made by the board of directors of the corporation.[39] When saving is forced upon the community by the use of commercial credit for the acquisition of capital goods, the decision to add to the equipment of industry is made, of course, by the purchasers of the equipment, not by those who must temporarily consume less in order that more capital can be produced. When the state collects funds by taxation for the purpose of building roads or bridges or otherwise adding to the capital of the community, the decision to levy the tax is made by the legislature and not by the persons who must pay the tax or who

[39] Nevertheless it is important to notice that it is ordinarily *possible* for a stockholder in a corporation to avoid being compelled to save against his wishes. One alternative is to sell his stock and to invest in a corporation which disburses a larger proportion of its earnings in dividends. A second alternative would be to sell *part* of his stock. If the management of the enterprise is wise in plowing back earnings into the business, the shares of the stockholders should soon increase in value because they now represent claims to more property and income than before. Assume that an investor owns ten shares which, before the reinvestment of earnings, were worth $100 each or $1,000 in all. Suppose that earnings to the amount of $10 per share are employed by the management to increase the property of the enterprise and that, as a result, the shares rise in value from $100 to $110. If the owner of the ten shares did not wish to increase his savings, he could avoid doing so by selling one of his shares for $110 and spending the proceeds on consumption goods. In this way he would keep the value of his investment in the enterprise practically unchanged — originally it was $1,000; now it is $990. It should be noted, however, that the investment of earnings would probably not cause an immediate increase in the value of the shares of the enterprise — the increase in value would probably not occur until the additional investment had raised the net earnings of the concern and this would probably not occur for some months. Consequently, stockholders who wished to avoid saving could not entirely do so.

But although these methods of avoiding saving are available, few stockholders are likely to use them. And yet if the enterprise had paid out more of its earnings in dividends, many of the stockholders would probably have spent most of the additional income on consumers' goods. The *actual*, though not the necessary effect, of the decision of the directors is to cause the stockholders to save more than they otherwise would.

must limit their consumption in order that more capital goods may be produced. Finally, when enterprises establish pension funds and sickness insurance funds for the benefit of their men, the contribution which the employees must make is determined, not by the men themselves, but by the management.

All of these forms of forced saving probably result in more saving than would occur if the decision to save or not to save were made by the individuals who must limit their consumption. But whether the result is to make the actual volume of saving more closely approximate the optimum amount depends upon whether most individuals, when left to themselves, tend to save too little or too much — if too little, then these forms of forced saving probably tend to make the actual amount more closely approximate the optimum amount;[40] if too much, forced saving probably tends to make the actual volume of saving less closely approximate the optimum. But do individuals, when left to decide for themselves, tend to save too much or too little — that is, more than the optimum or less than the optimum.

Unfortunately this question cannot be answered. It is probable that many, possibly most, persons save too little while they are young; but it is also probable that many persons spend too little on consumption goods when they are older and finally die in the possession of much property which they would have done better (from the standpoint of their own pleasure) to spend. But whether the net result is too much or too little saving, no one knows. The principal reason for believing that many persons save too little while they are young is the fact that their decisions to spend are determined in large degree by aggressive and often none too scrupulous salesmanship. As a result of being persuaded to spend too much for immediate consumption, they have less left for saving than they would have devoted to that purpose if the apportionment of their incomes between saving and spending had been the result of reflection and a careful examination of alternatives. On the other hand, many people in old age spend too little because they do not consume their principal. In part, this is because they wish to leave some-

[40] It is possible, of course, that these other methods may so greatly increase the volume of saving that it less closely approximates the optimum amount than it would if all decisions to save were made by the individuals who do the actual saving — that is, who limit their consumption.

thing to their children or for some charitable or public purpose, and this use of the principal may, of course, give the owner more satisfaction than any other. In part, the failure to spend the principal is due to the fact that no one knows how long he will live. In large degree, however, it is caused by habits and prejudices acquired earlier in life — habits and prejudices which were wise during the years that the principal was being built up but which, when continued into old age, simply prevent people from enjoying the savings of their youth. Most persons would probably gain more satisfaction from their property by setting aside the amount which they wish to bequeath to children, relatives, and charities, and to retain for emergencies, and then using the remainder to purchase a life annuity. But although the individual would be better off, the community would be worse off. Indeed, the rapid accumulation of capital during the last several centuries has in no small degree been made possible by the fact that many men in their old age have failed to spend the savings of their youth.

Thus far we have discussed how the volume of saving is affected by the fact that the decision to save is often made by persons who do not themselves do the saving — or, at least, who do not do an appreciable part of it. But it is not satisfactory to analyze the effect of this fact upon the *volume* of saving without also analyzing its effect upon the *distribution* of saving. Possibly the community as a whole tends to save too little, and possibly methods which concentrate the decisions whether to save or not to save among a few business managers or legislators tend to increase the total volume of saving. This may *seem* to be a desirable result and yet actually it may be undesirable. The mere fact that more saving is desirable does not make it desirable *however accomplished*. Possibly the increase in saving is achieved only by forcing a reduction of consumption among the persons who can least afford to consume less. In this event, the additions to the equipment of industry may not be worth their cost.

Here we encounter the gravest fault of the various methods of involuntary saving — they do not permit the benefits of saving to be equated against the cost. Suppose that a corporation saves by plowing back earnings. The stockholders, for the time being, receive smaller dividends. As far as most of the well-to-do stockholders are concerned, this may represent no serious privation — perhaps, in many cases, no sacrifice at all. But many of the stockholders may be persons of small means — too poor to save but a small part of their income. To compel them to save by investing most of the earnings of the enterprise instead of paying dividends may impose a real sacrifice upon these stockholders; it may compel them to save at a cost which the benefits do not compensate.

The same criticism applies to all the other forms of involuntary saving — the saving accomplished by compulsory pension and insurance schemes, by taxation, and especially by the use of commercial credit. The criticism probably applies least of all to compulsory pension or insurance plans because the contributions to these plans are usually adjusted so that the low-paid workers contribute less than the high-paid. Nevertheless, when all workmen in a plant are obliged to contribute to a pension or an insurance scheme, the payments are bound to be more burdensome and less beneficial to some workmen than to others. Consequently, there may be a small minority to whom the benefits of the insurance are not worth its cost. When the state increases taxes to obtain funds for certain public improvements, many taxpayers may derive no benefit from the improvements — in fact, some of them may be seriously injured by the improvements, as are railroads when they are taxed to build highways for competing motor busses and trucks. Finally, the saving accomplished by the expansion of commercial credit may force a limitation of consumption where it imposes a greater sacrifice than the benefits of the saving warrant. As a result of the expansion of credit, prices rise. The rise in prices may not cause the very rich to reduce their consumption — they may meet the rise simply by saving less. But the poor, confronted with substantially higher prices, find it necessary, not only practically to cease saving, but also to reduce their consumption appreciably. Hence it comes about that the increase in capital equipment is made possible largely by a curtailment of consumption among the persons who can least afford to do with less. Later, as a result of the productivity of the additional capital, the poor are better supplied with goods than ever. Nevertheless, the persons who must make the sacrifice have no opportunity to decide whether the chances for future gain warrant it.

XIV. Are Our Methods of Saving Fair?

Are our methods of saving fair? Were all saving the result of the decision of persons who do it, this question would probably not arise, but the large amount of involuntary saving in modern economic society makes the question one of importance. Saving may be forced upon the community, we have seen, either by the government or by private agencies.

The propriety of the state's using taxation to compel saving depends upon (1) the fairness of the specific taxes by which the state raises its funds and (2) the purposes for which the state spends its money.[41] The discussion of what is a fair tax can be advantageously postponed to Chapter XXVIII on The Support of the State. If we assume that specific taxes are fair, the propriety of any tax would appear to hinge upon the propriety of the expenditures of the state — are the expenditures for legitimate public purposes? What is a legitimate public purpose? The government is intended to protect and promote interests that are common to everyone in the community and to fulfill obligations which it is felt that the community owes to each of its members. What specific activities properly fall under these general headings is a matter of opinion, and government expenditures which seem proper to some persons may seem illegitimate to others.

To some forms of saving forced by private agencies there appears to be no serious objection. Many pension and insurance schemes are examples. The amount which each individual is compelled to save is small and is usually proportionate to his earnings, and the benefits which accrue to the contributors are often substantial.[42] Even the involuntary saving that is forced upon investors in an enterprise by the plowing back of earnings is not open to serious objection. Some plowing back of earn-

---

[41] In Chapter XXVIII on The Support of the State, it will be pointed out that the answers to these two questions are interdependent. One cannot determine what taxes are fair without knowing how the money is to be used.

[42] But the specific terms of many pension and insurance schemes are open to serious criticism.

It is true that the future is largely unforeseeable. In a dynamic world, with the future a mystery, it must be true that profits are in substantial degree a matter of luck. More completely than any other form of economic income, profits reflect man's imperfect ability to predict the future and consequently, in greater degree than any other form of income, they defy explanation by general rules. But the element of chance in profits does not mean that no explanation is possible. The world is not so chaotic that intelligent guessing about the future is impossible. Furthermore, despite the difficulty in judging the future, men are not without a working rule in deciding whether or not to become business owners. Because they find difficulty in forecasting the future, they tend to judge the future by the immediate past — in the absence of the ability to foresee changes, they act largely (though not, of course, entirely) upon the assumption that there will not be changes. This tendency to judge the future by the past is partly responsible, as we have seen, for the business cycle and for the alternating periods of under- and over-development of industries.[8]

It is not necessary, of course, for a man to become a business owner. There is always the alternative of lending his funds instead of investing them in business ownership; of working for hire instead of becoming an independent business man. Naturally there is bound to be a close relationship between profits on the average and in the long run and the return which men can obtain as lenders and as employees. If profits are low and the outlook is discouraging, fewer men will seek to become business owners and more will seek to lend their capital and to work for hire. The interest rate on loans and the rates of wages will tend to fall. As this occurs, the income left over for business owners will tend to rise. This decrease in the proportion of capital and labor which seeks business ownership will continue until the returns of business ownership are as attractive as those from lending and from working for wages. Likewise, if the returns from business ownership are more attractive than the returns from lending and from working for wages, men will shift from lending and working for hire to business ownership until the drop

[8] See pp. 456–458.

in profits and the increase in interest rates and wages destroy its greater attractiveness.   It is interesting to notice that, during recent years, there have been violent shifts in the preference of investors for lending and for buying shares of business owner-ship.   During the period 1922 to 1930, inclusive, for example, nearly three-fifths (57.3 per cent) of private security issues in the United States were either bonds or notes, and slightly more than two-fifths (42.6 per cent) were stocks.   But the intense speculation which developed in the stock market during 1928 and 1929 created a temporary preference for stocks.   In 1928, over half (54.3 per cent) of the domestic corporate issues were stocks and in 1929, nearly three-fourths (73.9 per cent).   In 1930, after the crash in the stock market, the proportion of stock issues fell to a little more than one-third.[9]

It will be observed that it has not been stated that business owners tend to receive the *same* return for their capital as do lenders or for their services as do employees.   What has been said is that business owners tend to receive *an equally attractive* return.   The position of business owners differs so much from that of lenders or hired managers that an equally attractive re-turn may be higher or it may be lower than the amount which they could obtain as lenders or as employees.   But sufficient statistical data are not available to enable us to compare the return of busi-ness owners, as a whole and in the long run, with the return re-ceived by lenders or the wages received by employees.[10]   It is pos-sible, however, to point out some of the things which tend to make the return of business owners different from that of lenders and wage earners.   First, we shall discuss the conditions which affect the return which business owners receive upon their capital, and then the conditions which affect the return which they re-ceive for their services.

V. The Return of Business Owners upon their Capital

Lenders of capital contract for a definite rate of interest upon their funds.   This interest must be paid whether the enter-prise is making money or not.   But the owners of a business con-

---

[9] *Federal Reserve Bulletin*, February, 1931, v. XVII, p. 67.

[10] It is entirely possible, of course, that business owners may receive a higher return on their capital than do lenders but a smaller compensation for their services than do wage earners.   Or the reverse may be true.

cern receive a return only when there is something left after all the expenses of the enterprise, including the interest on borrowed capital, have been paid. It is obvious that the owners assume a greater financial risk than the lenders of capital. How does this additional risk affect the return which business owners receive upon their investment? Does the extra risk so reduce the supply of capital seeking investment in ownership that owners on the average receive a higher return than lenders on the average? In a word, does the extra financial hazard of business ownership enable business owners to obtain an extra return for risk bearing?

Unfortunately the statistical data needed to answer this question are not available. It is worth noting, however, that the question is more complicated than might at first appear. Let us assume that, although men are not able to know whether a given enterprise will be successful, they are able to know precisely in what proportion of cases in the past a given rate of profit or loss has occurred. In the light of such knowledge, it is quite possible that men would divide their investing between lending and buying shares of ownership in such proportions that the chance of profits exceeding the current rate of interest would be exactly counterbalanced by the chance that they would be less. Many business owners would receive a higher return for their capital than the prevailing rate of interest, some would receive a smaller return, and some, of course, would suffer losses. The *average* return of *all* business owners, however, including those who lost money, would be precisely the same as the average return received by lenders.

But is it true that most investors are indifferent as between owning and lending provided only that the average return received by all owners and all lenders is the same? Possibly an overwhelming majority of investors place an exceedingly high value upon security. In this event, the few who are willing to assume the risks of business ownership may be able to obtain an *average* rate of return on their capital which is substantially higher than the average return on loans. But it is also possible that a large proportion of investors are willing to run great risks of loss in order to have even a small chance to make large gains. If this class of investors is sufficiently numerous, so much money may be seeking investment in business ownership and so little seeking investment in loans that the average return on funds invested in business ownership is lower than the average return on loans. We know that many investors are exceedingly cautious and place most of their funds in bonds or in seasoned and conservative common stocks and we know that many others are quite ready to take chances and are ready to put a large part of their resources in highly speculative securities, but we do yet not know whether the first class is so large that business owners receive more than lenders or whether the second class is so large that they receive less than lenders.

Thus far we have assumed that, although investors cannot foresee the precise outcome of any given business venture, they can judge rather accurately the *chances* of gain or loss and thus can compare rather accurately the advantage of becoming business owners and the advantage of lending. But this assumption, of course, is far from true. Prospective investors can know the chances of gain or loss only most imperfectly. They must make their decisions whether to become business owners or lenders on the basis of exceedingly fragmentary and unreliable information. This fact is itself of great importance in determining the relative return of owners and lenders, because, when the information at the disposal of investors is so unsatisfactory, their decisions must depend in large degree upon the bias of each investor, upon his optimism or pessimism, upon his disposition to take long chances or to play safe. From this it follows that the returns of business owners as a whole are probably less than the returns of lenders as a whole. Naturally it is the most optimistic investors, those who are inclined to exaggerate in their minds the chances of gain and to minimize the chances of loss, who are most likely to become business owners rather than lenders. But it is also the optimistic investors, of course, who are most likely to put their funds in enterprises which fail to yield the profits expected of them. When men are compelled to invest upon the basis of such scanty and unreliable data, it is quite probable that the small returns and the losses of the many optimistic investors who become business owners reduce the average return of all business owners to less than that received by lenders.

Another reason for suspecting that the average return of business owners on their capital is less than the return received by lenders is found in the tendency of investors to judge the prospects of profit in an industry by the profits of the existing enterprises. But the firms in business at any instant do not accurately indicate either the chances of gain or the dangers of loss. They are in the main enterprises which have succeeded in surviving because they are efficient. They do not include the many inefficient firms which have failed to survive. A comparison of the number of concerns which are making money at a given time and the number which are losing money does not indicate the proportion of all enterprises which attempted to make money and failed. In fact, it appears to be true that in most industries at most times a majority of the firms are making money, but it also appears to be true that in most industries only a minority of the enterprises which start succeed in surviving as long as ten years.[11] For example, the University of Nebraska School of Business found that, from 1900 to 1924, the average number of grocery stores going out of business in Lincoln each year was 26 per cent of the average number in business.[12] A study of retail trade mortality in Buffalo shows that, of the stores in existence in 1918, the following proportions were still in business ten years later: grocery, 15.9 per cent; shoe, 26.8 per cent; hardware, 29.8 per cent; and drugs, 45.1 per cent.[13] Out of 1663 hotels in 315 cities in 1900, 946, or 57 per cent, had ceased to exist as hotels in 1928.[14] Of 180 firms which engaged in the manufacture of automobiles between 1903 and 1924 only fifty-nine were still in business at the beginning of 1925.[15]

---

[11] Not all withdrawals from business represent failures but the vast majority of them do. An analysis of seventy-four retirements from the grocery business in Lincoln, Nebraska, in 1923 led to the conclusion that in nineteen cases the proprietor sold out with a gain, that in fifty cases he suffered a loss, and that in five the stores changed hands because of ill health, sickness, or death. " Some Aspects of Grocery Store Failures," *University of Nebraska Studies in Business, No. 14*, p. 8.

[12] *Ibid.*, p. 6.

[13] McGarry, E. F., " Retail Trade Mortality," *University of Buffalo Studies in Business, No. 1*, pp. 17, 35, 45, and 55.

[14] " Depreciation and Obsolescence in Hotels," *Report of the Depreciation Committee of the American Hotel Association*, 1928, p. 12.

[15] Epstein, R. C., " The Rise and Fall of Firms in the Automobile Industry,"

VI. The Return of Business Owners upon their Labor

It has been pointed out above that nearly ten million persons, or slightly more than one-fifth of all gainfully employed in the United States, are in business for themselves. Consequently, it is of great importance to ask how the return which these independent business men obtain for their services differs from that which they could obtain as employees. Is their return for their services more or less than the compensation earned by hired employees for similar services?

Most men who go into business for themselves supply part or all of their capital. The return which they receive from the business must be regarded as a return upon *both* their capital and their services. In order to isolate the return which they receive upon their services, it is necessary to determine what part of the return should be assigned to the capital. The return assignable to capital may be determined by the rate of interest commanded by long-term loans which represent about the same risk as the business owner's investment in his own enterprise. Suppose, for example, that an enterpriser has invested $50,000 in a business, that he receives a return of $6,500 a year, and that the return on investments of similar risk is about 6 per cent. In this case, the return on his investment may be put at $3,000 and the compensation for his services at $3,500.

But how does the compensation of business owners compare with the salaries or wages which they might command as employees? Again the confession must be made that the question cannot be answered. The necessary data are not available. It is true that, just as stockholders have a more speculative income than bondholders, so independent business owners, in a sense, have a less certain income than employees. It is possible, though not inevitable, that this additional risk may make men unwilling to become independent business men unless the average return is higher than the average income of employees of similar ability. But this is far from certain. In particular it is to be noted that although, in some respects, the financial risks of the independent business man are greater than those of the employee, in other

Harvard Business Review, January, 1927, v. V, p. 157. Separate companies operated by a single corporation were counted as individual units.

respects they are less. The business owner, it is true, gets paid last and, if nothing is left after expenses have been met, he gets nothing. But as long as the enterprise makes enough for the owner to live on, he is at least sure of a job. This is more than can be said of the employee. His job depends upon the whim of his superior or the need of the enterprise for men and can be taken from him at a moment's notice. In many industries at least, the danger of being laid off or discharged is greater than the danger of being unsuccessful in business and it is probable that thousands of men accept the hazards of business ownership in order to escape the still greater hazards of being hired employees subject to lay-off or discharge without warning. Possibly the greater security of business ownership renders men willing to continue as independent business men for substantially less than they could earn as employees.

The persons who go into business for themselves, just as the persons who purchase stocks rather than bonds, undoubtedly comprise an unusually large proportion of optimists, of willing chance-takers. These hopeful and willing chance-takers undoubtedly are led to start many enterprises under unfavorable circumstances and their losses may reduce the average return of all business owners for their services to a point below the salaries received by employees of similar ability.

An exceedingly important characteristic of the position of the independent business man is his so-called independence. It is fairly clear that in some respects the business owner has less freedom than a hired employee. It is true that he does not have to be at work at the stroke of a certain hour every day and work until another stroke. He can make his hours more or less to suit himself. But a move from one town to another is practically equivalent to going out of business and starting in again. Certainly the employee has far more freedom of movement. Even getting away on an extended vacation may be more difficult for the owner than for the employee. But some of the kinds of freedom which go with ownership, especially the freedom to decide policies and the authority to give orders instead of being compelled to take them, are very dear to some men.

Finally, a degree of prestige often goes with owning a business and this is attractive to many men.

When account is taken of all the men who prefer business ownership because of its greater security, those who prefer it because they are optimists and have great faith in their ability to make money, those who prefer it because it gives them greater freedom and authority, and those who prefer it because of the prestige which it confers, the probability seems strong that the number of men who become independent business owners is sufficient to reduce the average return for their services below the wages paid to employees of about the same ability. As has been said before, statistical proof of this belief is impossible. Nevertheless, for one important industry, agriculture, it is possible to make a rough comparison of the wages paid to employees and the part of profits which are left for business owners after a moderate return has been allowed on their investment. Such a comparison is contained in the following table. The estimates are those of Dr. W. I. King.[16]

Year	Income attributable to farmers and their families (per family)	Average annual earnings of wage earners attached to agriculture
1909	$50	$285
1910	542	277
1911	426	290
1912	818	298
1913	187	306
1914	726	301
1915	916	304
1916	−384	331
1917	136	407
1918	581	474
1919	786	567
1920	1,161	653
1921	−311	551
1922	509	489
1923	442	513
1924	165	516
1925	−64	526
1926	686*	535
1927	963*	533

* Preliminary estimate

The labor income was computed by deducting from the total agricultural income of farmers a return of 5½ per cent on the estimated investment in farms. In eleven out of the nineteen

---

[16] King, W. I., *The National Income and Its Purchasing Power*, pp. 146 and 312.

years, the labor income of farmers and their families exceeded the average annual earnings of farm employees. The average labor income of farmers and their families for the entire nineteen year period was $439 as against average annual earnings of $429 for farm laborers. This might be interpreted as indicating that independent business men in agriculture receive a slightly larger compensation for their services than do employees. But obviously a deduction must be made from the labor income of farmers and their families because of the fact that it is the compensation for services rendered by the *entire family,* not merely the farmer himself. It is conservative to assume that the combined services of the wife and children are at least one half as important as those of the farmer himself. If this assumption is accepted, then it appears that the average labor income of farmers for the entire period is substantially less than the average annual earnings of hired men — $293 as against $429. In thirteen out of the nineteen years, the farmers earned less than their employees.

But even if it be true that men are willing to become independent business men for less than they could command as employees, it does not necessarily mean that the ultimate consumer obtains goods for less than he otherwise would. In fact, the very eagerness of a multitude of men to be independent, even in the face of a return below that of employees, may in a few instances compel the consumer to pay more instead of less for goods. The reason has been explained in Chapter XV.[17] The multitude of small independent enterprises may prevent the development of large scale concerns and thus prevent the attainment of the economies of production in large business units. If some enterprises could become large enough, they might be able to undersell the small independent business men. But they may be prevented from becoming large by a process of gradual growth because of the impossibility of obtaining hired employees for as little as independent business men are willing to accept.

VII. Some Functional Aspects of Profits

Profits are assumed to perform two principal functions: (1) bringing about the distribution of production among different industries in accordance with the demand for it and (2) stimu-

[17] Pp. 338–343.

lating managerial efficiency. How well do they perform these functions?

Undoubtedly capital tends in a rough way to flow mainly into the industries where profits are large — where the demand for capital is greatest and where investors can obtain the highest return for their investment. This tendency is, of course, partly a result of the fact that men prefer to invest where the prospects for gain seem best. But it is also a result of the fact that much capital is obtained by the re-investment of earnings. When earnings are large, enterprises are *able* to plow back more. In addition, when the owners find that their enterprise is unusually profitable, they are more willing to permit a large part of the earnings to be kept in the business.

Despite the general tendency of capital to go where it will yield the largest return, huge amounts each year are invested where they yield little or no profit. For this there are several reasons. When capital is invested in established concerns, some estimate of future earnings can sometimes be made from past earnings. But in a large proportion of cases no accurate information concerning past earnings is available. Consider, for example, the single item of the allowance for depreciation. Unless this is known, one cannot judge the reliability of the income statement. And yet Mr. L. H. Sloan has pointed out that less than half of the industrial corporations give illuminating information on this point.[18] And even when accurate information concerning profits is available, it is not, of course, an infallible guide. In fact, as has been emphasized several times, the acceptance of past and present profits as a guide in expanding the capacity of an industry is almost certain to result in overexpansion. The history of investment shows that a sudden and spectacular increase in the profits of an industry is almost invariably followed by overdevelopment of the industry and the waste of vast amounts of capital, because investors insist on believing that large profits in the past indicate large profits in the future.

Far more difficult than the decision of whether or not to invest in an established enterprise is the decision of whether or not to invest in one that is just being launched. This decision must be made on the basis of so many unknowns that mistakes are

[18] Sloan, L. H., *Corporation Profits*, p. 59.

bound to be frequent. The majority of newly established concerns fail and every failure involves a more or less serious loss of capital. The number of persons who have funds to invest runs into the millions. Relatively few of them are skilled in judging investment opportunities and reliable advice is difficult to obtain because investment bankers, like other merchants, are inclined to recommend whatever they have on hand to sell.

Because of the fact that investment opportunities are often exceedingly difficult to appraise and because many investors are neither competent to appraise them nor able to seek reliable advice, many millions of dollars of securities which should never be sold are marketed each year. This statement does not refer to the out-and-out fraudulent issues but to the securities of legitimate enterprises which will never yield more than a trifling profit. The loss to the individual investors is, of course, obvious. What is perhaps more important but less obvious is the loss to the community. The community loses because, when capital is invested so that it yields little or no profit, it is probably making only a small and unimportant addition to the supply of goods.

But even capital which yields large returns to the owners may yield little or no return to the community. This is clear in case the capital is used to produce articles that are useless or harmful. But it is also true that capital which is highly productive in commodities which are badly needed may yield only a small return to the community. This seems paradoxical but the explanation is simple. A principal effect of the investment of new capital may be, as we have seen,[19] to put out of operation less efficient plants or machines. The gain to the community from the new investments is represented by the productivity of new capital *minus the loss of production from the old capital*.[20] This

---

[19] Pp. 344–346.

[20] The *future* as well as the present productivity of the capital must be taken into account in estimating the effect of new capital upon the community. Suppose that the introduction of a machine which will make 10,000 units a year and will last ten years puts out of operation a machine in another factory which will make 5,000 units a year and which would ordinarily run five more years before becoming useless. The value of the new machine *to the community* is obviously the present value of 10,000 units of product a year for ten years minus the present value of 5,000 units a year for five years. If labor and repair costs on the two machines are not the same, it would also be necessary, of course, to allow for these differences in computing the value of the machines.

is one reason why the desire of investors for the greatest possible profit does not necessarily guide new capital into the industries or regions where it will produce the largest return to the community.

Unquestionably one of the greatest problems in modern economic society is how to protect the interest of the community in the way that new capital is invested — how to prevent capital from being wasted by being invested in concerns which have little chance for success, how to prevent it from being invested in industries which, relative to other industries, are already overdeveloped, and how to prevent it from being invested where its principal effect is to drive out existing enterprises rather than to increase the total product available for consumption. Thus far the investment bankers, who perform the function of helping business concerns obtain capital and of helping investors find securities for their funds, have shown little capacity to deal with these major problems of investment policy.

How effective are profits as a method of stimulating managerial efficiency? Profits would appear to be most effective in the case of small enterprises where the owner and manager are one and where the manager, therefore, receives all of the profits. It is true that most of the small, one-man business concerns which abound in retailing and farming are notoriously poorly managed. This might be taken to indicate that profits are not an effective stimulant of good management, but the conclusion would be unwarranted. Most of the small enterprises in retailing and farming are poorly managed simply because good managerial ability is scarce. All that the low level of managerial efficiency in these industries proves, therefore, is that the incentive of profits is not capable of making good managers out of men who possess little managerial capacity.

But an outstanding characteristic of modern industry is the separation of ownership and management. The heads and principal executives of most large corporations own a very small proportion of the stock. The great bulk of the profits of the enterprise goes to persons who have little or nothing to do with the efficiency of the management. How do profits work under these conditions? Does the management which receives only a trifling part of the profits of an enterprise concern itself seriously with the efficiency of operations? Is the separation of ownership and management gradually rendering profits obsolete as a device for stimulating managerial efficiency?

As business enterprises go, the large corporations which are owned in the main by non-managers do not appear to be poorly administered. How much better they might be managed if the ownership were more largely concentrated in the executives, no one can say. Possibly the improvement in the efficiency of the management would be very great, perhaps there would be little or no improvement. At any rate, it seems clear that the separation of ownership and management does not prevent large enterprises from being well administered. It is desirable to notice some of the reasons why it does not.

In the first place, large enterprises can afford to pay enough to attract the best managerial ability. In the second place, when a concern employs hired executives, administrative capacity usually plays a large part in their selection and promotion. One reason why many small concerns are poorly administered is because the manager is not selected for his competency as a manager. Anyone who has saved enough or who can borrow enough can start a small enterprise if he wishes to and many persons who possess little managerial capacity wish to try the experiment of being their own boss. In the third place, even though managers own only a small part of the enterprise and receive only a small part of the profits, profits are an important measuring stick by which their competency is judged. Besides profits there are other measures of efficiency, such as unit costs and also physical measures. These indicators of administrative performance are powerful spurs to efficiency because upon the ability of managers to make a satisfactory record depends their success in holding their jobs and in obtaining better jobs. In the fourth place, hired managers work under the supervision of a board of directors. Some boards are far more competent and far better informed about the operations of their enterprises than others. To the newness of the corporate form of organization is largely attributable the fact that stockholders in many concerns have failed to appreciate the importance of having competent and interested directors and have permitted places to go as honors to men who have known little about the business and have had little interest in finding out. But a competent board which keeps itself well informed about the problems and operation of the enterprise is likely to be a powerful spur to the management. In the fifth place, managements are affected by competition, direct and indirect. The aggressive marketing methods of modern business expose nearly every concern to intense competition. Even if an enterprise is a monopoly, it is affected by the competition between commodities, for improvements in other commodities or reductions in their prices may cause consumers to shift their purchasing away from the good which a monopoly makes. The constant improvements which enterprises are making in their wares and the reductions which they are making in their prices compel each management to strive strenuously to make its products more salable and to cut its prices. Finally, a tremendous spur to managerial efficiency is created by the nature of modern industrial costs. Heavy fixed costs, we have seen, cause any falling off in sales to produce a disproportionate drop in profit. Consequently, managements must struggle energetically to prevent a drop in sales and when, in spite of all efforts to prevent it, a drop occurs, they must leave no stone unturned to counteract the effect on profits by discovering ways of cutting costs. In other words, when the aggressive marketing methods and the heavy fixed costs of modern business cause even a slight drop in managerial efficiency to produce such a disastrous drop in profits, the spur of ownership does not seem to be needed to produce alert and energetic administration. But despite the many conditions which tend to make for efficiency even among hired managers, there appears to be a steady tendency for enterprises to introduce profit-sharing schemes among their executives.

When we examine the conditions under which business concerns are managed most efficiently, it appears that, not the hope for more profits, but the fear of loss or of smaller profits is the stronger spur to efficiency. Evidence of this is abundant. The mere hope of gain was not sufficient to prevent policies and practices from being dominated by tradition and custom either in farming, where the individual enterprise is supreme, or in railroading, where ownership and management are separated. But the rise of competition from busses and motor trucks has given the managements of railroads the greatest incentive to raise their efficiency which they have had in over a generation, and the depression that has prevailed in many branches of agriculture since 1920 has caused farmers rapidly to improve their methods. Indeed, the downward trend in the general price level that has prevailed since 1920 has been a powerful stimulant to more alert, enterprising, and intelligent management in all branches of industry.

Thus far we have discussed profits as a stimulant of managerial efficiency without inquiring what kind of efficiency they encourage. Do they make managers efficient in doing things that are beneficial to the community or in doing things that are harmful to the community? The answer, of course, is that they do both — they encourage managers to do whatever is profitable, regardless of whether it is injurious or beneficial to the community. What is profitable depends, of course, upon circumstances. A monopoly, as a rule, finds it profitable to restrict output, competitors to increase output until additional production would cost more than the price which it would bring. The pursuit of profits may lead a concern either to adulterate its goods or to spend millions upon research to improve its product; it may lead some enterprises to spend vast sums upon the invention of improved machinery and others to spend huge amounts to prevent or delay the use of the new devices; it may lead some concerns to consume wantonly the lives of their employees by speeding up and by neglecting to establish safeguards against accidents and industrial diseases, or it may lead them to go to great expense to guard their employees against accidents, disease, or excessive fatigue. In order to make the institution of production for private profit work satisfactorily, it is important to make the conditions of industry such that it is profitable for enterprises to pursue policies that are beneficial to the community and unprofitable for them to pursue policies that are harmful. Much of the regulation of industry by the government has this for its purpose. Indeed, the guidance of economic activity by creating conditions which make it profitable for industry to pursue the policies which are socially advantageous, and unprofitable to pursue policies which are socially harmful is rapidly becoming a major function of government — comparable to the functions of protecting life and property and enforcing contracts.[21]

But in spite of everything that can be done to make the advantage of individual business enterprises coincide with the welfare of the community, there are bound to be a multitude of acts and policies which are profitable to business enterprises and yet harmful to the community. To restrain business men from seizing every opportunity to turn a penny regardless of the effect upon others, we must rely partly upon ethical and professional standards. It is doubtful, however, whether the restraints imposed by ethical and professional standards will be enough. The business manager of today is a partisan; he represents one class in modern economic society — the business owner. He is paid to manage industry so as to produce the largest return to business owners regardless of how the rest of the community is affected. It is true, as has been pointed out, that he sometimes puts his own interests ahead of those of the stockholders or business owners by whom he is employed.[22] Nevertheless, in the main, he represents the interests of business owners. As long as managers are partisans, as long as they represent one economic class rather than all economic classes, it would seem to be inevitable that industry will be managed in the interest of this class. No external control — whether it be competition, the law, or ethical standards — can entirely counteract the strategic advantage which business owners derive from the fact that they appoint the managers of industry. No external control can make the policies of partisan managers harmonize completely with the interests of the community. As long as the present form of industrial organization persists, the achievement of national prosperity must be more or less of an accidental by-product of the pursuit of private profit — a result of the fact that it often (though not always) pays business enterprises to pursue policies which are beneficial to the rest of the community.

The essential difficulty, be it noted, is not primarily with the institution of private profit itself; the difficulty is with the organi-

[21] In fact, the guidance of economic activity is really an extension of the government's function of protecting life and property. Workmen's compensation laws, for example, which give employers an incentive to prevent accidents are simply an additional way in which the government protects life.

[22] Pp. 144-145.

zation of industry and with the way in which the institution of private profit functions when the control of management is exclusively in the hands of business owners. Under another organization of industry, in which the management would be neutral instead of partisan, responsible equally to each of the three basic economic interests — property owners, wage earners, and consumers — the institution of profit would function very differently. Profits would still be useful in guiding the investment of capital and they would still be a valuable check upon some aspects of managerial efficiency. They would not, however, be the sole criterion of efficiency and they would not be the sole, or even the predominant, determinant of industrial policies. Inevitably the question arises: Might not the community possibly be better off under a form of industrial organization which would make managers neutrals instead of partisans, which would make them the servants, not merely of business owners, but equally of wage earners and consumers?

REFERENCES

Carver, T. N., *The Distribution of Wealth*, 1904.
Foreman, C. J., *Efficiency and Scarcity Profits*, 1930.
James, Gorton, Dennison, H. S., Gay, E. F., Kendall, H. P., Burritt, A. W., *Profit Sharing and Stock Ownership for Employees*, 1926.
Knight, F. H., *Risk, Uncertainty and Profit*, 1921.
Marshall, Alfred, *Principles of Economics* (eighth edition), 1920. Bk. VI, ch. VI and VII.

CHAPTER XXVIII

THE SUPPORT OF THE STATE

I. THE ISSUES. II. THE TAX SYSTEM OF THE UNITED STATES. III. HOW DOES THE GOVERNMENT SPEND ITS MONEY? IV. HOW SHOULD THE BURDEN OF TAXATION BE DISTRIBUTED? V. THE SHIFTING OF TAXES. VI. THE PRINCIPAL FAULTS OF THE TAX SYSTEM OF THE UNITED STATES. VII. THE GEOGRAPHICAL UNIT OF TAXATION. VIII. SUGGESTIONS FOR IMPROVING THE TAX SYSTEM.

I. THE ISSUES

The tax collections in the United States in 1928 amounted to $77.39 per capita.[1] This was over $180 per gainfully employed person. Many of our taxes we pay without knowing it. Taxes, as some one has said, are in our grocery bills, our house rent, in the price we pay for tobacco, clothing, and a multitude of other things that we purchase. Approximately 12 per cent of the national income is taken by the state in the form of taxation.[2] But the tax burden in the United States is substantially less than in European countries. In Great Britain, it is about 22 per cent of the national income; in France, about 17 per cent; in Italy, about 19 per cent.[3] The amount of the tax payments varies enormously among the states. In the case of state and local taxes, the high state in 1927 was Nevada, where the per capita collections were $86.39, and the low was Alabama, where the per capita collections were $17.68.[4]

The amount taken by the government in taxes has been growing rapidly. In 1890, tax collections in the United States were

---

[1] National Industrial Conference Board, *The Cost of Government in the United States, 1927–1928*, p. 64.

[2] *Ibid.*, p. 69.

[3] Patterson, E. M., "Europe in 1927," *Annals of the American Academy of Political and Social Science*, November, 1927, CXXXIV, p. 40.

[4] *The Cost of Government in the United States, 1927–1928*, Table 33, p. 73. Other high states were California ($78.16), New York ($76.10), Florida ($73.83); other low states were Georgia ($18.18) and Arkansas ($19.96).

about $13.88 per capita and constituted about 7 per cent of the national income.[5] In 1924, the state of New York collected under its general property tax more than 230 times as much as in 1840.[6] But the increase in taxes is far from a new phenomenon. In fact, it has been going on during most of the life of the nation. Between 1846 and 1855, for example, state and local taxes in New York more than doubled, and, in 1870, they were nearly eleven times as large as in 1846.[7] Nor is it necessarily to be deplored that a larger and larger part of the national income is being spent by the government today than formerly. The essential question is: Does the money bring a larger return when it is spent by the government than it would if it were spent by individuals? It is not improbable that many of the expenditures of the government (for education, roads, public health, recreation, security) yield more satisfaction than most of the expenditures by individuals. Nevertheless, it is obvious that, the larger the proportion of the national income which is taken by the government, the more important it becomes that the burden be fairly distributed. Likewise, the more important become the effects of taxes upon industrial activities. If unfairly and unwisely levied, heavy taxes may be exceedingly harmful to the economic life of the community.

The rapid growth in the demand for governmental services, in conjunction with the rapid industrial development of the country, has rendered the tax system of the United States badly out of date. The state and local governments in particular have met their needs largely by increasing old forms of taxes, especially taxes on real estate. But the industrial growth of the country has made incomes from real estate less and less important and has created many new forms of income which now largely escape taxation. In these days of large-scale industry, when America has become the greatest manufacturing country in the world, we are still attempting to support our government by a system of taxation which, for the most part, was designed for small rural communities without large manufacturing industries. Even

[5] *Ibid.*, pp. 44 and 64.
[6] Kendrick, M. Slade, "An Outline of the New York State System of Taxation," *Cornell Extension Bulletin 152*, p. 17.
[7] Lutz, H. L., *The State Tax Commission*, p. 23. A substantial part of the increase between 1846 and 1870 was caused by a rise in the general price level.

within New York State, the financial center of the country and the first state in value of manufactures, the state and the various local governments raise about 70 per cent of their total tax revenue by taxes on real estate.

We shall begin our study of the support of the state by a brief description of the tax system of the United States. Then we shall inquire into what constitutes a fair distribution of the burden of taxation. The person who pays a tax to the government is often not the person who really bears the burden. Frequently the taxpayer can shift the tax to some one else. What determines his ability to do this? To what extent and under what conditions can taxes not be shifted? It is impossible to collect the money necessary to support the state without penalizing to some extent desirable economic activities, such as working and saving. But a poorly planned system of taxation may discourage them far more than a wisely constructed system. In fact, a badly devised system of taxation may positively encourage industrial waste, such as the wasteful exploitation of natural resources. After examining the principles which determine the fairness of taxes, the possibilities of shifting the burden of taxes, and the effects of taxes upon industry, we shall undertake an appraisal of the tax system of the country. Is the burden distributed with reasonable fairness? Are some branches of industry or some forms of economic activity excessively discouraged? Are wasteful industrial policies encouraged? What changes are needed to adapt our system of taxation to this age of large-scale machine industry?

II. The Tax System of the United States

Practically half of the taxes in the United States are collected by the local communities, that is, by municipalities, counties, and school districts. About one-sixth are collected by the states, and slightly more than one-third by the federal government. The money is not always spent by the authority which collects it. Part of the federal revenues, for example, go to the states to subsidize road building, education, and other activities. Likewise, some of the revenues of the states are turned over to the local communities. During the fiscal year ending June 30, 1929, the state of Wisconsin collected nearly $42,000,000 in taxes, of which nearly half, or $19,530,000, was distributed by the state as aids to local communities.[8] In the main, however, the money is spent by the authorities who collect it. The tendency has been for the proportion of the taxes collected by the federal government to shrink and for that collected by the states and the local communities to increase. The change between 1890 and 1928 was as follows:[9]

	1890	*1928*
Federal	42.7 per cent	34.4 per cent
State	11.0	15.8
Local	46.3	49.8

The federal government derives practically all of its tax revenue from various forms of income and sales taxes, including in sales taxes the customs duties. Corporate and personal income taxes form nearly two-thirds of the total federal tax revenue, with the corporation income tax yielding 34.8 per cent of the total in 1928, and the personal income tax 30.9 per cent. Customs receipts, which for many years were by far the largest source of income for the federal government, yielded in 1928 only 17.2 per cent of the revenue. Sumptuary excises, such as the taxes on spirits, fermented liquors, tobacco, oleomargarine, opium, and other narcotics, yielded 12.7 per cent. Various other taxes — the estate tax, the corporation capital stock tax, and others — yielded 4.4 per cent of the revenue.[10]

Over four-fifths of the tax revenue collected by the states comes from four principal kinds of taxes — property taxes; business license and business income taxes; motor vehicle licenses; and sales and excise taxes. By far the largest source of revenue are the property taxes which, in 1927, yielded 34.7 per cent of the revenue; business license and business income taxes yielded 18.7 per cent; motor vehicle licenses, 18.4 per cent; and gasoline taxes, 12.2 per cent. Only sixteen states in 1927 had income taxes and these provided only 4.1 per cent of the tax revenue of all states. Every state except three levies an inheritance tax, but

---

[8] Wisconsin Tax Commission, *Report for Year Ending June 30, 1929*, pp. 233–235. About $9,000,000 was distributed as educational aids, $9,100,000 as highway aids, and $1,400,000 as charitable aids.

[9] National Industrial Conference Board, *The Cost of Government in the United States, 1927–1928*, p. 69.

[10] *Ibid.*, p. 82.

the rates in most instances are not high and these taxes provide less than 8 per cent of the revenue.[11]

Cities, counties, and school districts derive practically all of their revenue from property taxes. In 1928, the percentage was 92.8.[12] Licenses and permits yielded 4.2 per cent and other taxes 2.9 per cent. It must be remembered that the local units, especially the counties, usually receive from the states a substantial part of the automobile license fees and of the gasoline taxes.

In this brief survey of the tax system of the United States, three things stand out: (1) the extremely large proportion of revenue derived from property taxes; (2) the large proportion of revenue obtained from sales taxes and from corporate income and license taxes; and (3) the exceedingly small proportion of revenue derived from personal income taxes. Of the tax revenue collected by all governmental units in the United States — federal, state, and local — almost exactly half is derived from taxes on property and less than one-ninth from taxes on personal income. The taxes on property are, in the main, taxes on real estate. They are a heritage from the day when real estate was the principal source of income in the community and when, in consequence, it bore most of the cost of supporting the government. As the expenses of government have grown, various forms of business and sales taxes have been added, but the voters have been reluctant to permit direct taxation of their incomes and only the federal government derives a substantial part of its tax revenue from this source.

III. How Does the Government Spend Its Money?

The largest single expenditure of the government is the redemption of the public debt and the payment of interest on the debt. Of the total disbursements of the nation, the states, and the local governments in 1927, nearly one-fourth were for these purposes. Nearly one-fifth (19.2 per cent) were for education, slightly less (17.8 per cent) were for protection — police, military, and navy — and about one-seventh (14.0 per cent) for highways.[13] Only one-fourteenth (7.1 per cent) of all expenditures were for general administration.

---

[11] *The Cost of Government in the United States, 1927–1928*, pp. 94–97.
[12] *Ibid.*, p. 105.
[13] *Ibid.*, pp. 11–13.

The outlay of the national government for redemption of the debt and interest on the debt represents almost entirely payment of the cost of war. If these are included in the expenditures for protection, as they should be, 26.7 per cent of all disbursements went for protection. A substantial part of the debts of the state and local governments were incurred for school buildings and highways. If the payments on this part of the debt are added to the other outlays for education and highways, nearly one-fourth of all disbursements would be found to go for education and close to one-fifth for highways. Indeed the three major objects of protection, education, and highway transportation account for approximately two-thirds of the cost of government. In the cost of the recent war, in the demand of the community for more and better educational facilities, and in its demand for more and better highways, therefore, is to be found most of the explanation of the increasing share of the national income which goes to support the state. If the taxpayer grumbles because his tax bill has been rapidly rising, he can blame it on the war, the automobile, and the thirst, if not for knowledge, at least for more schooling.

IV. How Should the Burden of Taxation Be Distributed?

Approximately one-eighth of the national income, we have seen, goes to support the government. How should the burden be distributed? Should some entirely escape bearing part of the burden? Should everyone, no matter how large or how small his income, pay the same *percentage* to the government? Or should some pay a higher share of their incomes than others? Three ways of distributing the cost of government merit consideration. The cost might be distributed (1) on the basis of the benefits conferred by the government upon the individuals; (2) so that the sacrifice imposed on all persons would be the same; (3) so that it would fall upon the recipients of unearned incomes. An examination of these theories will indicate that each has merits and limitations and that none of them alone furnishes a satisfactory basis for distributing the cost of government.

It might seem fair to distribute the burden in proportion to the benefits conferred by the government. This principle encounters the obvious objection that the benefit usually cannot be measured. How ascertain the benefit which various individuals derive from the army, the police, the public health service? One of the purposes of government is to produce a well-ordered, peaceful, and healthful community. When the government gives protection against invasion, violence, fire, or disease it may, to some extent, confer special benefits upon certain persons but it is also benefiting the entire community. Even in the few cases where it is possible to measure more or less definitely the value of the service conferred by the police or the fire department upon certain persons, there is no way of measuring the value of a police department, the fire department, or the public health service to the community as a whole. And even if benefits could be measured, it would not do, as a general rule, to make taxes proportionate to them. Governments are used, in part, to meet certain basic needs which are so important that they must be satisfied regardless of the individual's ability to pay. Protection against violence and disease, a certain minimum of education, the support given to the blind, the insane, and other handicapped persons are examples of the moral claims which, it is felt, every individual has against the community. Were taxes assessed on the basis of the benefit received, many persons would be unable to pay their tax bills.

But the benefit theory of taxation should not be entirely discarded. The government makes some expenditures which confer special benefits and special favors upon certain individuals. In these instances, it is desirable to collect at least the cost of rendering the special service. The improvement of streets is a case in point. No doubt it would be unfair to assess the entire expense upon the abutting property, because the whole community benefits. Nevertheless, the abutting property should bear a substantial part of the cost. Otherwise municipal governments would soon find themselves contributing heavily to the financing of real estate developments. The provision of free roads by the government is another illustration. As long as roads were used for short local hauls, there was no serious problem. But now that motor trucks and busses compete with the railroads for long hauls, there is danger that the government, by subsidizing motor transportation through the gift of free roads, will encourage a method of transportation which, when all costs are taken into account, including the cost of building and maintaining the road, is more expensive than transportation by rail. This is why part of the expense of building, improving, and maintaining roads should be assessed against busses and trucks by licenses and gasoline taxes.

The principle of payment according to benefits received is not, we have seen, a satisfactory basis for most taxes. Another theory of taxation is the equality-of-sacrifice theory. According to this theory, the tax payments of all persons should represent the same sacrifice. This principle is consistent with the fact that the government is largely engaged in protecting the common interests of everyone in the community and in discharging certain moral obligations which, it is felt, the community has to the weak, the handicapped, and the unfortunate. In so far as the expenses of government are incurred, not for the purpose of conferring special benefits upon certain groups, but for the purpose of promoting the interests or of meeting the common obligations of all members of the community, it is only fair that every income receiver should bear the same burden as every other income receiver. In other words, equality of sacrifice seems the proper basis for distributing most of the costs of government.

But the equality-of-sacrifice theory encounters the same practical difficulty as the benefit theory. Just as it is impossible to compare the benefits conferred by government upon different men (except in a few cases where the government confers a definite pecuniary benefit), so it is also impossible to compare the sacrifice that a given payment would impose upon different individuals. No one knows how much a dollar means to different persons. We are accustomed to assume that a dollar means less to a rich man than it does to a poor man, but there is no way of proving this. It is entirely possible, for example, that a rich man, because he has numerous desires and numerous uses for money, would feel the loss of $10,000 far more than some poor men of simple tastes and few desires would feel the loss of $50. Because it is impossible to compare individual sacrifices, it is necessary, in applying the equal-sacrifice theory, to rely upon certain assumptions which seem fair and reasonable but which, nevertheless, cannot be proved to be either correct or incorrect.

The impossibility of measuring sacrifice has led many economists to prefer the principle of basing taxes upon ability to pay.

The expression " ability to pay " is in some respects superior to the expression "equality of sacrifice." It avoids creating the impression that sacrifice can be measured. But when one asks what is meant by ability to pay, one encounters the same difficulties that arise in applying the equal-sacrifice principle. Is the ability-to-pay principle satisfied when every man contributes the same percentage of his income in taxes? The courts of some states (Massachusetts and New Hampshire, for example) have held that uniformity in taxation requires that the same rate be levied upon incomes of all sizes.[14] If the rate is 3 per cent, it must be 3 per cent for all incomes. Few persons would probably agree that a poor man, receiving an income of say, $1,000, is able to pay a tax of $30 as easily as a man with an income of $100,000 is able to pay a tax of $3,000. After all, the man receiving $100,000 still has $97,000 left after paying his tax. A more convincing argument can be made for the conclusion that ability to pay is measured by what a man has left after he has paid his tax. For example, it might be argued that a man with an annual income of $100,000 is better able to pay a tax of $95,000 than is a man with an income of $5,000 a tax of one dollar, because, after paying $95,000, the first man would have $5,000 left to spend and the second man, after paying one dollar, would have only $4,999. But no one would regard it as fair to concentrate the expense of supporting the government exclusively upon the recipients of very large incomes.[15] We are forced into the conclusion that the ability-to-pay principle is tenable only when ability to pay means that each taxpayer, in paying his contribution to the support of the state, makes the same sacrifice. In the last analysis, therefore, the ability-to-pay and the equal-sacrifice principles are one and the same thing.

The equal-sacrifice or ability-to-pay principle appears to require that the rich pay a higher rate of taxation than the poor — in other words that taxes be *progressive*. The justification of a

[14] Even in these states, the courts permit the total exemption of incomes below a given amount and also an exemption for dependents.

[15] Nor would it be wise. The output of industry would be reduced, partly because the incentive of business leaders to do their best would be weakened and partly because the accumulation of capital would be substantially retarded. A large part of saving is done, we have seen, by recipients of large incomes. Since all but a small residue of each large income would be taken by the state, saving by the well-to-do would be greatly reduced.

progressive tax is the assumption that, as a general rule, a dollar means less to a man who possesses many of them than to a man who possesses few of them. It is taken for granted that a loss of 5 per cent of his income would be a greater burden to a man receiving $1,000 a year than to one receiving $100,000. The rich man would still have $95,000 to spend, but the poor man would have only $950. The assumption, let it be stressed again, cannot be proved to be either correct or incorrect. Nevertheless it seems to be fair and reasonable. Of course, even after one has arrived at the conclusion that the equal-sacrifice principle involves *some* progression in taxes, there arises the far more difficult question: How much? If incomes of $4,000 to $8,000 are taxed at 1½ per cent, should incomes of $100,000 or more be taxed at 10 per cent, or 20 per cent, or 33 per cent, or what rate? The answers of no two persons are likely to be the same.[16]

Some persons believe that the government should be supported either entirely or in part by taxing unearned incomes. The most common example of the tax on unearned incomes is the inheritance tax. Nearly all the countries of Europe have an inheritance tax and forty-five of the forty-eight states impose one. So also does the federal government. In some countries, the tax is steeply graduated on the largest fortunes. In Great Britain it runs up to 40 per cent. Andrew Carnegie advocated a tax of 50 per cent on very large estates.[17] The proposal of the single taxers is based upon the belief that the burden of supporting the government should fall upon unearned incomes. The single taxers believe that the predominating form of unearned income is that part of the rise in land values which results from the increase in population. Consequently, they propose to support the gov-

[16] In the case of the Federal income tax, for example, there is no tax on incomes of $1,500 a year or less in the case of single persons, or of $3,500 in the case of married persons. In addition, there is a personal exemption of $400 for each child under eighteen years of age or for each person incapable of self-support who is supported by the taxpayer. Upon the amount remaining, there is a tax of 1½ per cent on the first $4,000 of income, 3 per cent on the next $4,000, and 5 per cent above that. In addition, all incomes above $10,000 pay a surtax. The surtax begins at 1 per cent and rises by gradual increments until it becomes 20 per cent on the part of the net income in excess of $100,000. The Federal income tax provides for a credit of 25 per cent on all earned incomes (income from labor as distinguished from income derived from property) up to $30,000.

[17] Hunter, M. H., *Outlines of Public Finance*, p. 331.

ernment by a single tax upon the so-called unearned increment of land values.[18]   The proposal to levy a special tax on excess profits (that is, profits in excess of the normal rate) arises from the belief that very large profits are usually, in part at least, the result of luck.

The idea of supporting the government by taxing unearned income has many attractions.   But there are almost insuperable administrative difficulties in determining who are receiving unearned incomes and how much of their incomes is unearned. Consequently the taxation of unearned incomes has been confined almost entirely to inheritances.

From this brief analysis of alternative bases of taxation we may draw the following tentative conclusions: (1) that the activities of the government which advance the common interests of the community or which discharge the community's moral obligations should be supported by taxes levied as nearly as possible in accordance with the principle of equal sacrifice or of ability to pay — that is, taxes imposed at a higher rate upon large incomes than upon small; (2) that the governmental activities which confer special benefits upon certain groups in the community and which do not represent the discharge of moral obligations to those groups should be supported by taxes levied either in proportion to the benefit conferred (where that is measurable) or in accordance with the cost of rendering the service; and (3) that, to the extent that unearned incomes can be easily and accurately detected, they should be heavily taxed in order to lighten the burden falling upon earned incomes.

But these general principles alone are not safe guides in constructing a system of taxation.   *Every specific tax must be judged by the particular economic effects which it produces.*   A tax, for example, may appear to correspond with the principle of equal sacrifice and yet it may produce certain effects which make it highly undesirable.   Furthermore, there is much to be said for the conclusion that the government, in addition to taxing all recipients of income within its jurisdiction in accordance with the principles of equal sacrifice or benefits received, should also levy

---

[18] Although the desirability of taxing unearned income is the principal argument of the single taxers, they advance other reasons in support of their proposal.

at least a small tax on all tangible property within its jurisdiction (subject to a few special exceptions) whether owned by residents or nonresidents and upon all businesses conducted for profit. This would mean that nonresidents would be compelled to pay a tax for the protection of their property and that all business enterprises would make a contribution to the support of the state.[19] Such a system of taxation, as an entirety, would not, of course, correspond closely either to the benefit or to the ability-to-pay principle. It would not correspond to the benefit principle, because there would be no necessary or close connection between the amount of taxes paid and the benefits received. It would not correspond to the ability-to-pay or equal-sacrifice theory, because neither the taxes on tangible property nor those on business concerns are likely to be consistent with the equal-sacrifice theory. This is true of taxes on property because it is not practicable to make them progressive — that is, to impose a higher rate upon the property of large owners. Even less do taxes on business enterprises correspond to the equal-sacrifice theory. For example, a tax of one per cent on the net income of business enterprises would reduce by one per cent the profits received by every owner regardless of whether his income were large or small. Nevertheless, it would seem to be a sound principle that every person, every piece of tangible property, and every business (barring a few exceptions of a special character) should pay a contribution to the state.

V. The Shifting of Taxes

In appraising the fairness of a system of taxation, it is essential to discover who really pays the taxes. It has been pointed out that the people who actually hand over money to the government may not be the persons who really bear the burden. Political and administrative considerations often lead governments to concentrate the levy of taxes upon relatively small and easily discovered groups. It is fortunate that in most cases these persons can shift all or part of the burden to others. Were it not so, our system of taxation would probably be more unfair than it

---

[19] For a discussion of this topic see the *Preliminary Report of the Committee Appointed by the National Tax Association to Prepare a Plan of a Model System of State and Local Taxation*, pp. 4 and 5. This report is commended to the reader as an able and illuminating discussion of the proper structure of the tax system.

actually is. What determines whether or not the taxpayer can shift his taxes to some one else?

An example of a tax that is shifted easily and rather quickly is the sales tax, such as that now imposed upon gasoline by every one of the forty-eight states. It is not paid, for the most part, by either the manufacturers or the distributors of gasoline. It is paid, in the main, by the consumers. Yet the tax is collected by the government from the distributors of gasoline. Why are most distributors able to shift it to the consumers?

In seeking an answer to this question, the essential point to notice is that the tax is so levied that every additional unit of the product sold increases the amount which the seller must pay to the government. The tax, therefore, is precisely like any expenditure which varies with the volume of business done — like the wages of direct labor or the costs of the material contained in the article. In other words, it is one of the variable costs of production, and the seller of gasoline cannot afford to sell for a price which does not cover the tax. Consequently, he endeavors to limit his offerings to an amount which can be sold at such a price. The tax, therefore, has the effect of restricting the supply. In this, its effect is precisely the same as any other direct cost. Here we find the reason why the tax can be shifted to the consumer; *it can be shifted only because it affects the supply*.[20] If it did not affect the supply, the price would not be affected and no shifting would occur. The price can be raised and the tax shifted only because the tax results in a smaller supply.[21]

[20] To a small extent, the tax undoubtedly falls upon the owner of oil land. By raising the price and discouraging the consumption of gasoline the tax reduces the demand for crude oil and thus the price which the owners of oil land can obtain for their oil.

[21] It must not be assumed that a sales tax will cause the price of the commodity to be increased by the amount of the tax. In nearly every case, the increase in price will be less than the amount of the tax. The reason is that the costs of no two producers are alike. When the tax, by raising the price, reduces the quantity of the article that is demanded, the high cost producers are driven out of business. It is possible, although extremely improbable, that a sales tax will cause the price to rise by more than the amount of the tax. It has been pointed out (pp. 338–343) that cost of production per unit often depends upon the volume of demand and that a shrinkage in the volume of demand may limit the use of minute specialization and automatic machines and thus raise the cost of production. Were a tax on sales very high and the demand for the commodity highly elastic, it is possible that the tax might restrict demand so much as to raise substantially the unit cost of producing the commodity. In this event, the price might rise by more than the amount of the tax. Such cases are very rare, partly because most sales taxes are not large and partly

From this analysis it follows that taxes which do not affect the supply of a commodity, do not affect the price and, therefore, cannot be shifted. In order to make this clear, let us examine the possibility of shifting a tax levied upon the net income of a monopoly. A monopoly, it will be recalled, tends to sell its product at a price which yields the maximum net profit. The reason why a tax upon the net income of a monopoly cannot be shifted is because such a tax does not change the point of maximum net profit. Suppose that the tax is 5 per cent of the monopoly's net income. This means, of course, that, regardless of the price which the monopoly may charge, it has 5 per cent less to distribute to its owners. In the case of the illustration on page 361, for example, the monopoly finds that $1.20 would be the most profitable price because it yields larger net profits than any other price. A tax of 5 per cent would reduce the amount available for distribution to the owners of the monopoly from $1,500,000 to $1,425,000. But the tax would also reduce by 5 per cent the amount available for distribution at any other price. Consequently, a tax upon the net income of the monopoly would not make it profitable for the monopoly to restrict production any further and, therefore, would not make it profitable for the monopoly to raise the price.[22] Quite different, however, would be the effect if the tax were levied, not upon the net income of the monopoly, but upon each unit of product sold. In the latter case, the tax might change the point at which the monopoly gained the greatest profit.[23]

An interesting case is presented by taxes on land. Part of the value of land comes from the improvements which have been

---

because *small* changes in demand do not have much effect upon the methods of production which are most economical or the size of the plant which is most profitable.

[22] If the tax were so heavy that it reduced the return on capital in the monopolized industry to a point below the current rate of return, it would cause a shrinkage in the volume of capital devoted to the industry. This would reduce the output of the commodity and thus lead to a higher price. To this extent and under these circumstances, the tax might be shifted.

[23] In discussing the determination of a monopoly price, it was pointed out that monopoly price is more likely to be far above the competitive price when the direct costs of the monopoly are relatively high and fixed costs relatively low. The tax upon each unit of the product sold by the monopoly has the effect, of course, of increasing the relative importance of direct costs and, therefore, raising the price which the monopoly finds it most profitable to charge.

made to it. But part of the value is independent of the improvements — it is the value which land would have even if it were not improved by buildings, fences, drainages, and fertilizers. In so far as a tax is levied upon the unimproved value of the land, it cannot be shifted. The reason is obvious. It is plain that the tax cannot be shifted unless it enables landowners to obtain higher prices for the products of their land. Naturally, a landowner does not find it profitable to use his land less intensively simply because he must pay a tax upon it. He does not thereby escape part of the tax. Consequently, a tax upon unimproved land values does not reduce the output from land that is kept in use. On the contrary, the tax is likely to encourage the owner to cultivate his land more intensively and to make it produce more. But may not such a tax affect the total output from land by reducing the number of acres in use? In a few cases, where the tax exceeds the net income from the land, it may force some land out of use.[24] But a tax on land values increases the burden of keeping land out of use. Consequently, the *net* effect of the tax is likely to be to increase the amount of land in use and thus to increase the volume of production from land. In consequence, not only are landowners unable, as a general rule, to pass on a tax on the unimproved value of land, but the tax, by tending to push down the prices of the products of land, falls on the owners with double force.

But most land is improved and a large part of its value is derived from that fact. Naturally a tax on improvements tends to discourage men from making them and leads to a smaller output from land and to higher prices for the products of land.

---

[24] In some of these cases, the owners may permit the land to be sold for taxes. If no one is willing to purchase the land, it remains out of use in the hands of the state.

If land were always accurately assessed on the basis of its present and prospective net earnings, a tax on its value would not force land out of use, provided the tax rate were less than the current rate of interest in the community and provided also that the land were assessed on the basis of the net earnings before the payment of taxes. Extensive investigations, however, have shown that there is a strong tendency to overassess poor land. Assessors seem to feel that land is land and that even the poorest land must be worth an appreciable amount. Errors in assessment may force some of the poorest land out of use.

It should be noted, however, that accurate assessment of land on the basis of prospective earnings may *change* the uses of land. For example, accurate assessment of farm land near a growing city on the basis of its prospective earnings as suburban property may accelerate its abandonment as farm land.

Thus, to *some* extent at least, a tax on the value of the improvements to land can be shifted. But to *what* extent? This raises a more general question: To what extent is it possible to shift a general tax on capital values (other than unimproved land values) and upon what groups or classes does such a tax fall in case it is shifted?

Obviously if a tax upon capital did not affect the supply of capital, it would fall entirely upon investors. The extent to which it does not fall upon them depends largely upon how it affects the supply of capital. The immediate effect of the tax is, of course, to reduce the returns from capital by the amount of the tax. The tax is equivalent, therefore, to a drop in the rate of interest. In our analysis of the accumulation and the reward of capital, it was pointed out that a lower return on investments might conceivably increase the volume of saving.[25] In this event, a tax on capital would obviously fall entirely on investors — in fact, they would lose more than the amount of the tax, because the gross rate of return on investments (that is, the return before the deduction of taxes) would be reduced. But although a lower net return on investments might possibly increase the volume of saving, it would be *more likely* to diminish the volume of saving. To the extent that it did, investors would be able to shift a tax on capital by obtaining a higher gross return on their funds — that is, a larger return before the deduction for taxes. In the analysis of the accumulation and the reward of capital, reasons were given for believing that a drop in the rate of interest would not produce a substantial change in volume of saving. If this is correct, a tax on capital will fall *in the main* upon investors.

But to the extent that a tax on capital retards the increase in the supply of capital, it enables capitalists to obtain a higher gross return on their funds and falls, therefore, upon others. Who are these others? In part they are consumers, because, when the increase in the supply of capital is retarded, the increase in goods for ultimate consumption is also retarded. This, of course, tends to raise the prices which consumers must pay. In part they are wage earners, because the productivity of labor (and hence wages) depends, as we have seen, upon how much

[25] Pp. 689–691.

capital each employee has to help him in his work.[26]   When the growth of capital is retarded, therefore, the rise in wages is also retarded.   In precisely the same way, the productivity of land (and hence its value) depends upon the amount of capital that is available for use in connection with land.   In part, therefore, a general tax on capital falls upon landowners not merely as capitalists but also as landowners, because a smaller amount of capital per acre of land means a lower return on land.   In what degree a slower growth in capital retards the increase in wages or in the returns of landowners depends upon whether the productivity of labor or capital is much or little affected by small changes in the volume of capital per wage earner or per acre of land.

Of great importance in determining the shifting of taxes is the fact that the tax rates in no two states or in no two cities within the state are the same.   This variation in tax rates is important primarily in the case of taxes on capital and on business income.

In discussing the effect of different tax rates in different taxing jurisdictions, a distinction must be made between the case of capital or enterprises which compete with capital or enterprises outside the taxing jurisdiction and the case of capital and enterprises which do not compete outside the taxing jurisdiction.   An abnormally high tax on property in a city, for example, will tend to make house rents in that city higher than in neighboring cities. The reason is obvious.   Capital, of course, tends to be invested where it will yield the most attractive return.   If a city taxes houses more heavily than do its neighbors, the investment of capital in new houses tends to be restricted until rents are high enough to cover the tax and at the same time to yield the current rate of return on capital.[27]   By a converse course of reasoning, it could be shown that an abnormally low tax rate in a city tends

---

[26] See pp. 332–335 and pp. 615–617.

[27] Of course, if capital is not invested in houses in a city with a high tax rate, it is invested elsewhere, either in houses or other ways.   To the extent that high taxes in some jurisdictions prevent capital from being invested as advantageously as it might be, the burden of the tax falls partly upon the owners of capital and partly upon the community in general.   The community suffers because comparison in tax rates interferes with the ideal distribution of capital among localities and as between industries.

to attract capital, to increase the investment in housing there, and thus to make for lower rents.

Very different is the effect of an abnormally high or abnormally low rate of taxation upon capital or business enterprises which compete with capital or enterprises outside the taxing jurisdiction. The extra tax burden which must be borne by a part of an industry does not necessarily diminish the total output of the industry — it encourages the industry to grow more rapidly outside the high taxing jurisdiction than within it.[28] Consequently, the concerns which are more heavily taxed than their competitors cannot shift any part of the *extra* burden which falls on them. They must absorb it. But the conclusion does not necessarily follow that their profits are diminished by the extent of the extra burden. Managerial efficiency — and, indeed, human efficiency in general — is determined in no small degree by necessity. Within certain limits men tend to be about as efficient as it is necessary to be. When an enterprise has a handicap imposed upon it, the management is likely to exert itself in order to overcome the handicap. In many cases, the management will not be entirely successful and profits, to some extent, will suffer. Nevertheless, in most cases the handicap will be *partially* overcome. An extra tax burden which affects some competitors, but not all, will partly reduce profits and partly increase the efficiency of some concerns.

The fact that taxes can be shifted does not necessarily mean that they can be shifted at once. A decade or two may elapse before a tax which raises the cost of producing a commodity is completely shifted to the consumers. This is the reason why producers of gasoline strongly oppose increases in gasoline taxes. In view of the fact that the tax ultimately falls on the users of gasoline and the owners of oil lands, it might appear to be a matter of indifference to the refiners whether the tax is high or low. But any attempt to shift the tax to the consumer is bound either to reduce the consumption of gasoline or, at least, to retard the increase in consumption. This, naturally, is disadvan-

---

[28] If a high tax discourages enterprises from locating where the productivity of capital and labor is greatest, it will diminish the output of the industry and enable the heavily taxed concerns to shift part of the burden in the form of higher prices.

tageous to the refiners of petroleum.[29]   Part of their costs are
overhead expenses which go on more or less unchanged regardless
of whether sales are large or small.   A tax on gasoline, by checking consumption, therefore, reduces the profits of the producers
and the refiners.   Eventually, of course, the volume of capital invested in the petroleum industry will be adjusted to the amount
which can earn a rate of profit that is no less attractive than capital earns in other industries.   For a transitional period however, the tax may fall heavily upon the refiners.

How the burden of the tax is divided during the transitional
period depends upon (1) the nature of the tax, (2) the elasticity of the demand for the product, and (3) the elasticity
of the supply of the product.   As a rule, a tax on sales can be
shifted to consumers far more promptly than a tax on capital.
In the case of a tax on sales, each additional unit sold increases
the tax which must be paid.   Consequently, the tax gives enterprises an incentive to restrict output in order to raise the price.
Indeed, if costs were entirely direct, a sales tax would be shifted
to buyers instantaneously.   Only because costs are partly fixed
does the complete shifting require some time — concerns do
not find it profitable to restrict output at once by enough to cover
the tax, because smaller output means higher overhead costs per
unit.   The complete shifting of the tax occurs through an adjustment of the amount of capital invested in the industry.   A tax
on the capital, on the other hand, even though so heavy that it
substantially reduces profits, does not make it profitable for enterprises either to reduce their output or to shift to the production of other commodities.   Neither procedure would enable
concerns to escape part of the tax.   For this reason, the tax
falls upon producers until the volume of investment in the industry is adjusted (either by growth in the demand for the
commodity or by the failure of enterprises) to the amount which
will earn the rate of return that savers expect.   If the supply of
capital is inelastic, as it probably is, taxes on capital will always
fall, in the main, upon investors.

The elasticity of demand and supply affect the time required
to shift a tax.   The more inelastic the demand for a commodity
affected by a tax, the more promptly the tax can be shifted.   In

---

[29] Of course, many refiners are large owners of oil lands.

this case, a small decrease in supply relative to demand produces a pronounced rise in price. Consequently, only a small readjustment of the productive capacity of the industry is needed to bring about an increase in price sufficient to cover the tax and to permit investors to obtain the current rate of return on their funds. The more elastic the supply, the more promptly a tax is shifted because the more promptly the supply responds to a price which, in view of the tax, is no longer sufficient to yield the current rate of return on capital.

Because the time required to shift a tax depends in part upon how rapidly enterprises are able to raise the price of their products, shifting occurs most rapidly in the case of commodities for which the demand is rapidly growing.

Of the principal taxes levied in the United States today, the personal income taxes, the inheritance taxes, and that part of the general property tax which represents taxation of the unimproved value of land, are not shifted.[30] The sales taxes and excise taxes, such as those on gasoline and tobacco, are almost entirely shifted (though with some delay) to consumers and to the owners of petroleum and tobacco land. Betwixt and between these extremes are the general property tax, in so far as it represents taxation of man-made capital, the corporate income tax levied by the United States, and the business income taxes and business license taxes imposed by the states and the cities. This last group are all taxes on capital or on the income yielded by capital. The extent to which they are shifted depends, as we have seen, largely upon the elasticity of the supply of capital. Our conclusion that the supply of capital is inelastic leads in turn to the conclusion that in the main these taxes are not shifted.

VI. The Principal Faults of the Tax System of the United States

Unquestionably the outstanding fault of the tax system of the United States is the gross and glaring unfairness with which

---

[30] To a small extent and by a circuitous process even these taxes are shifted. They fall, for the most part, upon the rich who do most of the saving. Consequently, they undoubtedly reduce the volume of saving, retard the growth of capital, and enable the owners of capital (who, *as a class*, are the heaviest payers of taxes on incomes, inheritances, and property) to collect a slightly larger return on their investments.

the burden of supporting the state is distributed. Additional faults are the diversion of capital and labor into relatively unproductive pursuits and the encouragement of some wasteful economic activities.

How unfairly the burdens of taxation are distributed in the United States is roughly indicated by the percentage of income paid in taxes by persons in different income groups. Such an estimate, for state and local taxes, has been made by the National Industrial Conference Board. The estimate covers personal and business taxes, including taxes on property, paid by individuals. The estimate is too detailed to quote in entirety, but for selected income classes in 1924 it is as follows: [31]

Income class	Per cent of personal and individual business taxes to total income
Under $1,000	16.32
$5,000 to $6,000	4.22
10,000 to 11,000	3.61
50,000 to 60,000	3.38
100,000 to 150,000	3.04
1,000,000 to 1,500,000	2.37
5,000,000 and over	1.47

The estimate is probably subject to a fairly wide margin of error but the trend is unmistakable. The larger the income, the smaller the fraction taken by the states and local governments. A little more than 16 cents out of every dollar received by those with incomes of less than $1,000 a year are taken; less than a cent and a half out of every dollar received by those with incomes of $5,000,000 a year or more. In the case of the Federal government, the burden is more fairly distributed because about one-third of the revenue of the Federal government comes from the personal income tax which is levied on a progressive scale.

The unfair distribution of the burden of taxation is the result of three principal causes: (1) the nature of the taxes levied; (2) the overlapping of taxes, with the result that some incomes and some pieces of property are taxed more times than others;

[31] National Industrial Conference Board, *The Cost of Government in the United States, 1925–1926*, p. 128.

and (3) the administration of taxation. Inequality results because most of the taxes levied are not consistent with the equal-sacrifice or ability-to-pay test. The tax which can be most easily and accurately adjusted to the ability to pay is the income tax. Not only is income the most accurate index of ability to pay, but, in levying income taxes, it is easy to make allowances for the dependents whom the taxpayer must support and to vary the rate of tax with the size of the income.[32] But only about 31 per cent of the tax revenue of the Federal government, only about 4 per cent of the tax revenue of the states, and practically none of the tax revenue of the local communities is derived from personal income taxes. Of all the tax revenue collected in the United States, less than 11 per cent is derived from personal income taxes. On the other hand, over two-thirds of the Federal tax revenue is derived from the corporation tax, customs receipts, and various forms of excise taxes, and about 31 per cent of the tax revenue of the states comes from business license taxes or sales taxes.[33] None of these taxes falls upon persons in proportion to their ability to pay.

The corporate income tax, as we have seen, falls, in the main, upon investors. Its effect is to reduce, by a given percentage, the profits available for distribution to all stockholders in an enterprise, both large and small stockholders. The burden imposed by the tax has no close relation to the total income of the investor — it is determined by his holdings of corporate stock rather than by his income. Business income taxes, franchise

[32] Even income is not an entirely satisfactory measure of ability to pay. Two men may each have an income of $5,000 a year; one may derive his income from his services; the other from property. Although both have the same income, the latter is really much better off. He has a permanent source of income which (assuming that his money is conservatively invested) will continue after he has reached the age of retirement and even after his death. Consequently, he is under less necessity to save in order to provide for his old age and for his family after his death. The fact that a given amount of income from property is really greater than the same amount of income for personal services is recognized in some income tax laws by the imposition of a higher rate of taxation upon the so-called unearned income. In the case of the Federal income tax law, a reduction of 25 per cent of the tax is given on earned income up to $30,000 a year.

[33] But this is somewhat less unfair than it appears to be, because included in the 31 per cent are the gasoline taxes which, in 1927, yielded about 12.2 per cent of the state tax revenue. Gasoline taxes are almost entirely devoted to building and maintenance of roads. There is good reason, we have seen, for distributing this expense on the basis of the use made of the roads rather than on the basis of the ability-to-pay or equal-sacrifice principle.

taxes, and license taxes, such as are levied by many states, correspond to ability to pay no more than does the Federal corporate
income tax.   Business income taxes are essentially the same as
the corporate income tax, except that they apply to all enterprises, both incorporated and unincorporated.   Business franchise taxes and license taxes are usually computed upon the income, net or gross, of enterprises.   When the tax is computed
upon net income, it is essentially the same as a corporate income
tax or a business income tax and open to the criticisms which
apply to them.   When it is computed upon the gross income of
enterprises, it is even less closely related to ability to pay, because net income, of course, is by no means uniformly proportionate to gross income.

Sales taxes and customs duties (which are practically a peculiar form of sales tax), in so far as they fall upon purchasers,
are paid in proportion to expenditures for the commodities.
If a good is used by the poor in almost the same quantity as by
the rich, the tax will take a much larger proportion of the income
of the poor than of the income of the well-to-do.   Examples are
the import duties upon wool and sugar, and the excise tax upon
tobacco.   The poor consume almost as much of these products
as do the rich.   These taxes, therefore, are roughly comparable
to an income tax which takes a larger percentage of small incomes
than of large.

But more than one-third of the tax revenue of the states and
about nine-tenths of the tax revenue of local communities are
derived from taxes on property.   Does this not represent taxation in accordance with ability to pay?   If property were the only
source of income in the community, an *ad valorem* tax on property
would be roughly equivalent to a tax on incomes at a uniform
rate and would be open to objections that apply to such a tax.
"But," it may be asked, " is not property largely owned by the
well-to-do?   Does not a tax on property, therefore, represent
a concentration of the tax burden largely upon the more well-
to-do members of the community?   When over three-fourths of
the tax revenues of the states and local communities come from
the general property tax, do not the less well-to-do, who own little
property, escape taxation almost entirely? "

To some extent, although to a less degree than is usually supposed, taxes on property are shifted. To that extent there may be little relationship between the distribution of the burden and the ability to pay. But it is an erroneous assumption that the less-well-to-do are not important property owners. Among the largest of the low-income groups in the United States are the farmers. And yet farmers are important property owners. Especially are their property holdings large in proportion to their incomes. The result is that farmers, although a low-income group, are one of the most heavily taxed classes in the community.

In practical effect, the general property tax is a tax upon real estate — that is, a tax upon land and buildings. The reason is that, as a rule, little effort is made to assess personal property. In fact, about three-fourths of the property reached through the general property tax is real estate. In New York State the proportion is even higher — 98.6 per cent in 1929. In an agricultural community, real estate is a fairly satisfactory indicator of producing and earning power. But the development of the country has made income from real estate a smaller and smaller part of the national income. Nevertheless, because taxes on real estate were already in effect and because there has been strong opposition to new taxes, particularly to taxes on personal incomes, the rapidly growing expenses of the government have been met in large degree by increasing the burden upon real estate. In Massachusetts, real estate, which is estimated to represent about 35 per cent of the wealth of the state, provided 65.6 per cent of the tax revenue in 1928.[34] In New York, the man who obtains his income from real estate pays a high tax, and the one who obtains it from professional services or from a salary pays a low tax. In 1923, the tax burden on farms in regions of moderate land values in New York State was 12.75 per cent of the net income before deducting interest and taxes. Consequently, a farmer who made a profit (exclusive of interest and taxes) of $1,000 on his farm would pay about $127.50 in taxes. On the other hand, a salaried man with a wife and no children and with an income of $4,000 would pay under the New York income tax

[34] *Annual Report of the Commissioner of Corporations and Taxation*, 1928, p. 40.

only $3.75. In other words, he would pay less than one-thirtieth as much as a farmer who had only one-fourth the income of the salaried man.[35]

A second general source of inequality in distributing the burden of taxation is double or multiple taxation. Not all forms of multiple taxation are unfair. In fact, if everyone were affected alike by multiple taxation there would be no problem, for two taxes on the same property or the same income would be equivalent to one tax at a higher rate. But injustice obviously results when two taxes overlap not completely but partially, so that some persons are taxed twice and other persons only once. To illustrate: under a general property tax, a piece of land may be taxed because it is property, and a mortgage secured by the land may also be taxed because it is property. Obviously this is unfair because the mortgage is not a separate and distinct instrument of production; it is merely evidence of a claim against the land. If the practice is to tax mortgages, lenders will exact from borrowers a rate of interest high enough to cover the tax and to yield the current rate of return on investments. The result is that the landowner pays two taxes on the same property — one directly as a landowner and the other indirectly in the form of a higher interest rate on his mortgage.

What applies to mortgages applies in large degree to other forms of intangible property, such as stocks and bonds. To a substantial extent, they represent tangible property which is taxed. If the intangible property is also taxed, there is double taxation. For this reason, twelve states exempt most forms of intangible property and fourteen tax it at special low rates. Twenty-two, however, treat intangibles the same as tangible property.[36]

The tax laws abound with provisions designed to prevent double taxation, but when there are forty-eight states each levy-

---

[35] This comparison is presented by Professor M. Slade Kendrick in his excellent monograph, "An Outline of the New York State System of Taxation," *Cornell Extension Bulletin No. 152*, pp. 18–19.

[36] National Industrial Conference Board, *State and Local Taxation of Property*, p. 242. It should be observed, however, that where intangible property is legally taxable at the same rate as tangible property, the law is rarely enforced and intangibles escape taxation altogether.

Although mortgages and bonds represent tangible property, this may not be true of stock, which derives its value, not merely from the physical assets of the

ing a score or more of taxes upon persons, corporations, transactions, bequests, and property — often upon the property or transactions of non-residents as well as of residents — it is inevitable that there should be a myriad of instances of unfair multiple taxation. Indeed, to eliminate all unfair taxation would make many tax laws impossible to administer. Moreover, many states do not appear to be keenly interested in avoiding the imposition of unfair taxes upon non-residents. For example, some states exempt stock in domestic corporations from taxation, but not stock in foreign corporations. Space does not permit a more or less comprehensive list of the numerous forms of double taxation. Among the most important are the taxation of both tangible property and the intangible claims to it (only nine states, for example, in 1930, completely exempted mortgages from taxation), the taxation of the incomes both by the state in which the recipient of the income lives and by the state in which the business that produces the income is located,[37] and the taxation of bequests by several states.[38] Because there is often little relationship between the value of the physical property of a corporation, measured by cost, and the value of the enterprise as a going concern, many states impose corporate franchise taxes. Such a tax may be levied on the value of so-called " corporate excess "

---

corporation, but from its earning power — that is, from the efficiency of the management and the value of patents, trade names, etc. For this reason, there is a far stronger case for the taxation of stocks than of bonds or mortgages. Some states do not tax the owners of stock on their securities but do tax the corporation on the amount by which the value of its stock exceeds the assessed value of its physical property.

[37] New York and Wisconsin, for example, tax incomes received by non-residents from property within the state. In case the income recipient happens to live in a state which also imposes an income tax, there will be double taxation. In order to avoid this injustice, the income taxes of Delaware, Massachusetts, New Hampshire, and North Dakota exempt income earned or derived in the state but received by non-residents. But in a federal system, such as the United States, it may be necessary to discourage persons from escaping an income tax by establishing residence in another state which does not tax incomes. This is the practical justification for the New York and Wisconsin rule of taxing the non-residents for income derived within the state.

[38] The application of the inheritance tax to the stock of domestic corporations bequeathed by non-resident owners may result in double taxation, because an inheritance tax may be levied against the same property both by the state in which the decedent lived and by the state in which the property is located. Of the states having inheritance laws, all but eleven had by 1930 adopted a reciprocity provision by which the inheritance tax is not applied to the intangibles of foreign decedents who were residents of another state which had also adopted the reciprocity provision.

— that is, on the market value of the stock of the corporation minus an exemption for tangible property assessed within the state, for property located in other states, and for tax-exempt property owned by the corporation. Suppose that the stock of the corporation is worth $10,000,000 in the market, that the physical property tax in the state is assessed at $5,000,000, that physical property located in other states is worth $2,000,000, and that tax exempt bonds owned by the company are worth $500,000. There remains a taxable corporate excess of $2,500,-000. This may be taxed at the average rate of the general property tax within the state. It is obvious that if every state follows this method of assessment, a corporation may be taxed on its corporate excess in many states.

An important cause of inequality in taxation is the faulty administration of tax laws. Perhaps the most glaring faults are in the assessment of property. The method of assessment is a product of the days when the country consisted, in the main, of small rural communities where everyone knew everyone else and everyone else's affairs. In most states, assessors are still selected for each township by popular election and for a brief term of office. Only in six states are they appointed and these appointments are not on a merit basis. In no state, except in parts of Delaware and Maryland, does the term of office of the assessors exceed four years.[39] Nearly all states have created state tax commissions with some authority to supervise and review the work of the assessors. The authority of the tax commissions over the local assessors and their work varies greatly. It may be no more than authority to prepare forms for the assessors and to give advice. Or the commission may have authority to remove assessors and to make reassessments. The exact nature of the commission's authority to make reassessments is important — whether the commission may proceed on its own motion or must wait for a complaint; whether it may reassess only the classes of property specified in a complaint or whether it may order reassessment of all property in the district or any classes of property; whether it may simply order the local assessors to make a reassessment or whether it may make the reassessment with its own

[39] Coombs, Whitney, "Taxation of Farm Property," *United States Bureau of Agriculture, Technical Bulletin, No. 172*, p. 70.

agents. Only fifteen states give the state supervisory officials
(usually the tax commission) power to make reassessments on
their own motion and with their own agents. Ten other states
give the supervisory officials power to order reassessments.[40]
Unfortunately, these powers are rarely used.

The nature of the administrative machinery causes the highly
technical and difficult work of determining fair values for a great
variety of property to be performed by underpaid and part-time
assessors who depend upon election for continuance in office and
who, in consequence, are susceptible to pressure from political
machines and influential local interests. If the system of assessment had been deliberately planned in order to make it as inefficient and as unfair as possible, a better job could scarcely
have been done.

The assessments made by the local assessors serve as a basis,
not merely for taxes which go into the treasury of the local community, but for taxes which go to the state. The lower the ratio
of the assessments to real value of property, the smaller the
contribution which the township or county makes to the state.
Consequently, there is an incentive to underassess. In order to
prevent tax dodging by whole communities through the device
of underassessment, counties and states have established boards
and commissions with power to review assessments and to equalize them as between towns, cities, and counties. This prevents
gross inequalities in the appraisal of property *as between* counties or townships but it does not prevent glaring inequalities in
the appraisal of individual pieces of property *within* townships
or counties — inequalities due to the incompetency of the assessors or to political favoritism. Numerous studies of the ratios
of assessed values to real values have invariably disclosed wide
variation, with a distinct tendency to overestimate low property
values in relation to high property values.[41]

Although the most glaring fault in our tax system is the unfair distribution of the burden of taxation, this is by no means its
only fault. Many of our customs duties cause waste of labor

[40] *Ibid.*, p. 375.
[41] For a convenient summary of studies of this topic in Chicago, Colorado, Delaware, Iowa, Kansas, Massachusetts, New York, Oregon, and Pennsylvania, see a
paper by Professor M. Slade Kendrick, " A Comparison between Urban and Rural

and capital by diverting them into relatively unproductive pursuits. This will be discussed in the next chapter. Other taxes are undesirable because they encourage wasteful and uneconomical practices. A good example is the application of the general property tax to certain natural resources, such as standing timber. An annual tax makes it expensive to hold timber uncut. Consequently, it encourages reckless and wasteful cutting. Furthermore, an annual tax discourages the reforestation of cut-over land. When one considers that approximately thirty years is required to grow timber suitable for pulpwood and fifty years timber suitable for lumber, it is obvious that even a small annual tax renders reforestation prohibitively expensive. A few states, therefore, have replaced the general property tax on timber land with a severance or a forest crop tax. Such a law provides for a nominal annual payment and a larger payment at the time that the timber is cut.[42] The principle of the severance tax is applicable also to other natural resources — such as coal, oil, gas, and minerals in general. Rather than stimulate too rapid and wasteful development by imposing a heavy annual tax, it may be wise to base the tax on the rate of extraction.

VII. The Geographical Unit of Taxation

Of great importance is the question of the proper geographical unit for taxation and expenditure. In essence the question is whether the rich should be taxed in order to support the poor. And if so, in what degree? Should the rich manufacturing states in the East be taxed to build roads in the West or South? Should the wealthy parts of a state be taxed to build roads and to support schools in the poorer and less prosperous parts? Should the cities be taxed in order to build roads and to maintain schools in the country? The variations between geographical districts in wealth and income per capita are immense. For example, the

---

Taxation in Real Estate Values," *Annals of the American Academy of Political and Social Science*, March, 1930, v. CXLVIII, pp. 225–232.

[42] The Wisconsin law of 1927 permits the classification of lands devoted to growing timber as forest crop lands for a period of fifty years. Such lands are subject to an annual tax of 10 cents an acre plus a severance tax of 10 per cent of the value of the stumpage cut, payable at the time of cutting. For a discussion of some of the problems in administering the law, see *Report of the Wisconsin Tax Commission, 1930*, pp. 28–29.

National Bureau of Economic Research estimates that average income per capita in 1921 varied from $207 in Mississippi to $921 in New York. In six states (Alabama, Arkansas, Georgia, Mississippi, North Carolina, and South Carolina) it was less than $300; in seven (California, Illinois, Massachusetts, Nevada, New York, Rhode Island, and Wyoming), it was more than $700.[43] Within the various counties of the states, there are similar variations. In Wisconsin, for example, it was found that the county with the highest per capita value of taxable property had a figure three times as great as that of the county with the lowest per capita value.[44] It was also found in Wisconsin that, as a general rule, the counties showing the highest property values per acre, per capita, and per school census child were the counties showing the lowest tax rates.[45]

The essential nature of most taxes, it has been pointed out, consists in the fact that they are compulsory levies upon individuals for the benefit of all. The question of what is the proper unit for taxing and expenditure, therefore, raises the question of what is the group which may be regarded as sharing in the common benefits. Should the East be regarded as sharing in the benefits from roads in the West? Should city dwellers be regarded as sharing in benefits from roads in the country or from country schools? Another way of looking at the problem is to ask how far it is desirable to penalize people for living in poor and undeveloped regions. Should the children who happen to be born to families who undertake to farm the cutover land in the northern parts of Michigan, Wisconsin, and Minnesota be penalized by poor schools? Should the children of the farmers who (probably unwisely, in most cases) attempt to make a living by farming the poor land in the southern tier counties of New York State be penalized because of the poor business judgment of their fathers?

Wide differences of opinion are bound to prevail concerning what is the proper unit of taxation. To some extent all of us have interests in common. But what degree of interest is sufficient

---

[43] Leven, M., *Income in the Various States*, p. 267.

[44] Blough, J. R., " The Geographical Problem in Wisconsin Taxation," Wisconsin Tax Commission, *Bulletin No. 39*, p. 61.

[45] *Ibid.*, p. 71. The tax rates were computed on the estimated sale value of the taxable property.

to justify taxing everyone to promote the common interest? The people of Illinois, Iowa, and other inland states do not object to paying part of the cost of the navy, but many persons in New York, Pennsylvania, and other eastern states consider it unfair that the Federal government should collect money from them in order to help build roads in Nevada or Idaho or Wyoming. Should the navy be supported by the coastal states and should roads be built by each state or county for itself?

In a few cases, the problem of the proper unit of taxation can be settled by determining who receives the benefit from certain expenditures. The financing of the construction and maintenance of through roads in large degree out of state, rather than county, funds can be justified by traffic counts which indicate that a substantial part of the traffic on these roads is through rather than local. In other cases, the problem can be settled by what is the most efficient unit for spending money. If the state is a more satisfactory unit than the county for caring for the feeble-minded and the insane, then probably the cost should be collected through state taxes.[46] Likewise, since the state can build and maintain roads more efficiently than the counties, possibly the cost of building and maintaining through roads should be assumed by the state and met by state taxes.

The difficulties in determining what is the proper unit of taxation will retard but will not check the growing tendency for the Federal government to grant funds in aid of state projects and for the states to make substantial grants to the counties and towns. Most of the grants of both the Federal government and the states are for roads and education. The demand for both of these aids is certain to increase. As our standards continue to rise and as we demand better roads and better schools, it will become more and more burdensome for the poorer regions to supply them without help.

VIII. Suggestions for Improving the Tax System

Suggestions for improving the tax system fall under two principal heads: (1) improvements needed in the taxes themselves; and (2) improvements needed in tax administration.

---

[46] But it may be argued that, although the state should provide the facilities, each county should bear the cost of maintaining its own patients.

In the taxes themselves four principal changes are needed: (1) reduction of the unfair burden upon real estate; (2) adjustment of taxes more closely to ability to pay; (3) reduction in unfair multiple taxation; (4) the elimination of taxes which encourage wasteful economic practices.

The first two proposals are intimately related. If the tax on real estate is reduced, another tax or other taxes must be added or raised. It has been pointed out that, at the present time, the states and local communities take approximately 16 cents out of each dollar received by persons with incomes of less than $1,000 a year and about 2 or 3 cents out of each dollar received by persons with incomes of $100,000 or over. Would it not be fair to reduce the taxes on real estate and to make up for the loss of revenue by placing a heavier burden in the main upon the recipients of large incomes?[47] This could be done by the addition of a personal income tax. The personal income tax, more easily than any other tax, can be closely adjusted to ability to pay and yet, precisely for that reason, it has encountered stubborn opposition from the well-to-do and is used by only a minority of states. But the hope of reforming our system of taxation, of relieving real estate from its unfair burden, and of taxing the rich as heavily as the poor, depends upon the spread of the income tax.

The personal income tax also offers the principal hope for reducing unfair multiple taxation. The tax might well be used to replace or to reduce the numerous corporate franchise taxes and business income taxes which the states now impose. Such taxes do not fall upon investors in accordance with their ability to pay and they are prolific sources of unequal and multiple taxation.

---

[47] The value of real estate is the present value of its prospective net earnings. A reduction in the tax on real estate raises its prospective net earnings and thus increases its value. Consequently, a reduction in the tax amounts to a gift to land owners. Is not this unfair?

The principal reason for concluding that it is not, arises from the fact that taxes on real estate have been rising rapidly and from the fact that taxes on real estate in part cannot be shifted at all and in part can be shifted only very slowly. A reduction in these taxes, therefore, would relieve the real estate owner of the burden of recent tax increases which he is paying either because he has not had time to shift them or because they never can be shifted. In other words, tax reductions will merely give back to him what has recently been taken away from him. This reasoning would not, of course, justify abolishing taxes on real estate — it would justify abolishing the abnormal burden which rests upon it.

The elimination of taxes which encourage wasteful economic practices would include the gradual withdrawal of many customs duties with the exemption of timber and mineral land from the general property tax and the substitution of a severance tax.

Among the many improvements needed in the machinery for administering taxes, none is more urgent than an improvement in the work of the local assessors. The Wisconsin Tax Commission has made a vigorous effort to improve their work by thorough supervision and by distributing to them carefully prepared information about real estate values. But even a private employer, with absolute power to discharge on a moment's notice, does not expect good results from inefficient employees. As long as the work of the local assessor is only part-time, poorly paid, and of uncertain duration, men who have good jobs cannot afford to accept it, and it is bound, in large degree, to fall into the hands of incompetents.[48] No matter how conscientious and well planned the supervision of the state tax commission may be, it cannot entirely overcome the incompetency of the assessors.

In view of its highly technical nature, the work of assessment should be placed in the hands of full-time, well-paid experts, appointed as the result of civil service examination. In order to make the job a full-time one, it would be necessary to replace township assessors with county assessors. Appointments should be made by the state tax commission, and assessors should be subject to removal for cause by the commission.

Other changes are needed to improve the work of the state tax commissions. Many commissions need more authority to order reassessments of property — authority to act on their own initiative and with their own staff. Nearly all commissions need a larger and stronger technical staff. Membership on the commissions needs to be made more attractive by higher salaries and, in some cases, longer terms. Indeed the things which need to be done to improve the work of the tax commissions are strikingly similar to those which need to be done to improve the

[48] In Illinois, for example, township assessors are paid from $5 to $10 a day with a maximum of $1,000 a year. This is the usual method of compensating township assessors. National Industrial Conference Board, *The Fiscal Problem in Illinois*, p. 152.

work of the public utility commissions. America, which leads the world in developing improved methods of administration within *private* business enterprises, is amazingly tolerant of stagnation and of gross inefficiency in the field of public administration.

REFERENCES

Brown, H. G., *The Economics of Taxation*, 1924.
Comstock, Alzada, *Taxation in the Modern State*, 1931.
Dalton, H., *Principles of Public Finance*, 1923.
Jensen, Jens P., *Problems of Public Finance*, 1924.
Lutz, H. G., *The State Tax Commission*, 1918.
National Industrial Conference Board, *The Cost of Government in the United States, 1927–1928*, 1930.
National Industrial Conference Board, *State and Local Taxation of Property*, 1930.
National Tax Association, *Preliminary Report of the Committee Appointed to Prepare a Plan of a Model System of State and Local Taxation*, 1923.
Seligman, E. R. A., *Essays in Taxation*, 1925.

CHAPTER XXIX

INTERNATIONAL ECONOMIC POLICIES — RESTRICTIONS ON IMPORTS AND EXPORTS

I. The Importance of International Economic Policies Today

The inhabitants of each of the many countries of the world have formed the habit of thinking of themselves as having, in considerable degree, more or less common economic interests. Only to a far less extent, have they formed the habit of thinking of themselves as possessing common interests with persons who live beyond the national boundary line. This nationalistic bias in modern thought produces important effects upon economic policies. It leads each country to pursue policies which are intended to promote its national economic advantage. Sometimes countries seek to promote their interests at the expense of other nations; sometimes by coöperating with other nations.

What are the principal policies that nations pursue in order to advance their national economic interests? What are the results of these policies? Does the striving for national advantage leave nations better off or worse off? Or does it leave some nations better off and others worse off? Do some profit at the expense of others? What is the outlook for better organization of the world's economic life? for more coöperation between nations? What is the possibility of giving more adequate expression in national economic policies to the interests which all nations have in common?

These questions gain added importance from the fact that the efforts of nations to promote their economic interests often come in conflict with the needs of technology. The economies of large-scale industry can be fully achieved only when markets are large. The development of technology, therefore, creates the need for coöperation among nations in making possible larger markets. This coöperation is sadly lacking. On the contrary, nations have tended to restrict the size of markets by raising trade barriers higher and higher. Consequently, the world is far better organized for economic competition and conflict than it is for economic coöperation. Organizations with authority to represent the common economic interests of all nations exist in only rudimentary form, and efforts to create international coöperation come in conflict with powerful special interests within each nation, with ancient national traditions, and with national pride and prejudice.

Problems of international economic policy have been made increasingly important by the war. By substantially altering the trade relationships among nations, the war has compelled many nations to find new markets for their goods. Many European manufacturing countries in particular have had difficulty in finding outlets for their goods. Even before 1914, Europe was gradually becoming relatively less important as the workshop of the world. But the war enormously accelerated the industrialization of the United States, Canada, Australia, Japan, India, and China, and when the fighting ceased, Europe found that, to a large extent, her overseas customers were buying elsewhere or were manufacturing for themselves.[1] Within Europe, the war led to the creation of seven new countries. Some of these and some other countries, which had their political ambitions stimulated by territorial gains, have been eager to develop manufacturing and have imposed heavy duties on imports of manufactured

[1] The loss of trade by European manufacturing countries is shown by the following comparison of the exports of the United States, Great Britain and Germany. The figures are in millions.

	United States	United Kingdom	Germany
1913	$2,484	$3,089	$2,405
1925	4,910	4,478	2,211
1929	5,241	4,084	3,212

Between 1913 and 1929, there was a substantial rise in the price level. When allowance is made for this, it will be found that the physical volume of the exports of the United Kingdom and Germany was slightly less than in 1913. But the exports of the United States increased substantially. U. S. Department of Commerce, *Commerce Yearbook*, 1930, v. II, pp. 678–681.

goods. Finally, war and revolution have, temporarily at least, greatly diminished the buying power of Russia and other parts of the world. For all of these reasons, Great Britain, Germany, and other countries which obtain food to a large extent by exporting manufactured goods have had difficulty in finding markets for their products. This has meant chronic unemployment among millions of European factory workers and it has likewise meant chronic depression in many branches of agriculture in the United States, Canada, Australia, Brazil, and Argentina. The standard of living is lower than it should be, not because productive capacity is lacking, but because the world is still far from having solved the problem of building up trade relationships to replace those destroyed by the war. It is noteworthy that, whereas the commodity output of Europe in 1925 was about 5 per cent above 1913, its international trade was only about 94 per cent of 1913.[2]

Parallel with the tendency to impose restrictions upon imports has gone a tendency to impose them on exports. This has been encouraged by the fact that the industrial revolution has made many nations increasingly dependent upon foreign supplies of raw materials. Countries which possess a more or less complete monopoly of some raw materials have endeavored, by limiting exports, to collect a higher price from the rest of the world. About twenty commodities, including such important ones as coffee, long staple cotton, potash, rubber, sugar, and tin, are now or have recently been subject to control. What effects do these export controls produce, what problems do they create, and what are the possibilities of regulating them by international action?

The war and its aftermath not only violently changed the flow of international trade but also created grave monetary and financial problems — the problem of stabilizing currencies, the problem of collecting reparations from Germany, the problem of controlling the distribution (and possibly the value) of gold. In dealing with financial and monetary problems, nations have shown far greater disposition to coöperate than they have displayed in their highly restrictive tariff policies. When the war

[2] Patterson, E. M., "Europe in 1927," *Annals of the American Academy of Political and Social Science*, November, 1927, v. CXXXIV, p. 27.

closed, only the United States, among the leading nations of the world, remained on a gold standard. All of the currencies in Europe were paper, all fluctuated more or less violently in value, and some of them were rapidly depreciating. The problem of stabilizing the currencies was greatly complicated by the loss of trade which European countries experienced as a result of the war, by the enormous power of the United States to attract gold, and by the huge debts which many European countries — both combatants and non-combatants — incurred during the war. Some nations struggled with the problem of stabilizing their currencies for nearly a decade. In practically all instances, outside assistance has been necessary.

During the war, the leaders of the allied nations promised their people that Germany would be compelled to pay for the damage done by her armies. Consequently, one of the greatest problems of the post-war period has been that of collecting reparations from Germany. Indeed, it may be said that the attempt to collect reparations has been one of the most costly experiments in which post-war Europe has engaged. Mainly because of war hysteria and hatred of Germany but partly because the conditions limiting the capacity of a nation to pay reparations have not been clearly understood even by economic experts, the allies attempted to collect far more than Germany could pay. As a result, the economic recovery not only of Germany but of all of Europe was seriously retarded. Furthermore, so highly interdependent is our economic system, that the payment of reparations by Germany has been as harmful to one of the recipients, Great Britain, as to Germany herself. The history of the attempt to collect reparations is illuminating and important because it sheds light on the ability of victorious nations to shift some of the costs of war to the defeated nations and also on the ability of a victorious nation to collect reparations without serious injuries to itself.

During the last decade, the trend of prices the world over has been downward. In Switzerland, Sweden, the Netherlands, and Japan, the fall has been going on with only brief interruptions since 1921; in the United States, Great Britain, and Germany, since 1925; in France and Italy, since 1926. The effect of the decline is to increase the burden of the heavy debts which the war and reconstruction have imposed on many nations. With taxes absorbing nearly one-fifth of the national incomes in many countries, a drop of one-fifth in the price level, such as has occurred since 1925, is little short of a calamity. Governments cannot stand by and permit the drop to continue if a way can be found to prevent it. Some experts believe that coöperation among central banks might check the drop in prices. A preliminary step in creating machinery for coöperation has been taken in establishing the Bank for International Settlements. The immediate purpose of the Bank is to transfer reparation payments from Germany to the allied nations. Nevertheless the founders of the Bank visualized it as an agency for facilitating coöperation among central banks and for economizing gold. What are the prospects for effective international coöperation to check the downward trend in prices? What form might such coöperation take? What part might the Bank for International Settlements play? Are efforts to stop the drop in prices likely to succeed? Or are the causes of the drop too deep-seated to be reached by the instruments which the central banks and the Bank for International Settlements have at their command?

The importance of a better understanding of the problems of international economic policy is particularly important in the United States because the war has suddenly transformed us from the world's largest debtor nation to the second largest creditor nation. In addition, it has made us by far the most important source of current supplies of capital. But our position as a creditor nation is so new and our tradition of narrow nationalism is so strong that we do not know how to behave as a creditor nation. Few Americans understand how our prosperity is linked with the world's prosperity and how our policies affect the world's prosperity.

In this chapter, we shall discuss the efforts of nations to control the imports and exports of goods. In the following chapter, we shall analyze their efforts to cope with the monetary and financial problems of the post-war period.

II. The Development of Tariff Policies

It will shed light on the nature of tariff policies, and particularly on the problem of creating economic coöperation among nations, if we examine briefly the tariff history of the principal countries and notice some of the outstanding influences which have molded their commercial policies. Practically all of the leading countries of the world, with the exception of Great Britain and the Netherlands, pursue the general policy of protection. Even Great Britain has introduced a substantial degree of protection in the form of so-called " safeguarding " duties. During the first three quarters of the nineteenth century, the tendency was to relax restrictions on trade. The nearest approach to freedom of trade was probably reached in the sixties and seventies. During the last quarter of the century, the trend changed. Despite the fact that the development of modern technology has made large markets more needed than ever, the nations of the world have been surrounding themselves with higher and higher tariff walls. In fact, the restrictions on international trade today are, on the whole, greater than at any time since the eighteenth century.

Great Britain, it has been said, is one of two countries which still adheres to the general policy of free trade. The movement for lower duties developed among the manufacturers early in the nineteenth century. The Industrial Revolution developed far more rapidly in Great Britain than on the Continent because Great Britain was free from internal tariffs and did not suffer invasion or loss of colonial markets during the Napoleonic Wars.[3] Even as late as 1870, Great Britain produced half of the world's iron, three times as much as any other nation, and nearly half of the world's cotton textiles. Its foreign commerce was twice that of any rival.[4] The growth of manufacturing made Britain dependent upon foreign nations for part of its food supplies. Consequently, British manufacturers demanded the removal of the duties on foodstuffs and on raw materials used in manufacturing. Because of their superiority in manufacturing, British employers were ready to accept lower duties on their own products in return for lower duties on food and raw materials.

[3] Not until 1791 did France, as a result of the Revolution, abolish provincial tolls and duties. In Prussia, internal tariffs, of which there were nearly sixty affecting nearly 2,800 classes of goods, were not abolished until the reform of the administration after the Napoleonic Wars in 1818. Ashley, Percy, *Modern Tariff History*, p. 3.

[4] Moon, P. T., *Imperialism and World Politics*, p. 25.

The first great reduction in the British tariff occurred in 1842, when a severe depression focussed attention upon the fact that food was much higher in Great Britain than in continental countries. Duties were reduced on about 750 out of 1200 articles. In 1845, a second general reduction was made. The most important step occurred in 1846, when it was decided to eliminate, by several steps, the duties on wheat.[5] The prosperity of the fifties in England was attributed, rightly or wrongly, to the lower duties, and both political parties were converted to the policy of free trade. As a result of the Cobden-Chevalier treaty of 1860, additional duties were lowered or abolished. This treaty will be discussed presently. After the budget of 1860, only forty-eight articles were left in the tariff.[6]

In the German states, in contrast to Great Britain, the support for low duties came from the agriculturalists rather than the manufacturers, particularly from the large landowners of North and East Prussia. Prussia produced a surplus of grain. The landowners wished to have foreign markets open to their grain and to obtain manufactured goods on the best possible terms. The manufacturers desired protection, but they were not influential because manufacturing was undeveloped. Prussia, in reorganizing her finances in 1818 after the Napoleonic Wars, established one of the lowest tariffs in Europe. Raw materials were admitted free and there was an average duty of only about 10 per cent on manufactured goods.[7]

[5] The immediate occasion for this step was the failure of the Irish potato crop. At the same time that the duty on wheat was being eliminated, the duties on other articles, such as woolen, cotton, and linen goods, were reduced. It is interesting to notice that Peel, in proposing the abolition of the corn laws, asked all protected interests, manufacturers as well as agriculturalists, to sacrifice their protection for the common good and in particular called upon the cotton, woolen, and linen manufacturers " to set an example to others by relaxing voluntarily and cheerfully the protection they enjoyed." Page, W., *Commerce and Industry*, p. 161. The manufacturers, though strongly demanding the abolition of duties on foodstuffs, particularly wheat, were not adverse to having duties on their own products.

[6] *Ibid.*, p. 228.

[7] Ashley, Percy, *Modern Tariff History*, p. 3. Schmoller has expressed the opinion that this liberal tariff was possible only because Prussia was an absolute monarchy. His observation, which is referred to by Ashley, occurs in his *Grundriss der Allgemeinen Volkswirtschaftslehre*, v. II, p. 611. No doubt it is true that the relative independence of an absolute monarchy which is fairly well established and

An important step in the removal of trade barriers was the establishment of the German Zollverein in 1834. The Zollverein was a customs union of Prussia and most of the other states of Germany, except Austria. Duties between member states were abolished, a uniform tariff was maintained against the rest of the world, and the proceeds were divided among the member states in proportion to population. Many of the German states were so small (there were thirty-nine in all) that the need for the removal of barriers was obvious, and this need was the greater because Prussia levied transit duties on goods passing through her territories. Prussia's political ambitions made her willing to grant concessions in order to reach an agreement with the smaller states. Despite many difficulties and despite intense jealousy among the states, the union was finally accomplished.[8] It began with no duties on raw materials and with moderate duties on manufactured goods. After 1840, there was a distinct upswing in the rates. The cotton spinners and the manufacturers of iron, in particular, demanded protection from British competition. The ports of the North and the agricultural interests of Prussia favored free trade.[9] The negotiation of the Cobden-Chevalier treaty of 1860 between France and Great Britain gave the upper hand to the low-duty group within the Zollverein. With this treaty, France began the policy of two tariffs — a general tariff, applying to states with which France had no commercial treaty, and lower duties established by special conventions with states which made concessions to France. To gain admittance to the French market on the most advantageous terms, the Zollverein made a treaty with France which provided for reductions on 161 duties by the Verein, mostly on manufactured goods. In 1873, the newly established German Empire adopted the general policy of duties for revenue only. Some manufacturing interests, particularly the heavy iron and

---

does not fear overthrow enables it to refuse concessions to particular interests and to formulate a truly national policy.

[8] Great Britain and France attempted to prevent the formation of the union. It was fortunate that the extraordinary indifference of Metternich to economic problems kept Austria from attempting to prevent it.

[9] The manufacturing interests were not, however, united in demanding protection, for many users of machinery opposed the duties on iron and the cotton weavers opposed duties on British yarns. *Ibid.*, p. 18.

the spinning industries, were protectionist, as they always had been, but most of the influential Prussian landowners were still free traders.

In France, the Napoleonic Wars had brought into existence small iron and textile manufacturers who needed protection against British goods. The Restoration Monarchy protected them and other manufacturers by high duties or by prohibitions upon imports. Influential parts of the community, particularly the Paris merchants and the wine growers who were large exporters, advocated a less restricted policy, but the manufacturers, as generally on the Continent, were protectionists. Napoleon III was impressed by the reforms of Peel in England, and during the fifties he lowered many duties by decree. The most important step, however, was the Cobden-Chevalier treaty of 1860. The French system of prohibitions upon certain imports was about to expire in 1861. The British feared that the prohibitions would be replaced by high duties. One purpose of the treaty was to prevent this. But the treaty was not solely inspired by economic motives. The prospective annexation of Nice and Savoy aroused great resentment against France in England where some people feared that Napoleon III might emulate Napoleon I. Both parties desired the treaty in order to allay warlike feeling. Great Britain undertook to abolish all duties on manufactured goods and to reduce the tariff on wine and brandy; France to reduce the duties on English coal and coke, bar and pig iron, steel, worked metals, tools and machinery, yarns, and other manufactured goods.[10] When the system of prohibitions expired on October 1, 1861, France agreed to replace them with duties of not more than 30 per cent up to October, 1864, and of 24 per cent thereafter.[11]

Great Britain reduced its duties by a general act which affected all nations as well as France. France, on the other hand, made the reductions to Great Britain only. Other nations, in order to obtain the same terms as Great Britain, were compelled to negotiate special treaties with France. The result was a series of commercial treaties by which the other countries, in re-

[10] Page, W., *Commerce and Industry*, p. 226.
[11] Ashley, P., *Modern Tariff History*, p. 299.

turn for admittance to the French market on the same terms as Great Britain, offered reductions to France. It was this series of treaties, between France and Belgium, Italy, the German Zollverein, the Netherlands, Norway, Sweden, Switzerland, and others, which brought Europe as nearly to free trade as it has come.[12]

The beginning of the last quarter of the nineteenth century saw the policy of free trade or of moderate duties practiced by the three greatest powers of Europe — Great Britain, Germany, and France. During the last quarter of the century, however, a strong drift toward higher duties set in. The increases in duties were due partly to fiscal causes, partly to the demands of agricultural interests for protection against cheap American products, and partly to the growing influence of the manufacturers. The movement began in France. Here the immediate cause was fiscal. The government needed large sums to pay the indemnity and the interest on the large debt incurred in the Franco-Prussian War. Most branches of manufacturing in France had always been protectionist and the growing invasion of American wheat now caused many agricultural groups, except the wine growers, to demand higher duties.[13] In 1881, the tariff was raised slightly. The continued fall in the prices of wheat and other agricultural products during the eighties stimulated the demand for protection among the agriculturalists. In 1892, there were substantial increases in duties. This tariff remained substantially unchanged until 1910.[14]

In Germany, the movement for higher duties came from much the same reasons as in France — partly fiscal reasons and partly the demands of agriculturalists for protection. The rising expenses of the Empire led Bismarck to favor a higher tariff. More important, however, was the changing sentiment among the agrarian interests. The growth of urban population was chang-

---

[12] Under the " most favored nation clause " the reductions granted to one nation were automatically extended to all nations enjoying " most favored nation " treatment.

[13] Ashley, Percy, *Modern Tariff History*, p. 13.

[14] The tariff of 1892 contained two sets of rates, a minimum for nations which gave France the most favored nation treatment, and a maximum for nations which did not. The tariff of 1910 did not greatly change the minimum rates but, for bargaining purposes, it raised many of the maximum rates.

ing Germany from an exporter to an importer of grain. This, combined with the growing competition of the United States and the falling prices of grain, caused the Prussian grain growers to become protectionists. The iron and the textile manufacturers had always been protectionists and remained so. In 1880, a tariff was passed which gave moderate protection to both agriculture and manufacturing. After 1880, the growing power of the agrarian party resulted in substantial increases in the duties on farm products.

As Germany became an importer of foodstuffs and an important exporter of manufactured goods, the duties on food became a substantial handicap to German manufacturing because they increased the cost of living and made for higher money wages. During the late eighties and early nineties, therefore, the German manufacturers began to manifest serious opposition to the high duties demanded by the agrarian interests. Following the dismissal of Bismarck in 1890, Germany made a series of reciprocal treaties by which she reduced her duties on agricultural products to other countries in return for reductions in their duties on German manufactured goods. Such treaties were made with Austria-Hungary, Servia, Spain, Belgium, Italy, and Switzerland. They were bitterly opposed by the agrarian party in Germany.

The commercial treaties were to terminate on December 31, 1903. As a basis for bargaining in renewing the treaties, the agrarian interests, which had greatly increased their strength in the Reichstag, passed a new tariff which substantially increased many agricultural duties and, in the case of some farm products, limited the reductions which the government might make by treaty. When Germany raised her tariff for bargaining purposes, the other countries of eastern and central Europe did likewise. The new general tariffs and the new commercial treaties which granted reductions from them resulted, therefore, in a substantially higher scale of duties throughout central and eastern Europe.[15] They remained in effect until the outbreak of the war.

As might be expected, the United States, a new country without large manufacturing industries during its early years, has

[15] The negotiations of the new treaties were so protracted that the old treaties remained in effect until early in 1906.

pursued a policy of protection, especially with respect to manufactured products. It is interesting, however, to notice that the protectionist policy was less extreme during the first half of our history when manufacturing here was in its infancy than during the last half when we had become the largest manufacturing nation in the world. The tariff has reflected less the needs of industries than their political power.

The first tariff bill, passed in 1789, was primarily intended to provide revenue for the newly established national government, but it also reflected the desire to encourage manufacturing. The duties, however, were moderate in comparison with those levied today; the highest ad valorem duty was 15 per cent; most products paid 10 per cent or less. The Napoleonic Wars and the War of 1812 shut out foreign goods and gave great impetus to American manufacturing. After the restoration of peace, the newly established enterprises were threatened with extinction by the influx of foreign goods. A tariff was passed in 1816, which, though lower than the duties imposed during the war, was substantially above the pre-war level. The opposition of the powerful New England shipping interests and of the South kept the duties moderate. The South opposed protection, partly because it exported cotton, tobacco, and rice and feared that a protectionist policy might lead foreign countries to retaliate against its products. More important was the fact that the South employed slave labor and could not expect to develop important manufacturing. It was interested, therefore, in being free to purchase manufactured goods in the cheapest market.

The redistribution of representation in Congress after the census of 1820 increased the strength of the Middle Atlantic and Western States. The Middle Atlantic States wished protection for their manufactures and the West for its hemp, wool, and flax. The result was the tariff of 1824, a frankly protectionist act. It was followed by the act of 1828, the "tariff of abominations," which still further raised duties. This act was regarded as so outrageous that it was replaced in 1832 by a new law which reduced the duties to about the level of 1824.[16] A compromise in 1833 went even further and provided for the gradual reduction of all duties to a maximum of 20 per cent by 1842.

[16] The act of 1832, because of its very moderation, was regarded as permanently

A victory of the Whigs in 1840 and the fact that the treasury was facing a deficit led to an advance in the tariff in 1842, but in 1846 the Democrats made substantial reductions in the duties. Nevertheless the tariff of 1846 gave moderate protection. Woolens, leather, glass, and manufactures of iron paid 30 per cent, and cotton goods 25 per cent. This tariff remained in force for eleven years. The period was one of great prosperity and rapid growth of both manufacturing and agriculture. There was almost no demand for higher duties. In 1857, the growing surplus in the treasury led to a reduction in duties to the lowest point since the War of 1812. This reduction encountered practically no opposition either from manufacturers or within Congress.

Possibly the prosperity of the United States under a moderate tariff, such as that of 1846, might have led, as it did in Great Britain, to the continuance of a low-tariff policy. But this possibility was destroyed by the Civil War, during which were laid the foundations of the present extreme protectionist policy of the country. To meet the extraordinary war needs of the government, duties were substantially increased. In addition, excise taxes were levied on many products. To compensate for these taxes, duties on imports were raised still higher. When the war was over, most of the excise taxes and also the income tax, which had been enacted as war measures, were promptly repealed. But the tariff was scarcely touched.[17] Manufacturing had increased rapidly during the war and many manufacturers were opposed to lower duties. In addition, the South, which had been a stronghold of low tariff sentiment, was not represented in Congress for several years. Of course, when the excise taxes were abolished without repealing the compensating duties, the tariff was in effect

---

establishing the protectionist policy. This led South Carolina, on November 24, 1832, to declare the tariff acts of 1824 and 1828 null and void within the state as an exercise of power not granted to Congress by the Constitution. South Carolina declared that, in the event of the Federal government's attempting to enforce these laws, the state would withdraw from the Union. The firm stand of President Jackson and the unwillingness of other Southern states to follow South Carolina prevented trouble.

[17] An attempt to reduce the tariff by a moderate amount in 1867 failed; a few duties, such as those on wool, woolens, copper, and steel rails, were actually increased in 1867.

increased. There was some opposition to the high duties among the farmers in the West who received low prices for their produce and were far from prosperous but, except for a temporary reduction of 10 per cent in all duties in 1872, there was no general revision of the high war duties until 1883. But the tariff of 1883 was only a weak concession to the demand for more moderate duties and represented no real change in the rates.

Since 1883, there have been seven general tariff revisions. Two of them were downward, but at no time has the United States been without a high tariff, and the tendency has been to raise the rates. During the eighties, dissatisfaction with the high duties grew in the South and West where the farmers produced wheat, cotton, and cattle in excess of domestic needs. They could obtain only the world price for their products but were compelled by the tariff to pay higher prices for many manufactured goods. President Cleveland made the tariff the principal issue in the campaign of 1888, but the Republicans won by a small margin and passed the McKinley bill of 1890, which raised duties to new heights. The profound reaction against this bill enabled the Democrats to win the next two elections and, in 1894, they passed the Wilson tariff. The bill reduced many duties but it was essentially a protective tariff and, indeed, a high one.[18] The Wilson bill took effect shortly after an acute commercial crisis which was followed by a prolonged depression. The crisis was world-wide but the depression in the United States was greatly intensified by lack of confidence in our monetary system.[19] Nevertheless the fact that the reduction in the tariff was followed by depression encouraged the belief that prohibitively high duties

[18] Democrats in the Senate, who were interested in retaining high duties on products from their own states, joined with the Republican minority to raise the rates in the bill as it was passed by the House. President Cleveland regarded the action of the Democratic bolters in the Senate as a breach of faith and permitted the bill to become law without his signature.

[19] The United States had been practically (but not formally) on the gold standard. Falling prices which inflicted grave injustice on debtors led to the demand that the United States adopt a double standard (bimetallism) of gold and silver. This in itself might not have provoked great alarm but it was proposed to make the silver dollar only sixteen times as heavy as the gold dollar — a great overvaluation of silver because, by 1894, silver was worth less than one-thirtieth as much as gold. The possibility that investors in American securities might be paid in silver dollars that were worth less than gold dollars discouraged foreign capital from entering the United States and caused much of it to withdraw.

were necessary for prosperity and destroyed the low-tariff movement which had been gaining strength during the eighties. In
1897, the Republicans passed the Dingley bill which raised the
level beyond the McKinley bill.

The act of 1897 remained in force for twelve years — longer
than any other general tariff. The belief that the hard times of
the nineties were attributable to the Wilson bill discouraged the
demand for lower duties, and the rising price level, which brought
prosperity to the farmers in the South and West, reduced their
interest in the tariff. But dissatisfaction gradually developed,
especially because many persons believed that the tariff stimulated the growth of monopolies and trusts. There was an inde-
cisive revision in 1909, under the Taft administration, and a
distinct revision downward in 1913 when the Democrats passed
the Underwood bill. But the Underwood tariff, like the Wilson
tariff, was, in the main, a protective bill and many of the reductions in duties, although substantial, were merely nominal.[20]
Manufacturing costs in the United States were in many cases as
low as costs abroad and, even where costs here were higher, the
duties were high enough to be prohibitive. Lower duties did, of
course, limit the possibilities of monopolistic price-fixing by domestic producers and, in the case of some commodities, this was
no doubt important. The Underwood tariff remained in effect
until 1922.

The tendency to raise higher and higher trade barriers has
been greatly stimulated all over the world by the economic and
political conditions which followed the war.[21] The immense war

[20] A few important raw materials and semi-manufactured goods, such as wool,
coal, lumber, wheat, cattle, and sugar, were admitted free. The abolition of the
duty on sugar was to take effect gradually but it was never completely carried out
because Congress in 1916 amended the act to provide for the retention of a duty
of one and one-fourth cents per pound (one cent per pound on Cuban sugar).

[21] It was pointed out in Chapter XXI (p. 530) that, when depreciation occurs, the currency usually falls in terms of foreign currencies faster than in terms
of domestic prices. This makes it possible for holders of foreign currency to obtain
goods in a country with a rapidly depreciating currency on exceedingly favorable
terms. The demoralized condition of the currencies immediately after the war led
to the imposition of many restrictions upon both imports and exports — upon imports, by countries with relatively stable currencies which feared a flood of goods
from countries with rapidly depreciating currencies, and upon exports, by countries
with depreciating currencies which feared that they might be denuded of goods by
foreign purchases. In addition, countries with depreciating currencies often limited
or prohibited the importation of many non-essential articles. The purpose was to

debts and the heavy financial burdens imposed by pensions and by reconstruction compelled some countries to raise duties for fiscal reasons. Newly established countries or countries which came out of the war with large territorial gains and with strong national ambitions have been eager to develop manufacturing because it is the basis of military strength. The world-wide depression in some branches of agriculture has led many countries to raise their duties on agricultural products.[22] Some oriental countries — Turkey, Siam, Persia, China, and Egypt — whose tariffs had been controlled by western powers, have succeeded in freeing themselves from that control and have increased their duties. And not only have tariffs been rising, but the changes have occurred frequently and often without reasonable notice. The French tariff of 1892 remained substantially unchanged until 1910, the German commercial treaties of the early nineties were in effect until 1906, those of 1906 until 1914 or later. The relative stability of the pre-war years has disappeared. In 1925 and 1926, there were general revisions or material alterations in the tariffs of sixteen countries in Europe; in 1927, of ten; in 1928, of five; in 1929, of two.[23]

In the United States, as in the rest of the world, the protectionist movement has reached new heights in the post-war years. Immediately after the war there was fear that the European countries with depreciated currencies would flood the American market. New industries, such as the chemical industry, which had grown up during the war, demanded protection against the longer established ones in Europe. Finally, both the South and the Middle West, the traditional centers of low tariff sentiment, have been drifting in the direction of protection. The industrialization of the South — a process which was hastened during the

---

limit the demand for foreign currencies and then to check the depreciation of the domestic currency. As nations have succeeded in stabilizing their currencies, the system of prohibitions and licenses has been largely abandoned.

[22] But immediately after the war there was a shortage of foodstuffs and this led a number of countries — Czechoslovakia, Denmark, France, Germany, and Italy — to reduce their duties on foodstuffs below the pre-war level. Patterson, E. M., "Europe in 1927," *Annals of the American Academy of Political and Social Science,* November, 1927, v. CXXXIV, pp. 34–35. In a few cases also — Austria, Denmark, and France — the general level of the tariff was below the pre-war level, at least as late as 1925. *Ibid.,* p. 33.

[23] Chalmers, Henry, "Current Trends in Foreign Commercial Policy," *Annals of the American Academy of Political and Social Science,* July, 1930, v. CL, p. 131.

war — created a demand for the protection of its manufactures. Following the collapse of prices in 1920, many branches of agriculture were in the grip of a severe depression. Farmers were willing to grasp at any straw and many of them came to believe that higher duties on farm products might possibly help. The result was that in 1922 Congress passed the Fordney-McCumber bill which raised duties almost to the level of the Dingley tariff of 1897. Most of the increases were of little effect, either because the United States, with its rich resources and up-to-date equipment, could make most articles for less than foreign competitors or because the old duties were high enough to be practically prohibitive.

Despite the tariff of 1922, the depression in agriculture continued. More and more insistently the farmers demanded help from the government. Embarrassed by a demand which they did not know how to meet, politicians in the campaign of 1928 again suggested high duties as a remedy. Manufacturers took advantage of the situation to demand higher rates for themselves. The revision of 1930 pushed the tariff even above the levels of 1922. Again it must be stressed that most of the increases have little protective value. In the case of most agricultural products, the United States produces more than it consumes; in the case of many manufactured goods, production costs here are lower than abroad; in the case of many other manufactured goods, the old duties have been prohibitive.[24]

[24] The competing power of American industries is indicated by the fact that our share of export trade of the world increased from 12.3 per cent in 1913 to 15.8 per cent in 1929. *Commerce Yearbook*, 1930, v. II, p. 679. These figures, however, do not fully reflect the competitive strength of American manufacturing because the increase in our total exports has been held down by the decline in our exports of foodstuffs. The competitive power of our manufacturers is reflected in our increasing share in the imports of certain countries to which we sell largely manufactured goods:

	1913	1929
Australia	14.0 per cent	24.6 per cent
Asia		
China	6.0	18.0
India	2.5	8.7
Japan	16.8	29.5
Latin-America		
Argentine	14.7	25.4 [a]
Brazil	15.7	30.1
Chile	16.7	33.9
Cuba	53.6	60.8 [b]
Mexico	50.6	67.5 [b]

[a] 1927.   [b] 1928.

For several decades the United States has been producing more than 96 per cent of the manufactured goods which it consumes. In the year 1930, it was the greatest producer in the world of both manufactured goods and agricultural products; it possessed more and better equipment than any other country in the world. Its export trade exceeded that of any other nation. And yet, despite its general superiority, the United States maintains the highest tariff among the principal industrial countries of the world.

III. THE CASE FOR FREEDOM OF TRADE

What is the effect of a protective tariff? Does it increase or diminish the output of industry? Does it raise wages, as it is often said to do, or does it lower them?

Australia can raise wool for less than most parts of the United States; the United States, on the other hand, can make automobiles for less than Australia. If there were no barriers to the importation of wool into the United States and of automobiles into Australia, the United States would procure more of its wool from Australia and Australia would purchase more automobiles from the United States. But the United States imposes a high duty on wool and Australia a high duty on automobiles. What is the result? Our duty on wool diminishes our imports of wool and causes us to devote a larger part of our labor and capital to raising wool and less to other lines of industry. Likewise, the Australian duty on automobiles diminishes their imports of automobiles and causes them to devote more of their labor and capital to making automobiles. The American tariff on wool and the Australian tariff on automobiles, therefore, cause Australia to produce less wool and more automobiles and the United States to produce less automobiles and more wool. But since capital and labor are more productive in making automobiles in the United States than in Australia and since they are more productive in raising wool in Australia than in the United States, the net effect of the tariffs is to reduce the total output of both wool and automobiles.

This illustration makes clear the most obvious effect of protective tariffs. They interfere with the territorial specialization of industry. If there were no barriers to the movement of goods, the production of each commodity would tend to be concentrated in the places where the cost of production was least. The place where a commodity can be produced for least depends, of course, upon many factors — the proximity to raw materials, the location of markets, the availability of cheap and skilled labor. One location may be desirable for one reason, another location for another. Consequently, in the absence of trade barriers, all the output of the given commodity would not necessarily come from one place or region; it might come from many places where the commodity could be produced advantageously. To the extent that tariffs interfere with this ideal distribution of production, they reduce the output of industry.[25]

Not only do tariff barriers interfere with territorial specialization but they also limit the size of business enterprises, the use of machinery, and the specialization of labor within plants. The reason is obvious. Large and specialized plants which use much machinery and which minutely divide operations among many workers must have large markets. To visualize the effect of protective tariffs, imagine that each of the forty-eight states in

[25] Articles *tend* to be made in the places where they can be reproduced with the smallest expenditure of labor and capital, but this tendency is not entirely realized. Capital and labor are not distributed so that they can be used to the greatest advantage and, for various reasons, they are slow to migrate to places where they would be more productive. Consequently, the capital and labor of each country tend to go into the industry where the advantage of the country is greatest or its disadvantage least. Let us suppose that capital and labor are more productive *in all lines* in country A than they are in country B. Nevertheless, country A may import some commodities from country B. This can be easily demonstrated. Assume, for simplicity, that labor cost is the entire cost of production and that the entire output of the two countries is represented by two commodities — say, shoes and automobile tires. In country A, a pair of shoes can be produced with one day's labor and an automobile tire with two days' labor. In country B, where labor is less efficient, two days' labor are required to produce a pair of shoes and three to produce an automobile tire. Although country A is more efficient than country B in producing both commodities, its relative efficiency is greater in producing shoes than in producing tires — a given amount of labor in country A produces 100 per cent more tires and 50 per cent more shoes than in country B. Consequently, it will pay country A to use its limited supplies of labor in producing shoes, where its advantage is greatest, and to import tires from country B. This can be shown by comparing the values of the two products in the two countries. In country A, it will take two pairs of shoes (or the price of two pairs of shoes) to buy one automobile tire — because two pairs of shoes and one tire are each the product of two days' labor. In country B, it takes only one and one-half pairs of shoes (or the price of one and one-half) to buy one tire — because one and one-half pairs of shoes and one tire are the product of the same amount of labor. Under these conditions, the cheapest way for country A to get tires is to make shoes and to export them to country B (where shoes are worth more relative to tires than at home) in exchange for tires. This is why country B, though less efficient at making tires than country A, may, nevertheless, export them to country A.

the United States were surrounded by a high tariff wall. There would be no huge automobile plants, such as those in Detroit, no huge packing plants, such as those in Chicago and Kansas City, and no immense steel plants, such as those in Pittsburgh. Instead, there would be small automobile plants, small packing plants, small steel plants in every state. Kansas, for example, would have more automobile plants and more radio plants, but the people of Kansas would own fewer automobiles and fewer radios because of economies of large-scale production would be unattainable and automobiles and radios would cost far more than they do now. The United States, because of its very size, is probably less injured by protective tariffs than any country in the world.

An especially strong argument for free trade exists in the case of some easily exhaustible natural resources, such as petroleum. Other countries can produce some petroleum at less cost than some domestic producers. The duties not only prevent the ideal distribution of capital and labor and reduce the national income, but they may impose a hardship upon future generations by causing premature exhaustion of the domestic supply. Protective tariffs are often urged on the ground that certain domestic industries are needed for national defense. In the case of petroleum, however, national defense seems to require the conservation of the domestic supply. This means that we should satisfy our requirements as much as possible from abroad.[26]

It is evident that many industries in the United States could not pay the wages which they are now paying if the tariff on their products were removed or substantially lowered. The observation of this fact has led many persons to conclude that the tariff raises wages. It is true that the tariff makes possible higher wages than would otherwise be possible in *some* industries, but the *general effect* of the tariff, as actually applied, is to lower

[26] Under special circumstances, conservation of natural resources may be promoted by a tariff. For example, farmers may be wearing out soil through single cropping. Duties on agricultural products may accelerate the spread of diversified farming and conserve the fertility of the soil. This policy would impose a burden upon the present generation in order that future generations might have better soil. It must not, however, be assumed that, as a general rule, a tariff on agricultural products is necessary to conserve the soil. And even where uneconomical single cropping is practiced, it does not necessarily follow that a tariff will be effective in ending it.

rather than to raise wages.[27]   Labor's productivity depends upon the conditions under which it is employed and its wages, we have seen, depend in general upon its productivity.[28]   To the extent that the tariff causes capital and labor to be employed under unfavorable conditions, to the extent that it limits the use of machinery and the specialization of labor and equipment within business enterprises, it reduces the productivity of labor and thus reduces wages.   The industries where the existing wage level is possible only because of the tariff are precisely the industries where labor is relatively unproductive.   The tariff is usually regarded as helping domestic producers to compete with foreign producers.   This is only part of its effect.   It also helps some domestic industries in which labor and capital have a relatively low productivity to compete for men and funds with other domestic industries in which labor and capital have a greater productivity.   *In other words, it protects the less productive domestic industries against the more productive.*   At precisely the points where the tariff *appears* to be raising wages by enabling employers to bid more for labor, it is *in reality* lowering wages by diverting labor into relatively unproductive uses.

IV. The Case for Protection

No doubt protection, *as actually practiced,* often prevents the attainment of the largest possible output of goods at the lowest possible cost.   But this is not a conclusive argument against protection.   Diversity of industry itself may be desirable and the inhabitants of a country may prefer to sacrifice some income in order to achieve more diversity.   Protection is one way, although not necessarily the best way, of fostering diversification.

[27] It should be observed, however, that a tariff may possibly raise wages in some new countries which are rich in natural resources but which lack capital and labor. As will be pointed out in the next section, a tariff under these circumstances may cause capital and labor to migrate to the new country. If capital is more mobile than labor, then the effect of the tariff will be to increase the proportion of capital to labor in the new country and thus to raise wages. Of course, in the old countries from which capital and labor have migrated, labor may be more plentiful relative to capital and wages will drop. If capital were less mobile than labor, the effect of the tariff would be to lower wages in the country imposing the tariff. Whether or not wages would rise in the country from which labor was emigrating would depend upon whether emigration retarded the rate of population increase. There appears to be considerable doubt whether emigration from a densely settled region has much effect upon the population there.

[28] Pp. 605–617.

And, *under some circumstances,* tariffs, instead of interfering with the most productive distribution of capital and labor, may improve the distribution of resources.

Diversity may be desired for several reasons. National defense may be one. A predominantly manufacturing country may wish to avoid being too completely dependent upon foreign sources of food supply and may foster agriculture by a tariff; a predominantly agricultural country may consider it wise, from the standpoint of national defense, to encourage some branches of manufacturing, particularly the metal trades and the textile industry.[29] Diversity may be sought for cultural and political reasons. The inhabitants of a country may desire to preserve a balance between the urban and the rural population. A class of landowning farmers, for example, may contribute a stable and moderate element to the population and it may seem sound public policy to keep this class large by a tariff on agriculture. Cities and towns are centers of cultural life, and manufacturing industries offer many opportunities for technical and professional careers which agriculture does not provide. The inhabitants of a predominantly agricultural country may feel that the cultural life of the community will be improved by an increase in the urban industries or they may desire to open up professional opportunities for their children by fostering manufacturing.

Thus far we have assumed that the effect of tariffs is simply to change the distribution of capital and labor between industries. But tariffs may also be an instrument by which nations, particularly new countries with much land but with few inhabitants and little capital, compete for a larger share of the world's capital and population. By erecting high tariff walls, a country makes it profitable for capital and labor to enter. From the standpoint of the world as a whole and particularly from the standpoint of the capital and labor which are forced to migrate, the tariff may be burdensome. Perhaps capital and labor could earn more if they were not forced to move. But, from the standpoint

---

[29] But protective duties may hinder rather than promote national defense. This is particularly true of duties on minerals which, by shutting out foreign supplies, accelerate the exhaustion of the domestic deposits. It might be wise, from the standpoint of national defense, for the United States to abandon its duty on manganese and to conserve the limited domestic supply. And it would be an error of the first magnitude for the United States to hasten the exhaustion of its petroleum by shutting out imports.

of the people who are already on the ground, it may be advantageous to compel capital and labor to move into the country. The landowners obtain a larger market for dairy products, fruit, and vegetables; many retailers acquire more customers; doctors, dentists, and lawyers obtain more clients, building tradesmen obtain more work. Furthermore, by gaining in population and capital, the country becomes more powerful and thus more secure against invasion.[30]

It is not inevitable, however, that a protective tariff will reduce the productivity of industry. In at least three ways, it may increase productivity. In the first place, it must not be assumed that protection *invariably* brings about an uneconomical distribution of capital and labor. Under some circumstances it may have precisely the opposite effect. In fact, *carefully and judiciously applied,* protection may improve the distribution of resources and increase the output of industry. This is most likely to be true in the case of new and undeveloped countries. A country may be an ideal location in which to produce certain commodities, but it may lack labor and capital. Labor and capital are not perfectly mobile. They are even slow in migrating to locations where a commodity can be produced at less than prevailing costs. A tariff may help to overcome the inertia of labor and capital and to accelerate their movement to desirable locations. But after the new industry has become reasonably well established, the tariff should be removed. Otherwise it is likely to keep inefficient plants in business or lead domestic producers to form monopolies in order to take advantage of the duty.[31]

In the second place, protection may increase output by reducing the wastage of labor and capital which almost invariably attends the development of an industry in a new region. A new enterprise is usually at a disadvantage in competing with old ones because assembling and training a force is expensive and because the enterprise must acquire its customers by taking them away from old concerns — a difficult and often a costly process. Consequently, the mortality among new enterprises is usually high. Every failure involves a more or less serious economic

---

[30] This is an important consideration in Australian tariff and population policy.
[31] The argument that a tariff may be useful in assisting the establishment of new industries is known as " the infant industry " argument.

loss because some of the capital sunk in the concern may never be used again. By reducing the mortality among new enterprises, a tariff reduces the waste of capital. Of course, if the tariff is too high, it will do more harm than good by enabling inefficient concerns to survive. For this reason, a low tariff may be desirable but a high one undesirable.[32]

In the third place, a protective tariff may increase the output of industry by accelerating the rate of capital accumulation.[33] A tariff increases the profits of enterprises in the protected industries. But profits are a form of income which produces an unusually large amount of saving. In the United States, as we have seen, about 40 per cent of business profits are saved. To the extent that a tariff increases profits, therefore, it is likely to accelerate the accumulation of capital and thus to increase the output of goods. Allowance must be made for the fact that the tariff, while increasing the profits of some industries, may reduce the profits of others, especially of industries which lose export trade because of the tariff. Whether or not its *net* effect is to increase the volume of saving depends upon its net effect upon profits in all industries. Of course, the fact that it causes the community to save more does not in itself prove that the tariff is desirable. On the contrary, possibly the community would obtain a greater return from its expenditures if the distribution of income were not disturbed by the tariff.

In addition, a tariff may have indirect repercussions upon production which cannot be accurately judged and yet which may be of substantial importance. The encouragement of domestic industries which use many scientists and technical men — such as the electrical equipment industry or the chemical industry — may accelerate the development of science and technology within the country. This, in turn, may affect the technique and the productivity of a wide variety of industries.

[32] When we assert that the tariff may be a useful device because it accelerates the migration of capital and labor, we raise the question: "What is the most economical rate of migration?" Migration may involve considerable cost. Laborers, for example, may prefer not to leave their relatives and friends for a new land. Perhaps it would be desirable to have population distributed more uniformly over the globe. But on the generation which must break home ties and bear the cost of moving, the change imposes a burden.

[33] This point is developed by Dr. A. S. Johnson in "Protection and the Formation of Capital," *Political Science Quarterly*, June, 1908, v. XXIII, pp. 220–241.

V. The Cost of Individual Duties

In *theory,* the case for limited and judiciously applied protection is undoubtedly stronger than the case for absolute freedom of trade. But judiciously applied protection is exactly what we do not have. Tariffs in practice are the result of pressure from special interests and reflect the political influence of many small groups rather than the needs of the community as a whole. Majorities for tariff bills are created by trading or " log rolling." A member of Congress who wishes a high duty for an industry that is important in his district or state obtains the necessary votes by supporting high duties which other members of Congress desire. The result is that the tariff does not represent a truly *national* economic policy. It represents merely the efforts of various special interests to profit at the expense of the rest of the community. Duty after duty is put in the bill, not because it is desirable from the standpoint of the country as a whole, but because its inclusion helps to obtain votes for other duties. The common interests of all states and districts receive little consideration.

Although tariffs, as they are made, reduce rather than increase the national income, some duties are more burdensome than others. It is desirable to inquire what determines the burdens imposed by duties. The purpose of a protective tariff (as distinguished from a tariff for revenue) is, of course, to build up certain domestic industries. Some duties are more effective than others in stimulating domestic production. What determines how large a bill consumers must pay in order to create this or that domestic industry? Is the industry worth what consumers must pay for it? [34]

To begin with, it should be pointed out again that many duties in our tariff have little or no effect either in developing domestic industries or in burdening consumers, for the simple reason that the costs of most American producers are below the costs of

[34] A series of excellent analyses of the effects of important duties has been published by the Institute of Economics. Among them are: Wright, P. G., *Sugar in Relation to the Tariff*; Smith, M. A., *The Tariff on Wool*; Edminster, L. R., *The Cattle Industry and the Tariff*; Wright, P. G., *The Tariff on Animal and Vegetable Oils*; Berglund, A., and Wright, P. G., *The Tariff on Iron and Steel*.

most of their foreign competitors. The export trade of the United States is the largest in the world, and, during the last sixty years, it has been increasing more rapidly than that of our chief European competitors.[35] Nevertheless, on many of the commodities which we successfully export we impose high duties. Iron and steel products, automobiles, cement, corn, and wheat are examples.[36] The best that can be said of these duties is that, as long as they do not stimulate domestic producers to form monopolies, they do practically no harm. They do not in themselves raise the domestic price and they do not divert capital and labor to uneconomical uses and thus lower the national output and the standard of living. In some industries, however, they have led domestic producers to form monopolies in order to gain the benefit of the duty.

There is a second group of duties which has little or no effect upon domestic production, not because domestic costs are lower than foreign costs, but because domestic costs are so much higher (or because alternative lines of production are so profitable) that even a very high duty is not sufficient to create a domestic industry. The duty on olive oil is an example. The duty yields the government about $7,000,000 a year. It also encourages consumers to use substitutes for olive oil. But it does not produce an olive oil industry. The small district in California which produces olives supplies us with only 1¼ per cent of our olive oil. At one hundredth of the cost to the consumer, we could give the California industry the same benefit, in the form of a subsidy, and,

[35] Between 1872 and 1929, the exports of the United States increased about twelvefold, those of Great Britain less than threefold, and those of Germany about fourfold.

[36] It must not, of course, be assumed that the tariff on products which are exported has no effect whatever. The United States is a large country and a duty which is ineffective in most parts of the country may have some effect in seaboard cities. This is true, for example, of the duties on cement and corn. Furthermore, there may be several grades of a product and a duty which is ineffective on some grades may be effective on others. This is true of wheat. Although the United States raises more wheat than it consumes, most of the production is low-protein wheat. We import high-protein wheat to be mixed with low-protein in milling. The duty, ineffective for low-protein wheat, tends to raise the price of high-protein. In fact, by raising the price of high-protein wheat, the duty tends to reduce the price of low-protein wheat. But although there are probably few duties which have no effect whatever, there are many which have only a small effect. When there are marked seasonal variations in the output of the commodity (as in the case of butter) the duty may be effective during part of the year and not during other parts.

at the same time, obtain our olive oil from Italy for much less.[37] The duty on manganese is another example. In 1928, the duty yielded about $6,000,000. This protection brought about the production of approximately 47,000 tons of domestic manganese worth about $1,250,000. In other words, consumers of manganese were taxed in duties about $129 for every ton of domestic ore produced — worth about $25 a ton. An outlay of four dollars in taxes was necessary to bring about the production of one dollar's worth of domestic ore. A new duty which is likely to have about the same effect as the duties on olive oil and manganese is the duty of 7 cents a pound on long-staple cotton. This product can be grown in only a few regions. Practically all of our supply is imported from Egypt, but a small amount is grown in the Imperial Valley, California. The duty is not likely to produce an important expansion of the American industry; in the main it will simply be a tax on consumers.

These duties which, though high, are not high enough to create a domestic industry do not cause great waste of capital and labor because they do not divert capital and labor into relatively less productive channels. For this reason, they may be less objectionable than lower duties on other products which do reduce the national income by diverting capital and labor to less advantageous uses. The duties which fail to protect do, of course, produce revenue for the treasury. The duty on olive oil, for example, imposes a certain part of the cost of supporting the government upon those who like olive oil. People who do not happen to like olive oil do not pay this particular tax and, to that extent, escape supporting the government. People who are fond of olive oil pay a larger share of the cost of the government. But is this a proper basis for determining the contributions which men make to the support of the state?

Betwixt and between the duties which are ineffective because domestic costs are so much below or so much above foreign costs are the many others which make possible domestic industries that otherwise would not exist at all or that would not exist on such a large scale. It is these duties that divert capital and labor from

---

[37] Dennis, A. P., "American Economic Policy," *Annals of the American Academy of Political and Social Science*, July, 1930, v. CL, p. 162.

more productive into less productive employments and thus keep down the national standard of living. These duties, therefore, have a special claim on our attention. What determines how burdensome they are? If some domestic industry is desired, how large a one is it wise to create? Is it desirable to build up an industry large enough to satisfy the entire domestic demand? And if not, how large an industry is it wise to build up?

In the subsequent discussion, it is assumed that the tariff does not alter the total amount of capital and labor in the country either by attracting it from abroad or by reducing its migration abroad. In other words, the sole effect of the tariff, it is assumed, is to change the distribution of capital and labor among domestic industries. In this event, the burden of creating a domestic industry depends upon how much less productive capital and labor are when employed in the protected industry than they otherwise would be. In other words, the cost of the duty is measured by the reduction which it produces in the national income. If capital and labor are almost as productive in the protected industry as they would be in unprotected industries, the loss in national income and consequently the cost of creating the domestic industry are small. But if capital and labor are substantially less productive in the protected industry than in other industries, the domestic industry can be created only at the cost of a substantial loss in national income. In some cases, the lower productivity of capital and labor is so obvious and so great that even America, usually generous in granting protection, has not applied the policy. Rubber growing is an example. By using greenhouses, rubber could be produced in the United States. The cost, of course, would be enormous. Nevertheless, if a sufficiently high tariff were imposed, rubber would be raised here instead of imported. There are military arguments in favor of a domestic rubber industry. Were the United States engaged in land operations against a power which could seriously interfere with our shipping, the shortage of rubber would sooner or later become a serious problem. But despite the military importance of rubber, the American people have not been prepared to pay the cost of creating a domestic industry.[38]

[38] Nevertheless, a duty on rubber may yet become a political issue, for there is a possibility of developing several rubber-yielding plants which could be grown out-of-doors in some parts of the United States.

In some instances, there are more or less definite limits to our ability to develop an industry beyond a certain point. This is particularly true of agricultural and mineral products. Wool, sugar, cattle, and long-staple cotton are examples. The proper combination of land, labor, and climatic conditions may exist only in limited areas, or it may be profitable to produce a commodity only as part of a certain scheme of husbandry involving the combination of certain crops and animals. Consequently, duties above a certain point do little to encourage the industry. In such cases, the response of domestic production to duties of different amounts is represented by the following curve:

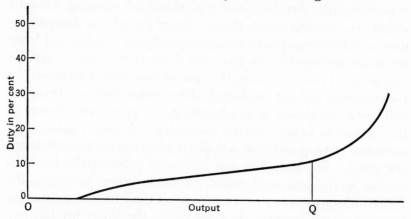

It will be observed that, up to a production of quantity OQ, small increases in the tariff produce large increases in domestic output. Beyond that point, output rises slowly in response to increases in the duty. If the policy of protection is to be applied at all, it is fairly obvious that (barring urgent considerations of national defense) the duty should be only sufficient to produce an output of approximately OQ. Beyond that point, the consumer must be taxed heavily in order to induce a small increase in domestic output. It would be far better to import whatever additional quantities may be needed.

In the case of a number of important commodities, the duty has been raised above the point where it is effective in producing a substantial increase in domestic output. The duty on wool is an example. Despite the high duty on wool (31 cents per pound on scoured wool under the tariff of 1922) about 37 per cent of our supply comes from abroad. In fact, the conditions of wool production have been such that during the last twenty years there has been no increase in the domestic output of wool.[39] The tariff has not increased the domestic industry and there is no prospect that it will. In the opinion of Dr. M. A. Smith, the duty could be reduced to 22 cents per scoured pound without greatly lowering domestic output.[40] If this is correct, then the duty above 22 cents is primarily a tax which compels the consumer to pay more but which has little effect upon domestic output and little effect in excluding foreign wool.

In discussing the effect of tariffs, it is frequently assumed that they raise the domestic price by the full amount of the duty — that a specific duty of 10 cents a pound, for example, will raise the domestic price by 10 cents a pound. This assumption, of course, is erroneous. A duty can affect the price of a commodity within a country only by affecting the total supply offered for sale in the domestic market. Some duties, as we have seen, have no effect upon supply and, therefore, none upon price. A duty, of course, shuts out that part of the imports which is produced at a high cost. If this happens to be only a small part of the total output (in other words, if the *foreign* supply of the commodity is inelastic), the effect of the duty upon supply will be slight, as the following illustration indicates:

Demand	Price	Supply before duty was imposed	after duty was imposed
183,000	60 cents	140,000 lbs.	120,000 lbs.
170,000	65	150,000	130,000
160,000	70	160,000	140,000
150,000	75	170,000	150,000
142,000	80	180,000	160,000
137,000	85	190,000	170,000

It is assumed that the entire supply comes from abroad and that a specific duty of 10 cents a pound is imposed. The effect of the duty, of course, is to reduce the supply that is offered at

[39] During the five-year period, 1903 to 1907, wool production in the United States averaged 294,500,000 pounds a year; during the five years, 1923 to 1927, 294,800,000 pounds.

[40] Smith, M. A., *The Tariff on Wool*, p. 292.

any given price to the amount that was formerly offered at 10 cents below the given price. After the imposition of the duty, for example, the amount that is offered at 70 cents is no more than formerly was offered at 60 cents. Before the imposition of the duty, supply and demand reached equilibrium at a price of 70 cents. The duty, by restricting the supply, raises the price to 75 cents. But notice that a duty of 10 cents is necessary in order to produce an increase of 5 cents in the price. If the effect of the duty were to create a domestic industry, the supply offered would be greater and the effect of the duty on the price would be even less.

The effect of a duty upon the supply of a commodity (and hence upon its price) depends upon (1) the elasticity of the foreign supply of the commodity; (2) the elasticity of the foreign demand; and (3) the elasticity of the domestic supply. The duty, of course, tends to reduce the price of the commodity abroad. If the foreign supply of the commodity is elastic (that is, if foreign production shrinks substantially when the price drops), the effect of the duty in raising the domestic price is accentuated. If the foreign demand is also elastic, the lower price abroad will cause a substantial increase in the foreign consumption of the commodity. This will also tend to reduce the supply of the commodity sent in from abroad and thus to increase the effect of the duty upon the domestic price. The higher domestic price tends, of course, to stimulate domestic production of the commodity. If a small rise in the domestic price produces a large increase in domestic output, the drop in imports may be largely counteracted and the effect of the duty upon the domestic price may be small. But if domestic supply is not responsive to an increase in price, then the duty will cause a greater drop in the total supply and a greater rise in the domestic price. In brief, the effect of a duty upon supply and, therefore, upon price is greatest when (1) the foreign supply and demand are both elastic; and (2) domestic supply is inelastic. Its effect is least when (1) the foreign supply and foreign demand are both inelastic and (2) when the domestic supply is elastic.

Thus far no account has been taken of the effect of the elasticity of domestic demand. A given change in supply will, of course, have a greater effect upon price when the demand is inelastic than when it is elastic.[41] It follows that the effect of a given duty upon the domestic price is greatest when the supply of the commodity is elastic and the demand for it inelastic, and the effect of the duty is least when the supply is inelastic and the demand elastic.[42]

VI. The Problem of Abandoning Protection

The question that confronts the United States today is not which to choose, protection or free trade. For over a hundred years we have been imposing high duties on most commodities which are or might be produced in the United States. Whether it would now be wise to abandon protection is a far different question from whether it was wise to adopt the policy in the first place. Laborers have acquired skill in certain trades, large investments of capital have been made in certain industries, and heavy debts have been incurred, all on the assumption that substantial protection would be given against foreign competition. Were duties suddenly and drastically reduced, many plants in some industries would be compelled to shut down and many men would be thrown out of employment. It is true that foreign countries would sell more to us and, consequently, also buy more from us and that our exporting industries would expand. It might be expected that the workers who were displaced by the withdrawal of protection would promptly find jobs in the growing exporting industries. But this would not necessarily follow, as we know well from experience with labor-saving inventions. The purchasing power released by the labor-saving inventions stimulates some industries to expand. But the workers displaced by the invention are often slow in finding employment in the expanding industries.[43] Even more difficult would be the transfer of capital from

---

[41] See pp. 286–287.

[42] To be completely accurate, account must be taken of the proportion of imports to domestic production. If imports are small, even a duty which is prohibitive will have little effect upon domestic price. For a mathematical analysis of the problem of estimating the effect of a duty upon the domestic price, see Wright, P. G., *The Tariff on Animal and Vegetable Oils*, Appendix B. See also Edminster, L. R., *The Cattle Industry and the Tariff*, Ch. IX.

[43] A study of 754 displaced men by Mr. Isador Lubin indicated that 410 had found permanent work. Of those who had obtained permanent work only one-ninth had found it within thirty days. Over one-half were unemployed for three months and almost one-fourth for six months. Of 344 who were still unemployed when

one use to another, because much equipment is built for special purposes. It is evident that the drastic reduction of some protective duties might diminish the national income by throwing much capital and many workers into idleness.

Does this mean that protection, once adopted, should never be abandoned? By no means. But the procedure that is wise depends upon conditions. Some duties, we have seen, give practically no protection, either because they are not needed or because they are not high enough to create a domestic industry. These should be promptly removed — before conditions change and wage earners and investors become dependent upon the duties.[44] Many other duties which do give needed protection are unnecessarily high. These duties should be lowered. But how far? In every industry there are a few plants with very low costs and a few with very high costs. The great majority of enterprises fall between these extremes. Surely the principle of protection does not require that duties be high enough to protect the small minority of high-cost plants, which are poorly managed, poorly equipped, or poorly located. If a duty is imposed at all, surely it should be no higher than necessary to protect the large group of intermediate cost plants — those which are well located, possess up-to-date equipment, and are reasonably well managed.

But should duties be reduced even below this point? In answering this question, a distinction should be made between industries which are needed for national defense and those which are not. It is difficult to see why a tariff should be permitted to divert

---

interviewed, 221 had been out of work for three months or more and 139 six months or more. *The Absorption of the Unemployed by American Industry*, p. 5.

[44] Wage earners and investors might become dependent upon the duty if the low-cost domestic plants were to form a monopoly and to raise prices. Then small, high-cost independent plants might spring up — plants which could only exist so long as the duty remained. Or a duty which had been ineffective because domestic costs were too far above foreign costs might become effective if domestic costs were to drop. Once a large number of plants became dependent upon the duty, it would be difficult to reduce or to remove it. Finally, a duty might become effective if domestic demand were to continue to expand and if domestic output could be increased only at substantially higher cost. In this event, the consumers would be compelled to bear a heavy burden in order to support a small expansion of domestic production. Mr. L. R. Edminster, in his excellent study, *The Cattle Industry and the Tariff* (pp. 242–267), concludes that expansion of the domestic demand for beef is likely, sooner or later, to make the duties on cattle and beef effective and that this will impose a substantial burden on the consumer without producing a large expansion of the domestic industry. Consequently, he believes that the duties should be removed.

capital and labor into relatively unproductive uses unless these uses have an important military value.[45]   If the military value of an industry is small, the duty should be reduced as rapidly as practicable.   The rapidity would depend upon how readily capital and labor can be transferred from the industry to other uses.   If they can be easily transferred, then the duty should be reduced rapidly.   Otherwise, it should be reduced slowly or the reduction should be offset by temporarily paying domestic producers a subsidy or a bounty.   The subsidy should be restricted, of course, to enterprises in operation at the time that the duty is reduced.

In case an industry has military importance, it may be desirable to retain a duty sufficient to preserve a fairly large domestic industry.   Or the duty might be removed entirely and domestic producers be helped by a bounty.   Bounties, it is true, are open to many objections.   They are a burden on the public; they tend to keep inefficient concerns in business; once granted they cannot be easily terminated and there is likely to be constant pressure for higher and higher bounties.   *But each of these objections applies with equal force to protective tariffs.*   In addition, bounties or subsidies have two important advantages over tariffs.   In the first place, a bounty enables even the most ignorant voters to see that the nation is being taxed to support a certain industry. Many voters have difficulty in seeing that this is being done when a protective tariff is imposed.   Because the nature of bounties is more easily understood than the nature of tariffs, public opinion is likely to be more intelligent concerning the desirability of continuing bounties than concerning the desirability of continuing customs duties.   In the second place, a bounty results in a more equitable distribution of the burden of supporting an industry. It places the burden upon the general public; a tariff imposes it upon the users of the product in proportion to their purchases. If national defense requires that wool raising be encouraged, why should the burden fall more heavily upon the people of the North, who are compelled to use more wool, than upon the people of the South?   Why should not everyone bear part of the burden regardless of whether he uses much or little wool? Would it be reasonable to impose the cost of building and main-

---

[45] An industry may have great military importance and not directly produce munitions.

taining battleships upon members of the community in proportion to their consumption of woolens?

It is true that mistakes in making tariffs are likely to be less costly than mistakes in granting bounties. Suppose that a duty is imposed on a commodity which needs no duty because it can be produced by domestic enterprises in sufficient quantities to meet the domestic demand and at less than the cost of production abroad. Unless domestic producers combine to form a monopoly, the duty simply has no effect. It causes no wasteful diversion of capital and labor to the less productive channels and it imposes no tax upon the consumer. But if a bounty were granted to an industry which needed none, the nation would be burdened by heavier taxes, and a wasteful diversion of capital and labor would be produced, because the bounty would encourage a larger development of the industry than would otherwise occur. No doubt, if the tariff were replaced by bounties, there would be many cases of this sort. On the other hand, the very nature of the bounties makes it certain that the government would grant them far more sparingly than it now grants duties. Consequently, the actual diversion of capital and labor into less productive channels would probably be smaller under a system of bounties than it is at present under the tariff.

VII. How Can the Method of Making Tariffs be Improved?

In preparing the tariff bill of 1930, the Ways and Means Committee of the House of Representatives heard 1,131 witnesses and the Finance Committee of the Senate, 1,232. The testimony, exhibits, and statistical material furnished to the committees, including 2,750 pages furnished by the Tariff Commission, ran to more than 50,000 printed pages.[46] The bill contains more than 3,300 items. It consumed the major portion of the Senate's time for nine months. No one in Congress can form a just estimate of the economic effects of most of the 3,300 rates. One bill was passed by the House and a very different bill by the Senate. The real bill was hastily made by a small conference committee representing the two Houses. Its method, in the main, was to settle differences by granting the higher rate.

It is obvious that Congress is not the proper body to make

[46] *United States Daily,* February 22, 1930, pp. 1 and 3.

the tariff. It is no more fitted to fix the import tariff on thousands of products than it is to fix the railroad tariff on thousands of commodities between thousands of localities. And if it were decided to use bounties rather than duties, it is obvious that Congress would be incompetent to determine what industries should receive bounties and how large the bounties should be.

The obvious inability of Congress to judge accurately the effects of duties upon tens of thousands of commodities led in 1916 to the creation of a bipartisan Tariff Commission to aid Congress in fixing rates. The Commission was originally given no authority to fix rates. Indeed it was not even given the duty of recommending definite rates to Congress. It was simply a fact-finding body with the duty of investigating the effects of duties upon labor and industry and the " conditions, causes, and effects relating to competition of foreign industries with those of the United States." Despite the fact that the original Commission consisted of a distinguished personnel, including two of the foremost economists of the country, Congress did not seek aid of the Commission in fixing the rates in the Emergency Tariff of 1921 nor in the Fordney-McCumber Act of 1922.[47] The Fordney-McCumber Act, however, enlarged the powers of the Commission. It was felt that, in a rapidly changing world, there should be a way of promptly adjusting duties to changing conditions. Consequently, the Commission was given the duty of recommending to the President increases or decreases of not more than 50 per cent in existing rates, upon finding that those rates were less than sufficient or more than sufficient to equalize the difference in the cost of production here and abroad. But the Commission might not recommend that a commodity which was on the free list should be made dutiable or that an article which was dutiable should be placed on the free list. The President, if he approved the recommendation of the Commission, might put it into effect by decree.

As the appointments of the original Commissioners expired, President Harding and President Coolidge filled the places, for the most part, with tariff lobbyists and men who, for one reason or another, were interested in maintaining high duties on certain

---

[47] The Commission did have considerable influence upon many of the technical aspects of the bill — matters of nomenclature and classification in particular.

commodities.[48]   Consequently, it is not surprising that the Commission failed to improve the tariff and that the so-called " flexible " provision resulted almost exclusively in higher rates.[49] Some of the men appointed by Presidents Harding and Coolidge had brought the Commission into such disrepute that it had little influence upon the tariff act of 1930.   In order to give President Hoover an opportunity to make some new appointments, the Smoot-Hawley Act abolished the old Commission and created a new one with substantially the same powers.

How should the tariff be made?   The problem falls into two principal parts: (1) what body should fix the duties; and (2) what principles should be followed in fixing them.

The task of fixing duties is obviously one which Congress is not fitted to perform.   However unfortunate our experience with the Tariff Commission has been, it is evident that a Commission, with an able technical staff, is essential.   The only question is whether the *complete* authority to fix rates should be given to the Commission or whether the authority of the Commission should be limited by some outside body.   At the present time, as we have seen, the Commission may recommend to the President changes of not more than 50 per cent in rates, and if he approves, he may put the recommendation into effect.   Many persons believe that acceptance of the Commission's recommendations should depend upon an act of Congress rather than upon presidential approval.   Several leaders of the Democratic party have made this proposal.   They would still have the Commission base its recommendations on the difference between the cost of production at home and abroad, but they would not limit the Commission to recommending changes of no more than 50 per cent in rates.   In order to prevent the trading of votes in Congress, it is suggested that any bill having for its object the carrying out

[48] For an excellent and impartial analysis of the history of the Tariff Commission and of the type of men appointed to the Commission by Presidents Harding and Coolidge, see Wright, P. G., *Tariff-Making by Commission,* a publication of the Rawleigh Tariff Bureau.

[49] Of the thirty-seven rate changes, five — on bobwhite quail, paintbrush handles, mill feeds and bran, cresylic acid, and phenol — were decreases, and thirty-two — including such important products as pig iron, plate and window glass, and linseed oil — were increases.   In the case of the important duty on sugar, President Coolidge refused to put into effect a decrease recommended by the Commission.

of a recommendation of the Commission shall include no item not included in the report of the Commission and shall not be amended to include other duties. In other words, the proposal is that tariff *as a whole* shall never come before Congress again. Congress would be invited only to change individual schedules and those only on recommendation of the Tariff Commission.

Congress is an exceedingly busy and cumbersome body and its rules permit a few members, if strategically situated, to delay for months or years legislation desired by the majority. Consequently, it is probable that Congress would not act promptly upon the recommendations of the Commission and that in many cases it would fail to act upon them at all. Mr. David J. Lewis, a former member of the Commission, has suggested, therefore, that the recommendations of the Commission should become automatically effective if not disapproved by Congress within a limited period — Mr. Lewis suggests thirty days.

In view of the fact that Congress is not competent to determine import duties, why should it be permitted to veto the decisions of the Commission? Would it not be wiser to delegate the task of making the tariff to the Tariff Commission as completely as the task of determining railroad tariffs has been delegated to the Interstate Commerce Commission?

What rule or rules should guide the Commission in fixing duties? The present rule, "difference in cost of production at home and abroad," is not satisfactory. Differences in costs cannot be satisfactorily ascertained because no two plants either in this country or abroad have the same costs.[50] And even if differences in costs could be accurately ascertained, the rule would be unsatisfactory because it takes no account of the effect of the duty upon consumers, other industries, the economic life of the country as a whole, or international relations. In the case of the Interstate Commerce Commission, the general rule is that rates must be "reasonable." The Commission has the task of determining what are reasonable rates. The same general rule might be applied to the tariff. If Congress believes that the basic policy of the country should be protection, it might simply de-

[50] In addition, there are insurmountable difficulties in obtaining accurate cost figures from individual plants.

clare that the policy of the United States is to give " reasonable " protection to domestic industries whenever that can be done without (1) unduly burdening consumers; (2) hindering the development of another branch of domestic industry; (3) seriously injuring our export trade; (4) substantially hindering foreign countries from meeting their obligations to us; and (5) dangerously accelerating the exhaustion of non-replaceable natural resources. This rule would be highly indefinite but it would be no more so than the rule which now governs the Interstate Commerce Commission. The very indefiniteness of the rule would be an advantage because it would give the Commission opportunity to exercise considerable discretion and to determine, in the light of circumstances, what duty is reasonable.[51]

It would be desirable to supplement the general rule of reason with several additional principles. The burden of clearly proving the need for protection should rest upon the industry which seeks it. Every enterprise receiving protection or asking for it should be required to furnish the government with full information concerning its costs, the prices and terms on which its products are sold, and labor conditions in the industry. In view of the grave danger that the tariff will be used to protect inefficiency and incompetency in management, it is important that efficiency be made a requirement for protection and that no duty be granted unless the industry can show that its methods and equipment are up-to-date. Finally, the Tariff Commission should have authority to revoke duties when they are abused and used to shelter domestic monopolies. In order to assist the Commission in enforcing this provision, the recipients of protection should be required, upon request, to give complete information concerning their sales methods and concerning the existence of any agreements or understanding among competitors in the industry.[52] In case it were decided to protect industry by subsi-

[51] There is much to be said for the creation of the office of consumers' counsel who would have the duty of representing the consumers' interests before the Tariff Commission.

[52] It should be expected that a large proportion of the applications for protection will be rejected. On this point the experience of Great Britain under the Safeguarding of Industry Act is illuminating. The procedure provides for inquiry by the Board of Trade which determines whether the industry making application has a *prima facie* case. If the decision is in the affirmative, the Board of Trade sets up an impartial commission to make a further investigation. Out of forty-eight applications, twenty were referred for investigation, and a duty was granted in only eight.

dies rather than by duties on imports, the task of determining the need for subsidies and of making recommendations to Congress could be given to a commission with a staff of technical experts.

VIII. The Control of Raw Materials [53]

Although restriction of trade has usually taken the form of restraints upon imports, there has been a growing tendency for governments to impose restrictions on exports, especially exports of raw materials. The development of a dense population in America and western Europe, with relatively high purchasing power in comparison with most of the world and with a rapidly growing demand for many raw materials, has encouraged countries which possess a monopoly or a near-monopoly of certain products to take advantage of their position. Controls began to develop before the end of the nineteenth century but they have become particularly important since the war. Wallace and Edminster list twenty instances of control.[54]

Most of the controls take the form of an export tax. In some instances, as in the Japanese control of silk, the government may advance credit to enable the producers to withhold part of the supply. In still other instances, the government itself has purchased and withheld part of the supply, as in the purchase of coffee by Brazil, of long-staple cotton by Egypt, and of cocoa by Ecuador. Finally, the state may enforce measures designed to limit the output of the commodity.

For a valuable analysis of tariff-making procedure in the British Empire and France, see Chalmers, H., " Tariff Making in Great Britain and the Dominions," *Annals of the American Academy of Political and Social Science*, January, 1929, v. CXLIX, pp. 68–97 and Stuart, G. H., " Tariff Making in France," *ibid.*, January, 1929, v. CXLIX, pp. 98–106.

[53] This account is based almost exclusively upon Wallace and Edminster's *International Control of Raw Materials*, which is the result of an extensive study made for the Institute of Economics. For an excellent brief discussion of the subject see Edminster, L. R., " Control of Exports of Raw Materials: an International Problem," *Annals of the American Academy of Political and Social Science*, July, 1930, v. CL, p. 89 ff.

[54] Wallace, B. B., and Edminster, L. R., *International Control of Raw Materials*, p. 13. These controls are: natural camphor, cinchona bark, citrate of lime, coffee, long-staple cotton, Greek currants, Kauri-gum, mercury, nitrate, pearlshell, potash, pulpwood, quebracho, rubber, sandalwood, oil, silk, sisal, sugar, sulphur, and tin. The list is not intended to be complete. Not all of these control schemes are still in effect. The sugar control and the rubber control, for example, were abandoned in 1928. In 1931, however, an international sugar control scheme was established.

An important purpose of some controls is to obtain revenue for the state at the expense of foreign consumers. For many years the Chilean government derived about half of its revenues from its high export duty on nitrate. In a few instances the purpose is to promote domestic manufacturing by enabling domestic plants to obtain the raw material for substantially less than their foreign competitors. The Canadian restrictions on pulpwood are an illustration. The most important and frequent purpose of export controls, however, is to enable the domestic industry to collect a monopoly price and thus to help the country prosper at the expense of the rest of the world.

From the standpoint of the country that enforces a control scheme, the device may be desirable, precisely as a monopoly may be desirable from the standpoint of the monopolists. And just as there are monopolies which are able to raise the price only slightly above the level of cut-throat competition, so there are control schemes which have not succeeded in raising the price to an exorbitant level. From the standpoint of the world as a whole, however, the objection to schemes for controlling exports is the same as that which applies to any monopoly — it tends to produce both an uneconomical distribution of capital and labor and an inequitable division of income. But it is interesting and important to notice how short-lived have been many of the control schemes and what disastrous results some of them have brought in the countries which fostered them. The enforcement of a high monopoly price naturally encourages the expansion of the industry abroad and the search for substitute products or for processes of making the product synthetically. Nitrate, camphor, rubber, and coffee are illustrations. The high price of nitrate stimulated the efforts to develop an alternative supply. Chile once had a world monopoly but today synthetic and by-product nitrate constitute over three-fourths of the world supply. The high price of natural camphor encouraged the development of the synthetic product which has now largely displaced the natural product. The British control of rubber broke down after a few years because it stimulated rapid expansion of rubber growing in the Dutch East Indies.[55] The Bra-

[55] But in the meantime it kept price of rubber at over a dollar a pound for several years and cost American consumers about $400,000,000. In view of the huge

zilian coffee control accelerated the growth of the industry in Columbia and Central America and this no doubt accentuated the recent collapse in the price of coffee. But because many controls have broken down after several years, it must not be inferred that the problem of controls is self-solving. Many of the controls may be exceedingly burdensome while they last; even temporary success encourages attempts to reconstruct them after a breakdown; and, possibly most important of all, failure of a national control may lead to an attempt to construct an international control — as in the case of nitrate, potash, mercury, tin, and sugar. Quite apart from their economic effects, control schemes may generate dangerous political friction between nations.

IX. The Possibility of Removing or Diminishing Barriers to Trade

No doubt the world as a whole would be better off if there were a general reduction of restrictions on imports and exports. The World Economic Conference of May, 1927, which has been described by Sir Arthur Salter as " probably the most elaborate and ambitious attempt which has yet been made to examine the economic situation of the world " declared that " the time has come to put an end to the increase in tariffs and to move in the opposite direction." It was hoped by many persons all over the world that the Conference would mark the turning point in tariff policies. The fact that practically the whole world was represented — including non-members of the League of Nations, such as the United States, Russia and Turkey — gave great weight to the findings of the Conference. And yet, the hopes based on the Conference have not been realized. Following it, in 1927, numerous and substantial reductions were negotiated between pairs of countries and extended by the most-favored-nation clause. During 1928, too, there was a halt in the process of raising tariffs; but in 1929 and 1930, the process was resumed. The leadership in this unfortunate policy was taken by the United States, a country which already possessed one of the highest

indebtedness of the rest of the world to the United States and our high tariff policy, it was perhaps fortunate that the rest of the world was able to use this means of paying its debts to us. Of course, it was burdensome to millions of small consumers in the United States.

tariffs in the world. During most of 1929 and the first half of 1930, the United States was engaged in building a new and still higher tariff wall. This provoked a cycle of retaliatory increases. Alarmed by these increases, Great Britain and other countries proposed an international tariff holiday during which no existing duties would be increased. The League of Nations Assembly, in its meeting in September, 1929, recommended that a conference to discuss such a holiday be convened at an early date. The conference met at Geneva on February 7, 1930, and remained in session for a number of weeks. Opposition from business interests manifested itself and the meeting accomplished practically nothing. Plainly the experience of the last several years offers little hope that restrictions on imports and exports will be substantially moderated.

An attractive ideal is the reciprocal reduction in duties — that is, a reduction in some duties by one nation in return for a reduction in other duties by other nations. On at least two occasions, as we have seen, reciprocal reductions have been the means of substantially lowering the barriers to trade. The first occasion was in the sixties when the series of reciprocal treaties growing out of the Cobden-Chevalier treaty substantially reduced duties throughout Europe. The second occasion was in the nineties, when Germany entered into a series of reciprocal treaties with countries in Central Europe. Under the most-favored-nation rule which regulates the duties between most countries, a reduction in a duty granted to one nation is automatically extended to all others enjoying most-favored-nation treatment.

But the method of reciprocal reductions encounters serious obstacles. The reductions, of course, are made as a result of bargaining, and hence there is a tendency to erect high tariffs for bargaining purposes. This was clearly shown when the German treaties of the nineties came up for renewal shortly after the turn of the century. Possibly a more piecemeal process of reciprocity, carried on independently of general tariff revisions, would be more effective in the long run in reducing trade barriers. An important obstacle to reciprocal reductions, whether piecemeal or general, is found in the most-favored-nation treatment now generally accorded by nations to each other and in the tariff policy of the United States. The prohibitive duties levied by the United States upon important European exports has made many European countries determined not to lower their duties upon American products. But if one European nation makes a concession to another, the concession is automatically extended by the most-favored-nation principle to all countries of the world, including the United States, to which the country gives most-favored-nation treatment. Impressed by the relationship between the immense free trade area in the United States and the growth of mass production here, they see that our immense domestic market permits our enterprises to use methods of production which would not pay in smaller markets and which give us important advantages in export trade. They are eager to gain the same advantages for their own industries. As industrial technique develops, the competitive handicap of small economic units is likely to become greater and greater. Consequently, during the last several years, there has been a growing discussion of a European customs union, or, at least, of mutual reduction in duties within Europe. At the meeting of the League of Nations Assembly in September, 1929, M. Briand suggested for practical consideration a United States of Europe. Such a union, it is hoped, would lead to mutual reductions in duties. In 1930, an agreement for closer economic coöperation was effected between Roumania and Jugoslavia. A conference of Balkan nations was also held at Athens looking toward the creation of a Confederation of Balkan States.

The possibility of a general European customs union, or even of regional unions, must be regarded as remote. A customs union must collect the customs revenues for all of its members and distribute these revenues to them. It means, therefore, that the members must sacrifice a large part of their financial independence. Few countries are prepared to take this step. And mutual reductions in duties, it has been pointed out, are hindered by the most-favored-nation principle and the tariff policy of the United States. Recognizing these difficulties, a writer in *The Round Table* has proposed tariff reductions through regional preferential arrangements — such as a European preferential system.[56]

[56] " The United States of Europe," *The Round Table,* December, 1929, v. XX,

Such regional agreements would require that the interpretation of the most-favored-nation principle be modified to exempt from its application reductions in duties made under plurilateral conventions intended to improve the economic relations among the participating countries. In other words, reductions in duties made under such conventions would not be extended, under the most-favored-nation principle, to non-participating nations. The participating countries would agree to make no increases in their duties either during the period when the agreement was being negotiated or during the life of the agreement. This restriction would apply to duties upon the products not only of participating nations but also of non-participants, unless outside states made increases in their duties which, in the opinion of a suitable authority, such as a committee of the League of Nations, created a new situation. The participants in the preferential arrangement would agree to make reductions of a certain percentage in the duties levied upon the products of other participants. These reductions would not apply to the products of non-members. It would probably be desirable to exempt from the scheme certain duties intended primarily for revenue — such as duties on tea or coffee. In view of the fact that some countries have much higher tariffs than others, it might be desirable to classify the participating countries into " high-tariff countries," " moderate-tariff countries," and " low-tariff countries " and to provide for a larger percentage of reduction in the duties of high-tariff countries than in the duties of either moderate- or low-tariff countries and a somewhat smaller reduction in the duties of low-tariff countries than in the duties of the other two classes.

The key to the world tariff situation is possessed by the United States. With our bargaining position strong because of our enormous domestic market in which other nations desire to sell, it lies within our power, through reciprocity treaties with other countries, to bring about substantial reductions in their duties on many of our exports. Through the action of the most-favored-nation clause, these reductions would apply to other nations. Just as the United States has been a leader in pushing

---

pp. 79–99. The above discussion of regional agreements is based largely upon the proposal outlined in this article.

up trade barriers, so, in view of its great buying power, it could be a leader in reducing them. Possibly the time will come when the growing export trade of American manufacturers will lead Congress to create a body to negotiate reciprocal treaties. At the moment, however, the vision and the courage necessary to support this proposal are lacking both among the business men and among the politicians of the United States.[57]

What can be done to moderate or to prevent restrictions on the export of raw material. Wallace and Edminster see hope in international agreements. They believe that the first requirement is an international agreement dealing with the basic principles that are fair.[58] Such principles might be formulated by an international conference on government control and access to raw materials. Wallace and Edminster believe that it would be desirable to establish a special body to interpret the principles agreed upon and to settle the technical questions that would arise in applying general principles. Thus there would gradually be built up a body of fair practices. A beginning was made in the fall of 1927 when there was signed in Geneva a convention for the abolition of import and export prohibitions and restrictions.[59] The convention is not limited to raw materials and it contains many exceptions. It does not, for example, apply to export duties. It does, however, contain an agreement to reduce existing restrictions and prohibitions to a minimum and not to establish new restrictions and prohibitions, and it establishes a procedure for settling disputes between nations. At the same time, two conventions were signed by representatives of twelve countries providing for the concurrent abolition of restrictions on the export of hides, skins, and bones. These conventions cover export duties. In the case of hides and skins, the signatory powers agreed to abolish all duties except so-called statistical

[57] Mr. L. R. Edminster justly points out the need for caution in accepting this rather pessimistic description of the outlook for a reduction in trade barriers. He says: "Surely we must hope and work for something better and if we remember that in a comparatively short period of time England turned from a policy of protection all the way to free trade, we cannot be too certain that a general change of opinion with reference to the merits of prohibitive protectionism will not take place in the United States during the next decade or two."

[58] Wallace, B. B., and Edminster, L. R., *International Control of Raw Materials,* pp. 336–343.

[59] *Ibid.,* pp. 329–330.

duties, that is, duties imposed primarily for the purpose of collecting trade statistics. In the case of bones, a maximum limit is set on export duties.[60]

Whether or not much progress can be made against export restrictions by coöperative action remains to be seen. As long as the principal manufacturing countries pursue a high protective policy, they are likely to have difficulty in convincing the producers of raw materials that restrictions of trade are undesirable. In so far as restrictions can be removed by international agreement, progress would appear to depend largely upon the ability and the willingness of the manufacturing countries to offer concessions in exchange for concessions.

On the whole, there appears to be little immediate prospect for substantial reductions in trade barriers. The world as a whole no doubt loses because of tariffs, but many countries gain. As transportation becomes cheaper and as the use of electric power grows, the number of commodities which can be manufactured in one country for about the same cost as in other countries increases. By accepting the burden of paying 15 or 25 per cent more for some commodities, a country can compel industries to establish themselves within its borders. To the extent that these industries are built with foreign rather than domestic capital and manned with foreign labor, the country increases its capital and its population. The country is stronger and many of the inhabitants are richer. The inhabitants may be right in considering the tariff a low price to pay for more capital and more people.

Under the circumstances, many countries, especially new ones, are bound to pursue a policy of restriction unless offered attractive terms for abandoning it. But who is to make them an offer? The three nations which would profit most from a general reduction in duties are probably Great Britain, Germany, and the United States. Great Britain already pursues a general policy of free trade and has little or nothing to offer other countries in exchange for a reduction in duties. The United States, which has much to offer, is still dominated by an economic philosophy which was appropriate to a new country, rich in

[60] Wallace, B. B., and Edminster, L. R., *International Control of Raw Materials,* p. 331.

natural resources but poor in capital and labor. It will be a long time before the people of the United States escape from the domination of their traditional outlook and see what they might gain from a policy of reciprocal reductions. Germany, acting alone, scarcely possesses the bargaining power to produce a pronounced effect upon the tariffs of the world. And as for the raw material controls, however disadvantageous they may be to the world, they are not necessarily harmful to the nations which impose them.

REFERENCES

Annals of the American Academy of Political and Social Science, January, 1929, v. CXLIX, No. 230, " Tariff Problems of the United States."

Ashley, Percy, *Modern Tariff History*, 1926.

Culbertson, W. S., *International Economic Policies*, 1925.

Donaldson, John, *International Economic Relations*, 1928.

Gregory, T. E. G., *Tariffs — A Study in Method*, 1921.

Grunzel, Josef, *Economic Protectionism*, 1916.

Marshall, Alfred, *Industry and Trade* (fourth edition), 1923.

Page, T. W., *Making the Tariff in the United States*, 1924.

Taussig, F. W., *Some Aspects of the Tariff Question* (second edition), 1916.

Wallace, B. B., and Edminster, L. R., *International Control of Raw Materials*, 1930.

CHAPTER XXX

INTERNATIONAL ECONOMIC POLICIES — MONETARY AND FINANCIAL PROBLEMS

I. INTERNATIONAL COÖPERATION IN STABILIZING CURRENCIES AND IN RESTORING THE GOLD STANDARD. II. THE REPARATION PROBLEM. III. THE PROSPECT FOR COÖPERATION AMONG NATIONS IN CHECKING THE FALL IN PRICES.

I. INTERNATIONAL COÖPERATION IN STABILIZING CURRENCIES AND IN RESTORING THE GOLD STANDARD

It was pointed out in the preceding chapter that the most urgent economic problem of Europe at the end of the war was the stabilization of its currencies. When the war ended, no budget in Europe had balanced for a number of years. The inability of most countries to meet their expenses either by taxation or by borrowing had compelled them to inflate the currency.[1] Even after the war had ceased, most nations were still unable to balance their budgets and thus inflation continued. Practically all governments in Europe were subjected to one or more kinds of extraordinary expense. Military operations did not cease with the end of the major conflict. There were numerous minor wars — one between Poland and Russia, another between Greece and Turkey, civil wars in Finland, Hungary, Germany, and later, in 1923, the French occupation of the Ruhr. Some governments made heavy expenditures for reconstruction; some were compelled to pay reparations; all of the former belligerents had enormous war debts on which the annual interest charges were heavy. In many countries there was a serious shortage of food and the government was compelled to import it at public expense.[2]

---

[1] Inflation took various forms. In some instances, the governments simply issued paper money; in others, the government sold treasury notes or treasury bills to the central bank in return for credits from the bank. In other words, governments went through the form of borrowing from the bank.

[2] The causes of the food shortage were various. In some eastern countries, food production was retarded by the seizure of large estates by the peasants. The

The industrial dislocations produced by the war, and accentuated in many instances by the peace treaties and the post-war tariffs, reduced the markets of many countries and created severe un-employment. Governments were compelled to support the un-employed by relief works or by doles and this, of course, added to the budget deficits.

The budget deficits were self-perpetuating. It is true that, as prices rose, the service of the internal debt became less burden-some. But other government expenses increased and, most im-portant of all, the yield of taxes lagged far behind the rise in prices. The rapidly depreciating currencies fell in terms of foreign currencies more rapidly than in terms of internal prices. This made it expensive to import goods and restricted the yield of customs duties. Inflation, of course, enormously increased profits, and governments attempted to obtain revenue by levying heavy taxes on profits and the incomes derived from them. But such taxes are not effective in balancing the budget in times of inflation. Profits and incomes can be taxed only some months after they have been received. If, in the meantime, the currency has greatly depreciated, the original tax rate becomes an exceedingly low one. Suppose, for example, that it were planned to tax profits 50 per cent. If, between the time that the tax was imposed and the time when it was collected, the value of the currency had dropped in half, the real rate of taxation would drop to 25 per cent.[3] In some countries (Germany, for example) the currency

---

peasants produced less when working for themselves than when working under the direction of landlords. Food production was also limited by the lack of fertilizers and by the fact that, during the war, farm equipment had been permitted to deterio-rate. Some countries had difficulty in procuring food because tariff barriers made it difficult for them to sell their manufactures. The inflation of the currency itself was a cause of food shortage because peasants preferred to hold their surplus crops rather than sell them for a rapidly depreciating currency. Finally, wars and internal military operations interfered with the output of food. The scarcity of food led some governments to requisition supplies and this discouraged peasants from pro-ducing and caused them to conceal the food which they had on hand. Even as late as 1922, German food output, for example, was substantially below 1913. Moul-ton and McGuire conclude that Germany's consumption of foodstuffs in 1922 was inadequate to maintain efficiency. They estimate that her consumption of wheat in 1922 was 55 per cent of 1913; of rye, 60 per cent; of potatoes, 99 per cent. Meat consumption was about two-thirds of 1913. Moulton, H. G., and McGuire, C. E., *Germany's Capacity to Pay*, pp. 132–133.

[3] In Germany, during the inflation between 1919 and 1923, the government's receipts averaged only about 25 per cent of its expenditures. Angell, J. W., *The Recovery of Germany*, p. 29.

depreciated so rapidly that taxpayers found it advantageous to delay payment and to pay the penalty for being delinquent. Thus, many countries found themselves in a vicious circle in which a budget deficit was creating inflation, and inflation, in turn, was creating a budget deficit.

Even in the face of progressive depreciation of the currency, some European countries slowly made progress in building up their industries. But rapidly depreciating currencies were disastrous to economic life in many ways. Naturally they were a serious handicap in restoring the international trade upon which practically all European countries were in large degree dependent, because, with the value of currencies constantly changing, foreign trade became in large degree a speculation in exchange. In addition, the fact that depreciation occurred in terms of relatively stable foreign currencies (such as the dollar and the pound) more rapidly than in terms of domestic prices made imports relatively expensive and made it more difficult for the country to obtain badly needed raw materials and equipment from abroad. Most serious of all, however, were the effects of rapid depreciation upon the internal economic life of the countries. Whole classes of the population were practically dispossessed by the drop in the purchasing power of their incomes and were thrown on the state for support. Wages and salaries in some cases lagged so far behind other prices that wage earners and salary workers were unable to purchase sufficient food. Furthermore, the peasants, because they did not have a good opportunity to spend money promptly before it depreciated, hoarded their crops and brought only enough to market to meet their immediate needs for cash. Thousands of city dwellers were unable to procure sufficient food, undernourishment and slow starvation were widespread, and tuberculosis and other diseases of poverty were rampant. The technical efficiency of industry suffered because the lag in wages made labor cheap in relation to other goods and discouraged the use of labor-saving methods.

A long step toward stabilizing the currency of a country would be taken by the government's balancing its budget and thus ceasing to issue paper money in one form or another. This would end the rapid rise of internal prices and eliminate the worst evils of inflation. It would not, however, prevent more or less substantial fluctuations in the value of the currency in terms of foreign currencies, and these fluctuations would seriously handicap foreign trade.[4] In order to assist in the restoration of foreign

[4] In order to understand the fluctuations of the value of a currency in terms of foreign currencies, it is necessary to understand what determines the value of currencies in terms of other currencies. When all countries are on the same metallic standard (gold, for example), the explanation is very simple. One British pound, for example, contains as much gold as 4.8665 American dollars. As long, therefore, as the British and American banks will pay out gold to their depositors and as long as the British and American governments do not restrict the exportation (or importation) of gold, the value of the pound in terms of dollars will not fluctuate from $4.8665 by much more than the cost of shipping gold between Great Britain and the United States. The reason is obvious. Suppose that large imports into Great Britain relative to exports from Great Britain create a large demand by British importers for drafts (exchange) on New York. The British banks are able to meet this demand in part by buying from British exporters bills drawn against American importers. (For an explanation of this process, see pp. 240–242.) But British exports are not sufficient to meet the entire demand for drafts payable in dollars. Naturally the price of drafts on New York goes up. But it does not go up beyond the cost of shipping gold from London to New York for the simple reason that banks (or anyone else) can replenish balances in New York simply by shipping gold. Cable transfers may, of course, command a slight premium over the cost of shifting specie because they represent speed.

Suppose, however, that Great Britain is not on the gold standard — as it was not during the war — and that British banks will not pay out gold to their depositors and that the British government will not permit the exportation of gold from the country. Suppose that heavy imports compel British buyers to make large payments in dollars and that British exports do not furnish sufficient drafts on New York to meet the demand. What happens to the value of the dollar in terms of the pound? Obviously it goes up — just as any price goes up when the article becomes scarce in relation to demand. But in this case the rise does not stop when it has increased by the cost of shipping gold — for the simple reason that the refusal of the banks to pay gold and the refusal of the government to permit its exportation make it impossible for any one to make payments in the United States by shipping gold. Under the circumstances, the only alternative for those having obligations to meet in the United States is to bid for drafts payable in dollars. The large demand for dollars (the result of large imports into Great Britain) and the small supply (the result of small exports from Great Britain) may cause the price of dollars, in terms of pounds, to rise very high. In fact, although one British pound will ordinarily buy about $4.866 in United States currency, there were times during the war when the dollar was so valuable relative to the pound that one pound would buy less than four dollars. And for some years after the war (before the pound was stabilized in 1925), a pound would purchase less than $4.50.

It is obvious that the ability of British exporters to sell drafts payable in dollars at a high price in pounds tends to make exporting more profitable. It is likewise obvious that the necessity of importers' paying a high price in pounds for dollar exchange tends to make importing less profitable. The rise in the dollar in terms of pounds, by discouraging imports and encouraging exports, tends to bring the demand for dollar exchange and the supply of dollar exchange into equilibrium and to check a further increase in the price of the dollar in terms of pounds.

As long, however, as gold cannot be exported, there is no telling how low the

trade, it was important that currencies be given a definite value by being made convertible into gold or relatively stable foreign currencies at a definite rate of exchange. It was recognized very clearly that there were grave dangers involved in the return to the gold standard. The price level had risen enormously since the pre-war days. Consequently, there was serious doubt whether sufficient gold was available to provide reserves under a gold standard for the volume of credit that would be needed to support the post-war price level. If the reserves were insufficient and credit were curtailed, the resulting fall in prices would be exceedingly burdensome to the debt-ridden countries of post-war Europe. An appreciation of this danger led some economists, notably Mr. J. M. Keynes, to oppose the restoration of the gold standard and to advocate a " managed currency," that is, a currency which would be adjusted in volume so as to maintain a steady domestic price level.[5] This scheme would involve more or less serious fluctuations in the exchange rates but Mr. Keynes and his followers felt that this disadvantage would be more than outweighed by the advantage of a stable internal price level. Most business men, statesmen, and economists, however, felt that it was imperative to stabilize foreign exchange rates in order to restore international trade. Consequently, they were willing to risk a fall in prices in order to reëstablish the gold standard. Some experts thought that the stock of gold which had accumulated in the United States during the war and the years immediately following would sooner or later lead to an inflation of commodity prices here. This would reduce the exports of the United States and increase its imports, gold would flow out, and thus Europe would acquire enough gold to sustain a price level much above pre-war.

In devising a plan for stabilizing a currency, one of the most important and difficult decisions is to determine the value at which to stabilize. It is important that the point selected shall be

domestic currency may fall in terms of foreign currencies. That depends upon the relationship between imports and exports. The impossibility of predicting the value of the domestic currency in terms of foreign currencies is the worst handicap imposed upon foreign trade by the absence of a common metallic standard. It makes foreign trade a hazardous speculation for both importers and exporters.

[5] For a discussion of this proposal see Chapter XXI, pp. 533–536.

neither too high nor too low. Most experts would probably agree that France stabilized the franc at too low a value and that Great Britain stabilized the pound at too high a value. If the point of stabilization is too low, an injustice is done to creditors; furthermore, so much gold may be attracted from abroad that other countries may have trouble in maintaining the gold standard. On the other hand, if the point of stabilization is too high, even graver difficulties are encountered. The higher the point of stabilization, the larger the reserve that is necessary to maintain the value of the currency. Stabilization at too high a value produces a drop in the domestic price level. When Great Britain stabilized the pound at the pre-war value of $4.866 instead of, say at $4.50, a shipment of British goods quoted at £1,000 cost, in dollars, $4,866 instead of $4,500. Naturally this made it more difficult for British exporters to sell abroad. Suppose that, before the pound was stabilized, the British exporter had been getting the business in competition with American and German competitors by offering a given quantity of his goods for £1,000 or $4,500. If, after stabilization, he continued to accept $4,500, he would receive in British currency only £925. This might be insufficient to cover his costs. Consequently, in order to continue to sell at $4,500, it would be necessary for him to reduce his costs, possibly by reducing wages. This is one reason why stabilizing at too high a value tends to reduce the domestic price level. On the other hand, the effect of stabilization at $4.866 instead of $4.50 was to encourage imports. The reason is obvious. With £1,000, an English importer could purchase $4,866 worth of goods abroad instead of $4,500 worth. This would help him to undersell domestic producers. This is another reason why stabilization at too high a value tends to reduce the price level. If the excess of imports over exports is too large, the foreign balances and credits of the government and of the central bank may be insufficient to meet the domestic importers' demands for foreign exchange. As a result, the external value of the country's currency may drop and the stabilization scheme will break down.

When domestic prices fall as a result of the currency's being stabilized at too high a value, buying is, of course, on a hand-to-mouth basis because everyone is waiting for lower prices. This means that industry is depressed, production drops, unemployment increases, and the standard of living temporarily falls. The government may be compelled to support many of the idle. This, of course, increases the difficulty of maintaining a balanced budget.

But in modern economic society, with many prices more or less closely regulated by the government, by monopolistic groups, by trade associations, and by trade unions, it is not safe to assume that the domestic price level will adjust itself promptly and smoothly to the new external value of the currency. In the meantime, the competitive position of exporting industries may be seriously impaired. This also creates unemployment and adds to the fiscal burdens of the government. The process of adjusting domestic wages to the higher domestic value of the currency is likely to result in costly strikes and to diminish the efficiency of industry by producing bad industrial relations. The losses suffered by business enterprises before the adjustment of the internal price level has been completed make domestic industry, for the time being at least, an unattractive field for investment, and new savings tend to be invested abroad. This retards the economic development of the country. Furthermore, the outflow of capital (and the consequent demand for foreign exchange) may dangerously deplete the foreign balances of the government and the central bank and threaten the success of the stabilization scheme.

Sooner or later, the internal price level is adjusted to the external value of the currency. But the effects of stabilizing at too high a value still persist. For the lower level of internal prices increases the burden of the national debt upon taxpayers and of private debts upon business enterprises. The government will have much more difficulty in balancing the budget and business concerns may have trouble in meeting foreign competition.

But how could the poverty stricken governments of Europe restore the gold standard? The very inflation of the currency, which began as a *result* of a failure of the governments to balance their budgets, had become a *cause* of their inability to balance them. And how could the debt-ridden governments of post-war Europe, unable to collect enough revenue to meet their expenses, obtain sufficient gold or foreign exchange to enable holders of domestic currency to exchange it at any time for gold or foreign currencies at a fixed rate?

Obviously outside help was in most cases essential. Once such help was obtained on a substantial scale, it might be possible both to balance the budget and to maintain the domestic currency at a constant value in relation to gold or to stable foreign currencies. The success of a scheme of stabilization depends in large degree upon the ability of the government to create the belief that the plan will succeed and this, in turn, depends upon the amount of help which the government is able to obtain. Once men have confidence that the value of the currency will be maintained, they no longer rush to convert their cash into goods as rapidly as possible, the volume of spending diminishes, and the rise in prices is halted. All of this, in turn, assists the government to balance its budget and thus to avoid issuing more paper money. And this, of course, strengthens the confidence in the value of the currency. Finally, confidence in the success of the stabilization plan contributes to the success of the scheme by drawing back funds from abroad. Naturally no one wishes to hold a currency which is rapidly depreciating in value. Consequently, one characteristic of a period of depreciation is a flight from the undesirable currency. Enterprises or persons who find it necessary or convenient to have ready cash purchase foreign exchange and thus transfer their balances abroad. During the post-war period of inflation, many Europeans bought dollars and, after Great Britain stabilized her currency, pounds. When confidence in the domestic currency is restored, many of the balances held abroad return. Their return creates a demand for the domestic currency, and relieves the government or the central bank from the necessity of expending its resources to maintain the value of the currency. In fact, the return of expatriated funds may be so rapid (and consequently the foreign demand for the domestic currency may be so large), that the external value of the domestic currency may rise above the intended point of stabilization.[6]

The help which nations obtained in order to stabilize their

---

[6] This may create a difficult and dangerous situation by encouraging imports and discouraging exports and thus creating unemployment. When France succeeded in re-

currencies usually took one of two forms. In some cases — in Great Britain, Belgium, Italy, and others — it took the form of a contingent credit which could be drawn upon, if necessary, to buy the currency and thus to keep up its value.[7] In other cases — in Germany, Austria, and Hungary, for example — the help took the form of a loan. Germany received a loan from a group of central banks. In Austria and Hungary, the stabilization was carried out under the auspices of the Financial Committee of the League of Nations. The financial condition of Austria was so desperate that a foreign loan could be obtained only by the allied nations' relinquishing the priority of their claims against her and guaranteeing a portion of the stabilization loan.[8] A plan for stabilizing the Spanish peseta in 1931 was worked out in coöperation with the newly created Bank for International Settlements.[9]

The coöperation in stabilizing currencies was not limited to making loans or granting contingent credits. It was reflected to

---

establishing confidence in the franc in 1927, the return of funds to France was so large that the Bank of France had difficulty in keeping down the external value of the franc to the point at which it was planned to stabilize the currency.

Although the immediate effect of the return of balances from abroad may be to increase unemployment by encouraging imports and discouraging exports, its subsequent effect may be to cause a boom, a rise in domestic prices, and a gain in employment. The return of the foreign balances is likely to increase domestic gold holdings and to stimulate business by making for lower interest rates. Furthermore, some of the balances are likely to be spent either for goods or for securities and thus to stimulate domestic business.

[7] When the pound was stabilized, the Reserve Bank of New York extended a credit to the Bank of England and the British Treasury obtained additional credit from private American bankers. These credits were not used. Nevertheless they were available to buy pounds and thus to prevent the price of pounds from falling below $4.866 — the pre-war parity and the point at which it had been decided to stabilize the pound.

[8] In order to stabilize the exchanges between the time when the agreement with Austria was made and the time when the proceeds of the stabilization loan became available, the Bank of England made an advance to the newly established Austrian National Bank. The Bank of England also made a special advance to the newly organized national bank of Hungary in order to stabilize the exchanges until the stabilization loan could be floated.

[9] It is impossible in this brief discussion of international economic policies to describe and explain in detail the various steps taken to achieve stabilization. In several cases, as has been indicated, new central banks were established. It was essential, of course, to do everything possible to eliminate the budget deficits that were compelling governments to issue more and more paper money. Unnecessary public employees were dismissed and some state undertakings which had been losing money were converted into private companies.

a pronounced degree in the discount policies of the central banks, especially the Federal Reserve Banks. Obviously the attempt of Great Britain to raise the pound to the pre-war parity of $4.866 and to hold it there would have been, if not impossible, at least far more difficult had interest rates in New York been too high relative to London. The relatively high New York rates would have attracted funds from London. The dollar would have become more valuable relative to the pound and the pound less valuable relative to the dollar. Indeed, the pound might have dropped so much below $4.866 and gold have left London in such quantities that Great Britain would have been compelled to forbid the exportation of gold, and thus to abandon the gold standard, in order to protect her bank reserves.

The need for coöperation from the Federal Reserve Banks in keeping down interest rates in New York was made doubly great because of the extraordinary power possessed by the United States during most of the post-war decade to attract gold from the rest of the world. This persistent flow of gold into the United States was due to a number of causes — to the fact that the United States had, during the war period, suddenly shifted from the largest debtor nation in the world to the second largest creditor nation, to the remarkable ability of the United States to expand its foreign trade in the face of European competition (largely the result of more rapid technical progress in the United States), and partly to a combination of circumstances which prevented the large influx of gold into the United States from raising commodity prices, discouraging exports, and encouraging imports.[10] The two most notable instances of coöperation on the part of the United States occurred in 1924 and 1927. In 1924, the Federal Reserve Banks prepared the way for restoration of the gold standard in Great Britain in the spring of 1925 by an easy money policy which put rates in New York below rates in London and encouraged a flow of funds to London. Partly as a result of this policy, the United States lost gold for about five months late in 1924 and early in 1925. Again in the summer of

---

[10] The flow of gold to the United States was broken for about five months late in 1924 and early in 1925. The total net gain in the gold holdings of the United States between 1920 and 1929 was over $1,300,000,000.

1927, following a meeting in New York of Governor Norman of the Bank of England, Governor Schacht of the Bank of Germany, Deputy Governor Rist of the Bank of France, and Governor Strong of the New York Federal Reserve Bank, rediscount rates in the United States were reduced from 4 to 3½ per cent. The purpose evidently was to help the London market. The British had made the mistake of stabilizing the pound at too high a value. Largely as a result, the excess of imports over exports increased from $3,246,000,000 in the three year period 1922–1924 to $5,453,000,000 in the three years 1927–1929.[11] Under these conditions, high money rates were necessary to prevent heavy losses of gold. The position of London, which had been weak since 1925, was made worse by the *de facto* stabilization of the franc in 1927. With confidence in the franc restored, large French balances began to leave London. The loss of gold threatened to destroy the gold standard in Great Britain. By reducing rediscount rates in the United States, the Reserve Banks caused funds to move from here to both London and Paris, and stopped, for the time being, the gold movement from London to France.[12] A third notable instance of international coöperation occurred in the fall of 1930, after the gains of the Hitlerites in the German elections produced a flight from the mark and there were fears for the continuance of the gold standard in Germany. American, British, Italian, and other bankers bought marks in order to support the exchanges and maintain confidence in the

[11] *Commerce Year Book*, 1930, v. II, p. 579. Restoration of the gold standard in Great Britain occurred in April, 1925. The year 1926 is omitted from the comparison because the general strike in that year interfered with exports and made the import balance abnormally large.

[12] Between September, 1927, and October, 1928, the net losses of the United States by export and earmarking were about $500,000,000. *Report of the Secretary of the Treasury*, 1928, p. 78. (By earmarking is meant transfer of gold to the possession of foreigners without removing it from the vaults of the bank which has been holding it. Earmarked gold held by a Reserve Bank for a foreign bank does not, of course, count as part of the reserve of the Reserve Bank.) More than half of the gold lost by the United States in 1927 and 1928 by export and earmarking went to France but large amounts also went to Argentina and Brazil which had recently established the gold standard. Italy and Poland, which were also returning to the gold standard at this time took smaller amounts. The low money policy of the United States in 1927 was of great assistance in facilitating the return to gold all over the world. Unfortunately it stimulated speculation in the security markets and thus later attracted gold. But the fact that the Reserve Banks were unable to prevent inflation in 1928 and 1929 does not necessarily prove that the low rate policy of 1927 was unwise.

mark until the period of hysteria had passed. France refused to participate in this operation.[13]

II. The Reparation Problem

It was stated in the preceding chapter that the attempts of the allies to collect more than Germany could pay seriously retarded the economic recovery of Europe as a whole. It was also stated that the reparation payments by Germany have probably been more injurious to Great Britain than to Germany herself. Obli-

[13] In the *Report of the Secretary of the Treasury*, 1928, p. 354, will be found a list of the dates when the gold standard was restored. In some instances actual stabilizations preceded the official restoration of the gold standard by some time. In the case of France, for example, *de facto* stabilization preceded legal stabilization by about eighteen months. The dates on which the gold standard was restored are as follows:

Salvador	January 15, 1920
Latvia	August 3, 1922
Austria	January 3, 1923
Colombia	July 23, 1923
Costa Rica	March, 1924
Sweden	April 1, 1924
Germany	October 11, 1924
Lithuania	1924
Great Britain	April 28, 1925
Australia	April 28, 1925
New Zealand	April 28, 1925
Hungary	April 28, 1925
Danzig	April 28, 1925
Netherlands	April 28, 1925
Dutch East Indies	April 28, 1925
Switzerland	May, 1925
South Africa	May 18, 1925
Albania	September 2, 1925
Czechoslovakia	1925
Finland	January 1, 1926
Chile	January 11, 1926
Canada	July 1, 1926
Guatemala	July 6, 1926
Belgium	October 25, 1926
Brazil	December 18, 1926
India	April 1, 1927
Estonia	May 3, 1927
Ecuador	August 10, 1927
Argentina	August 26, 1927
Poland	October 13, 1927
Italy	December 22, 1927
Norway	May 1, 1928
Greece	May 4, 1928
France	June 25, 1928
Bolivia	August, 1928

gations of Germany have already been reduced twice and are now about one-third of the original amount. Nevertheless, it is probable that they are still too large and that it will be necessary again to reduce them. In fact, it is probable that most nations would be better off if Germany were entirely relieved of the obligation to pay reparations. What determines the ability of a country to pay reparations? What happens when an attempt is made to collect more than a nation can pay? Why may payment do as much harm to some creditor nations as to the debtor nation?

Economic experts are still in disagreement concerning what determines the ability of a nation to pay reparations. One thing, of course, is clear: that only to a limited extent can payment be made in gold. No nation in the world possesses sufficient gold to pay the sums that have been asked of Germany. Before the war, Germany was the second largest creditor nation in the world. During the war, she lost or sold most of her property located abroad. Some of her remaining property was later sold to pay reparations, but her foreign holdings were small in comparison with the demands upon her. This means that Germany must pay in the main by exports of goods, including, of course, the intangible services rendered to foreigners by her banks, insurance companies, and transportation companies. In other words, her capacity to pay is determined by her ability to develop an excess of exports over imports.

Before the war, Germany had an excess of imports over exports. This excess represented in the main the income from her large foreign investments. There have been two views among economists concerning Germany's ability to develop an excess of exports over imports. One view has been that the very process of making payments would automatically create the necessary excess of exports over imports. In other words, according to this view, Germany's ability to pay is limited by the amount which she can raise by taxation. There is no problem of transferring this amount to the creditor nations. The opposing view has been that Germany's ability to pay is limited by the amount which she can transfer without demoralizing the exchanges. This amount might be far less than she could collect by taxation.

The view that there is no transfer problem and that Germany

can pay as much as she can collect in taxes may be summarized as follows: In order to make payments, the German government must either purchase exchange on other countries or ship gold. Naturally this increase in the demand for bills payable in foreign countries will raise the price of bills. After the price has risen beyond a certain point, it will be cheaper to export specie than to purchase foreign bills. The outflow of specie will diminish bank reserves in Germany, raise interest rates, discourage borrowing, and lead to a drop of prices in Germany. On the other hand, the export of specie will increase reserves, lower interest rates, and raise prices abroad. Germany, therefore, will become a cheap place in which to buy, a bargain counter, so to speak. Exports from Germany will increase and imports into Germany will decrease. This process will continue until the excess of exports is sufficient to enable the German government to pay reparations without shipping cash.

In support of this argument, attention is directed to the experience of the United States during the nineteenth century. Until about 1873, the United States was importing capital in such volume that new borrowings exceeded interest and dividend payments on United States securities held abroad. During this period, the imports of the United States exceeded exports. By about 1873, however, the payments of dividends and interest on old capital exceeded new borrowings. As a result, the trade balance of the United States gradually changed from an excess of imports to an excess of exports. It is argued that Germany's balance of trade would adjust itself no less smoothly to the new situation created by her obligation to pay reparations.

Perhaps the most serious objection to this theory is that it fails to take account of time. The United States, for example, did not suddenly wake up one morning to find itself confronted with the problem of instantaneously developing an export balance of half a billion dollars a year. Gradually the annual dividend and interest payments of the United States to foreign security owners crept up on the new borrowings of the United States from abroad and finally passed new borrowings. As this occurred, the balance of trade also gradually shifted from an excess of imports to an excess of exports. But could Germany create, almost overnight, a substantial excess of exports? The conclusion that she could assumes that foreign demand for German goods would respond promptly and on a large scale to lower prices in Germany — in other words, that the external demand for the particular kinds of goods which Germany is prepared to supply is highly elastic or at any rate is ready to shift promptly from other producers to Germany at a relatively small drop in the German price and that other producers will not be able to meet the cuts made by Germany.

Possibly these conditions might exist. On the other hand, it seems even more probable that the actual situation may be very different. Because of tariffs, transportation costs, and other barriers to trade, the external demand for most German products may be exceedingly inelastic. In the latter event, the outflow of gold from Germany would not be effective in producing a large favorable balance of trade. It would simply cause Germany to lose her gold supply. The heavy gold losses would reduce the lending power of the German banks and hence the ability of German exporters to give the credits that are customary in international trade. This would be a serious obstacle to the growth of exports. The continued loss of gold would eventually compel Germany to declare an embargo on further gold exports. The demand in Germany for foreign currencies in excess of the demand for German marks in foreign countries and the impossibility of exporting gold from Germany would cause the foreign currencies to rise in terms of the mark and the mark to sink in terms of foreign currencies.

Some economists have argued that the rapid depreciation of the mark would in itself assist Germany in developing an export balance and, therefore, in making reparation payments, because, as the German currency would drop more rapidly in terms of foreign currencies than in terms of domestic prices, Germany would become a cheap place in which to buy. But the economists who believe that Germany's capacity to pay is limited by her ability to transfer payments without demoralizing the exchanges point out that the rapid depreciation of German currency in terms of foreign currencies would greatly hinder German foreign trade. It would, for example, increase the cost of raw materials imported from abroad — a serious handicap to all German exporting industries which depend upon foreign raw materials. The higher price level produced by the depreciation of the currency would create a shortage of working capital, because the volume of working capital that would be sufficient at a low price level would not be sufficient at a high one. Shortage of working capital would be a handicap to German enterprises in extending credit to their customers. Finally, and perhaps most important of all, as the currency depreciated and as exchange rates mounted, foreign trade between Germany and the rest of the world would become largely a speculation in exchange and this would discourage both importing and exporting.

What light does experience shed on the two theories of Germany's capacity to pay? The Treaty of Versailles did not state the amount which Germany would be required to pay but it established a Reparation Commission which was authorized to determine the amount not later than May 1, 1921.[14] In the meantime, Germany was to pay 20,000,000,000 gold marks ($4,760,000,000) on account. On April 27, 1921, Germany's obligation was fixed at 132,000,000,000 gold marks ($31,000,-000,000) plus 4,000,000,000 gold marks to reimburse Belgium for her war debt. At a conference in London in May, 1921, the allied nations drew up a schedule of payments. Germany was to pay annually 2,000,000,000 gold marks ($576,000,000) and 26 per cent of the value of her exports. In addition, she was to make certain payments in kind. By September, 1921, Germany had paid a billion gold marks under the London schedule. But Germany did not succeed in collecting enough by taxation to meet her obligations. Consequently, it was necessary for the government to inflate the currency. Moreover, the demand of the government for foreign exchange to make reparation payments caused a rapid depreciation of the mark in terms of foreign currency. In December, 1921, the mark had sunk to 160 to the dollar, but the domestic price level had not risen in proportion. This made Germany a cheap place in which to buy. It did not, however, result in the creation of an export surplus. On the contrary, the depreciation of the mark became greater and greater. During the year 1922, the Reparation Commission

---

[14] The Commission was to be composed of a representative each from Great Britain, France, Italy, Japan, Belgium, Jugoslavia, and the United States. As the United States rejected the entire treaty, it was never represented.

found it necessary to grant Germany short delays in the schedule of payments. France, however, insisted that Germany lacked the will to pay and was evading her obligations. By November, 1922, the mark had sunk to over 8,000 to the dollar.

The temporary expedients which Germany had been using to meet her obligations became exhausted by 1922.[15] But instead of a surplus of exports over imports, she still had an excess of imports. On January 9, 1923, the Reparation Commission, by a vote of three to one (the British delegate voting in the negative), declared Germany in willful default on gold deliveries. Two days later French and Belgian troops occupied the Ruhr. But this did not enable the allies to collect more from Germany. On the contrary, the attempts of Germany to finance passive resistance on the Ruhr accelerated the depreciation of the currency and accentuated the disorganization of German economic life. By November, 1923, the mark was worth only 4,200,000,-000,000 to the dollar. At last the French were able to see that they were demanding more than Germany could pay, and, in consequence, getting almost nothing. The Reparation Commission, therefore, appointed a committee of experts to determine how much Germany could pay. This was the Dawes Committee, which, on April 9, 1924, submitted its report to the Reparation Commission. On August 16, 1924, the report was adopted.

The attempts of the allies to collect reparations from Germany prior to 1924 did not test Germany's ability to develop

---

[15] During the four-year period, 1919–1922 inclusive, Germany's adverse trade balance was about 12,800,000,000 marks. The rapidly changing value of the mark during this period makes the exact size of the trade balance difficult to estimate. How did Germany meet this large deficit? About 1,000,000,000 gold marks were derived from the sale of foreign investments still held by Germany at the end of the war. To a substantial extent, Germany met the deficit by selling German marks to foreign speculators. Speculators bought the marks for several cents or less each. Many speculators expected to be paid the pre-war value of the mark which was 23.8 cents. The total sales of marks are uncertain, but it is probable that they amounted to approximately 8,000,000,000 marks. The depreciated German exchange also led to the purchase by foreigners of property in Germany, such as urban real estate, the securities of German companies, and German municipal bonds. It has been estimated by Moulton and McGuire that by the end of 1922 approximately 8,000,000,000 gold marks of German property had been purchased by foreigners. Much of this, however, was paid for with paper marks which had been previously acquired by foreigners. A discussion of how Germany met the adverse trade balance for the period 1919 to 1922 will be found in Moulton, H. G., and McGuire, C. E., *Germany's Capacity to Pay*, pp. 56–97.

an export surplus equal to the amount which she might be able to raise by taxation, because during this period the German payments were not limited to the amount which she could raise by taxation. The budget was not balanced, and most of the exchange purchased by the German government was bought by inflating the currency. It may be argued with considerable force that the inflation of the currency, by its demoralizing effect upon German industry, was itself an important cause of Germany's failure to develop an export balance. In addition, the German export trade was hampered by the tax of 26 per cent which was imposed by the London Agreement.

The first test of Germany's capacity to pay as much as she could raise by taxation, while still maintaining a substantially balanced budget, occurred under the Dawes Plan.[16] The Dawes Plan provided for the stabilization of the German currency and the restoration of the gold standard in Germany (with the help of a foreign loan). Certain revenues of the German government were definitely assigned to reparations. In addition, certain revenues from the German railways and from several of the larger industries were definitely pledged to the payment of reparations. It was recognized, however, that even with the budget balanced and the currency stable, Germany might not be able, without demoralizing the exchanges, to transfer to the creditor nations all that she succeeded in collecting by taxation. Consequently, the Dawes Plan provided that the obligation of Germany ended when she collected the money by taxation and turned it over to the Agent General for Reparations. The task of transferring German payments to the creditor nations was placed in charge of a Transfer Committee. In order not to endanger the stability of German currency, the Committee was authorized to suspend or curtail remittances in accordance with the capacity of the exchange market to absorb them.

The Dawes Plan did not fix the total amount which Germany was to pay. It fixed the annual payments but did not stipulate for how many years they were to continue. The first payment was 1,000,000,000 gold marks — less than half the amount pro-

---

[16] During the period of the Dawes Plan, the German budget was not balanced. The unbalanced budget did not destroy the stability of the currency because the deficits were not large and were met partly by long-term loans.

vided in the London schedule of May, 1921 — but Germany was granted a loan of 800,000,000 gold marks to be applied on the first payment. This made the first payment only 200,000,000 gold marks. The payments were to rise gradually to 2,500,000,-000 gold marks ($595,000,000) in the fifth and following years. The plan also provided that they were to be readjusted in accordance with an index of Germany's ability to pay and also in accordance with changes in the value of gold, provided the value of gold changed by more than 10 per cent.

Germany promptly paid all of her obligations under the Dawes Plan and the payments were transferred to the creditor nations without demoralizing the exchanges. But she did not succeed in developing an export balance. In fact the German payments were possible only because Germany borrowed on a large scale from abroad. By the end of the fourth year of the Dawes Plan, Germany had paid about $1,302,000,000 but had borrowed over $1,550,000,000. In other words, Germany was not *reducing* her indebtedness abroad; on the contrary, she was increasing her indebtedness and she was paying reparations by shifting her indebtedness from foreign governments to private purchasers of German securities.

The Dawes Plan was obviously a temporary arrangement. It did not specify how long the annual payments were to continue. Without knowledge of the total amount of her debt, Germany lacked a proper incentive to keep her finances in order. Furthermore, the plan was practically a receivership for Germany. Certain German revenues were pledged for payment and the execution of the plan was placed in charge of an Agent General for Reparations, who might be regarded as the receiver. Naturally such arrangements were offensive to Germany. Although the payments were substantially smaller than those specified in the London Agreement of 1921, it soon became apparent that the full payments, which were to become effective after five years, were larger than could be transferred. Finally, the creditor countries wished to raise money by the sale of bonds against Germany's obligation to pay. This they could not do as long as the transfer protection provisions of the Dawes Plan made it uncertain whether or not the owners of such bonds would receive their interest. Consequently, in the fall of 1928, it was decided to appoint another committee of experts in hopes of working out a more permanent settlement of the reparation problem. This committee became known as the Young Committee. Its report, known as the Young Plan, was accepted, with slight modifications, by the governments in the fall of 1929.

The Young Plan reduced the annual payments from 2,500,-000,000 gold marks ($595,000,000), the standard payment under the Dawes Plan, to an average for the first thirty-seven years of 2,050,600,000 gold marks, a reduction of slightly more than 20 per cent. But the annuities begin at 1,707,900,000 gold marks or about $400,000,000 — approximately one-third less than the standard payments under the Dawes Plan. Each annuity is divided into two parts. One part, amounting to $157,-000,000, is not postponable; the remainder may be postponed for a period not exceeding two years in case of special economic difficulties. This is necessary to guard against periods of world depression during which German exports might drop substantially. The payments are to diminish after thirty-seven years and to cease after fifty-nine years.[17] The present value of the annuities is approximately $9,000,000,000, which is less than one-third of the obligation of $33,000,000,000 originally imposed upon Germany by the Reparation Commission in the spring of 1921.

One of the principal purposes of the Young Committee was to end the financial tutelage of Germany, to remove the humiliation of external control of her finances. To this end, the Young Plan abolished the Reparation Commission and its subsidiary machinery, including, of course, the Transfer Committee. But it was desirable to provide some agency to receive and transfer the

[17] The government of the United States has always declined to recognize the relationship between reparation payments from Germany and the payments by Great Britain, France, Italy, and others of the allied countries on account of money borrowed from the United States during the war. But the Young Plan is so drawn that the two can be easily connected. To begin with, the German payments run for the same period as the allies' payments to the United States. For the first thirty-seven years, the German payments to the allies are about 50 per cent greater than the payments of the allies to the United States. The Young Plan provides that, in the event of a reduction in the payments of the allies to the United States, Germany shall receive a reduction in her payments to the allies. During the first thirty-seven years, this reduction shall be two-thirds of any reduction granted by the United States; during the last twenty-two years, Germany shall receive the full benefit of any reduction made by the United States.

German payments. It was important that the transfer should not demoralize the exchanges; it was important also that Germany should not be able to default in the payments to one power and continue those to another; it was important that the receipt of reparation payments should not permit one nation to hoard gold at the expense of the rest of the world and to use the claims acquired from Germany to put pressure on other nations in international negotiations. The agency proposed by the Young Committee to fulfill these purposes was an international bank to be known as the Bank for International Settlements.

The charter and by-laws of the bank were established by a treaty signed at The Hague on January 20, 1930. The bank is located at Basle, Switzerland. Its capital is $100,000,000. The shares may be held by private persons. Fifty-six per cent of the shares have been allotted in equal amounts to the seven countries represented on the Young Committee — Belgium, France, Germany, Great Britain, Italy, Japan, and the United States. But the shareholders have no voting power — this is in the hands of the central banks. Each bank votes in proportion to the number of shares held in its country. Japan and the United States, however, are represented on the board of directors by private banks instead of central banks.[18] In an attempt to keep down political influence in the bank, the statutes provide that no person may be a director who is also a government official.

It was the intention of the Young Committee that the Bank should be more than a mere agency for receiving and transferring the German payments. The statutes of the Bank specify that one of its objects shall be to promote coöperation between central banks in administering the world's gold supply and in solving the world's credit problems. However that may be, its immediate and primary purpose is to receive and transfer the reparation payments. The Bank is authorized to receive deposits, to buy and sell gold coin or bullion, to discount, purchase, and sell bills of exchange and other short-term paper, to make advances to or borrow from central banks against gold, bills of exchange, or

---

[18] In the case of Japan, the central bank is not represented because the great distance between Japan and Basle makes direct representation inconvenient. In the case of the United States, the reason is the isolationist policy of the government which has made the government unwilling to permit any official connection between the Federal Reserve system and the Bank for International Settlements.

other approved securities, and to buy and sell exchange, and negotiable securities. There was fear among the central banks that the Bank for International Settlements might become a super-central bank, that it might seriously compete with the central banks, interfere with their operations, and possibly, in some instances, defeat their policies. To prevent these results the statutes impose certain restrictions upon the activities of the Bank. It is prohibited from conducting any financial operation in any country in case the central bank of that country objects.[19] In addition, it is prohibited from issuing demand notes in any form and from accepting bills of exchange; it may not acquire control of any business enterprise; and, finally, it may not open accounts in the names of governments or lend to governments. This last prohibition compels governments to do business with the Bank for International Settlements through the medium of the central banks.

Will Germany be able to meet the obligations imposed upon her by the Young Plan? Thanks to the post-war inflation, the public debt of Germany, including her reparation obligations, is less than that of France and is only one-third that of Great Britain, which has only two-thirds the population of Germany. But paying reparations, as we have seen, is not primarily a problem of raising the funds by taxation; it is a problem of building up an export surplus. It has been pointed out that for many years preceding the war Germany imported more than she exported. During the six years ending in 1929, she made remarkable progress in building up her exports and in 1929 achieved for the first time a small export surplus.[20] *If Germany can obtain sufficient time,* pos-

---

[19] If the central bank of the country is not directly represented on the board of directors of the Bank for International Settlements, steps shall be taken to afford the central bank an opportunity to express dissent.

[20] German imports and exports of merchandise between 1924 and 1929, expressed in millions of dollars, were as follows:

	Imports	Exports
1924	$2,163.5	$1,560.6
1925	2,942.2	2,211.1
1926	2,380.3	2,478.6
1927	3,380.6	2,566.3
1928	3,335.1	2,924.0
1929	3,203.0	3,211.6

U. S. Department of Commerce, *Commerce Year Book*, 1930, v. II, pp. 678–679. These figures do not include intangible services bought or sold by Germany.

sibly she can build up an export surplus sufficient to enable her to meet her obligations under the Young Plan. But it will probably take ten years at least. Will Germany's credit permit her for ten years more to meet a substantial part of her obligations by borrowing? Time alone will tell. Although borrowing abroad enables Germany, for the time being, to pay reparations and (in so far as the loans are used for productive purposes) to increase her output of goods, it also compels her to make large interest payments to her creditors and thus increases the size of the export balance which she must eventually develop. If Germany could produce raw materials such as rubber, petroleum, or cotton, she would probably succeed in promptly developing a substantial surplus of exports. As it is, nearly three-fourths of her exports are finished goods upon which most countries impose heavy duties. Her success in paying reparations will depend in large degree upon the tariff policies of other nations. Possibly Russia, by developing a large export trade in petroleum, timber, and raw materials, will be able to purchase large quantities of German manufactures. The success of Germany in paying reparations will also depend in large degree upon the movement of the general price level. Within a year after the adoption of the Young Plan, prices fell so much as to make the actual burden of the payments greater than would have been the burden of the payments under the Dawes Plan at the previous price level. If the trend in price level continues sharply downward, then there is small chance that Germany will succeed in meeting her obligations.[21] The United States, in settling war debts owed to it by the allied nations, cancelled a substantial portion of them, partly because of the belief that the debtors could not pay the full amount.[22] Nevertheless, for the first thirty-seven years of the Young Plan, Germany is under obligation to pay 50 per cent more than Great Britain,

[21] It will be recalled that the Dawes Plan provided for an adjustment of the annual payments when gold changed in value 10 per cent or more. This provision was not included in the Young Plan. The reason for its exclusion was the fact that there is no corresponding provision in the debt settlements between the allied nations and the United States. The allies are counting on their receipts from Germany to meet their obligations to the United States and are unwilling to permit a reduction in Germany's payments without assurance that there will be an equivalent reduction in their payments to the United States.

[22] Moulton and Pasvolsky estimate that the debts were reduced about 43 per cent. Moulton, H. G., and Pasvolsky, L., *World War Debt Settlements*, p. 9.

France, Italy, and ten other nations together are paying to the United States. Would it be surprising if Germany alone were unable to pay so much more than all of the allied nations are paying to the United States?

How has the payment of reparations affected the creditor nations? Germany several times has offered to " work out " part of her debt by sending workers into France to restore the devastated regions. To a small extent this has been done. But the French labor unions, in particular, were opposed to the competition from German labor. On October 6, 1921, France and Germany signed an agreement whereby France consented to receive from Germany for a period of fourteen years free construction materials to the amount of not more than one billion marks a year. But only negligible amounts of materials have been requested and accepted. France preferred to do the work with French labor and materials and to charge the cost to Germany.[23]

These cases illustrate the dilemma which, in our interdependent economic order, confronts a nation that seeks to collect an indemnity from another. The allies insist that Germany pay reparations, but Germany must pay in goods and, when she does, she competes with the producers of those same goods in the creditor countries and possibly reduces employment in the industry. If labor were not specialized, the displaced men would probably soon find work in other industries. But because workers have special skill which fits them for certain tasks and not for others, they are slow to find other jobs. The payments received by the creditor countries, therefore, may not be net gains; they may be offset in part by the increase of unemployment in the creditor countries and by the loss of production resulting from it.

The effect of the payment of reparations has not fallen upon all of the allies alike. France, Italy, and Belgium, on the whole, have probably profited from the payment of reparations. On the other hand, it seems fairly clear that Great Britain has been injured. Germany was required to pay reparations in part by delivering ships to the allies. But the loss of their ships led the Germans to build new and better ones to replace them. This helped to create an excess of shipping capacity which, in turn,

[23] *Ibid.*, p. 16.

caused prolonged depressions and severe unemployment in the British shipbuilding industry. The British paid for their ships partly through unemployment in their shipyards and partly through lower earnings of their shipping companies, as a result of the excess capacity of shipping. Germany has been required to make large coal deliveries to France and Italy. This has been beneficial to France and Italy but ruinous to the British coal industry and to other British industries which found their markets reduced by the miners' loss of purchasing power. In addition, the British taxpayers have been taxed more heavily in order to pay doles to the unemployed miners. The burden of paying reparations to France and Italy, therefore, has fallen partly upon the British miners and the British taxpayers.

III. The Prospects for International Coöperation in Checking the Fall in Prices

The economists and financial experts who recommended the restoration of the gold standard after the war were well aware that the existing supply of gold might be insufficient to support the prevailing price level and that a general return to gold might lead to a decline in the price level which would be extremely burdensome to the debt-ridden countries of Europe. It was realized that the effect upon prices would be intensified if the central banks hoarded gold. The Genoa Economic Conference of 1922, which recommended the return to gold, warned specifically against the danger of " simultaneous and competitive efforts of countries to secure metallic reserves " and pointed out the desirability of coöperation among the central banks in economizing gold.

Despite the fact that the prospect of a decline in prices was clearly foreseen, it has not been possible to avoid a downward trend. In 1929, the level of wholesale prices in the United States was 7 per cent under 1925; in Great Britain, 14 per cent; and in Germany, 4 per cent. In France, prices declined 10 per cent between 1926 and 1929. The causes for this decline are in dispute. Some economists believe that the downward trend in prices since 1925 has been due either to a shortage or to a maldistribution of gold. During the three years, 1926 to 1928, for example, it is estimated that the amount of new gold available for monetary purposes has been about $250,000,000 a year, or approximately 2 per cent of the world's stock of gold money.[24] It is estimated that the physical production of commodities in general has been increasing at from 3 to 4 per cent a year.[25]

In 1929, the central banks and governments of the world possessed more than twice as much gold as in 1913 — $10,290,638,-000 as against $4,932,445,000.[26] Nevertheless, the price level in 1929 was less than 40 per cent above 1913. This does not look like a gold shortage. In reply it is said that, although the gold holdings of the central banks and governments are far greater than before the war, the direction of gold movements has tended to compel a restrictive credit policy and thus to force down prices in some countries, especially Great Britain and Germany. Ever since war days, there had been an almost continuous flow of gold to the United States. Beginning in 1926, a large flow started toward France.

That the decline in prices has been caused by a shortage or a maldistribution of gold is doubtful. There are other explanations which seem more satisfactory. In Great Britain, the necessity of adjusting the price level to the pre-war value of the pound, the idle productive capacity, the persistent unemployment have all had more effect in pushing down prices than the bank rate and a mildly restrictive credit policy. As for the world price level, it has been influenced by revolutions, by the overproduction of certain raw materials which seriously diminished the purchasing power of many countries, and, in 1929, by the shortage of funds available for long-term investment in some parts of the world because of the diversion of savings into speculation on the New York exchange.[27]

[24] Kitchin, Joseph, *Review of Economic Statistics*, May, 1929, v. XI, pp. 64–67.

[25] The physical production of the world cannot be accurately measured and this estimate must not be accepted as very exact.

[26] This great increase was made possible in large degree by the withdrawal of gold from hand-to-hand circulation and its replacement by bank notes.

[27] When the prices of raw materials, such as wheat, wool, rubber, sugar, coffee, dropped, the purchasing power of some countries was, of course, diminished. But did not the drop in the prices of raw materials simply leave the rest of the world more money to spend for other things? Would not the prices of these other things increase in response to the growth in demand and would not the general price level remain substantially unchanged?

Such a result is possible but it apparently did not occur in this case. On the contrary, the violent drop in the prices of raw materials apparently produced hesitation, caution, and a disposition to postpone the making of commitments. This

But although it is not clear that the downward trend in prices has been due to the shortage or the maldistribution of gold, it *is* clear that if the output of gold lags behind the physical production of commodities and especially if gold continues to pile up in the United States and France, prices in other countries are likely to be forced downward. The prospects are that gold output will lag behind the production of commodities in general. The principal source of gold is South Africa, and the South African output is apparently more likely to diminish than to increase. Furthermore, the problem of gold distribution is steadily becoming more acute because, throughout 1930, both the United States and France continued to attract gold at the expense of the rest of the world.[28] By the end of the year, these two countries held nearly three-fifths of the gold in the possession of governments and central banks. If gold continues to pile up in the United States and France, the effects of the deficiency in gold output will be greatly accentuated.

It should be observed that, at the time of writing (early in 1931), it is difficult to judge the world gold situation. Possibly the situation *appears* to be much worse than it really is. Although the United States continued to gain bullion during 1930, it did not attract gold from Europe as it had done prior to 1927. In fact, there is strong reason to believe that the influx during 1930 was due to rather temporary causes, particularly the severe drop in the prices of many raw materials which affected the incomes of such countries as Argentina, Australia, Brazil, and Japan (from all of which the United States gained gold heavily in 1930), and the severe depression which temporarily destroyed the market for foreign investments in the United States. When the prices of raw materials recover and when confidence in investments has been restored, it would not be surprising to find that the flow of specie into the United States had greatly diminished or had

---

meant unemployment and loss of production. Thus the fall in the prices of raw materials (and some other products) started a cycle of price reductions.

[28] During the year from November, 1929, to November, 1930, the United States and France gained $654,000,000 in monetary gold; the entire world gained $605,-000,000. The gains of the United States and France, therefore, more than absorbed the gains of the rest of the world. Most European countries gained gold. Losses were experienced by the producers of raw materials which had severely dropped in price — Argentina, Australia, Brazil, and Japan.

ceased. And, in somewhat less degree, the same statement applies to France.[29]

The fear of a gold shortage and of a further drop in prices has provoked the proposal that the central banks of the world and the Bank for International Settlements coöperate to control the flow of gold between countries and to devise ways and means of economizing gold reserves. What are the prospects that the central banks and the Bank for International Settlements can achieve these objectives?

As far as the flow of gold into the United States and France is concerned, the possibility of stopping it appears to be largely beyond the power of the central banks and the Bank for International Settlements. The causes are too deep seated to be reached by the instruments which the banks have at their command. The flow of gold into France has been due to a combination of circumstances. For some time after the stabilization of the franc, there were enormous transfers of balances from London and New York to Paris — balances which had fled from France when the franc was depreciating. The fact that France receives slightly more than half of the German reparation payments gives her immense power to attract gold. The French in the past have been heavy investors abroad. During the last few years, however, the French investors have been reluctant to send their money abroad and the French government, in addition, has been conservative in permitting the listing of foreign securities on the Paris Bourse.[30] Finally, gold has been flowing into France because of certain characteristics of the French money market. Checking accounts are not widely used in France. This

---

[29] But from a long-time point of view the outlook is not so promising. Although the *immediate* effect of a resumption of foreign investment by the United States would be to reduce our imports of gold, the *ultimate* effect would be to produce annual dividend and interest payments to us which exceeded our new investments. This, in conjunction with our high tariff policy and the large amounts payable to us under the inter-allied debt settlements, would be likely to produce a flow of gold to the United States. In addition, the large reparation payments to France are likely to produce a strong tendency for specie to gravitate to France.

[30] The government has apparently been governed by political and diplomatic considerations. By permitting the listing of investments in nations which are more or less French satellites and not permitting the listing of securities from other nations, it has used French capital to support French diplomatic policy. The net effect, however, has been merely to diminish French investment abroad.

means that when French citizens hold money without investing it, it is likely to be kept in their homes rather than in banks. It would be possible for the French banking system to meet this demand for cash without importing gold (1) if the Bank of France were permitted to engage in open market operations or (2) if there were a broad and active discount market. The banks might acquire notes from the Bank of France either by selling it acceptances or government securities through the open market or by rediscounting commercial paper. But the Bank of France is not permitted to engage in open market operations.[31] And although the commercial banks in France can discount at the Bank of France, they prefer not to do so.[32] When they need notes in order to meet the demand of their customers for cash, the banks prefer to convert foreign balances into gold, import the gold, take the gold to the Bank of France, and secure notes for it.[33]

The flow of gold into the United States was also produced by a combination of circumstances. The United States maintains one of the highest tariffs in the world, a tariff which on most manufactured goods is practically prohibitive.[34] Consequently, it is exceedingly difficult for other nations to sell us anything but raw materials. At the same time, the United States is the second largest creditor nation in the world. Immense sums are due us each year on account of investments which we have made abroad. In the third place, technical progress has apparently been more rapid in the United States than in any other country, except possibly Germany. Not only has this made it more difficult for other nations to sell to us, but it has caused our export trade rapidly to expand and has thus increased our power to draw specie.

But why has not the large flow of gold into the United States and France automatically checked itself by producing a rise in

---

[31] Possibly the Bank of France would not be willing to discourage the flow of gold by purchasing acceptances or securities. There are diplomatic advantages for France in a dominant gold position in Europe.

[32] The Bank of France is not purely a banker's bank. It does a commercial banking business in competition with the purely commercial banks. And it charges its competitors, the private banks, 2 per cent above the market rate for discount.

[33] From June, 1929, until February, 1931 (the time this is written), the Bank of France itself did not import gold. Its foreign bill holdings were not diminished. The gold was imported by the private banks.

[34] It is pointed out in the preceding chapter that the United States produces nearly 97 per cent of the manufactured goods which it consumes.

prices and thus producing an excess of imports over exports. To some extent, the influx of gold has affected prices. After March, 1930, for example, the prices in France held about even, although in other countries they were falling. But the main reason why the movement of specie into France has not affected prices more promptly and in greater degree is because cash has been hoarded on a large scale. As for the United States, a peculiar and extraordinarily interesting combination of circumstances has prevented the inflation of commodity prices.[35] When the post-war movement of gold into the United States started in the latter part of 1920, the member banks were heavily in debt to the Federal Reserve Banks — by over $2,500,000,000.[36] The first gold imports were largely used by the member banks to reduce their indebtedness at the Reserve Banks. As the banks reduced their indebtedness, credit became cheaper, but the drop in interest rates was undoubtedly far less than would have occurred if the gold imports had put the banks in possession of large surplus reserves. But although credit did gradually become cheaper, yet it did not produce inflation of commodity prices. The memory of severe inventory losses in 1920 and 1921 prevented enterprises from using cheap credit to build up large inventories. This created a " buyers' market " and compelled producers to pass on to buyers in lower prices a large part of the savings accomplished by technical progress. The fact that technical progress was rapid accelerated price reductions and encouraged buyers to persist in their policy of carrying small inventories. And the fact that prices were falling put terrific pressure upon producers to discover more new ways of cutting costs. The whole price level in the United States was held down, in substantial degree, by the low purchasing power of the farmers, and the purchasing power of the farmers was held down by the fact that the prices of several major farm products, such as wheat and cotton, are determined by the world demand rather than merely demand in the United States.[37] To this extent, the price level in the

[35] Some economists believe that there was inflation in the United States even when prices were slightly falling.

[36] This indebtedness had been incurred during the inflation of the war and the years immediately following.

[37] Because of the fact that the United States produces wheat and cotton in excess of the domestic demand.

United States was influenced by the same conditions which were depressing the price level in other countries. Commodity prices were also held down by the fact that Americans tended to spend their increased purchasing power, not, in the main, for commodities that enter into international commerce, but for various kinds of personal services.[38] Finally, the abundance of gold and cheap credit did eventually produce violent inflation in the security market. The effect of this inflation, however, was to attract gold from abroad, because funds came in to speculate in securities.

If the tendency for gold to pile up in the United States and France cannot be prevented by the central banks or the Bank for International Settlements, how can it be controlled? The peculiar tendency of France to meet its needs for more hand-to-hand currency by importing gold might be diminished by permitting the Bank of France to engage in open market operations and by the development of a broader and more active discount market. The development of a discount market would depend upon the willingness of the Bank of France to make discounts on more favorable terms. But more fundamental correctives of the pull of France and the United States upon the world's gold supply are needed. A reduction in the obligation of Germany to the allies under the Young Plan and of the allies to the United States on account of the war debts would help. In various ways the large export balance of the United States may be diminished. Reductions in the tariff of the United States by the Tariff Commission under the authority of the flexible clause may help to increase imports. Possibly the world will be more successful in

[38] It is a striking fact that although money expenditures in the United States in 1929, as measured by debits to individual accounts, were 57 per cent above 1919, manufacturers obtained for their goods only 10 per cent more dollars than in 1919. And in order to collect 10 per cent more dollars from the public, manufacturers were compelled to supply the public with about 42 per cent more goods. These facts indicate how much the American consumer preferred to spend his money for commodities and services other than manufactured goods. It should be mentioned, however, that there is at least one important exception to the statement that Americans did not greatly increase their expenditures for goods entering into international trade. That exception is automobiles. Both domestic expenditures for automobiles and the exports of cars increased substantially. But the growing domestic demand, instead of discouraging exports by raising the price of cars, seems to have had the opposite effect. It made for the economies of mass production and hence helped to lower the price, to increase exports, and (because the demand for cars, especially the foreign demand, is elastic) to increase the power of the United States to attract gold.

its efforts to escape dependence upon American cotton. Possibly the growth of population in the United States and the spread of diversified farming will eliminate the United States as an important exporter of wheat. Possibly a shift in the expenditures of American consumers will push up the prices of commodities here. Possibly other countries will compete more successfully with the United States in the export trade. The greatest help of all would be for Great Britain to develop stronger competitive power in international trade. Ever since 1925, her exports have been diminishing. Even in 1929, which, for the most part, was a prosperous year, British exports were $400,-000,000 less than in 1925.[39] The slow technical progress of British industry, the strength of the British trade unions (which prevents British manufacturers from adjusting wages to the fall in prices), the individualism of British manufacturers (which has retarded the reorganization of many industries, the concentration of production into the most efficient plants, and the shutdown of high-cost plants), and the failure of the British to develop new products have all combined to prevent Great Britain from holding her own in exporting. By greater success in competition with the United States, Great Britain would tend to prevent gold from flowing here and, at the same time, would experience less difficulty in holding her own gold. Possibly the gold distribution problem will be solved by a substantial increase in the scale of foreign investments by France and the United States.[40] Whether

---

[39] The failure of British exporters to hold their trade in competition with Germany and the United States, is shown by the following comparison of exports. The figures are in millions of dollars.

	Great Britain	United States	Germany
1925	$4,478	$4,910	$2,211
1929	4,084	5,241	3,212

[40] The central banks and the Bank for International Settlements, through their prestige and influence, may be able to accelerate the movement of French and American funds into foreign investment. An attempt to exert this type of leadership is represented by an address of Mr. G. M. McGarrah, President of the Bank for International Settlements, before the American Club at Paris on February 12, 1931, in which he said: "The Bank for International Settlements endorses the conviction that under the present economic conditions the pressing requirement of the Americans to ameliorate world trade and business is an active expansion of long-term credits and foreign lending which, in turn, demands political tranquillity and stability, both national and international to render them practically possible." New York *Times*, February 13, 1931, p. 8. Mr. McGarrah specifically advocated reopening the Paris market to foreign long-term securities. Unfortunately the recent experience of many American investors with foreign countries has been far from favorable.

this would be more than a temporary solution would depend upon whether the foreign investments produced exports sufficient to pay the interest and dividends payable to the investors. Here, of course, the high tariff of the United States may create difficulty.

The very fact that the causes of the maldistribution of gold seem to be largely beyond the control of central banks makes it important that ways and means be devised for economizing gold. How might it be economized? There are several methods. Reforms in some banking systems — the French and Argentine, for example — would reduce the tendency of those markets on certain occasions or under certain circumstances to draw gold from the rest of the world. Mr. Keynes has suggested that the reserve requirements of all central banks be subject to a variation of 20 per cent upward or downward upon recommendation of a committee of the central banks.[41] As central bank policies are determined largely by whether the banks have much or little gold in excess of their reserve requirements, a flexible reserve line might prove exceedingly useful in preventing a gold shortage from unduly affecting bank policies.[42]

A widely discussed plan of economizing gold is the gold exchange standard. By the gold exchange standard is meant that the central bank would stand ready to redeem paper currency, not in gold bullion, but in foreign gold standard currencies. In other words, part (or all) of the reserve of the central bank might exist in the form of short-term bills payable in gold-standard currencies, such as the dollar or the pound. For example, a continental central bank, instead of maintaining a gold reserve equivalent to $50,000,000, might keep a reserve of $35,000,000 in bullion and $15,000,000 in short-term bills payable in pounds or dollars. Obviously, the bank would be in a position to increase its cash on short notice by selling some of

---

[41] Keynes, J. M., *A Treatise on Money*, v. II, p. 317.

[42] A strong case can be made for the conclusion that legally fixed *gold* reserves represent hoarding of gold and that, if the reserves of central banks are to be regulated by law, the rule should take the form of prescribing certain proportions of quick assets (bills with near maturities) which should be held against certain liabilities. As a matter of fact, many central banks are not required to hold reserves against deposits. The legal reserve requirements often apply only to note issues.

its foreign bills. At the same time, $15,000,000 in gold would be released for use as reserves elsewhere.

As a matter of fact, the gold exchange standard is in wide operation today. The central banks of Austria, Belgium, Chile, Czechoslovakia, Equador, Egypt, Estonia, Greece, Hungary, Italy, Latvia, Peru, and Russia are permitted to hold all or part of their reserves in foreign balances and bills. And the gold exchange holdings of central banks are very large. Early in 1931, they were between $2,000,000,000 and $3,000,000,000. The Bank of France alone held about a billion in bills on foreign money centers. And yet, gold was not being economized. The reason is that gold exchange may be used either to economize gold or to hoard it — that is, large foreign balances may be employed to prevent the loss of gold.[43] To economize gold through the use of foreign exchange holdings, the holdings must be permitted to take the place of some gold bullion and the bullion must be permitted to leave the country and to accumulate in the markets against which the exchange is payable. This has not been done. Continental banks hold immense quantities of London exchange, but London does not have a proportionate amount of gold and during much of the time during recent years has kept what she has only with difficulty.

Gold may also be economized through the operations of the Bank for International Settlements. One way in which the Bank may help to economize gold is by assisting central banks to meet seasonal fluctuations in the demand for credit. It is hoped, according to President McGarrah of the Bank, that an increasing proportion of the Bank's funds will consist of the foreign exchange reserves of the various central banks.[44] In the fall of 1930, such reserves represented about one-third of the assets and liabilities of the Bank.[45] The Bank uses its resources to move

[43] The tendency for gold to leave the country could be counteracted by the bank's selling its exchange holdings abroad.

[44] McGarrah, G. W., "The First Six Months of the Bank for International Settlements," *Proceedings of the Academy of Political Science*, January, 1931, v. XIV, p. 243.

[45] The Bank does not publish the interest rate that it pays for deposits. President McGarrah states that it is feared that the rate would be mistaken for something in the nature of a world discount rate. The Bank pays one average rate for all currencies.

capital from countries where interest rates are low to countries where interest rates are high and credit is scarce. If the central banks can count on help from the Bank for International Settlements to meet temporary increases in the demand for credit, they *may* feel that they can safely conduct their business on the basis of smaller reserves. Whether the central banks actually will be willing to operate with smaller reserves, only time will tell.

A second way in which the Bank for International Settlements may help to economize gold is by preventing seasonal fluctuations in the demand for currencies from producing shipments of gold. The demand for the currencies of many countries, particularly countries which are large exporters of agricultural products, fluctuates violently. During the crop exporting season, when the country is being paid for its goods, the exporters are likely to have large quantities of bills payable in foreign currencies (usually pounds) which they wish to convert into their own domestic currency. As a result, the price of the domestic currency in terms of foreign currencies, let us say pounds, rises very high — so high that it may become profitable to meet the demand for the domestic currency by shipping gold from London. The Bank for International Settlements is prepared to make this shipment unnecessary. In order to avoid going into the open market and buying exchange — and thus pushing the price of a currency so high that gold shipments might occur — the Bank has arranged to acquire credits on the books of central banks by transferring bills from its own portfolio to the central bank in question.[46] In this manner, the Bank for International Settlements acquires a credit in the exporting country. It uses its credit to supply the demand for the domestic currency — in other words, it helps exporters to acquire their own currency by purchasing from them the foreign bills which they have acquired through exporting their goods.[47] By thus offering the domestic currency in exchange for foreign currencies — say, pounds — the Bank for International Settlements prevents the price of the domestic currency from becoming so high in terms of pounds and thus tends to prevent the shipment of gold. But why may this help to economize gold? Simply

[46] McGarrah, G. W., *Ibid.*, p. 245.

[47] By an indirect process, the Bank for International Settlements is inducing the central bank to invest a larger proportion of its resources in foreign bills instead of drawing gold from abroad.

because if the central banks feel that they will be protected against seasonal gold losses by the Bank for International Settlements, they may be content with smaller reserves. But again, it must be stressed, only time will tell whether or not central banks will be content with smaller reserves.

In the third place, the Bank for International Settlements may help to economize gold by lending to central banks. The economy which would be effected by this practice is obvious, particularly if the central banks were permitted to count their credits on the books of the Bank for International Settlements as part of their reserves, because it would not be necessary for the Bank for International Settlements to have a dollar of gold in reserve for every dollar of credit granted to central banks. This, of course, would be simply a particular form of the gold exchange standard.

But the Bank for International Settlements could not lend to the central banks on a substantial scale unless it possessed large resources. The Bank, however, is small. In February, 1931, its total resources were only $359,181,000.[48] Over a score of banks in the United States are larger than this — some of them six times as large. Plainly it would be ridiculous to expect such a small bank to have an appreciable influence upon the world credit situation. Mr. Keynes has suggested that, "in order to set a standard and a fashion," all central banks be expressly allowed to hold at least half of their legal reserves in balances with other central banks or with the Bank for International Settlements.[49] Unfortunately, this suggestion, though not without merit, does not strike at the heart of the difficulty, which is the hoarding of gold by central banks. The abandonment of hoarding presupposes the development of a certain confidence among nations, because gold is hoarded, not only for economic, but also for political reasons. On the Continent in particular, gold has always had

[48] *Federal Reserve Bulletin*, April, 1931, p. 215.
[49] *A Treatise on Money*, v. II, p. 317. Lending to central banks by the Bank for International Settlements would raise many difficult questions. What rate should the Bank for International Settlements charge? Should it charge the same rate to all central banks despite the various interest rates among various markets? Would embarrassment be created for the Bank in case applications for credit for some banks provoked similar applications from other central banks which did not need credit? For a discussion of these questions, see Paul Einzig, *The Bank for International Settlements*, Ch. IX.

a political as well as an economical significance. Large stocks of gold have been maintained as part of the equipment for war. Continental central banks have been ever ready to acquire gold, but always reluctant to release it. London, the credit center of the world in pre-war days, conducted its enormous operations on a much smaller gold base than either Paris or Berlin, which were much less important centers. Despite the Locarno treaty, the Kellogg-Briand Pact, and the moral influence of the League of Nations, it is doubtful whether Continental nations have reached the point where they are ready to abandon hoarding of gold against the possibility of war. Perhaps, if the price level continues to fall, the growing burden of the public debts will produce a change in their attitude. Then the central banks of Europe may be willing to deposit a substantial part of their gold " abroad " in the Bank for International Settlements and the Bank may become large enough to exercise a real influence upon world credit conditions.

REFERENCES

Angell, J. W., *The Recovery of Germany*, 1929.
Cole, G. H. D., *Gold, Credit and Employment*, 1930.
Einzig, Paul, *The Bank for International Settlements*, 1930.
Keynes, J. M., *A Treatise on Money*, 1930.
Kisch, C. H., and Elkin, W. A., *Central Banks*, 1930.
Moulton, H. G., and McGuire, C. E., *Germany's Capacity to Pay*, 1923.
Patterson, E. M., and others, " Europe in 1927," *Annals of the American Academy of Political and Social Science*, November, 1927, v. CXXXIV.

PART IV

SOME CONSTRUCTIVE SUGGESTIONS

CHAPTER XXXI

SOME CONSTRUCTIVE SUGGESTIONS

I. SOME ISSUES. II. THE CONTROL OF POPULATION. III. THE PROVISION OF MORE ADEQUATE MARKET INFORMATION. IV. PROVIDING INDUSTRY WITH MORE ACCURATE COST ACCOUNTING. V. IMPROVING THE REGULATION OF PUBLIC UTILITIES. VI. THE CREATION OF MORE PUBLIC UTILITIES. VII. MAKING ECONOMIC FORTUNE LESS OF A GAMBLE. VIII. GREATER RECOGNITION OF NEEDS IN THE DISTRIBUTION OF INCOME. IX. A GREATER VOICE FOR LABOR IN THE DIRECTION OF INDUSTRY. X. A GREATER VOICE FOR CONSUMERS IN THE DIRECTION OF INDUSTRY. XI. A PLANNED ECONOMY. XII. MAKING MANAGEMENT NEUTRAL INSTEAD OF PARTISAN.

I. Some Issues

The nineteenth century was a period of daring social experimentation on a gigantic scale. A large part of the world took the bold step of trusting the more or less uncontrolled pursuit of self-interest to build an industrial system which would serve the community. It must be confessed that the experiment was successful to a surprising degree — certainly to a degree that few men in the seventeenth or eighteenth centuries would have predicted. Instead of simply resulting in chaos indescribable, the institution of economic freedom produced an astounding increase in the output of industry and an equally unprecedented rise in the standard of living of the population. It is natural to attribute the increases in output and consumption to the system of industrial organization. To some extent the economic system is entitled to credit. Even if one suggests that the spectacular increase in production during the last century is mainly due to the application of science to industry and the settlement of rich areas in the United States, Canada, South America, Australia, and Africa, the reply can be made with much truth that the use of science by industry and the migration of Europeans into new lands have both occurred more rapidly and on a wider scale because each individual has been, in the main, free to seek profit in whatever

849

ways he wished and wherever he thought that he could find it. But however successfully freedom and capitalism have increased the output of industry, no one would contend that the present scheme of economic organization is perfect.

There are six basic tests by which we may appraise an industrial system: (1) by its productivity; (2) by the costs at which production is obtained; (3) by the fairness with which income is distributed; (4) by the effect of the industrial system upon security; (5) by its effect upon liberty; and (6) by the extent to which industrial activities are guided by the general interests of the community rather than by the special interests of small groups.

Modern industry undoubtedly satisfies the productivity test better than any of the others. Relative to past ages, output is large, and it is growing rapidly. Nevertheless, it is far less than it might be, because the available labor supply and plant equipment are not kept steadily employed. Moreover, the costs of operation are unnecessarily high. Consider, for example, the enormous waste of capital because of the fact that a large part of the savings each year are invested where their principal effect is to drive capital out of use rather than to increase the total output of industry. Even more serious are the excessive human costs of production. The reason is an unbalanced condition which gives business enterprises an extraordinarily powerful incentive to reduce money costs but only a weak incentive to reduce human costs. Consequently, it is often profitable for managements to reduce money costs by permitting human costs to rise. The question of what distribution of income is fair will probably always provoke disagreement. Nevertheless, it is generally agreed that gains and losses should not be merely a matter of luck. In modern economic society, with its violent fluctuations in prices and its rapid changes in markets and methods, both gains and losses are in a substantial degree determined by chance. Perhaps the greatest shortcoming of modern industry is its failure to provide security. This affects business men, investors, and wage earners alike. In large degree, insecurity is the result of the dynamic character of modern industry. We have not yet learned how to introduce more productive methods without at the same time creating great economic hazards.

Probably the claim which is most frequently made on behalf of modern industry is that it provides more liberty than could any other arrangement. But much liberty in modern economic society is appearance rather than reality. Certainly it is not liberty when a rise in the price level robs creditors of half of their property or when a fall doubles the burden of debtors. The modern workman is said to be free because he possesses the right to quit his employer at any time. His ancestors did not all enjoy this right. But from the mere fact that the worker is free to quit, may we infer that he has liberty? Most workers have no direct voice in making the shop rules under which they work. Is that liberty? And much of the consumer's liberty is a delusion. The consumer, it is true, is free to spend his money as he sees fit, but in many cases he knows precious little about what he is buying. He has the same liberty as a voter who is perfectly free to vote for any candidate on the ballot but who is not able to discover what the candidates stand for.

Finally, it cannot be said that the activities of industry are guided by the general interests of the community rather than the special interests of small groups. Our examination of the position of consumers and the position of wage earners in modern industry has indicated that these two groups have little opportunity to give effective expression to their interests. As a rule their interests have relatively little effect upon industrial policies. Modern industry is operated primarily for the benefit of property owners. It does the things which happen to be profitable to investors regardless of whether they are harmful or beneficial to consumers, wage earners, or the community in general.

However great may be the superiorities of industry today over the economic systems of past ages, it is plain that we are confronted with problems of great difficulty and delicacy — how to increase the productivity of industry, to reduce its costs of operation, particularly the scandalously high human costs, how to make income more dependent upon accomplishment and less upon luck, how to make the policies of industry more sensitive to human needs, such as the desire for security and liberty, and how, in general, to make industry more of an instrument for social service and less of an instrument for private profit by which some men gain at the expense of the community. All of this must be done while the machinery is going at full speed and with-out impairing the initiative and energy which underlie industry's unprecedented productivity.

Many of the specific methods by which the operation of in-dustry might be improved — such as ways and means of reducing the severity of business cycles and of stabilizing the price level, have been discussed in preceding chapters. In this final chapter, it is intended to outline several of the general methods by which industry might be made to yield more satisfactory results.

II. THE CONTROL OF POPULATION

The achievement of economic progress requires that popu-lation increase less rapidly than the output of goods. There would be little point in taking steps to increase the output of industry or to divide it more evenly if the inevitable effect were a proportionate growth in population. A principal reason for being optimistic concerning the possibility of economic progress is the fact that during the nineteenth century a rapid rise in income failed to produce an increase in the birth rate. In fact, as we have seen, during the last fifty years most European countries and the United States have had a declining birth rate in the face of rapidly rising income.[1] Indeed, the rise in income, or at least the causes which produced it, seem to have been partly responsible for the decline in the birth rate.

But although the gain in economic well-being has been greatly facilitated by a drop in the birth rate, it is nevertheless true that families are largest among the least well-to-do class in the com-munity — among those who can least afford to have children and who can give their children least in the way of educational ad-vantages and industrial training.[2] As long as the occupational

---

[1] In Germany, France, and England, the birth rate has already dropped so low that each woman does not on the average have two children who in turn have chil-dren. This means that the population is not maintaining itself and that a decrease is bound to occur unless the birth rate rises. Cf. Kucyzinski, R. R., *The Balance of Births and Deaths*, p. 4.

[2] The 1920 census shows that the average number of children born to women according to the occupation of the husband was as follows:

Professional occupations	2.3
Managers in manufacturing	2.5
Laborers in manufacturing and mechanical industries	3.7
Miners	4.3

Thompson, Warren S., " Natural Increase of Population," *Population Problems*, pp.

groups which command the lowest income multiply most rapidly, their earnings are bound to remain low. Progress in solving the problem of poverty hinges largely upon a reduction of the birth rate among wage earners and farmers. Possibly modern marketing methods and competitive consumption can be relied upon to raise the standard of living and to reduce the birth rate among these classes. Nevertheless, the fact that the problem of poverty cannot be effectively solved until there is a lower birth rate among the least well-to-do stands as one of the most impressive arguments for abolishing the legal barriers which at present prevent responsible agencies from giving information concerning birth control.

III. The Provision of More Adequate Market Information

Our examination of modern industry has made very plain the terrific responsibility which the system of free private enterprise imposes upon the individual. Upon a myriad of decisions concerning what to buy and what to sell, and at what prices to buy or at what prices to sell, made by millions of individuals, depends the working of the economic order. If these decisions are made wisely and on the basis of reasonably complete and accurate information, the system of free private enterprise may work fairly well. But naturally, the operation of the system cannot be better than the decisions of those who determine what it does. If these decisions are made by men who are ignorant of the relevant facts or who do not know how

---

47–48. Unfortunately, these figures throw no light on whether unskilled workers have larger families than skilled workers. In Great Britain, the effective fertility rate (as indicated by the number of children living per male in the occupational class) does not vary greatly as between the skilled and unskilled workers. This is indicated by the following table:

Upper and middle classes	.96
Skilled workmen	1.49
Intermediate	1.41
Unskilled workmen	1.41
Textile workers	1.13
Miners	1.63
Agricultural laborers	1.47

The figures are based on the 1911 census and indicate the number of children of members of the class per occupied male (married or not) over 15 years of age. McIver, R. M., "Trend of Population with Respect to a Future Equilibrium," *Population Problems*, p. 292.

to interpret them, we must expect industry to act as if it were guided by ignorant men. We must expect large sums of capital to be wasted by being invested in enterprises that are unwisely conceived and in industries that are already overdeveloped; we must expect vast quantities of goods to be produced for which there is no profitable demand; we must expect miscalculations and mistakes from time to time to bring about a general breakdown in the process of exchange and industrial stagnation on a broad scale; we must expect consumers to spend huge sums on worthless or next to worthless goods, or at least on goods which yield little or no satisfaction to the buyers. All of this, of course, is precisely what we do find. It is of basic importance, therefore, in improving the operation of free private enterprise, to make accurate and comprehensive market information constantly and easily available to all buyers and sellers. Not until this is done, not until it is possible for individuals to buy and sell intelligently, can we expect free private enterprise to work satisfactorily — as if it were directed by men of good judgment.

This means that the facilities for collecting and distributing market information must far surpass those which now exist. At present, most of the market information that is collected is intended for business men. But even business men are far from adequately supplied with market facts. Relatively few trades and industries possess adequate statistics concerning productive capacity in existence or in course of construction, stocks of goods in the hands of retailers, wholesalers, and manufacturers, and the volume of unfilled orders. In most instances, this information can best be collected through trade associations, but in some cases the help of government agencies may be needed.

Reliable market information, however, is needed not only by business men but also by investors, wage earners, and consumers. Investors must not be compelled to buy securities largely on the basis of balance sheets and income statements which are often next to worthless. Investment bankers cannot be relied upon for information concerning securities because, like all merchants, they are bound to puff their wares. Investors must undoubtedly organize to provide themselves with reliable and unbiased information. In time, an investors' organization of such prestige and strength may develop that companies seeking funds will find it necessary to submit to an audit by the accountants of the investors' association. Some help may come from the government supervision of accounting. No supervision by the government, of course, would eliminate the need for a strong protective organization of investors. Nevertheless, it would help for the government to require all corporations engaged in interstate commerce to submit to the same control and publicity of accounts that is now required of the railroads.

To provide job seekers with reliable information concerning vacancies, wages, and working conditions in different plants requires the development of a chain of efficient public labor exchanges. Closely connected with them must be vocational guidance bureaus for helping the boys and girls who are entering industry for the first time. The vocational guidance bureaus will also need to help many adult workers find new occupations. This will be necessary not only because of technical changes which permanently reduce the demand for certain classes of labor but also because, as population grows more slowly, it will be less possible to meet changes in the demand for labor solely by guiding into the new occupations young persons who are just entering industry.

The problem of supplying market information to consumers has already been discussed.[3] One way is to spread the practice of selling goods in retailing on the basis of official grades. This would require that the Department of Commerce do for manufactured goods what the Department of Agriculture has already done for many agricultural products, and it would require that both departments do what they can to encourage the use of grades in retailing. Obviously it is a gigantic task to work out grades for manufactured goods and it is also a permanent task because, as products change and new ones are invented, new grades must be established. In many cases, however, it is not practicable to standardize quality so that products can be sold by grade. To provide information concerning such commodities, consumers need organizations of their own which maintain testing laboratories and which report to their members on the quality of different brands, just as the testing laboratory of a corporation

[3] Pp. 575-591.

furnishes reports to the purchasing department. Until consumers are able to buy on the basis of grades or tests, they will be at the mercy of advertisers and salesmen who have a selfish interest in selling one brand rather than another, and a large part of consumers' money will be wasted.

This brings us to what may be designated as the dilemma of free private enterprise. As market information becomes more accurate and complete and as competition, in consequence, becomes more intense, competitors are bound to organize in order to protect themselves. For example, when wage earners are provided with exact and easily accessible information about wages and conditions in different plants, it is fairly certain that employers will combine, far more effectively than they do now, to control competition among themselves for labor. Then the organization of wage earners will become more imperative than ever. And when consumers are given reliable information concerning the quality and prices of the products of rival firms, enterprises will combine to regulate competition among themselves. Of course, many such combinations exist today, but the control which they find it necessary to impose is relatively weak in comparison with what would be necessary if the ultimate consumer knew prices and quality.[4] But strong combinations to control competition among producers would necessitate some method of protecting consumers — either organizations of consumers to bargain with producers over prices and quality or the regulation of monopolistic combinations by the government. No one knows what form of control will develop. It seems certain, however, that the next generation will see basic changes in the organization of industry. Business enterprises, investors, wage earners, and consumers will insist upon more accurate and more comprehensive market information; this, in turn, will provoke the organization of many combinations to control competition; and the rise of monopolistic combinations, more effective than most of those which are now in existence, will provoke efforts to control them.

[4] It is not probable that the Sherman anti-trust law would prove a serious obstacle to the formation of combinations. It would be possible, for example, for enterprises to combine into three or four large concerns which could easily maintain a gentlemen's agreement covering prices and quality.

IV. Providing Industry with More Accurate Cost Accounting

Industry cannot be expected to operate satisfactorily unless its policies are based upon a reasonably complete and accurate system of cost accounting. This, modern industry does not have. Our analysis of the buying and selling of labor has indicated that wage earners are unable to take proper account of many things which affect the human cost of production — such as the risks of unemployment, accident, or industrial disease. Consequently, the plants which have the most irregular employment and the highest accident and sickness rates are compelled to pay little more for labor than plants with much better records. In other words, the labor market fails to translate many human costs of production into money costs for employers. The result is that business enterprises pursue policies which are faulty and uneconomical because managers base their decisions upon a system of accounting which does not report all costs. Industry will not have accurate cost accounting and managers will not have a proper basis for determining business policies until the costs of unemployment, accident, and industrial disease fall upon enterprises, at least to a substantial extent, in proportion to the number of lay-offs, accidents, and cases of industrial disease among their men. It is of basic importance in improving our economic system to provide industry with a reliable and trustworthy system of cost accounting.

The distribution of more adequate market information would help the labor market to translate human costs into money costs, but it would not be sufficient. Many job seekers would be in too weak a bargaining position to insist upon very much extra compensation for working in plants or at jobs where the risks of unemployment, accident, or disease are unusually high. Furthermore, a large proportion of wage earners would not be likely to take the trouble to discriminate carefully between jobs. Consequently, if human costs are to be translated effectively into money costs, the law must give the victims of accidents, industrial disease, or unemployment a claim against their employers for compensation. At present, it is almost universally recognized that a large part of the costs of industrial accidents should fall upon employers. In 1930, forty-four states and four territories had workmen's compensation laws and there were also several compensation acts covering employees under Federal jurisdiction.[5] Unfortunately, however, most compensation acts permit the money costs of industrial accidents still to fall in the main upon the injured men. Partly this is because the compensation required by most acts is woefully inadequate. Partly it is because most compensation acts are too narrow in scope. Many occupations are excluded on the ground that they are " safe." But a man who loses an arm or a leg in a non-hazardous employment gains little consolation from being told that he lost it in a safe occupation. Practically none of the workmen's compensation acts apply to agriculture. This is a grave omission because farming is hazardous and accidents are numerous. Agriculture is excluded simply because the employers in the industry have too many votes.

Compensation for industrial disease is in a rudimentary stage in the United States. Only eleven states, three territories, and the Federal government now provide such compensation, and most of these provide it for a few diseases only.[6] No state at the time of writing (early in 1931) requires that employers pay compensation to victims of lay-off.

It is not ordinarily appreciated that when we permit the production costs represented by accidents, industrial disease, and unemployment to fall upon wage earners and the rest of the community rather than upon business enterprises, we are encouraging industry to use methods and to pursue policies which result in an unnecessary number of lay-offs, accidents, and cases of disease. *Indeed, we are practically subsidizing accidents, disease, and unemployment.* Today we say to industry in effect: " Lay off as many men as you desire. The cost of maintaining them

---

[5] The four states without workmen's compensation acts in 1930 were Arkansas, Florida, Mississippi, and South Carolina.

[6] *Monthly Labor Review*, September, 1929, v. XXIX, p. 570. The cost of compensating occupational disease does not appear to be high. Wisconsin has a blanket law covering all occupational diseases. When the workmen's compensation act was amended to require compensation for industrial diseases as well as for industrial accidents, the premiums paid by employers were increased uniformly by one cent per $100 of payroll. Such a large surplus was accumulated that the extra cent was taken off and Wisconsin, with universal coverage for industrial diseases, makes no additional assessment.

will fall upon the community not upon you." Suppose that we said to industry: " Don't worry about your transportation bill, the community will pay it for you." Naturally every enterprise would economize on inventories and would avoid interruption of production by ordering raw materials by express. The transportation bill of industry would soar. As long as the community, rather than industry, pays most of the cost of accidents, industrial disease, and unemployment, business executives will not be extraordinarily vigilant in watching these costs, and the accident, disease, and unemployment rates will be high.

V. IMPROVING THE REGULATION OF PUBLIC UTILITIES

How well competition works as a regulator of industry depends, we have seen, upon the nature of the particular industry. In some industries, such as the railroad, electric light and power, gas, street railway, telephone, and others, competition works so badly that it has been superseded, as we know, by the policy of publicly regulated monopoly.[7] These industries are known as public utilities. The maximum (and, in some cases, the minimum) prices which they may charge are regulated by public authority. New enterprises may not enter these industries without the consent of the regulating bodies and, in some cases, extensions of existing plants may not be made without that consent. Nor may enterprises withdraw from business without the approval of the regulating authority. About one-tenth of the wealth of the United States, we have learned, is invested in public utilities. Just as it is important to improve the control of industry by competition, where competition is the principal regulating agency, so it is important to improve control by public authority, where that is the regulating instrument. And the public regulation of industry is gravely in need of improvement. Only in the case of the Interstate Commerce Commission and of a few state commissions, does it approach a tolerable degree of efficiency. Improvement in the effectiveness of regulation is partly a matter of improving the personnel of the regulating commissions and strengthening their technical staffs and partly a matter of en-

[7] To some extent, competition has been superseded by public ownership and operation. This is more true of Canada, Australia, and European countries than of the United States.

larging and clarifying the authority of the commissions. The
technical staffs of practically all commissions should be greatly
increased in size, should be given much higher compensation, and
should be protected by civil service laws. The terms of office
of the commissioners should be lengthened in many states, the
salaries substantially increased, and appointment by the governor
substituted for election by the people. And, of course, the public
utilities themselves should be deprived of much of their present
influence over political appointments. The president of the
Connecticut Light and Power Company, the largest utility
in the state, is Republican national committeemen and " boss "
of Connecticut, and the president of the Pennsylvania Railroad was recently Republican national committeeman from
Pennsylvania.

A more competent and a more numerous regulating personnel
would vastly improve the efficiency of regulation, but in most
states the legal authority of the commissions over the utilities
needs to be broadened. The inadequate authority of the commissions was discussed in Chapter XVIII.[8] Seven of the commissions, for example, have not authority to regulate electric
light and power companies, seven need authority to control the
accounts of the companies which they regulate, and nearly all
need to be empowered to begin cases on their own initiative.
Almost no commissions have access to the books of the holding
companies which control the local utilities and charge them for
managerial and engineering services. The increasing interstate
transmission of gas and electricity and the decision of the United
States Supreme Court that the states have no authority to regulate the price of gas or electricity entering into interstate commerce make it highly probable that Federal regulation will be
necessary.[9] Finally, there is the problem of the rate-base. If
rates are to be readjusted to changed conditions promptly and
without enormously expensive and burdensome litigation, a base
must be established which will be shown at any moment by the
accounts of the company — if the accounts have been properly
kept. Unfortunately, the courts, with whom the decision ulti-

[8] See pp. 397 and 425–427.
[9] *Kansas National Gas Company Case,* 265 U. S. (1924), 298 and *Public Service
Commission of Rhode Island* v. *Attleboro Steam and Electric Company,* 273 U. S.
(1927) 83.

mately rests, have manifested little appreciation of the administrative problems of regulation.[10]

VI. The Creation of More Public Utilities

In the face of the gravely inadequate regulation of public utilities, it may seem preposterous to propose that additional industries be regarded as public utilities and regulated as such. Nevertheless there are several industries in which competition has failed as a regulative force no less than in the railroad, electric, or gas industry. The petroleum industry is a conspicuous illustration. The proposal to treat this industry as a public utility and to permit the drilling of no wells except with the permission of the government and subject to conditions imposed by the government is not a popular one because it might diminish the overproduction of petroleum and raise the price of gasoline. In few industries, however, has competition caused more grievous waste than in oil producing. Petroleum and gas usually occur together and the oil, under pressure, has absorbed part of the gas. The recovery of the maximum amount of oil depends upon skillful utilization of the gas pressure to force the oil to the surface. Since the gas tends to separate from the oil as soon as the pressure is reduced, recovery of all of the oil is impossible. The amount obtained depends partly upon the location and the number of the wells and partly upon the rate at which the oil and gas are allowed to escape. Under the present method of development, which may be described as competitive robbery, each land owner or lessee endeavors to draw as much oil as possible from beneath the adjoining land.[11] The result is that both the location and the number of wells are determined by property lines rather than by geological conditions and that in many cases the number of wells is far too numerous. More serious still is the fact that oil and gas are not allowed to escape at the optimum rate

[10] It has been proposed (by the Pennsylvania Giant Power Survey Board and the Massachusetts Public Utility Commission) that utilities be offered a contract binding them to accept rate regulation on a prudent investment rate-base. The privilege of condemning property under eminent domain would be denied companies which refused. They would also be denied new charters and mergers of municipal franchise grants.

[11] For an excellent discussion of this topic see Stocking, G. W., *The Oil Industry and the Competitive System*, Ch. VIII and IX. The following account is based upon Stocking.

which will yield the maximum ultimate recovery of petroleum but
at a much more rapid rate — due, of course, to the fact that each
landholder is seeking to get the oil before his neighbors do.   It is
estimated that present methods of exploitation leave from 40 to
90 per cent of the petroleum underground.[12]   In drilling for oil,
sand strata containing only gas may be encountered.   It is possible to seal the gas strata and to conserve the gas by drilling with
a mud-laden fluid in the hole.   But this slows down drilling operations and, in the race for oil, speed is all important.   So the gas
may be allowed to escape into the atmosphere.[13]   And likewise
the so-called " wet " gas, which comes, not from gas sands, but
from the same strata as the oil and which is released in increasing
quantities as the flow of oil reduces the pressure, has in many
cases been allowed to waste into the air.   This gas is often rich
in the more volatile petroleum elements and can be made to
yield natural-gas gasoline.   And yet in the competitive rush for
oil, many producers neglect to install plants for treating the
" wet " gas and recovering gasoline.

Here clearly is an industry in which competition is a calamity
rather than a beneficent regulating force.   And yet public control
of the industry is bound to be difficult in the extreme.   Federal
regulation would undoubtedly be far more satisfactory than control by the states, but this would require a constitutional amendment because the authority of Congress over interstate commerce does not permit it to control the methods by which goods
are produced.   Despite the obstacles to effective regulation, however, here plainly is an industry in which control by public
authority is urgently needed.

VII. Making Economic Fortune Less of a Gamble

It is undeniable that making a living in modern economic society is, in large degree, a gamble, and that success or failure is

---

[12] *Ibid.*, pp. 142–143.

[13] Stocking quotes V. H. Manning, former director of the United States Bureau
of Mines, on the waste of gas in the Cushing, Oklahoma, field in 1913. " Not only
was the gas allowed to waste, but such tremendous volumes of this inflammable material hung over the oil fields that automobiles were not allowed to enter, and in many
cases disastrous fires were started, resulting in loss of life and property."   *Ibid.*, p.
179.   Mr. R. S. Blatchley of the Bureau of Mines estimated that the waste of gas
in the Mid-Continent field prior to 1913 was enough to supply the state of Oklahoma
for sixty years at the then current rate of consumption.   *Ibid.*, p. 179.

often a matter of chance. The element of chance in the distribution of income cannot be eliminated entirely but it can be reduced, and the task of reducing it may well be regarded as a major function of the state, comparable with the suppression of violence and fraud and the enforcement of contracts. More abundant and more accurate market information would, of course, itself diminish the importance of chance. Unforeseeable changes in the price level are a major source of unearned income and undeserved losses. Stabilization of the price level would be an important step in reducing the element of chance in economic life. Inherited wealth is another major source of unearned income. Mr. Josiah Wedgwood has estimated that in Great Britain before the war nearly twice as much wealth was acquired by individuals through inheritance as through saving.[14] His estimates, though carefully made, are necessarily rough. Furthermore, the importance of inheritance in a relatively new country, such as the United States, is probably far less than in an old country, such as Great Britain. Nevertheless, the returns from the Federal inheritance tax indicate that between $2,000,000,000 and $2,500,000,000 of property is acquired annually by inheritance from estates large enough to be taxable under the Federal law.[15] This does not include gifts to public and charitable institutions and it does not include the large acquisitions from estates of less than $100,000, which are exempt from the Federal estates tax.[16] The acquisitions of individuals by inheritance are probably at least one-third as large as the annual savings by individuals. Just as it was once necessary to make war on the inheritance of political power, so now it is necessary to make war on the inheritance of economic power.

[14] Wedgwood, Josiah, *The Economics of Inheritance*, pp. 105–126, especially p. 119.

[15] The net estates (that is, the gross estate less debts, charitable and public bequests, funeral and administrative costs but inclusive of other exemptions permitted under the law) during recent years have been as follows:

1924	$1,888,032,000
1925	2,255,949,000
1926	2,418,217,000
1927	2,408,912,000
1928	2,569,230,000

Statistical Abstract of the United States, 1930, p. 210.

[16] In 1928, the number of returns under the Federal law was only 8,079. *Ibid.*, p. 210.

It has been pointed out that the Federal government and forty-five of the states now tax either bequests or estates, but the rates are not high. In fact, taking the United States as a whole, inheritance taxes are lower than in any other industrial country. Unfortunately, in 1926 the rates on the Federal estates tax were lowered and the exemption was raised from $50,000 to $100,000. The maximum rate of 40 per cent on estates of over $10,000,000 was reduced to 20 per cent.[17] In 1928, the total tax revenue of the Federal government and the states from inheritance taxes was only 7.3 per cent of the net value of the estates reported under the Federal estates tax.[18] A progressive tax rising as high as 50 per cent on large estates or bequests, such as Andrew Carnegie suggested, would not be unreasonable.[19] The inheritance tax is not

[17] The Federal government allows a credit of 80 per cent of the Federal tax on all payments of estate, inheritance, legacy, or succession taxes actually made to any of the several states.

[18] Computed from data in National Industrial Conference Board, *Cost of Government in the United States, 1928–1929*, pp. 88 and 96, and *Statistical Abstract of the United States*, 1930, p. 210. Most estates are exempt from the Federal tax. Net value is used here as defined in footnote 15. It is higher than taxable value, because taxable value is net value minus certain exemptions.

[19] It would probably be desirable to graduate the rates according to the size of the *bequest* rather than the size of the entire estate.

It is often objected that taxes on estates or bequests would cause dissipation of capital. Capital consists of concrete things — buildings, machines, railroads, and other instruments of production. Obviously an inheritance tax, no matter how heavy, does not cause the existing buildings, machines, and railroads to disappear. But if the tax does not affect the amount of capital already in existence, does it not retard the growth of capital? Executors of estates or heirs may be compelled to sell a large part of the estate in order to acquire funds to pay the tax. The property is purchased by men who have saved and who have money to invest. In other words, a substantial part of the new savings of the community are used, not to finance the creation of new capital but to purchase property forced on the market by the inheritance or estate tax. Apparently the growth of capital is retarded.

Whether or not this actually is the net effect of the tax depends upon a number of circumstances. The inheritance tax may, to some extent, keep down the amount which the government must raise by other taxes. If taxpayers in general find themselves less heavily taxed, they may save a little more. This will partly compensate for the new savings that are invested in property forced upon the market by the inheritance tax. If heirs are given a reasonable period to pay the tax (say five years), they may prefer to pay it out of income rather than by selling part of the property. In such cases, the effect of the tax may be to cause the heirs to spend a large part of the income of the estate in meeting the tax rather than on high living. Finally, the effect of an inheritance tax upon the growth of capital depends upon how the government uses the money. Obviously the growth of capital is not retarded if the government spends the money, not for current operations, but for buildings, roads, and other items of capital expenditure. There is nothing, of course, to prevent the government from providing a program of public works to be financed solely out of the proceeds of the inheritance tax.

well adapted to such a small political unit as the American state because, when applied to a relatively small population, its yield fluctuates too much from year to year. It should be abandoned by the states but used, with higher rates, by the Federal government. Of course even a tax as heavy as Andrew Carnegie advocated would fall far short of eliminating bequests as sources of unearned income, but it would diminish the evil.

VIII. Greater Recognition of Needs in the Distribution of Income

In the main, we have seen, goods are distributed in modern economic society on the basis of ability to pay for them. But some things, such as police and fire protection, roads, parks, and elementary and secondary education, are provided by the government without charge. Food, shelter, and medical attention too are provided in extreme cases, but as charity and not as a matter of right. It is desirable that the distribution of goods on the basis of needs should be substantially increased. In fact, it seems a sound general principle that all men should receive the necessities of life before some men are permitted to enjoy luxuries. Especially does this seem a sound principle when one considers the nature of production. Recipients of large incomes often believe they are entitled to what they receive because they have acquired it by hard work and business acumen. But the present generation cannot be said to have earned the income which it receives. That income is as large as it is because countless preceding generations have built up technical knowledge, have cleared land, drained swamps, opened mines, and accumulated capital. Only a minute part of the work and the saving necessary to produce the present output of industry has been done by the generation which consumes that output. All of us are the heirs of the ages in things economic no less than in things cultural.

In view of the fact that most of the output of the present generation was made possible by past generations and that we all, therefore, reap what we did not sow, no one is in a position

---

On the whole, it seems plain that the government can levy inheritance taxes without seriously retarding the growth of capital. Experience alone can reveal how far it would prove desirable to go in raising the inheritance tax. It may be desirable to have a society in which capital is growing less slowly but in which wealth is distributed more justly.

to object if a substantial fraction of the product is regarded as the common property of us all. Consequently, if a man is willing to work and unable to find employment because not enough jobs exist, or is prevented from working by physical or mental disability, should he not receive at least the requirements of a bare existence without the slightest taint of charity? The case for more extensive distribution on the basis of needs is especially strong when one considers the claims of wives and children. Why should they be deprived of adequate nourishment or shelter or medical care simply because they happen to be the dependents of a man who is a poor workman or who is unemployed or who is incapacitated by illness or accident? Even if the man himself is in some degree responsible for his misfortunes, why should his family be penalized?

But to assert that as a general principle more recognition should be given to needs in the distribution of income is one thing; to apply the principle is quite another. Just how should greater recognition be given to needs? This would appear to involve the guarantee of a minimum wage, the payment of unemployment benefits to men out of work through no fault of their own, more adequate compensation for industrial accidents and industrial diseases, and ample provision for rehabilitating men who suffer industrial accidents, and, if necessary, training them for new occupations. Medical and hospital care are so important that they should be available to everyone at all times at only nominal cost. The Committee on the Cost of Medical Care reports that in this country 15 per cent of the 2,400,000 births each year are attended by midwives rather than by physicians. It also reports that in the Mulberry district of New York, where hospitals and doctors are numerous, 16 per cent of the persons confined at home on account of sickness and 22 per cent of those too sick to be at work, though out of bed, secured no medical care from physicians.[20] Among 11,000 persons disabled by sickness, the Metropolitan Life Insurance Company found that 25 per cent were not attended by physicians.[21] It is estimated that only 20 per cent of the people in the United States go regularly to a dentist for examination and repairs. Certainly no one should be permitted

---

[20] *The Five-Year Program of the Committee on the Cost of Medical Care*, p. 9.
[21] *Ibid.*, p. 23.

to enjoy luxuries while others lack proper medical attention. Free medical and hospital care would not need to interfere with the employment of private physicians by those who prefer them. It would simply mean that the state would compete, through clinics and hospitals that are free or practically free, with the institution of the private physician. Each person would be free in each case to choose between hiring his own physician and using a private hospital and using the clinical and hospital facilities offered by the state. And, finally, there is the matter of provision for old age. A substantial proportion of those who are destitute at old age are so through no fault of their own. The premature loss of steady work through industrial accident, sickness, technical changes, strike, the merger of business enterprises, or the bankruptcy or retirement of the employer, accounts for a large part of the destitution in old age. In view of the fact that we have all gained by inheritance a large part of our ability to produce and that economic life is more or less of a gamble, there is a strong case for granting pensions at public expense to those who find themselves without means of support in old age. For the most part, these are the persons who have had more than their share of misfortune. A pension merely helps to even the balance. The other alternative is the poorhouse, which costs the government nearly as much and imposes a stigma, often undeserved, upon its inmates.

No doubt most people (though not all) who have children are performing a service to the community. Family allowances to cover a substantial part of the expenses of birth and through the early years of childhood appear to have a place in an equitable system of distribution. The theory of family allowances is easy to justify. But the operation of such a scheme raises practical questions of the utmost gravity. The obvious difficulty would be to restrict the allowances to parents fit to have children. It would be important to grant allowances only in cases where both parents, after submitting to thorough physical and mental examinations, were found to be fit. Indeed, it would be important to refuse allowances in case either parent fell into the lowest third of the population in intelligence. In case both parents rated exceptionally high in intellectual and physical qualifications, the allowance might be made larger. But it seems certain that many generations must pass before it would be politically possible to administer a scheme of family allowances with proper discrimination.[22]

IX. A Greater Voice for Labor in the Direction of Industry

The obstacles which make it difficult for wage earners in selling their labor to discriminate in favor of enterprises which offer the best wages and working conditions mean that wage earners are bound to be an exceedingly weak influence in modern industry as long as they are mainly dependent upon this one method of exercising a voice. Workmen's compensation acts, compensation for industrial disease, and laws defining minimum standards of safety and sanitation in factories, mines, and other working places counteract, in some degree, the inability of wage earners to make their influence felt in the labor market. But there are many things which laws cannot do — they cannot protect workmen against arbitrary discharge, compel the management to relieve laid-off employees before employing outsiders, prevent favoritism in promotion or in the distribution of overtime work, prevent excessive speed of work, control the cutting of piece rates, protect pieceworkers against the multitude of conditions which interfere with their earning capacity, or guard the interests of wage earners in a hundred and one other situations. Trade unions appear to be needed in order that the workmen in the vast enterprises of modern industry can acquire liberty and security — liberty to participate in determining the conditions under which they shall work and security against arbitrary treatment by the management. At present, as we have seen, only about one-seventh of the workers engaged in manufacturing, mining, transportation, and building construction are organized.[23] Not until wage earners achieve a far greater degree of organization will they gain an effective voice in the direction of industry.

The organization of trade unions must in the main be accomplished by the wage earners themselves with little help from the outside. Indeed, organizations, to be worth much, should be spontaneous growths, not hothouse plants. Nevertheless, in

---

[22] An excellent discussion of family allowances will be found in P. H. Douglas' *Wages and the Family*.

[23] Pp. 176–177.

view of the encouragement which the state has given the organization of capital, it might seem fair for the government to lend a helping hand to labor organizations. The government has encouraged the organization of capital in several ways. It has given corporations the special privilege of limited liability; through the Department of Commerce it has encouraged business enterprises to form trade associations; it has assisted farmers to form coöperatives. Recently it has established the Federal Farm Board, which is assisting farmers to develop marketing associations "owned and controlled by the several producers of agricultural commodities" that will be " large enough . . . to exercise effective control over the marketing of a considerable proportion of each commodity." [24] Possibly it would be wise for the government to establish a Federal Labor Board which would seek to organize trade unions among the wage earners as the Federal Farm Board is seeking to organize coöperatives among farmers.

If the state does not help labor to organize, certainly it should not hinder. The obligation to maintain strict neutrality is doubly compelling in view of the assistance that the government has given to capital. Unfortunately, the record of the state has too often been one not of neutrality but of hostility to the efforts of labor to organize. The establishment of a union usually involves a strike (or a lockout), for few employers are willing to have their employees organize. It would seem elementary that proper neutrality on the part of the state would involve the prohibition of the use of private guards by either side in an industrial dispute. The provision of police protection should be the monopoly of the state. And yet instances are numerous in which employers have been permitted to hire armed guards, often thugs supplied by detective agencies, who, under the guise of protecting property have seized every opportunity to intimidate strikers. Nor should the government permit the swearing in of deputy sheriffs who are paid their salaries either by the employers or by the unions. Many coal operators have used this device for recruiting armed forces with which to crush strikes. Proper neutrality by the state would also involve a radically different attitude on the part of the authorities—

[24] *First Annual Report of the Federal Farm Board*, p. 3.

the police, the sheriffs, and the militia. Often they lose sight of the fact that it is their duty to protect the rights of the strikers no less than those of the employers. The ordinary activities of the strikers, such as the holding of meetings or parades, are prohibited by police order upon flimsy pretexts; strike leaders are railroaded out of town with the connivance of the police; pickets are clubbed or arrested even though engaged in no unlawful activities; strikers are terrified by being herded into jail and held for a few days with no charges preferred against them. Then the jail is emptied and filled with a new group, likewise to be held and let go. Even the courts in many cases have forgotten their neutral position. They have not hesitated, after an *ex parte* hearing only, to issue sweeping temporary restraining orders against all manner of innocent activities of the strikers.[25] Often the evidence offered in support of the application for the order is of the flimsiest and most unreliable sort — nothing more than affidavits by the armed guards of the employer. Legislation to hold the courts to a more cautious procedure in the issuance of temporary restraining orders and injunctions is badly needed.[26] Finally, proper neutrality on the part of the state would involve legislation against the so-called " yellow dog " contract. This is a written individual contract by which each employee of an enterprise stipulates that he is not a member of a trade union and agrees that during his term of service with the firm he will not become or agree to become a member of a labor organization. Despite the fact that these contracts are terminable by either party at will, the United States Supreme Court has held that, when an enterprise has made

[25] The material on the attitude and actions of the civil authorities during strikes is so voluminous that it is difficult to select references from it. The report of the Interchurch World Movement, *Public Opinion and the Steel Strike,* is to be recommended. See especially Chapter III by George Soule, entitled " Civil Rights in Western Pennsylvania." Additional material will be found in: " Investigation of the Strike in the Steel Industry," *Hearings before the Committee on Education and Labor, United States Senate, 66th Congress, 1st Session, pursuant to S. Res. 188 and S. Res. 202.* A mine of material will be found in the various Congressional hearings on the Michigan copper strike, the Paint and Cabin Creek Coal Strike in West Virginia, and the recent coal strike in western Pennsylvania.

[26] For abundant material on this subject see: " Limiting the Scope of Injunctions in Labor Disputes," *Hearings before a Subcommittee of the Committee on the Judiciary, United States Senate, 70th Congress, 1st Session.* A lucid and comprehensive discussion of the problem of the injunction in labor disputes will be found in Frankfurter, F., and Greene, N., *The Labor Injunction.*

such contracts with its workers, the attempts of union representatives to organize the employees are an unjustifiable interference with contractual relationships and are actionable. On the ground that a suit for damages would be an inadequate remedy, courts of equity issue injunctions forbidding union agents from attempting to extend their organizations into enterprises where the " yellow dog " contracts exist. It is safe to say that a *statute* forbidding unions to pursue their organizing activities would promptly be held unconstitutional. Nevertheless, by the ingenious device of the " yellow dog " contract, employers have succeeded in doing what the legislatures could not — in making organizing activities, however innocent in themselves, illegal. As a result of injunctions issued to protect " yellow dog " contracts, it is now illegal for the miners' union to do any organizing work throughout large parts of Pennsylvania, West Virginia, and Kentucky.

The government can probably extricate itself from the partisan position into which it has been manoeuvered through the enactment of a statute declaring these contracts contrary to public policy. Wisconsin, Ohio, and several other states have already passed such a law.[27] This means that the courts of these states (assuming that the constitutionality of the acts is sustained) will not enforce " yellow dog " contracts either by injunctions or by hearing damage suits based on the contracts.

X. A GREATER VOICE FOR CONSUMERS IN THE DIRECTION OF INDUSTRY

In view of the fact that industry is operated to the end that men may consume, it is remarkable and unfortunate that consumers, as such, have so little to say about what industry does. As has been said several times, the inability of consumers to exercise more influence is a major source of industrial waste. The reasons for the consumer's inability to exercise influence through the ordinary process of buying and selling were discussed in Chapter XXII, and some of the ways and means by which he might acquire a more effective voice were suggested. It was pointed out that the consumer needs two types of organiza-

---

[27] It is interesting to notice that the governor who signed the bill in Wisconsin was himself one of the largest manufacturers in the state.

tions — organizations to do for him what testing laboratories do for manufacturers and organizations to keep in close touch with the work of the government in protecting consumers, to help improve the administration of the laws intended to protect the consumer, and to help close the wide gaps in the protection which the law now gives. The consumer lives in a world in which other great interests are more or less completely organized — labor, the farmers, and especially the business men, who are banded together into nearly a thousand national trade associations representing every variety of manufacturing, mining, transporting, wholesaling, retailing, and banking. The consumer alone in this world of organization is unorganized. The reasons for being optimistic about the economic future of the United States are many. A principal reason for tempering one's optimism is the failure of consumers to organize.

XI. A Planned Economy

Attention has frequently been called to the fact that the activities of modern industry are determined for the most part by the decisions of millions of individuals each of whom is thinking of his own interests rather than of the common good. As a result, the interests which men have in common are often neglected. Each individual and each business enterprise may be fairly efficient in the pursuit of private gain and yet the economic system as a whole may be wretchedly operated — precisely because there is no one or no organization to give proper attention to the pursuit of the general welfare. Naturally the question arises: Could we not do better by setting definite goals and organizing to achieve them? During the last generation the art of management has developed rapidly and has achieved marvelous results within individual business enterprises. But why should management be practiced only within business concerns? If it is good for them, may it not be good for larger units — for entire industries or for the economic system as a whole? Should we not extend the principles of planning and control that have been developed within individual enterprises over a wider area? Why not have a planned or a managed economy?

This suggestion is not a new one. The need for a planned economy has always been an important part of the Socialist philosophy. But the need has been recognized outside of Socialist circles. Bismarck conceived of an economic parliament which would advise the government in economic matters, and for a brief time, about 1881, an economic council existed in Germany. Interest in the idea of a managed economy was greatly stimulated by the national control of economic activities during the war, by the grave economic problems of post-war Europe and by the constant example of a planned economy in Russia. The new German constitution of 1919 provided for a National Economic Council. In Great Britain, Sir William Beveridge and later the Liberal Industrial Inquiry suggested an economic general staff to assist in formulating national economic policies. France established a national economic council in 1925. In the United States, the severe depression of 1930 and the apparently favorable progress of the Russian Five Year Plan suddenly stimulated great interest in a planned economy. The idea was endorsed by the American Federation of Labor at its Boston Convention in October, 1930, and it was a principal topic of discussion at the annual meeting of the Taylor Society in December, 1930.

Before we undertake to analyze the possibilities and the problems which national planning presents, let us notice the extent to which central planning or guidance is already in operation today. Zoning ordinances are perhaps the most widespread form. They require that the use of real estate shall correspond to a plan for the entire city. The simplification and standardization work of the Bureau of Standards is another example. Competing enterprises do not formally bind themselves to limit their production to a certain standard of sizes. Nevertheless, when a series of sizes is accepted by a group of producers or a trade association as standard, most enterprises confine their output to the standard sizes. In 1920, the Interstate Commerce Commission was given the task of drawing up a plan for consolidating the railroads of the country into a few large systems. In December, 1929, after much delay, a plan was approved by the Commission (with some dissenting votes) and published. The Federal Farm Board may be regarded as applying the idea of national planning to agriculture. It has endeavored to persuade farmers to reduce the acreage devoted to certain crops, such as wheat and cotton — guidance similar to that which has been given for some years by the Bureau of Agricultural Economics. It has also undertaken the task of drastically reorganizing the whole machinery for marketing farm products by establishing for each principal agricultural commodity a national coöperative or sales agency. If the Board's plans succeed, the machinery for marketing many agricultural products will be radically transformed and a host of middlemen will be eliminated. The Federal Reserve Board also may be regarded as a planning body, for it has the responsibility of formulating and executing a national credit policy. Recently a board has been established to introduce forward planning into the construction activities of the Federal government so that public building may be concentrated so far as possible into times when the volume of private building is small.

How would a National Planning Board be constituted? How would it function? What might it accomplish? What problems and difficulties would it create?

The German Economic Council (which is provisional only) consists of 326 members representing a wide variety of economic groups.[28] The German Council is so large that it has not held plenary sessions since 1923. It functions through eleven committees and nine sub-committees. The two principal standing committees are on economic affairs and social policies. Each consists of thirty members. The French Economic Council consists of forty-seven delegates who are divided into three principal groups — nine from the group of population and consumption, eight from the group of capital, and thirty from the group of labor. But the thirty labor delegates include eleven representing management.

For a National Economic Council in the United States, Dr. L. L. Lorwin has suggested a body of one hundred members

[28] Sixty-eight represent agriculture and forestry; 68, industry; 44, banking, commerce, and insurance; 24, transport and public utilities; 36, artisan classes; 30, consumers; 16, officials and professors. In addition, there are 24 members who are appointed as leaders or technical experts. Within each group, such as agriculture or industry, the delegates are evenly divided between employers and employees. Lorwin, L. L., " France-Germany Have Economic Councils," *Journal of Electrical Workers and Operators*, January, 1931, v. XXX, p. 11. The above account of the German and French councils is based, in the main, upon Dr. Lorwin's article.

which would meet in plenary session for about ten days or two weeks once a year and which would operate, in the main, through committees. A permanent staff of technical experts would work under the direction of these committees.[29] Dr. Lorwin suggests that Congress, in authorizing the creation of the Economic Council, specify the representation to be given different economic interests, such as agriculture, business, and labor, and that the Secretaries of Agriculture, Commerce, and Labor be given the task of preparing a list of organizations which would be representative of the different economic interests of the country and which would be expected to send delegates to the Council. Dr. Lorwin suggests that the delegates serve two years and that half of the Council be changed each year.

Mr. George Soule has suggested a more elaborate organization. He proposes an Economic General Staff, a small research body composed of economic experts, which would collect information about what is going on, forecast what is likely to happen, devise policies and agencies of control to fulfill national purposes, and make recommendations to a larger body, the National Economic Council. The latter would be a delegate body representing industries, occupations, and the administrative agencies of the national and local governments. The function of the National Economic Council would be to make plans for the development and the operation of industry and to persuade enterprises and governmental bodies to accept these plans.[30] Subordinate to the Economic Council, Mr. Soule proposes three boards or commissions. One would have to do with the guidance of new investments. A second would have the task of organizing the labor market and of adjusting the labor supply to changes in the geographical and occupational demand. A third would plan the geographical distribution and location of industries and the uses of various types of land.[31]

The composition of a National Planning Board or a National Economic Council is likely to arouse intense controversy. In fact, failure to settle this issue has, up to 1931, prevented the

[29] *New Republic*, April 29, 1931, v. LXVI, pp. 296–297.
[30] *Ibid.*, March 4, 1931, v. LXVI, p. 62.
[31] *Ibid.*, March 11, 1931, v. LXVI, pp. 89–90.

provisional Economic Council in Germany from being constituted upon a permanent basis. The most desirable organization for the Council would depend upon the functions which it was expected to perform. If one of its major tasks were the stabilization of business and the control of the business cycle, the Council would need to meet frequently — at least four times a year. Otherwise its decisions and its advice would come too late. A Council meeting four times a year, and oftener at special call, would have to be small — not more than forty or fifty members. For each member there should be an alternate to assure full representation of each interest at every meeting. On the other hand, if the major task of the Council were the preparation of long-time plans and policies, an annual meeting would suffice and the Council could be much larger. On the whole, a larger body primarily concerning itself with long-term plans would seem to be preferable. For one thing, the preparation of permanent policies rather than the study of current developments would be a more suitable task for the National Economic Council, because such a body could not make really informed decisions concerning current problems on short notice. In addition, it would be difficult to give adequate representation to the multitude of economic groups in the country in a body of less than one hundred members. If possible, however, the size should be kept down to that number. Four principal interests should be represented — consumers, capitalists, wage earners, and farmers. It might be desirable, as Dr. Lorwin has suggested, also to give special representation to economic research, because economists would be in a favorable position to help reconcile conflicting points of view in the Council. The term of the members should be not less than four years. The Council should have a permanent secretary, who should not be a member, and a permanent research staff of economists and statisticians. In the present state of our knowledge and experience, it is plain that a National Economic Council should be advisory only. After it had demonstrated its fitness for greater power and responsibility, more authority might gradually be conferred upon it.

What could a purely advisory National Economic Council accomplish? Could it prevent depressions? Could it prevent the great overdevelopment of industries? If a Council had been in existence as early as 1920, could it have checked the great overdevelopment of the textile industry, the shoe industry, the coal industry, the petroleum industry, the automobile industry, and others? Could it have solved the farm problem? Could it have prevented the dizzy speculation of 1928 and 1929? Could it have prevented the depression of 1930 or substantially reduced the severity of the depression? Could it have prevented our foreign trade from being injured by a general upward revision of the tariff in 1930?

Our experience with planning must prevent us from entertaining high hopes concerning the results which a National Economic Council or Planning Board might accomplish. Consider the record of the principal planning bodies that we now have — the Federal Reserve Board, the Federal Farm Board, and the Interstate Commerce Commission. All of these bodies have done much good and are worth continuing, but each has committed major errors. Take, for example, the work of the Interstate Commerce Commission in devising a plan for consolidating the railroads. This task was far less difficult than many problems which would confront a National Economic Council, and the Interstate Commerce Commission took nearly ten years for the work. It found the task difficult and asked to be relieved of the responsibility. The scheme of consolidation finally submitted by the Commission in the fall of 1929 proposed many systems which can only be described as weird or grotesque. This does not necessarily mean that national planning is not worth attempting but it does mean we must not expect it to accomplish too much.

The current interest in national planning has been largely inspired by the great industrial depression of 1930–1931. Such spectacles as millions of men on the verge of starvation when farmers are feeding wheat to cattle and the Farm Board has 200,000,000 bushels with which it does not know what to do impel men to ask whether we cannot organize production so that industry will operate more smoothly and steadily. But paradoxically, it seems plain that a National Economic Council would be most helpless in dealing with the very problem about which it would be expected to do most — the problem of stabilizing business. The reason has already been indicated. In order to stabilize business, decisions concerning policies must be made before it is too late. Unless the Board could meet frequently and arrive at decisions promptly, it would not act when action was most needed. But a body large enough to be representative would be too large to meet frequently. Nor could this difficulty be solved by breaking up the larger body into committees of fifteen or twenty, which would meet quarterly or on special call. No doubt it would be necessary for the Council to have committees on special problems and undoubtedly there would be one to promote the stabilization of business. But a committee by its very nature is unwilling to take the responsibility for public decisions which might fail to command fairly unanimous support in the parent body.[32]

In order to visualize more clearly just what a National Economic Council might do to stabilize business, let us suppose that one had been in existence since the end of the war or longer. Obviously the Council could have done relatively little about the international causes of the depression of 1930 — the various influences which, by the winter of 1930–1931, had sent sugar in Cuba down to nearly a cent a pound, rubber to 7 or 8 cents a pound, wheat in Liverpool to the lowest price in over three hundred years, coffee to the lowest price in twenty-eight years, or silver to 27 cents an ounce. But what would it have done about the internal causes? Would it have induced the Federal Reserve Board to act more promptly and vigorously in curbing speculation in 1928 and 1929? Would the Council have appreciated the relationship between world prosperity and the ability of foreign nations to borrow in the United States and have taken a vigorous stand against the practical destruction of the bond market in the United States during 1929? It will be recalled that when the Federal Reserve Board issued a warning against speculation in January, 1928, President Coolidge answered by expressing the opinion that brokers' loans were not too high but simply reflected the prosperity of the country. In the face of this presidential statement, would the National Economic Council have supported the Federal Reserve Board and encouraged

[32] This is not true when the committee is making a confidential report to the parent body but it is emphatically true when the committee takes a public position.

it to pursue a strong policy in curbing speculation? Throughout 1928 and most of 1929, there raged a vigorous controversy concerning whether it was proper for the Reserve Board to concern itself with the stock market and the prices of securities so long as there was ample credit for business at reasonable prices. Would the National Economic Council itself have taken a definite stand on this issue? Is it not probable that the members would have been so evenly divided that no action would have occurred?

Nevertheless, a National Economic Council might be of *some* help in stabilizing business. There are three principal things which it might do. In the first place, it might see that business men receive the market information which, as we know, they so badly need in order to avoid overproduction. In the second place, it might be a powerful influence in inducing the Federal government, the states, and the cities to plan public works for years in advance and to concentrate construction as far as possible during periods of depression by doing part of the program ahead of time. During the depression of 1930, there was much pretence that the ordinary construction work of the government represented an expansion of public works. It was possible for politicians to mislead the public because there were no reliable statistics on government building. By collecting accurate information on the volume of public works and particularly on the extent to which a long-time program was being constructed ahead of schedule, the Council might do much to compel the government to increase its building during depressions. In the third place, the Council might help in handling certain weak situations which invariably develop after prosperity collapses. The weak spots are not necessarily the same in different depressions. Among those which characterized 1930 was a severe drop in the demand for residential building. To a substantial extent, the causes of this situation were beyond control after the depression started. Nevertheless, an Economic Council might have done something to help sustain both the willingness of men to buy houses and their ability to obtain the funds. This problem, incidentally, serves well to illustrate how the Council would be hampered by the infrequency of its meetings. Assume that it met once a year in October or November shortly before the

opening of Congress. Assume also that an appropriate committee of the Council had become promptly aware of the drop
in residential building; that the committee, with the help of the
technical staff of the Council, had studied the problem and prepared a report for consideration by the full Council at its meeting in October or November, 1930. Assume that the report
was accepted. Nevertheless, a year of depression and the entire
building season of 1930 would have passed before the Council
could have acted.

A National Economic Council is likely to be most useful in
formulating long-term plans and policies for industry and in
dealing with problems which do not require quick decisions.
In the field of long-term plans and policies, what might a Council
accomplish?

One of the greatest wastes in modern industry results, we
have seen, from the investment of capital in such ways that it
adds little or nothing to the national income. Capital may add
little to the national income because it is invested in concerns that
are unwisely planned and can produce only at high cost, because it
is invested in an overdeveloped industry which cannot operate at
capacity, or because it is so invested that it drives too much other
capital out of operation. There is little gain to the community,
for example, in building a cotton mill in the South, which compels
other mills in New England to shut down. There may be a slight
gain to the community, because the new mill may be more productive than older mills which it replaces. But the country would
be better off if the capital were so invested that its principal
effect would not be to drive other capital out of operation.

Could a National Economic Council prevent these enormous
wastes in the investment of capital? Had it been in existence
during the last decade could it have restrained the flow of additional funds into overdeveloped industries, such as textiles, oil,
coal, shoes, and others? A fact which is often overlooked is that
these industries have grown in part because low-cost enterprises
have found it profitable to expand regardless of the effect upon
the rest of the industry. It is obvious that a National Council
would have great difficulty in preventing this kind of expansion.
Nevertheless, it might do something. The overdevelopment of

industries is not *entirely* a matter of expansion by low-cost enterprises. Almost invariably large profits in an industry are followed by overdevelopment. Of great help in preventing this
would be a more critical and cautious attitude on the part of
prospective investors, an insistence by them on rather complete
information concerning investment opportunities, and a refusal
to invest where the enterprises seeking funds decline to provide
satisfactory information about their finances. The National
Economic Council could, *if it would,* do much to stimulate a more
critical and cautious attitude among investors. It might encourage security owners to organize associations of their own to collect financial facts. It might help to focus attention upon dangerous situations where overdevelopment seemed to be occurring.
A specific warning by the Board against investing in any except
low-cost enterprises in certain overdeveloped industries would
make it more difficult to sell the issues of weak concerns in these
industries. Of course, as efforts to predict the saturation point
in the demand for automobiles have indicated, it is often difficult
to determine just how much expansion represents overdevelopment. Eventually the Board might feel safe in having its technical staff prepare each year an estimate of the maximum amount
of new capital which could advantageously be absorbed by certain major industries. There would be obvious difficulties in
preparing such estimates because the amount of capital which
industries could use would depend largely upon where and how
it was invested and at what cost it could produce. Nevertheless,
it might be possible to prepare a fairly satisfactory estimate and
this would undoubtedly help to encourage more discriminative
investing. This would be particularly true if the estimate were
supplemented by quarterly reports of the amount of new capital
which had been raised by the industry.

A National Economic Council could, if it would, sponsor more
effective organization of the labor market. Of all the major markets, scarcely any is so primitive, so lacking in facilities, as the
labor market. It is the only major market where the peddler
is still supreme. And yet human services are peculiarly difficult
to market, partly because men are less mobile than commodities,
partly because every worker is more or less unique in what he is

willing and able to do, and partly because many jobs are unique. The facilities that are needed in the labor market are far more elaborate than is usually realized. Public employment exchanges, though a necessary part of the machinery of the labor market, are not enough. They are not capable of handling all the problems. Consider the problem of blind-alley jobs. How many blind-alley jobs are there? In what occupations do they exist? How can outlets for these jobs be created? Some industries, because of their technique, inevitably hire far more boys than they can possibly promote. The flow of boys out of these industries should not be left to chance. It needs to be guided in order to make sure that the boys do not remain in the industry too long and that, when they leave, they obtain desirable work. Another important problem results from the fact that in 50,000 to 70,000 cases each year, industrial accident destroys the worker's ability to pursue his former occupation. A well organized labor market should be prepared to retrain many of these men for new occupations. Closely allied to this problem is that of the displacement of men by machines. It often happens that machines are introduced so gradually that some plants are hiring new men in the very occupation from which the machines are expelling them in other plants. Every new machine which substantially displaces labor should be the subject of immediate study, and a program for meeting the problem should be prepared. How many men is a machine likely to displace and how rapidly? How can the influx of workers into the shrinking occupation be stopped? How can the enterprises which need men in the occupation obtain them from other plants which are installing machines and laying off men? Into what other pursuits can the displaced men be most advantageously transferred?

All of this points to the need of a body which is capable of furnishing leadership in dealing with such problems as blind-alley jobs, vocational rehabilitation, technological unemployment, and many others. The logical body would appear to be a Federal Labor Board composed of six or seven men of standing in industry and in the labor movement, with possibly the Secretaries of Commerce and Labor as ex-officio members. A National Economic Council could undoubtedly persuade Congress to create a Federal Labor Board. From time to time the Council would find it convenient to refer problems to the Board for study.[33]

In order that we may make the most advantageous use of our land, there is need of a comprehensive study of land utilization, including an investigation of the best uses of land in areas of low income. The expansion of agriculture into new regions is making it uneconomical to farm some land where operating costs are high. An attempt should be made to determine what land is worth farming and what is not. Some farms could advantageously be put into forests. It happens that more forest land is needed because we are consuming timber about four times as fast as we are growing it. The immediate task of making a land survey should undoubtedly be handled by such bodies as the Federal Farm Board, the Bureau of Agricultural Economics, and the several states. Nevertheless, the impetus for a comprehensive survey could well come from the National Economic Council. In order to encourage the conversion of unprofitable farm land into forests, changes in the method of taxing such land are needed. This need was discussed in Chapter XXVIII.[34] The support of the National Economic Council would help induce more states to change their methods of taxing forest land.

The National Economic Council could help reduce the enormous wastes in marketing goods. It might be willing, in a mild way at least, to encourage the practice of selling by grade in retailing. Possibly it would be willing to support proposals to strengthen the laws which are designed to protect consumers and to improve the administration of these laws. Possibly it might be able to bring about a mutual and simultaneous reduction in advertising expenditures by competitors. Expenditures for advertising, as many persons have pointed out, are comparable to expenditures for armaments. The more one competitor spends, the more his rival must spend. A simultaneous reduction of advertising budgets by half would be advantageous to all competitors and might, in some cases, eventually be reflected in

[33] This discussion of a Federal Labor Board is based upon my article "Orderly Marketing for Labor," in the *New Republic*, August 6, 1930, v. LXIII, pp. 342–344. Acknowledgement is made for permission to draw liberally upon the article.

[34] Pp. 755–756.

slightly lower prices to consumers. Possibly a National Economic Council might be willing to take a stand against some of the more anti-social methods of advertising, such as desecration of the countryside by billboards. Possibly plans might be worked out under the sponsorship of the Council by which competitors in different industries would gradually and simultaneously reduce their use of billboard advertising. Or a plan might be worked out by which a given percentage of the highway mileage (say half) would be reserved for the enjoyment of motorists free from billboards or by which certain areas of unusual beauty should be kept free of billboards.

In addition to these problems, there are a multitude of others which the National Economic Council might help to solve. There is the problem of neutralizing the railroad terminals in large cities so that the tracks of each road would be open to the locomotives of all roads — a difficult and an important problem. There is the problem of more effectively regulating public utilities, of overhauling our system of taxation (particularly state taxes) in order to shift the burden from the poor, upon whom it now falls most heavily, to the rich. There is the problem of creating a tariff which represents the interests of the community as a whole rather than merely the special interests of a multitude of small groups. And, of course, there are scores of additional problems.

Up to this point, the discussion has pertained to what a National Economic Council could do *if it would*. But how much would it be *willing* to do? Probably not very much. A consideration of the sort of men who would compose the Council indicates that it would be a cautious and a conservative body. Capital would be represented by delegates from such bodies as the United States Chamber of Commerce, the National Association of Manufacturers, the American Bankers' Association, and the Investment Bankers of America; labor, by delegates from the American Federation of Labor, the railroad brotherhoods, some of the independent unions, and employee representation plans. Nothing radical would be sponsored by either of these general groups. The representatives of the farmers and of the consumers might be less conservative, but few of them would be positively radical. Furthermore, it must be remembered that the Council, as a matter of general policy, would probably refuse to commit itself publicly to the support of policies which failed to command fairly unanimous support from its members. This practice would undoubtedly be wise, and yet it would mean that the Council would move slowly, for no radical departure from existing arrangements could command unanimous support or anything approaching it.

All of this does not mean that a National Economic Council would be useless. It does mean, however, that the Council would achieve results very gradually. Moreover, it means that a Council would deeply disappoint many persons who expect quick and dramatic accomplishments from national planning. Indeed, it is probable that a Council would be badly discredited in the eyes of many of its friends after it had been in existence for two or three years or less. Suppose, for example, that a Council were established now, in the spring of 1931. The farmers would immediately expect it to solve the farm problem. But there is relatively little that it could do to help the farmers and that little it could achieve only very slowly. Labor would expect it to do something about technological unemployment, and yet the Council could do little. Everyone would expect the Council to stabilize business, and yet business cycles would continue to occur very much as always.

This suggests a question of considerable importance. Is there not the danger that a National Economic Council would be a formidable bar to economic experimentation. One of the great needs of the United States is a form of unemployment insurance which would place a substantial part of the cost of maintaining idle wage earners upon industry. If the National Economic Council had been in existence in 1931, it might have encouraged the creation of private, voluntary schemes of unemployment insurance, but almost certainly it would not have encouraged compulsory schemes. In fact, it might have thrown the weight of its prestige and influence definitely against compulsory unemployment insurance. Probably it would be wise for some communities to experiment with various forms of public ownership of municipal utilities. Public ownership might take various forms.

It might be ownership without operation or it might be ownership with operation. There are great possibilities of inventing various forms of public corporations which would put the control of the utilities in the hands of various business, labor, and consumers and which would render them independent of control by politicians. The opportunities for invention here are no less real than those which exist in the realm of mechanics. Yet it is scarcely to be expected that a conservative body such as a National Economic Council would help to discover ways by which the public might advantageously own its utilities. Indeed, there is danger that the Council might throw its influence strongly against experimentation with public ownership in any form.

XII. Making Management Neutral instead of Partisan

This survey of ways and means of improving our economic society has omitted the most important of all. By far the greatest waste in modern industry is the failure of thousands of able men who direct the large business enterprises of the country to contribute to the creation of sound national economic policies.[35] As was pointed out in Chapter XXVII, the country is full of men who know how to run factories, railroads, public utilities, stores, and banks and yet only a handful of these thousands of able men are willing and able to make contributions to the creation of wise national economic policies. One of the great problems of the day, for example, is the creation of a wise policy of public utility regulation. And yet how much have the able executives at the head of the country's utilities contributed to solving the problem of regulating utilities? It is not too much to say that in most cases they have hindered rather than helped in solving this problem. In other words, so far as this particular problem is concerned, the public has almost completely lost the use of the abilities of the leaders in the public utility industry. Another great problem is the creation of a wise national railroad policy, and yet out of several score railroad presidents, few have given important help in solving this problem. Consider, for example, the failure of railroad leaders to work out a solution of the problems of railroad consolidation or of terminal unification. From the thousands of able manufacturers in the country,

[35] Pp. 726–727.

how much help does the nation obtain in formulating a wise tariff policy? Instead of helping, most manufacturers fight hard to create a tariff which gratifies special interests at the expense of the community.

What is the reason for the failure of business managers to make a greater contribution to the creation of wise national economic policies? Plainly it is not lack of ability, because business managers constitute one of the ablest groups in the community. This, indeed, is precisely the tragedy in the situation — that the help of such an able group should, to a large extent, be lost to the community in solving its economic problems. The failure of business men to make a larger contribution to the creation of wise economic policies is a result of the position which managers occupy. They are not free men. They are not neutrals, hired to serve all interests alike. They are employed by stockholders to promote the interests of the stockholders. Their task is to produce a favorable income statement and balance sheet for particular enterprises at the end of each year. If they fail to do so, they know that the stockholders will find other managers.

The community cannot afford to permit the abilities of the men in the managerial professions to be appropriated almost exclusively by the owners of capital. If the managers of industry are to apply their talents to solving the economic problems of the community instead of merely to making money for a small group of property owners, they must be neutrals — equally the servants of the owners of capital, wage earners, and consumers. This does not necessarily mean that representatives of the workers and consumers must sit upon the directing boards of our great railroads, steel corporations, and automobile plants. The form of organization which will most effectively give representation to all interests must be discovered by experimentation. What may be best in one industry may not be best in another. But it does mean that a clear distinction must be drawn between the *government* of industry and the *management* of industry. The function of the government of industry is to determine policies, that of management to execute them. Today the distinction between the two is blurred because the owners of capital control both the government and the management of industry. The government of industry must cease to be the exclusive affair of the owners of capital; it must be shared equally with the two other basic economic interests — the wage earners and the consumers. Management must become the task of neutral, professional administrators whose duty is to execute impartially and loyally the policies which the governing bodies formulate.

At the beginning of this survey of industry in the United States, the opinion was expressed that the supreme economic problem of the day is how to acquire some degree of control over our economic system — such control as is possible in a world where the consequences of acts can be only imperfectly foreseen. In concluding this survey, the opinion may be expressed that the problem of achieving control is primarily one of making the management of industry neutral instead of partisan and of creating, over and above management, a form of industrial government which will give fair representation to the three basic economic interests, workers, property owners, and consumers.

REFERENCES

Carver, T. N., *Essays in Social Justice*, 1922. Chs. IX, X, XIV, XV.
Clark, J. M., *Social Control of Business*, 1926.
Donham, W. B., *Business Adrift*, 1931.
Downey, E. H., *Workmen's Compensation*, 1924.
Keezer, D. M., and May, S., *The Public Control of Business*, 1930.
Liberal Industrial Inquiry, *Britain's Industrial Future*, 1928.
Tawney, R. H., *Equality*, 1931.
Thomas, Norman, *America's Way Out*, 1931.

INDEX

INDEX

A

Accidents, industrial, 8, 69–70, 101, 858

Accounting concepts, terms, and devices, 25–32

Accounts: control of, 397–398; payable, 26, 27, 28; receivable, 26, 28

Adie, David C., 420

Advertising: a recent development, 553; and quality, 560–561, 564; and special brands, 560; effects of, 555–557; expenditures, control of, 175; expenses of, uneconomically large, 559; extent of, 554; monopoly created by, 357; National Economic Council and, 884; misleading, protection of consumer against, 582–587; trade associations and, 171; unrest created by, 181; "word-of-mouth," 570–571

Agnew, P. G., 81

Agreements: gentlemen's, 351; trade, *see* Trade Agreements

Agricultural coöperatives, *see* Coöperatives

Agricultural prices: fluctuations in, 428–431; effect on farmers' incomes, 440–441; stabilization of, 388, 428–447

Agriculture: motorization of, 312, 313; National Economic Council and, 883; revolution in, 88; Secretary of, 576, 875; uncertainties in, 207, 209–211. *See also* Agricultural Prices; Farmer; Federal Farm Board

Alaskan Government Railroad, 376

Albrecht, A. E., 577

Amalgamated Association of Street and Electric Railway Employees, 355

Amalgamated Clothing Workers, 191

Amateurs: buying largely done by, 541–542; speculation by, 218–219

American Association of Wholesale Opticians, 565

American Federation of Labor, 183, 873

American Gas Association, 580

American Home Economic Association, 589

American Institute of Baking, 170

American Photo-Engravers' Association, 311, 354, 365

American Public Health Association, 589

American Standards Association, 577

American Sugar Refining Company, 131, 358

American Telephone and Telegraph Company, 9, 13, 122, 131, 362

American Tobacco Company, 158, 359

Angell, J. W., 811

Apprentice training: by trade associations, 171; union policies concerning, 191, 192, 193, 657–658

Arkwright, Richard, 89

Ashley, Percy, 768, 770, 771

Ashley, W. J., 88

Assets: current, 25, 28–29; fixed, 25, 28–29; in balance sheet, 25–29

Atchison, Topeka, and Santa Fé Railroad, 163

Authority, delegation of, in large business units, 136

Automobile industry, output of, 7

B

Bailey, W. B., 622

Balance sheet, 25–30

Baltimore and Ohio Railroad, 131, 162, 363

Bank for International Settlements, 766, 818, 831, 837, 840, 844, 846; as device for economizing gold, 843–846

Bankers' acceptance, 229; advantages of, 233–234; rate, 687

Bankers' bill, 229, 230, 231, 241; advantages of, 233–234

Banks: central, *see* Central Banks; central reserve city, 248–249; commercial, *see* Commercial Banks; country, 248–249; investment, 227; national, 248–249; number of, 124; reserve city, 248–249; savings, 227; warnings of, and control of business cycle, 473, 475–476. *See also* Federal Reserve Banks

Bargaining, collective, *see* Collective Bargaining

Bargaining power: disturbed by business cycle, 454–455; inequalities decreased by market information, 278; of labor,